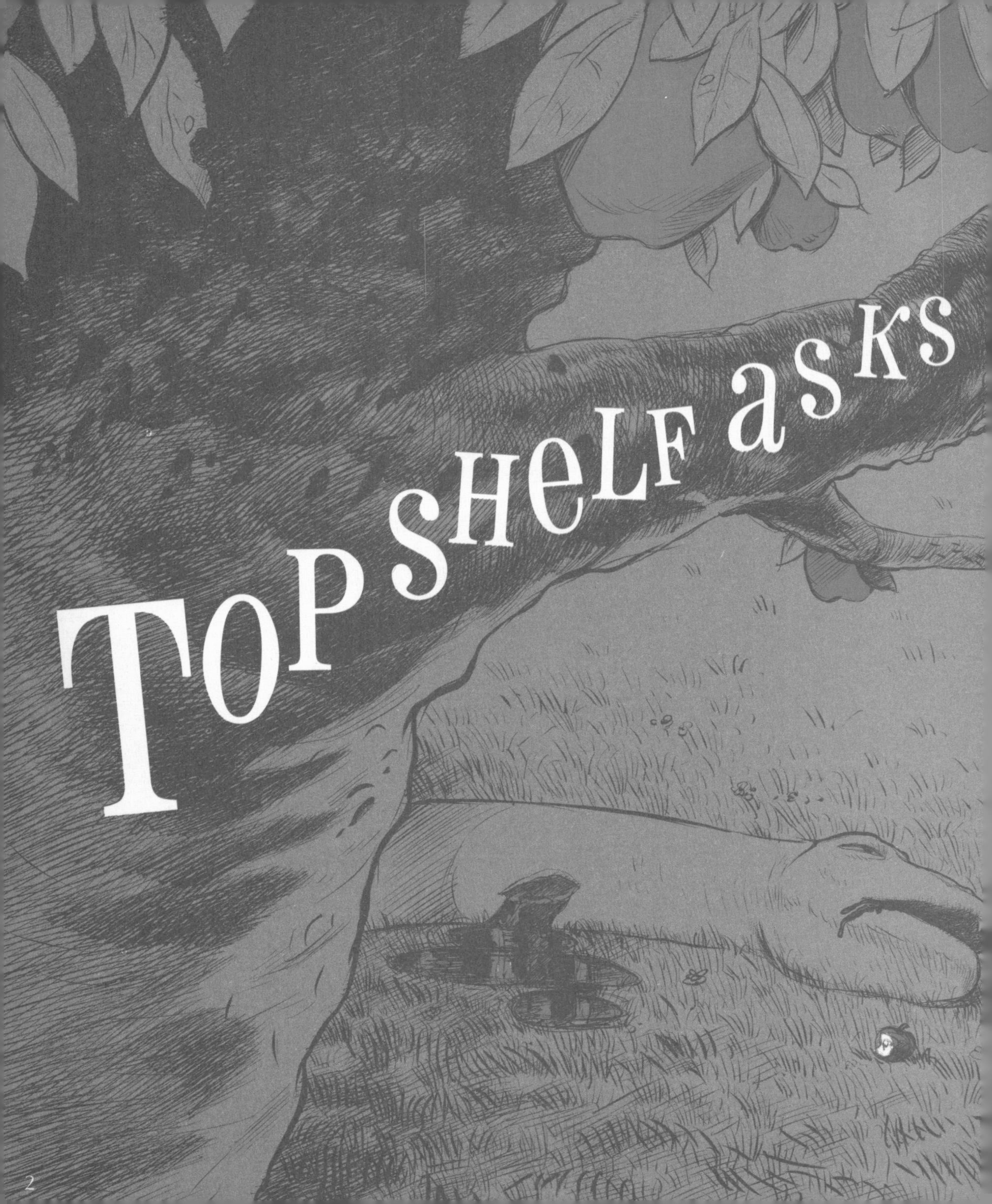
TOP SHELF asks

THE Big QUESTIONS

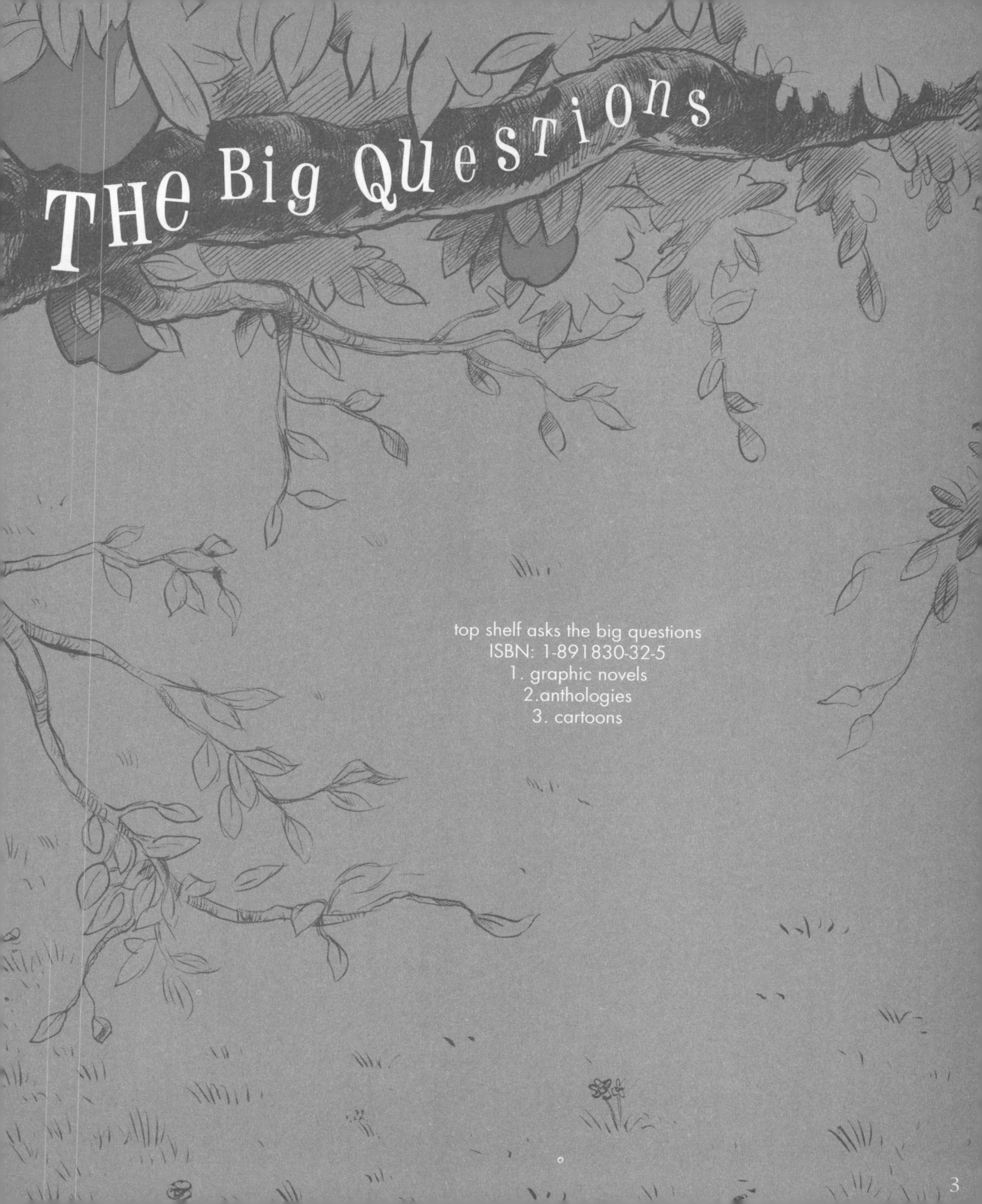

top shelf asks the big questions
ISBN: 1-891830-32-5
1. graphic novels
2.anthologies
3. cartoons

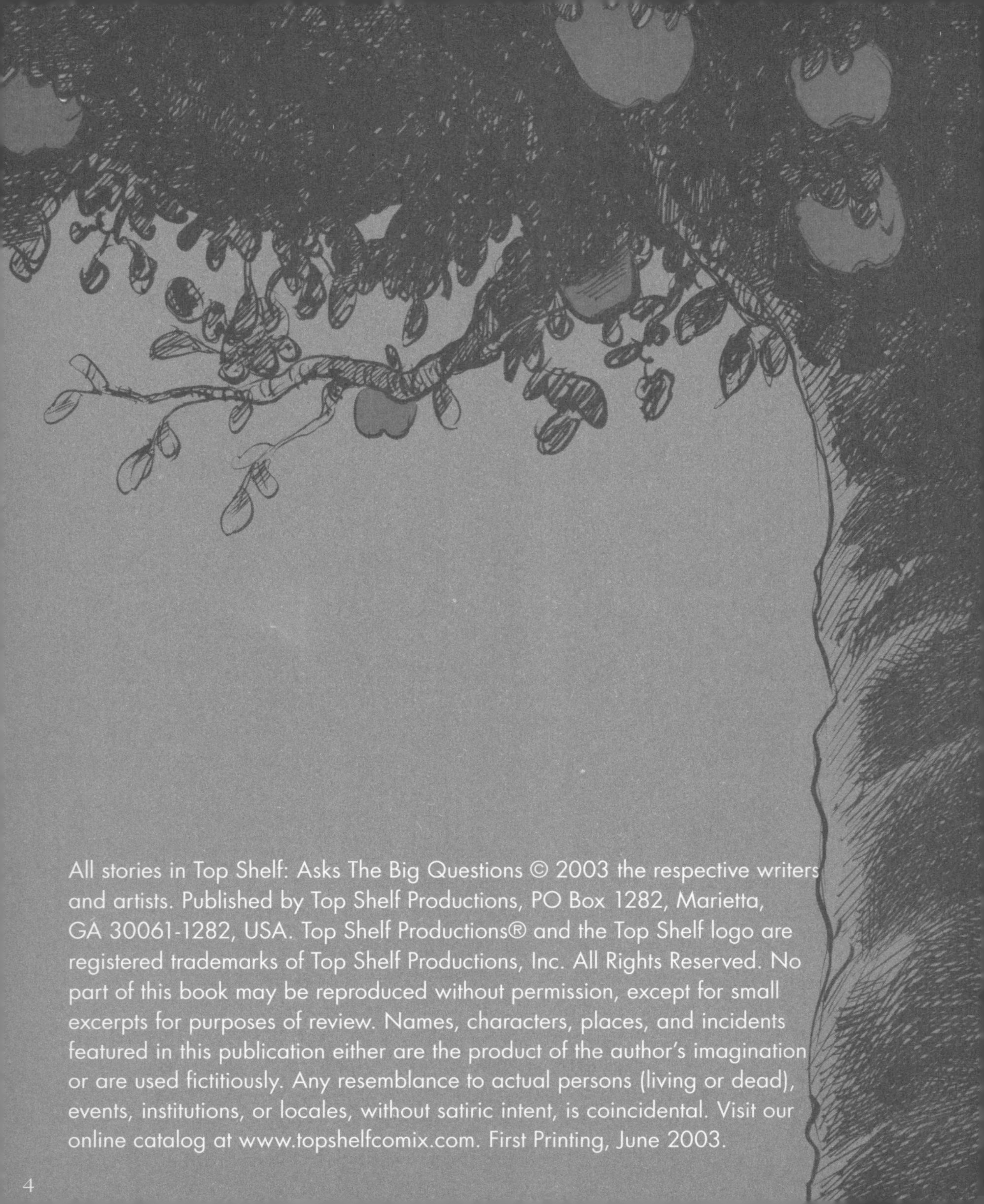

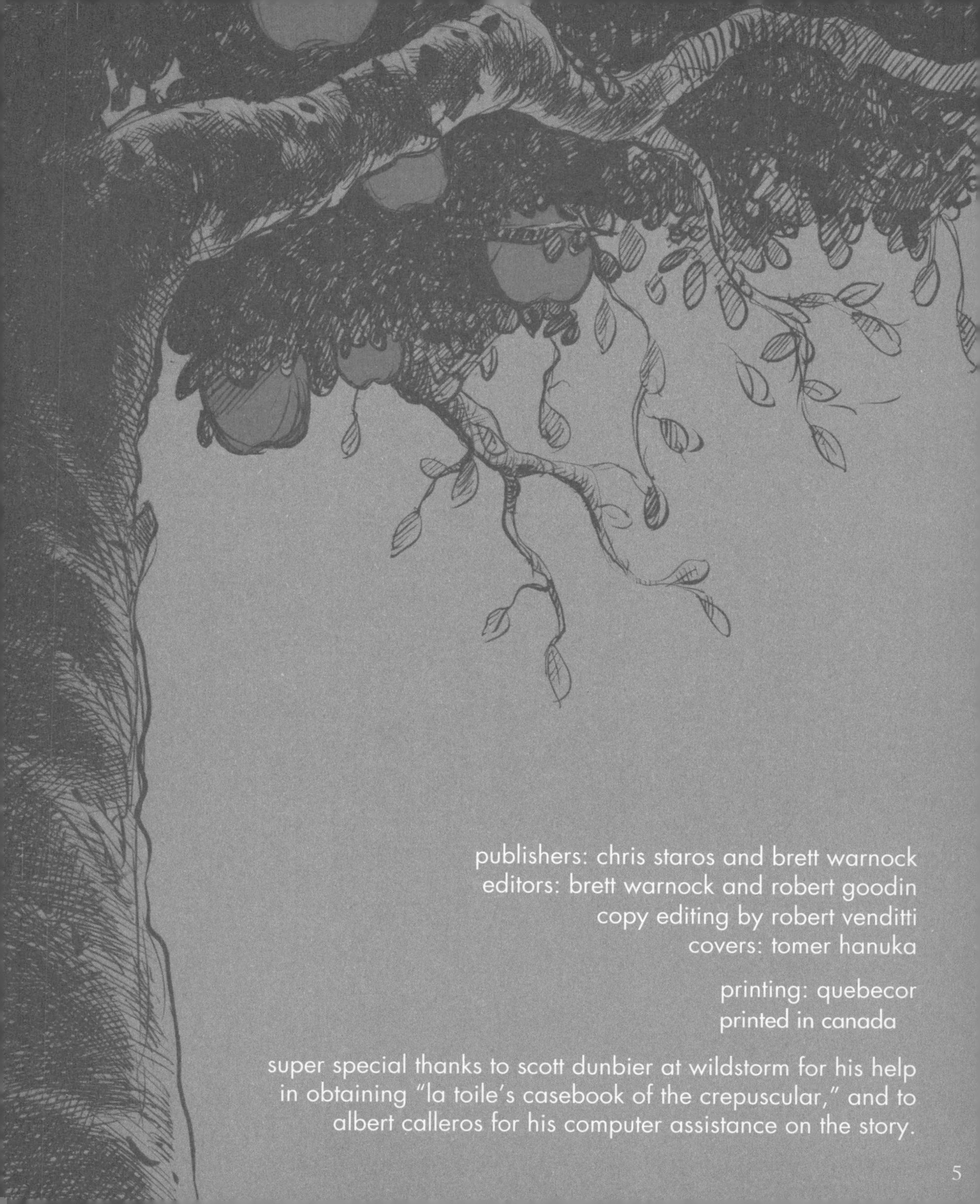

publishers: chris staros and brett warnock
editors: brett warnock and robert goodin
copy editing by robert venditti
covers: tomer hanuka

printing: quebecor
printed in canada

super special thanks to scott dunbier at wildstorm for his help in obtaining "la toile's casebook of the crepuscular," and to albert calleros for his computer assistance on the story.

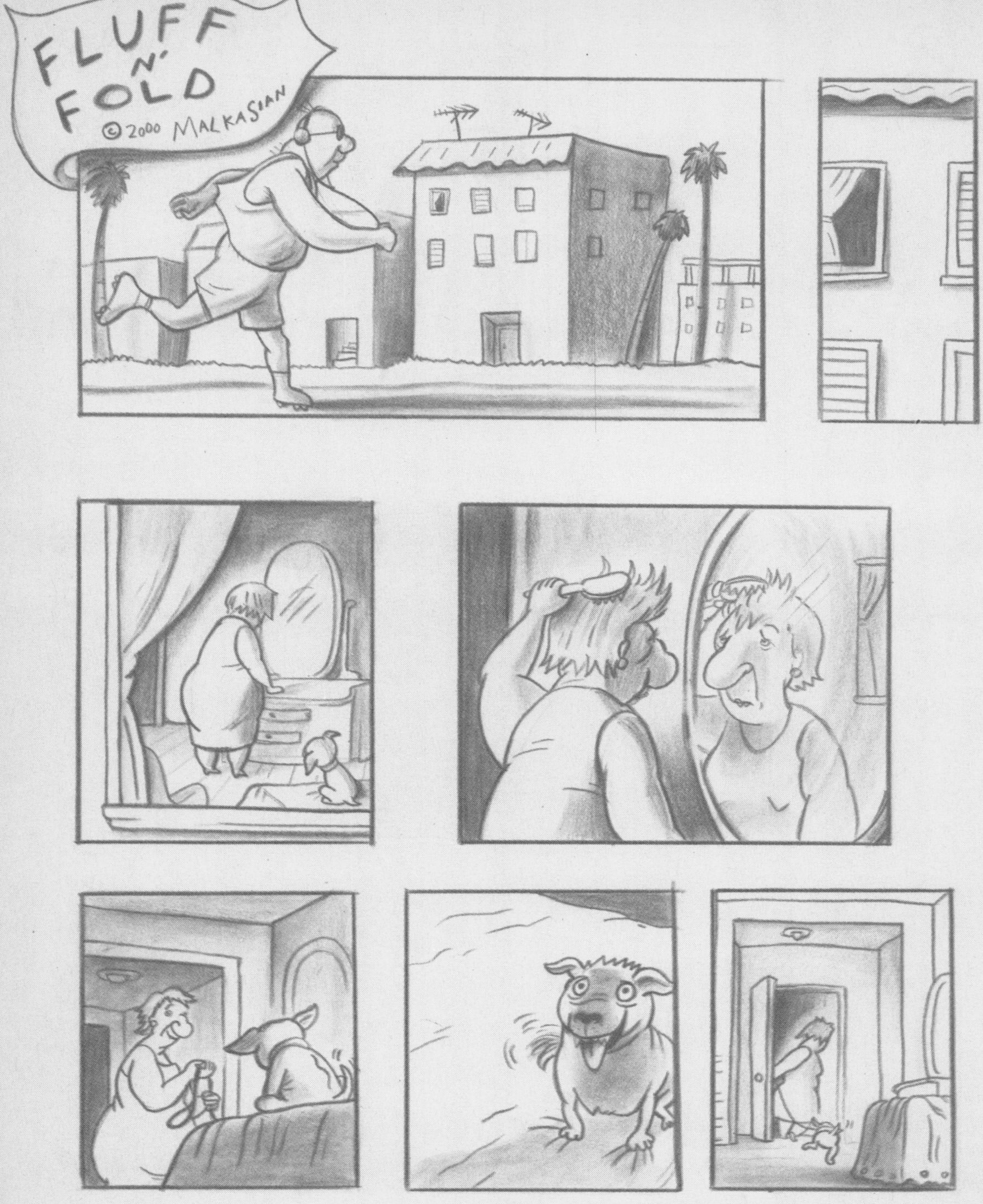
FLUFF N' FOLD
©2000 MALKASIAN

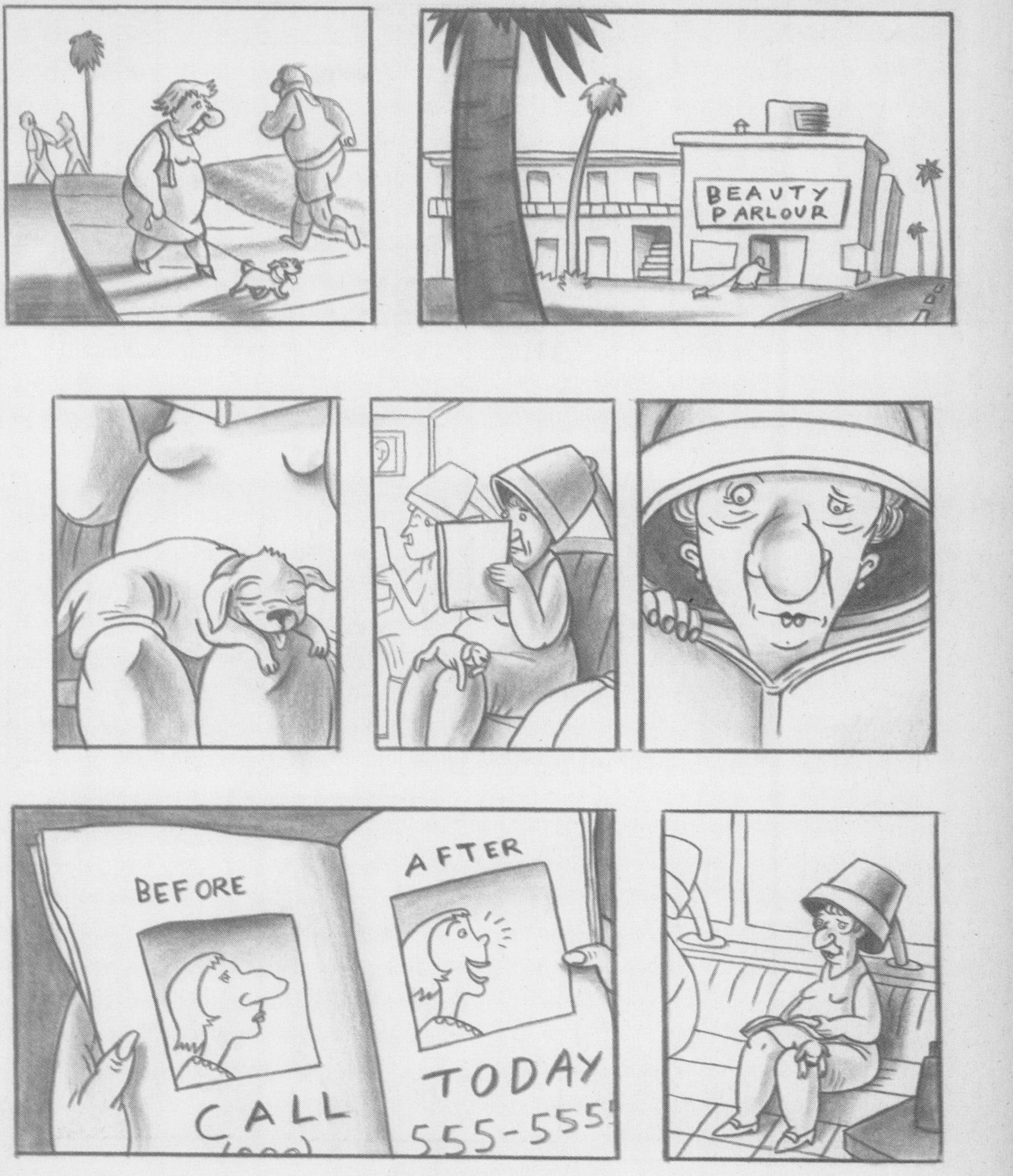
BEAUTY PARLOUR
BEFORE
AFTER
CALL
TODAY
555-555

YIP! YIP! YIP!
YIP! YIP! YIP! YIP! YIP! YIP! YIP! YI YIP! YIP! YI
GRRR RRRR

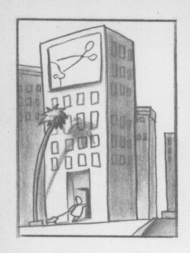

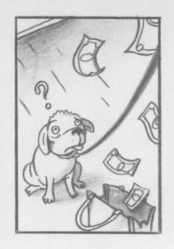

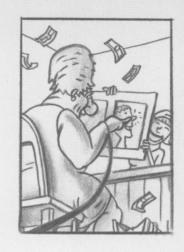

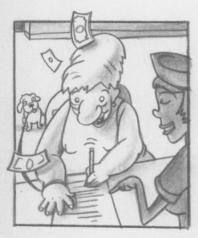

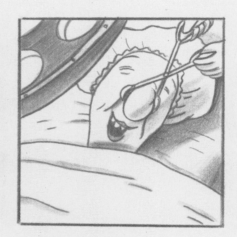

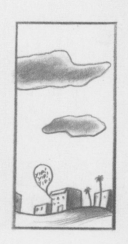

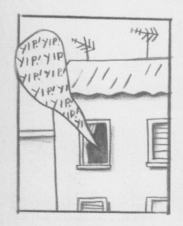

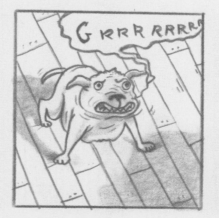

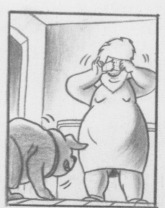

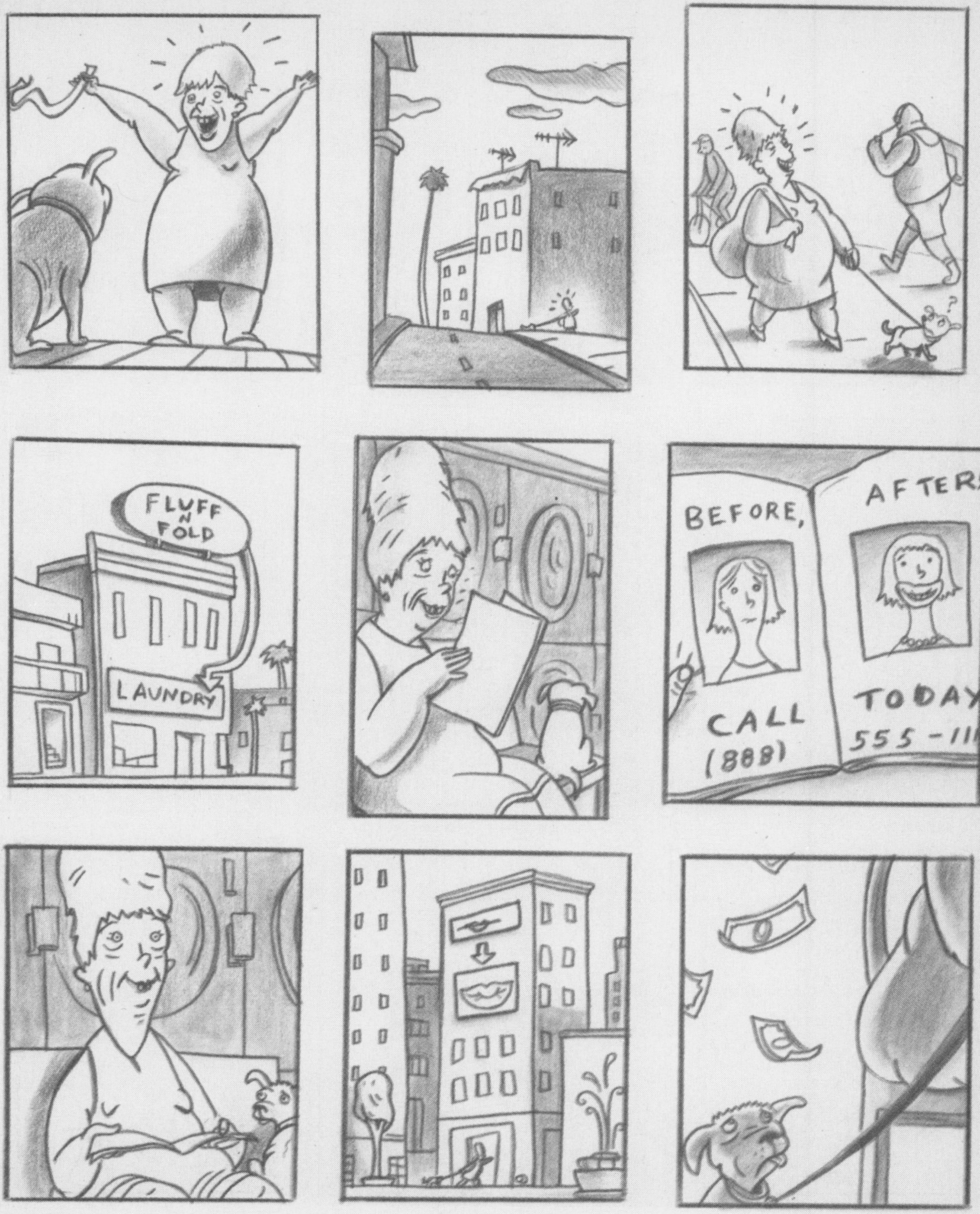
FLUFF N FOLD
LAUNDRY
BEFORE,
AFTER!
CALL
(888)
TODAY
555-11

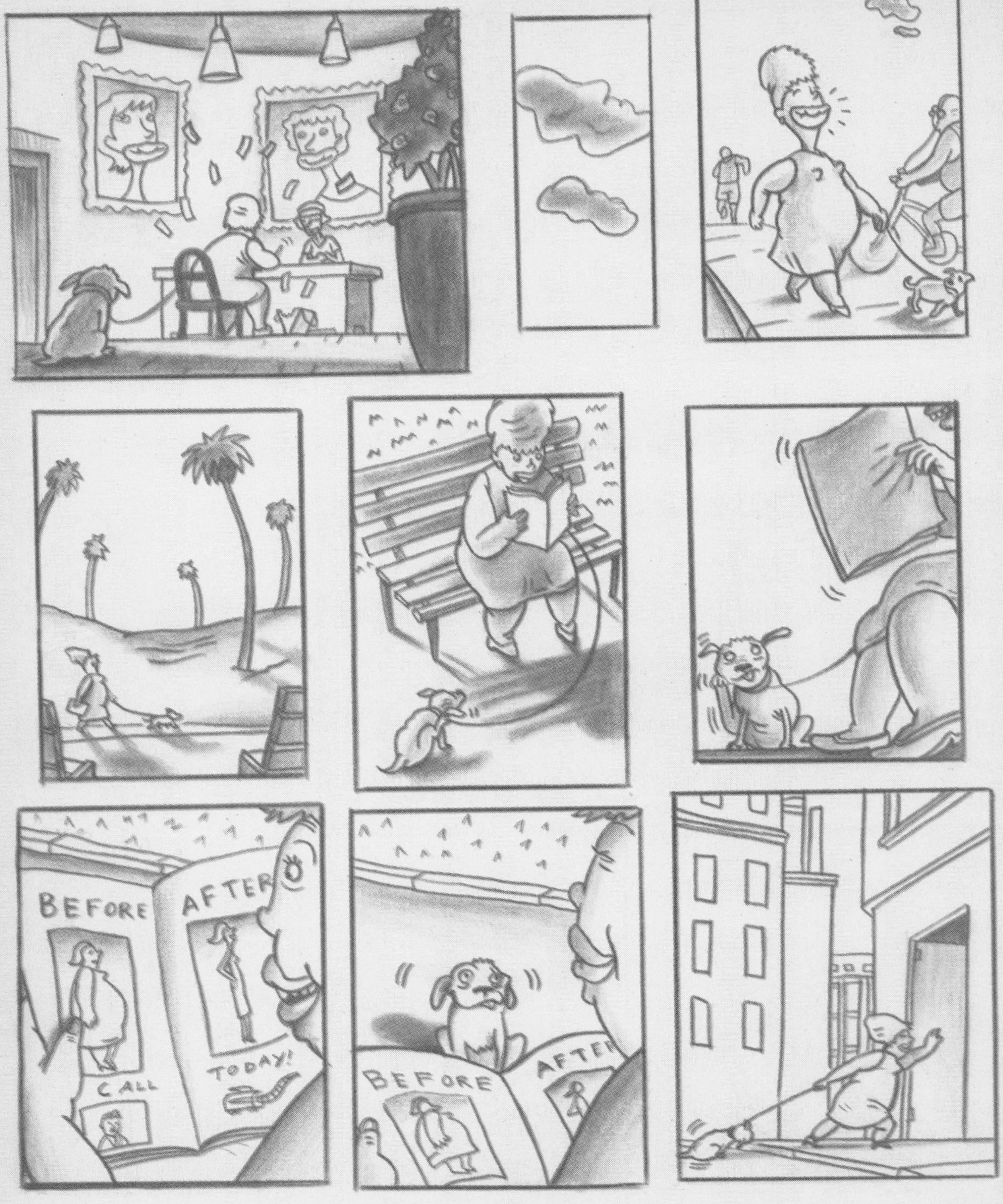
BEFORE
AFTER
CALL
TODAY!
BEFORE
AFTE

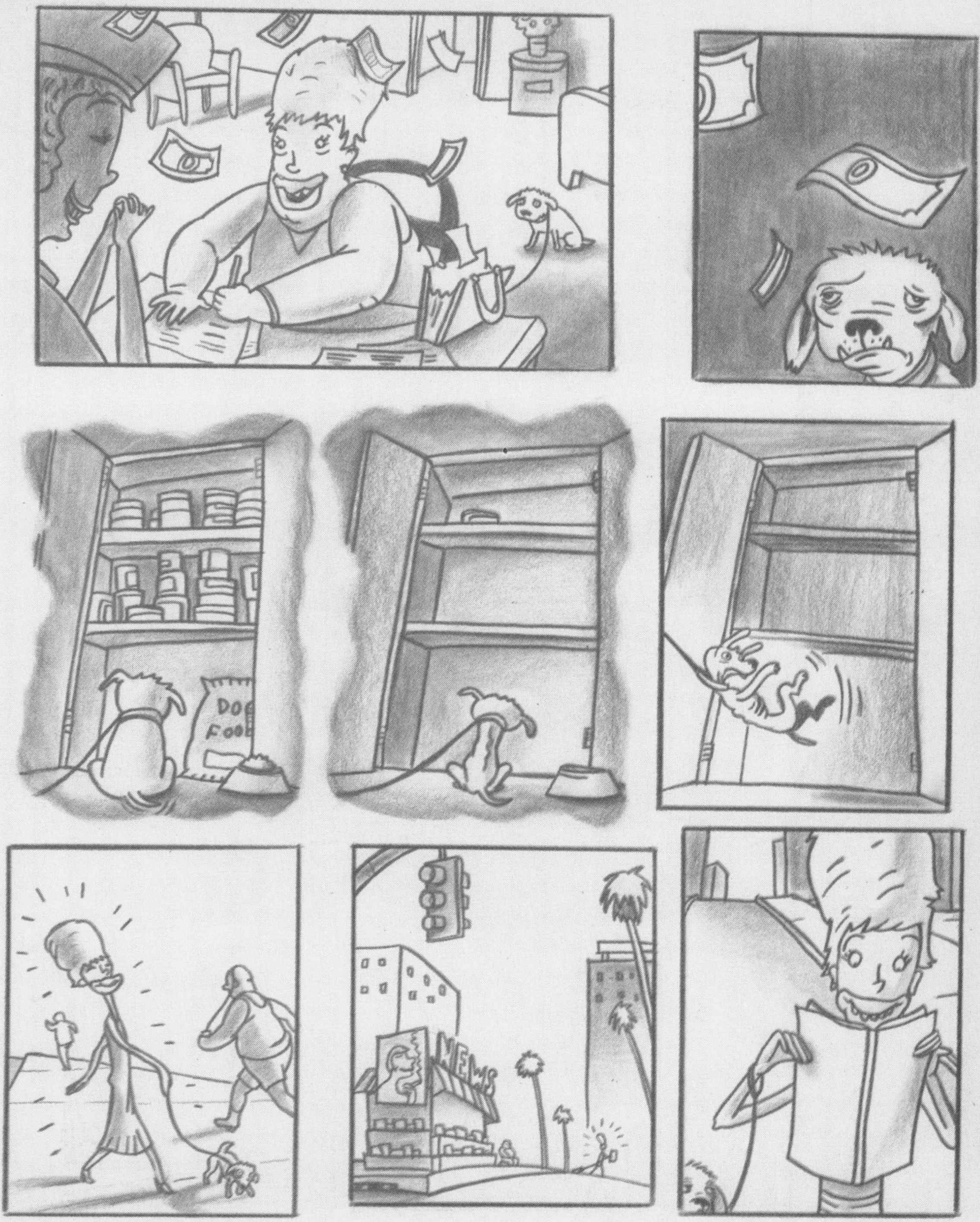
NEWS

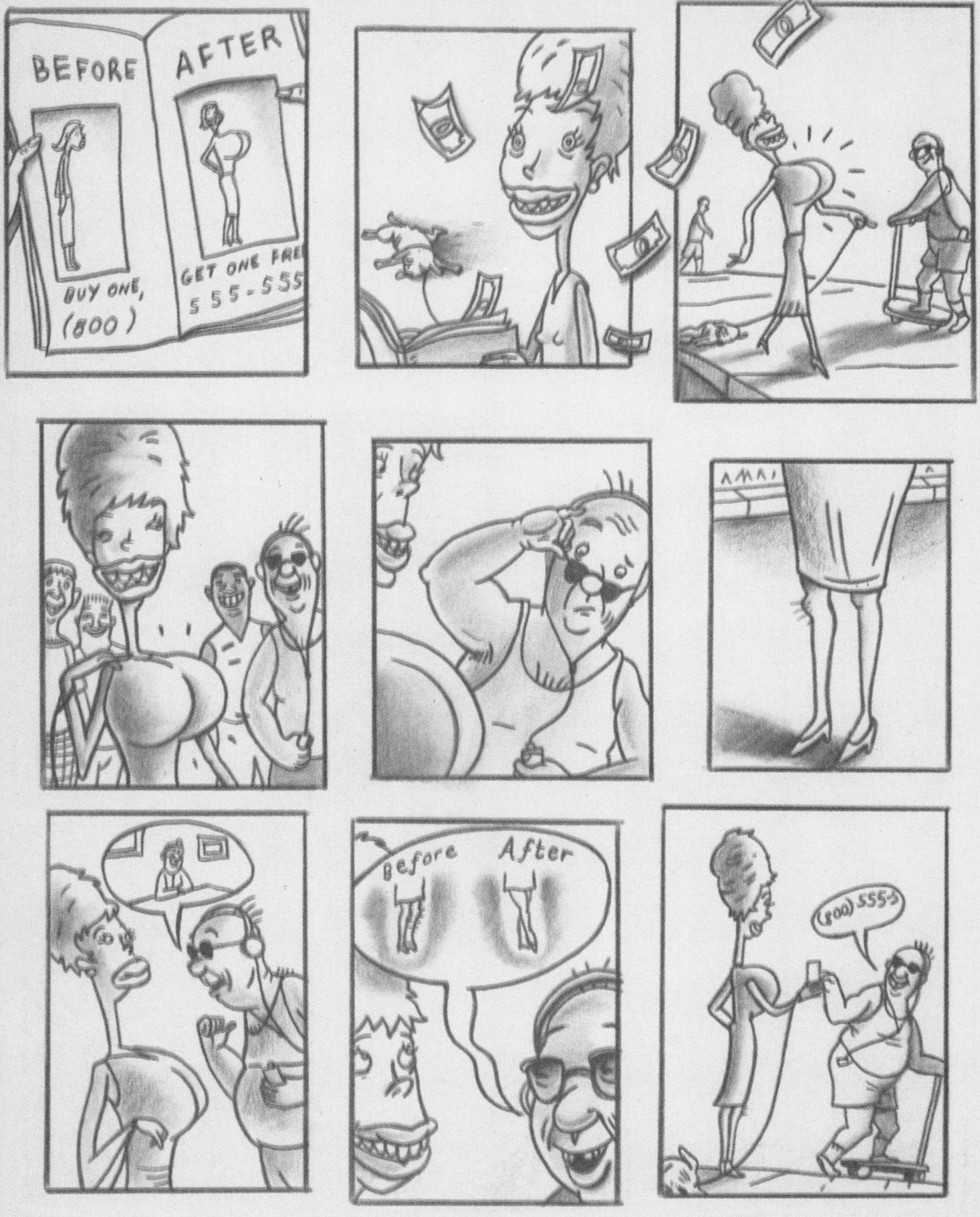
BEFORE
AFTER
BUY ONE,
(800)
GET ONE FRE
555-555
Before
After
(800) 555-5

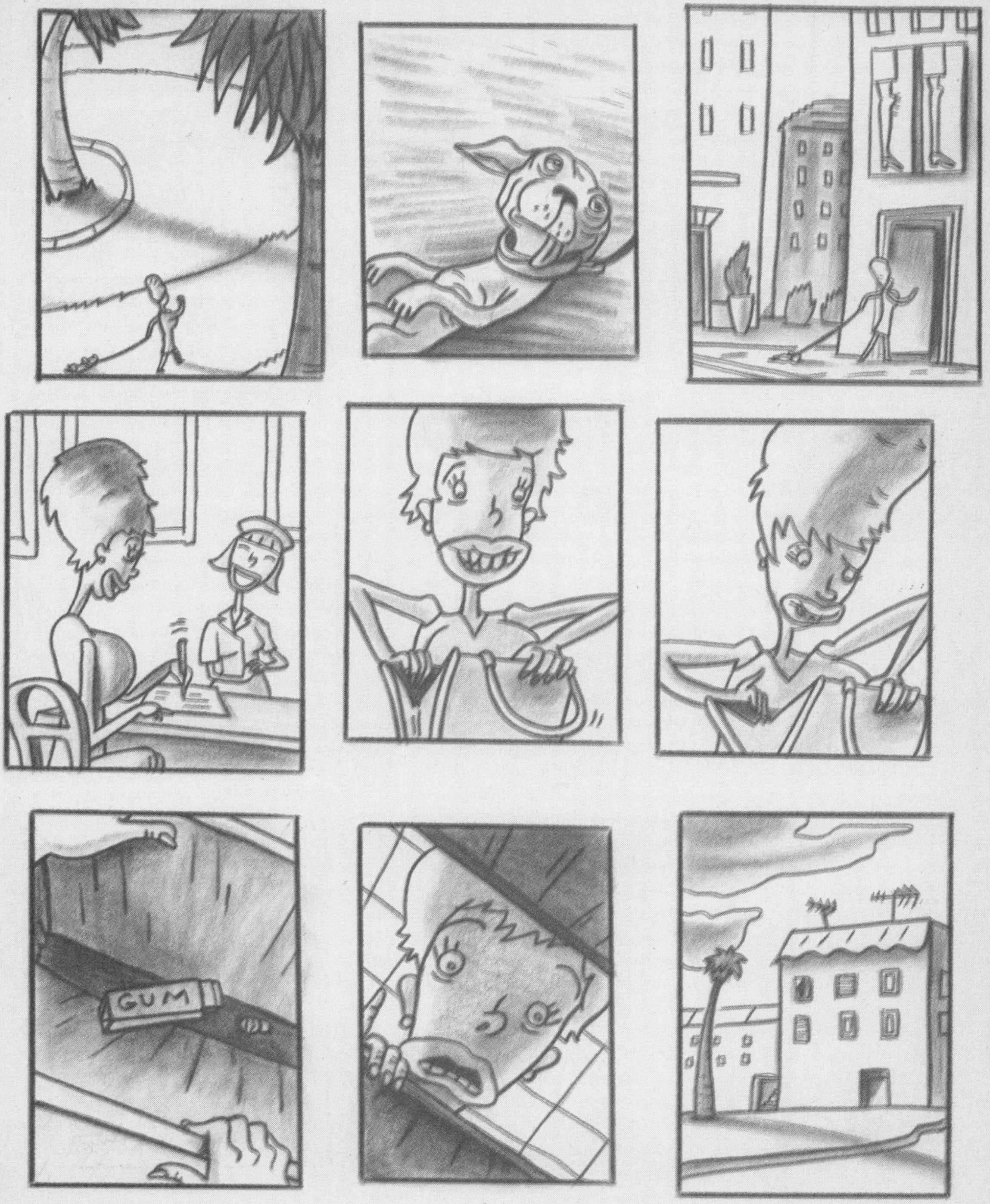
GUM

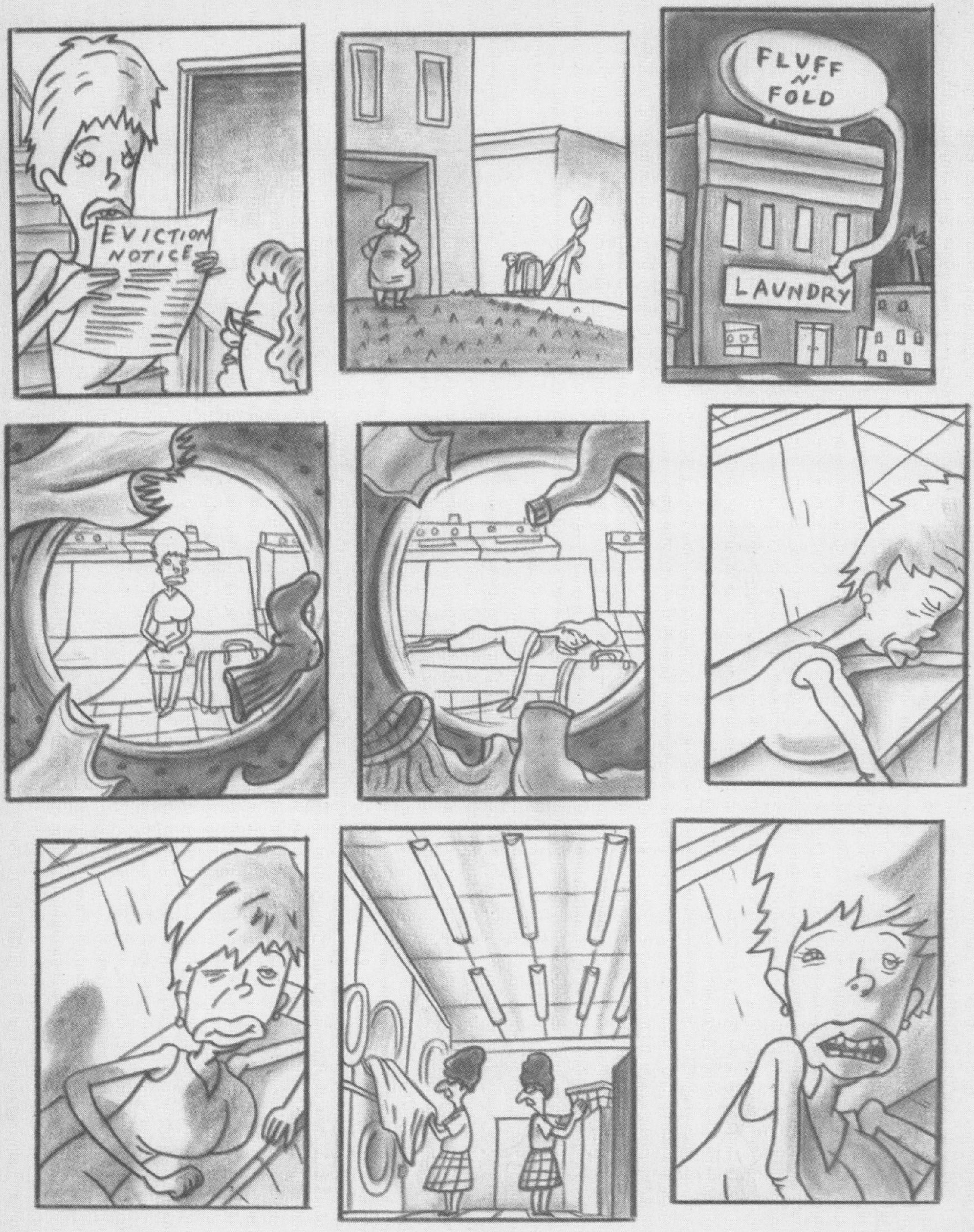
EVICTION NOTICE
FLUFF N' FOLD
LAUNDRY

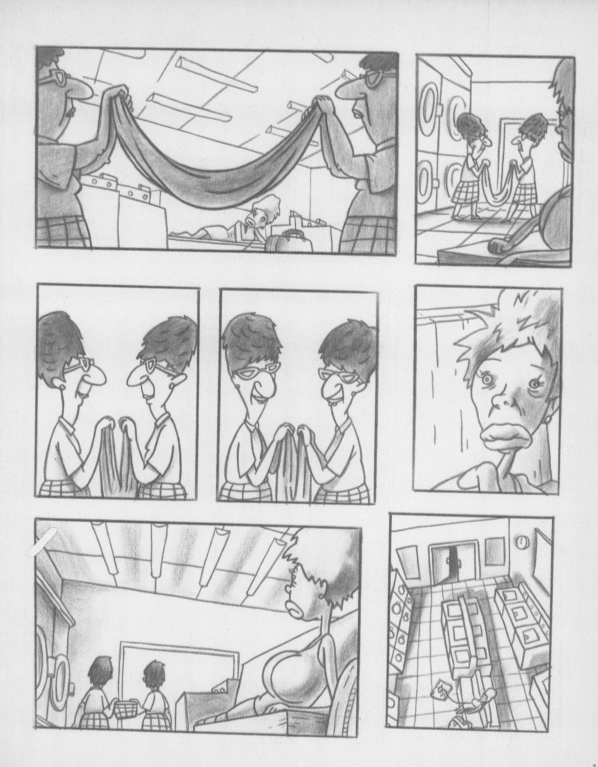

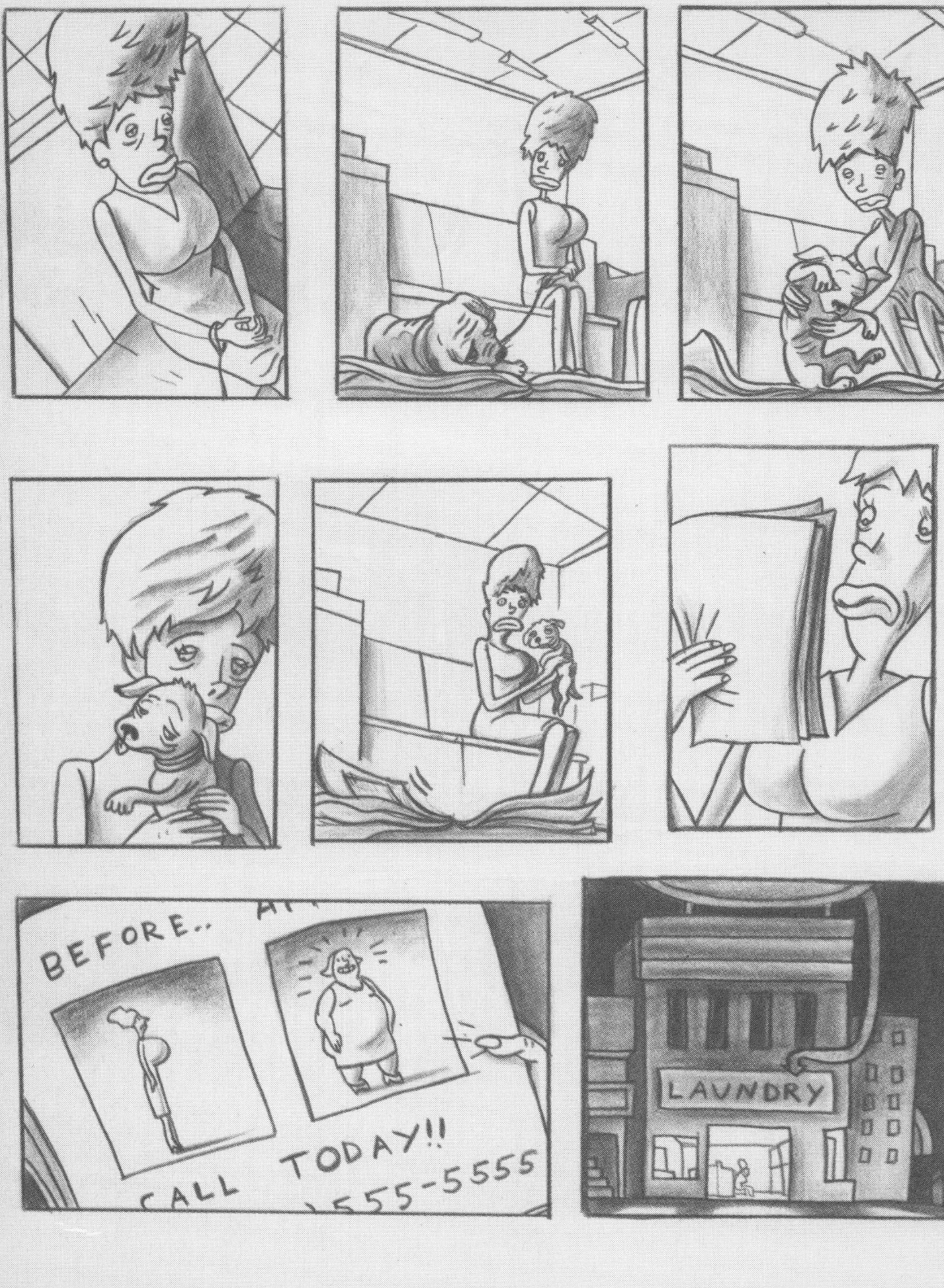
BEFORE..
CALL TODAY!!
555-5555
LAUNDRY

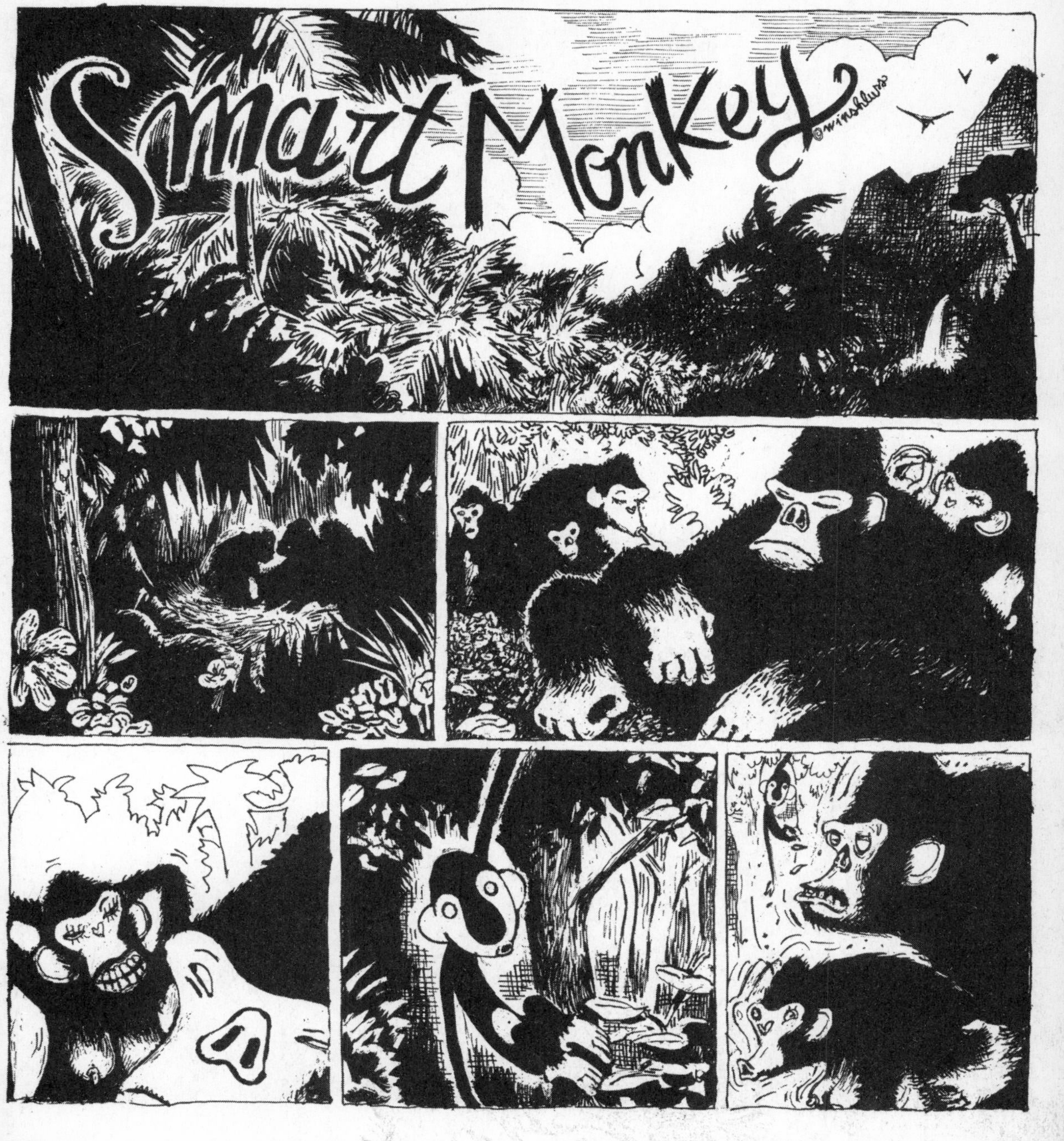
Smart Monkey
©winshluss

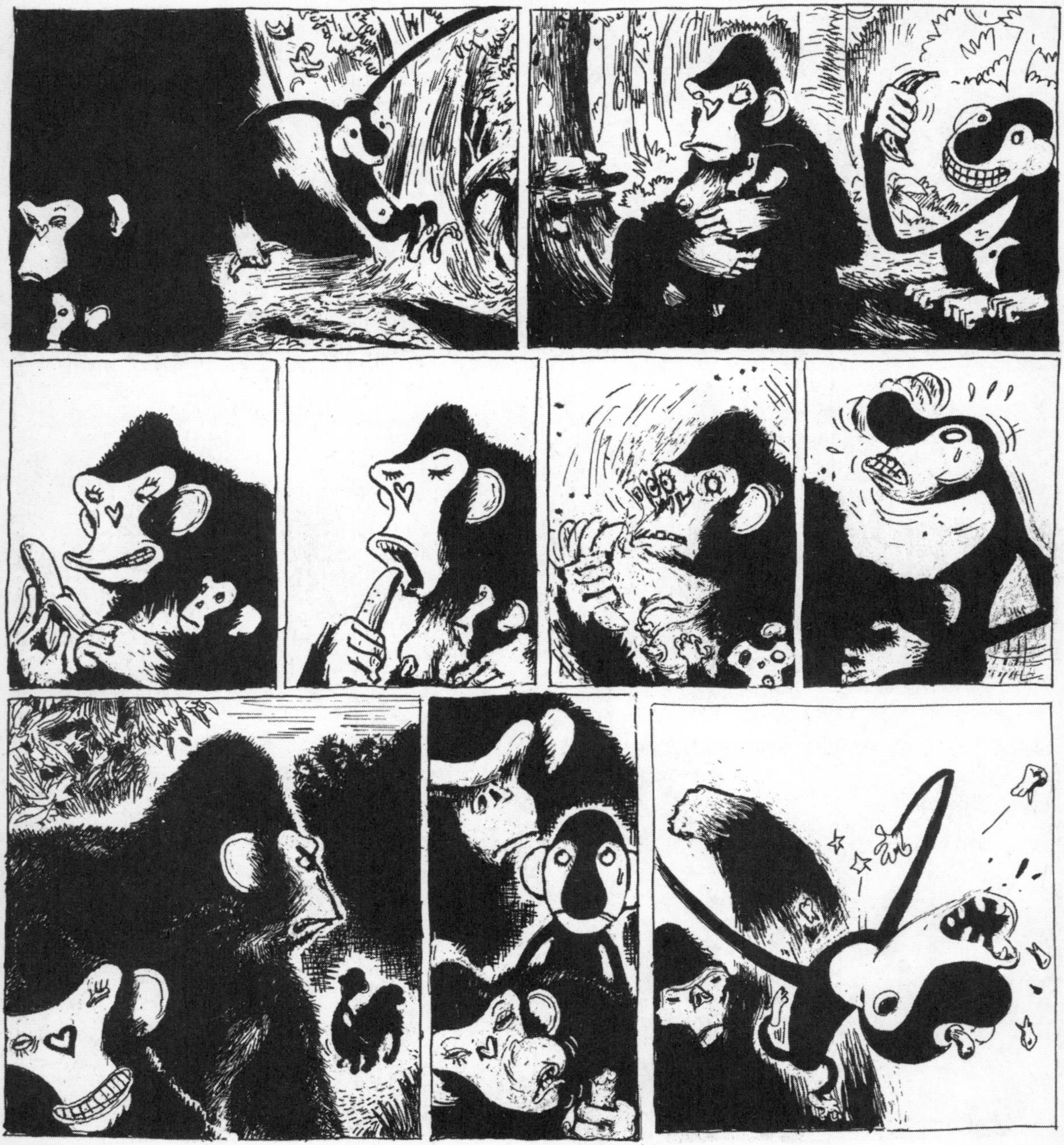

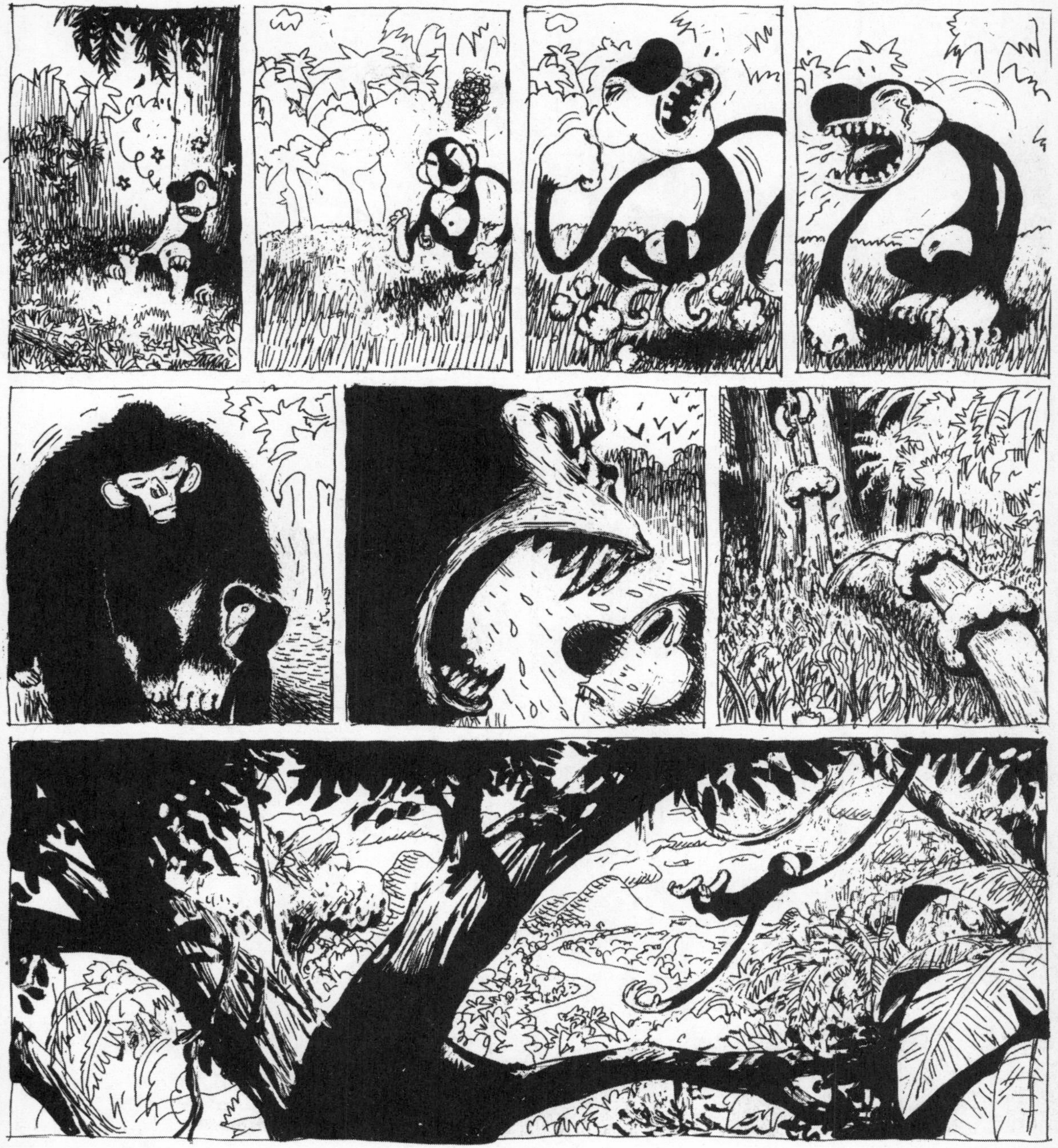

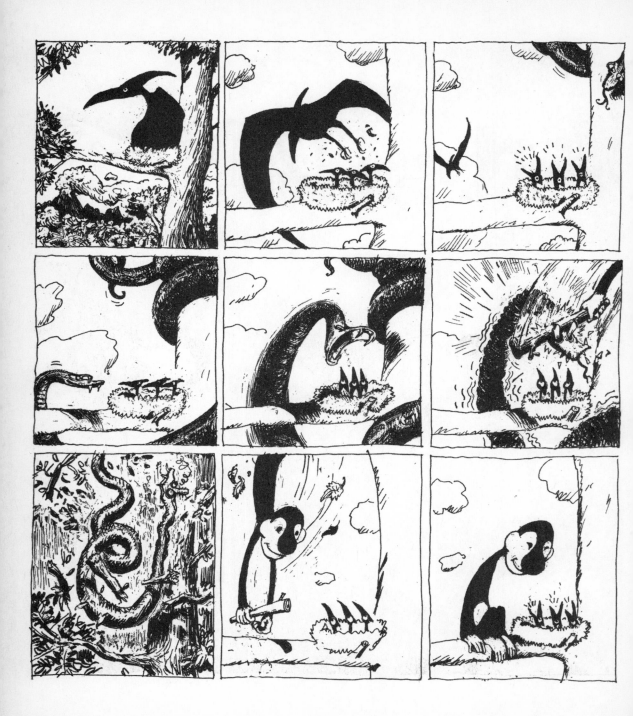

20

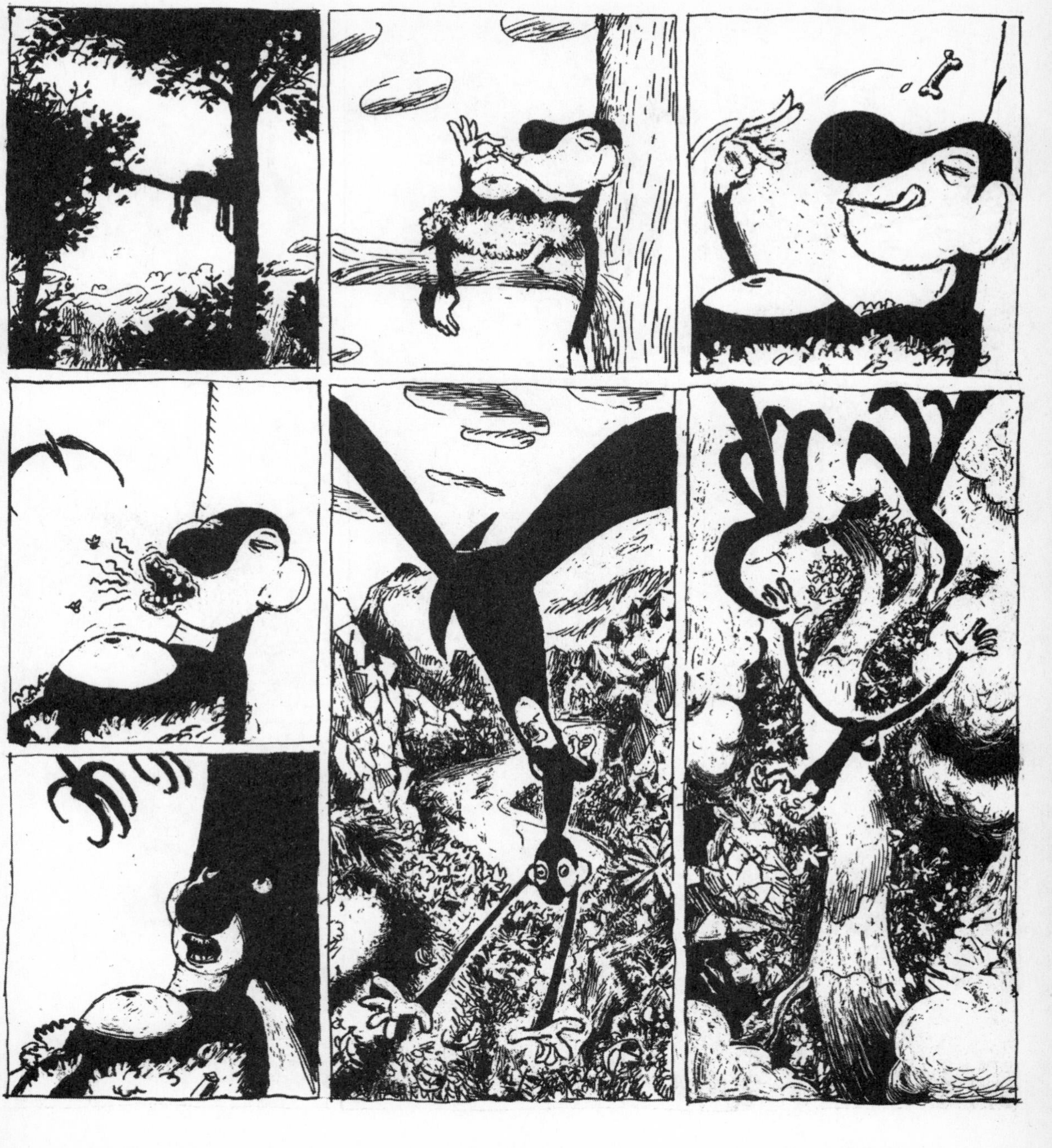

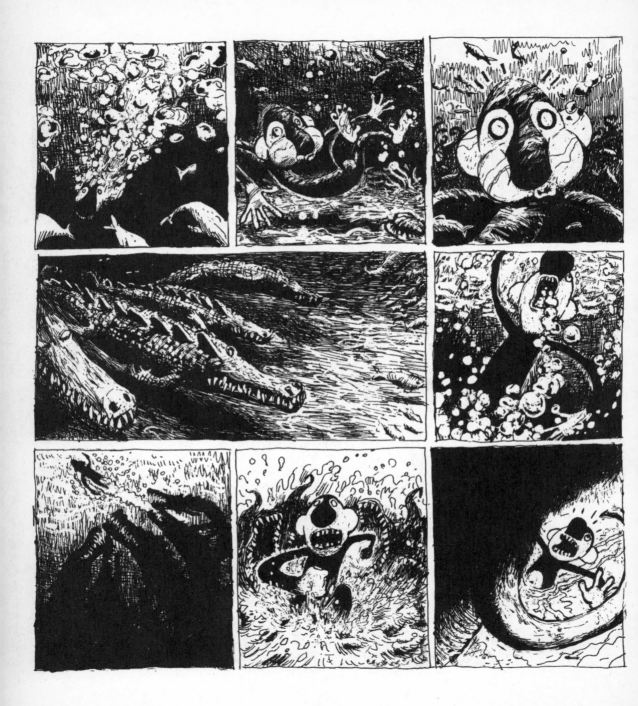

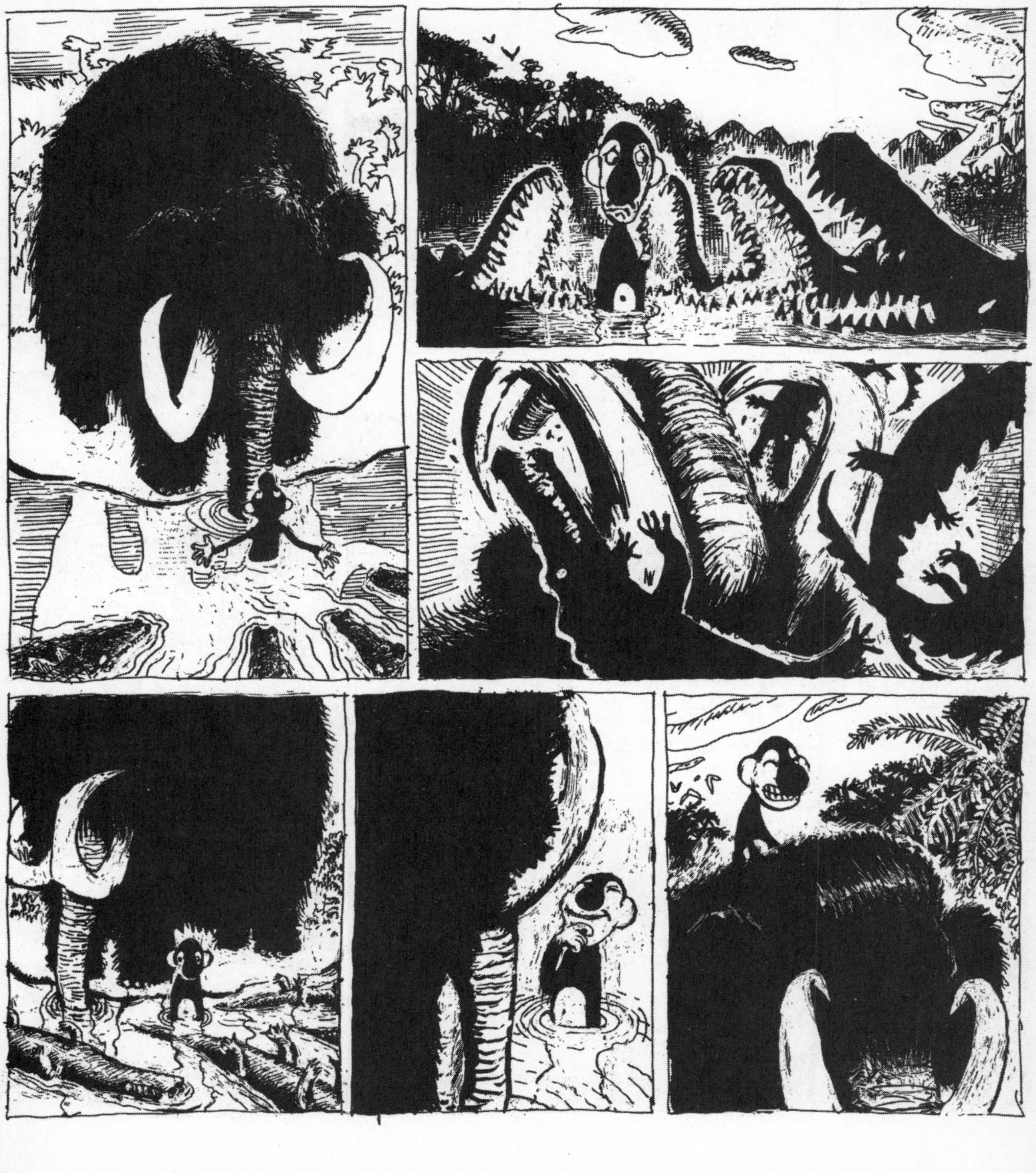

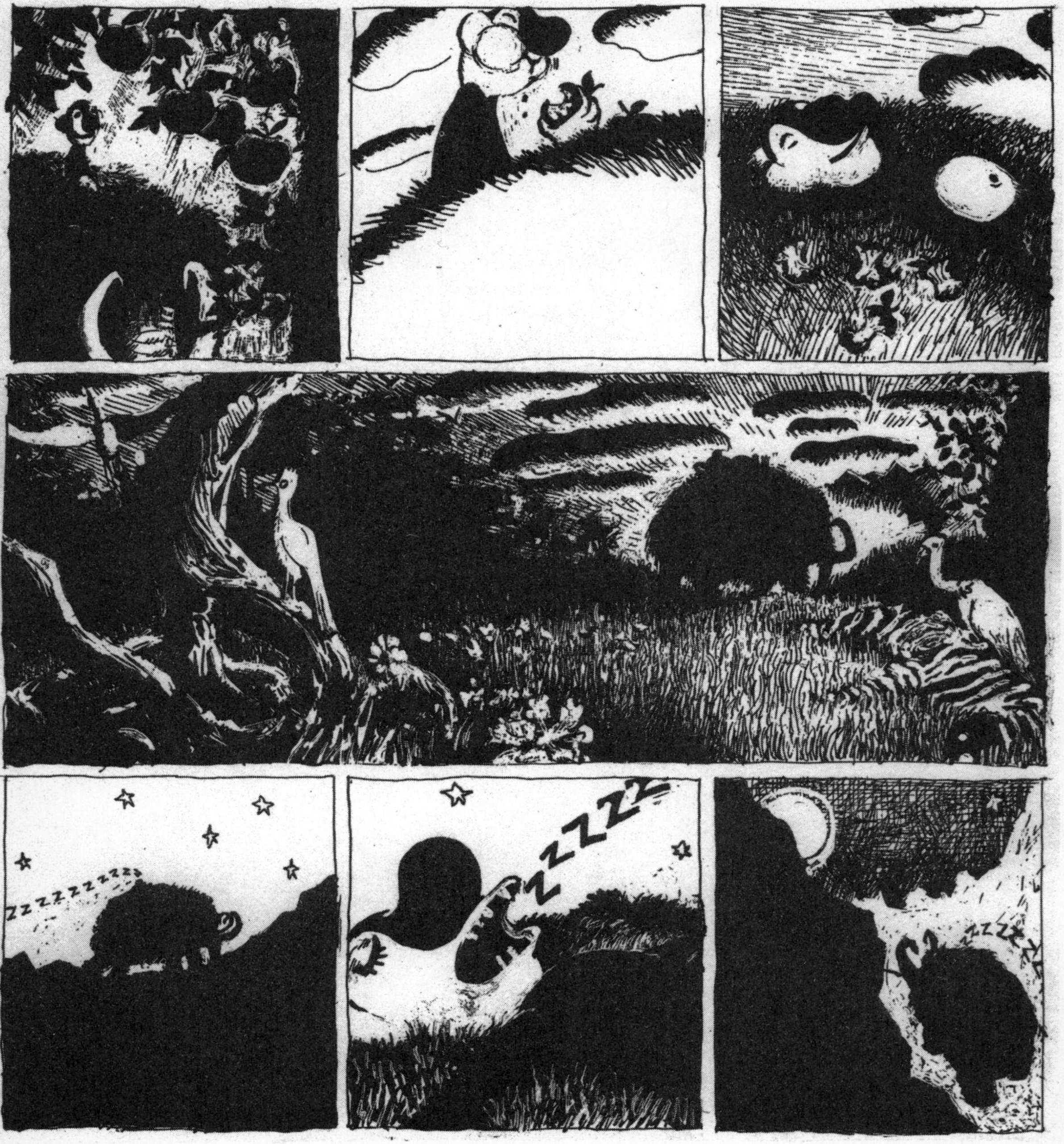

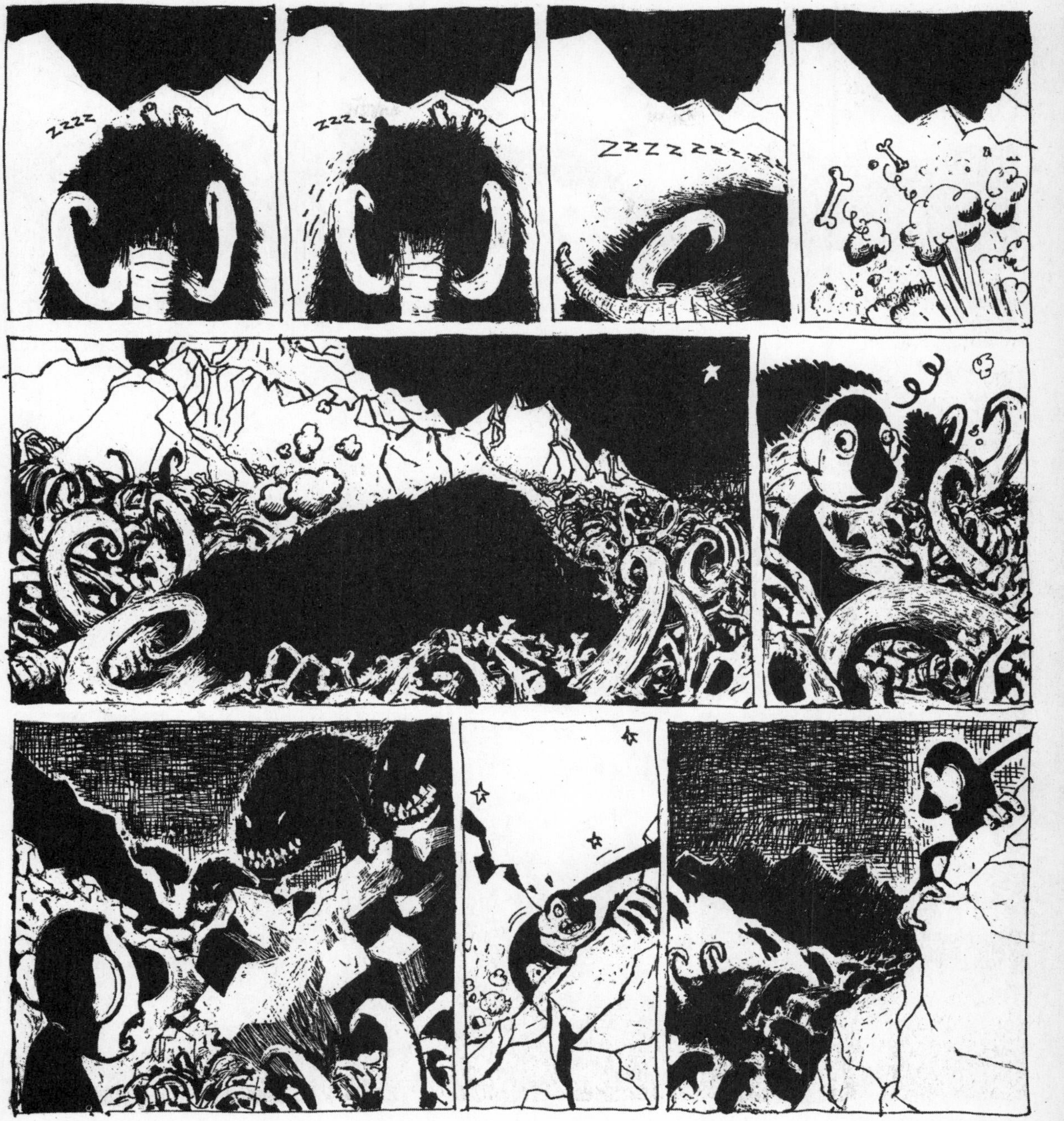
ZZZZ
ZZZZ
ZZZZZZZZZ

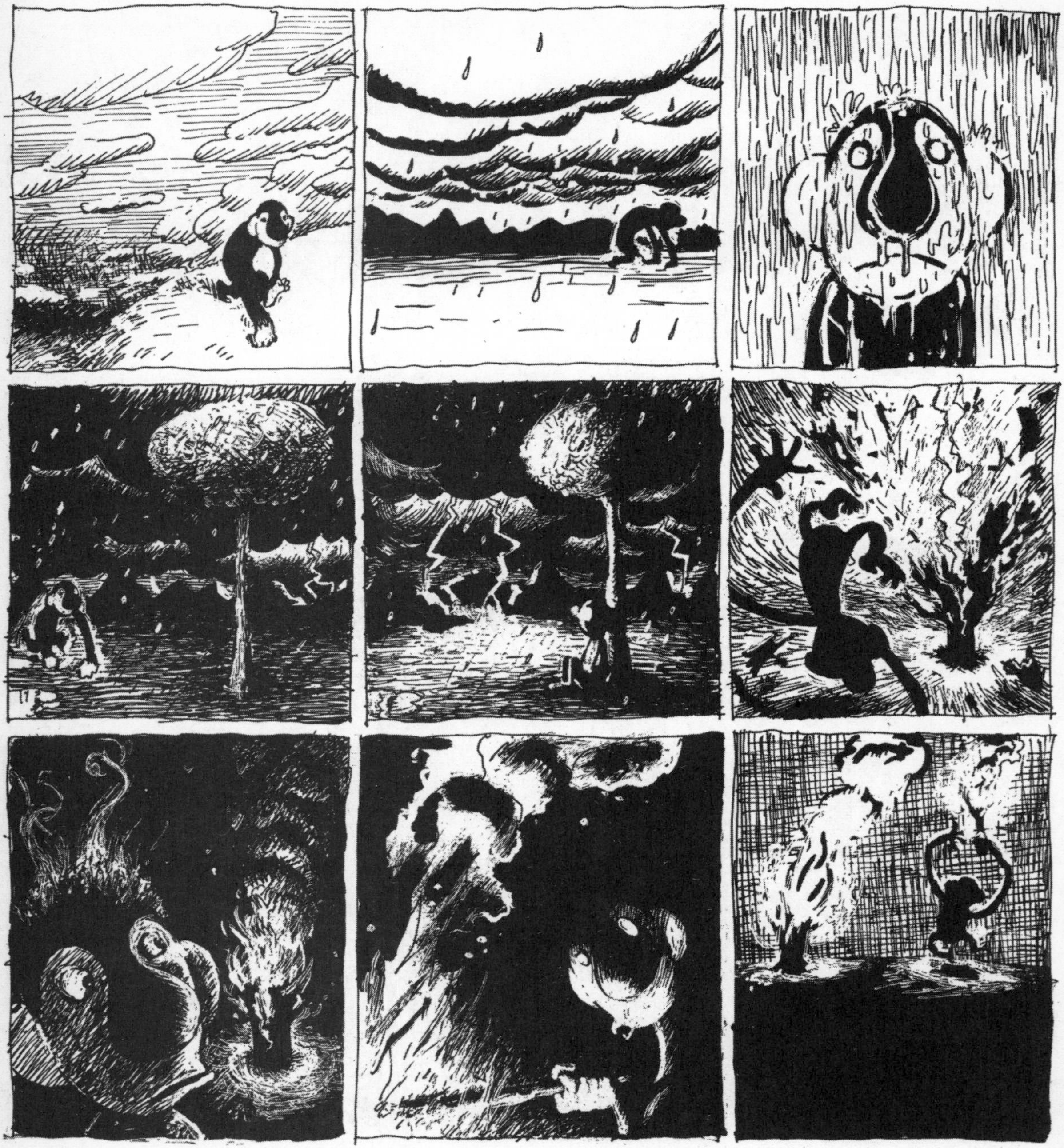

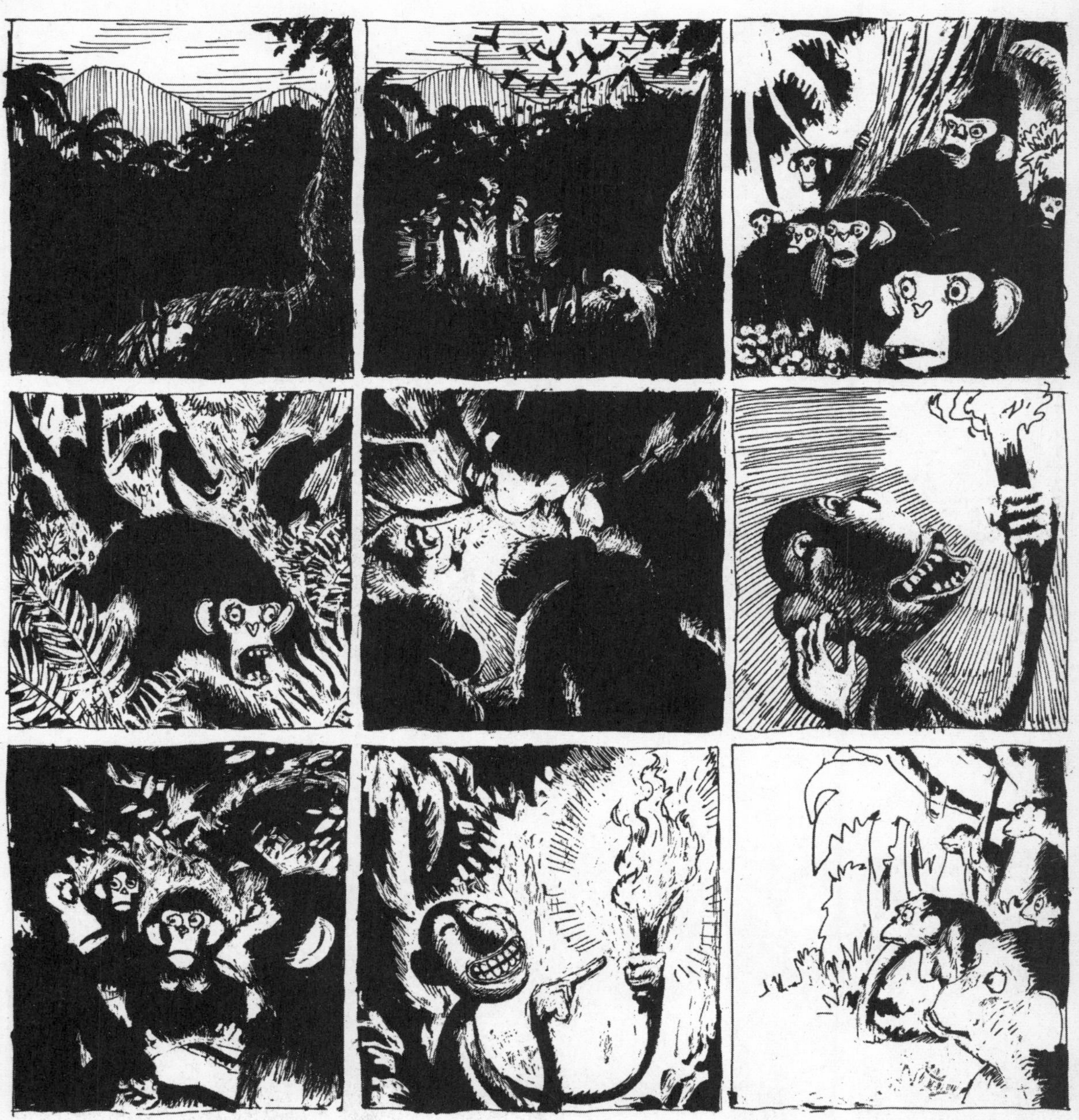

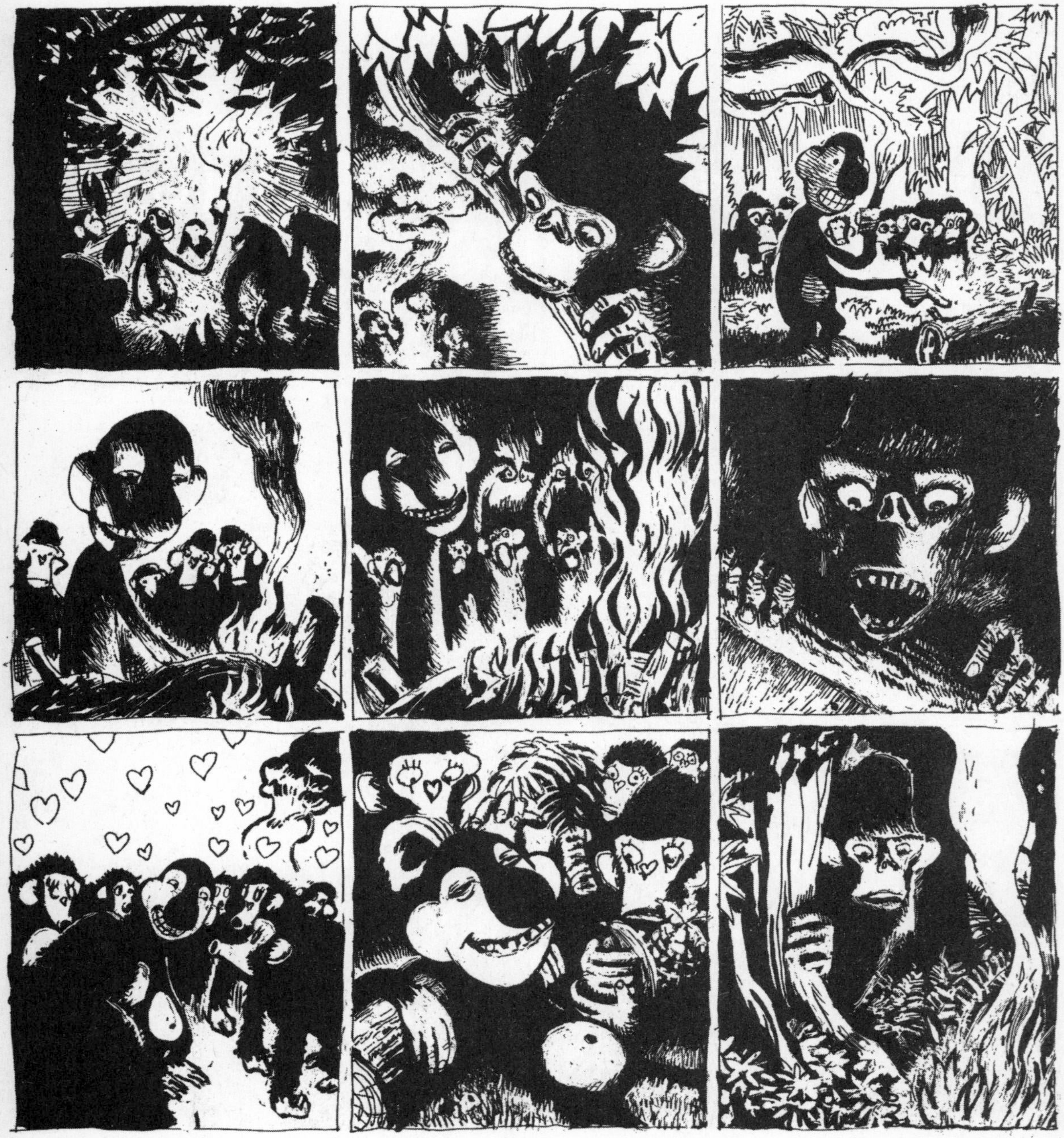

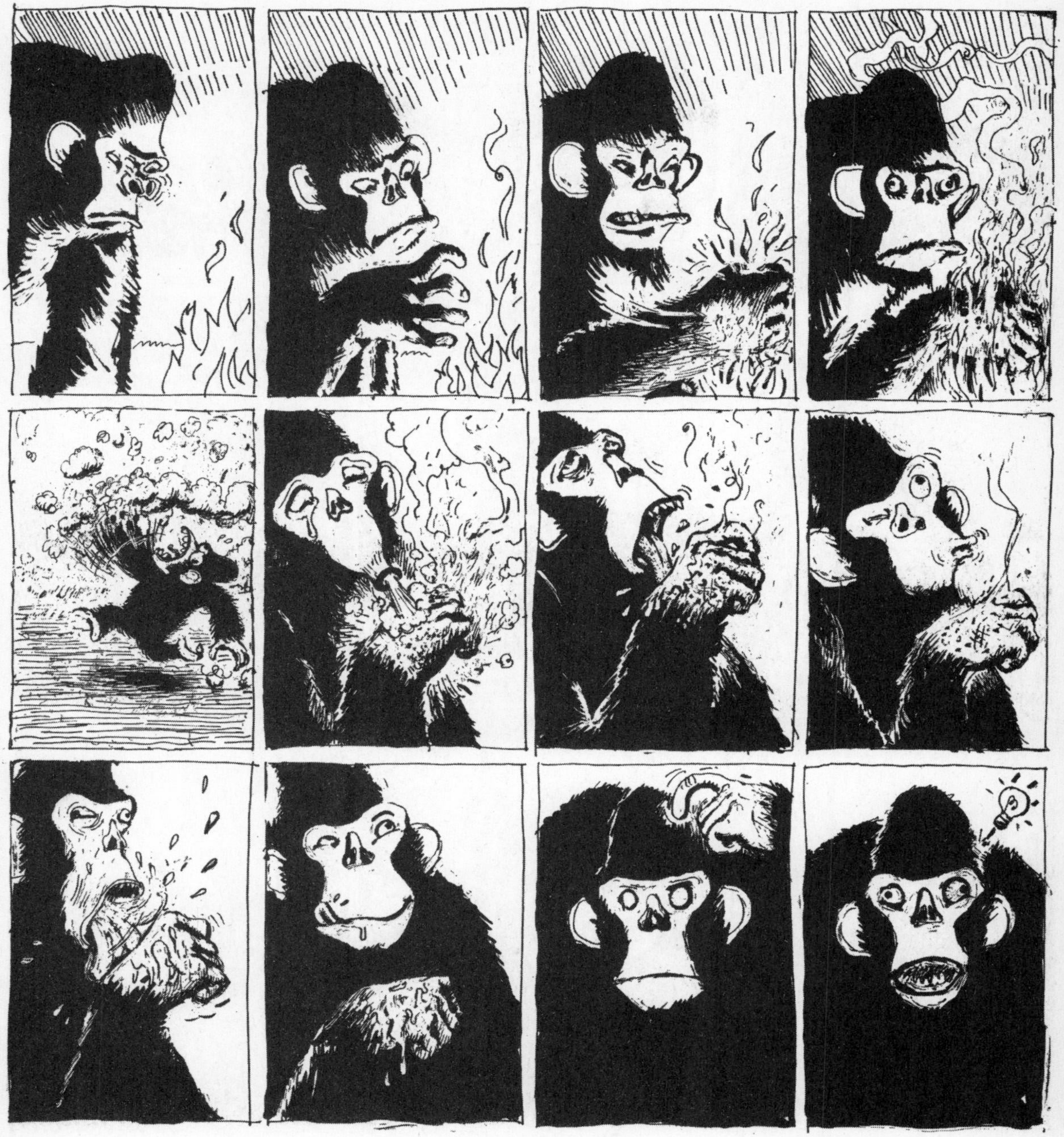

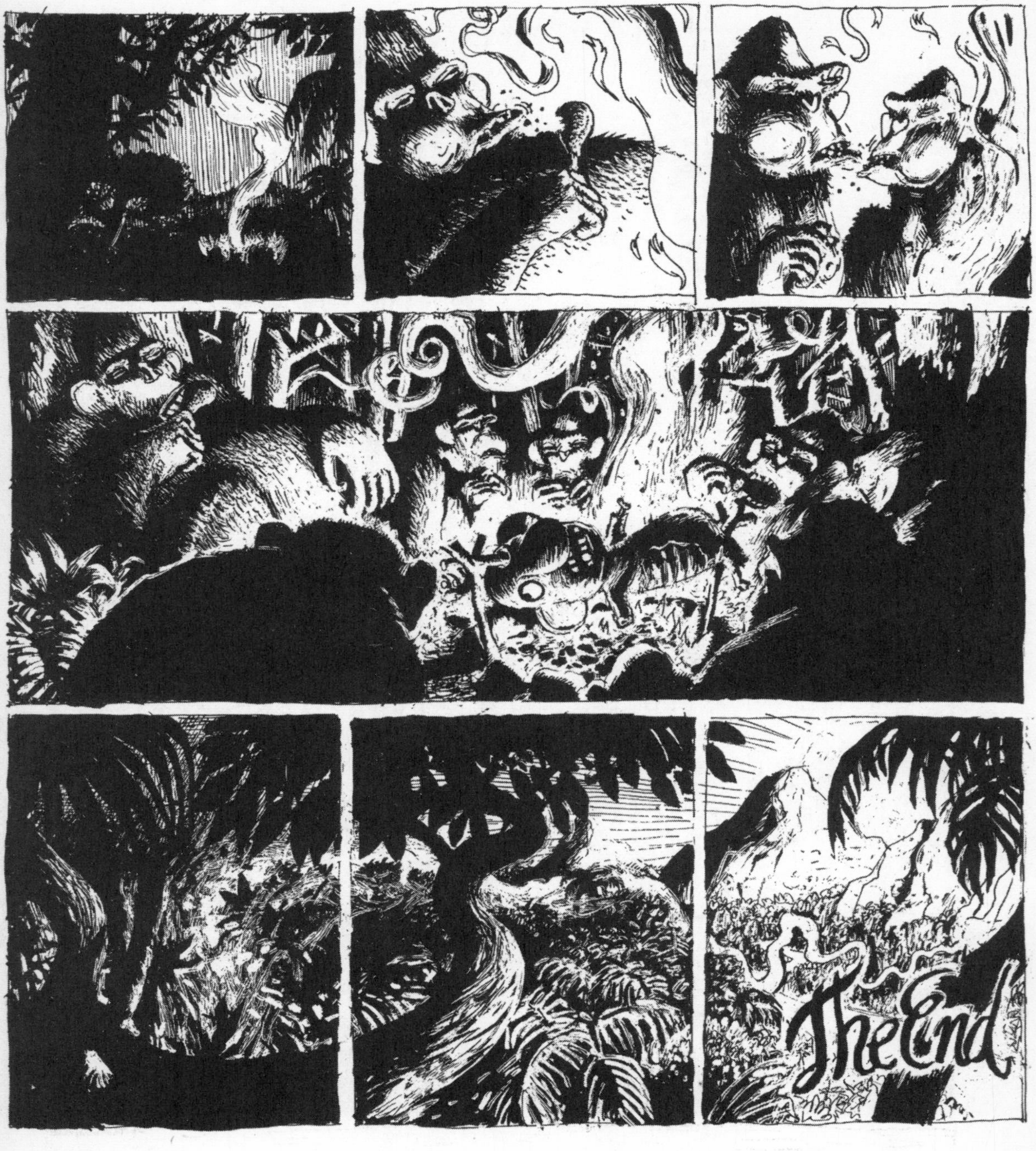
The End

(Bird in a Boat)

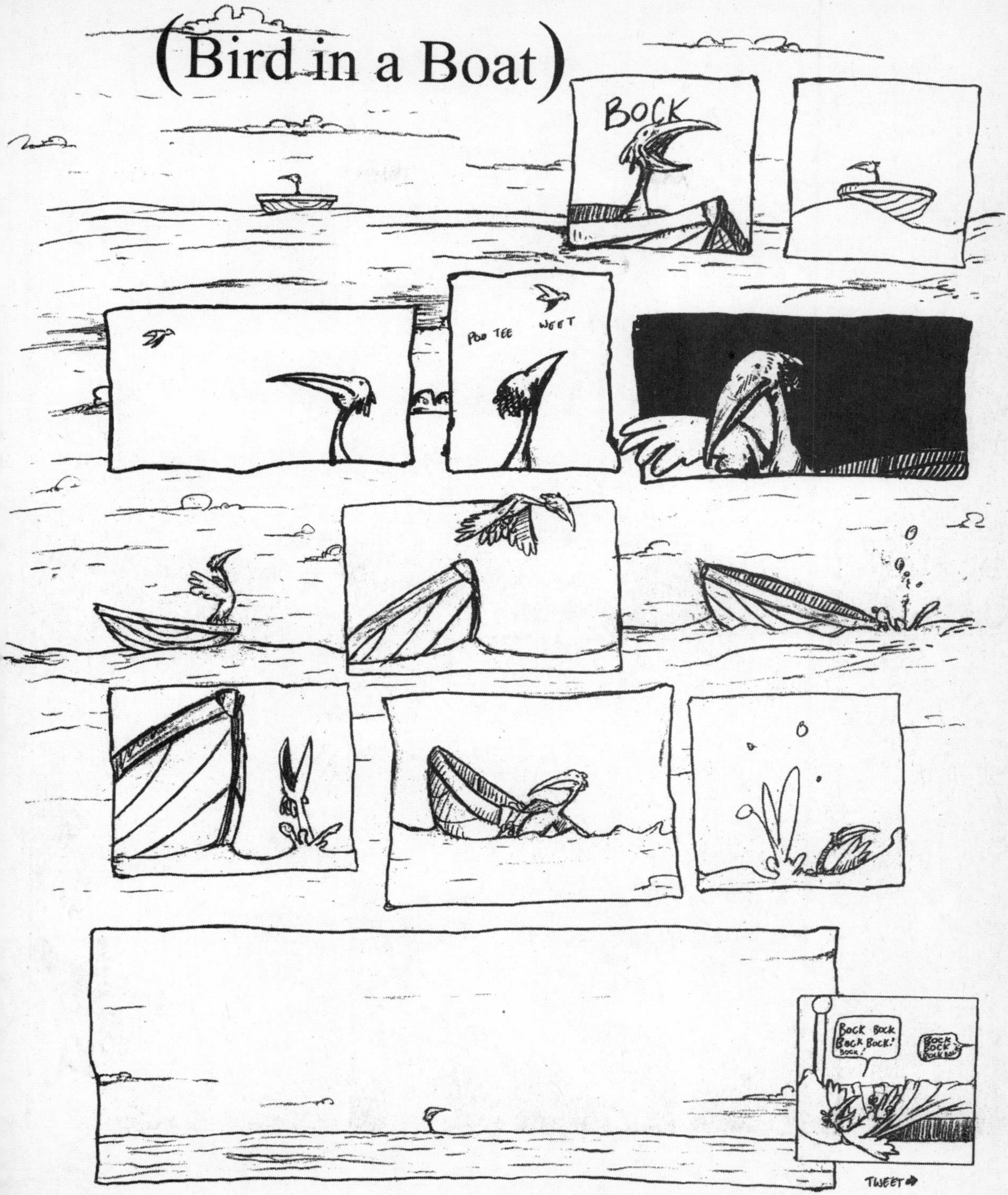
BOCK
POO TEE WEET
BOCK BOCK BOCK BOCK! BOCK!
BOCK BOCK BOCK
TWEET

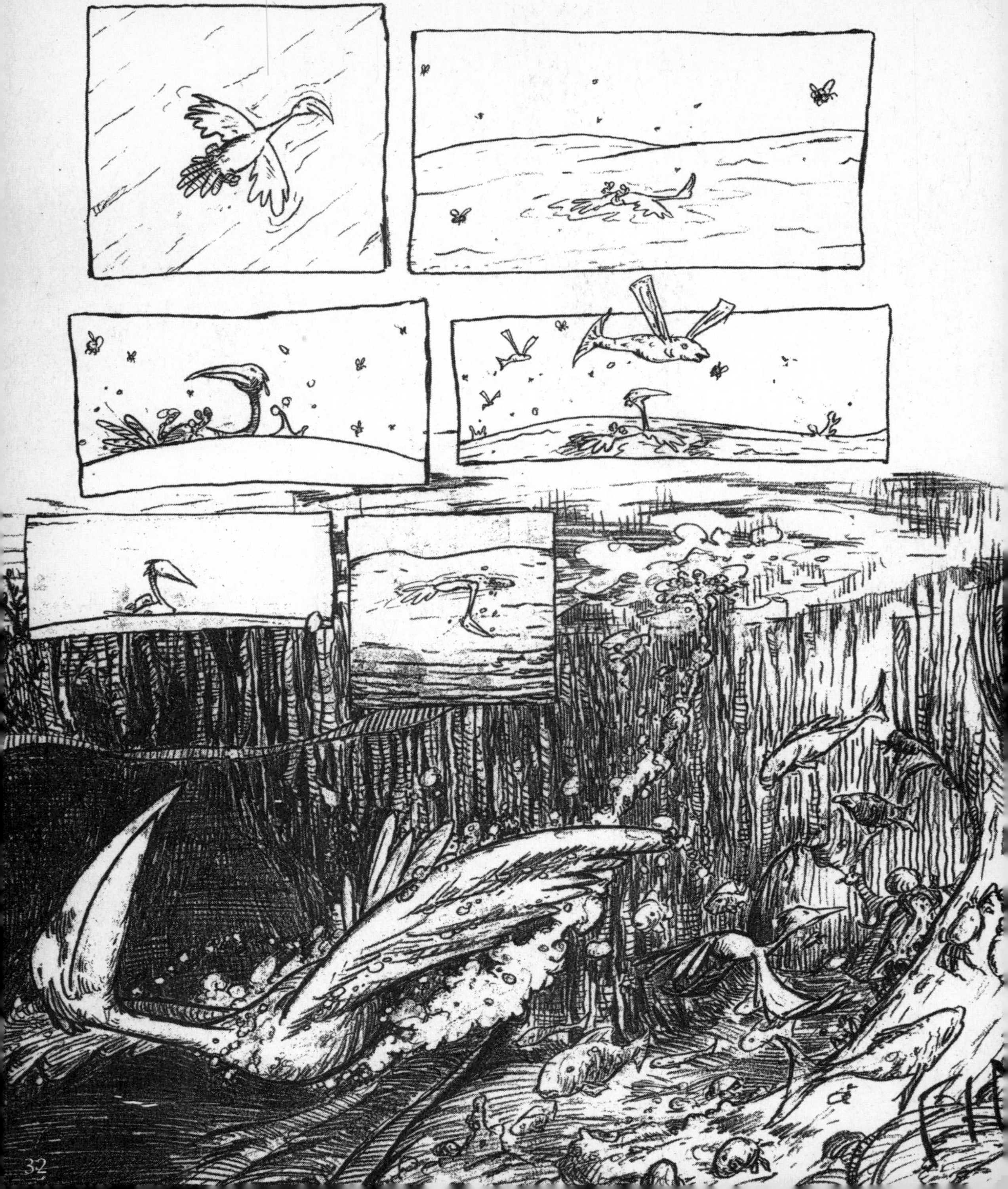

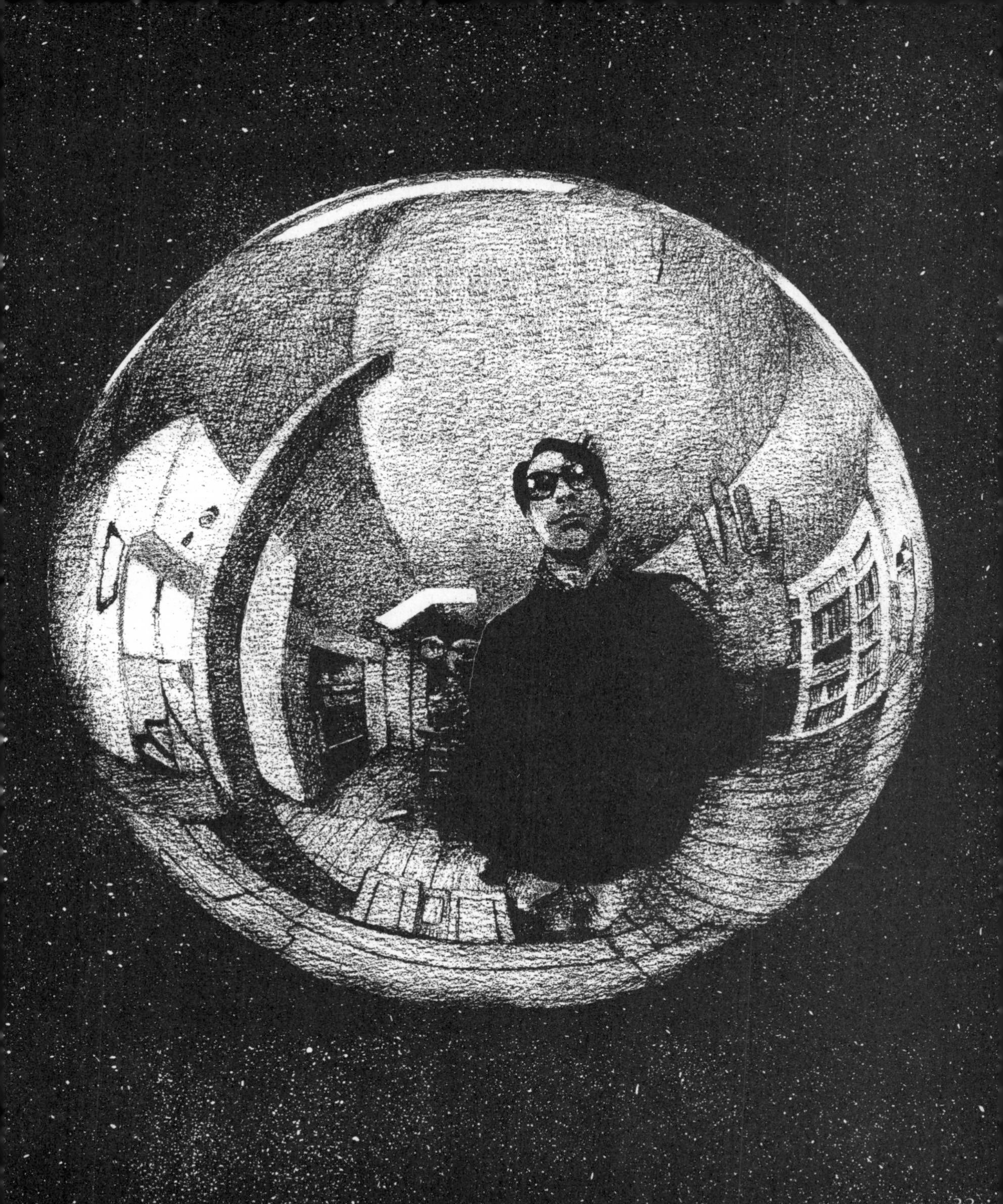

Ladies & Gentlemen... David Chelsea

David Chelsea grew up in Portland, Oregon, but he matriculated 2,600 miles and four time zones away, in New York City. He knows from good cups of coffee and tall, green January trees and he knows how to draw rain in all its soggy splendor, but he's also witty enough, sophisticated enough—urbane enough to have a long-running gig as an illustrator for the *New York Observer*. ¶ Which is not to say Portland is not witty, or sophisticated, or even urbane. It rains in New York after all, where one can get a good cup of coffee, and there are evergreen trees in Central Park—a park designed by Frederick Law Olmstead, whose son, John Olmstead, designed Portland's immense Forest Park. ¶ David Chelsea is an illustrator whose artistry and craft are unmistakable, whether you're looking at his loopy, playful caricatures, or marveling at the solidity of the gorgeous old Portland houses that he tosses off in the background. You can walk into his drawings and up to one of those houses, knock on the front door, step inside and marvel at the architectural detail. ¶ And yet—David Chelsea keeps coming back to comics. Not for the spandex and capecapdes, no; he never went through a Batman and Spider-Man phase, so there's no boyhood nostalgia for him to mine. (Find a cartoonist of the comic book variety and mention "George Perez." You're going to hear something giddily nostalgic, or dismissive [if grudgingly appreciating his ability to render the costumes of 100 different superheroes in one monster splash page], but you're going to hear something. David Chelsea says, "George who?") Chelsea's forebears are older and further afield: *National Lampoon* humor strips, a smattering of the underground, and our shabbily genteel royalty—those newspaper strips grudging accorded the status of "classic" by the mainstream, for all that the strips insist on expatriating themselves to the lowly genre of comics: *Pogo*, *Krazy Kat*, *Little Orphan Annie*. You can see their influence in his linework, and you can hear it in the rhythms of his dialogue—a faint whiff of the anachronistic, almost apocryphal. ¶ But this isn't the slumming of a successful mainstream artist, putting on genre trappings for a lark. Chelsea's comics are vivid, vital, important; *David Chelsea in Love* was one of the earliest and is still one of the best of the influential wave of autobiographical comics—sweet, funny, at once cruelly honest and generously nostalgic. And *Perspective!* isn't just the clearest textbook available on a tricky technique that's resisted centuries of explication; it's also the one true successor to Scott McCloud's seminal *Understanding Comics*, in that *Perspective!* demands we pay attention to just what comics can do and be, as nonfiction, as essays, as powerful engines of instruction. ¶ Portland and New York, comics and fine illustration, grotty caricatures and finicky spherical perspective paintings; thesis, antithesis, synthesis. Opposites attract, because if you look closely enough, you find they aren't opposites at all.

—Kip Manley, 2003

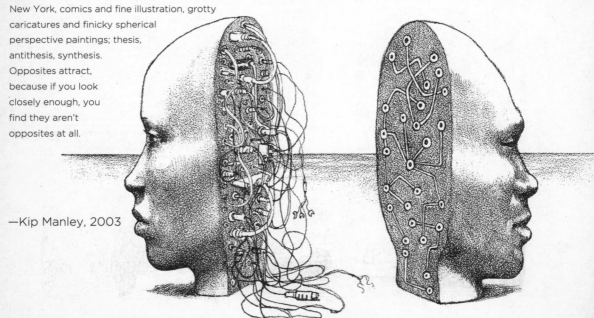

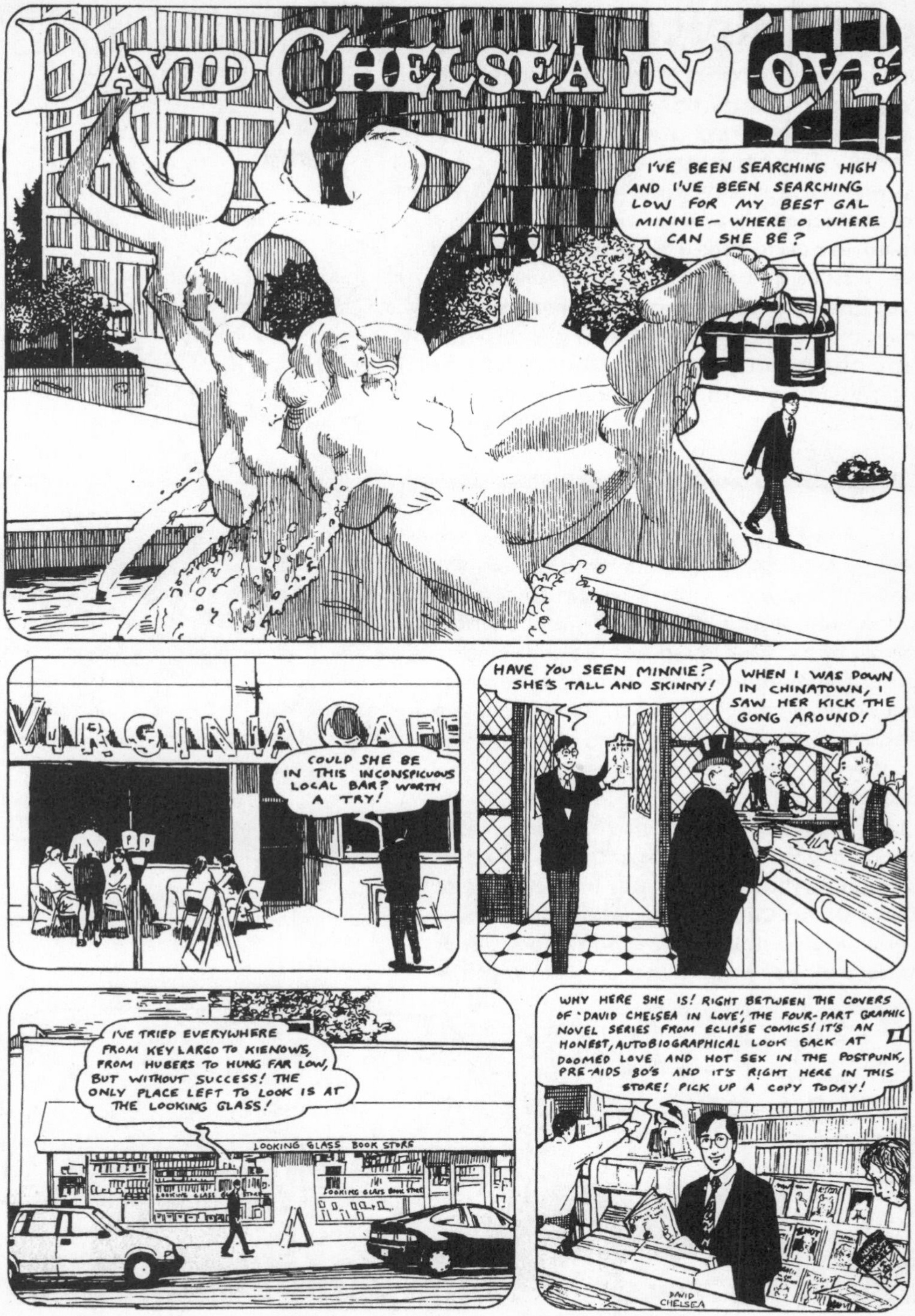
DAVID CHELSEA IN LOVE
I'VE BEEN SEARCHING HIGH AND I'VE BEEN SEARCHING LOW FOR MY BEST GAL MINNIE— WHERE O WHERE CAN SHE BE?
VIRGINIA CAFE
COULD SHE BE IN THIS INCONSPICUOUS LOCAL BAR? WORTH A TRY!
HAVE YOU SEEN MINNIE? SHE'S TALL AND SKINNY!
WHEN I WAS DOWN IN CHINATOWN, I SAW HER KICK THE GONG AROUND!
I'VE TRIED EVERYWHERE FROM KEY LARGO TO KIENOWS, FROM HUBERS TO HUNG FAR LOW, BUT WITHOUT SUCCESS! THE ONLY PLACE LEFT TO LOOK IS AT THE LOOKING GLASS!
LOOKING GLASS BOOK STORE
WHY HERE SHE IS! RIGHT BETWEEN THE COVERS OF 'DAVID CHELSEA IN LOVE', THE FOUR-PART GRAPHIC NOVEL SERIES FROM ECLIPSE COMICS! IT'S AN HONEST, AUTOBIOGRAPHICAL LOOK BACK AT DOOMED LOVE AND HOT SEX IN THE POSTPUNK, PRE-AIDS 80'S AND IT'S RIGHT HERE IN THIS STORE! PICK UP A COPY TODAY!
DAVID CHELSEA

David Chelsea: This half of the floor was my room as a kid. So I used to spend time in this little room.

John Weeks: Right. Must be great that you can come back to your family home and all that. Not so many people have that sort of continuity.

DC: Most people assume that it must be "weird." "It must be weird for you to like, live in the same house that you grew up in." ¶ The answer I have for that is that I moved out in 1978, and my parents didn't preserve my room as a shrine to my teenage years. They rented rooms out, eventually every unemployed musician/actor/deadbeat in Portland passed through this house, so it became like a legendary clubhouse.

JW: What you've labeled "the penniless intelligentsia?"

DC: My parents just needed to make ends meet. So renting out rooms was the tradition in the family. Eighteen years while I was in New York, I would come out and visit and the place would be just full of all these strangers. So that kind of wiped out the memories I had of it being a family home. ¶ When we moved in we fumigated, we did a full renovation, just did our best to obliterate the traces of when this was a flophouse. So now it's on its third life.

JW: Like this house, you've also had multiple incarnations, in your comics. *David Chelsea in Love*, "David Chutney" the performer in *Welcome to the Zone*, David Chelsea the artist in *Perspective!*, now you've got this new book about your acting days in the works. What I liked about the

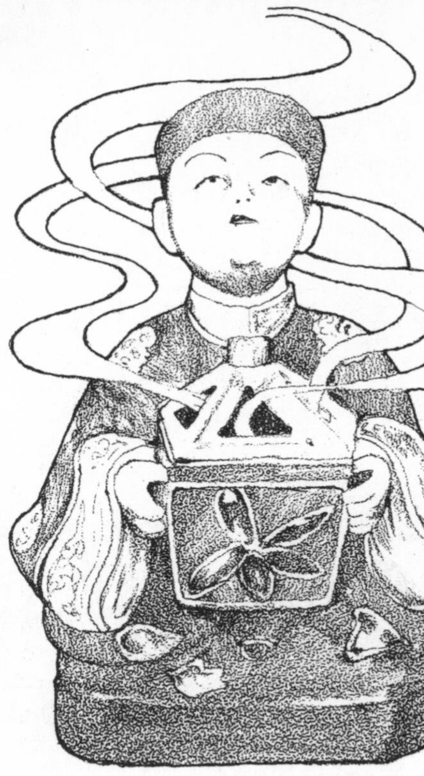

Page 34: Illustration for an article on the differences between the male and female mind, from the *Portland Tribune*.

Page 35: Promotional giveaway intended to publicize both Chelsea's first book and his favorite Portland bookstore. Similar pieces were commissioned for stores in New York, Los Angeles and Chicago.

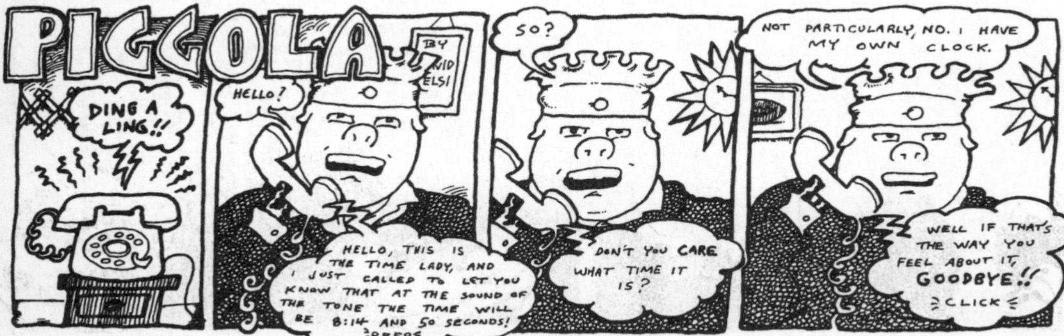
PIGGOLA
DING A LING!!
HELLO?
HELLO, THIS IS THE TIME LADY, AND I JUST CALLED TO LET YOU KNOW THAT AT THE SOUND OF THE TONE THE TIME WILL BE 8:14 AND 50 SECONDS!
BEEP
SO?
DON'T YOU CARE WHAT TIME IT IS?
NOT PARTICULARLY, NO. I HAVE MY OWN CLOCK.
WELL IF THAT'S THE WAY YOU FEEL ABOUT IT, GOODBYE!!
CLICK

Pages 36-37: Typical early strip starring Piggola from the mid-70's. Unpublished.

Page 36: Illustration from the *New York Observer*.

Page 37: Butt-cleavage illustration, from the *New York Observer*.

Page 38: Woody Allen caricature from the *New York Observer*.

Page 39: Alfred Hitchcock, from the *New York Observer*

Pages 40-41: Lobster illustration from the *New York Observer*.

Page 42: Original sketchbook version of an episode from *David Chelsea In Love*, circa 1982, and a version from the series handed out at performances, later redrawn yet again for the graphic novel.

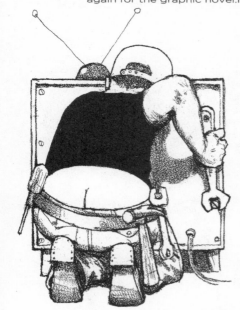

first was that it seemed to be a real, cohesive graphic novel, as opposed to the more common collection of short vignettes that's lumped together and labeled a graphic novel.

DC: Are those so uncommon?

JW: Graphic novels? It's a term that's been applied to everything; "The Spider-Man Graphic Novel."

DC: (Laughter)

JW: *David Chelsea in Love* is closer to the reality of what the term aspires to. ¶ Not to set you up as "Mr. Craft" here, but you have picked up a fair bit of technique. To get the chops you have now under your belt, what did you grow up reading, what schools did you go to—what paths led to your technical acumen?

DC: What I grew up reading has very little to do with how I'm drawing now. When I was a kid I was a fan first of *Mad*, and then *Zap*—actually I went through a period where I was reading a lot of *Archie* comics. ¶ But mostly it was *Mad*, then *Zap* and the *National Lampoon*. I never really went through a phase when I was reading superheroes. It had something to do with that I was going to a hippie school where everyone read *Zap Comics*. It was very uncool, very fascist, very normal-plastic-Disney to like superheroes, so nobody did. ¶ It was the Metropolitan Learning Center, an A.S. Neill type "free school," which actually still exists. It's in Northwest Portland, the old Couch school building. Learning was strictly voluntary, so I got to skip gym for eight years.

JW: Wow.

DC: I barely took math or science, mostly I spent my time there in the art room drawing comic strips. They were mostly *Zap* imitations. ¶ There were a couple of friends of mine, we did jam strips, our character was Piggola, who was this—he was kind of like Wonder Wart-

MAMA MIA! IF THAT TIME LADY IS RIGHT, MY CLOCK IS TWO HOURS FAST! I'D BETTER RESET IT!
DING A LING!!
SKRITCH
SKRITCH
HELLO?
SUCKER!

hog but he didn't have any super powers, and he wore this kind of silly crown-like hat. Just kind of bad-taste adventures. ¶ I would hang out at the library and take out those big collections of *Pogo* and *Krazy Kat*, *Little Orphan Annie*. I was into some of the early newspaper strips. Including *Little Nemo*. ¶ What I didn't realize at the time was how unusual my background was. When I got seriously into doing my own comics in the 90's, and started meeting other comics people, I was shocked to discover that all of them, meaning the mainstream *and* the alternative, they're all ex-fanboys.

JW: Meaning superhero fanboys?

DC: Even a guy like Peter Kuper, he told me he spent the Seventies putting together a fanzine, and he was very proud of getting Frazetta and Kirby originals printed in it.

JW: My gawd.

DC: I may be slagging some people, I don't know about everybody, but my experience is scratch an alternative cartoonist, and (under the surface) you'll find a fanboy.

JW: Well I do know Pete Bagge's claimed that he's never gone through a superhero phase, but aside from him, and everybody working at *Fantagraphics*...

DC: Whenever the *Journal* wants to come out with something like a tribute to Jack Kirby, they can get quotes from everybody, they can get quotes from Chester Brown. You ask me about Kirby, I never heard about Kirby 'til I was thirty years old and read about his dispute with Marvel in the *Village Voice*.

JW: So what's your problem, anyway?

DC: The problem is hanging out with comics people, I kind of feel like a Jew listening to an argument between lapsed and believing Catholics, I just don't know the doctrine.

JW: So perhaps you have a different doctrine.

DC: My doctrine is the Church of Crumb; it all kind of derives from Kurtzman. This whole schism occurred somewhere between Kurtzman and Eisner. Of course, I grew up on the Sixties *Mad*, which Spiegelman and his ilk will tell you is "no damn good," it's the Fifties *Mad* that Kurtzman edited personally that's good. But y'know, I didn't have a choice of what was available

Page 43: An illustration from a series that ran in the *New York Observer* for a while, the Bridget Jones-like diary entries of a fictional New York fashionista Phyllis Stein—actually written by *Observer* fashion reporter Billy Norwich. In this episode, Phyllis visits Windsor Castle.

Page 44: "For several months in 1999 I illustrated a series in the *New York Post* on what life would be like in the new millennium. This drawing ran with one about the future of cars. Unfortunately, this job ended when the new millennium actually arrived."

Page 45: Illustration from the *New York Post* for an article on feng shui in your kitchen.

Page 46-47: 'Mass Transit' and 'Toolbox.' Two of a series of column header illustrations commissioned by the *Portland Tribune*.

Page 48: Richard Nixon a la William Steig, from the *Portland Tribune*.

Page 49: "My computer worked harder than I did on this illustration for a *Portland Tribune* editorial on the mayor's latest highway plan. The streetmap was scanned in sections and put in perspective in Photoshop, and the scissors, the only part of the image actually drawn on paper, were traced directly off scans of two real pairs of scissors, scanned and pasted in as a separate layer."

for my influences.

JW: There were certainly reprints of all that Fifties stuff I'll bet you must have seen.

DC: The first artist I ever seriously tried to copy was David Levine. People like B. Kliban and M.K. Brown were heavy teenage influences, and as I've gotten more into comics I've found I'm very much out on a limb here.

JW: With this influence of Kurtzman and all the *Mad* greats; I recall you went to SVA (The School of Visual Arts, in Manhattan). Did you gravitate to that because folks like Kurtzman and Eisner taught there?

DC: (Ruefully) No, by then I had "left cartooning behind." I was interested in being an illustrator, I actually enrolled in SVA because I heard vaguely it was Milton Glaser's pet school. ¶ I wasn't very impressed with it and I dropped out my freshman year. I was already getting illustration work as a freshman, taking my work around: "This art school is crampin' my style."

JW: It must have been gratifying to get illustration work that young.

DC: It was, and as a result there are probably things I never learned, but basically I have no big regrets. ¶ What is it Dan Clowes calls it? "Day care for twenty-year olds?" He's a fine one to talk, I think he actually got his degree—but he was on scholarship. He went to Pratt.

JW: You made the big move when you were young. You spent a year hanging out in Portland after High School, drawing and hanging out with theatre folks...

DC: You must have got this from *David Chelsea in Love*.

JW: That's right.

DC: I though this was worth mentioning. How would anybody know this? No, go on. People know things about me that I've forgotten because I did this graphic novel about myself.

JW: Comics have a great way of imprinting things in your memory, that's why they're such great teaching tools. You read it as text, you see a picture, and it's that right brain/left brain reinforcement that gets the details of your life

stamped on someone else's cerebellum.

DC: I did go to college a year after high school. Somewhere along the line though I was promoted a grade, so I was the same age as everyone else when I went.

JW: It must have been a big change going from quiet rainy Portland to bustling New York, though you already had a bit of bohemianism under your belt.

DC: Yeah, it was. But I liked New York, and it certainly put Portland in perspective.

JW: And these are the years that are covered in *David Chelsea in Love*.

DC: And actually if you look back on it, they were pretty bleak years.

JW: (Laughter)

DC: Being this lonely freelancer with roommates and living on my cash flow.

JW: You made it sound like fun, maybe it's a tribute to your technique.

DC: Most of the time, not working and looking for work. Being a freelance artist, unless you're really good...

JW: You've gotta hustle.

DC: You've gotta hustle, and there are people who are much better at hustling than I was. I made enough money most of the time to not have to borrow money from my family.

JW: Hustling for money, hustling for art, hustling for love. ¶ You summed up an era in your life, maybe that period of time too—what you've termed the "Pre-Aids Eighties." It's certainly a different kind of sexual etiquette, I think. Some of what people get up to in your books would be considered unconscionable now.

DC: (Laughs) Like what?

JW: Not using condoms, multiple partners.

DC: (Laughs) Well, I haven't been dating post-AIDS, but I suspect that people nowadays get more sex in than is strictly good for them.

JW: I think the real strength of your book is the depiction of a social milieu, which you seem to be looking towards doing in most of your works. You're summing up a scene. It's one of the most comics/visual art literate autobiographical stories that I can think of. Comics greats sit next to classical painters, Mexican Fotonovelas, stuff like *Alley Oop*, Winsor McCay, Crumb, Annie Liebowitz...

DC: This is my background as an illustrator. If you look

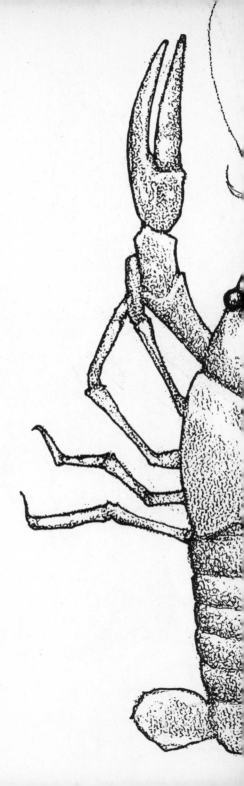

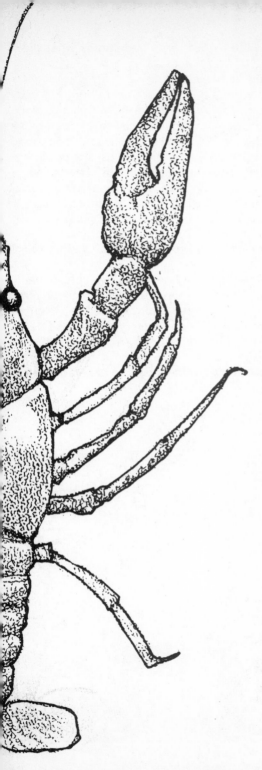

around my studio I have several files devoted to my "clipping morgue." If you get an illustration job, say you have to draw chopped liver in a scale, then you have to find reference for a scale. If you're not gonna be going to the library all the time, it's good to have a picture of a scale sitting around in a nice little file labeled "scale."

JW: I'm disillusioned. So you're not namechecking those people because you like them, you're also using them as a shortcut.

DC: Exactly, that's what illustrators do. With some of them it's more obvious than others, but an "illustrator" is often a very fancy kind of collagist. There are illustrators who are actually collage artists. It all starts with photo reference. ¶ Well, not all, but it all seems to come around to photo reference eventually. So because I have all this reference already, it seemed very easy to incorporate that.

JW: Right. It may have been easy for you to incorporate this visual reference you worked hard to assemble and access—what about accessing your personal life? Was it difficult to negotiate what scenes got in, and what got cut? 'Cause some of this stuff is very explicit.

DC: Nobody else got a vote. At the time I was young and fearless and had nothing to lose, also what I had seen was R. Crumb and Harvey Pekar and a little bit of Joe Matt. I hadn't seen much autobiographical stuff before I started on the book. ¶ In order to play in those leagues, you have to lay yourself out there.

JW: Was there an element of catharsis in getting this story out of your system?

DC: Yes, yes. I'm far less angry about this, a failed romance I had about seventeen or eighteen years ago, having had the book published, than I was before. Then I was burning with a story to tell. Now, it's water under the bridge.

JW: How did people in the book take it? What were the responses you got? Nobody's threatened to beat you up, I hope.

DC: Nobody's threatened to beat me up. Probably most of the people in the book haven't seen it. ¶ The one person who had a very strong negative response was my sister Anny. I'm still not exactly clear on what she objects to. She said [hurt tone] "You showed me doing stuff in that book I'm not really proud of." I guess she was under the impression that I'd soften it somehow. I still don't really understand what she's embarrassed about.

JW: And the person that the central character "Minnie" is based on?

DC: Well, true to form, she's had different responses. When I first let her know about it, I said, "You don't have to look at it if you don't want." She said, "No, no, I want to see it, I'm trying to work out a stand-up routine, and I think there might be some material I could use." So I sent it to her and she thought it was very funny. She said she really liked the Sam Shepard scene. I hadn't been that much in touch with her in the years before that. Then we kind of got to be friends, she got to be very good friends with my wife, and they used to hang out together with her kids. After about a year, suddenly she decided she was angry about it, really enraged about what I'd put in the book, didn't want to be friends anymore, so then we weren't friends. ¶ After a year or so she softened and said, "Okay, we can be friends again" and we were friends, sort of wary friends 'cause you get burned enough times; my wife said, "Okay, now I realize she is like she was in that book."

JW: I believe you've mentioned that your wife Eve has laid down some edict that she'd like to be off-limits for future treatment on that score.

DC: Um, yes, certainly nothing as explicit as what I did in *David Chelsea in Love*. ¶ Basically I started doing very primitive versions of the book even during the timeframe the book covers. Whenever a girlfriend of mine would start seeing those strips in my sketchbook, she'd say "You're never going to put me in one of those." And make me promise. I promised every woman I've been involved with since then, that I'm not gonna do a number on her. ¶ I'm pretty much restricted in material up to about Nineteen Eighty-Four.

JW: So it started in your sketchbook I guess. You submitted some strips to (Fantagraphics publisher) Gary Groth and Art (*RAW*) Spiegelman.

DC: Somebody from *Raw* wrote me and said it was "Perfect for the *National Lampoon*, but not for us." Pete Bagge also turned me down when he was editing *Weirdo*.

CHAPTER SEVENTEEN
THE FOURTH OF JULY
HEY DAVID LETS GO MEET MINNIE AFTER SHE GETS OFF WORK!
OK
Y'KNOW, VERA, I'M GOING TO TURN OVER A NEW LEAF
OH?
I'M GOING TO STOP MAKING ALL THOSE SNIDE JOKES THAT ALWAYS MAKE MINNIE FURIOUS. WATCH TO SEE I DON'T
OK
WANT TO MAKE A BET ABOUT HER MOOD? I SAY SHE'LL BE IN A GOOD ONE
I'M NOT GOING TO TOUCH THAT ONE

CHAPTER 24: THE FOURTH OF JULY
HEY DAVID, LETS GO MEET MINNIE AFTER SHE GETS OFF WORK!
OK
Y'KNOW, VERA, I'M GOING TO TURN OVER A NEW LEAF.
OH?
I'M GOING TO STOP MAKING THOSE SNIDE REMARKS THAT ALWAYS MAKE MINNIE FURIOUS. WATCH TO SEE THAT I DON'T.
OK
WANT TO MAKE A BET ABOUT HER MOOD? I SAY SHE'LL BE IN A GOOD ONE!
I'M NOT GOING TO TOUCH THAT ONE.
POW

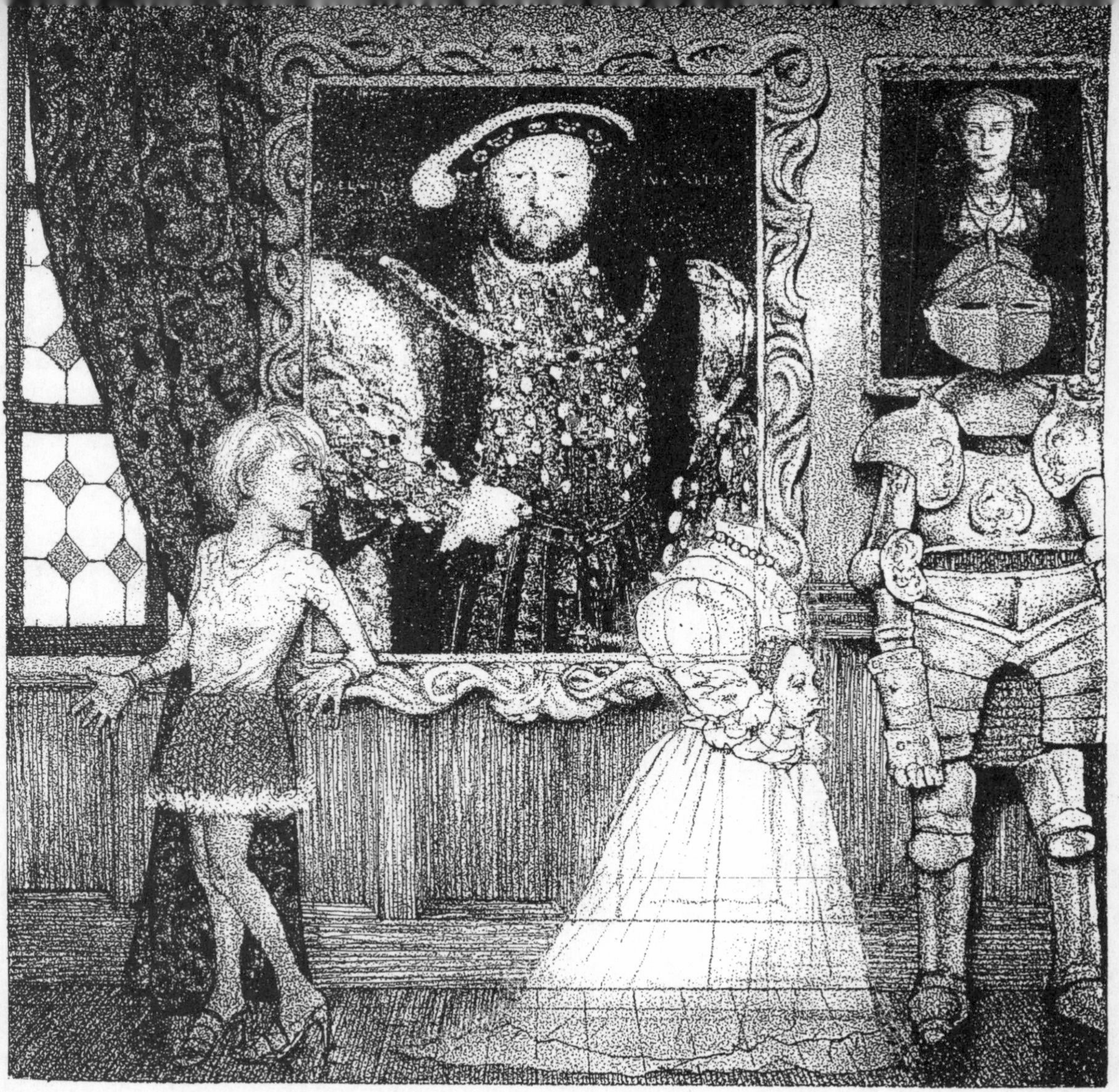

JW: So you were going to pitch it as an alternative newsweekly strip?

DC: Groth saw it, and he wasn't interested in the newsweekly type approach. I actually give him full credit, he was the one who said "This should be a graphic novel." And when I read his letter I said "Jeez, I've gotta do this whole thing over on spec." ¶ I didn't have anything better to do so I started working on it as a graphic novel.

JW: And then after the first thirty pages it got picked up by Eclipse.

DC: I kept sending work to Groth and he kept saying nice things about it, but he never sent me a contract. So I thought I'd better send it around somewhere else.

JW: One of the last books Eclipse did.

DC: Yeah, it would have been better if I'd been picked up by Fantagraphics—cause (laughs) they're still going.

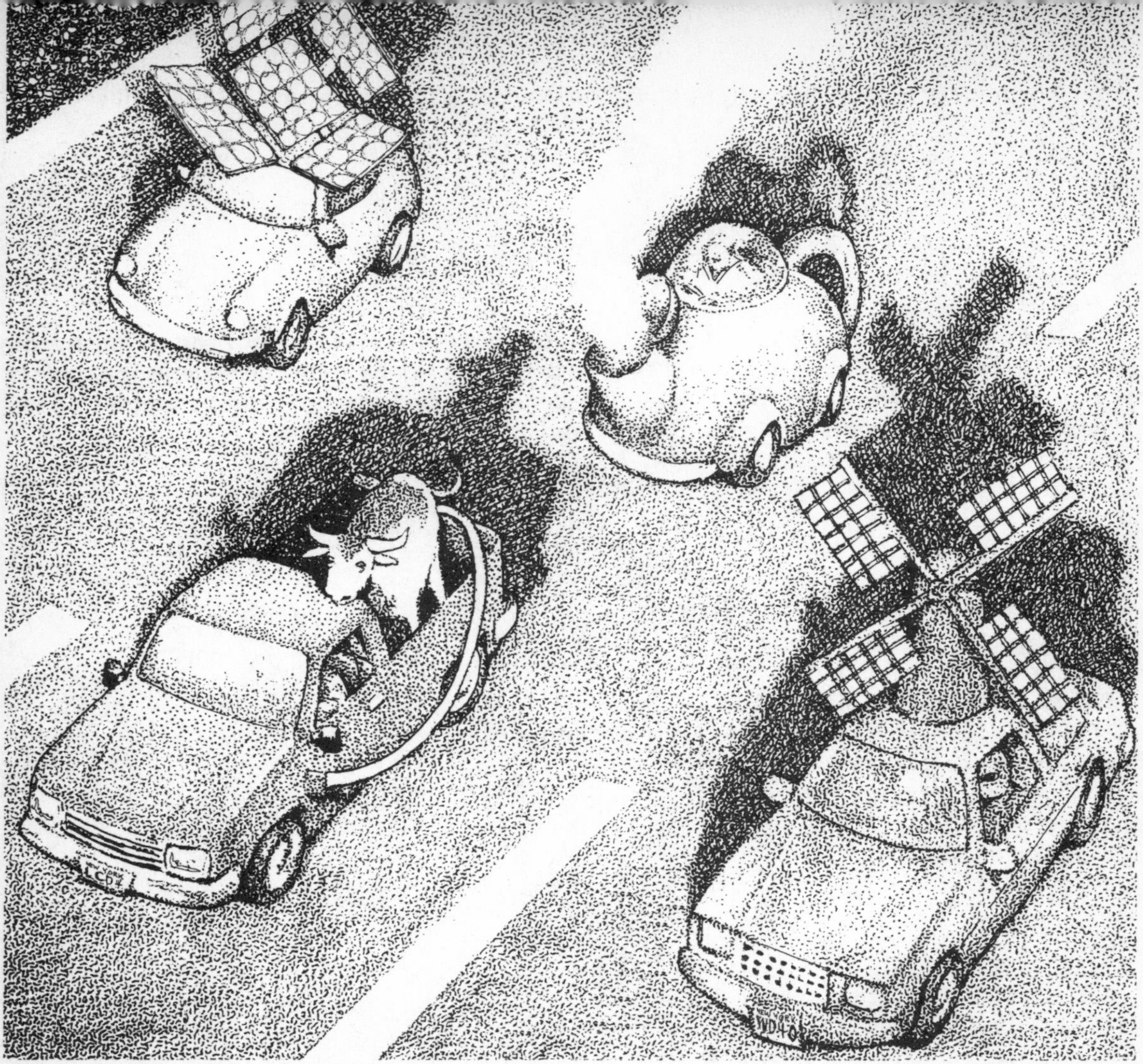

JW: Eclipse also published your earlier version, the weekly strips. They printed them in the weekly *Comics Buyers' Guide*; a readership more of fanboys instead of your urban sophisticate target audience.

DC: They printed them as a part of their weekly ad page. I didn't really appreciate it at the time, I was like, "Well, it's not costing them anything, since they buy that page every week anyway." ¶ But in fact, probably more people know my work from those ads. I hadn't realized how ubiquitous the *CBG* was in the industry.

JW: So they don't know you from *Details*, they don't know you from the illustration work you've done?

DC: Illustration is completely ephemeral, it wraps fish. It's just a peculiarity of our culture. ¶ People respond to cartoonists, they stick *Cathy* and *Dilbert* up on our refrigerators. Even if someone is completely blown away by an illustration, they will usually not think to cut it out and stick it on their wall.

JW: The only person looking for the name of an illustrator in a magazine is another illustrator, or an editor.

DC: Or a peculiar kid like me whose mom was a graphic designer. Anyway, when I first started going to comics conventions...

JW: "You're the *In Love* guy."

DC: Yeah! Distributors and retailers would all know me. I think a lot of people weren't aware that the comic was anything different. Many probably thought it was a collection of those *CBG* strips. ¶ Eclipse never throws out its leftovers, so my strip had a second life.

JW: Not only do you have two totally different careers as a comics creator and an illustrator, you've also been a performer, in I guess what has been termed the "Anti-Folk" scene, the subject of your second graphic novel, *Welcome to the Zone*. This one was printed as a graphic novel, no chapter breaks, it wasn't serialized beforehand.

DC: I was always something of a ham, but my first ten or so years in New York I didn't do anything about it. When I was a teenager I used to be part of this alternative theater in Portland called The Storefront Theater, I was in the "beating heart of show business," somehow when I got to New York I just stopped doing that. ¶ Eventually I got to be friends with people who were performance artists and poets. One fellow that I knew slightly had an open mike every week, and I went down and did some of the doggerel poems that I'd written over the years. It took me three weeks to use up all the poems I'd written over the last fifteen years. So I started doing new stuff, and it just started to be a habit for me.

JW: So these were spoken word performances?

DC: Mostly spoken word, also songs. As I got into it there were more and more songs.

JW: Like a cabaret thing.

DC: Exactly. So I would write new lyrics to "Walk Don't Run." I started writing my own songs. Eventually I graduated from the open mikes to doing shows, opening for some other acts at local performance clubs. ¶ I was really in over my head, for a while I was working with a band. I had no musical background whatsoever, don't play an instrument, can't read music, can barely keep in

the same key.

JW: But this was the Anti-Folk world, where everything was acoustic, few had much more than a guitar anyway.

DC: I didn't even have that.

JW: Punk without amps.

DC: Right.

JW: Brenda Kahn, Cindy Lee Berryhill, Michelle Shocked...

DC: Some of them got signed. Funny thing about that scene is that it seemed to be only the women that ever got any success out that. It was mostly guys, but...

JW: There's John S. Hall (of King Missile), Beck...

DC: Beck might have been part of that after I left. Much much younger than I am. There's still some kind of vestige of that scene going on in the East Village. This guy—Lach—I think still has this open mike going.

JW: The Fort.

DC: The last time I was in New York it was still going.

JW: So *The Zone* is your surreal take on the East Village scene.

DC: My dish on it. What *Zone* reminds me of—looking at these comics you forgot here the other day—is Jeff Nicholson's rant on the Small Press Scene. [Jeff Nicholson's *Small Press Tirade*].

JW: That one gives me a headache.

DC: Just beating up on himself and everyone else for being such amateurs, unable to make any money selling their xeroxed mini-comics. That's pretty much what I was doing, beating up on everybody for being such losers.

JW: This is one thing I've noticed in your work. You don't take a very strong political or

aesthetic stance, but you really seem to enjoy skewering hypocrisy and pompousness. If there's one thing that you nail to the wall, it's people that are false.

DC: I actually think I'm harder on naiveté. Yes, the people in *The Zone* are very naive in that they believe that they're getting somewhere. I'm very blatant about how all of them are losers and no one's getting anywhere! They're all just kidding themselves and they should just go out and get a job at Kinko's or something.

JW: They're all ambitious enough to cheat someone out of their performance slot if, say, they think Bob Dylan is in the audience.

DC: Exactly. One comic you didn't mention is one of my few anthology pieces, called "Gay Catholics: Silliest People in the World." Again, they seem impossibly naive. You believe in a church that says you go to hell. What's not to understand?

JW: Hypocrisy and naiveté. Hey, is Tompkins Square Park located near the Lower East Side?

DC: It's in the Lower East Side. That's where there was a famous riot in 1988, the shining moment of East Village activism. What was the predicating issue? A rock concert that went on too late.

JW: So the police had to break it up and bust heads.

DC: Yeah, the police went out of control and really did bust some heads. It was a little bit like Chicago, a really ugly crowd. Tompkins Square Park, for a certain generation of East Village Activists, is kind of like Spain is for lefties, or Berkeley's free speech movement is for Sixties radicals.

JW: You also hint at the flyering issue which was pretty big in the Eighties.

DC: Actually a woman I know did a flyer for her boyfriend; it was his band—no, it was for his marbling business. He had a studio that did faux marbling. And she, out of the goodness of her heart, (and because she was a doormat), printed up flyers and stuck them to lampposts.

JW: And promptly got arrested.

DC: And got stuck with a twenty-three hundred dollar fine because they fined you for every single flyer they found.

JW: Even if your name is on the flyer, how can they prove you've put 'em up? What if it's a promoter?

DC: One of my flyers got cited for this, I put the address and the number of the club I was playing at. Actually it was a comic strip on how to get to the place. That got cited. The police only found one of them. They were gonna fine Dixon Place (the club) fifty dollars. The woman, Elly Covan, who ran the place called me up and told me about this and I said "Oh, I'm sorry, I'll pay the fifty dollar fine." She said "No, I'm gonna fight this." ¶ She went down and she showed up in court—and she beat the rap.

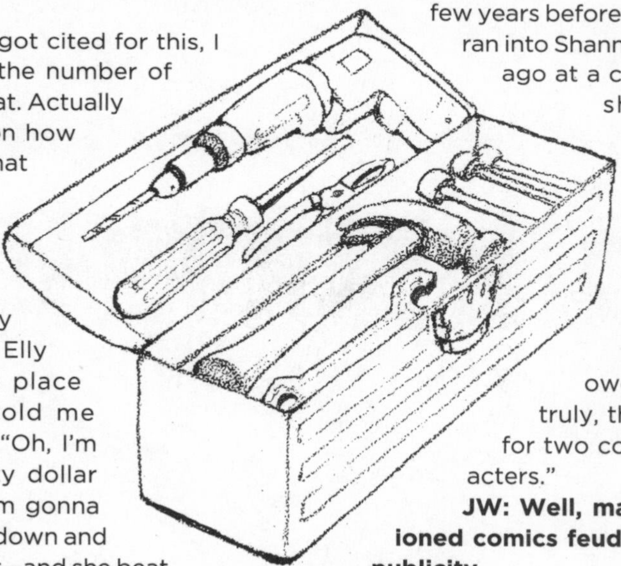

JW: I remember hearing of it with the case of Bob Z, another punk (punk folkie even?) guy, which was a big deal in *Factsheet Five*.

DC: This is all ancient history, eventually that law was overturned. It was a cash cow for the Sanitation Police for a while.

JW: Right. "Sanitation Police." Someone who pops up in *Welcome to the Zone* is Mugg, and he also makes an appearance in your latest book, the *Perspective!* book.

DC: Yeah, Mugg is just a character I had in this soup kitchen that went around feeding the homeless whether they wanted to be fed or not. Mugg is the character who has the hot coffee pouring out of his head. ¶ For some reason people really responded well to Mugg. He's got this sort of W.W. Denslow fixed grin, smiling face.

JW: A little manic, but friendly.

DC: So when I was casting about for some character to be the interlocutor for *Perspective!*, I kind of settled on him...

JW: ...as a coffee-swilling comics artist.

DC: *Welcome to the Zone* was published a few years after *Too Much Coffee Man* was published, but my proposal was knocking around a few years before *Too Much Coffee Man*; I ran into Shannon Wheeler a few years ago at a comics convention, and showed him an early proposal for *Welcome to the Zone*. "Just in case people come to you and say 'Chelsea's ripping you off.' This is something I've been working on for a few years and it owes nothing to you—and truly, the world is big enough for two coffee cup headed characters."

JW: Well, maybe a good old-fashioned comics feud could get you a little publicity.

DC: (Laughter) Besides, Mugg doesn't have a coffee cup on his head—his head is a coffee cup. There's a difference!

JW: Okay, so: perspective. Why bother? Why learn it? Especially if you're a cool alternative comics creator. What's in it for me? That's what I want to know.

DC: (Laughs) Well, I regard perspective as having saved me from slavish dependence on the photograph. As an illustrator with a fairly realistic style, which is what I was in the early Eighties; I was actually a student of Jim McMullan. After I dropped out of SVA, I took his illustration class in night school for a few years. ¶ His work is very

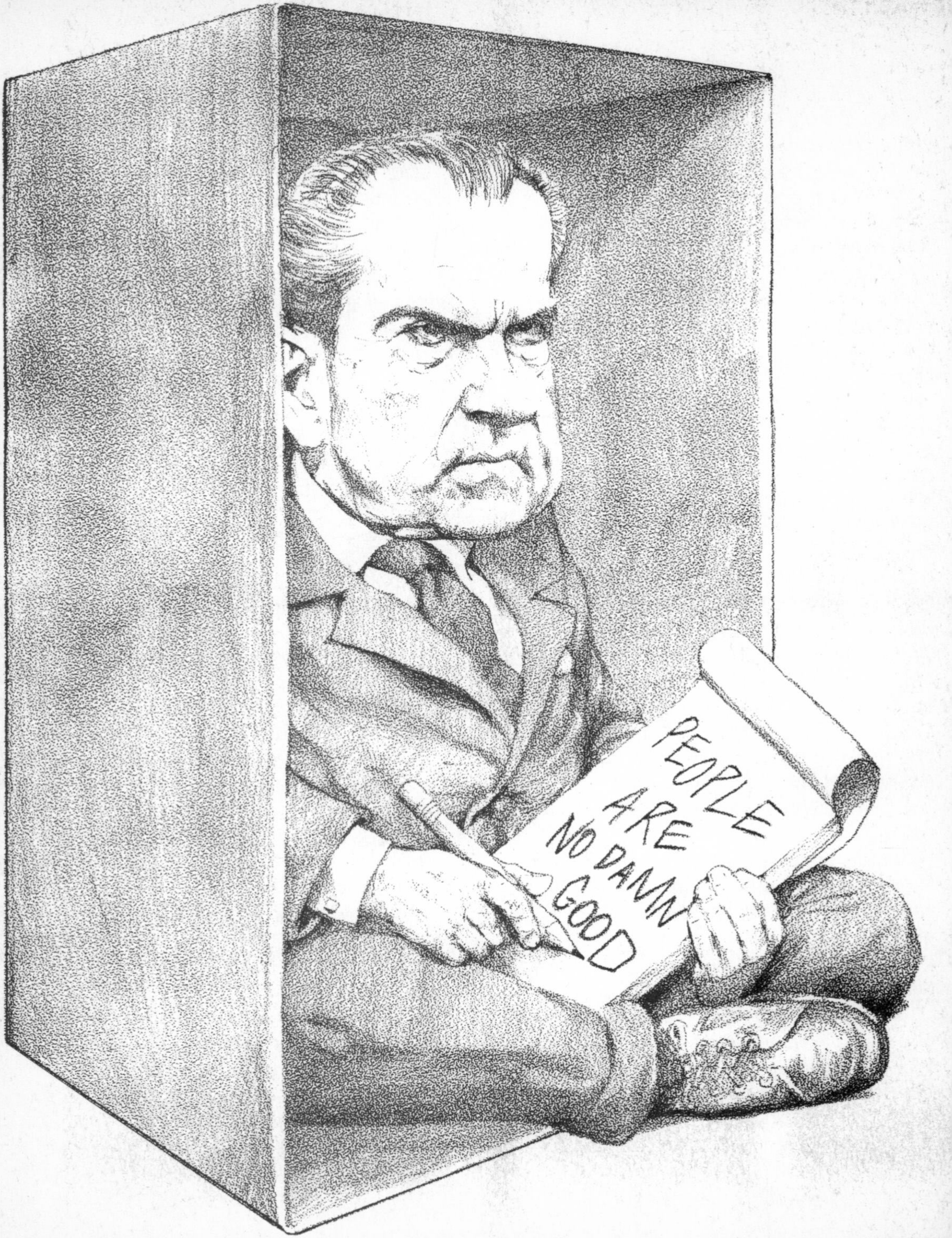
PEOPLE
ARE
NO DAMN
GOOD

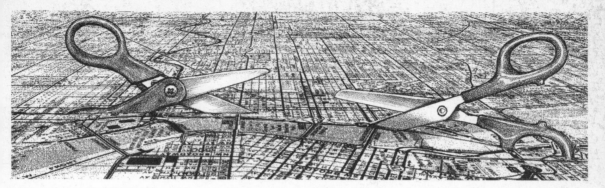

nice, pretty, puddled watercolor, mostly based on photo reference. So it has that underlying reality. I was trying to do something in the same style. I was finding that it was very hard to find photo reference for everything. ¶ I had a job where I had to show some murder victims lying on a tile floor. I didn't know how to do the floor. I could do it in one point perspective, but that was kind of boring. I hadn't gotten far enough in Art School to do two point perspective, so I knocked on the door of the woman in the next apartment, I knew she was a graphic designer. "Do you have any books on perspective?" ¶ She had this one book which was called *Architectural Graphics*, by Frank Ching, which did have some instructions on how to set up perspective. Going through this book, laboriously, step-by-step, I managed to set up a plausible scene, with the tile going the right way. ¶ Something just clicked, I got hooked. I started getting more books on perspective, eventually I found a class where I could learn perspective, and it just got more and more interesting to me.

JW: You can do tricks.

DC: Yes. Well, Winsor McCay knew this, it was very important for him to know perspective. He said something along the lines of, "You waste a lot of brain power trying to get the look of things just right if you don't know perspective." But if you do, then you can simply ask yourself, "What is the point of view from which I'd like to draw this thing?" ¶ Later I studied anatomy, and learned a lot that way. But to me perspective is even more important. It made a dramatic improvement in my work, more or less overnight.

JW: The anatomy stuff in that last chapter—Camp Meat N' Greet, Sub-Nudist Colony...very surreal.

DC: The reason why I did that anatomy chapter was that originally I'd done that chapter in a nudist camp. My wife looked at it and said, "Oh, you with the nudity again. If you have so many people naked, school libraries aren't going to buy the thing." I figured I'd go a step further and take everyone's skin off, there's nothing to "raise the blush of shame to the cheek of modesty."

JW: There are plenty of illustratorly creators working in comics, even in alternative comics. Jim Woodring worked at Ruby and Spears [animation company], and has done a fair bit of commercial illustration.

DC: He's done work at Microsoft.

JW: Yeah, these "chat avatars" where you become a Woodring character and interact with others. I saw this at an internet kiosk in a New Zealand hostel and it blew my mind. If anybody could pull off working with the Great Satan, it would be him.

DC: It's nice that he's put his name on it. A lot of the commercial work I do...

JW: It's anonymous.

DC: It's very anonymous, and I don't care who knows it.

JW: You pay your bills doing commercial work. What are some of the various magazines you've worked for?

DC:"Eclectic" would probably be the best word for the illustration career I've had. I've worked for big city newspapers like the *New York Times*, the *New York Post*, and the *Wall Street Journal*; children's magazines like *Ladybug* and *Scholastic*; obscure trade magazines like *Chemical Engineer* and *Geriatric Nursing*; and a whole raft of porn rags, from *Hustler* to *Leg Show*. For the last five or six years, I've had the security of steady work from a couple of newspapers where I'm more or less a regular—the *New York Observer* back east, and the *Portland Tribune* here, which after years of scrambling for freelance jobs feels like winning the lottery.

JW: Are you repped by agents, or do you do it yourself?

DC: No, just phone around, send work out. Most of the time no response. Being a freelance illustrator is like being a Don Juan, one in ten will say yes. In my case maybe one in a thousand.

JW: But you have to make the effort or nobody will respond.

DC: Well it gets a bit easier once you have a bit of a track record; illustration is almost a business without a memory, but having been around for twenty years, it's easier than when I was starting out. The work I do is better, I'm more likely to get repeat business.

JW: Who are the artists you swear by, and who do you swear at?

DC: I've always liked Drew Friedman's work, I think it's at a very high level. The *New York Observer* has him doing the big color cartoon that appears on the front page. Me, I do the little cartoons that appear on the calendar page. So I have something to aspire to.

JW: Size.

DC: What about people who do caricature— I still like David Levine's work—Steve Brodner is probably the best caricaturist working today. There's a guy named Daniel Adel; these names won't mean anything to anybody.

Page 50: Bob Dylan, from the *New York Observer*.

Page 51: 'Diving in the Hudson,' from the *New York Observer*.

Page 52: 'Millennium' illustration from the *New York Post*.

Page 53: Steven King, from the *Portland Tribune*.

Pages 54-55: Previously unpublished strip from the early 90's, drawn for a comics anthology which expired before the issue this was supposed to appear in could come out. This sort of thing has happened to me so often I've taken to calling myself "The Anthology Killer."

Pages 56-57: Illustrations from the Irvington Home Tour. Irvington was kind of a slummy, run-down neighborhood when I was growing up here in the 60's and 70's, but gentrification has made it historic—we even have street signs now that say "Historic Irvington" on them—and I guess moving back into the exact house I grew up in is my version of upward mobility. Every year there is a tour of some of Irvington's historic homes for charity, and since my wife is on the committee I usually wind up doing drawings for the brochure gratis. Once in a while this does lead to paying work, when someone sees the art in the brochure and commissions a picture of his own house.

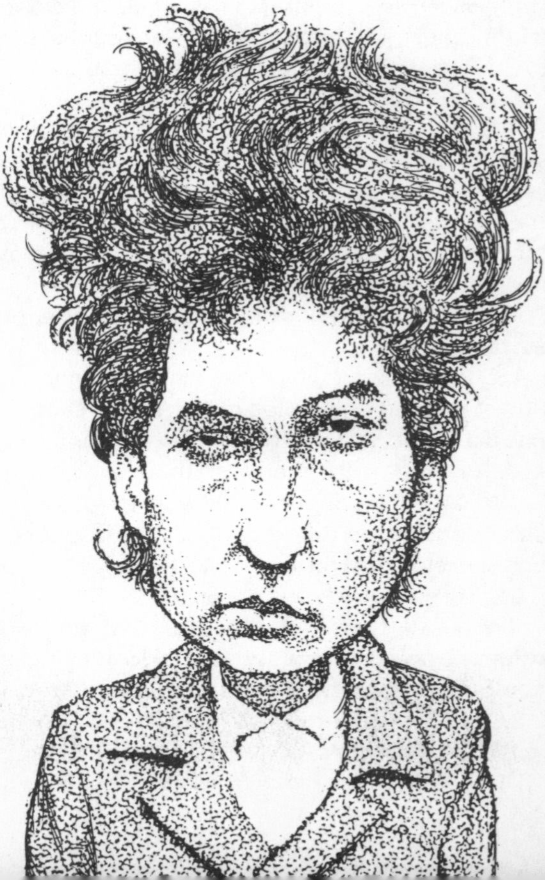

JW: Well maybe they can learn.

DC: Daniel Adel is a very good caricaturist. We have a book my six-year-old really used to like, *The Book That Jack Wrote*, which is kind of in his caricature style, but has the cow that jumped over the moon, *Humpty Dumpty*, things like that. Wonderful kind of juicy oil painting style. ¶ There's another caricaturist I like, C.F. Payne—works in pastels, colored pencils, his stuff is really good too.

JW: There are not a lot of people with an illustrative sensibility who can do comics with a good visual storytelling vocabulary: panel transitions, motion, narrative cues. They know how to make a good drawing but they don't know the visual grammar of comics. So I have to compliment you on that.

DC: Thank you. Who do I like in comics: Rick Geary I like, Kyle Baker. I like Dave Cooper. I really haven't been reading comics much; in New York there was Jim Hanley's Universe which was four blocks away from me. Since I did a signing once, they gave me a 40% discount. So I had a strong comics habit with them. ¶ When I moved to Portland, I'm not getting any discount, there's one decent comics shop in town, but it's a car ride away. I didn't even learn to drive a car for the first year I was here. I just kind of fell out of the habit, and don't miss it. Which makes me a big hypocrite, since I'm still aspiring to a place in the comics business and hoping to find readers, and I can't be bothered to be one myself ●

Born in Alabama shortly after the much-vaunted Summer of Love, Kip Manley has since set foot on five of the world's seven continents. He currently lives in Portland, Oregon, and knows entirely too many cartoonists; he even married one. In what little spare time he can find (under the couch cushions; in the pockets of freshly laundered pants, a little fuzzy from the drier) he continues his reckless experiments with em-dashes and semicolons.

John Weeks has drawn comics and chronicled comics lifestyle in his native USA, Australia, New Zealand, Indonesia and most recently Cambodia, where he currently resides. His sporadic *QuickDraw* has been printed wherever he sets foot. Recent efforts include *QuickArse* with Kirrily Schell (*Wide Arsed Mole*), and the upcoming mini *Spirit House*. Catch him at www.qdcomic.com

•Stand-Alone Books: *QuickDraw* #1-4 (1996-2000), *World of Sleep* 1996, *East Timor Funnies* 1997, *QuickArse* (with Kirrily Schell—2002), *Spirit House* (latest effort).
•Anthologies assembled: Founding member *Pure Evil* #1 (1997), *Nice* Anthology (1998).
•Comics Anthologies/comic contributions: *Big Smoke* (1996), *Votze* (1997), *Motherwort* (1998), *Froth* (various, 1997-2001), *Kumquat* (1998), *Pantry* (1999), *Sure* (with Angelo Madrid—1999), *Pure Evil* #1,#3 (with Greg MacKay—1998, 1999), *Comic Universe* (web site) 1998, *Satan Lives With Me* (2000), *Impulse Freak* #2 (2001), *Strip Jams* (2001), *Rubberneck* (Insert in *Pure Evil* #6, 2002).
•Zine contributions: *Ms .45* (1997), *Astrogrrl* (1997), *Farrago* (East Timor Funnies insert, University of Melbourne, 1997), *Moosiczine* (1998), *Il Draino* (1998), *Warm Cola* (1998), *Beanz Baxter* (1999), *Ozmosis* (1999)
•Comix Reviews & Writing: Dylan Horrocks Interview (*Indy Online* 1998), Q-Ray Interview (*Comics Quarterly*, 1998), Weeksy Newsletter (email newsletter, 2000-2001). http://www.qdcomic.com/blog/
•Exhibitions: Pure Evil, Melbourne (1998), Introduction, Cutnpaste Traveling Zine Exhibition http://cutnpaste.va.com.au, Whitney Biennial 2000 (for QuickDraw Web Site), Introduction, Comic Book Lifestyle, Exhibition, Melbourn, http://www.lindenarts.org/show_020417/index.html, Inside Out Exhibition 2002 Melbourne, Open Walls, Java Cafe, Phnom Penh.

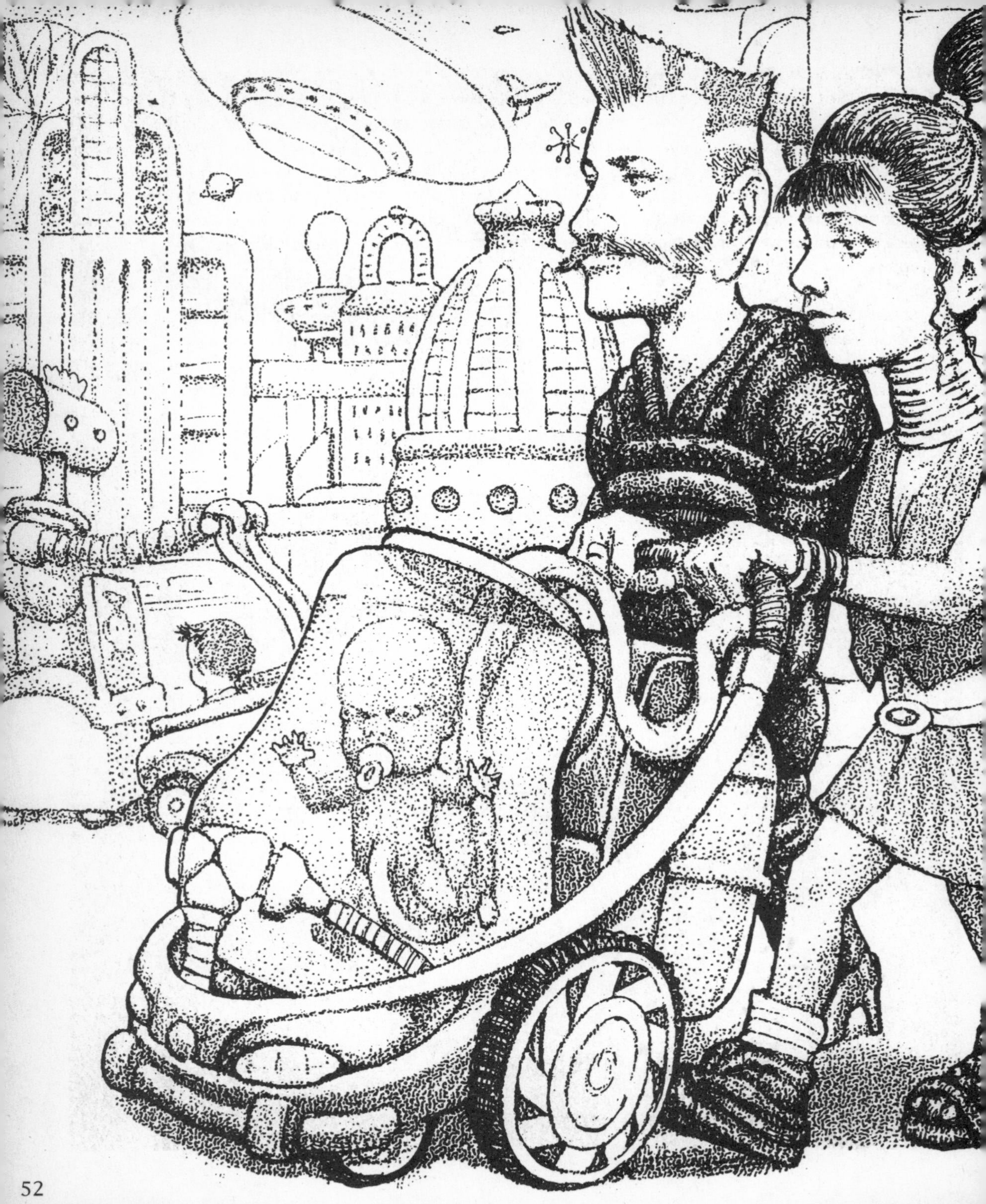

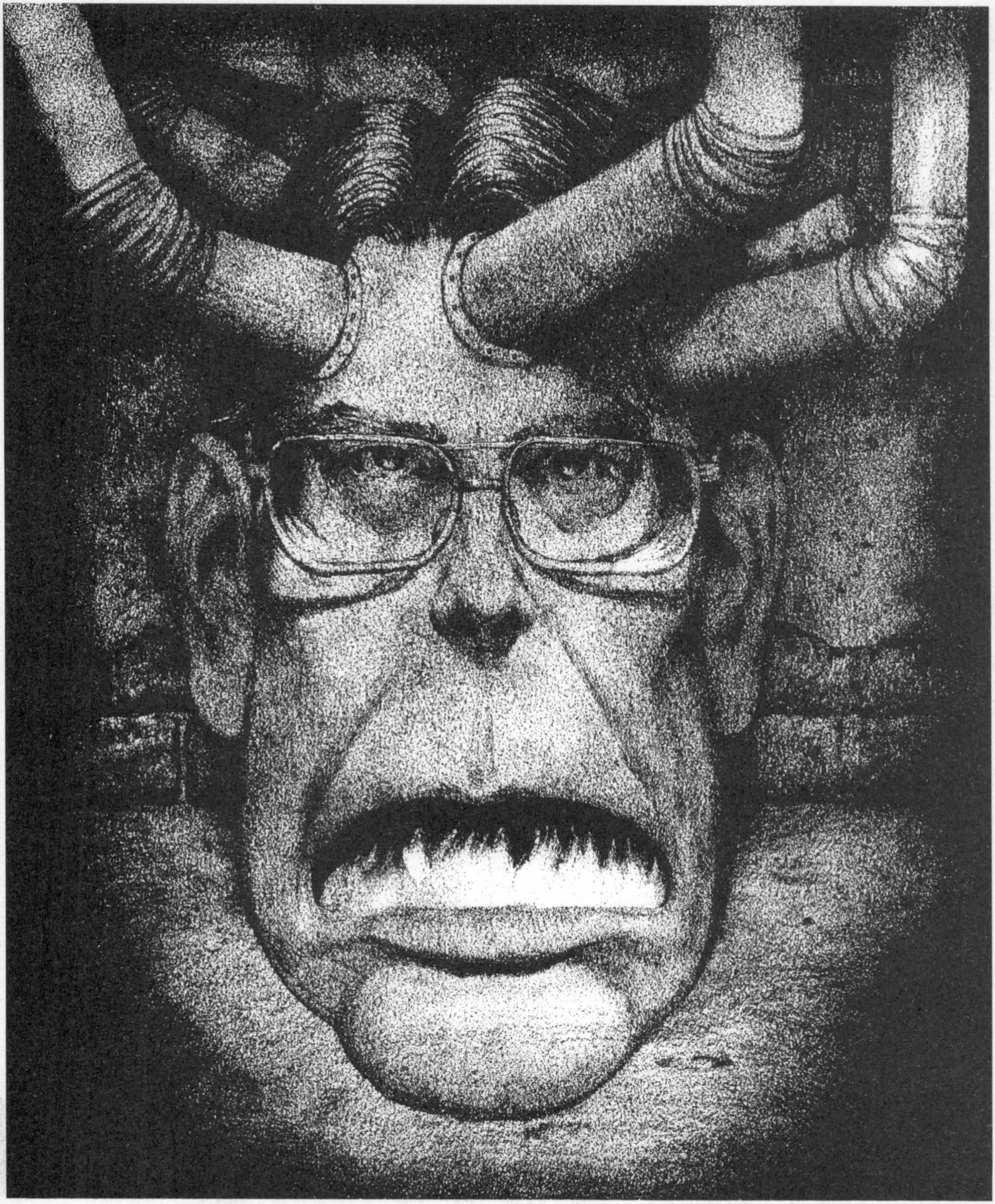

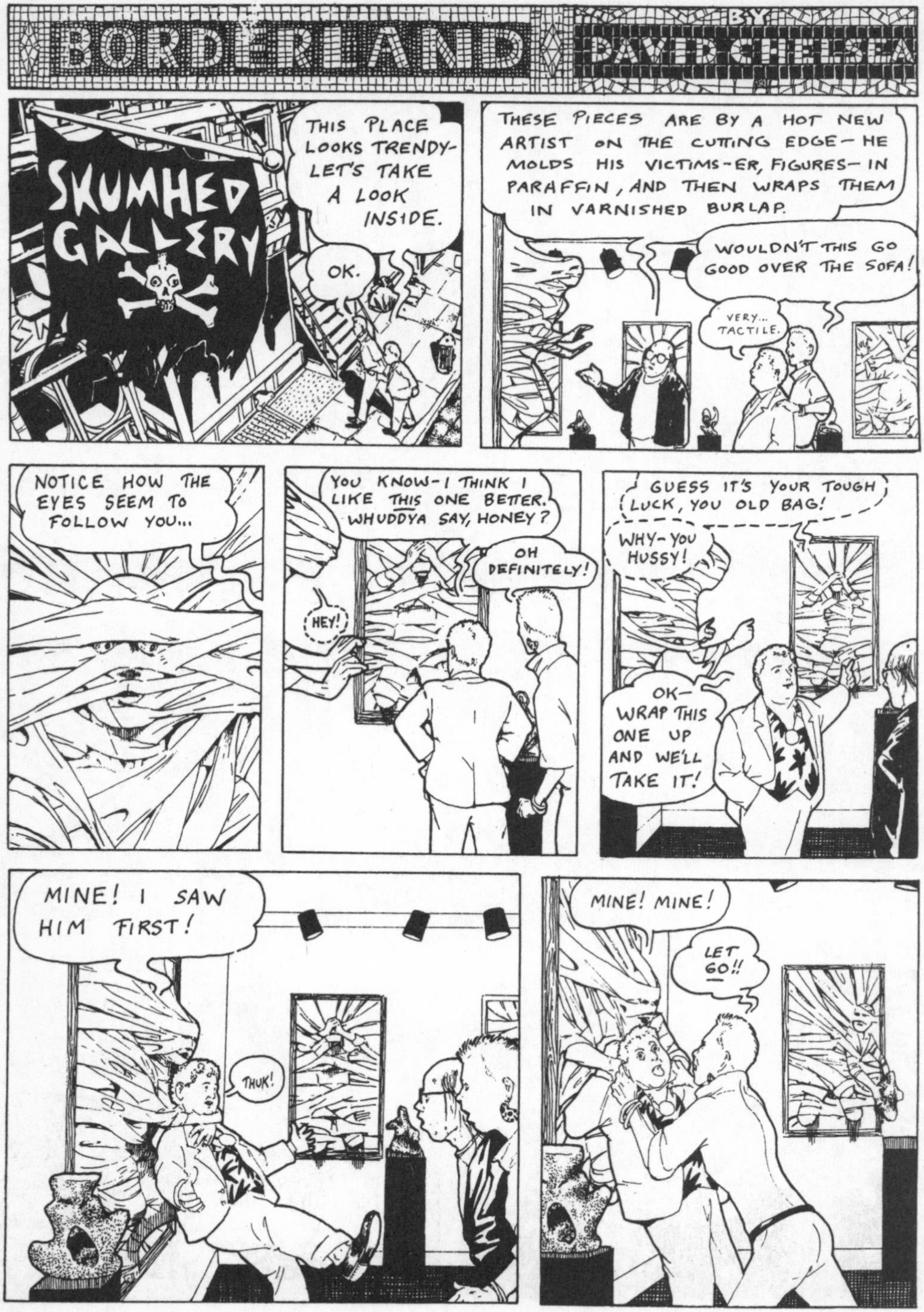
BORDERLAND
BY DAVID CHELSEA
SKUMHED GALLERY
THIS PLACE LOOKS TRENDY- LET'S TAKE A LOOK INSIDE.
OK.
THESE PIECES ARE BY A HOT NEW ARTIST ON THE CUTTING EDGE- HE MOLDS HIS VICTIMS-ER, FIGURES- IN PARAFFIN, AND THEN WRAPS THEM IN VARNISHED BURLAP.
WOULDN'T THIS GO GOOD OVER THE SOFA!
VERY... TACTILE.
NOTICE HOW THE EYES SEEM TO FOLLOW YOU...
YOU KNOW- I THINK I LIKE THIS ONE BETTER. WHUDDYA SAY, HONEY?
HEY!
OH DEFINITELY!
GUESS IT'S YOUR TOUGH LUCK, YOU OLD BAG!
WHY- YOU HUSSY!
OK- WRAP THIS ONE UP AND WE'LL TAKE IT!
MINE! I SAW HIM FIRST!
THUK!
MINE! MINE!
LET GO!!

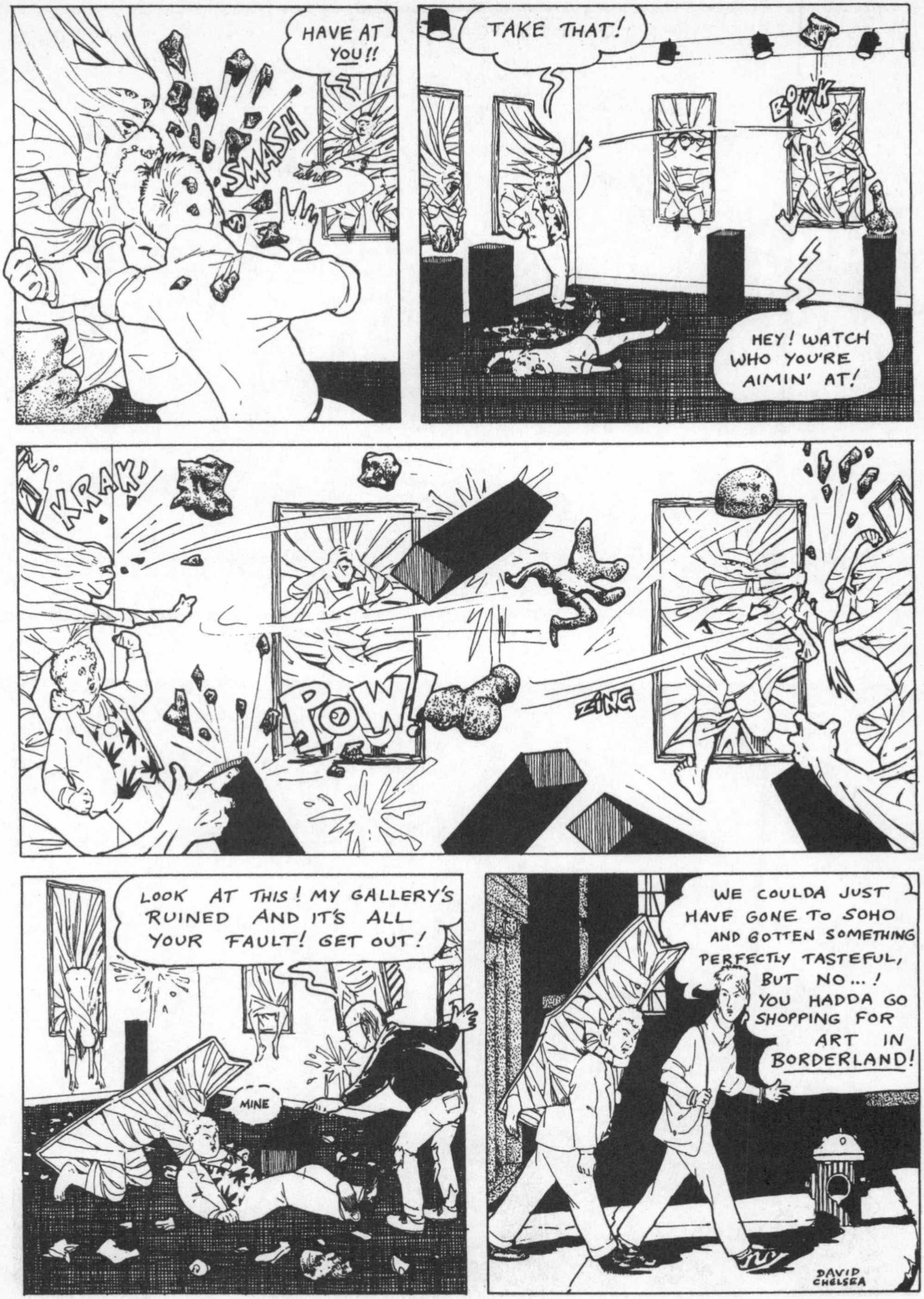
HAVE AT YOU!!
SMASH
TAKE THAT!
BONK
HEY! WATCH WHO YOU'RE AIMIN' AT!
KRAK!
POW!
ZING
LOOK AT THIS! MY GALLERY'S RUINED AND IT'S ALL YOUR FAULT! GET OUT!
MINE
WE COULDA JUST HAVE GONE TO SOHO AND GOTTEN SOMETHING PERFECTLY TASTEFUL, BUT NO...! YOU HADDA GO SHOPPING FOR ART IN BORDERLAND!
DAVID CHELSEA

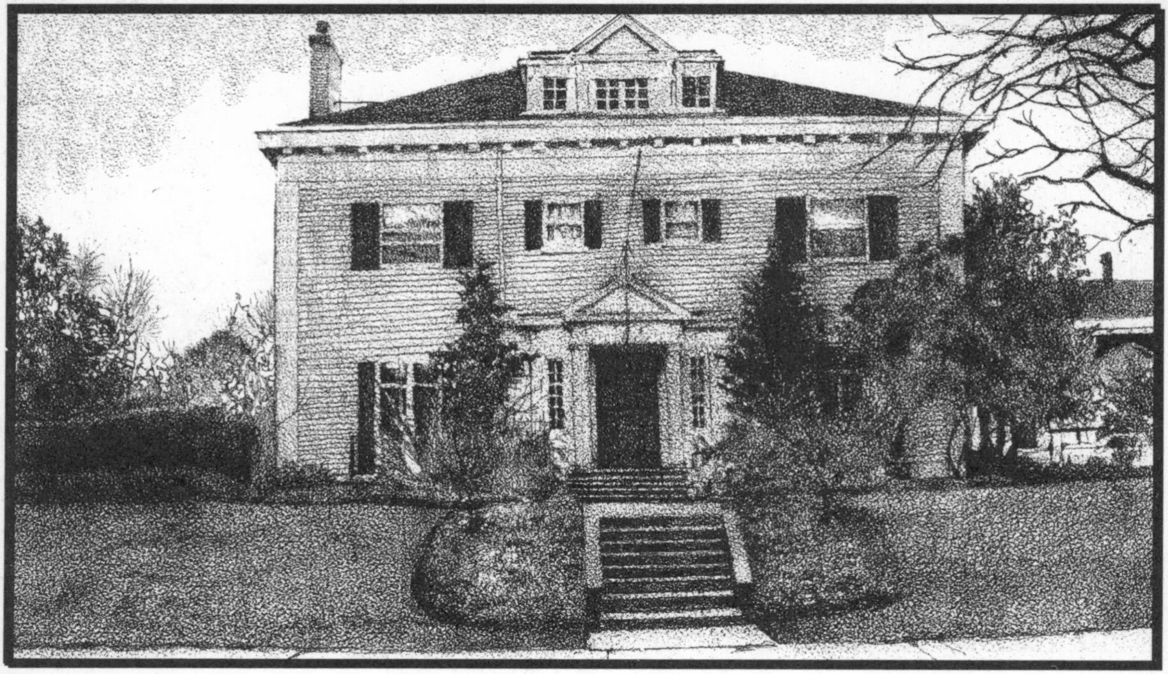

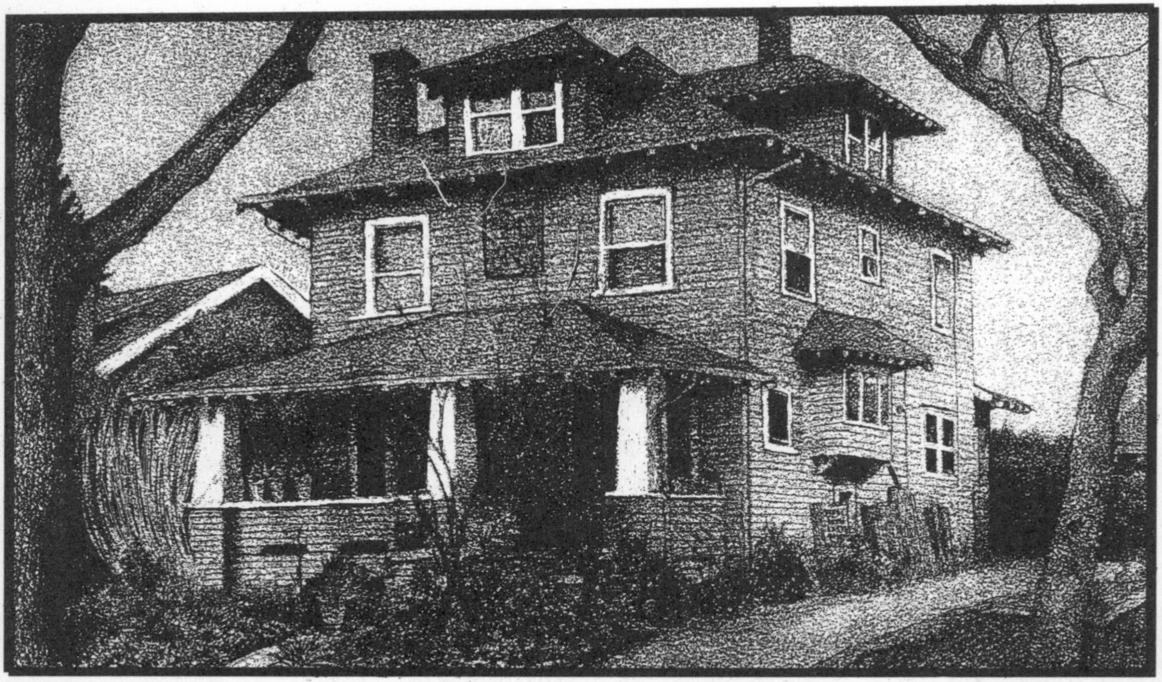

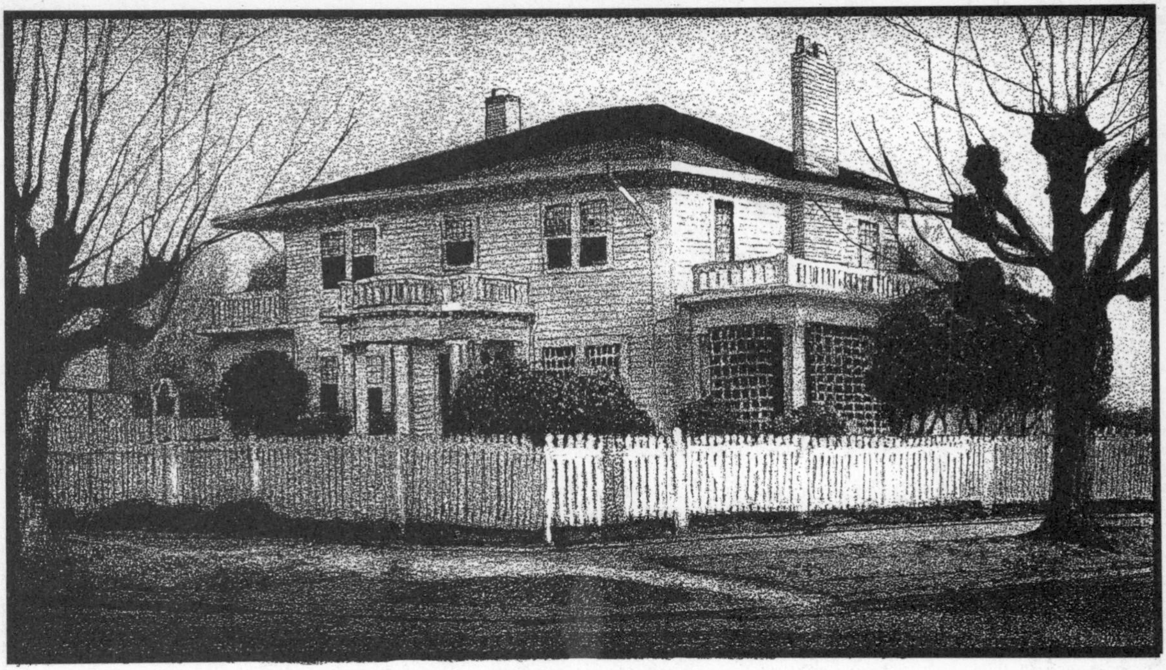

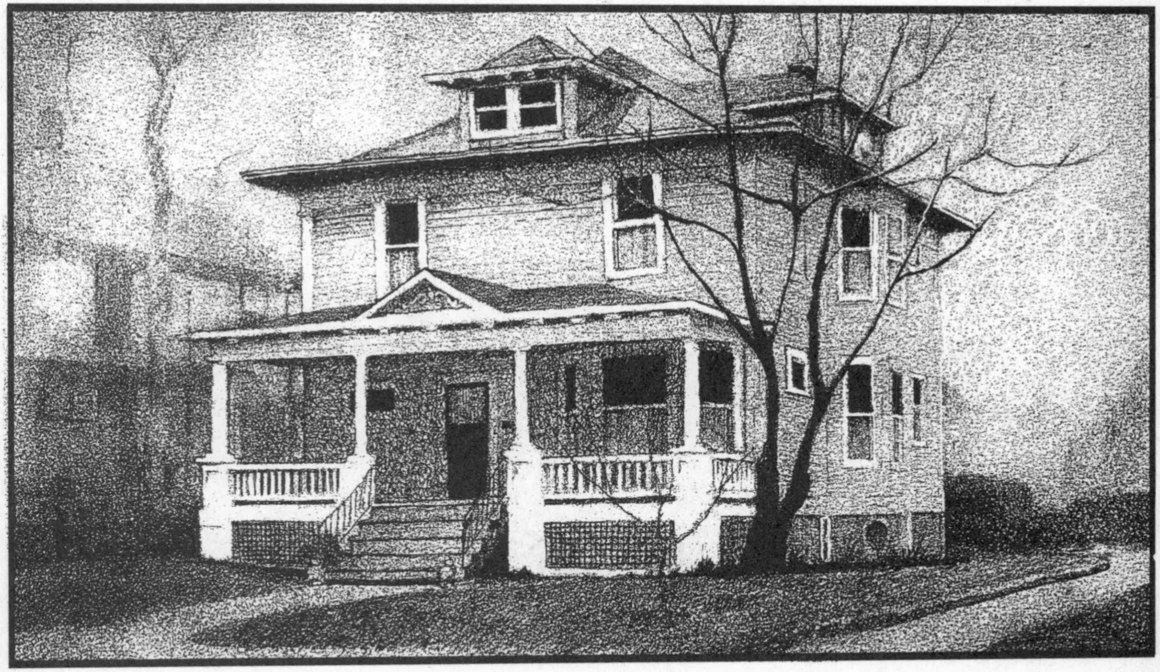

Words by Lewis Carroll

Humpty Dumpty's Song

Images by David Chelsea

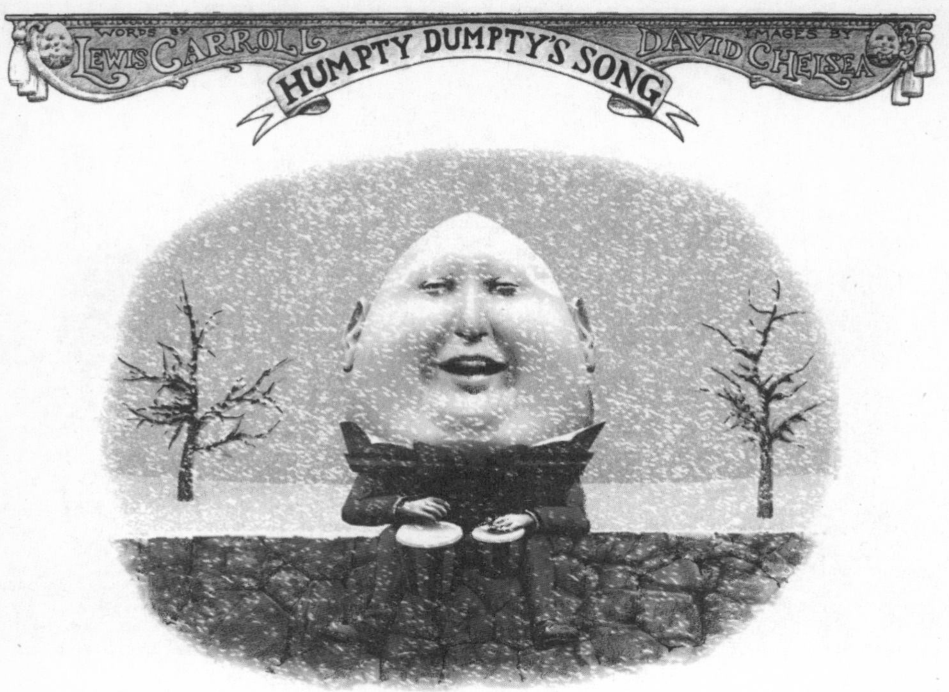

In winter, when the fields are white,
I sing this song for your delight.

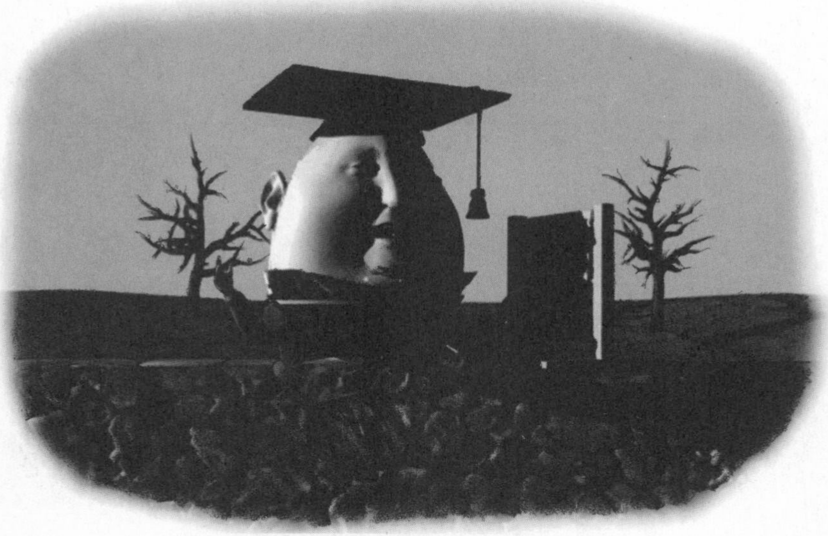

In spring, when woods are getting green,
I'll try and tell you what I mean.

In summer, when the days are long,
Perhaps you'll understand the song:

In autumn, when the leaves are brown,
Take pen and ink and write it down.

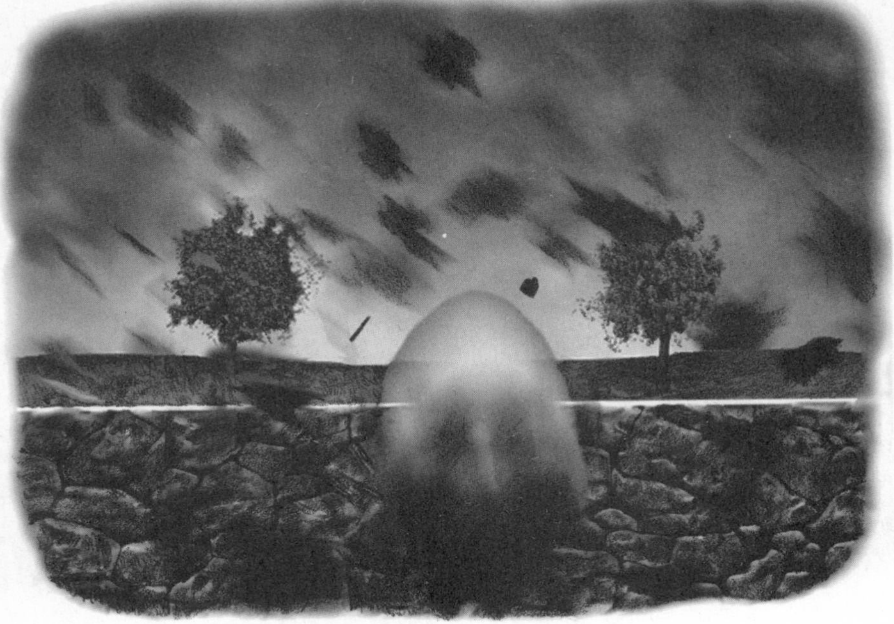

I sent a message to the fish.
I told them,

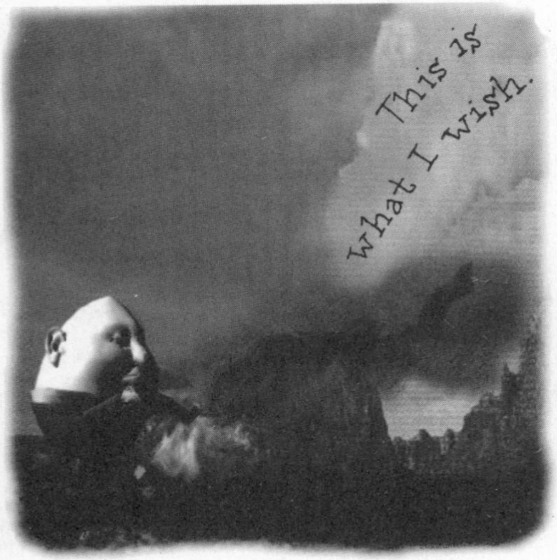
This is
what I wish.

The little fishes of the sea,
They sent an answer back to me.

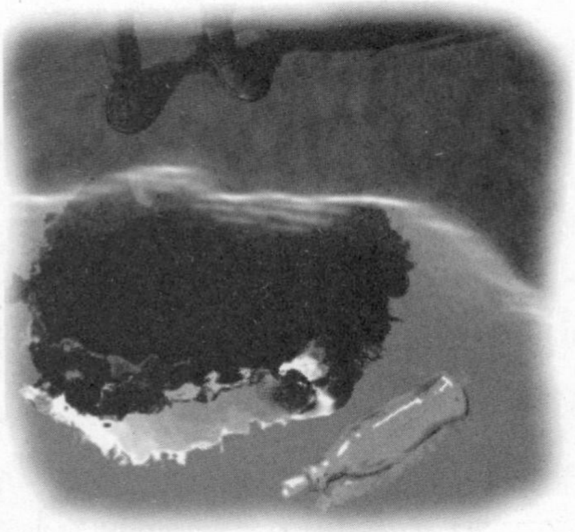

The little fishes' answer was
"We cannot do it, Sir, because---"

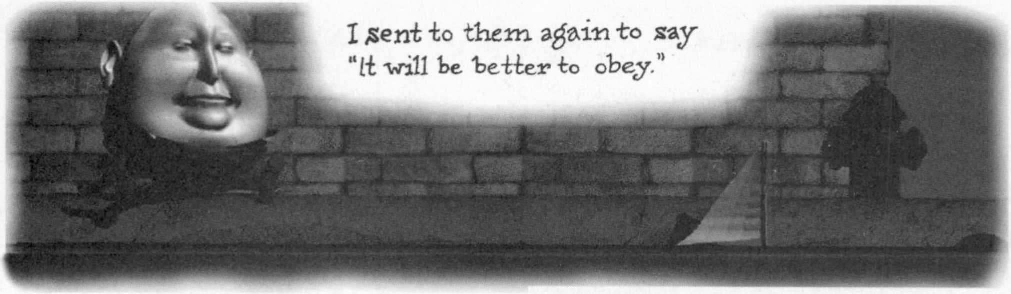
I sent to them again to say
"It will be better to obey."

The fishes answered

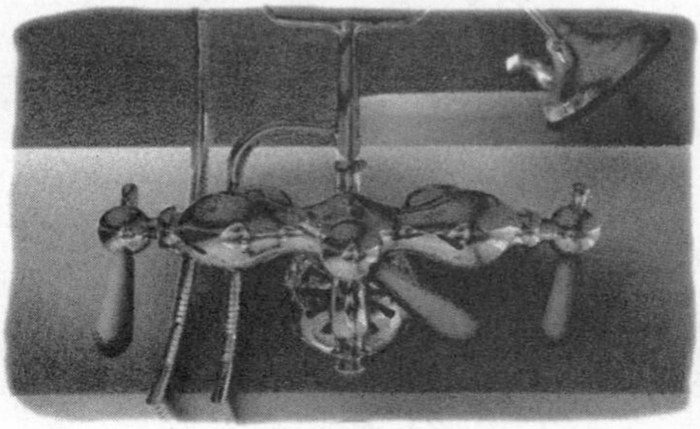

with a grin,

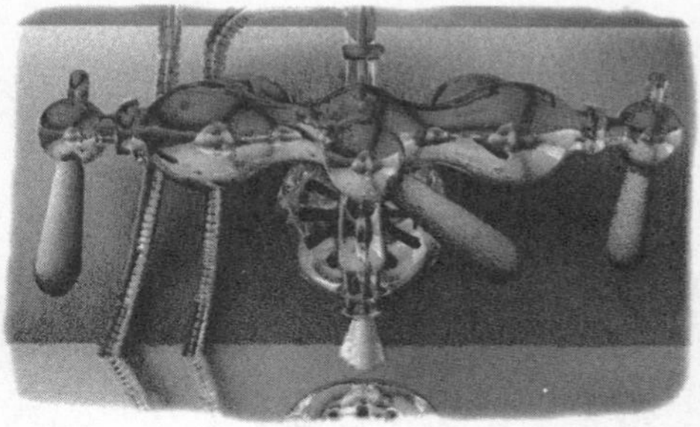

"Why, what a temper you are in!"

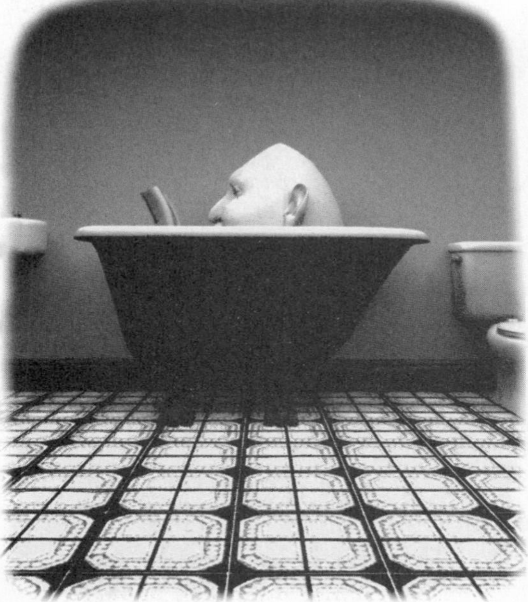

I told them once, I told them twice:
They would not listen to advice.

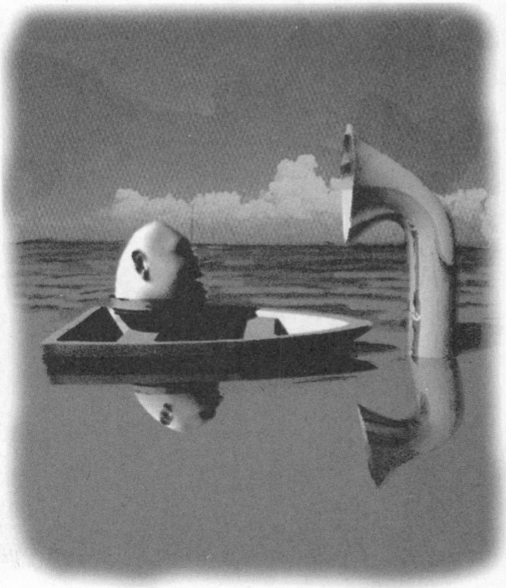

I took a kettle large and new,
Fit for the deed I had to do.

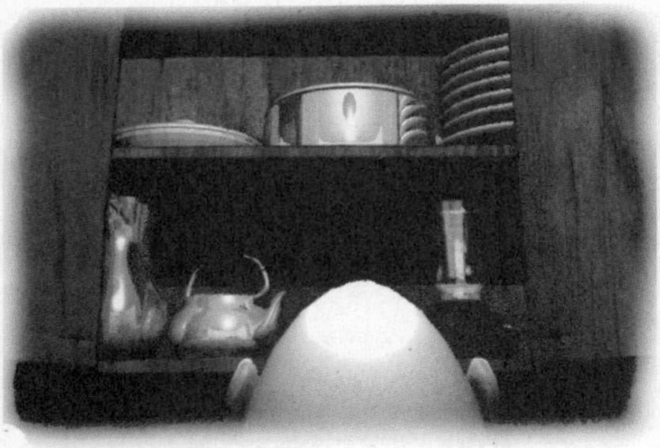

My heart went hop, my heart went thump;
I filled the kettle at the pump.

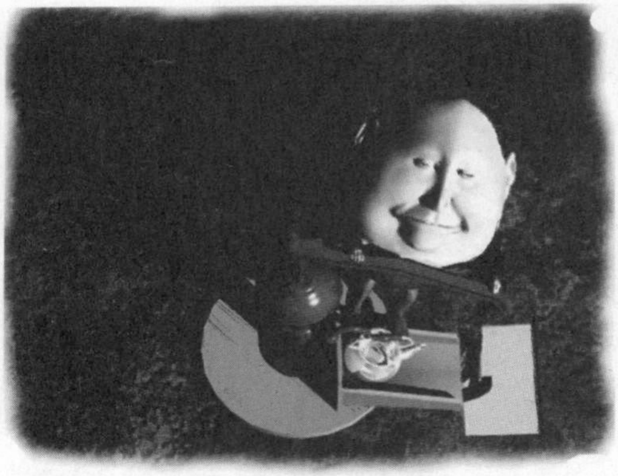

Then someone came to me and said,

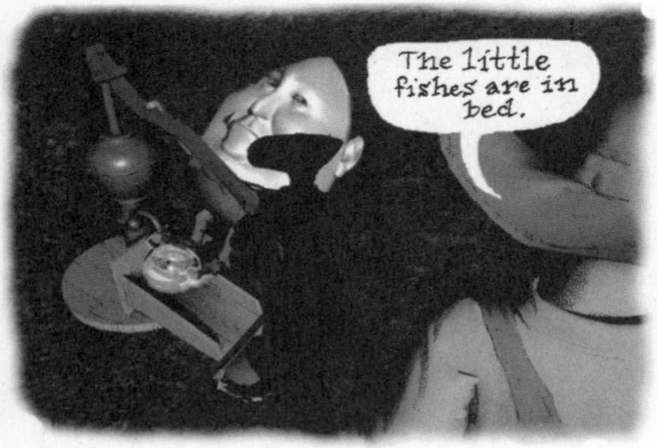
The little fishes are in bed.

I said to him, I said it plain,

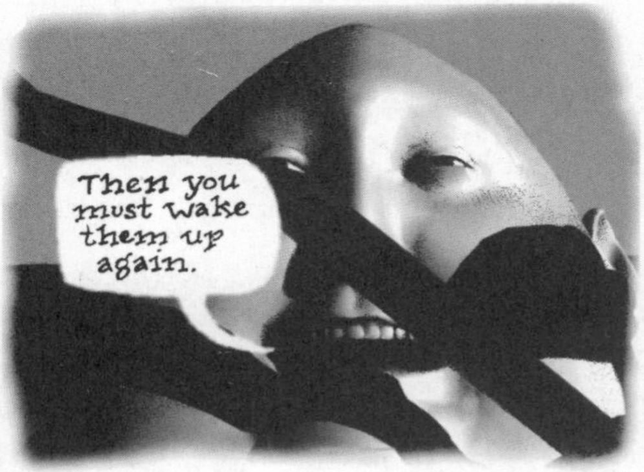
Then you must wake them up again.

I said it very loud and clear;
I went and shouted in his ear.

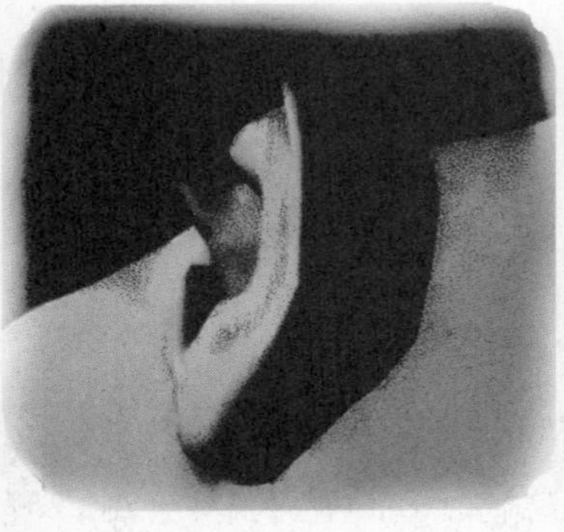

But he was very stiff and proud.
He said,

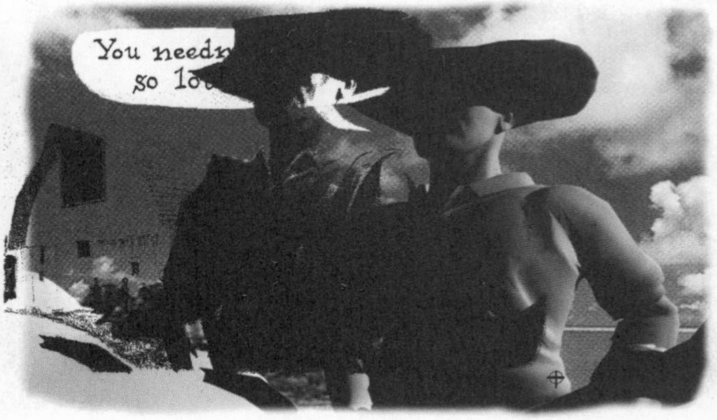
You needn
so lo

And he was very proud and stiff.
He said,

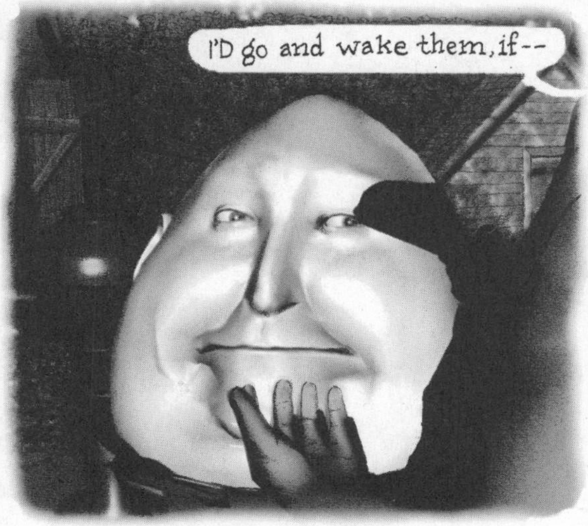
I'D go and wake them, if--

I took a corkscrew from the shelf.
I went to wake them up myself.

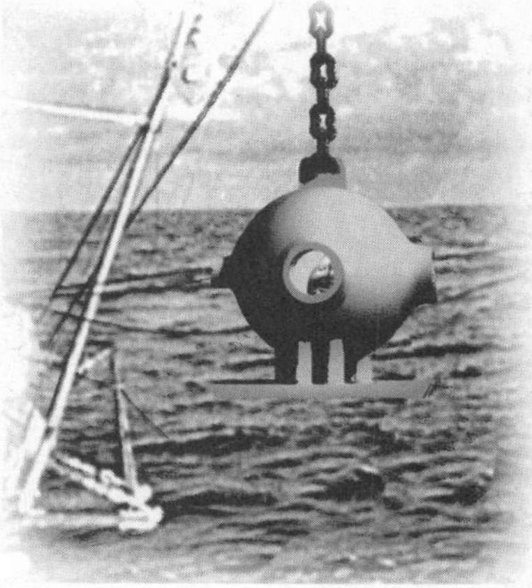

And when I found the door was locked,
I pulled and pushed and kicked and knocked.

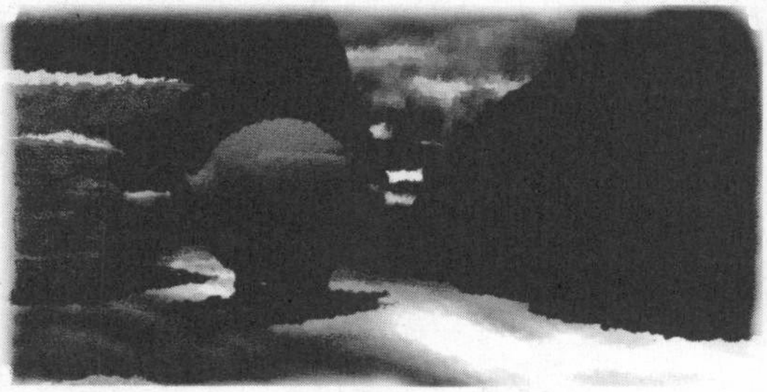

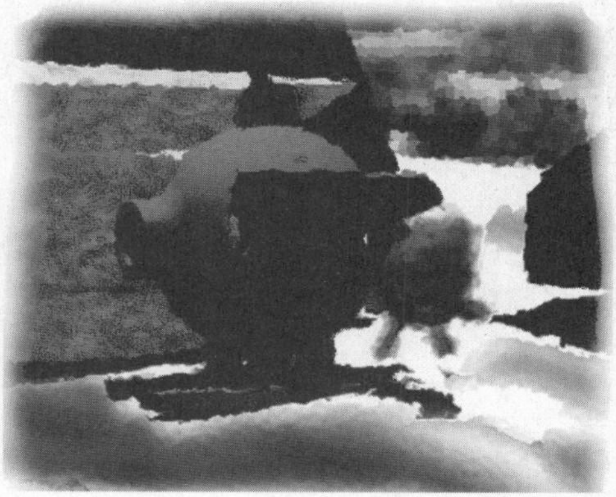

And when I found the door was shut,
I tried to turn the handle, but---

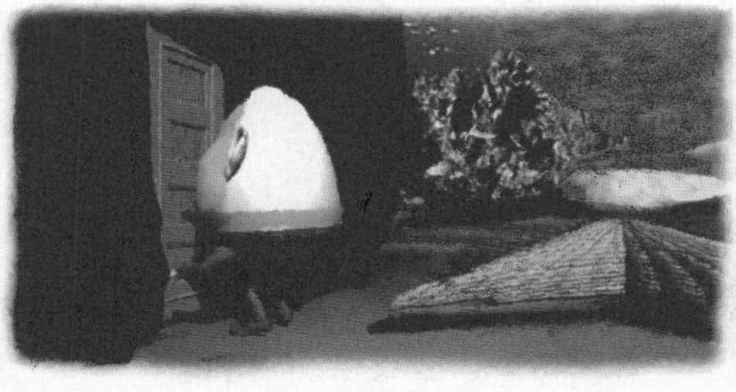

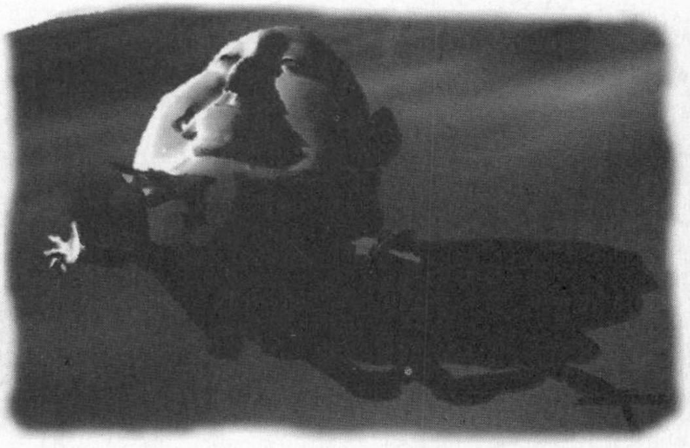

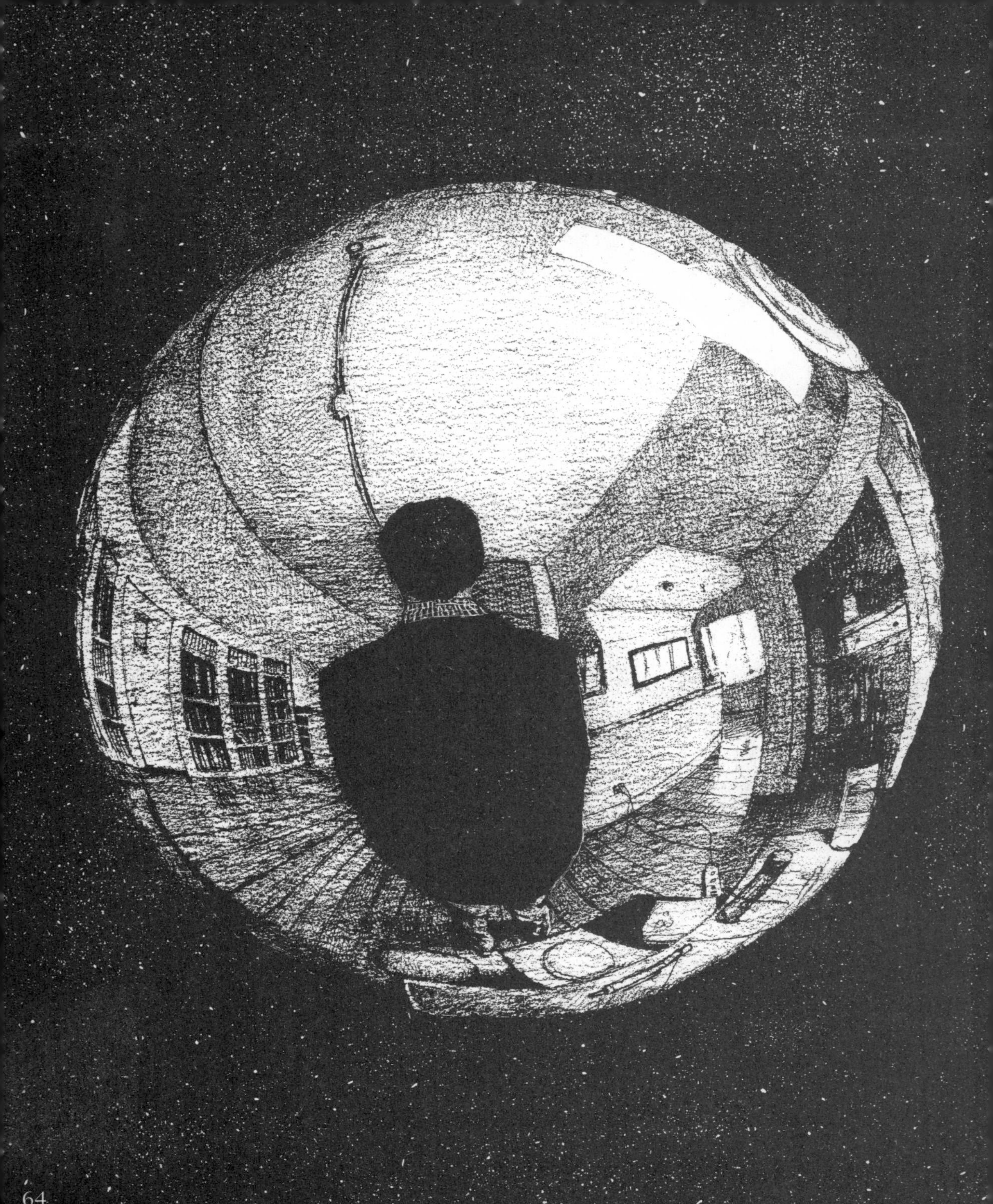

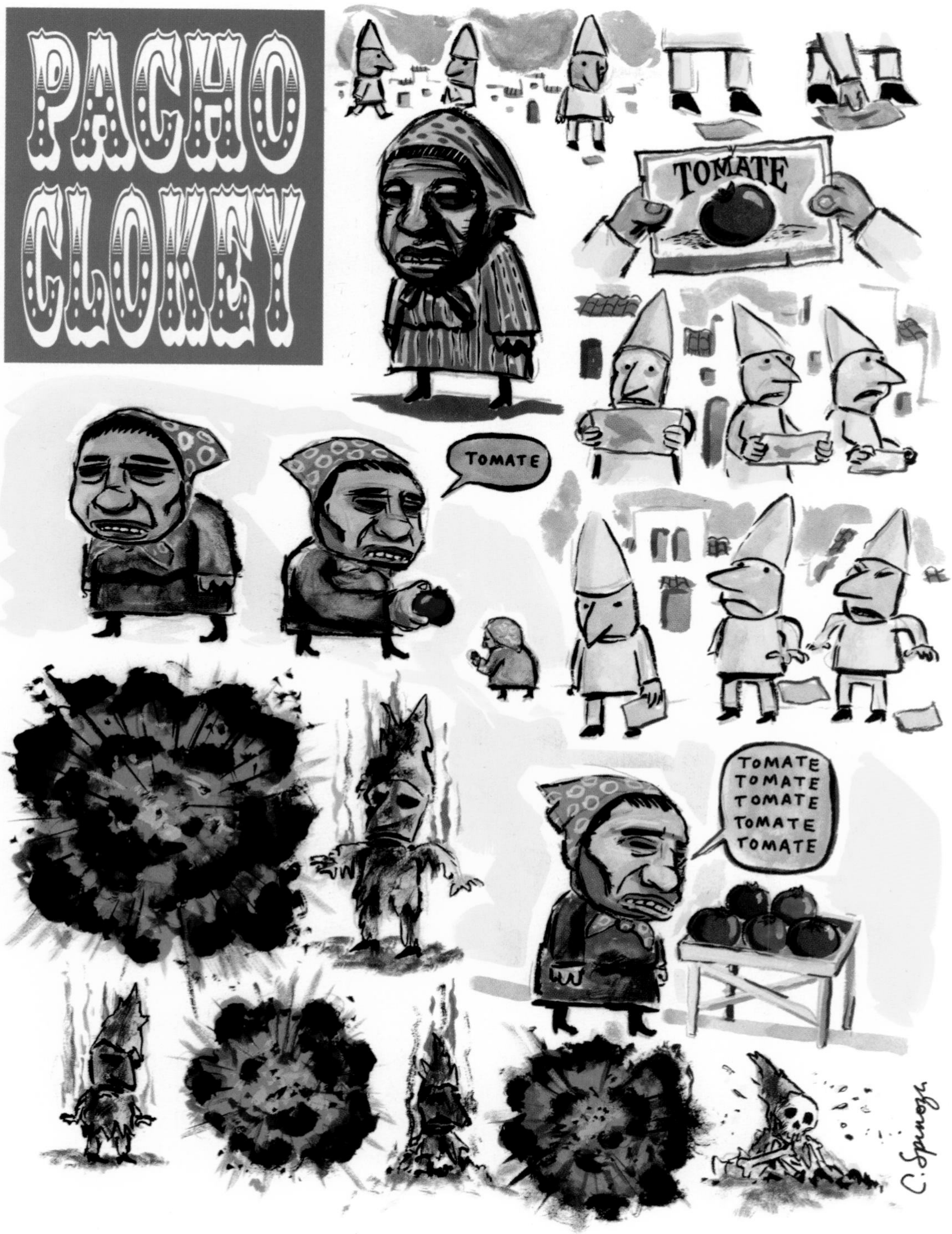
PACHO CLOKEY
TOMATE
TOMATE
TOMATE
TOMATE
TOMATE
TOMATE
TOMATE
TOMATE
C. Spinoza

They flew to the Moon!

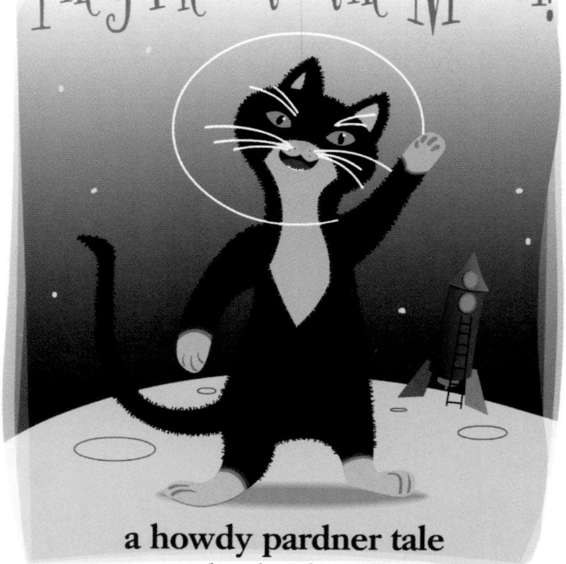

a howdy pardner tale

andrew brandou 2000

One day, Peeps the cat woke up and strrrrretched her back. "Today I'll fly to the moon," she said.

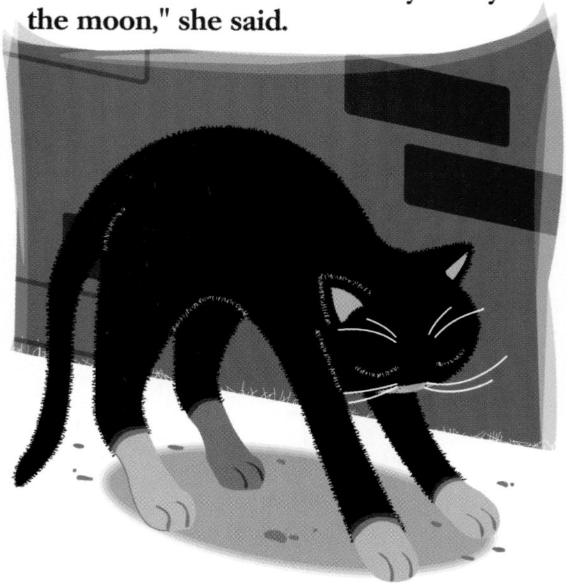

But a cat can't fly to the moon alone; she needs a little help. Walking along, she came upon a dog and asked "Would you like to fly to the moon with me?" "Uhhhm...I'm not sure," replied the dog.

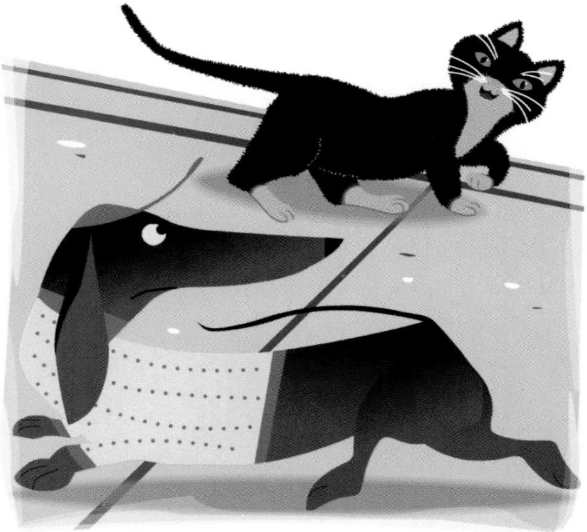

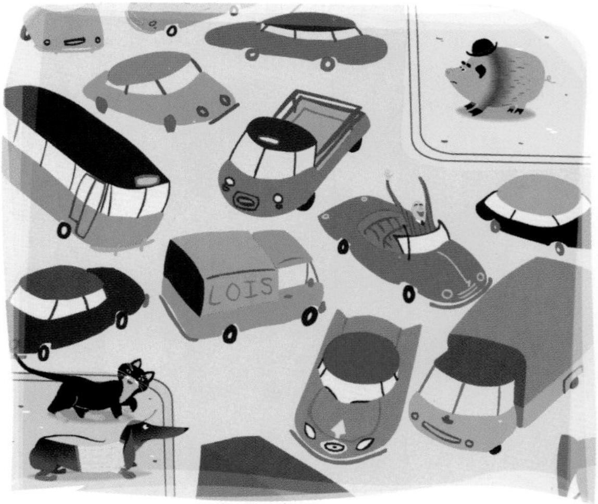
LOIS

Peeps saw a pig across the street. "I'll go ask Mr. Pig," she said. "How will you get across the street? Will you fly?" asked the dog. Peeps looked at the dog with a puzzled expression, and walked across the street.

"Hello Mr. Pig, would you like to fly to the moon with me?" asked Peeps. "Not me kid! How do ya make money doing that?" "Yeah," the dog chimed in," that's a dumb idea!"

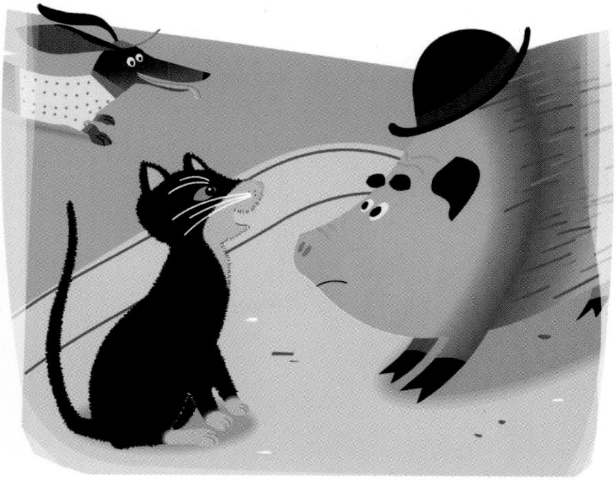

"Fine," said Peeps "I'll go ask the donkey." Peeps crawled through the donkey's fence. "Cat, you are an imbecile!" called Mr. Pig. "Yeah!" yelped the dog.

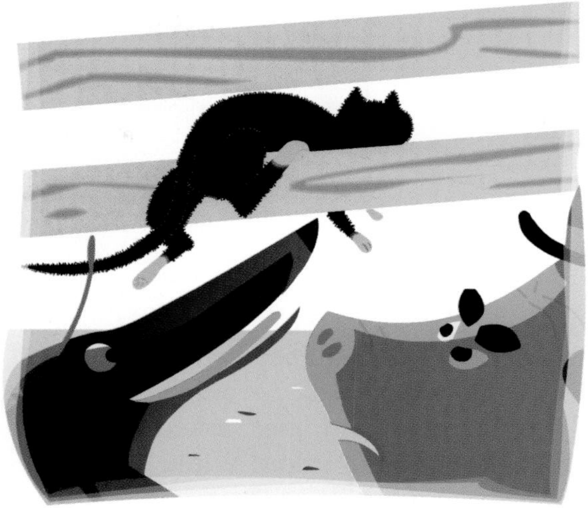

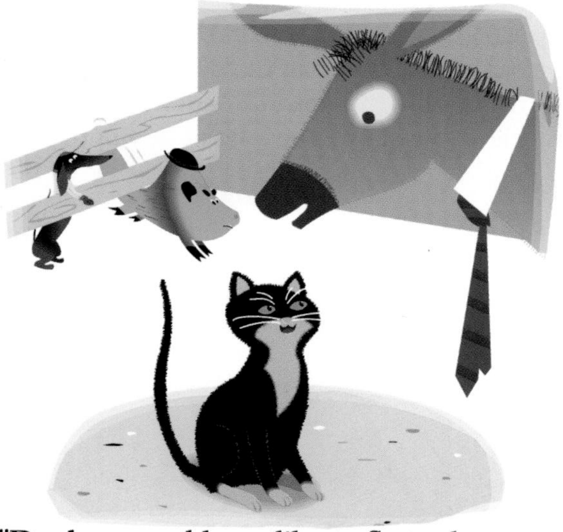

"Donkey, would you like to fly to the moon with me?" asked Peeps. "Well, let me see here…"the donkey hemmed and hawed. "Don't do it!" squealed Mr. Pig and the dog as they struggled beneath the fence.

"Donkey, that cat can't fly to the moon! She couldn't even get us over the fence!" snorted the pig. But the donkey had already made up his mind. "I can't fly anywhere unless I'm in charge!"

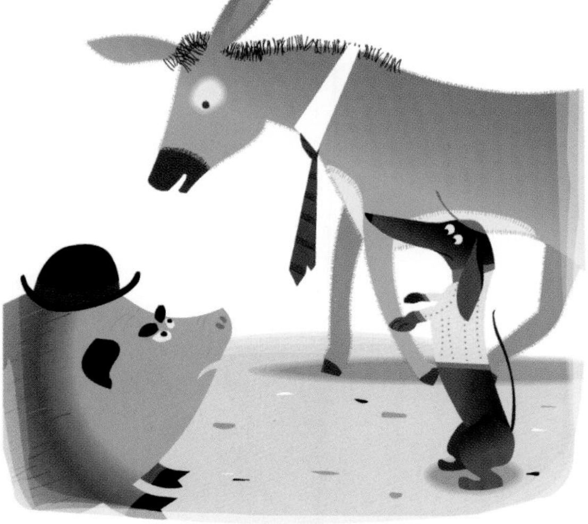

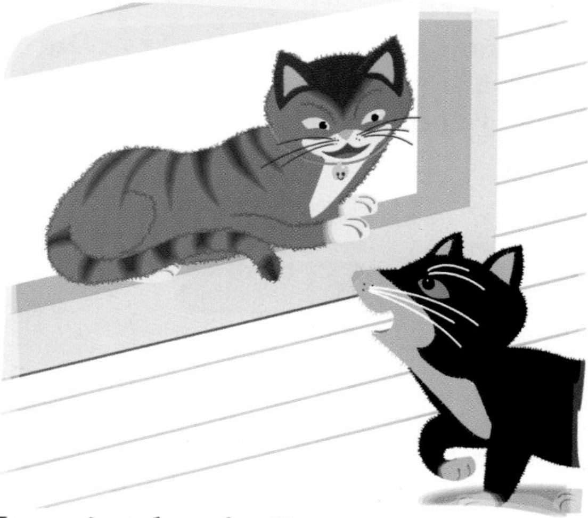

It was just then that Peeps saw a cat named Wink in a windowsill. "Would you like to fly to the moon with me?" asked Peeps. "Fly to the moon?" asked Wink, "I've always wanted to fly to the moon. Sure!"

"Whaaaaaat?!" The donkey brayed. "Cats. This is why they're all penniless," sighed the pig. The dog just watched as Peeps and Wink started for the rocket.

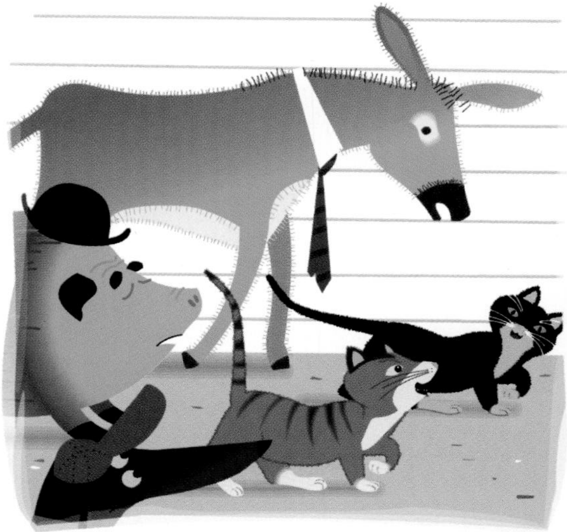

"Who are these other animals?" asked Wink. "I dunno. Ever since I said I was gonna fly to the moon they've been following me around," said Peeps.

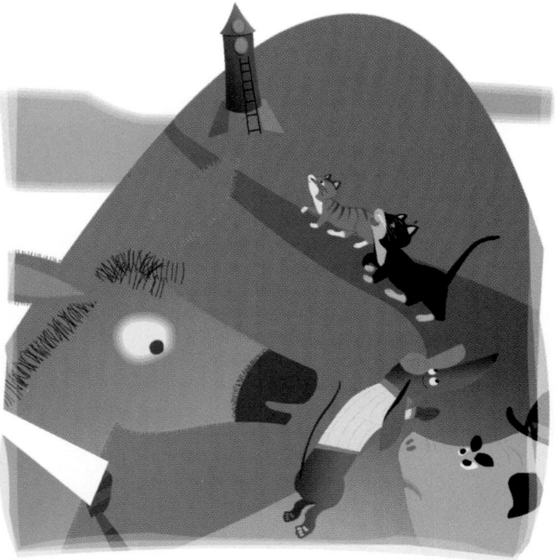

As Peeps and Wink climbed aboard the rocket, the other animals mocked them from below. "Fools! Dreamers!" they cried. Suddenly the rocket began to shudder and then…

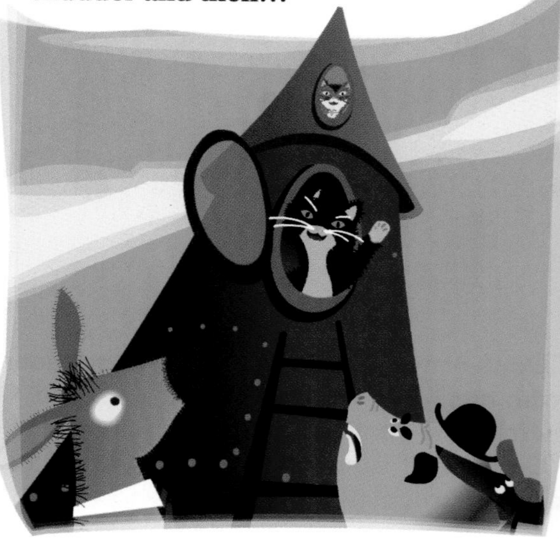

blast off!!!

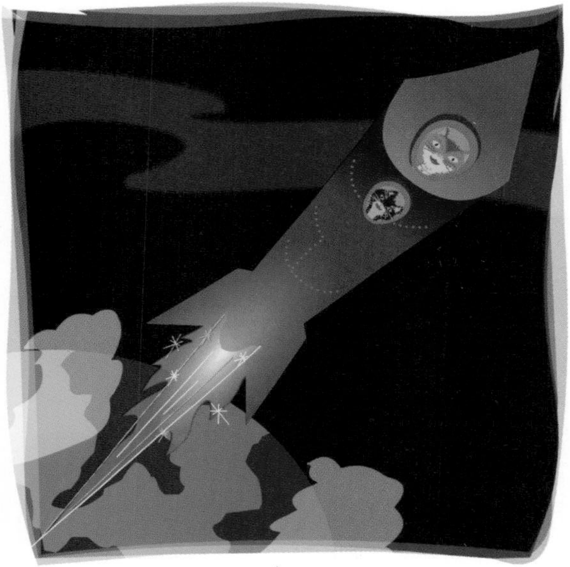

For a moment, the other animals were puzzled, but in a flash, they knew what to do! They got out their cell phones and started talking very fast!

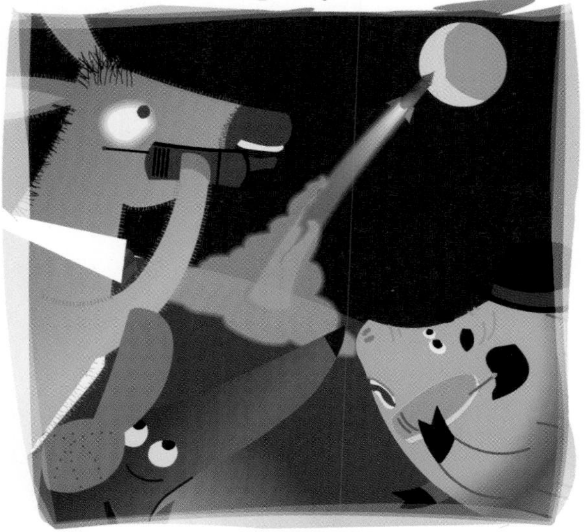

Right away reporters and spectators gathered. The donkey boasted, "I put my heart and soul into this project, I was glad just to do my part." The dog critiqued, "If I had gone along, the flight would have been much more fantastic." And the pig profited by selling t-shirts printed with the phrase "I saw them fly to the moon!"

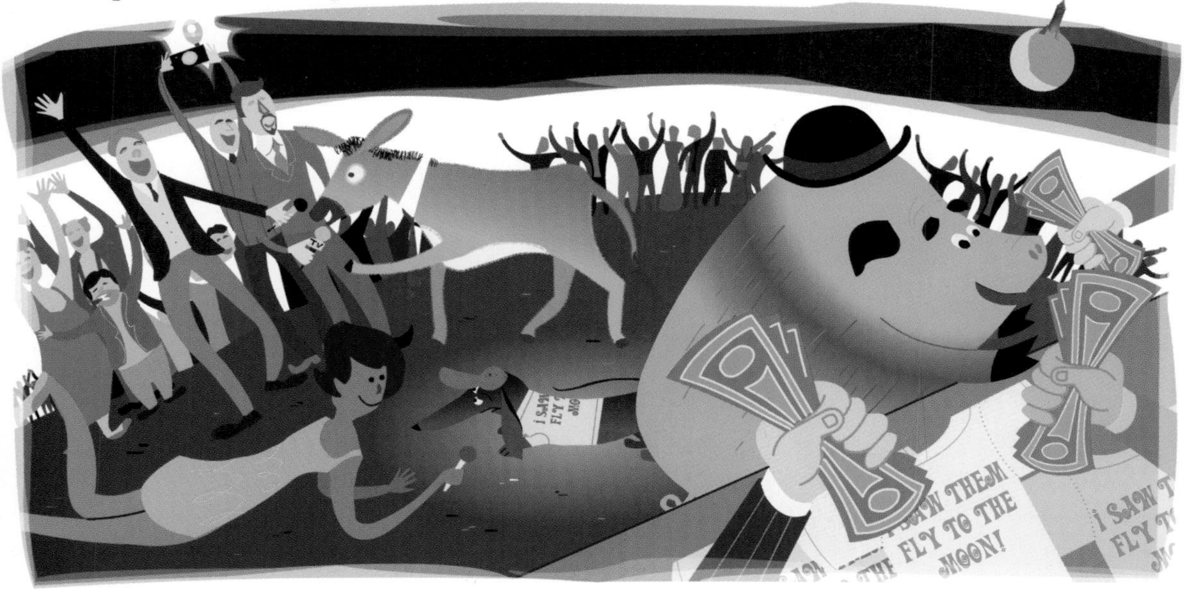
I SAW THEM FLY TO THE MOON!

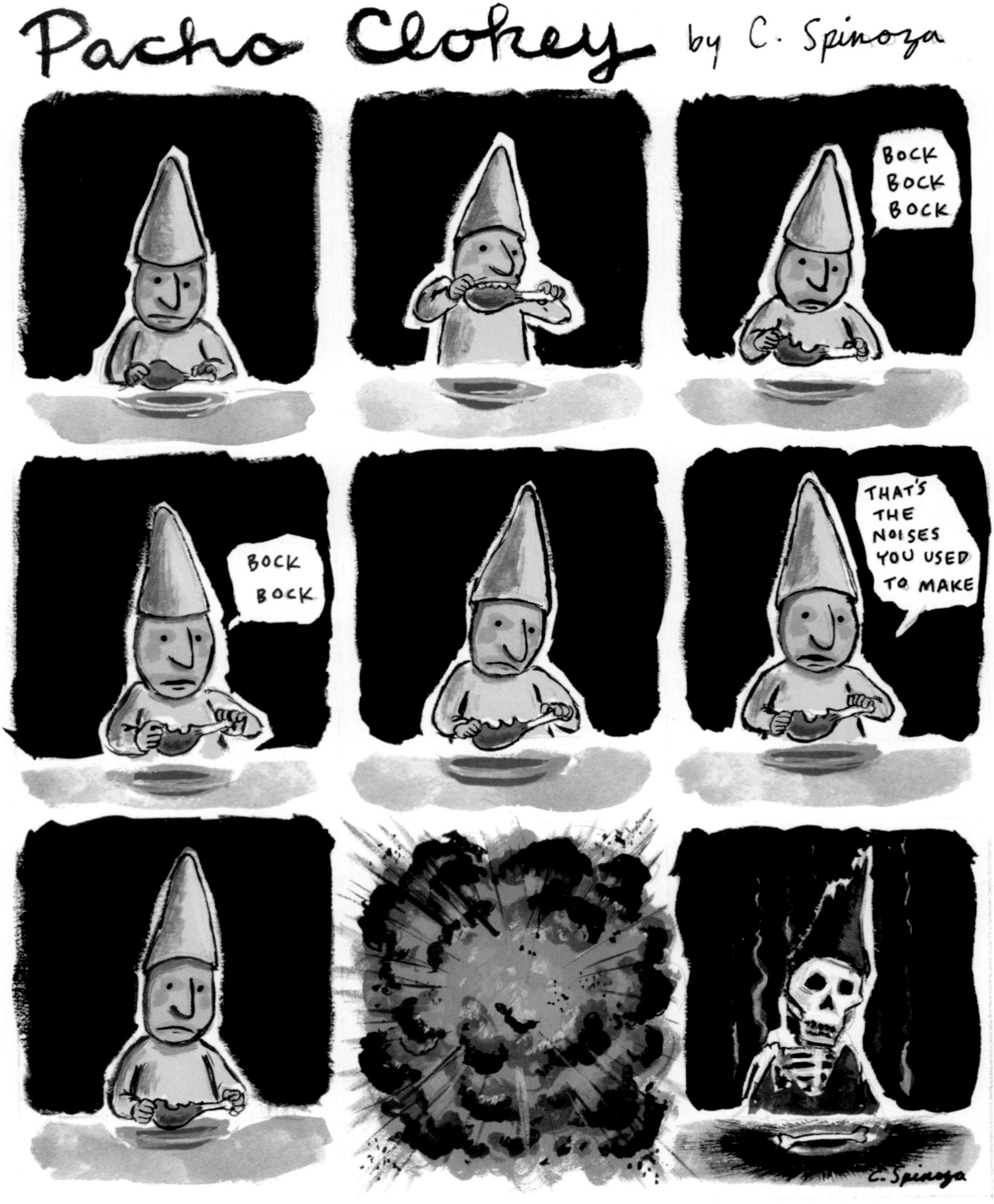
Pacho Clokey by C. Spinoza
BOCK BOCK BOCK
BOCK BOCK
THAT'S THE NOISES YOU USED TO MAKE
C. Spinoza

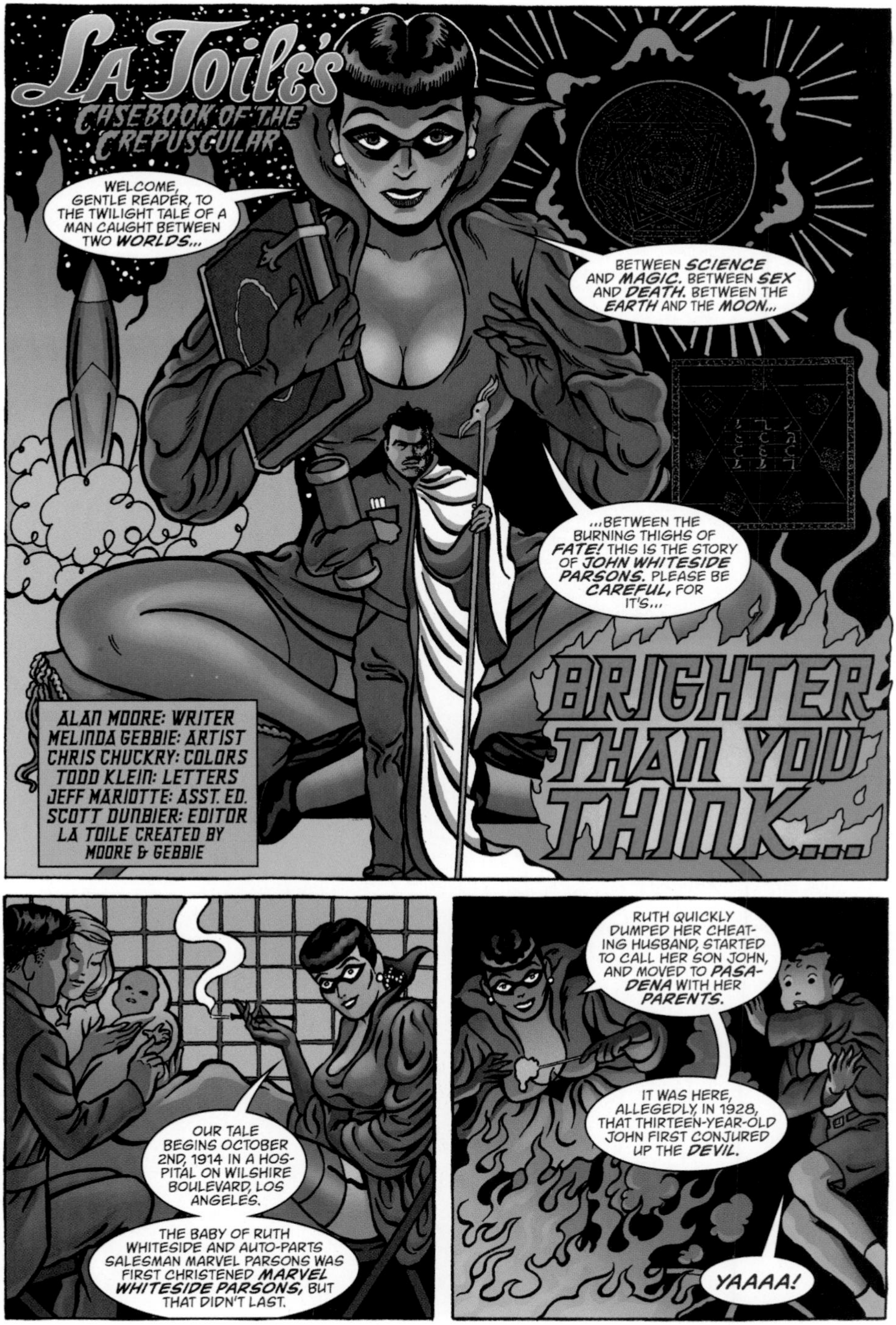
LA TOILE'S
CASEBOOK OF THE CREPUSCULAR
WELCOME, GENTLE READER, TO THE TWILIGHT TALE OF A MAN CAUGHT BETWEEN TWO WORLDS...
BETWEEN SCIENCE AND MAGIC. BETWEEN SEX AND DEATH. BETWEEN THE EARTH AND THE MOON...
...BETWEEN THE BURNING THIGHS OF FATE! THIS IS THE STORY OF JOHN WHITESIDE PARSONS. PLEASE BE CAREFUL, FOR IT'S...
BRIGHTER THAN YOU THINK...
ALAN MOORE: WRITER
MELINDA GEBBIE: ARTIST
CHRIS CHUCKRY: COLORS
TODD KLEIN: LETTERS
JEFF MARIOTTE: ASST. ED.
SCOTT DUNBIER: EDITOR
LA TOILE CREATED BY MOORE & GEBBIE
OUR TALE BEGINS OCTOBER 2ND, 1914 IN A HOSPITAL ON WILSHIRE BOULEVARD, LOS ANGELES.
THE BABY OF RUTH WHITESIDE AND AUTO-PARTS SALESMAN MARVEL PARSONS WAS FIRST CHRISTENED MARVEL WHITESIDE PARSONS, BUT THAT DIDN'T LAST.
RUTH QUICKLY DUMPED HER CHEATING HUSBAND, STARTED TO CALL HER SON JOHN, AND MOVED TO PASADENA WITH HER PARENTS.
IT WAS HERE, ALLEGEDLY, IN 1928, THAT THIRTEEN-YEAR-OLD JOHN FIRST CONJURED UP THE DEVIL.
YAAAA!

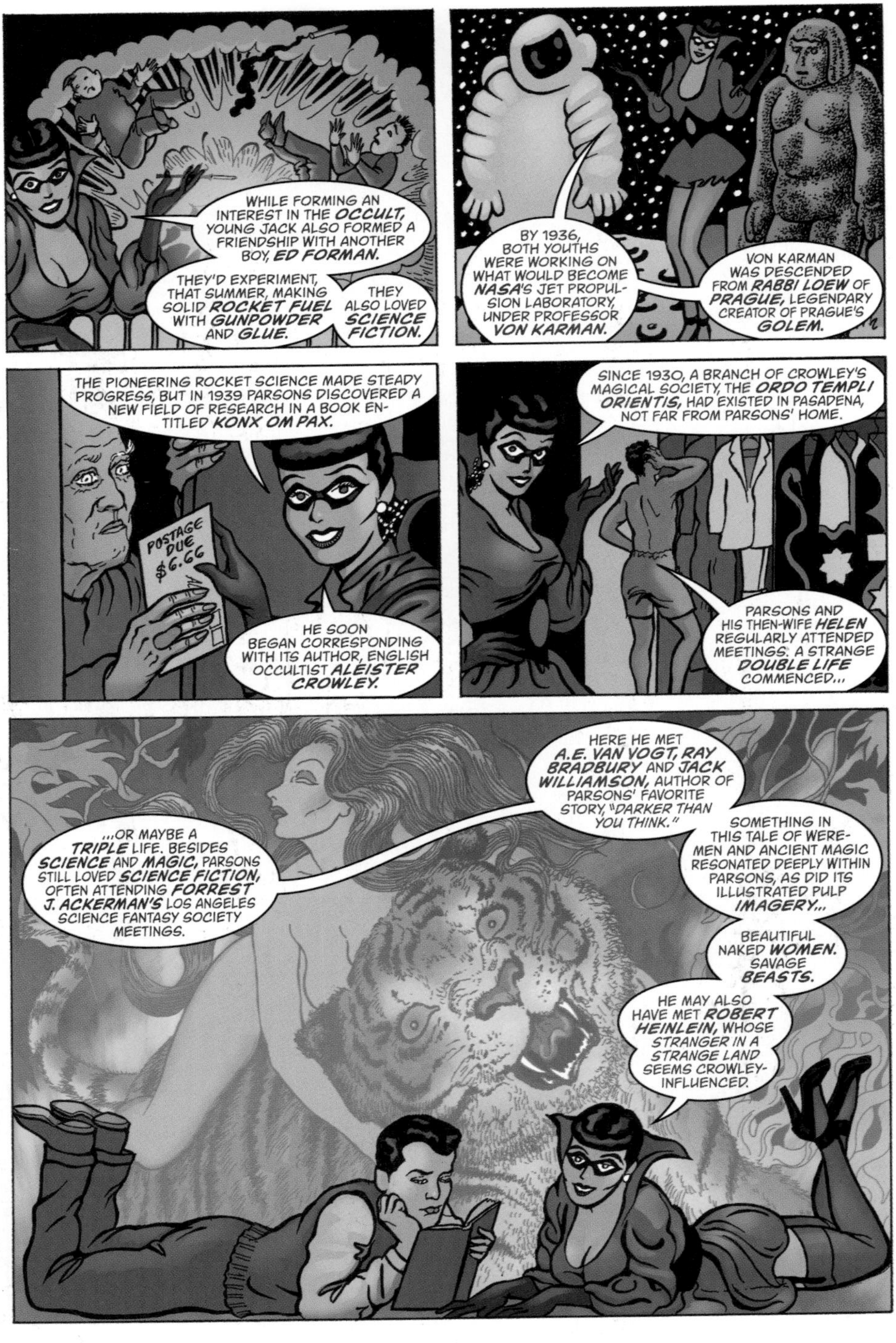
WHILE FORMING AN INTEREST IN THE OCCULT, YOUNG JACK ALSO FORMED A FRIENDSHIP WITH ANOTHER BOY, ED FORMAN.
THEY'D EXPERIMENT, THAT SUMMER, MAKING SOLID ROCKET FUEL WITH GUNPOWDER AND GLUE.
THEY ALSO LOVED SCIENCE FICTION.
BY 1936, BOTH YOUTHS WERE WORKING ON WHAT WOULD BECOME NASA'S JET PROPULSION LABORATORY, UNDER PROFESSOR VON KARMAN.
VON KARMAN WAS DESCENDED FROM RABBI LOEW OF PRAGUE, LEGENDARY CREATOR OF PRAGUE'S GOLEM.
THE PIONEERING ROCKET SCIENCE MADE STEADY PROGRESS, BUT IN 1939 PARSONS DISCOVERED A NEW FIELD OF RESEARCH IN A BOOK ENTITLED KONX OM PAX.
POSTAGE DUE $6.66
HE SOON BEGAN CORRESPONDING WITH ITS AUTHOR, ENGLISH OCCULTIST ALEISTER CROWLEY.
SINCE 1930, A BRANCH OF CROWLEY'S MAGICAL SOCIETY, THE ORDO TEMPLI ORIENTIS, HAD EXISTED IN PASADENA, NOT FAR FROM PARSONS' HOME.
PARSONS AND HIS THEN-WIFE HELEN REGULARLY ATTENDED MEETINGS. A STRANGE DOUBLE LIFE COMMENCED...
...OR MAYBE A TRIPLE LIFE. BESIDES SCIENCE AND MAGIC, PARSONS STILL LOVED SCIENCE FICTION, OFTEN ATTENDING FORREST J. ACKERMAN'S LOS ANGELES SCIENCE FANTASY SOCIETY MEETINGS.
HERE HE MET A.E. VAN VOGT, RAY BRADBURY AND JACK WILLIAMSON, AUTHOR OF PARSONS' FAVORITE STORY, "DARKER THAN YOU THINK."
SOMETHING IN THIS TALE OF WERE-MEN AND ANCIENT MAGIC RESONATED DEEPLY WITHIN PARSONS, AS DID ITS ILLUSTRATED PULP IMAGERY...
BEAUTIFUL NAKED WOMEN. SAVAGE BEASTS.
HE MAY ALSO HAVE MET ROBERT HEINLEIN, WHOSE STRANGER IN A STRANGE LAND SEEMS CROWLEY-INFLUENCED.

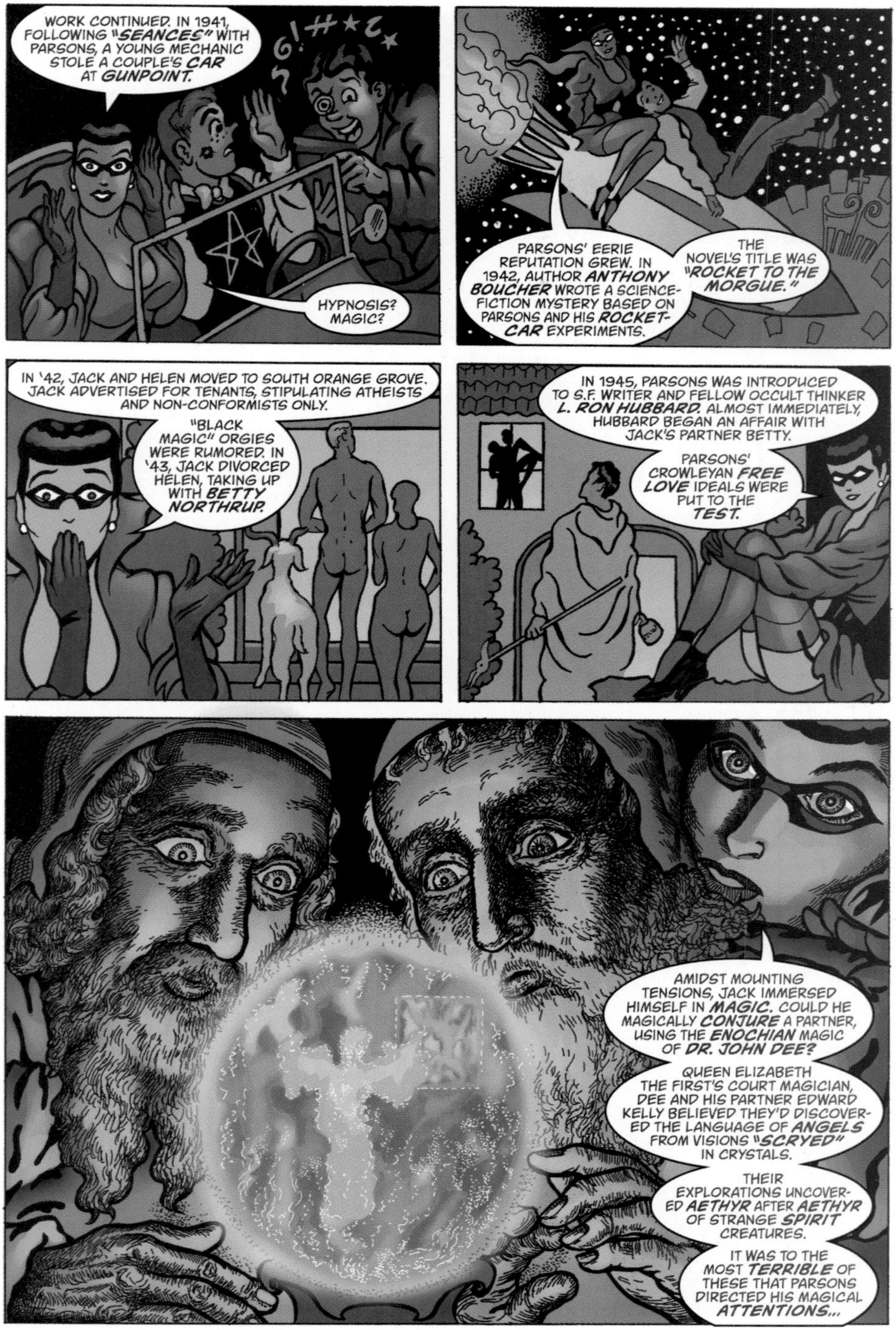
WORK CONTINUED. IN 1941, FOLLOWING "SEANCES" WITH PARSONS, A YOUNG MECHANIC STOLE A COUPLE'S CAR AT GUNPOINT.
HYPNOSIS? MAGIC?
PARSONS' EERIE REPUTATION GREW. IN 1942, AUTHOR ANTHONY BOUCHER WROTE A SCIENCE-FICTION MYSTERY BASED ON PARSONS AND HIS ROCKET-CAR EXPERIMENTS.
THE NOVEL'S TITLE WAS "ROCKET TO THE MORGUE."
IN '42, JACK AND HELEN MOVED TO SOUTH ORANGE GROVE. JACK ADVERTISED FOR TENANTS, STIPULATING ATHEISTS AND NON-CONFORMISTS ONLY.
"BLACK MAGIC" ORGIES WERE RUMORED. IN '43, JACK DIVORCED HELEN, TAKING UP WITH BETTY NORTHRUP.
IN 1945, PARSONS WAS INTRODUCED TO S.F. WRITER AND FELLOW OCCULT THINKER L. RON HUBBARD. ALMOST IMMEDIATELY, HUBBARD BEGAN AN AFFAIR WITH JACK'S PARTNER BETTY.
PARSONS' CROWLEYAN FREE LOVE IDEALS WERE PUT TO THE TEST.
AMIDST MOUNTING TENSIONS, JACK IMMERSED HIMSELF IN MAGIC. COULD HE MAGICALLY CONJURE A PARTNER, USING THE ENOCHIAN MAGIC OF DR. JOHN DEE?
QUEEN ELIZABETH THE FIRST'S COURT MAGICIAN, DEE AND HIS PARTNER EDWARD KELLY BELIEVED THEY'D DISCOVERED THE LANGUAGE OF ANGELS FROM VISIONS "SCRYED" IN CRYSTALS.
THEIR EXPLORATIONS UNCOVERED AETHYR AFTER AETHYR OF STRANGE SPIRIT CREATURES.
IT WAS TO THE MOST TERRIBLE OF THESE THAT PARSONS DIRECTED HIS MAGICAL ATTENTIONS...

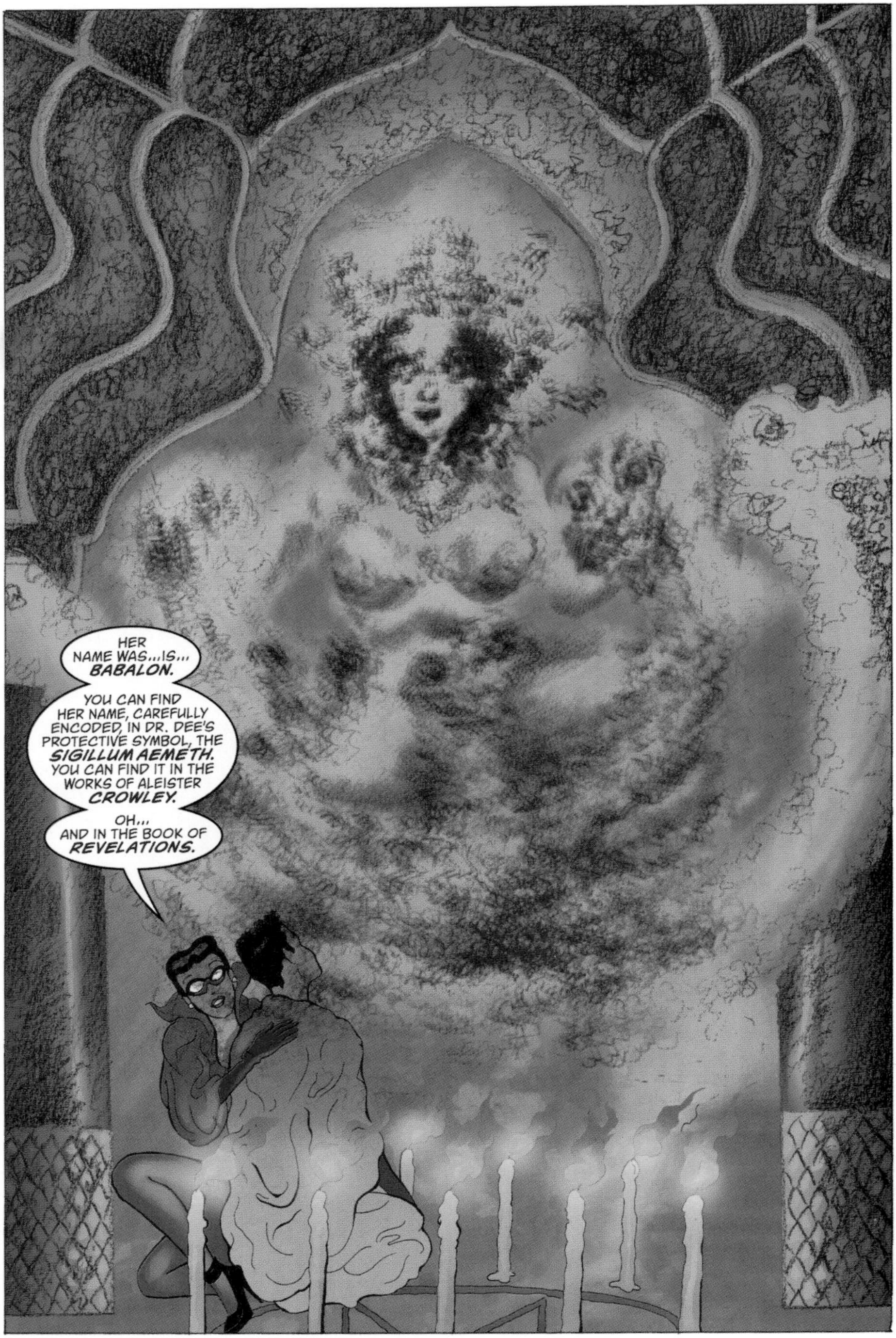
HER NAME WAS...IS... BABALON.
YOU CAN FIND HER NAME, CAREFULLY ENCODED, IN DR. DEE'S PROTECTIVE SYMBOL, THE SIGILLUM AEMETH. YOU CAN FIND IT IN THE WORKS OF ALEISTER CROWLEY.
OH... AND IN THE BOOK OF REVELATIONS.

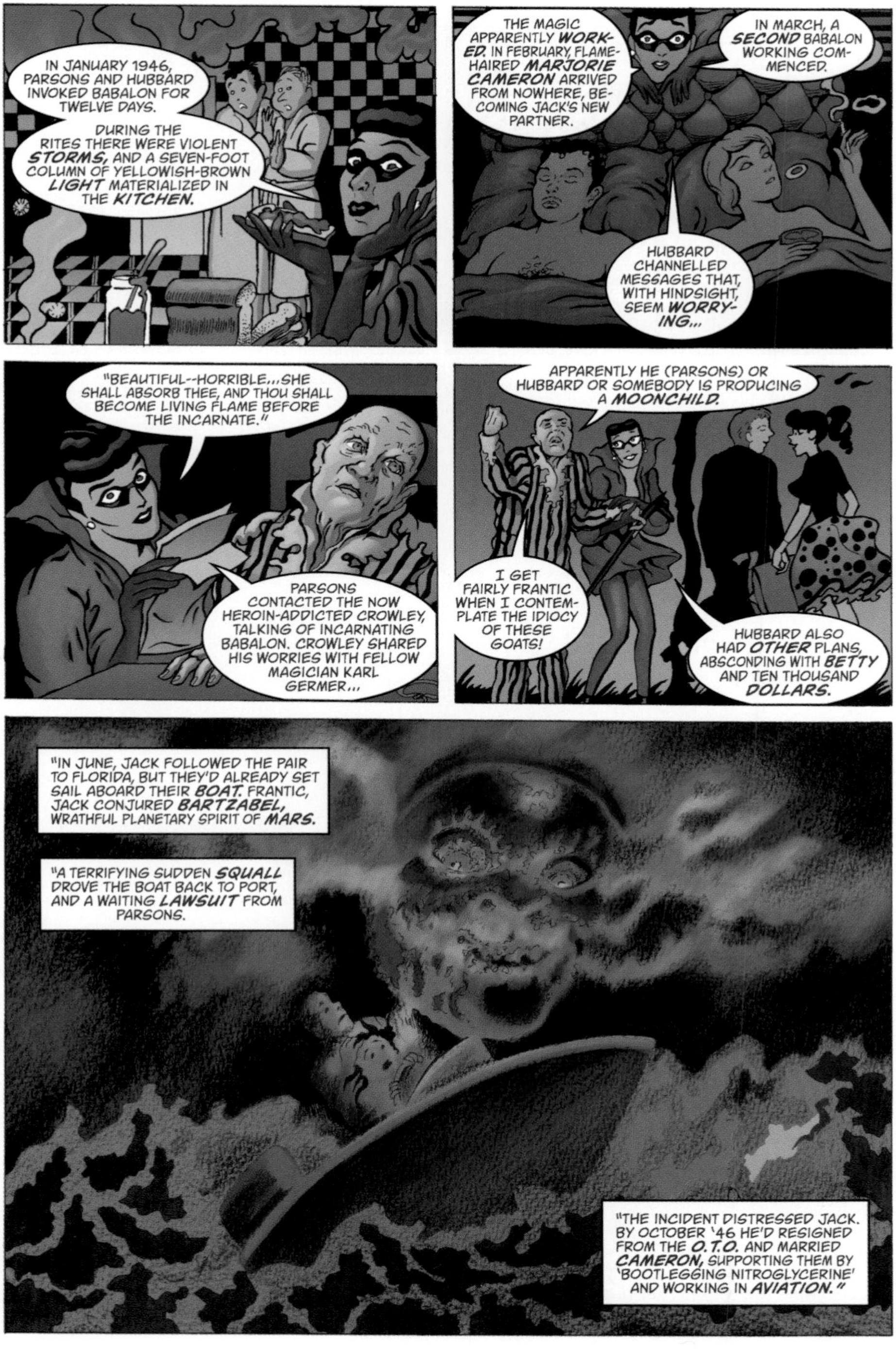

IN JANUARY 1946, PARSONS AND HUBBARD INVOKED BABALON FOR TWELVE DAYS.
DURING THE RITES THERE WERE VIOLENT STORMS, AND A SEVEN-FOOT COLUMN OF YELLOWISH-BROWN LIGHT MATERIALIZED IN THE KITCHEN.
THE MAGIC APPARENTLY WORKED. IN FEBRUARY, FLAME-HAIRED MARJORIE CAMERON ARRIVED FROM NOWHERE, BECOMING JACK'S NEW PARTNER.
IN MARCH, A SECOND BABALON WORKING COMMENCED.
HUBBARD CHANNELLED MESSAGES THAT, WITH HINDSIGHT, SEEM WORRYING...
"BEAUTIFUL--HORRIBLE...SHE SHALL ABSORB THEE, AND THOU SHALL BECOME LIVING FLAME BEFORE THE INCARNATE."
PARSONS CONTACTED THE NOW HEROIN-ADDICTED CROWLEY, TALKING OF INCARNATING BABALON. CROWLEY SHARED HIS WORRIES WITH FELLOW MAGICIAN KARL GERMER...
APPARENTLY HE (PARSONS) OR HUBBARD OR SOMEBODY IS PRODUCING A MOONCHILD.
I GET FAIRLY FRANTIC WHEN I CONTEMPLATE THE IDIOCY OF THESE GOATS!
HUBBARD ALSO HAD OTHER PLANS, ABSCONDING WITH BETTY AND TEN THOUSAND DOLLARS.
"IN JUNE, JACK FOLLOWED THE PAIR TO FLORIDA, BUT THEY'D ALREADY SET SAIL ABOARD THEIR BOAT. FRANTIC, JACK CONJURED BARTZABEL, WRATHFUL PLANETARY SPIRIT OF MARS.
"A TERRIFYING SUDDEN SQUALL DROVE THE BOAT BACK TO PORT, AND A WAITING LAWSUIT FROM PARSONS.
"THE INCIDENT DISTRESSED JACK. BY OCTOBER '46 HE'D RESIGNED FROM THE O.T.O. AND MARRIED CAMERON, SUPPORTING THEM BY 'BOOTLEGGING NITROGLYCERINE' AND WORKING IN AVIATION."

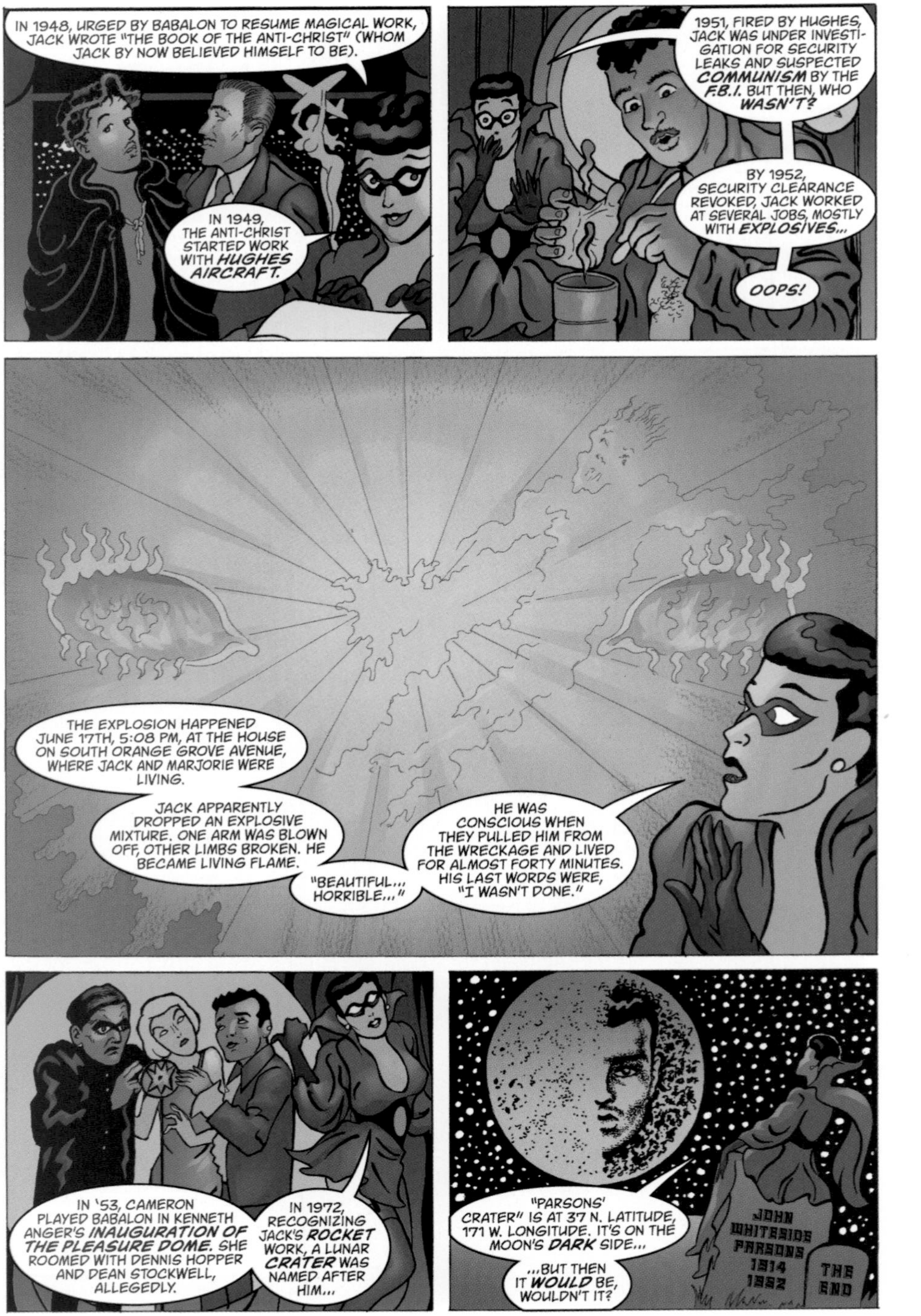
IN 1948, URGED BY BABALON TO RESUME MAGICAL WORK, JACK WROTE "THE BOOK OF THE ANTI-CHRIST" (WHOM JACK BY NOW BELIEVED HIMSELF TO BE).
IN 1949, THE ANTI-CHRIST STARTED WORK WITH HUGHES AIRCRAFT.
1951, FIRED BY HUGHES, JACK WAS UNDER INVESTIGATION FOR SECURITY LEAKS AND SUSPECTED COMMUNISM BY THE F.B.I. BUT THEN, WHO WASN'T?
BY 1952, SECURITY CLEARANCE REVOKED, JACK WORKED AT SEVERAL JOBS, MOSTLY WITH EXPLOSIVES...
OOPS!
THE EXPLOSION HAPPENED JUNE 17TH, 5:08 PM, AT THE HOUSE ON SOUTH ORANGE GROVE AVENUE, WHERE JACK AND MARJORIE WERE LIVING.
JACK APPARENTLY DROPPED AN EXPLOSIVE MIXTURE. ONE ARM WAS BLOWN OFF, OTHER LIMBS BROKEN. HE BECAME LIVING FLAME.
"BEAUTIFUL... HORRIBLE..."
HE WAS CONSCIOUS WHEN THEY PULLED HIM FROM THE WRECKAGE AND LIVED FOR ALMOST FORTY MINUTES. HIS LAST WORDS WERE, "I WASN'T DONE."
IN '53, CAMERON PLAYED BABALON IN KENNETH ANGER'S INAUGURATION OF THE PLEASURE DOME. SHE ROOMED WITH DENNIS HOPPER AND DEAN STOCKWELL, ALLEGEDLY.
IN 1972, RECOGNIZING JACK'S ROCKET WORK, A LUNAR CRATER WAS NAMED AFTER HIM...
"PARSONS' CRATER" IS AT 37 N. LATITUDE, 171 W. LONGITUDE. IT'S ON THE MOON'S DARK SIDE...
...BUT THEN IT WOULD BE, WOULDN'T IT?
JOHN WHITESIDE PARSONS 1914 1952
THE END

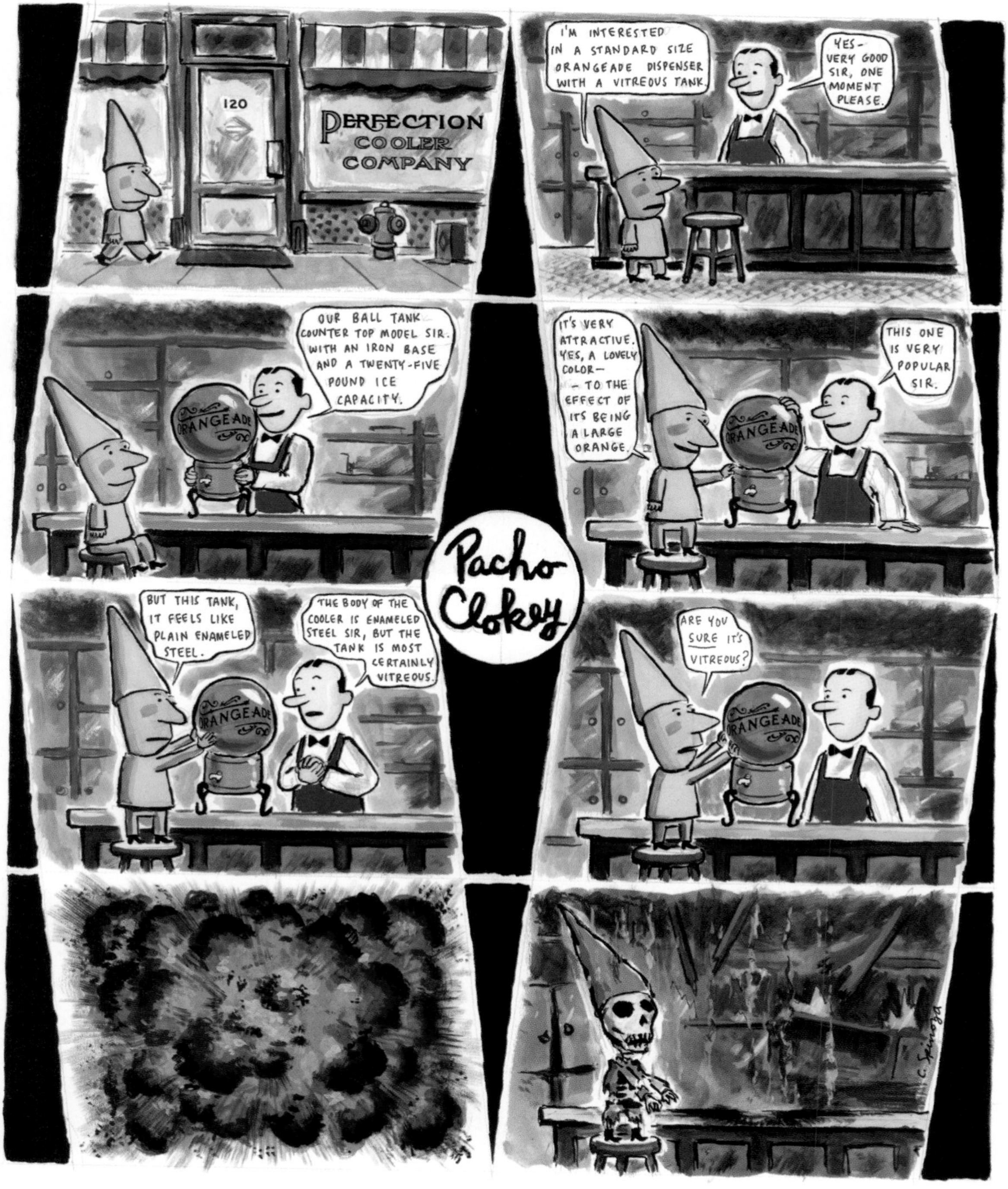
120
PERFECTION COOLER COMPANY
I'M INTERESTED IN A STANDARD SIZE ORANGEADE DISPENSER WITH A VITREOUS TANK.
YES- VERY GOOD SIR, ONE MOMENT PLEASE.
OUR BALL TANK COUNTER TOP MODEL SIR. WITH AN IRON BASE AND A TWENTY-FIVE POUND ICE CAPACITY.
ORANGEADE
IT'S VERY ATTRACTIVE. YES, A LOVELY COLOR— — TO THE EFFECT OF ITS BEING A LARGE ORANGE.
THIS ONE IS VERY POPULAR SIR.
Pacho Clokey
BUT THIS TANK, IT FEELS LIKE PLAIN ENAMELED STEEL.
THE BODY OF THE COOLER IS ENAMELED STEEL SIR, BUT THE TANK IS MOST CERTAINLY VITREOUS.
ARE YOU SURE IT'S VITREOUS?
C. Spinoza

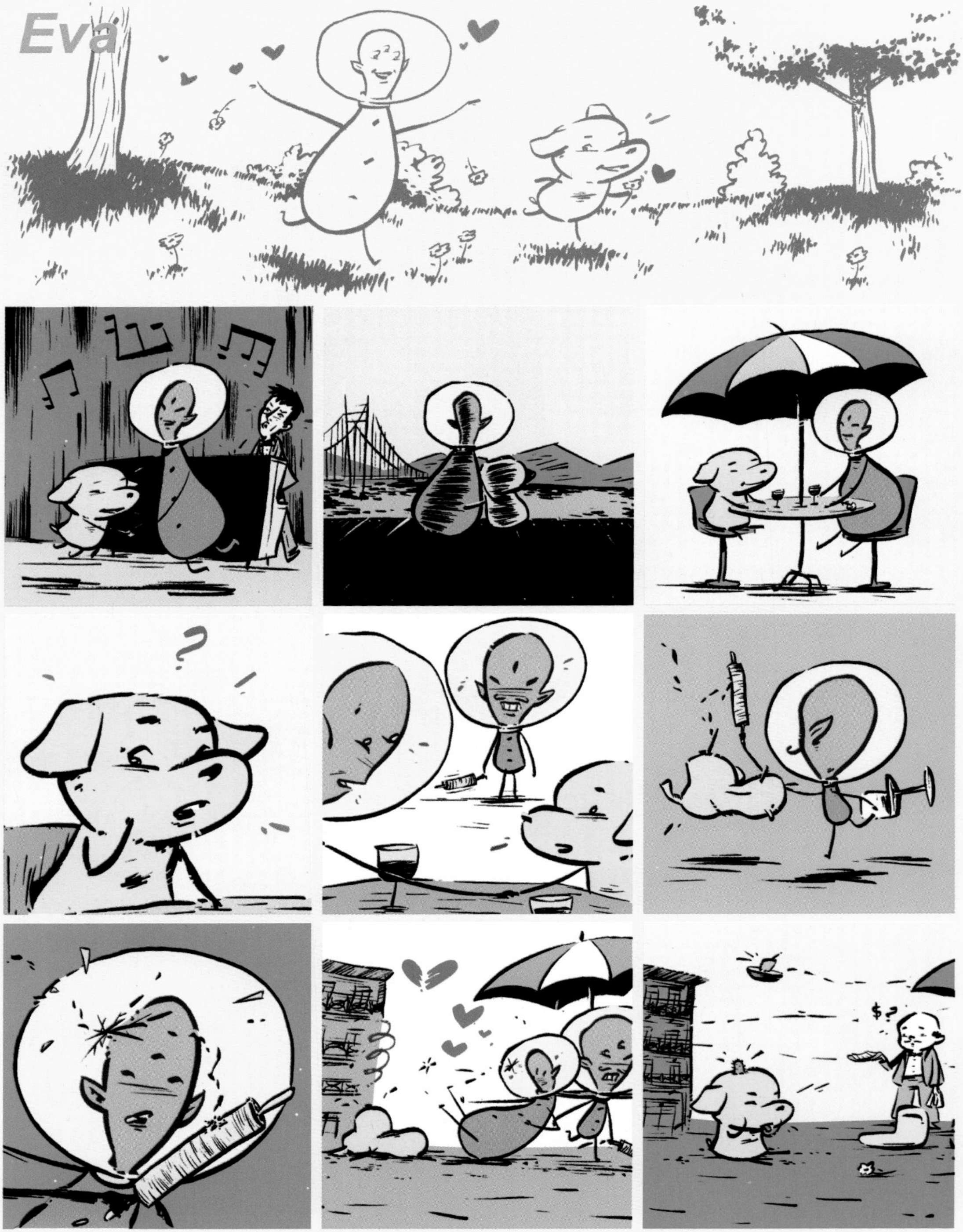
Eva
$?

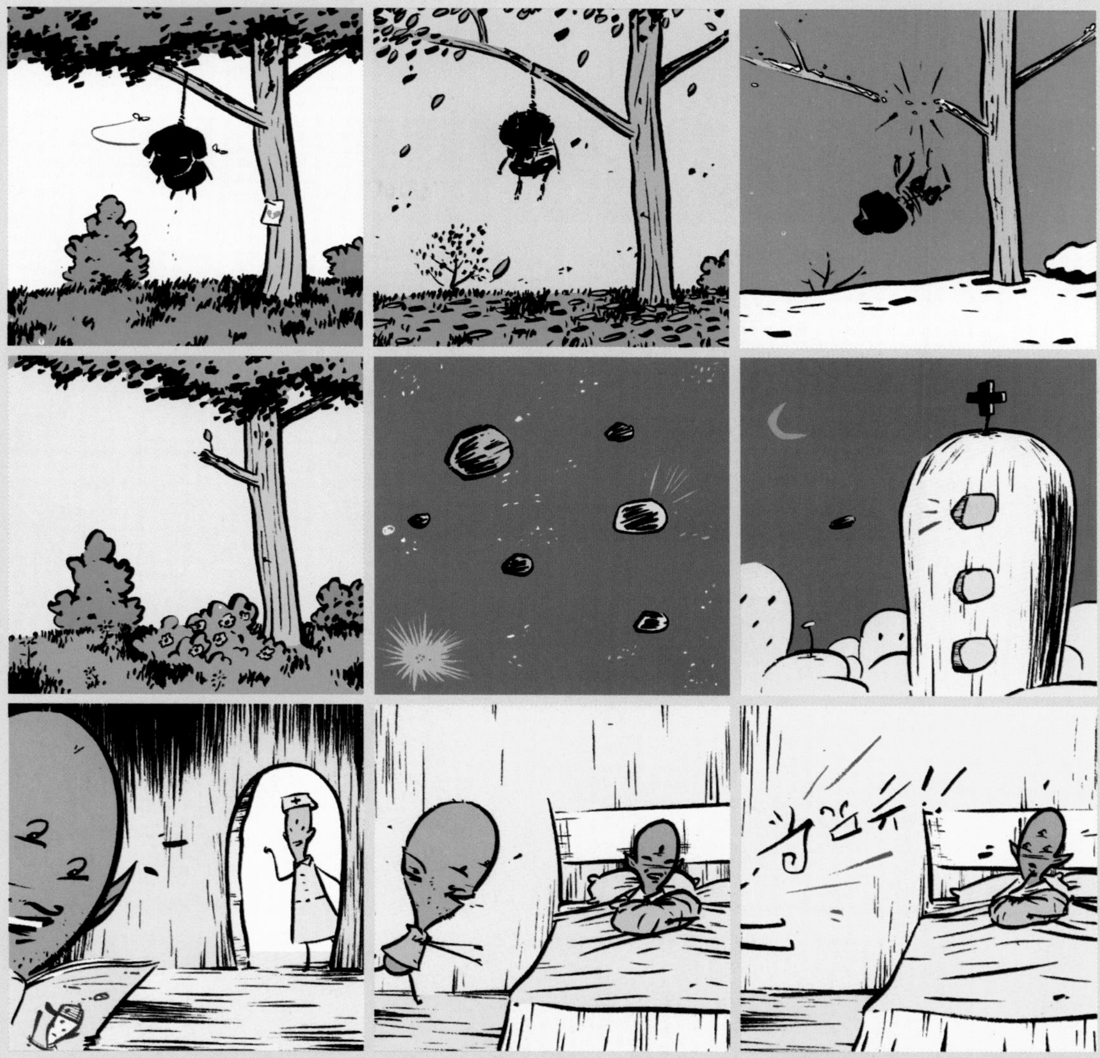

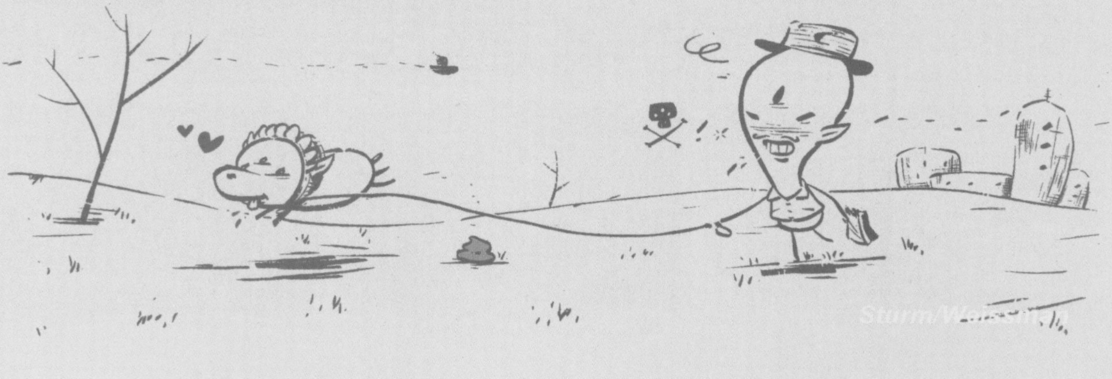
Sturm/Weissman

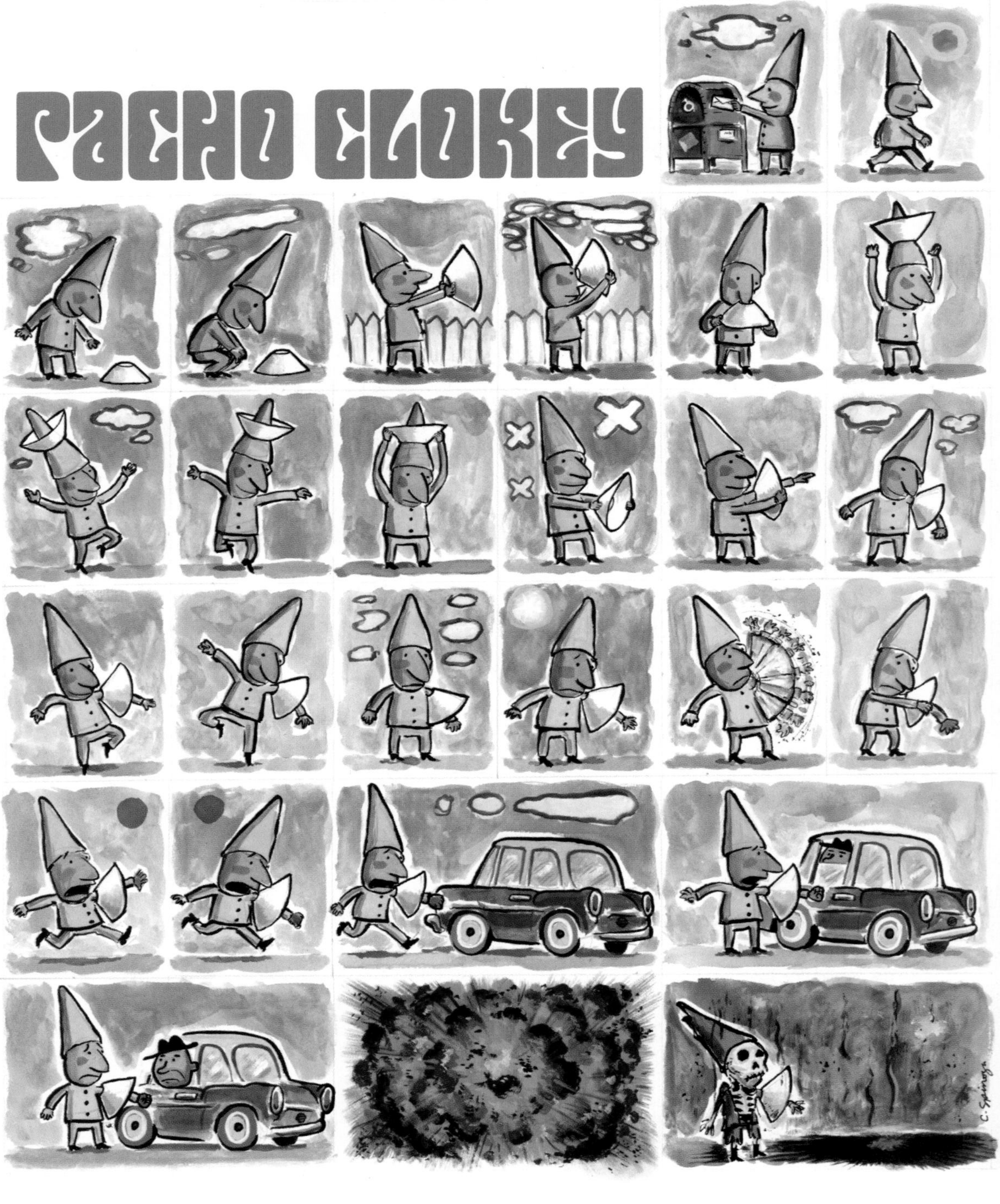
PACHO CLOKEY
C. Spinoza

PEANUTS
A CARTOONISTS' TRIBUTE

Many of the pages that follow originally ran in the Austin American-Statesman, under the editorship of Jeff Salamon, while others were created especially for this archive.

Many thanks to the contributing artists; to Jeff Salamon for this idea in the first place; and to Ian Lynam, for the splendid design and layout assistance for this section.

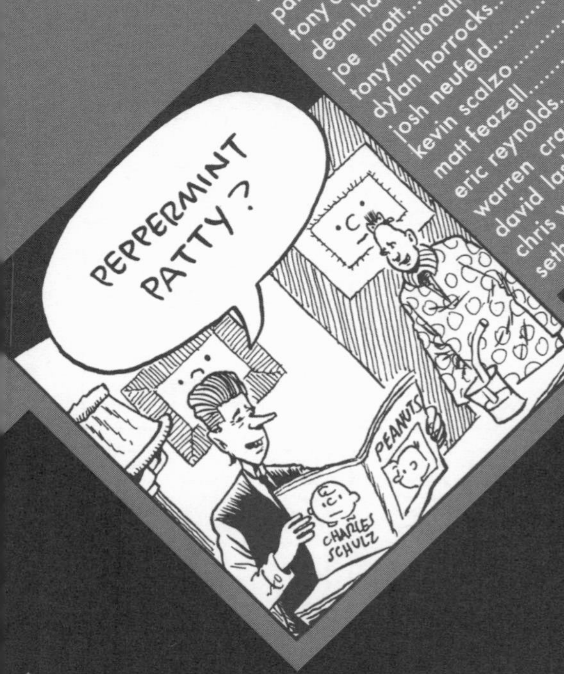

PEPPERMINT PATTY?
PEANUTS
CHARLES SCHULZ

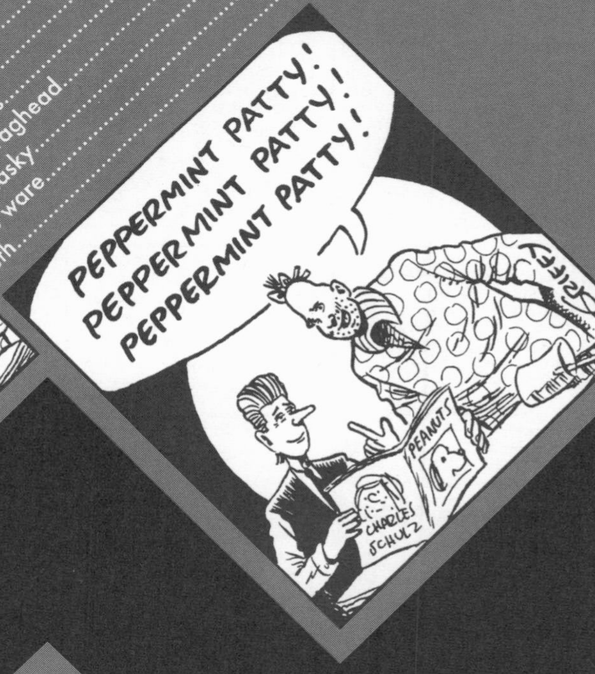

PEPPERMINT PATTY! PEPPERMINT PATTY! PEPPERMINT PATTY!
PEANUTS
CHARLES SCHULZ

Table of Contents

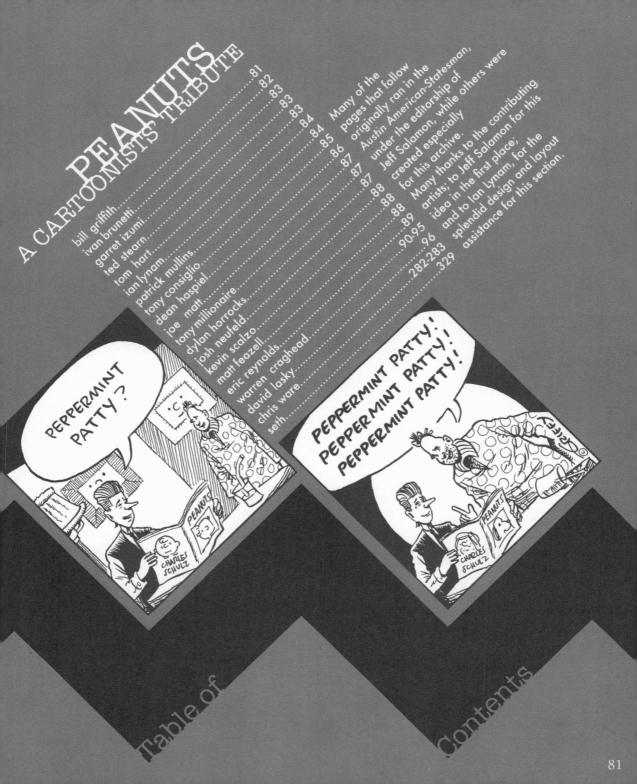

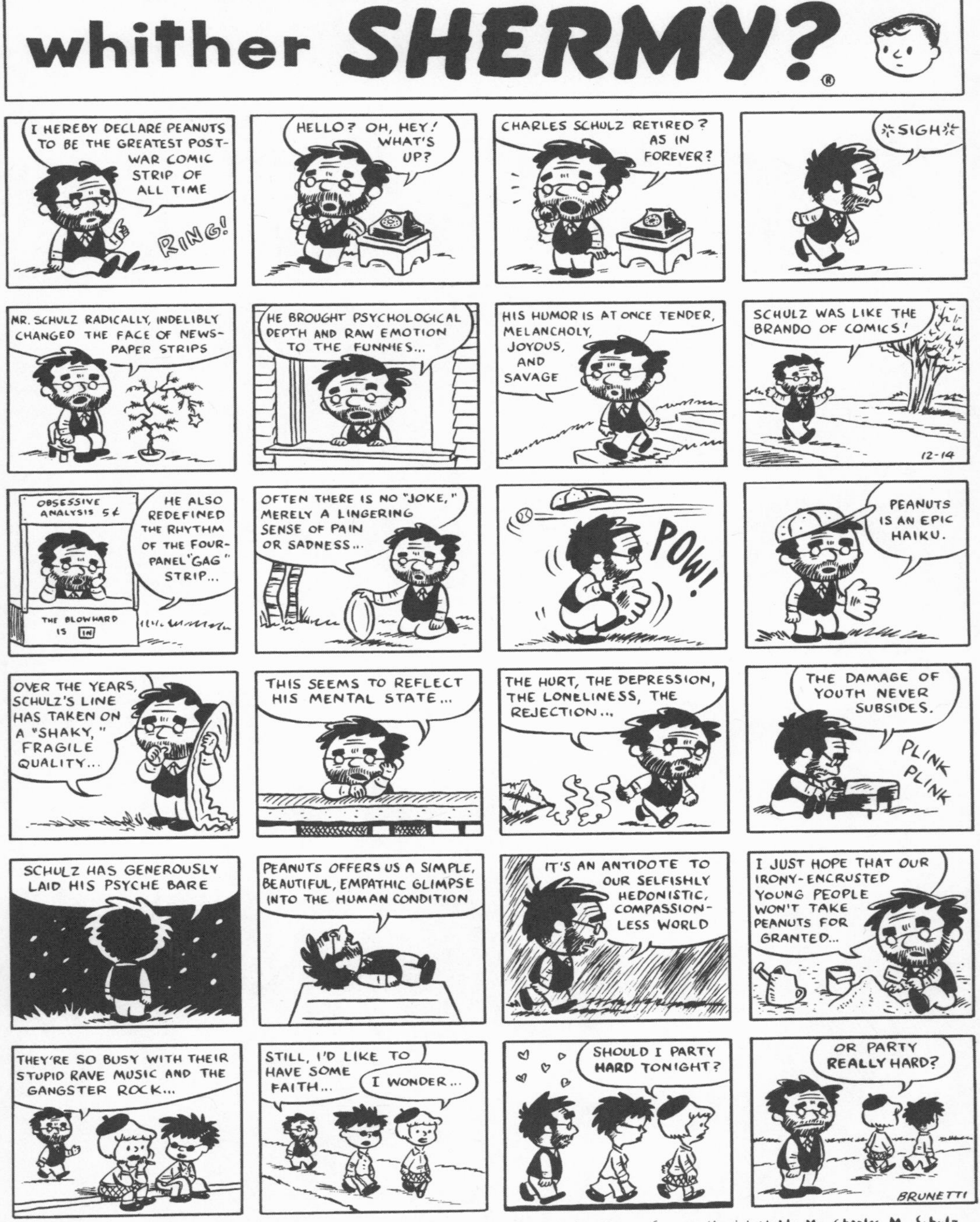

whither SHERMY?
I HEREBY DECLARE PEANUTS TO BE THE GREATEST POST-WAR COMIC STRIP OF ALL TIME
RING!
HELLO? OH, HEY! WHAT'S UP?
CHARLES SCHULZ RETIRED? AS IN FOREVER?
SIGH
MR. SCHULZ RADICALLY, INDELIBLY CHANGED THE FACE OF NEWSPAPER STRIPS
HE BROUGHT PSYCHOLOGICAL DEPTH AND RAW EMOTION TO THE FUNNIES...
HIS HUMOR IS AT ONCE TENDER, MELANCHOLY, JOYOUS, AND SAVAGE
SCHULZ WAS LIKE THE BRANDO OF COMICS!
12-14
OBSESSIVE ANALYSIS 5¢
HE ALSO REDEFINED THE RHYTHM OF THE FOUR-PANEL "GAG" STRIP...
THE BLOWHARD IS IN
OFTEN THERE IS NO "JOKE," MERELY A LINGERING SENSE OF PAIN OR SADNESS...
POW!
PEANUTS IS AN EPIC HAIKU.
OVER THE YEARS, SCHULZ'S LINE HAS TAKEN ON A "SHAKY," FRAGILE QUALITY...
THIS SEEMS TO REFLECT HIS MENTAL STATE...
THE HURT, THE DEPRESSION, THE LONELINESS, THE REJECTION...
THE DAMAGE OF YOUTH NEVER SUBSIDES.
PLINK PLINK
SCHULZ HAS GENEROUSLY LAID HIS PSYCHE BARE
PEANUTS OFFERS US A SIMPLE, BEAUTIFUL, EMPATHIC GLIMPSE INTO THE HUMAN CONDITION
IT'S AN ANTIDOTE TO OUR SELFISHLY HEDONISTIC, COMPASSIONLESS WORLD
I JUST HOPE THAT OUR IRONY-ENCRUSTED YOUNG PEOPLE WON'T TAKE PEANUTS FOR GRANTED...
THEY'RE SO BUSY WITH THEIR STUPID RAVE MUSIC AND THE GANGSTER ROCK...
STILL, I'D LIKE TO HAVE SOME FAITH...
I WONDER...
SHOULD I PARTY HARD TONIGHT?
OR PARTY REALLY HARD?
BRUNETTI

NOTE: Respectful thanks and sincere apologies must go to Mr. F. C. Ware, Ms. Shannon Wright, and of course the inimitable Mr. Charles M. Schulz.

The funny pages without *Peanuts* seem heartless, gutless, and soulless. Mr. Schulz's comic strip was inseparable from his life, each flowing seamlessly into the other. His masterful calligraphy directly manifested a rich, intense, internal world, somehow at once wistful, tortured, and joyful.

It was as if Mr. Schulz had splintered his psyche into each of his different characters. Perhaps he was trying to understand, even transform, himself in some fundamental way, shattering himself into Charlie Brown, Lucy, Linus, Schroeder, Snoopy, Rerun, etc., and then rebuild himself by structuring the various scenarios in the strips, much in the same way that a computer builds models based on a few components by shifting one parameter per iteration. Eventually, these models accumulate into a reconfigured, more complex, cohesive structure. Perhaps at some point, a profound, grand self-awareness may develop. Kind of like the human mind and, well, the universe itself.

Every line, every space, every word, every mark of every *Peanuts* strip is charged with Mr. Schulz's very essence, imbued with the depth and core of his being. Thus, *Peanuts* is and shall remain as alive as you or I, for Mr. Schulz's sincerity, humanity, faith, empathy, pain, struggle, and strength have indelibly etched his work into immortality, merging with the singular universal consciousness that permeates and, in fact, defines our existence.

In short, *Peanuts* is *Art*, pure and simple and without pretense, the way it should be.

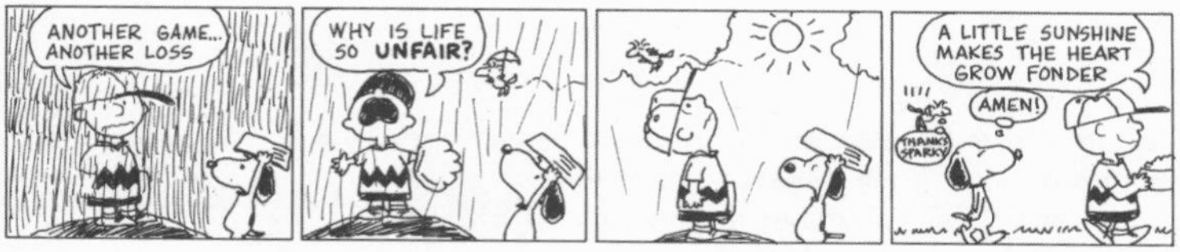
ANOTHER GAME... ANOTHER LOSS
WHY IS LIFE SO UNFAIR?
A LITTLE SUNSHINE MAKES THE HEART GROW FONDER
AMEN!
THANKS SPARKY

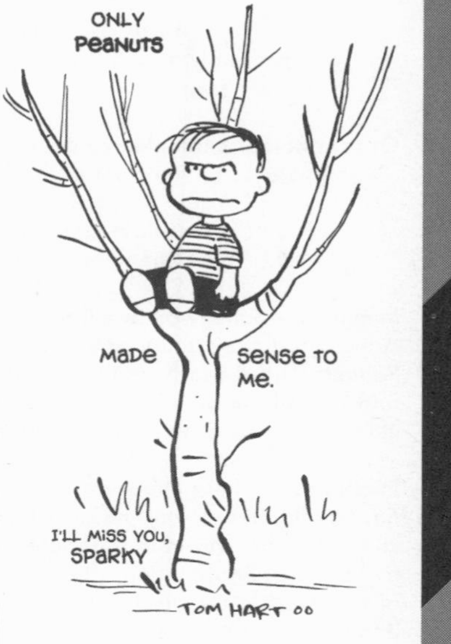
ONLY PEANUTS
MADE
SENSE TO ME.
I'LL MISS YOU, SPARKY
—TOM HART 00

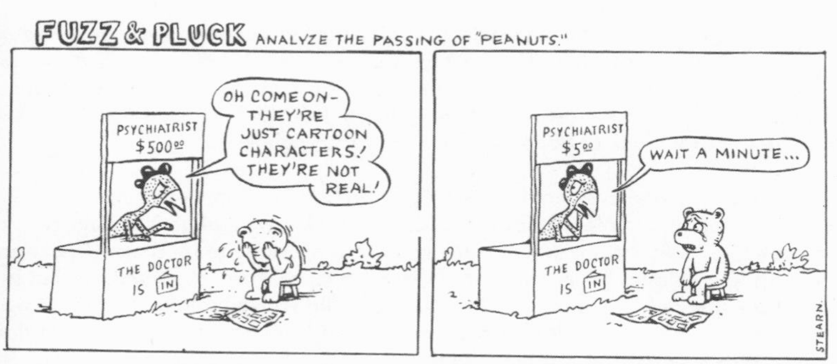
FUZZ & PLUCK ANALYZE THE PASSING OF "PEANUTS."
PSYCHIATRIST $500.00
OH COME ON- THEY'RE JUST CARTOON CHARACTERS! THEY'RE NOT REAL!
THE DOCTOR IS IN
PSYCHIATRIST $5.00
WAIT A MINUTE...
THE DOCTOR IS IN
STEARN

Meet Me at the Doghouse
by Patrick Mullins

I didn't grow up reading *Peanuts*, or at least I have no memory of it affecting me when I was a kid. I remember the TV specials and the merchandise, but the strip itself made no impression on me until my late teen years. At this later date I'm not sure what got me started on it; however, I am pretty sure of why I've stuck with it though. There's something strange at work in those little strips that becomes apparent only when you read them in bulk. If you pay attention, you can learn something.

The strips centered on the human characters' catalogue—in a very blunt, matter of fact style that's stopped just short of meanness by their creator's obviously caring demeanor and gentle humor—seemingly every possible variation of disappointment, mistreatment and misunderstanding available to a human being. Which, in itself is nothing particularly notable. Human folly has been a topic of art and literature since the beginnings of art and literature.

Before I go any further, let me say that I'm not in any way denying the sweetness of Charles "Sparky" Schulz's work, or attempting to portray *Peanuts* as purely pessimistic. What I'm asserting is that what initially makes the strip stand out from the 'cheap laffs' usually associated with newspaper comics is the fact that more often than not *Peanuts'* subjects are the small scale negative experiences that both ironists and optimists refer to as "character-builders." Everyone learns something, but it's usually something they'd rather not know. There is, of course, more to it, but we'll get to that later.

In the meantime, consider this scene by way of example:
Peppermint Patty and Charlie Brown are sitting beneath a tree in repose.
        P.P.: "Chuck, do you think a girl who is ugly has as much chance for happiness as a girl who is beautiful?"
        C.B.: "Of course! For one thing, you have a nice personality and..."
        P.P.: "What makes you think I was talking about myself, Chuck? Trapped you, didn't I, Chuck? That's alright... It was a dirty trick... Actually, I guess I *was* talking about myself, so what you were saying was probably true. But what makes you think I was talking about myself, Chuck?."
        C.B.: (sigh)

Or for another example, my personal favorite from the everyone-goes-home-a-loser variety of *Peanuts* strips:
Rerun knocks on the door of the Brown household; Sally answers.
        R.: "Would you like to buy some handmade Valentines to give to your friends?"
        S.: "I don't have any friends." (Shuts door in Rerun's face.)
        R.: "Well, then you shouldn't have answered the door!"

In much the same way that the small scale of the form and the characters amplify the impact of an individual *Peanuts* comic, the ongoing nature of the strip adds another dimension: the characters keep going. No one ever gives up in *Peanuts*. Those overly mature children plod along at an even keel no matter what happens, saved from depression and/or malaise by a healthy dose of slapstick candy. Like most of us here in the real world, they exist wholly in their little environment, and keep on despite the apparent lack of hope for any sort of transcendence.

In contrast to these little *every* men and women playing yet another losing baseball game, Sparky Schulz offers up Snoopy the beagle and his almost-constant companion, Woodstock the bird. Snoopy knows that he is a dog. He knows that he lives in a doghouse; he knows he's dependent on "the little round-headed kid" to feed him. The important thing is, Snoopy doesn't care about his lousy status. While the rest of the *Peanuts* cast are immersed in what is given (and it's not much), Snoopy lives in a variety of imaginary worlds made of *what* is available and what he wants it to be. Its not just a doghouse, it's a Sopwith Camel, it's the locker room where Joe Cool hangs out, it's where the Great Author works on his masterpiece, *It Was A Dark and Stormy Night*.

What's truly inspiring about this fantasyland lifestyle is that it occasionally succeeds in drawing in the other (human) characters. The Flying Ace is grounded in occupied France, and who should appear but Marcie, speaking perfect French, on cue. Charlie Brown puts on the airs of a waiter when Snoopy and Woodstock pretend the doghouse is a restaurant. Even the physical universe bows to their wishes sometimes—in one strip Woodstock literally dances up a little storm cloud. Their environment is correspondingly more expansive. These little animals get around. Snoopy makes solo voyages to the desert (to visit his brother Spike) and the surface of the moon; with Woodstock and the rest of the Beagle Scouts, he regularly goes on long hiking excursions. The children stay at home, or close by.

Did Schulz intentionally set up this dichotomy between drab reality and imagination? By all accounts, he was at least mildly depressed for most of his life, so I would be surprised if he wasn't on some level conscious of the contrast between his human characters' attachment to a disappointing existence and the animals' happy fantasy lives. Either way, whether he meant to or not, this is what Sparky Schulz gave to me: sympathy, and some useful suggestions for a way out. You can keep trying to kick that football; I'm only here temporarily, grounded behind enemy lines, and once my Sopwith Camel is up and running, I'll be on my way.

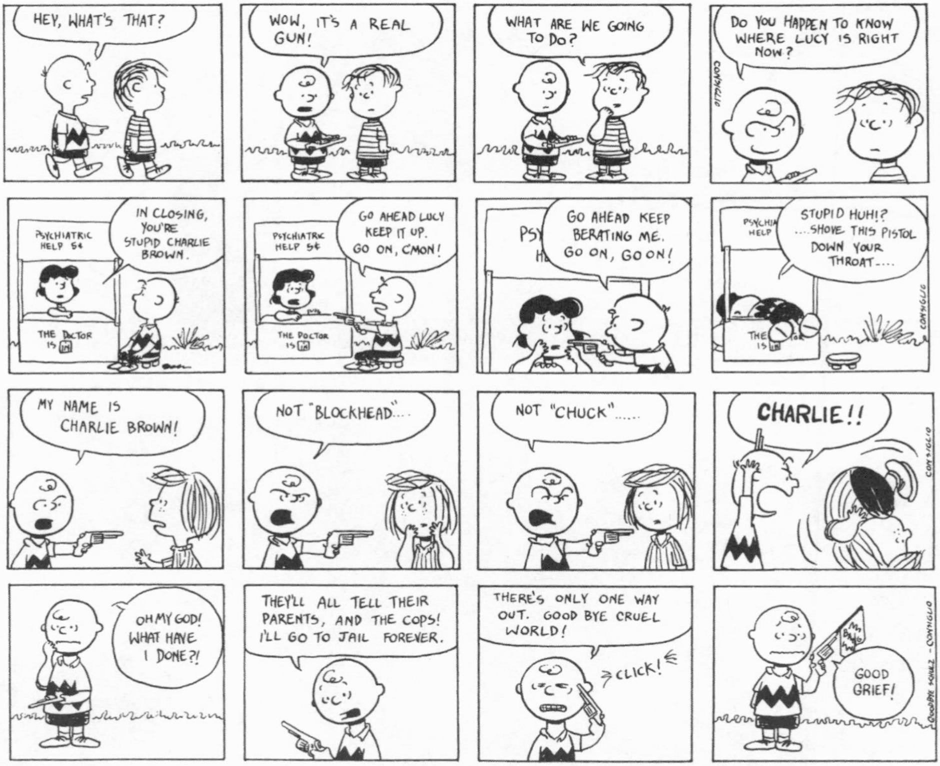
HEY, WHAT'S THAT?
WOW, IT'S A REAL GUN!
WHAT ARE WE GOING TO DO?
DO YOU HAPPEN TO KNOW WHERE LUCY IS RIGHT NOW?
PSYCHIATRIC HELP 5¢
IN CLOSING, YOU'RE STUPID CHARLIE BROWN.
THE DOCTOR IS IN
GO AHEAD LUCY KEEP IT UP. GO ON, C'MON!
GO AHEAD KEEP BERATING ME. GO ON, GO ON!
STUPID HUH!? ....SHOVE THIS PISTOL DOWN YOUR THROAT....
MY NAME IS CHARLIE BROWN!
NOT "BLOCKHEAD"...
NOT "CHUCK"......
CHARLIE!!
OH MY GOD! WHAT HAVE I DONE?!
THEY'LL ALL TELL THEIR PARENTS, AND THE COPS! I'LL GO TO JAIL FOREVER.
THERE'S ONLY ONE WAY OUT. GOOD BYE CRUEL WORLD!
CLICK!
GOOD GRIEF!

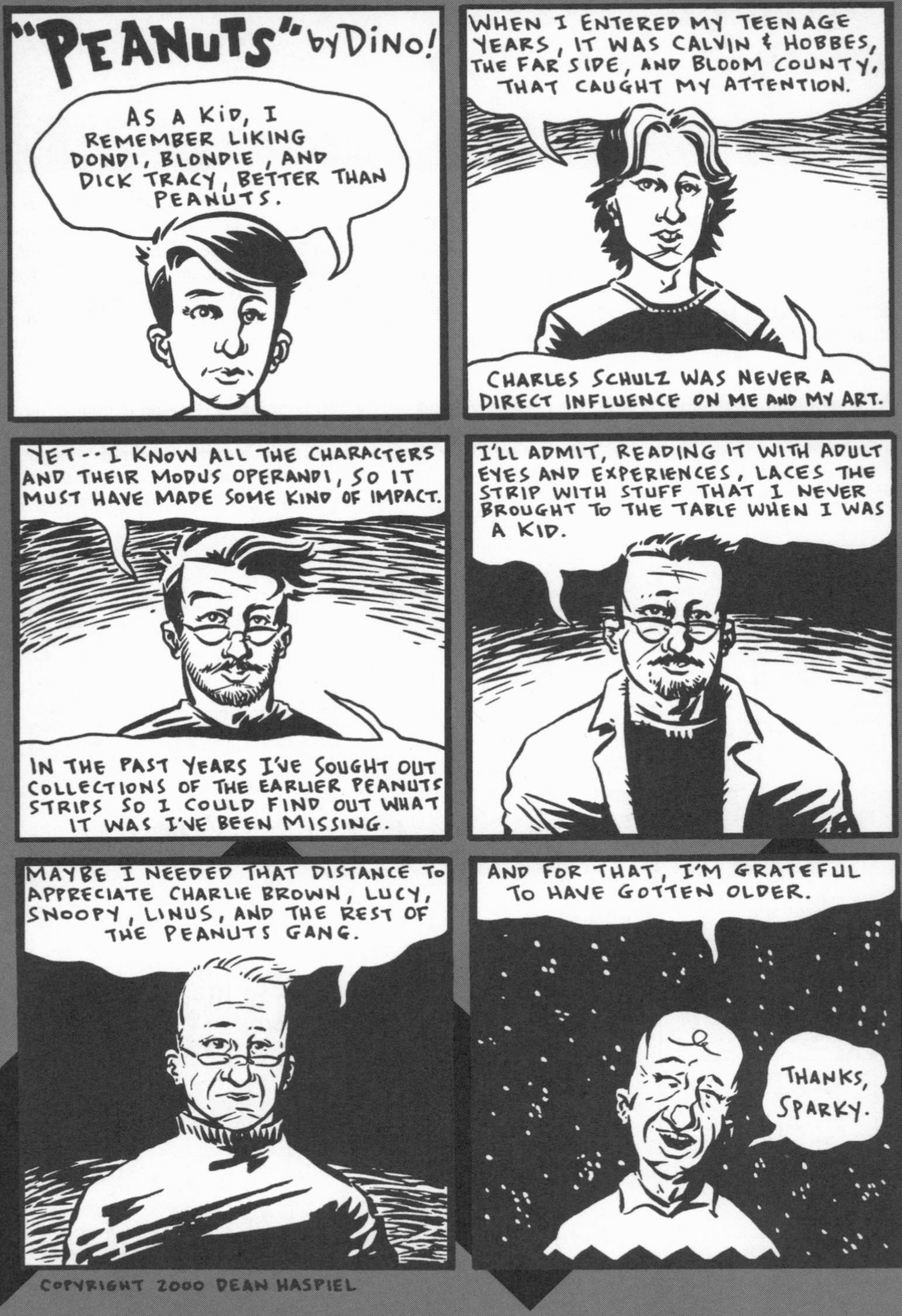
"PEANUTS" by DINO!
AS A KID, I REMEMBER LIKING DONDI, BLONDIE, AND DICK TRACY, BETTER THAN PEANUTS.
WHEN I ENTERED MY TEENAGE YEARS, IT WAS CALVIN & HOBBES, THE FAR SIDE, AND BLOOM COUNTY, THAT CAUGHT MY ATTENTION.
CHARLES SCHULZ WAS NEVER A DIRECT INFLUENCE ON ME AND MY ART.
YET--I KNOW ALL THE CHARACTERS AND THEIR MODUS OPERANDI, SO IT MUST HAVE MADE SOME KIND OF IMPACT.
IN THE PAST YEARS I'VE SOUGHT OUT COLLECTIONS OF THE EARLIER PEANUTS STRIPS SO I COULD FIND OUT WHAT IT WAS I'VE BEEN MISSING.
I'LL ADMIT, READING IT WITH ADULT EYES AND EXPERIENCES, LACES THE STRIP WITH STUFF THAT I NEVER BROUGHT TO THE TABLE WHEN I WAS A KID.
MAYBE I NEEDED THAT DISTANCE TO APPRECIATE CHARLIE BROWN, LUCY, SNOOPY, LINUS, AND THE REST OF THE PEANUTS GANG.
AND FOR THAT, I'M GRATEFUL TO HAVE GOTTEN OLDER.
THANKS, SPARKY.
COPYRIGHT 2000 DEAN HASPIEL

ST. PAUL, MN. 1932
SPARKY! PUT DOWN THOSE "FUNNIES" AND COME HELP YOUR FATHER.
I WAS JUST READING ABOUT FRANK KING, DAD. HE DRAWS THAT COMIC STRIP, "GASOLINE ALLEY" AND HE MAKES $1000 A WEEK!
$1000 A WEEK? THAT'S CERTAINLY A LOT OF MONEY. YESSIREE...
SOMEDAY I'M GONNA DRAW A COMIC STRIP AND I'M GONNA MAKE $1000 A WEEK TOO!!
GOOD FOR YOU, SPARKY. GOOD FOR YOU...
CLOSED
© JOE MATT

MAAKIES
WHY, DRINKY CROW! YOU SEEM TO BE EVEN MORE DRUNKEN THAN USUAL TODAY! WHAT IS THE OCCASION?
GRIEF AND MOURNING IS THE OCCASION, UNCLE GABBY...
ARE YOU MOURNING THE LOSS OF YOUR FUNNY PAGES DOG FRIEND, "SNOOPY?"
I WILL MISS THE LITTLE FELLOW, WITH HIS RIDICULOUS GLASSES OF "ROOT BEER," BUT NO, THAT'S NOT IT...
IS IT THE DEMISE OF THAT MASTER OF THE ABSURD, MR. DON MARTIN?
HE COULD DRAW A PLATE OF SPAGHETTI WITH MUSHROOM SAUCE LIKE NOBODY'S BUSINESS, BUT NO, I GRIEVE FOR ANOTHER...
OUR CAPTAIN, COMMANDER OF THE ORDER OF THE BRITISH EMPIRE, PATRICK O'BRIAN HAS PASSED...
NO!
BOOM BOOM BOOM BOOM BOOM BOOM BOOM BOOM BOOM BOOM BOOM BOOM BOOM BOOM BOOM BOOM BOOM BOOM BOOM BOOM BOOM
MILLIONAIRE@MINDSPRING.COM
PSYCHOLOGY
TO CLEAN HER PUKE OR NOT TO CLEAN HER PUKE...
IS CLEANING UP AFTER HER AN ACT OF KINDNESS OR SUBMISSION?
ALL I'LL PROBABLY GET OUT OF IT IS ACCUSATIONS OF WEAKNESS...HMM...
OH WELL...
MOP MOP
HEY! WHAT ASSHOLE STOLE MY BARF!

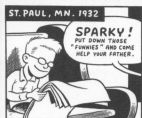

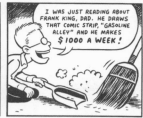

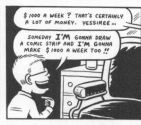

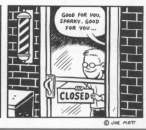

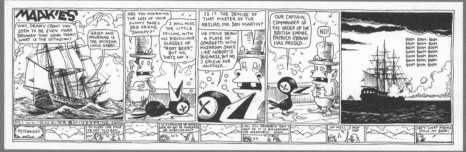

An appreciation by Dylan Horrocks

A funny thing happened a few years ago when I was writing the ninth issue of my comic book *Pickle*. The story was set at a costume party and, to my surprise, I knew immediately who the main character Sam Zabel would be dressed up as: Charlie Brown. It seemed so obvious and so appropriate that it got me thinking. See, I'd never realized it before, but in many respects Sam is Charlie Brown, grown up: a bit hopeless, prone to melancholy, self-deprecating and yet utterly free of cynicism. In fact, the more I thought about it, the clearer it became that the male leads in my own comics are mostly just variations on the basic Charlie Brown riff—and most of the heroines include a healthy pinch of Lucy. Sure, I'd grown up reading (and endlessly re-reading) *Peanuts*, but I confess I'd stopped following it a long time ago. Now I suddenly understood what a huge influence Schulz had been on me; not just on my work (it took practice to replicate that wobbly line from his later strips) but also on me as a person. Charlie Brown gives all us hapless square pegs, non-macho boys and perpetual losers a voice; we understand that in spite of Snoopy's show-stealing antics, Lucy's petty victories, Schroeder's talent and Linus' intelligence, the real hero will always be Charlie Brown. Because for all his constant failures, his lousy luck and his sheer ordinariness, he's a good man. So now that it's over, I realize how precious *Peanuts* is to me and, I believe, how important for our culture. Thank you, Sparky, from the bottom of my heart. You are a good man, Charlie Schulz.

SIGH
—DYLAN HORROCKS

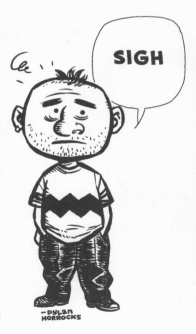

SPARKY'S LAST PITCH

Josh Neufeld

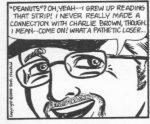

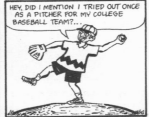

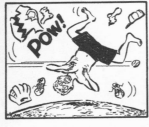

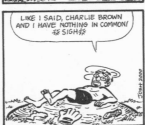

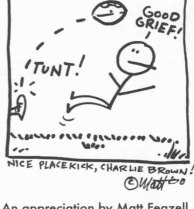

"PEANUTS"? OH, YEAH--I GREW UP READING THAT STRIP! I NEVER REALLY MADE A CONNECTION WITH CHARLIE BROWN, THOUGH. I MEAN--COME ON! WHAT A PATHETIC LOSER...
HEY, DID I MENTION I TRIED OUT ONCE AS A PITCHER FOR MY COLLEGE BASEBALL TEAM?...
POW!
LIKE I SAID, CHARLIE BROWN AND I HAVE NOTHING IN COMMON! *SIGH*
JOSH 2000

GOOD GRIEF!
TUNT!
NICE PLACEKICK, CHARLIE BROWN!

An appreciation by Matt Feazell

The *Des Moines Register* printed the first newspaper comic strips I ever saw. One of the strips they carried was Schulz's *Peanuts*. Back when it was popular but not mandatory (Snoopy was still a dog), it was an early influence on my cartooning, since it was the first comic strip that I had noticed that had recurring characters with distinct personalities.

I can still remember waiting for Charlie Brown to catch that long high fly ball with all his teammates surrounding him on the pitcher's mound, giving him encouragement or verbal abuse depending on whose character was setting up the punchline that day. Schulz stretched out the gag over many days... and got at least one grade school kid in Iowa to pay serious attention to the comics page for the first time.

12:15 SATURDAY NIGHT * BY KEVIN SCALZO * ©2000
....AND SO AT 9:45 PACIFIC COAST TIME-ON THE EVE OF THE LAST PEANUTS.....
AAUGH!!
OWOO!
SNIFF
WE MISS YOU SPARKY!

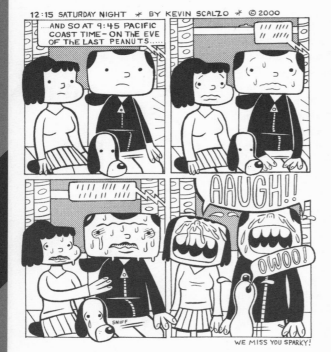

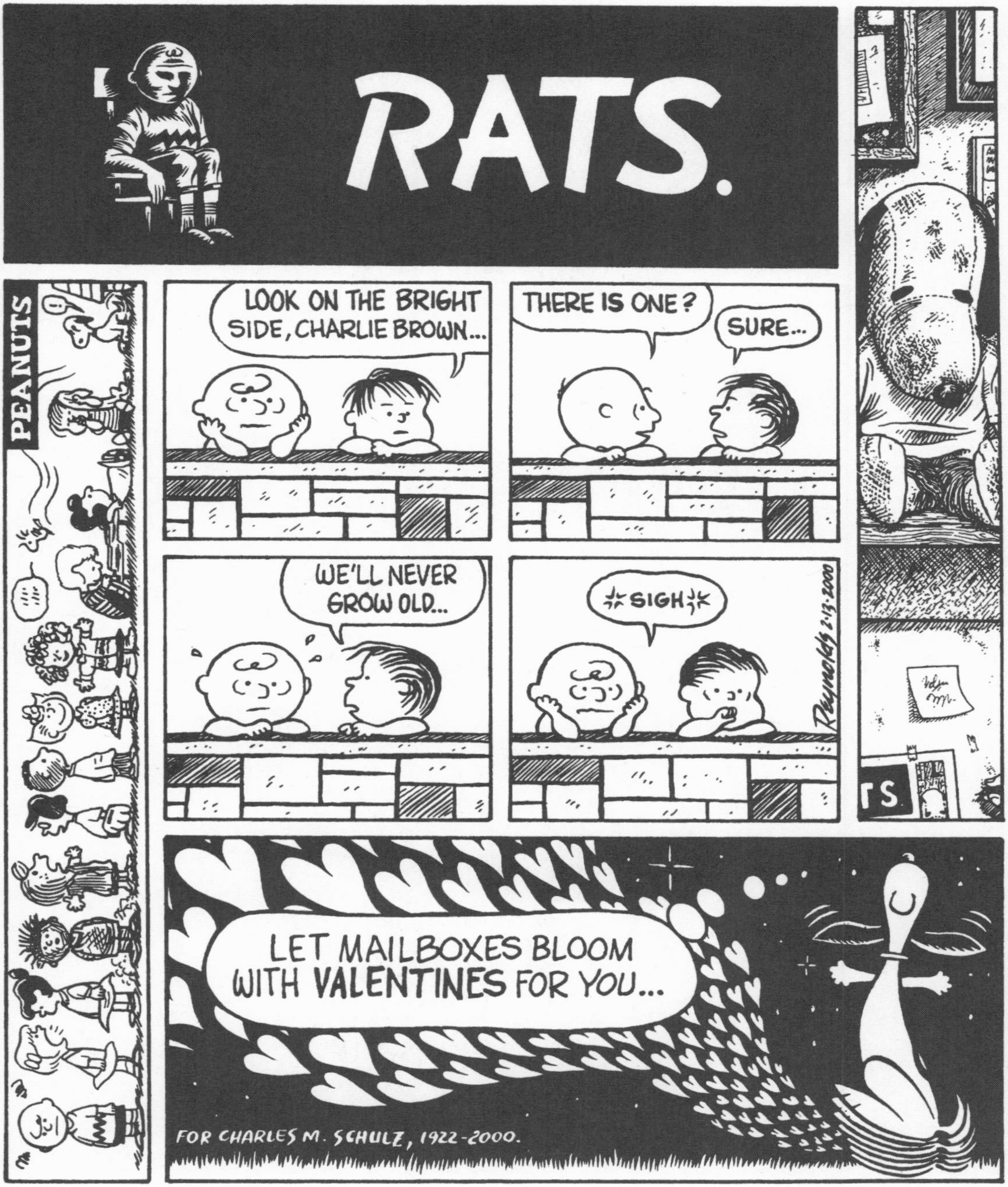
RATS.
PEANUTS
LOOK ON THE BRIGHT SIDE, CHARLIE BROWN...
THERE IS ONE?
SURE...
WE'LL NEVER GROW OLD...
SIGH
Reynolds 2-13-2000
LET MAILBOXES BLOOM WITH VALENTINES FOR YOU...
FOR CHARLES M. SCHULZ, 1922-2000.

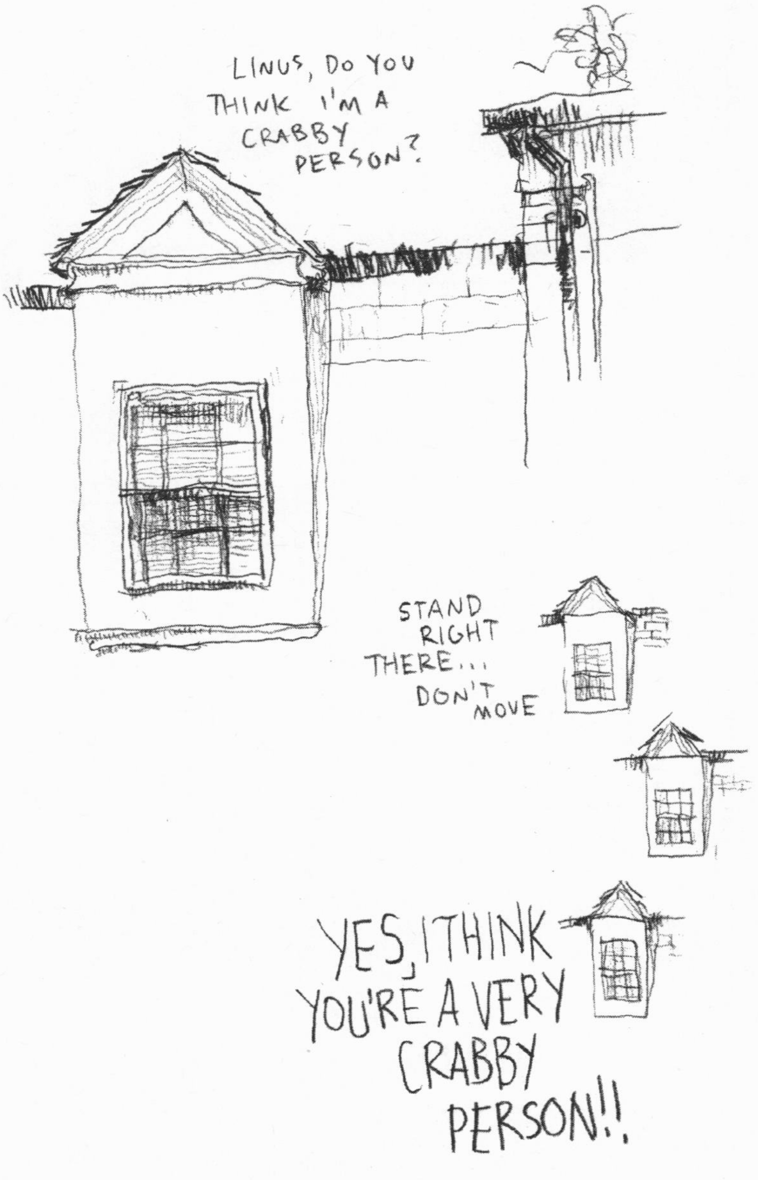
LINUS, DO YOU THINK I'M A CRABBY PERSON?
STAND RIGHT THERE... DON'T MOVE
YES, I THINK YOU'RE A VERY CRABBY PERSON!!

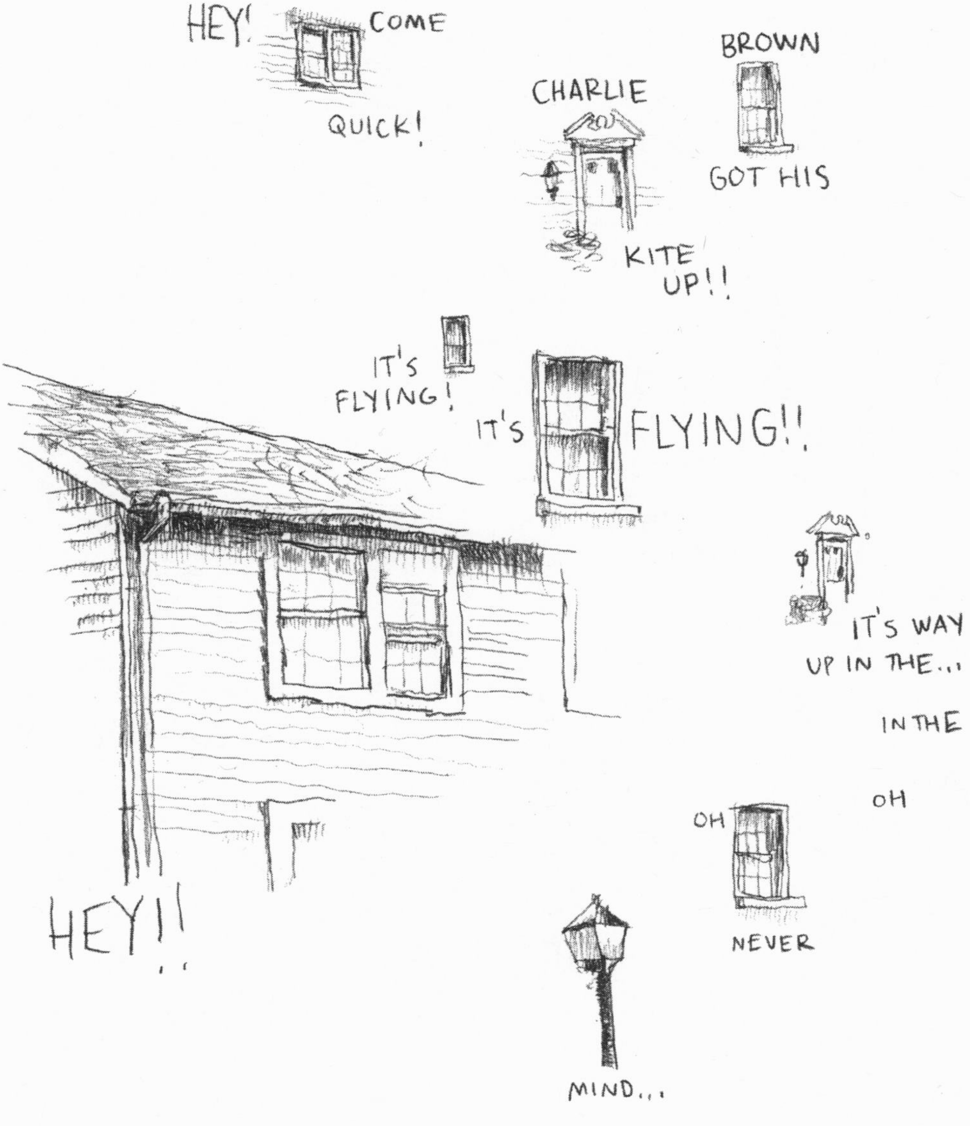
HEY!
COME
QUICK!
CHARLIE
BROWN
GOT HIS
KITE
UP!!
IT'S
FLYING!
IT'S
FLYING!!
IT'S WAY
UP IN THE...
IN THE
OH
OH
NEVER
MIND...
HEY!!

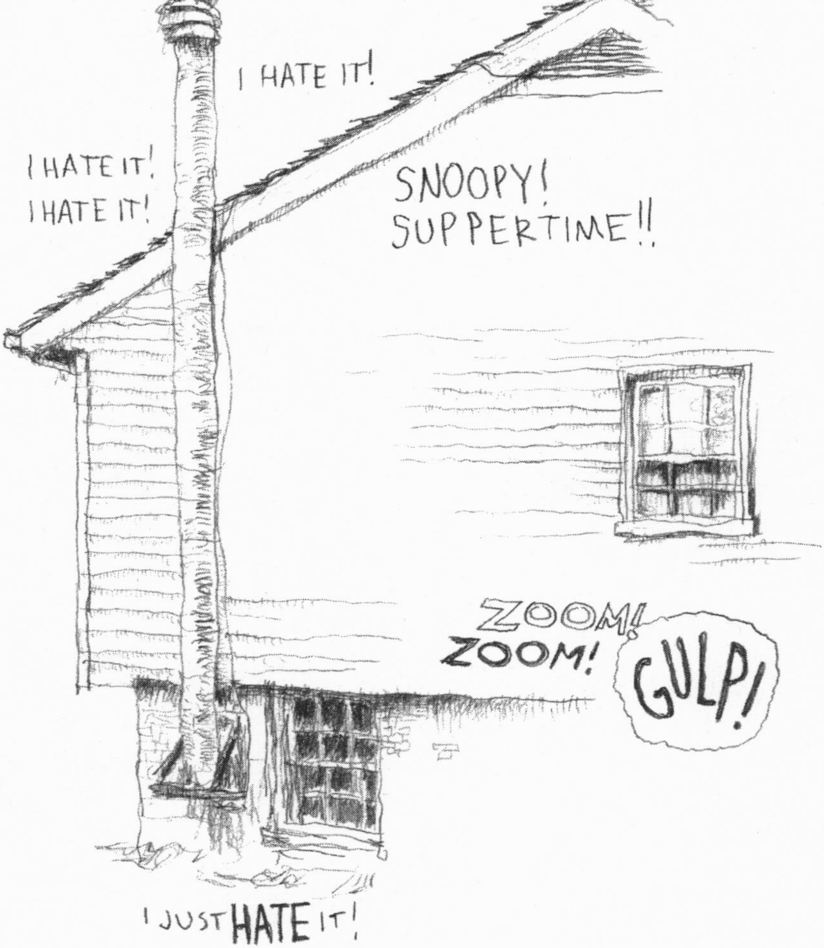
I HATE IT!
I HATE IT!
I HATE IT!
SNOOPY! SUPPERTIME!!
ZOOM! ZOOM!
GULP!
I JUST HATE IT!

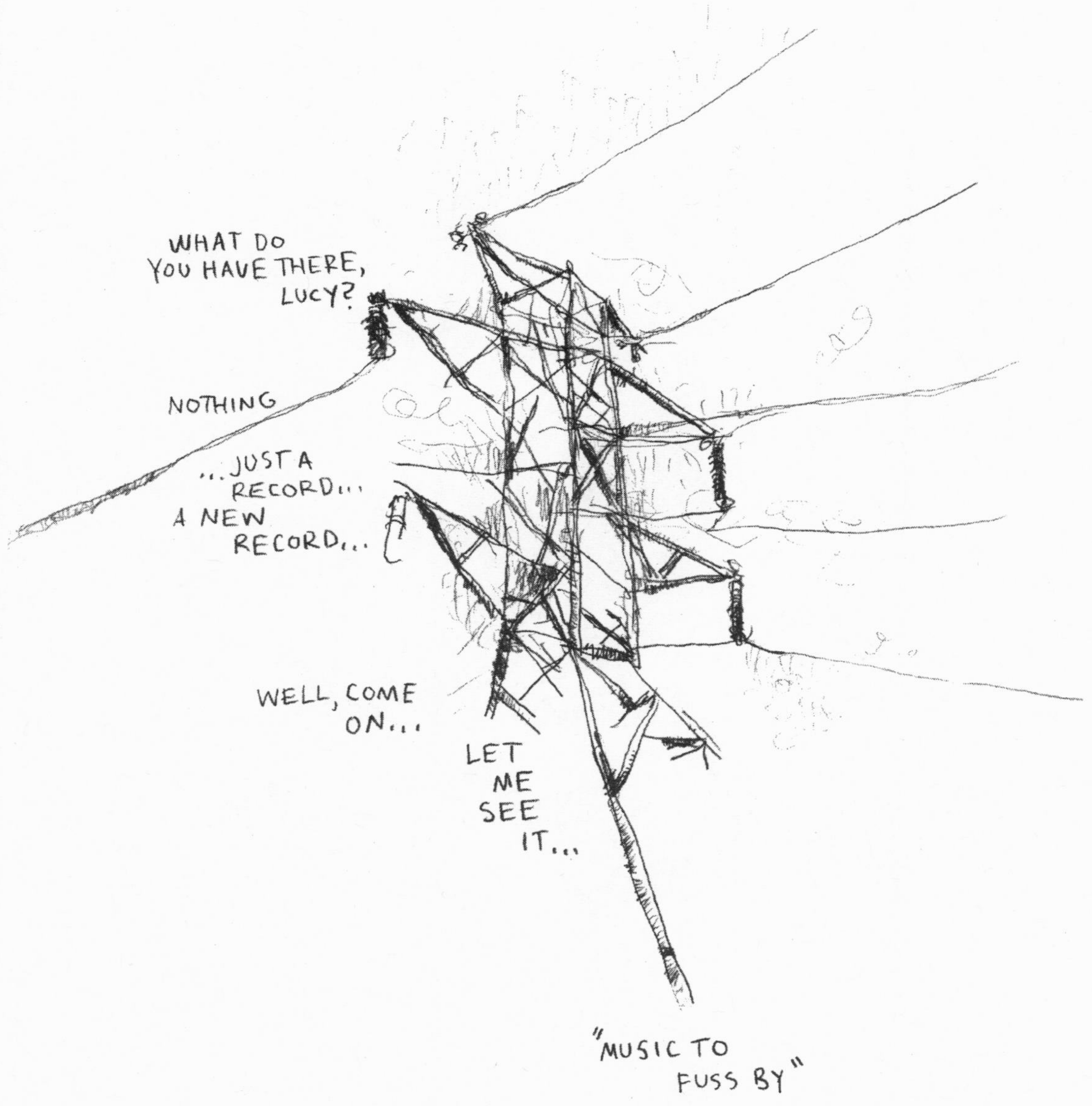
WHAT DO YOU HAVE THERE, LUCY?
NOTHING
...JUST A RECORD... A NEW RECORD...
WELL, COME ON...
LET ME SEE IT...
"MUSIC TO FUSS BY"

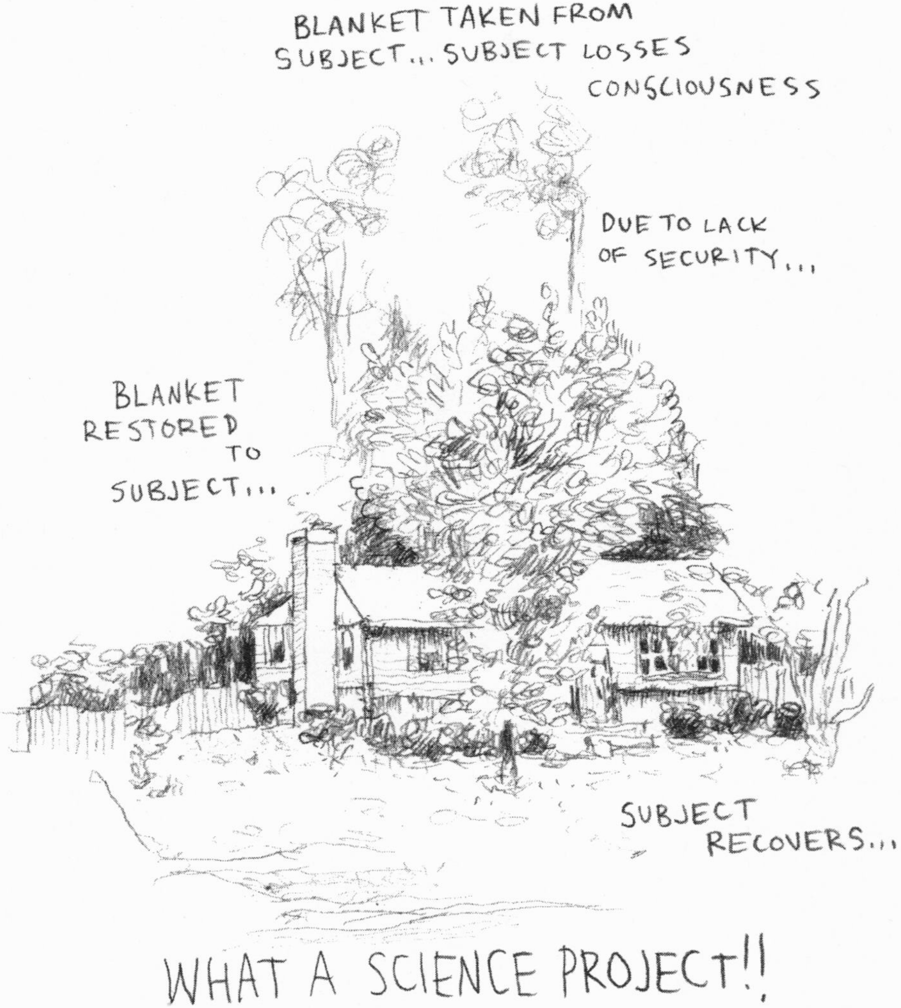
BLANKET TAKEN FROM SUBJECT... SUBJECT LOSSES CONSCIOUSNESS
DUE TO LACK OF SECURITY...
BLANKET RESTORED TO SUBJECT...
SUBJECT RECOVERS...
WHAT A SCIENCE PROJECT!!

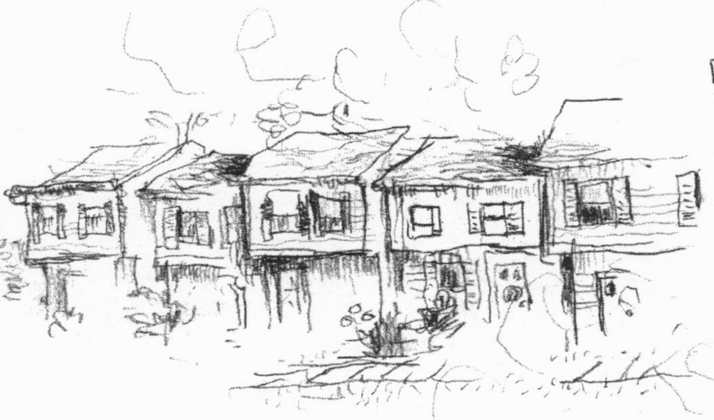
DO YOU KNOW WHAT HOLDS THE STARS UP, LINUS?

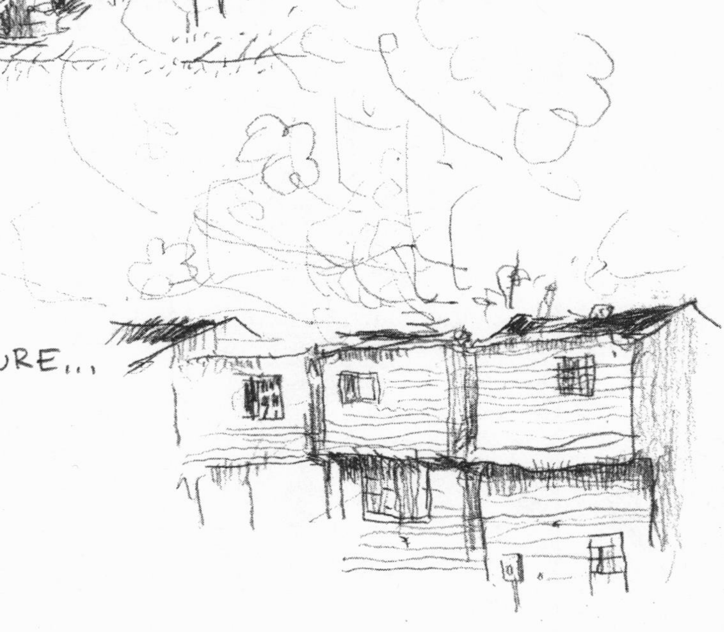
WELL, I'M NOT SURE...
THUMBTACKS?

thanks mister sparky.
love warren.
also thanks a(leaf)w.

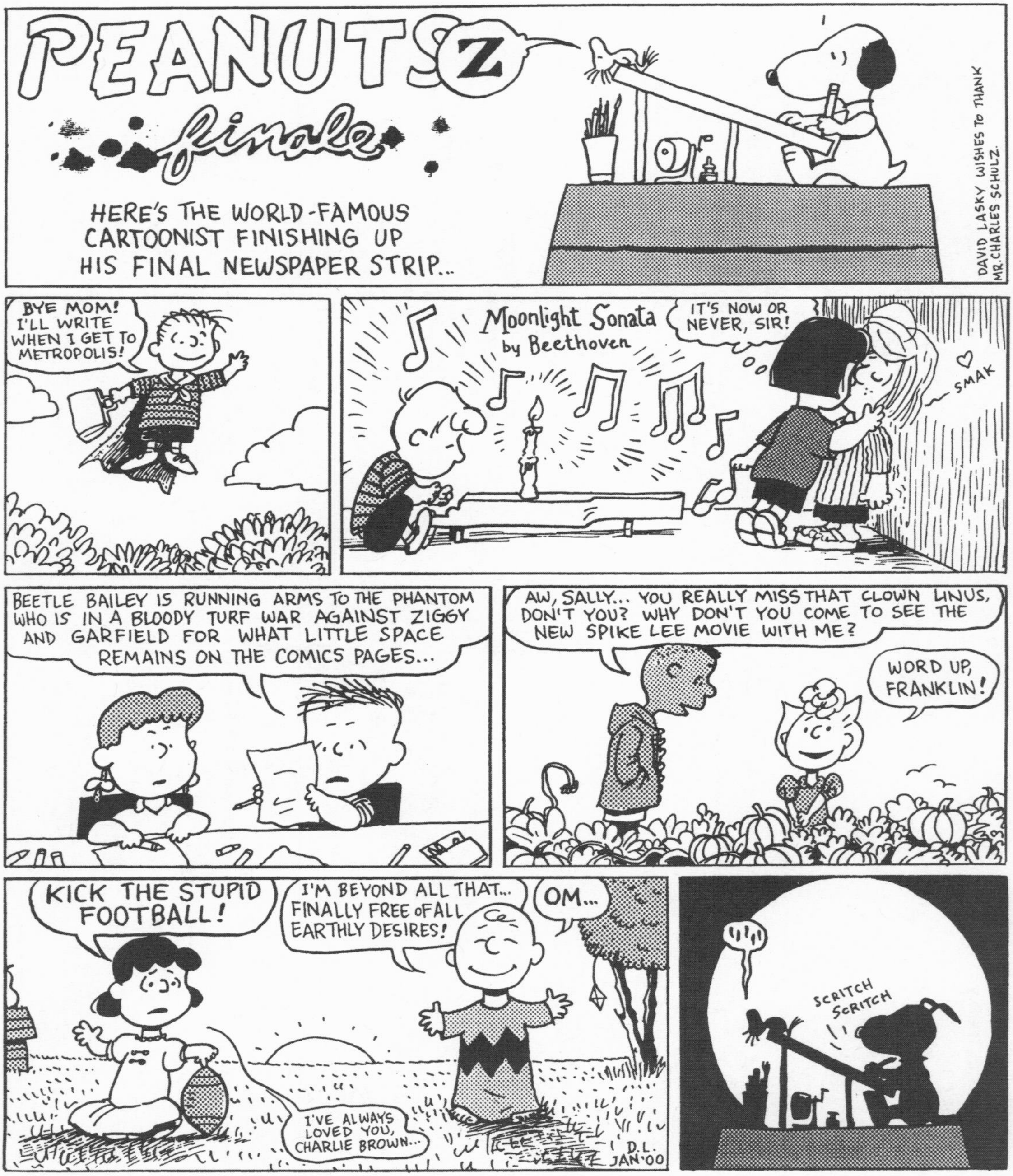
PEANUTS Z
finale
HERE'S THE WORLD-FAMOUS CARTOONIST FINISHING UP HIS FINAL NEWSPAPER STRIP...
DAVID LASKY WISHES TO THANK MR. CHARLES SCHULZ.
BYE MOM! I'LL WRITE WHEN I GET TO METROPOLIS!
Moonlight Sonata by Beethoven
IT'S NOW OR NEVER, SIR!
SMAK
BEETLE BAILEY IS RUNNING ARMS TO THE PHANTOM WHO IS IN A BLOODY TURF WAR AGAINST ZIGGY AND GARFIELD FOR WHAT LITTLE SPACE REMAINS ON THE COMICS PAGES...
AW, SALLY... YOU REALLY MISS THAT CLOWN LINUS, DON'T YOU? WHY DON'T YOU COME TO SEE THE NEW SPIKE LEE MOVIE WITH ME?
WORD UP, FRANKLIN!
KICK THE STUPID FOOTBALL!
I'M BEYOND ALL THAT... FINALLY FREE OF ALL EARTHLY DESIRES!
OM...
I'VE ALWAYS LOVED YOU, CHARLIE BROWN...
D.L. JAN '00
SCRITCH SCRITCH

MAhLER

"TNT"

The LAST HOURS before a fight are the worst...

TODAY everything is different...

I'LL TAKE the MONEY...

I'LL be on the floor...round 4.

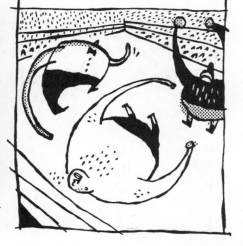

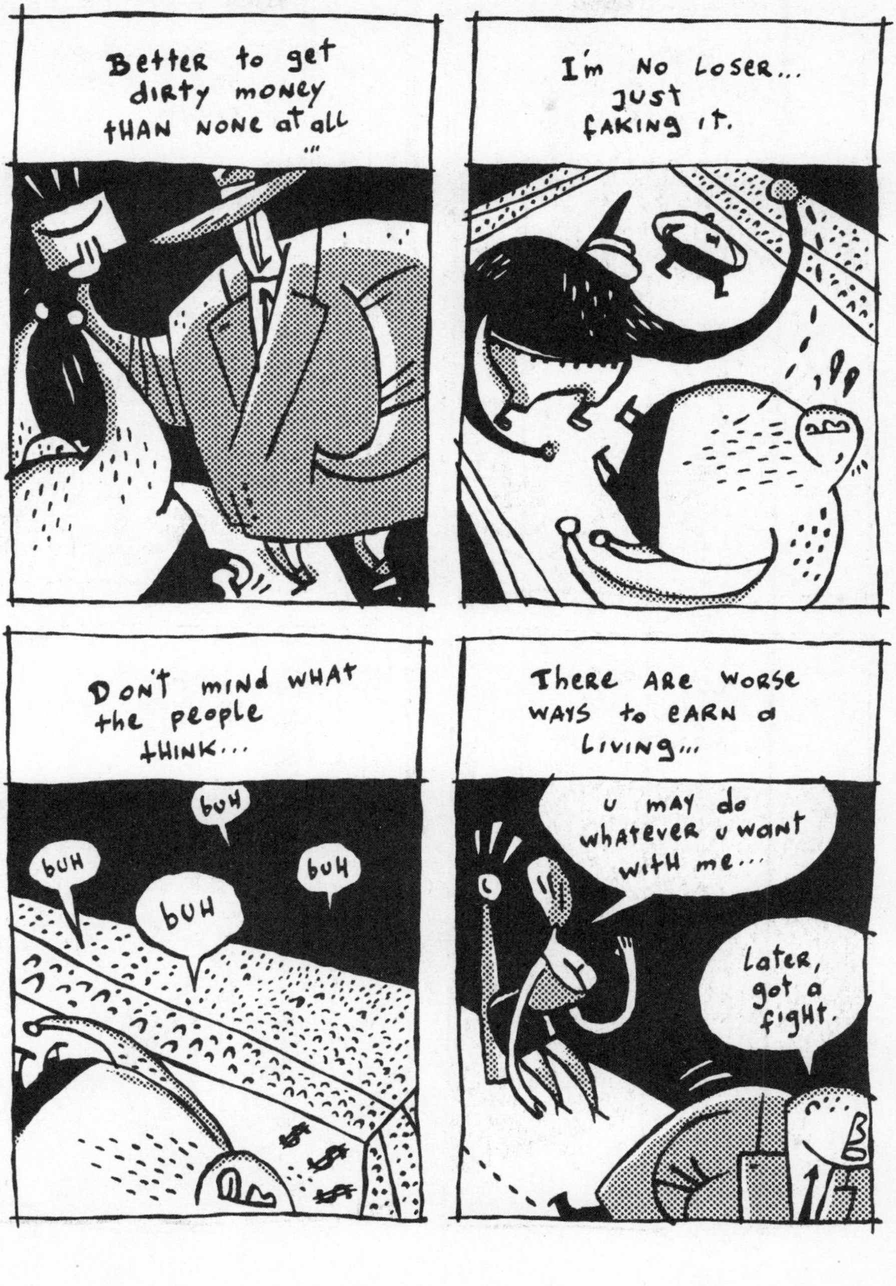
Better to get dirty money THAN NONE at all ...
I'm NO LOSER... JUST fAKING it.
DON'T mind WHAT the people think...
buH
buH
buH
buH
There ARE WORSE WAYS to eARN a LIVING...
u MAY do whatever u want with me...
Later, got a fight.

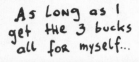

As Long as I get the 3 bucks all for myself...

and REMEMBER: Not a WORD...

A YEAR ago, CARLOS WOULD HAVE GOTTEN his SHARE...

CAN'T be WITH you DURING THE FIGHT... got a dATE...

The ONLY thing he did was keep the WOMEN FROM me ...

you got to understand ... you NeeD YOUR animal INSTINCTS for the FiGHT...

FoR tHAT, he took 2 thirds of everyThing...

okey dokey.

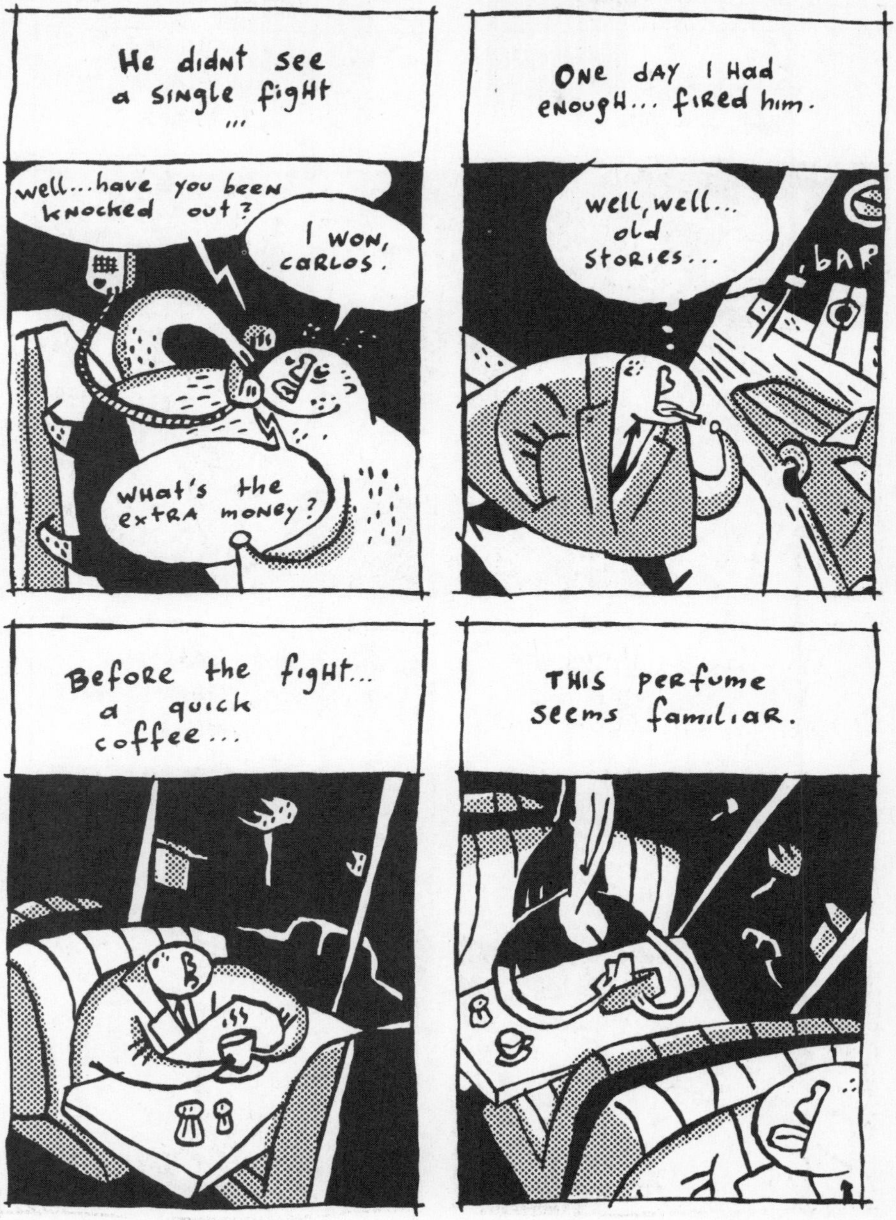
He didnt see a single fight ...
well...have you been knocked out?
I won, Carlos.
What's the extra money?
One day I had enough... fired him.
well, well... old stories...
BAR
Before the fight... a quick coffee...
This perfume seems familiar.

Smelled it every day.
Always had a good nose...
hi vanessa ... all alone?
...Despite the many punches I got on it...
I was already paying, TNT...
...only got problems breathing... when theres moist weather...
come on... stay awhile... for talkin'!
ok then.

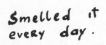

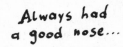

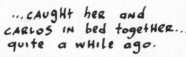

"...and... TNT...
still boxing?"

...CAUGHt HER and
CARLOS in bed togetHER...
quite a while ago.

whether it WAS his
Kind of REvenge, OR
some Kind of love-affair...

I don't
WANT to
Know...

Anyway... this was the end...
and you?
"Think I got to go now, TNT...
you... are frightening me
Actually, I never did hurt a woman...
hey... wait a minute
"Got a fight today... always get one free ticket..."
maybe you want to come...
that's sweet of you, TNT... but I don't think so.

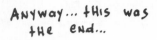

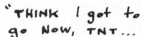

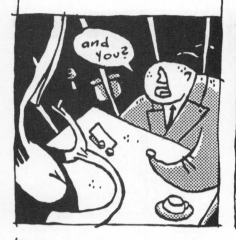

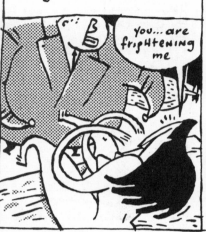

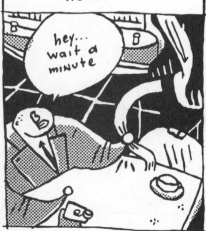

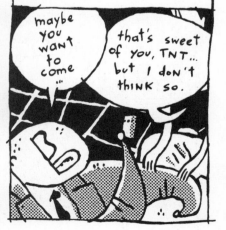

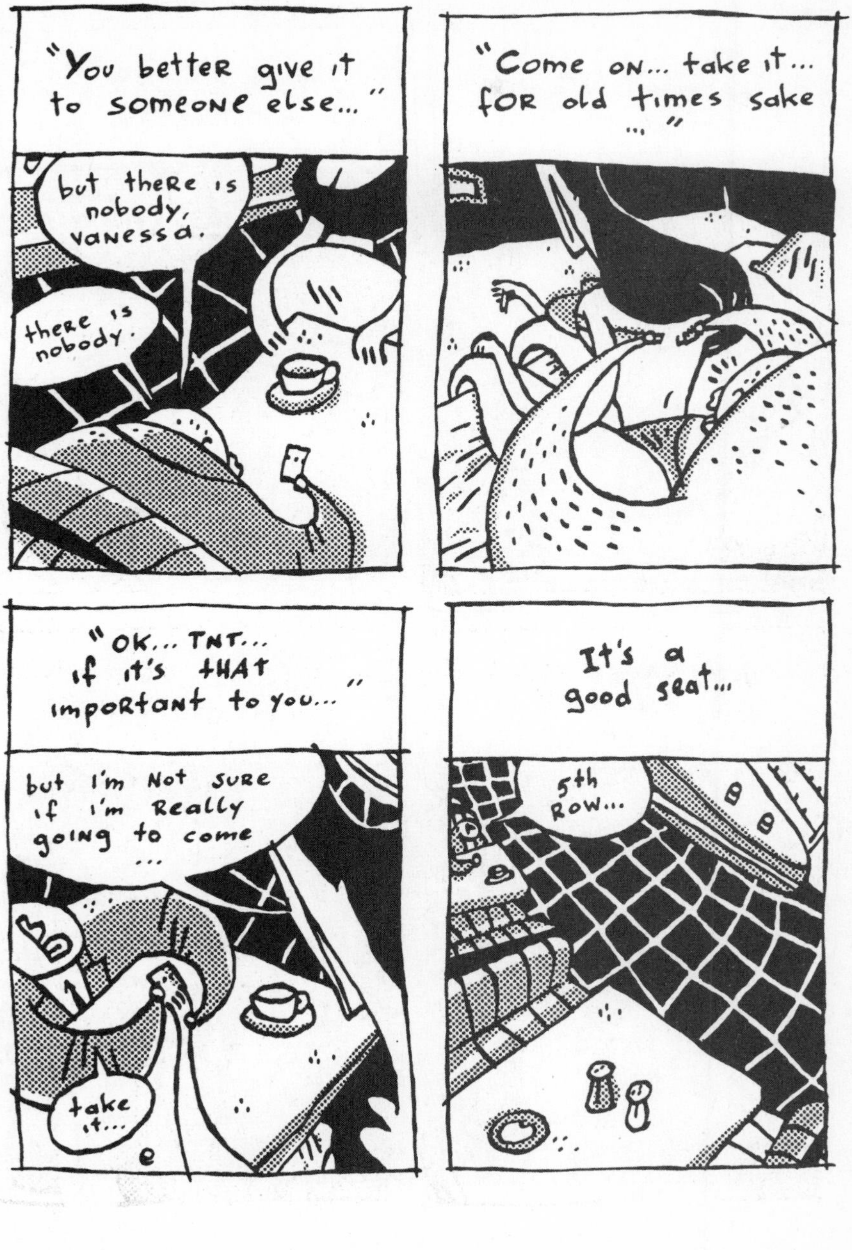
"You better give it to someone else..."
but there is nobody, vanessa.
there is nobody.
"Come on... take it... for old times sake ..."
"OK... TNT... if it's THAT important to you..."
but I'm Not sure if I'm Really going to come ...
take it...
It's a good seat...
5th Row...

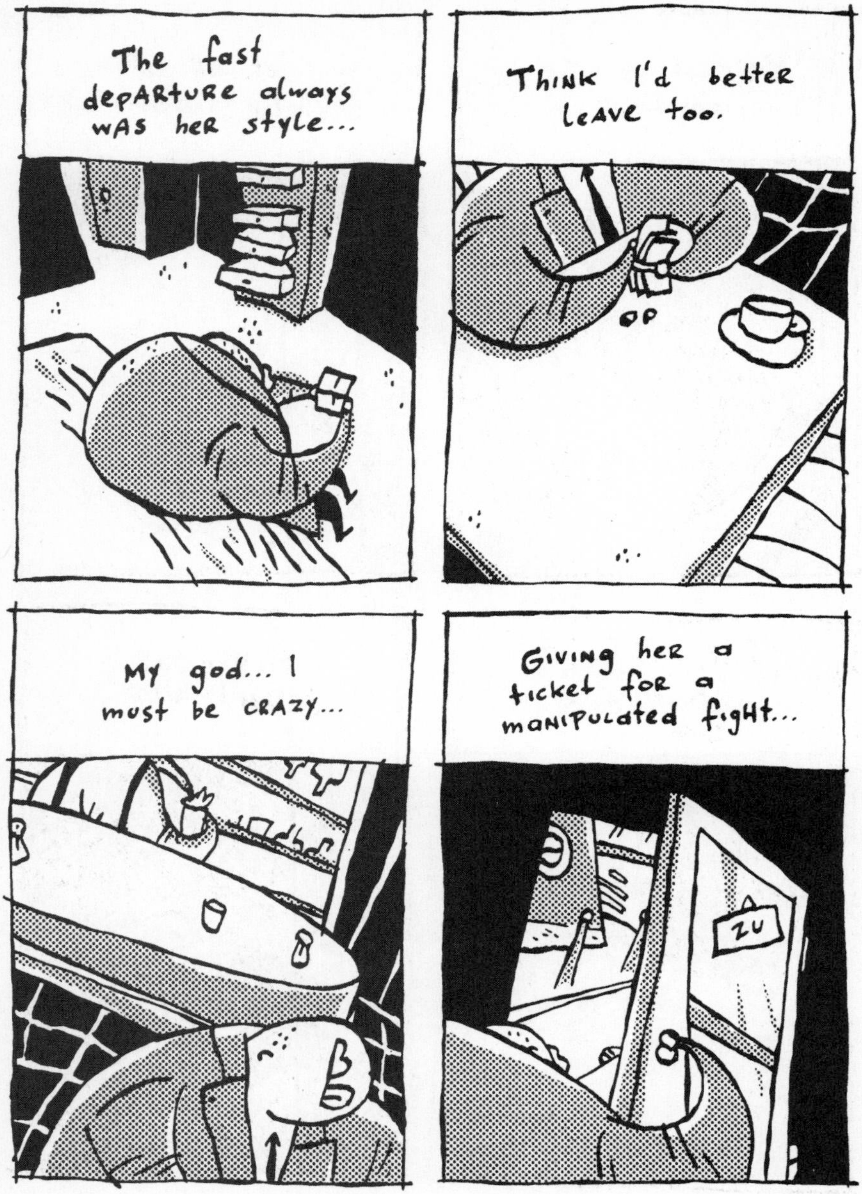
The fast departure always was her style...
Think I'd better leave too.
OP
My god... I must be crazy...
Giving her a ticket for a manipulated fight...
ZU

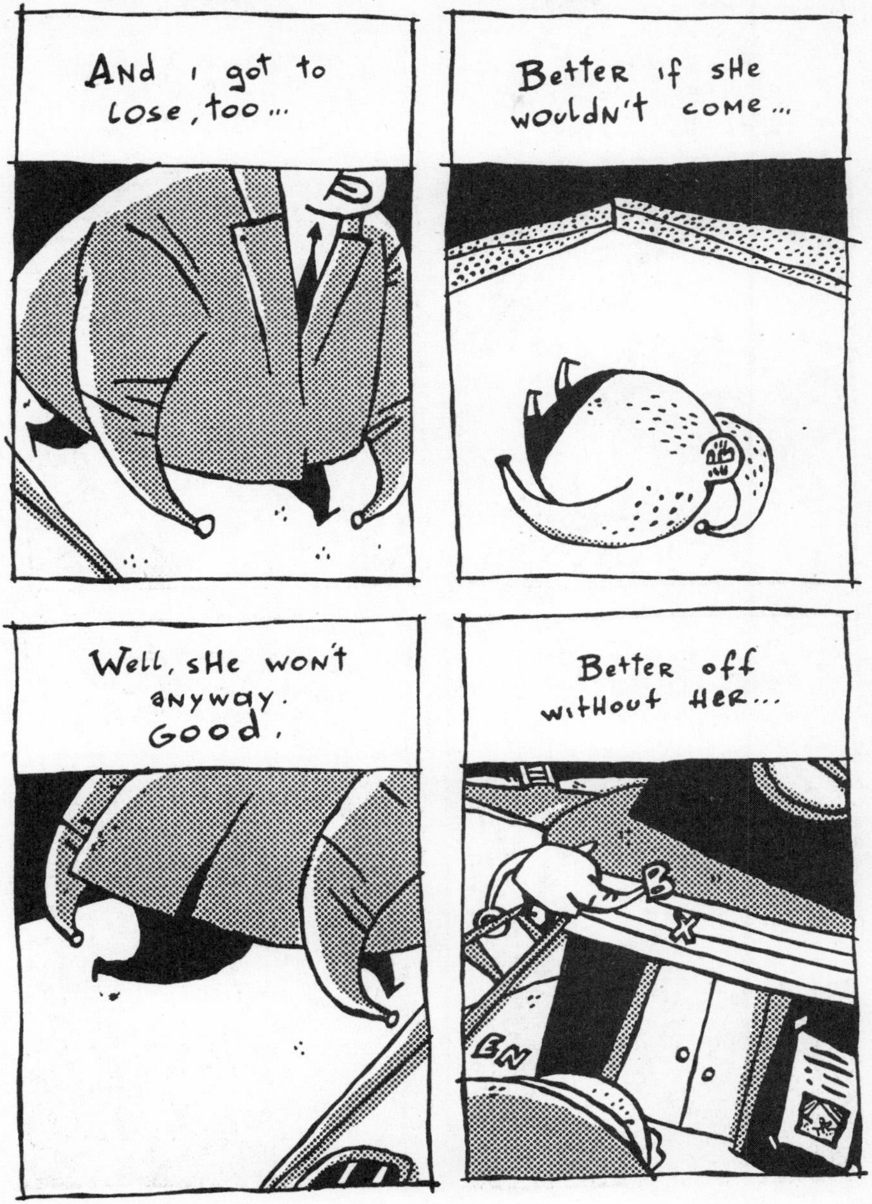
AND I got to lose, too...
Better if she wouldn't come...
Well, she won't anyway. Good.
Better off without her...
EN

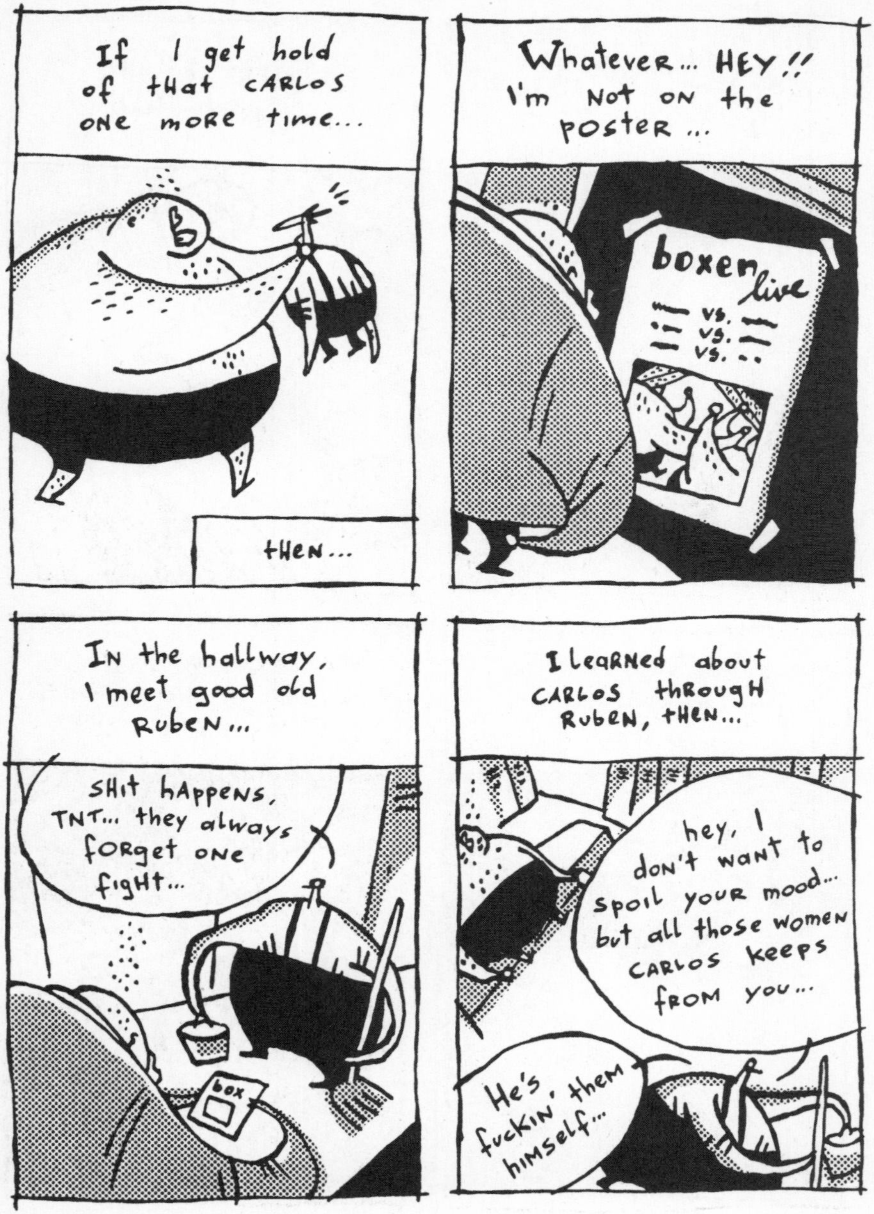
If I get hold of that CARLOS one more time...
THEN...
Whatever... HEY!! I'm NOT ON the poster...
boxen live
VS.
VS.
VS.
IN the hallway, I meet good old RUBEN...
SHIT HAPPENS, TNT... they always forget one fight...
box
I LEARNED about CARLOS through RUBEN, THEN...
hey, I don't want to spoil your mood... but all those women CARLOS keeps from you...
He's fuckin' them himself...

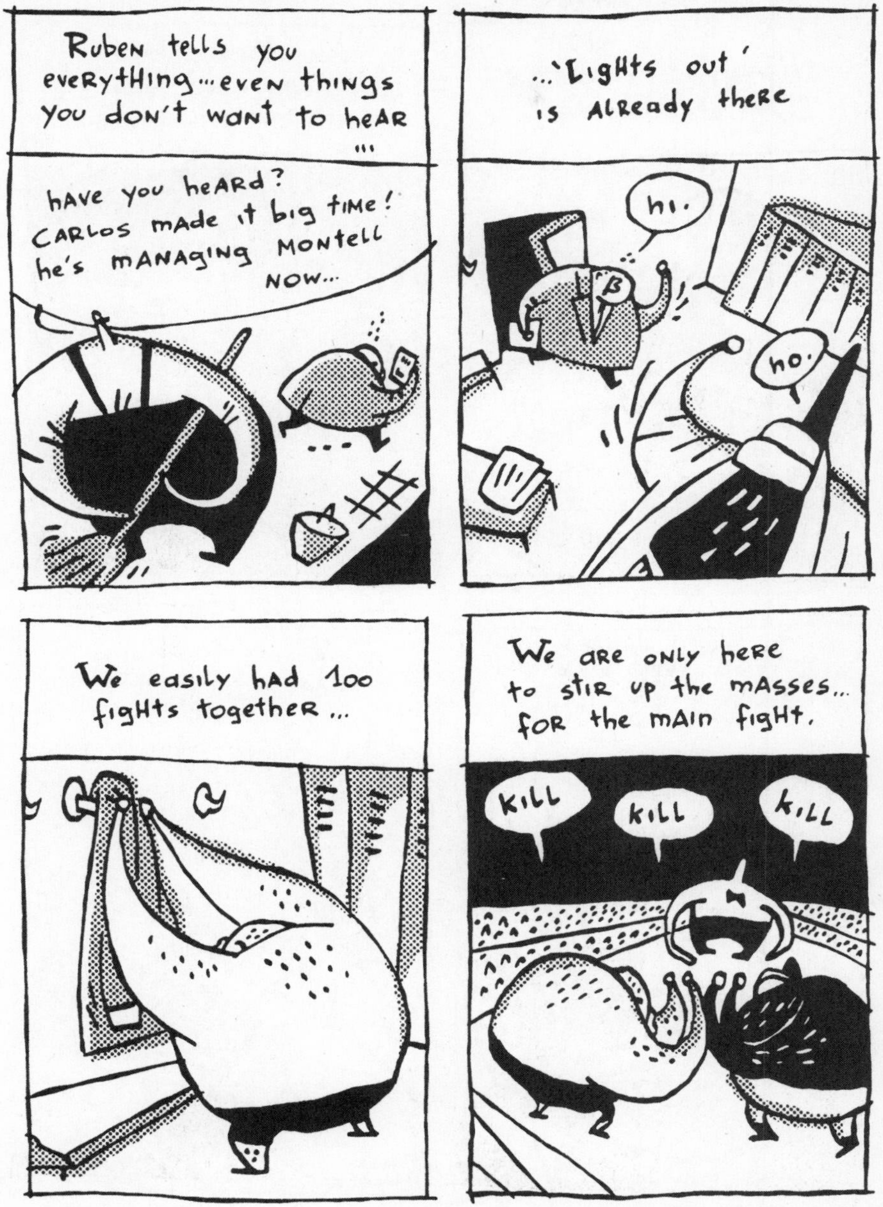
Ruben tells you everything... even things you don't want to hear ...
have you heard? Carlos made it big time! he's managing Montell now...
...
...'Lights out' is already there
hi.
ho.
We easily had 100 fights together...
We are only here to stir up the masses... for the main fight.
KILL
KILL
KILL

Nobody's interested in who's winning ...
KILL
KILL
KILL
KILL
KILL
Very strange that someone would pay 3 bucks just to see me lose ...
KILL
I think 'Lights Out' doesn't even know about it ...
Well, in fact he doesn't know about anything anymore ...

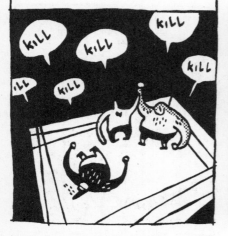

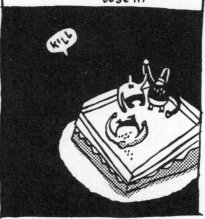

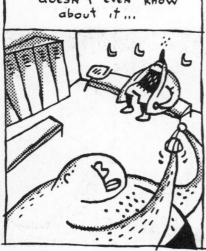

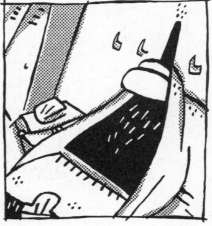

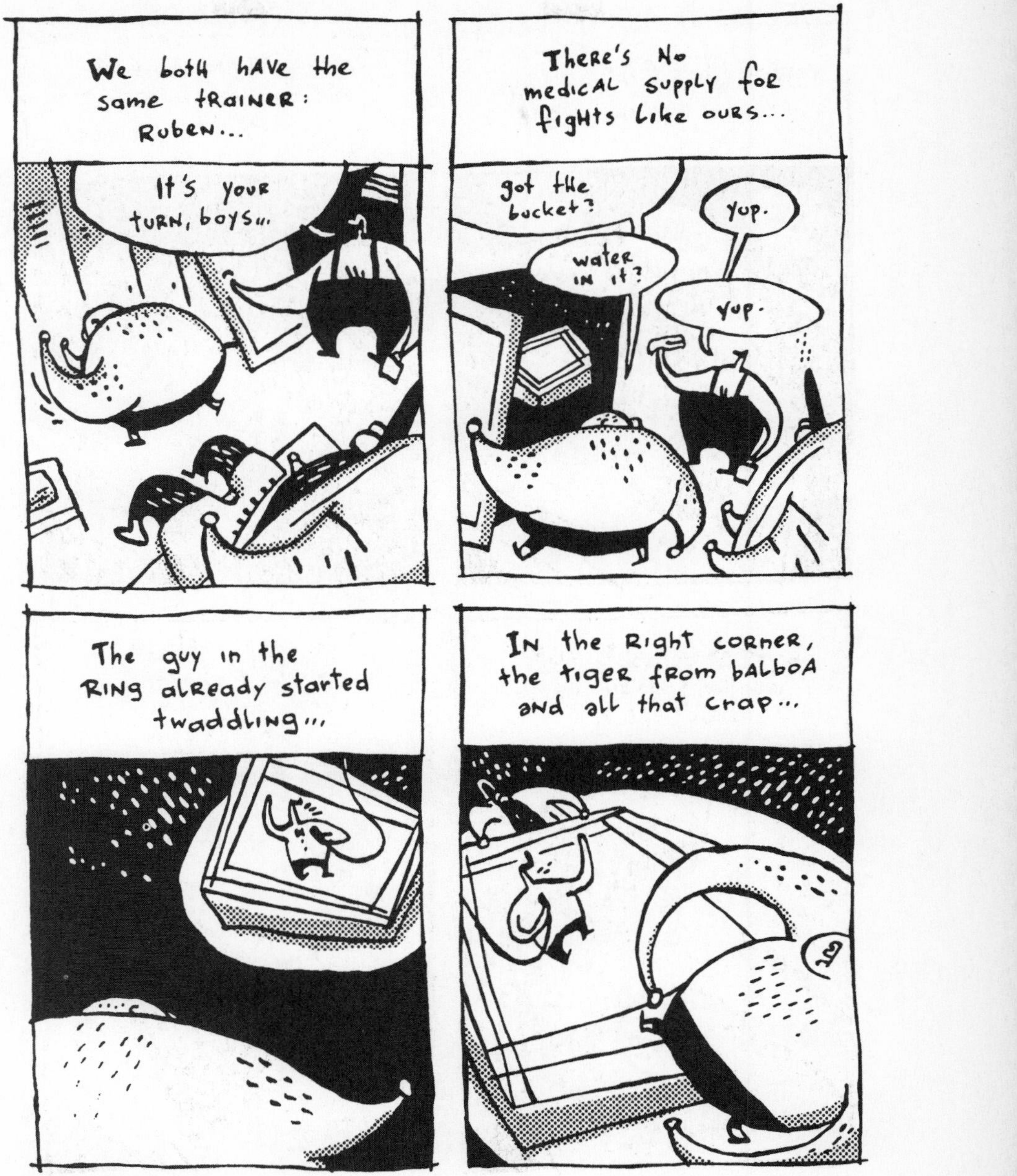

We both have the same trainer: Ruben...
It's your turn, boys...
There's no medical supply for fights like ours...
got the bucket?
yup.
water in it?
yup.
The guy in the ring already started twaddling...
In the right corner, the tiger from Balboa and all that crap...

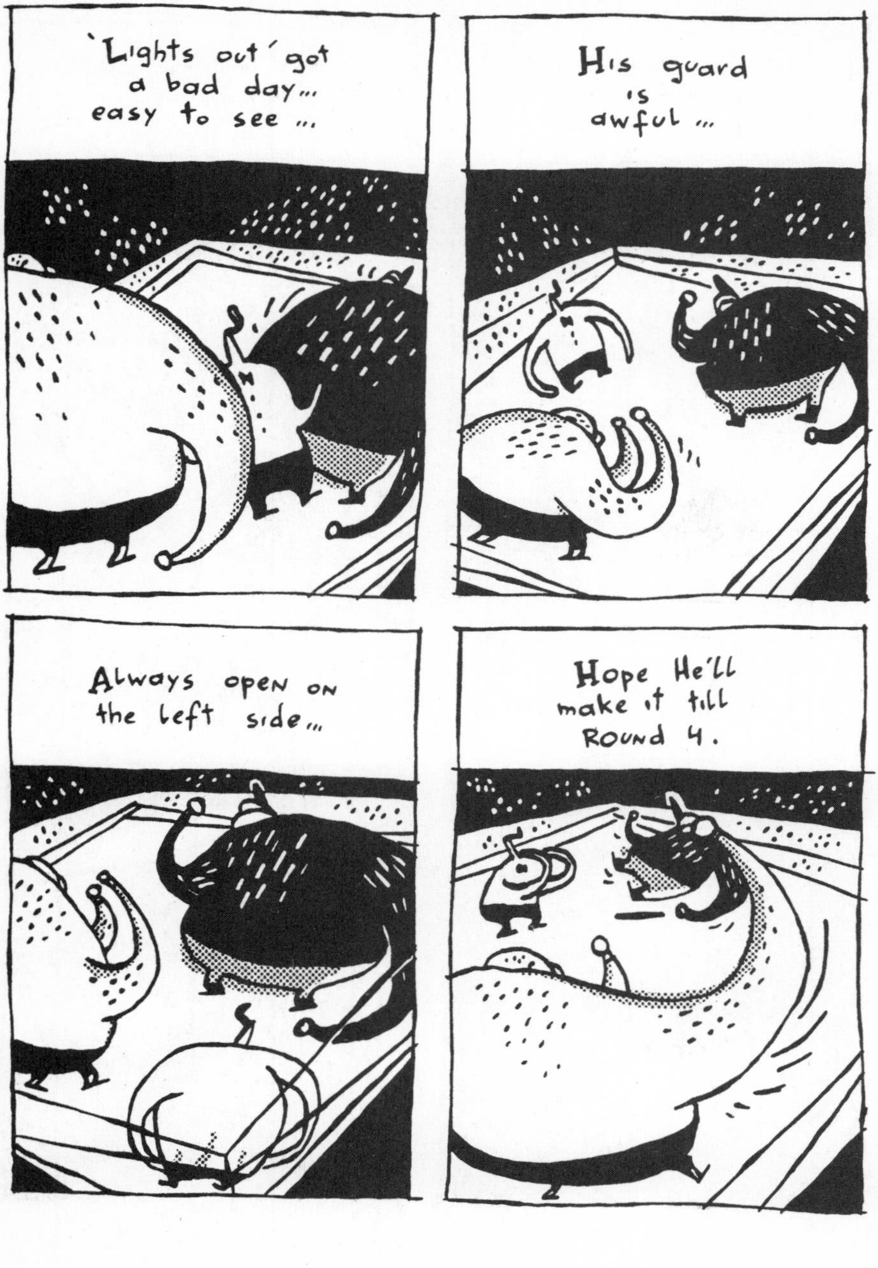
`Lights out´ got a bad day... easy to see ...
His guard is awful ...
Always open on the left side...
Hope He'll make it till Round 4.

The gong carries us into ROUND 2.
Got to look after 'Lights out'. He's in bad shape.
OK.
Ruben knows how to bring a boxer back on his feet...
hey, 'lights out'... how many fists have you got?
well... two.
then why don't you use them both?
'Lights out' is standing more firmly on his feet now...
Anyway... if that doesn't seem faked...

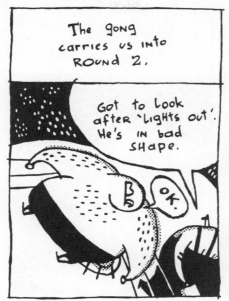

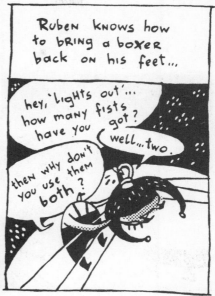

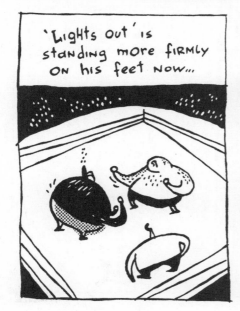

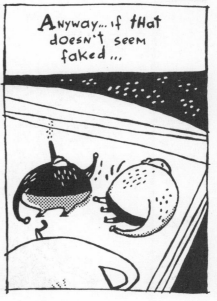

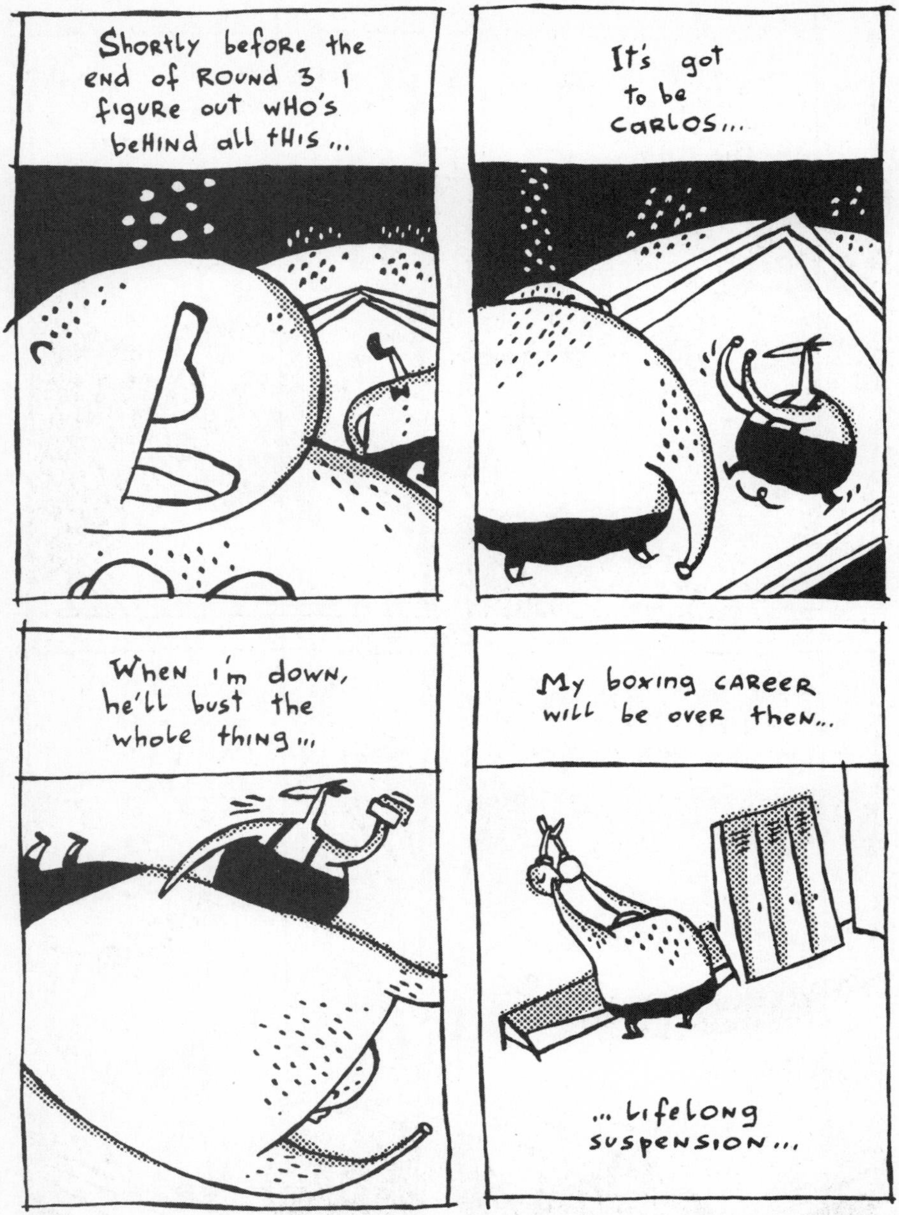
Shortly before the end of ROUND 3 I figure out WHO'S beHIND all THIS...
It's got to be CARLOS...
When i'm down, he'll bust the whole thing...
My boxing CAREER will be over then...
... Lifelong suspension...

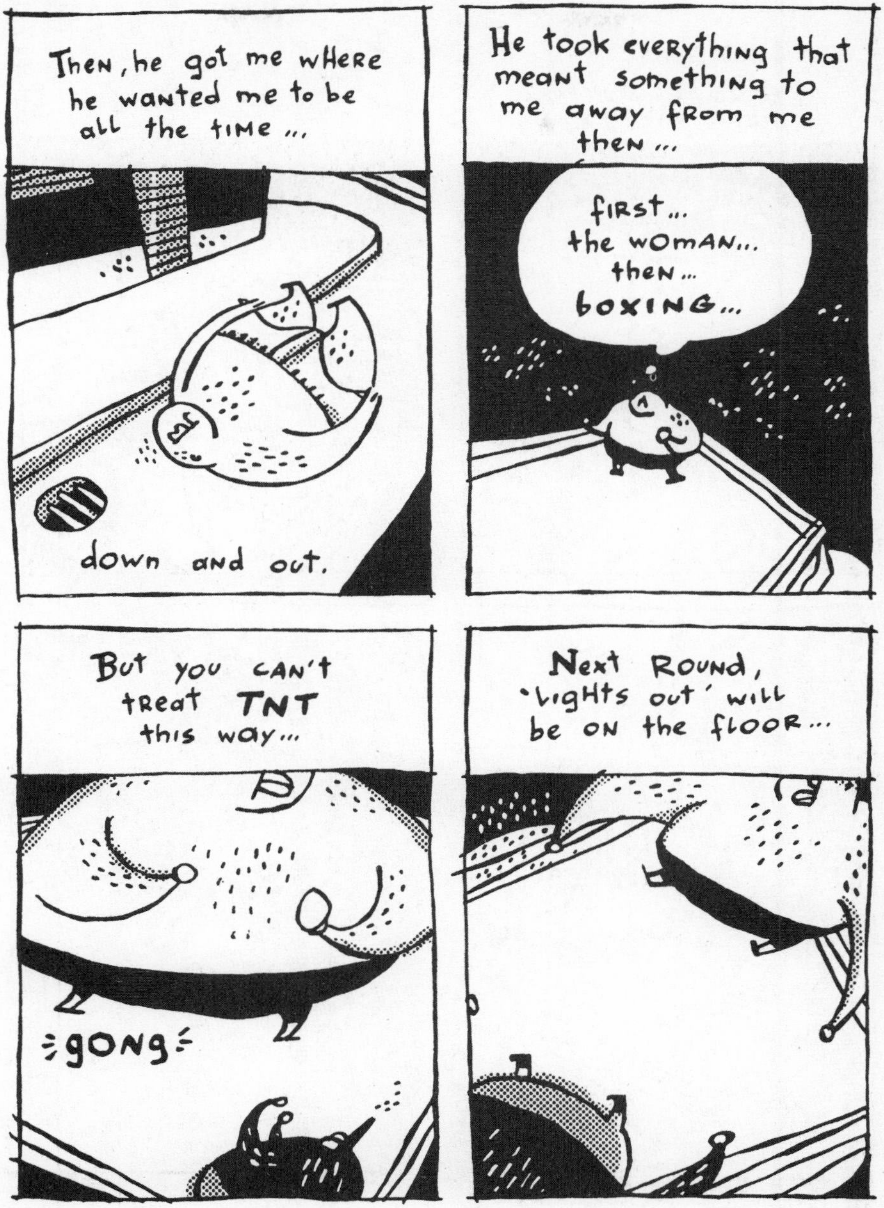
Then, he got me where he wanted me to be all the time...
down and out.
He took everything that meant something to me away from me then...
first... the woman... then... boxing...
But you can't treat TNT this way...
gong
Next Round, 'lights out' will be on the floor...

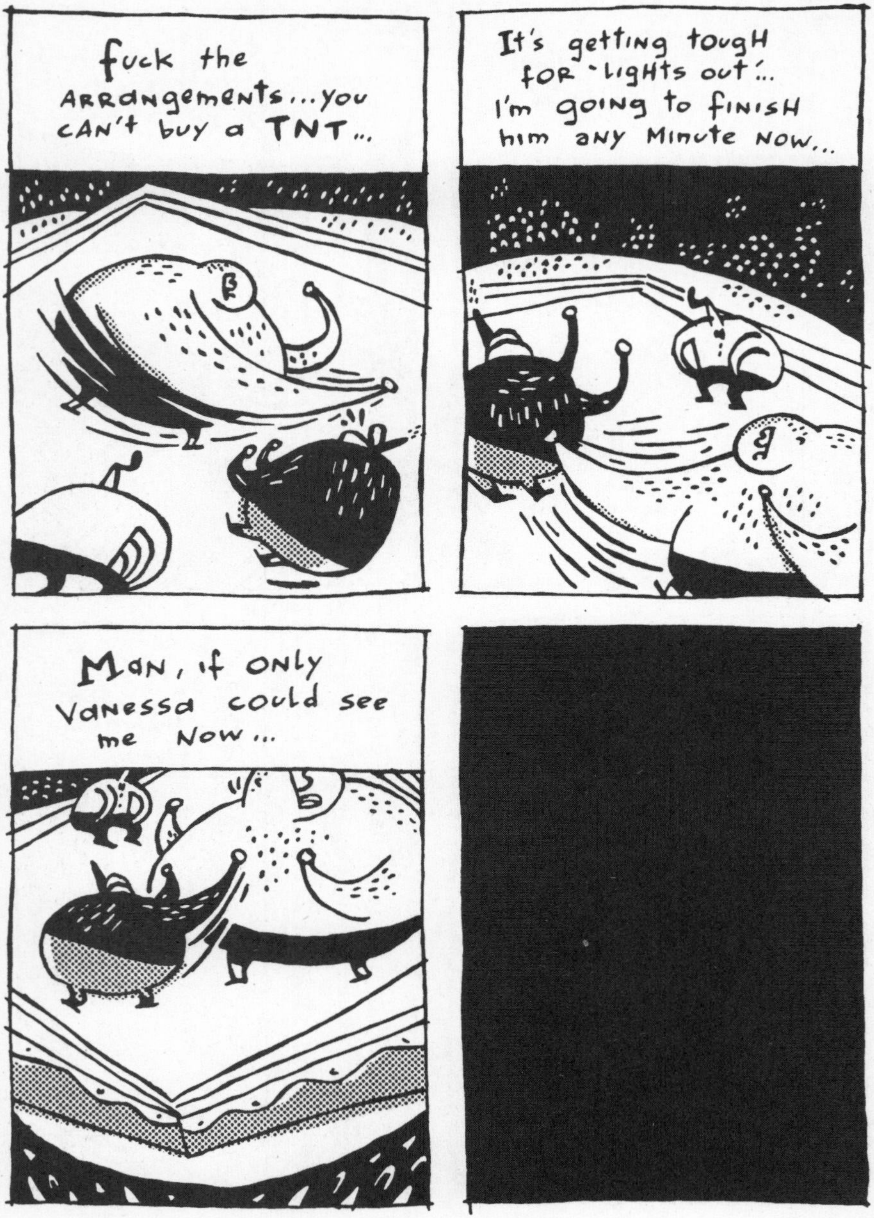
fuck the ARRANGEMENTS...you CAN'T buy a TNT...
It's getting tough for 'Lights out'... I'm going to finish him any minute now...
Man, if only Vanessa could see me now...

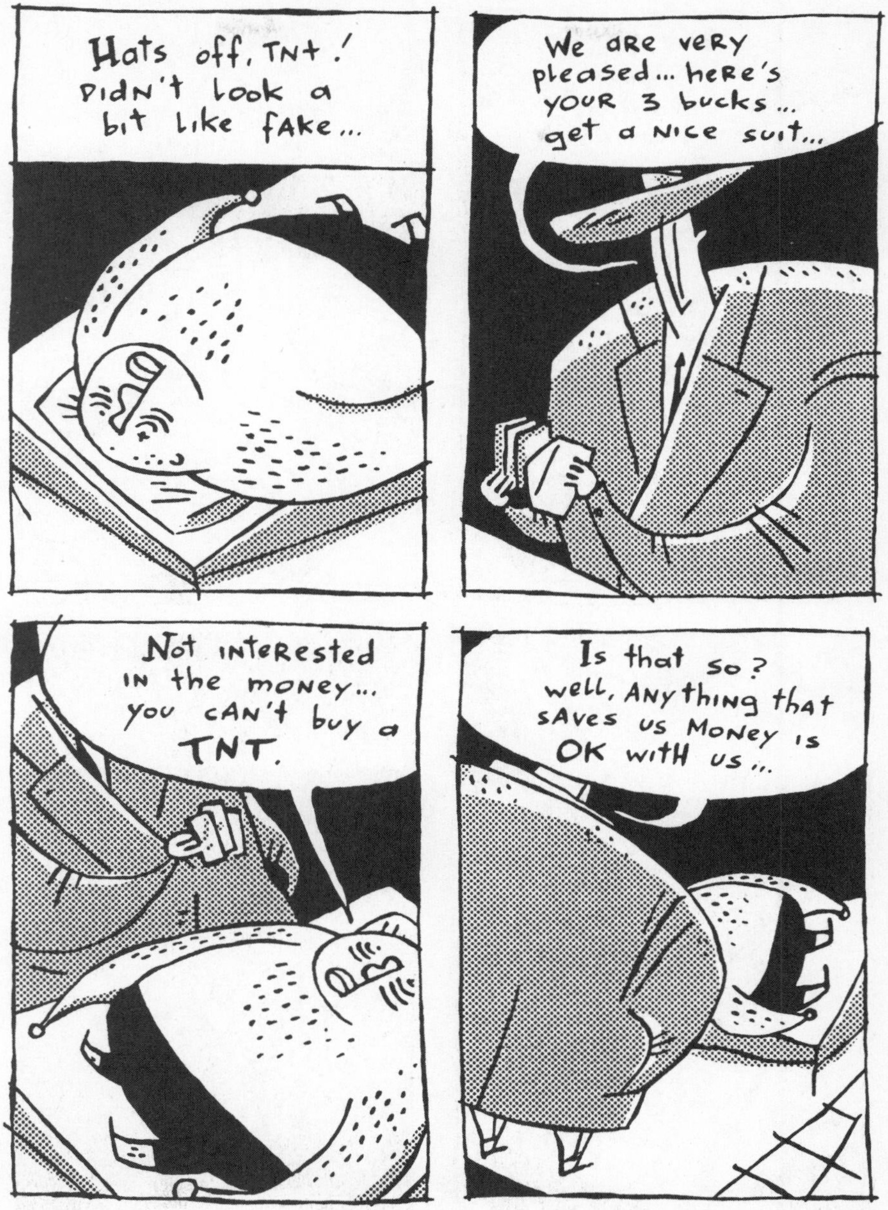
Hats off, TNT! Didn't look a bit like fake...
We are very pleased... here's your 3 bucks... get a nice suit...
Not interested in the money... you can't buy a TNT.
Is that so? well, Anything that saves us Money is OK with us...

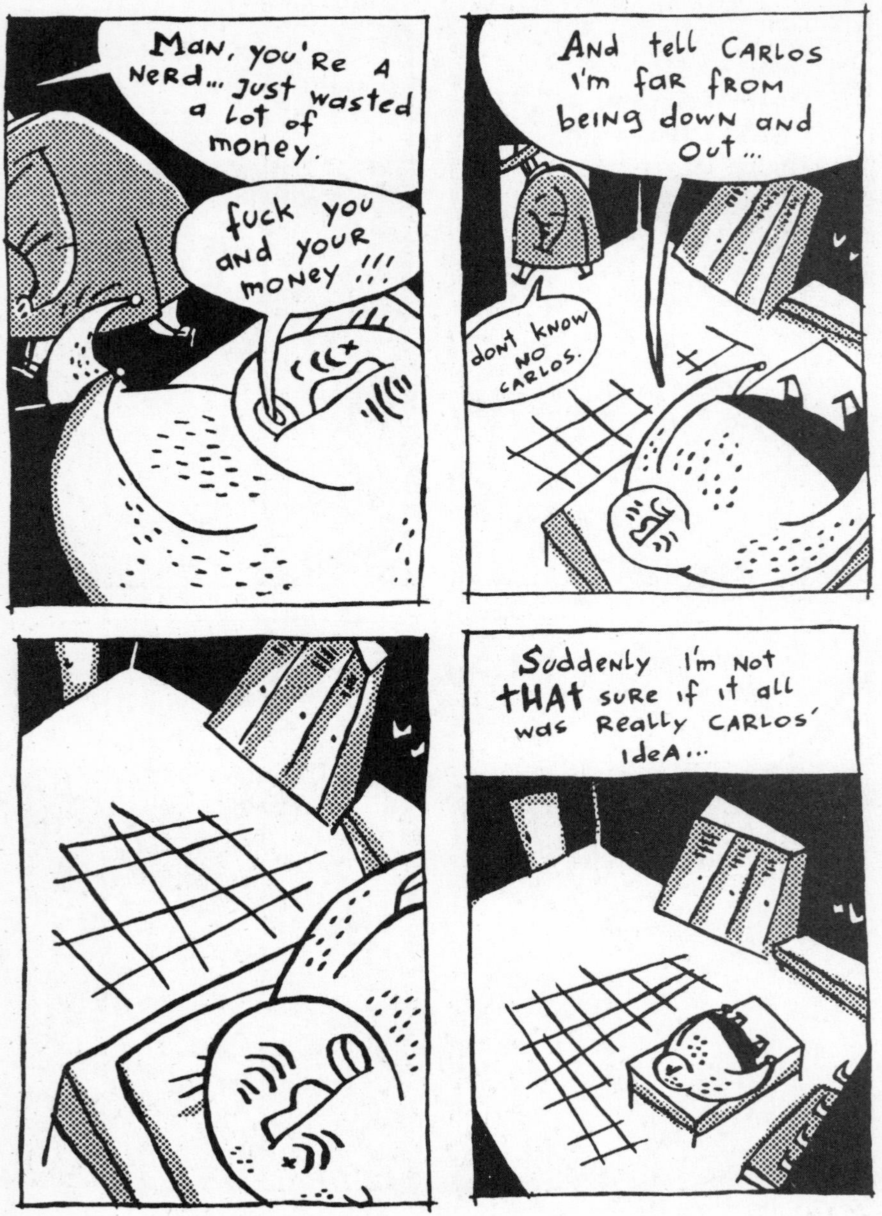
Man, you're A NERd... Just wasted a Lot of money.
fuck you and your money !!!
And tell CARLOS I'm far FROM being down and Out...
don't know NO CARLOS.
Suddenly I'm Not THAT sure if it all was Really CARLOS' ideA...

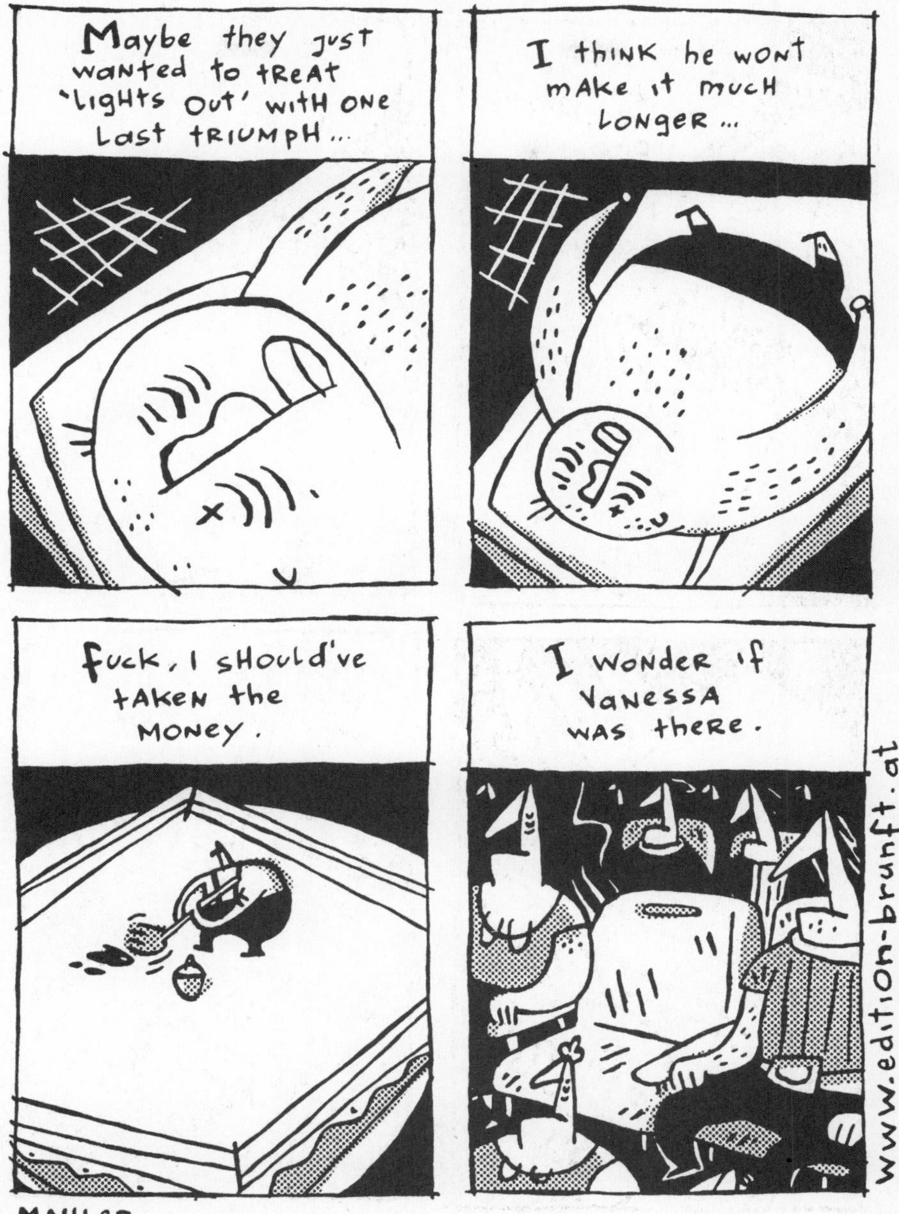
Maybe they just wanted to treat 'lights out' with one last triumph...
I think he wont make it much longer...
fuck, I should've taken the money.
I wonder if Vanessa was there.
www.edition-brunft.at
MAHLER

Portraits

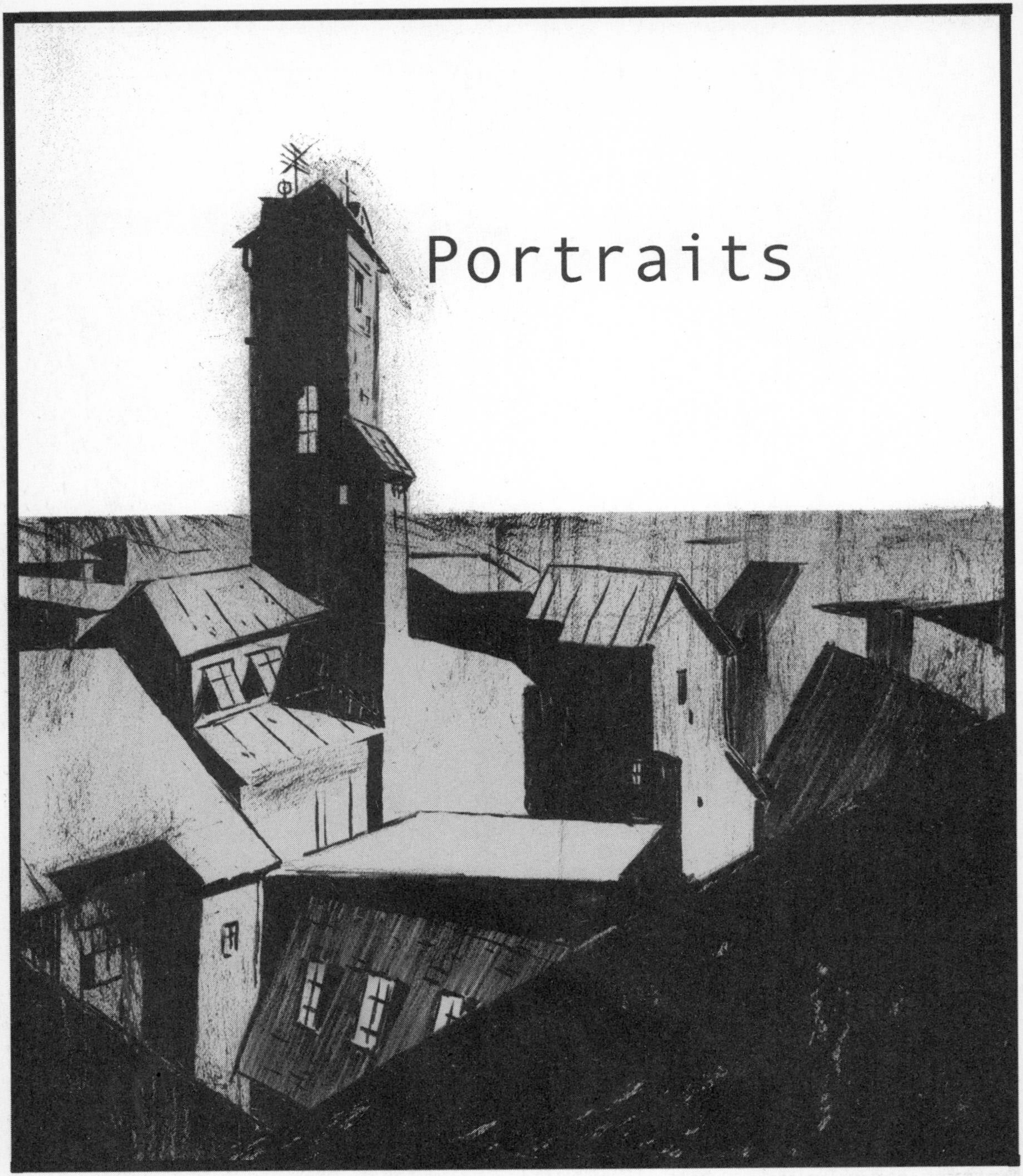

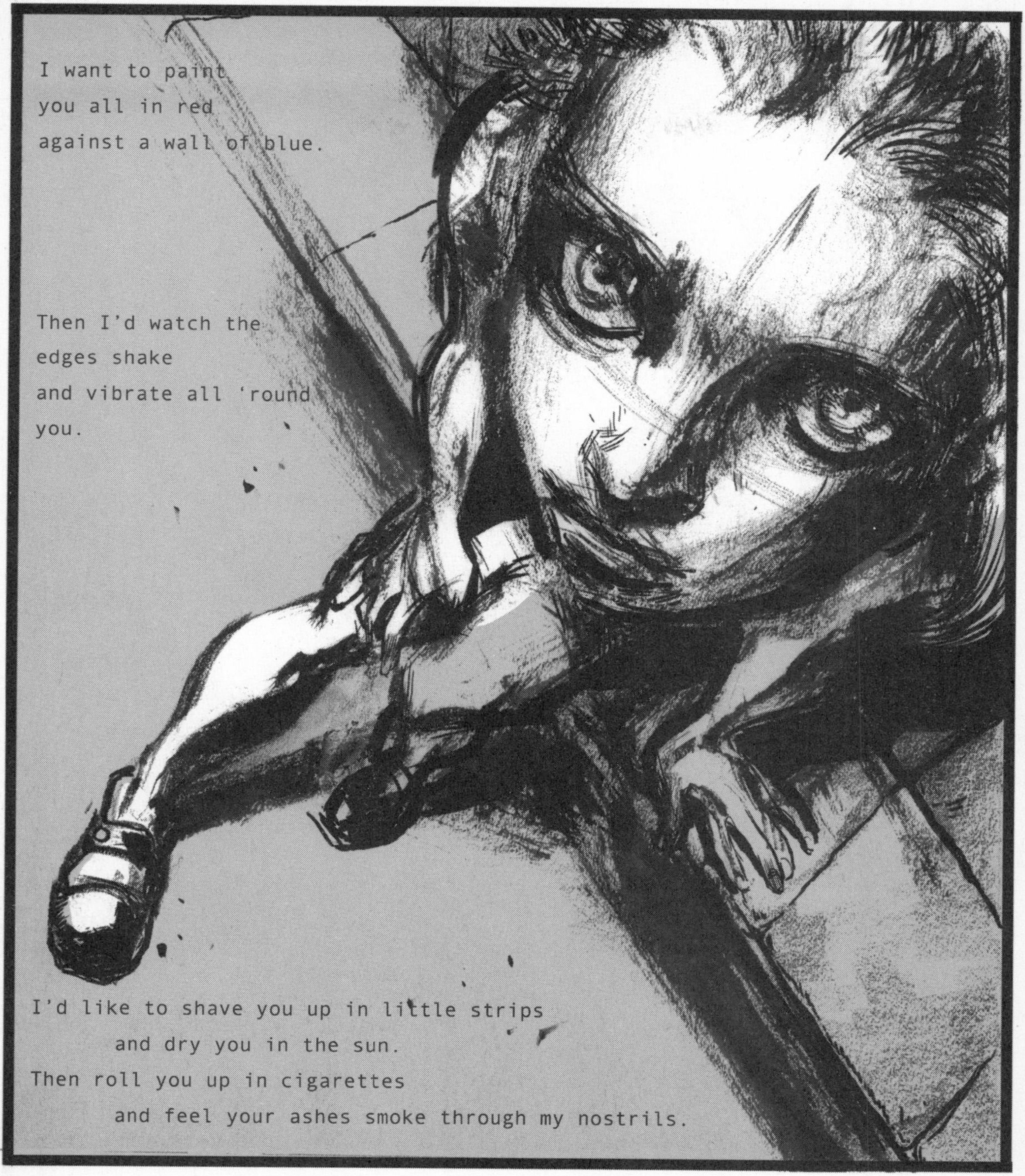
I want to paint
you all in red
against a wall of blue.
Then I'd watch the
edges shake
and vibrate all 'round
you.
I'd like to shave you up in little strips
and dry you in the sun.
Then roll you up in cigarettes
and feel your ashes smoke through my nostrils.

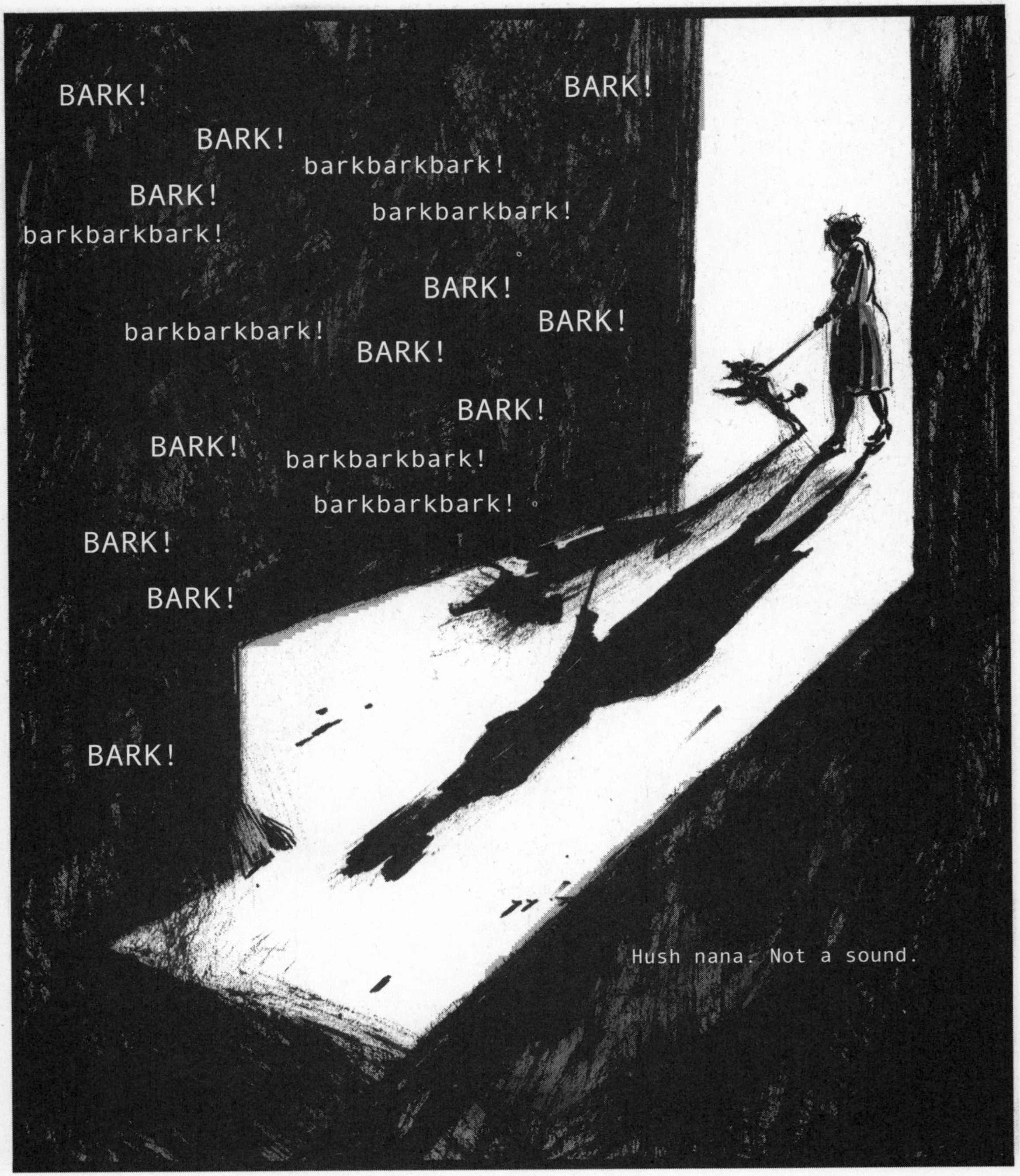
BARK!
BARK!
BARK!
barkbarkbark!
BARK!
barkbarkbark!
barkbarkbark!
BARK!
barkbarkbark!
BARK!
BARK!
BARK!
BARK!
barkbarkbark!
barkbarkbark!
BARK!
BARK!
BARK!
Hush nana. Not a sound.

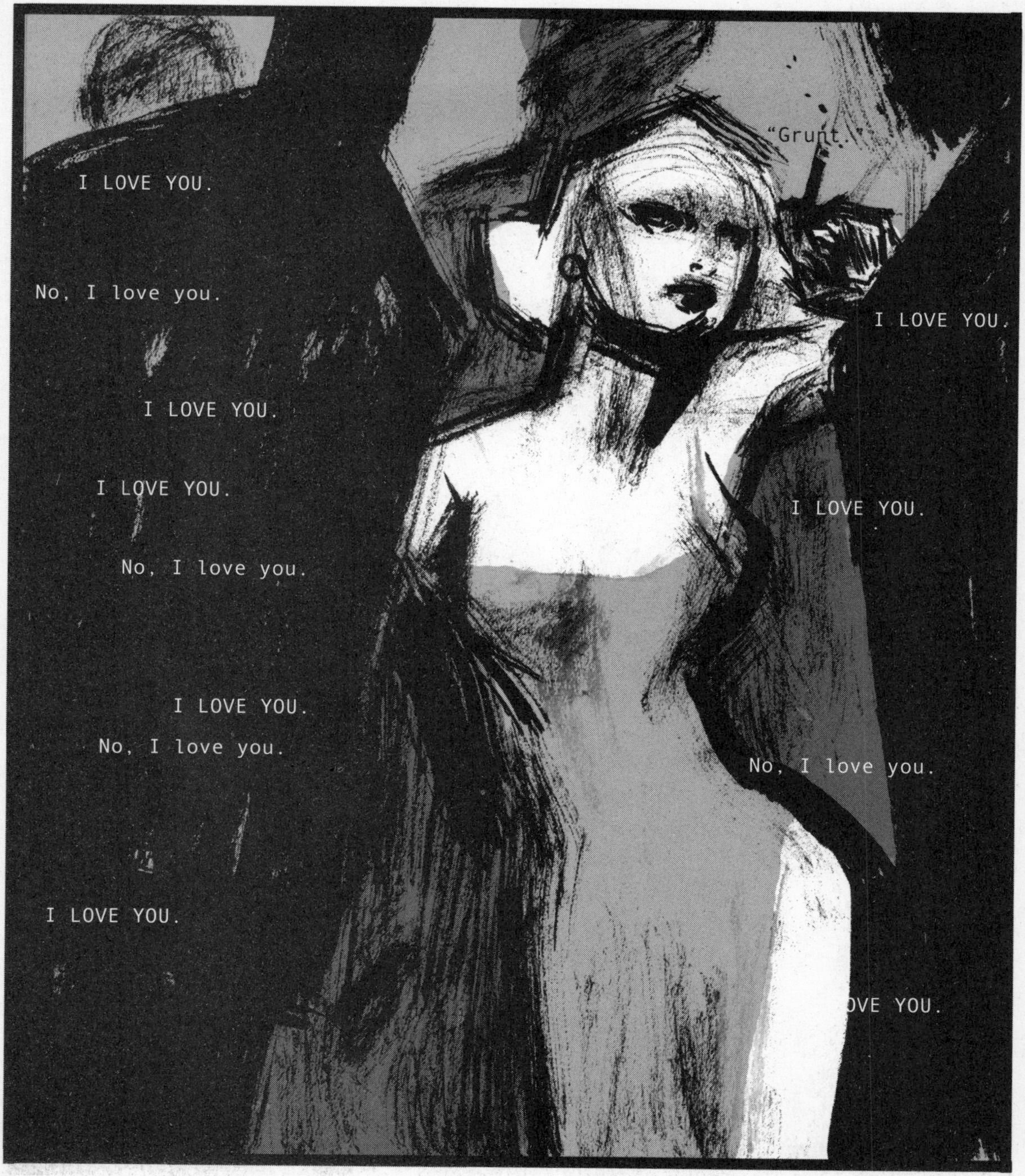
"Grunt.
I LOVE YOU.
No, I love you.
I LOVE YOU.
I LOVE YOU.
I LOVE YOU.
I LOVE YOU.
No, I love you.
I LOVE YOU.
No, I love you.
No, I love you.
I LOVE YOU.
OVE YOU.

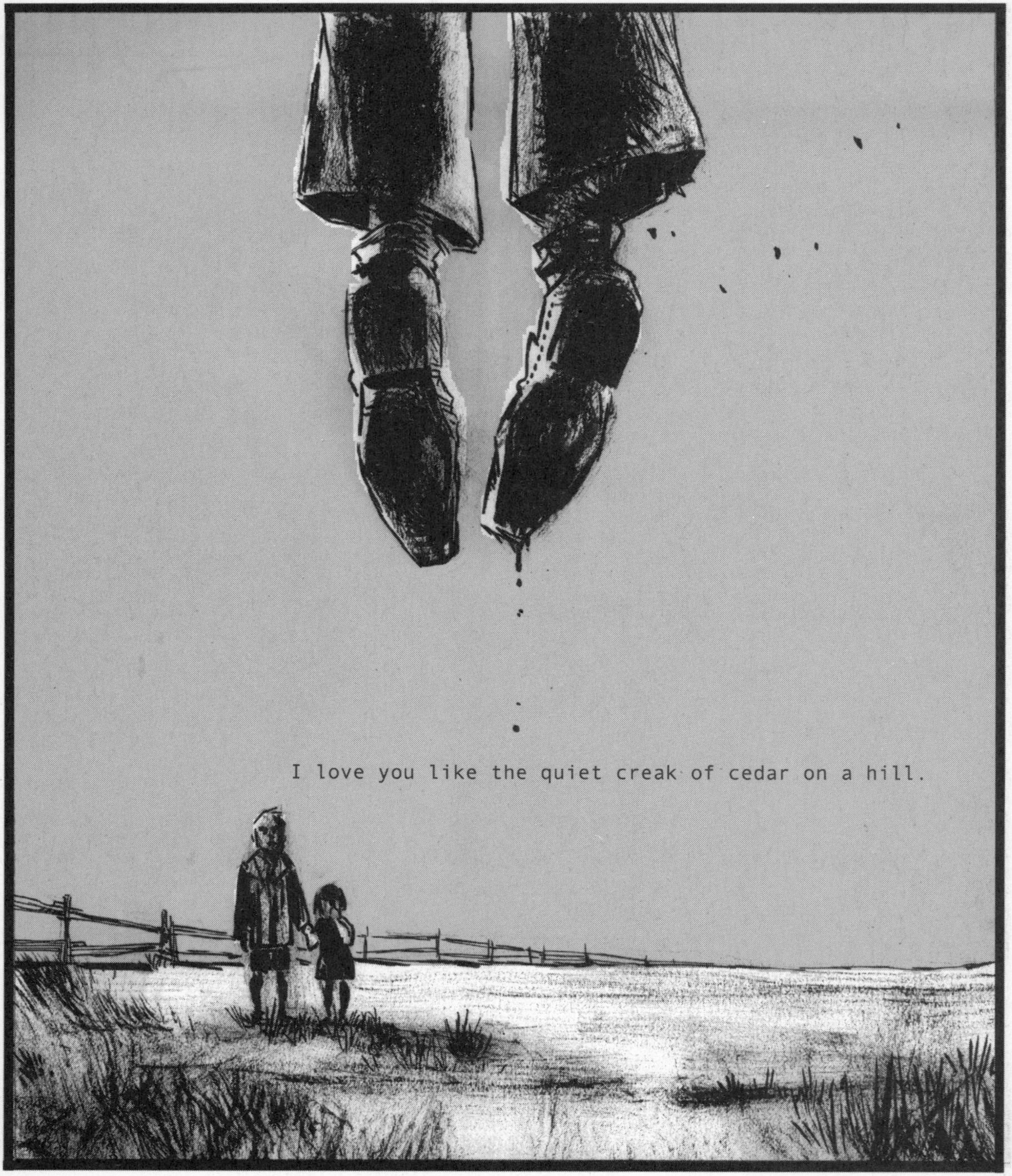
I love you like the quiet creak of cedar on a hill.

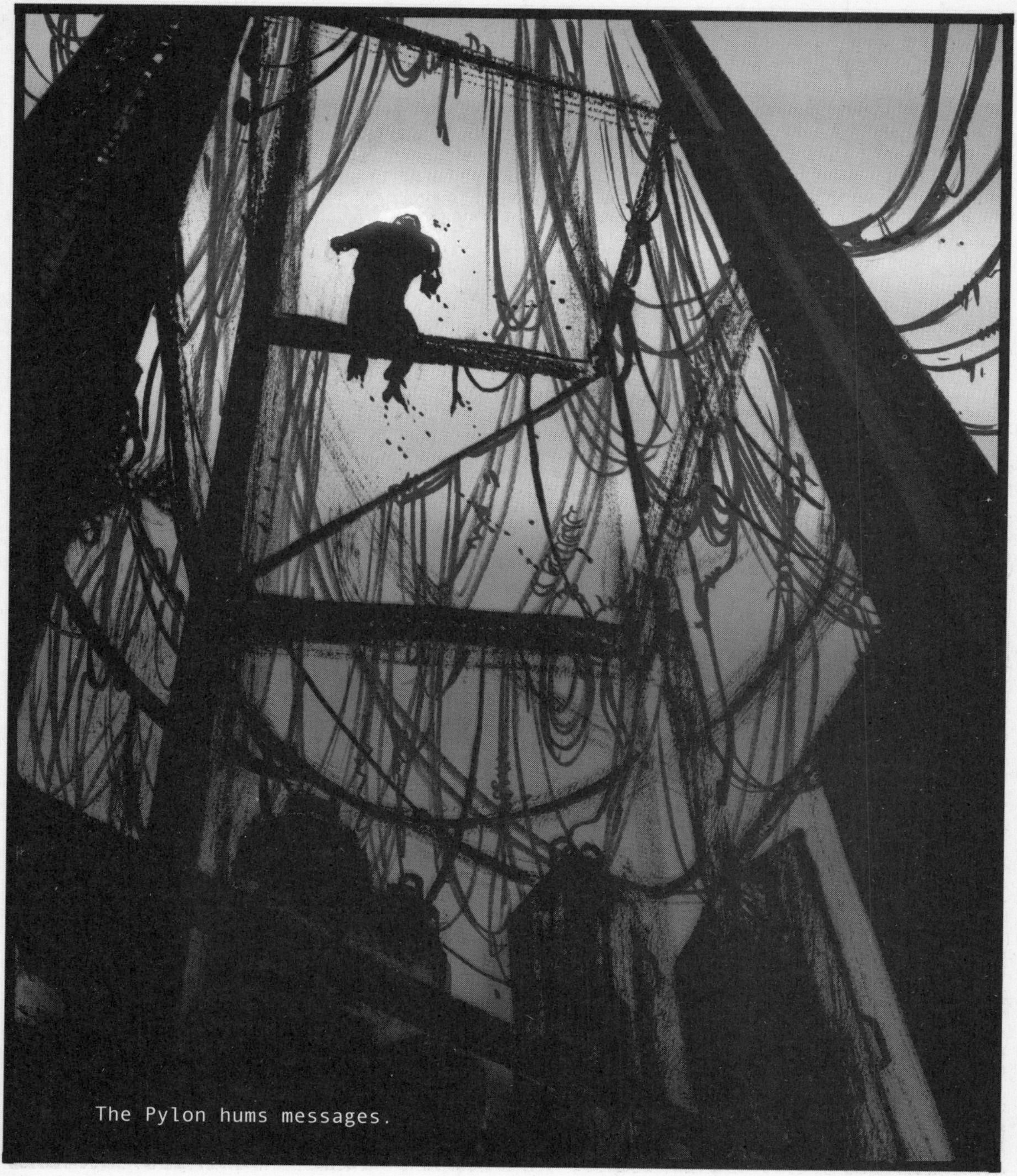
The Pylon hums messages.

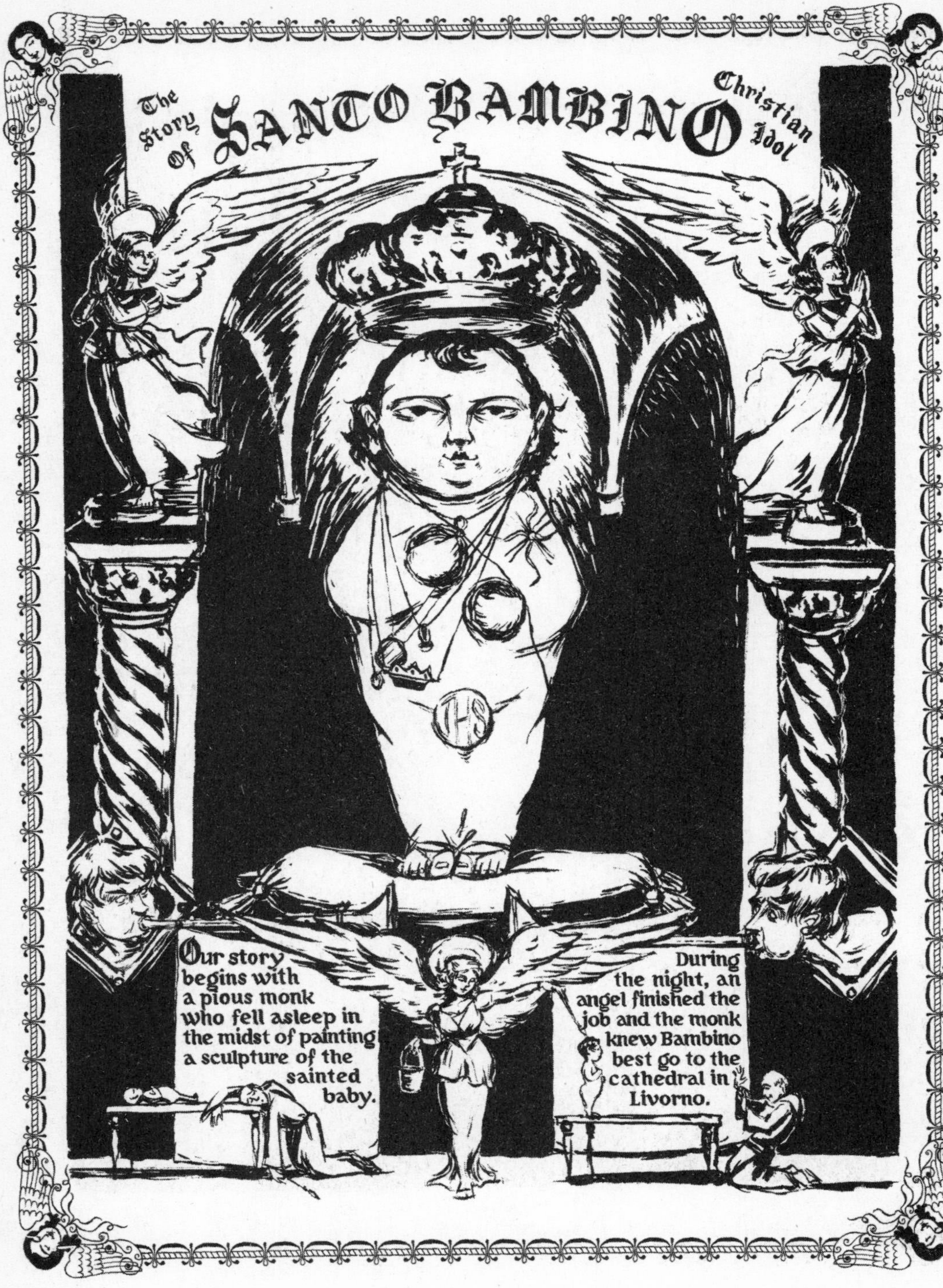
The Story of SANTO BAMBINO Christian Idol
Our story begins with a pious monk who fell asleep in the midst of painting a sculpture of the sainted baby.
IHS
During the night, an angel finished the job and the monk knew Bambino best go to the cathedral in Livorno.

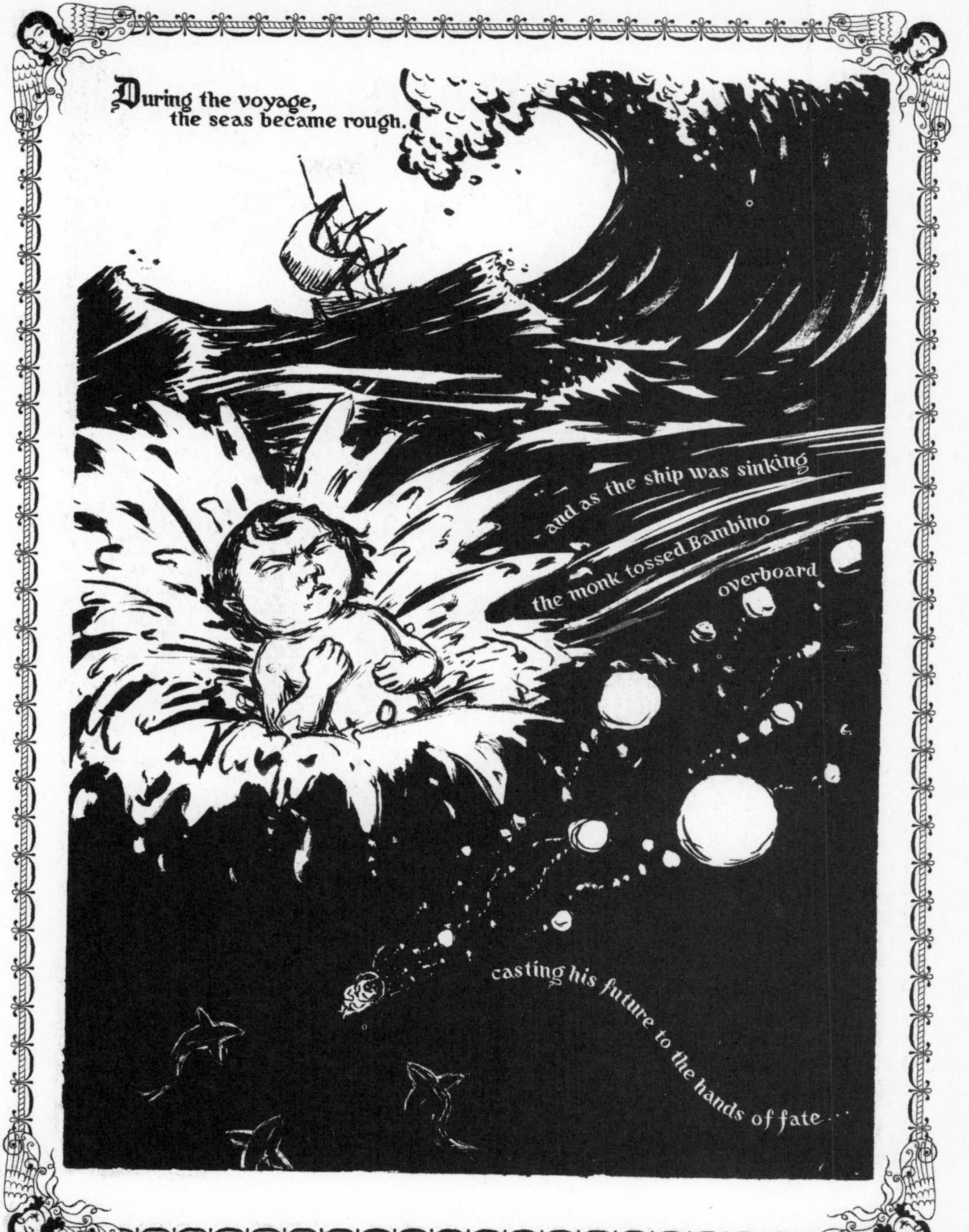
During the voyage,
the seas became rough.
and as the ship was sinking
the monk tossed Bambino
overboard
casting his future to the hands of fate...

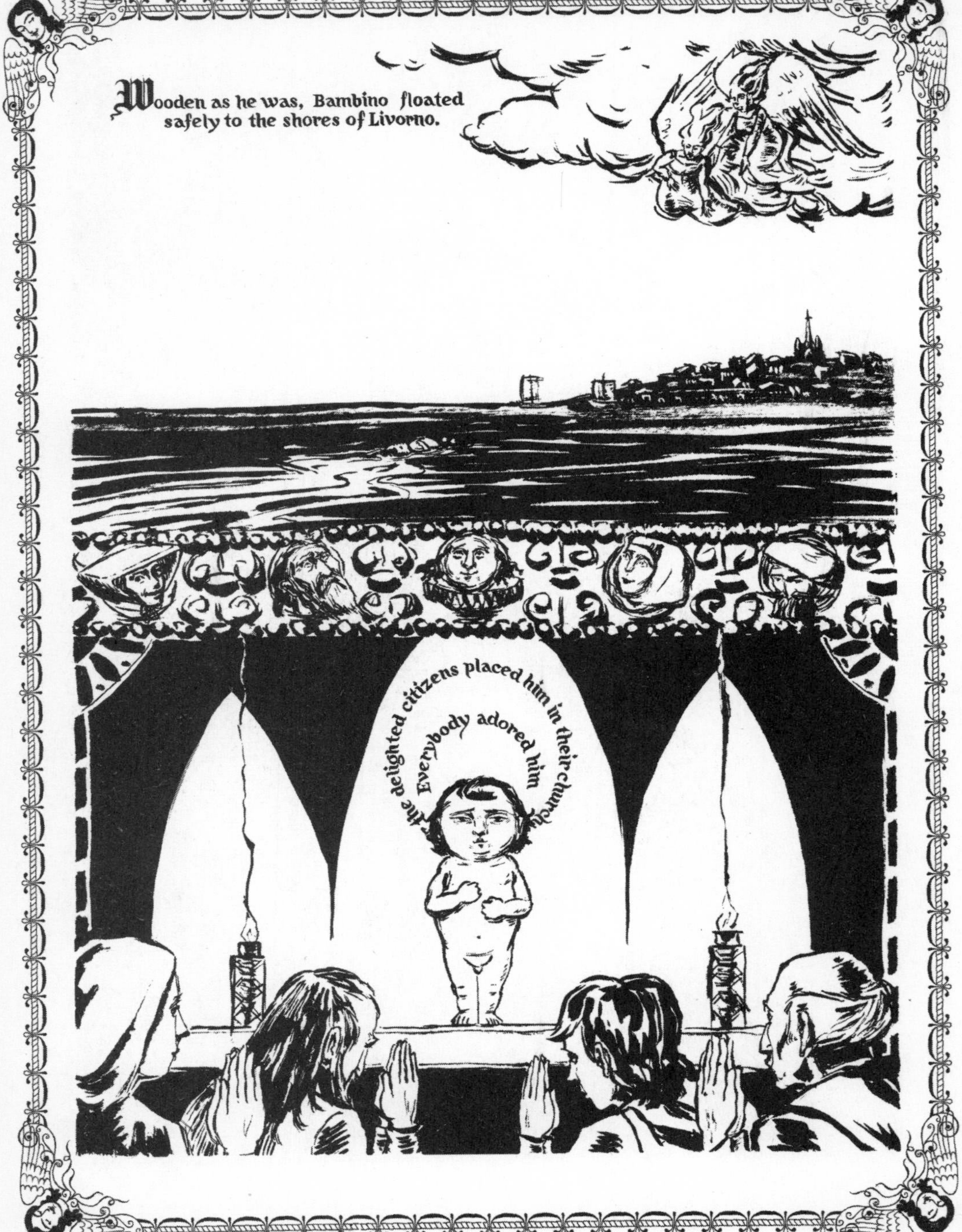
Wooden as he was, Bambino floated safely to the shores of Livorno.
the delighted citizens placed him in their church
Everybody adored him

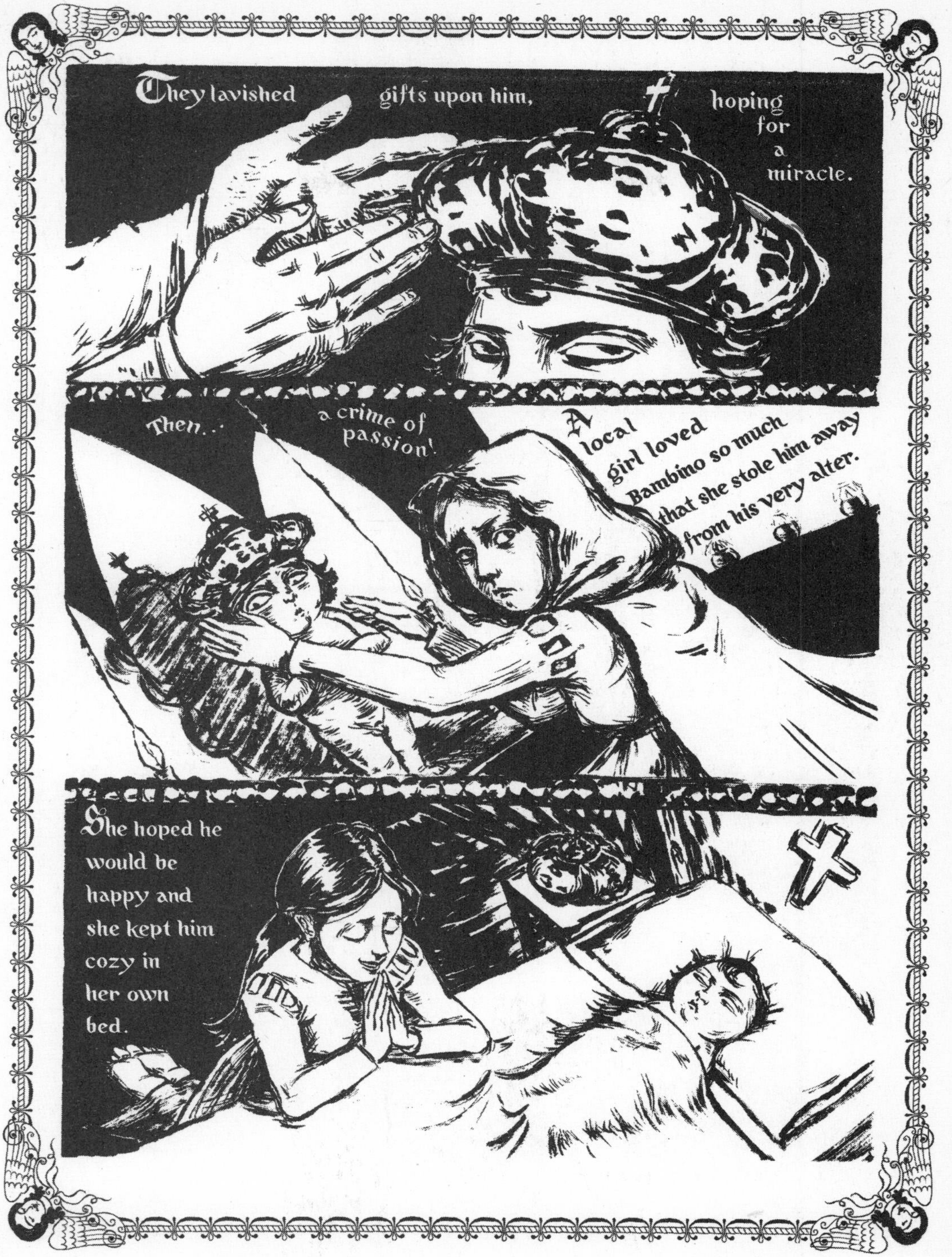
They lavished
gifts upon him,
hoping for a miracle.
Then...
a crime of passion!
A local girl loved Bambino so much that she stole him away from his very alter.
She hoped he would be happy and she kept him cozy in her own bed.

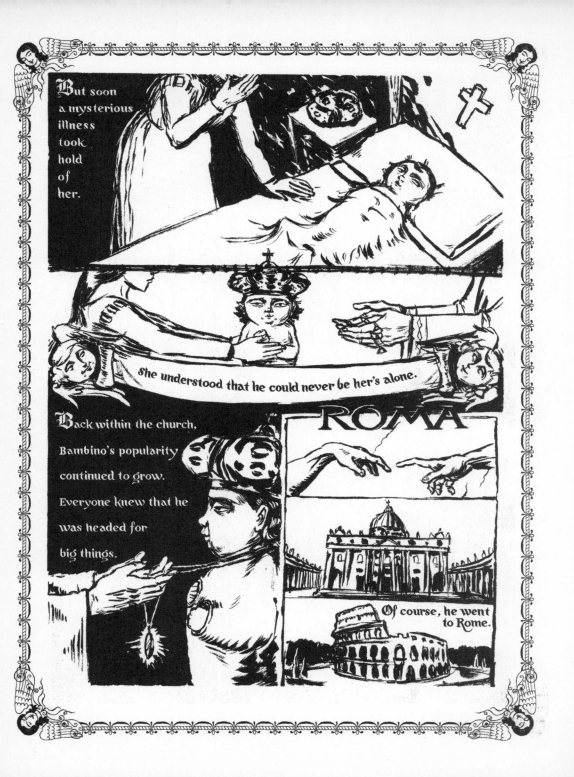

But soon a mysterious illness took hold of her.

she understood that he could never be her's alone.

Back within the church, Bambino's popularity continued to grow. Everyone knew that he was headed for big things.

ROMA

Of course, he went to Rome.

130

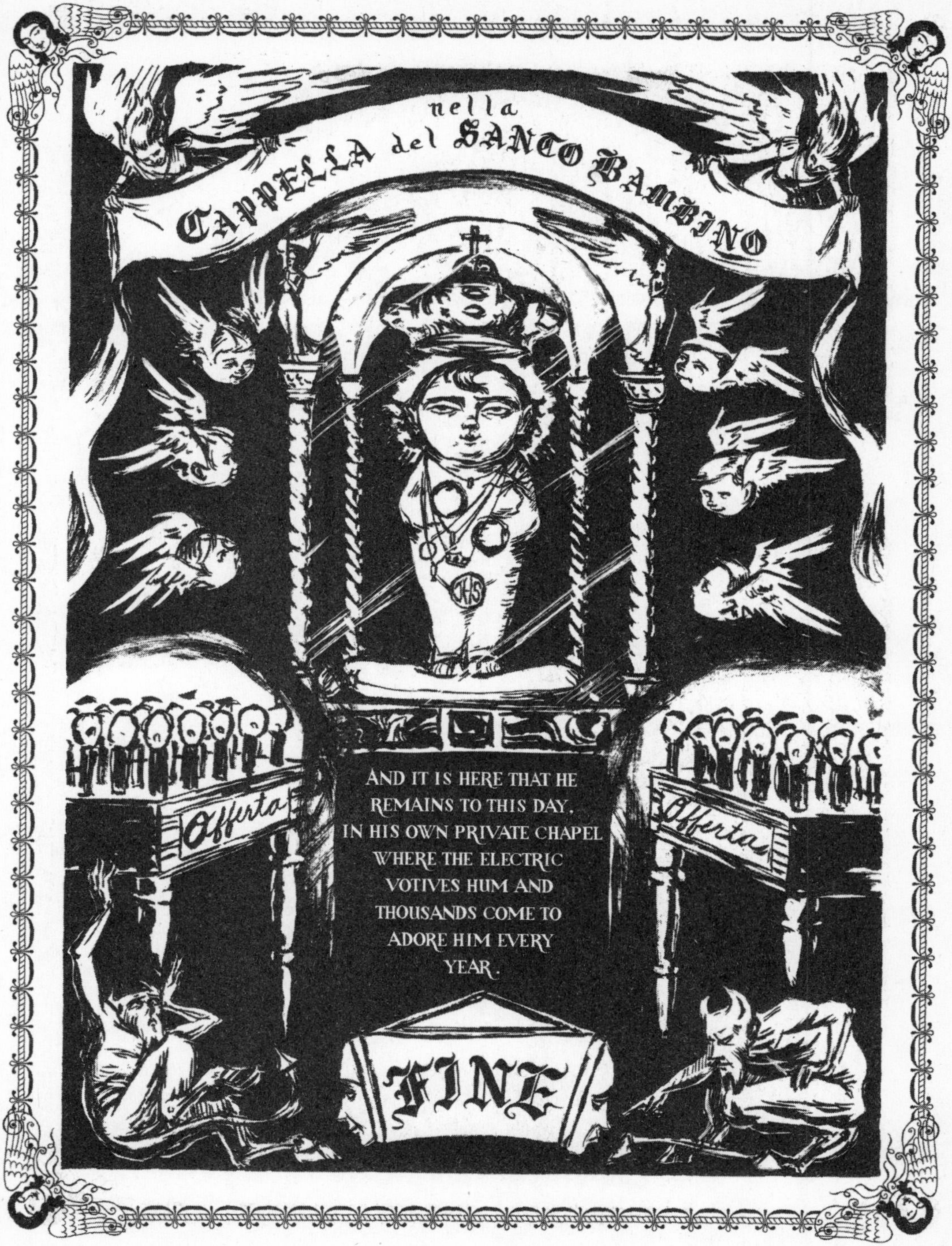
nella
CAPPELLA del SANTO BAMBINO
IHS
Offerta
Offerta
AND IT IS HERE THAT HE REMAINS TO THIS DAY, IN HIS OWN PRIVATE CHAPEL WHERE THE ELECTRIC VOTIVES HUM AND THOUSANDS COME TO ADORE HIM EVERY YEAR.
FINE

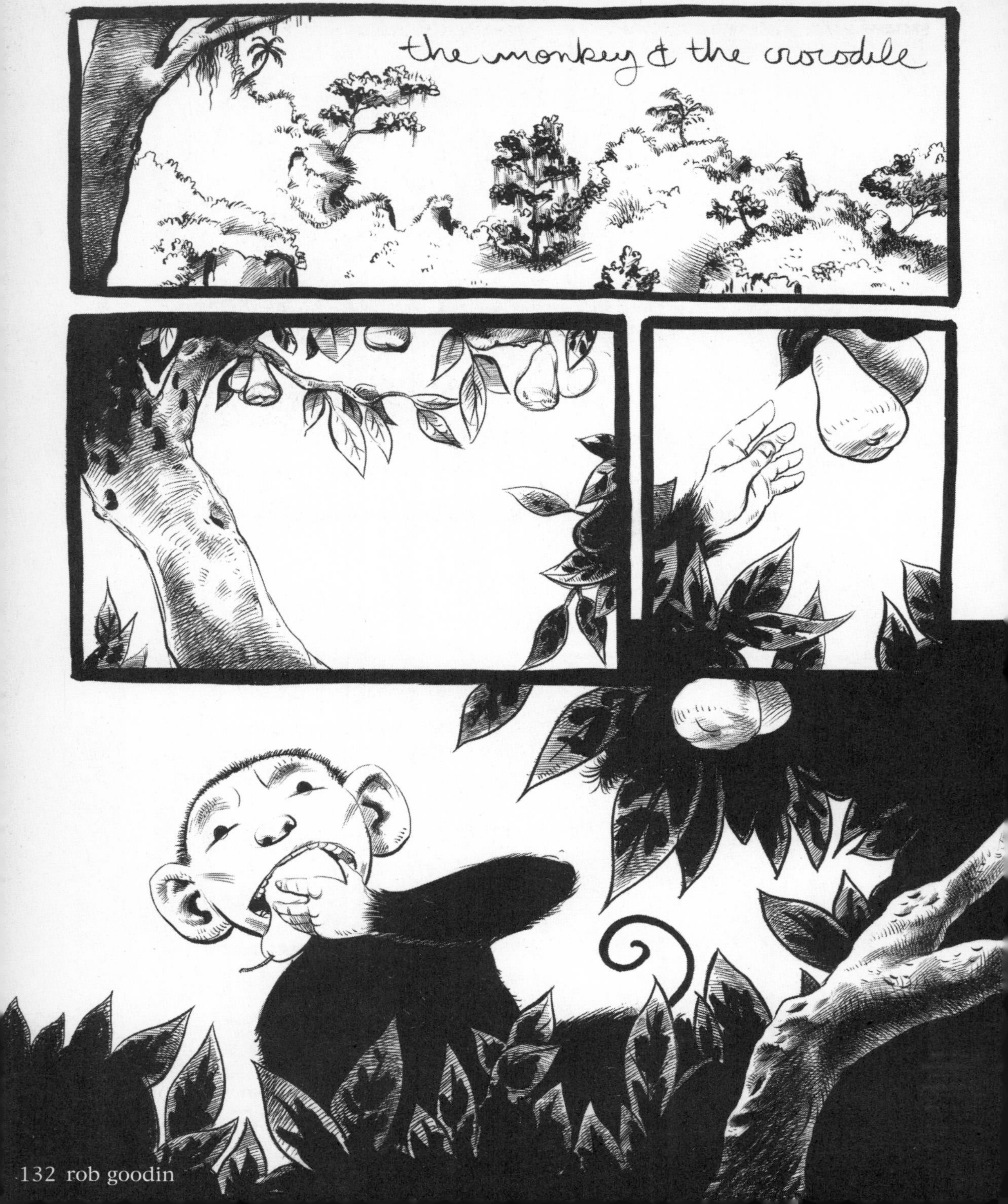
the monkey & the crocodile

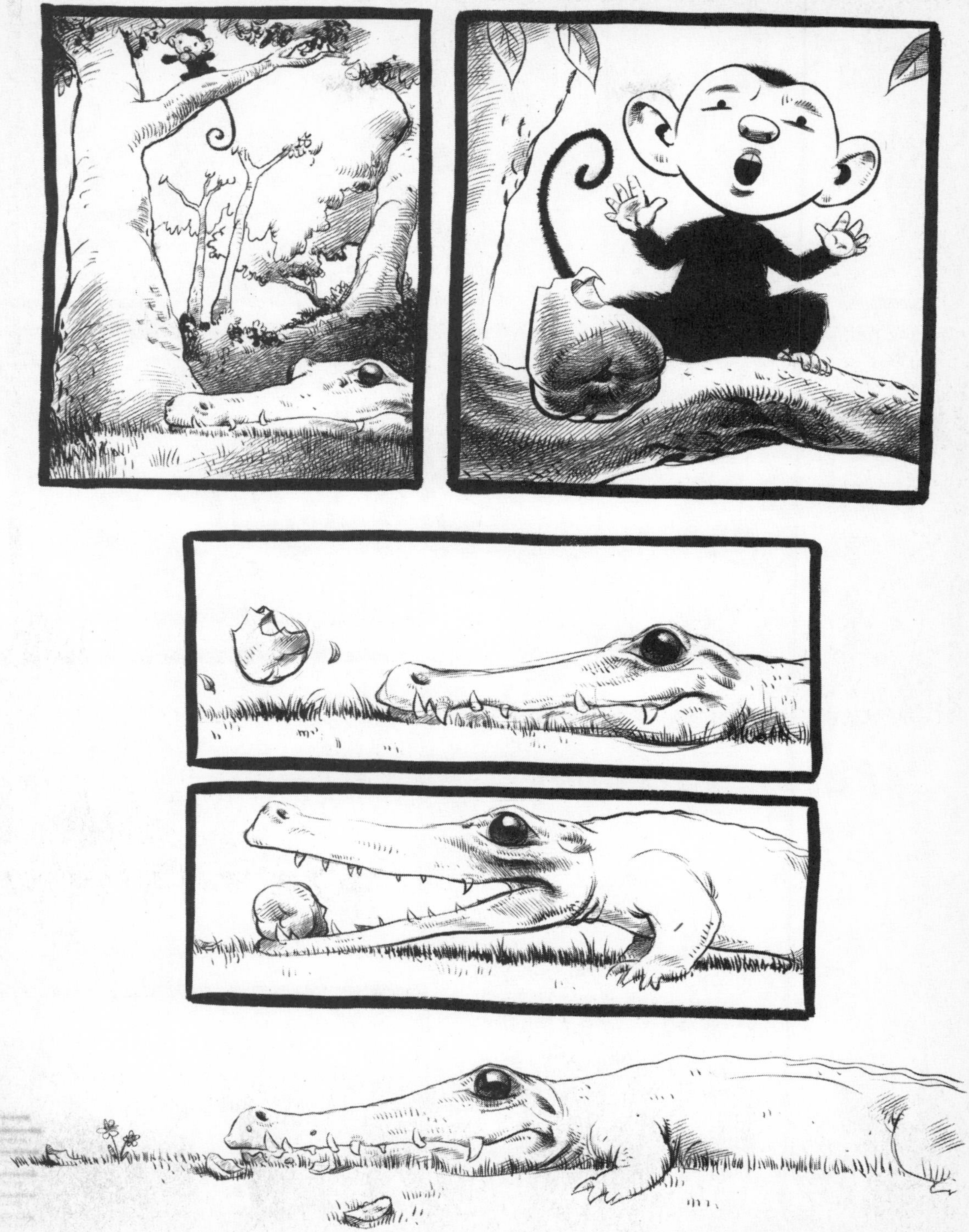

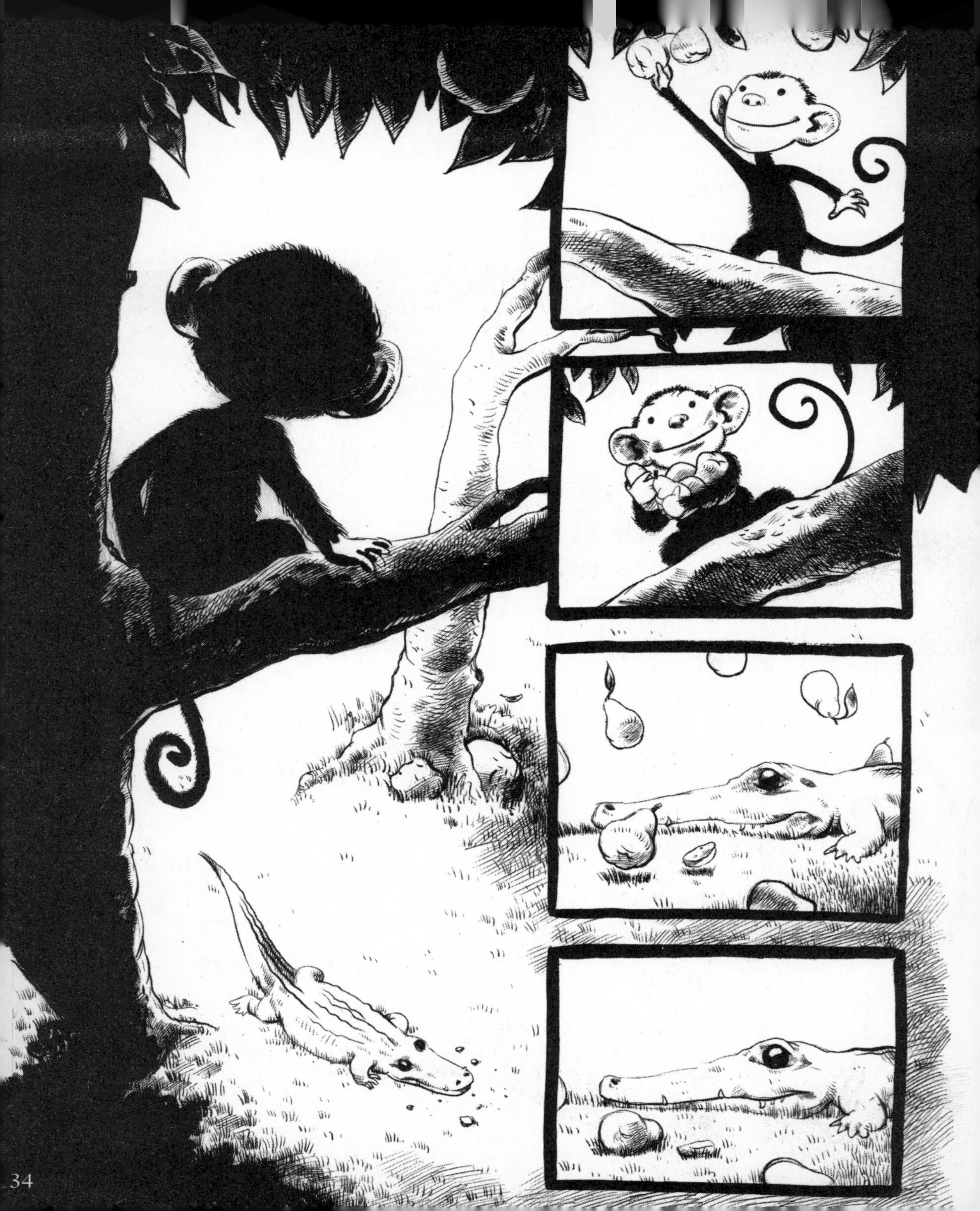

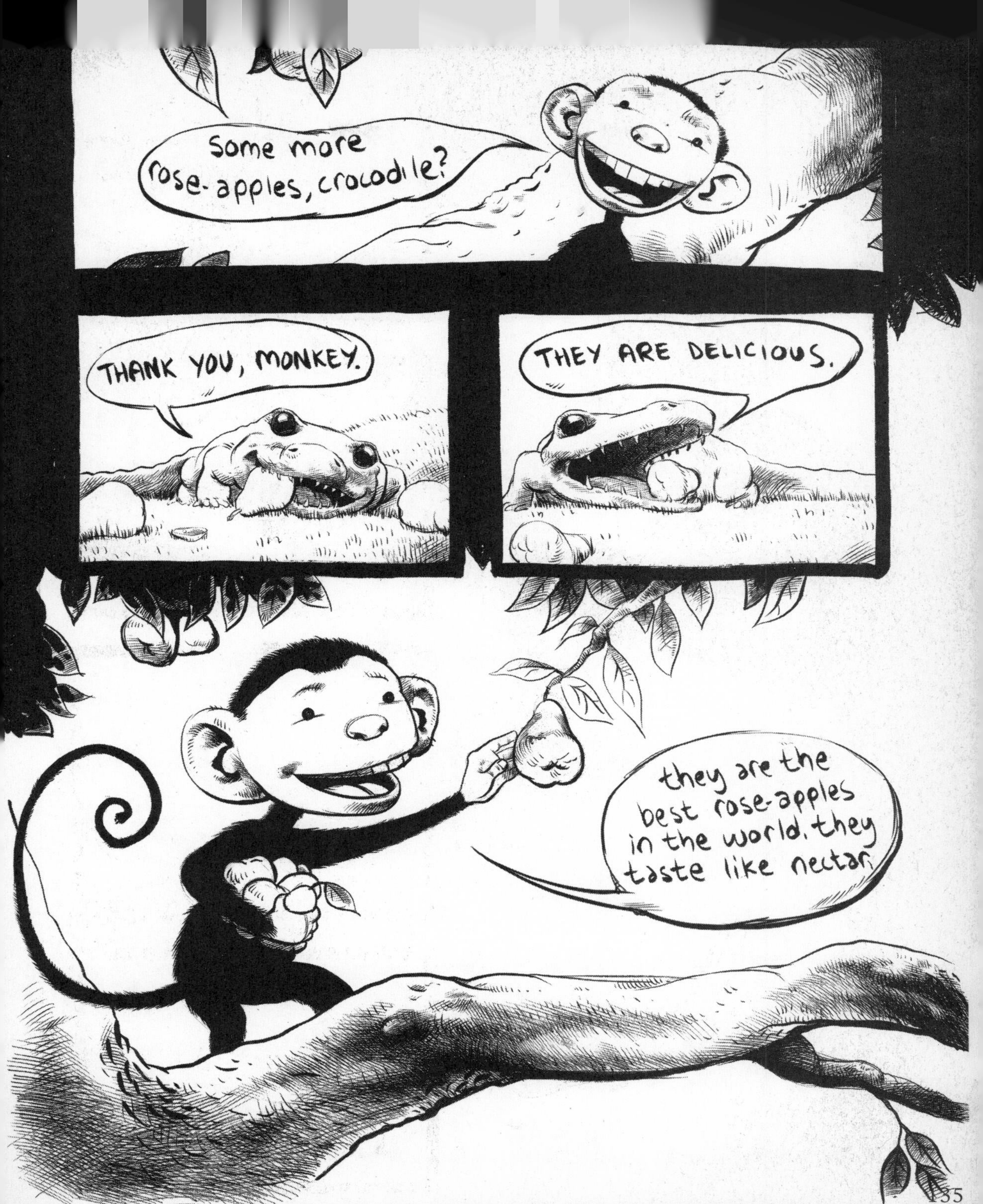
Some more rose-apples, crocodile?
THANK YOU, MONKEY.
THEY ARE DELICIOUS.
they are the best rose-apples in the world. they taste like nectar.

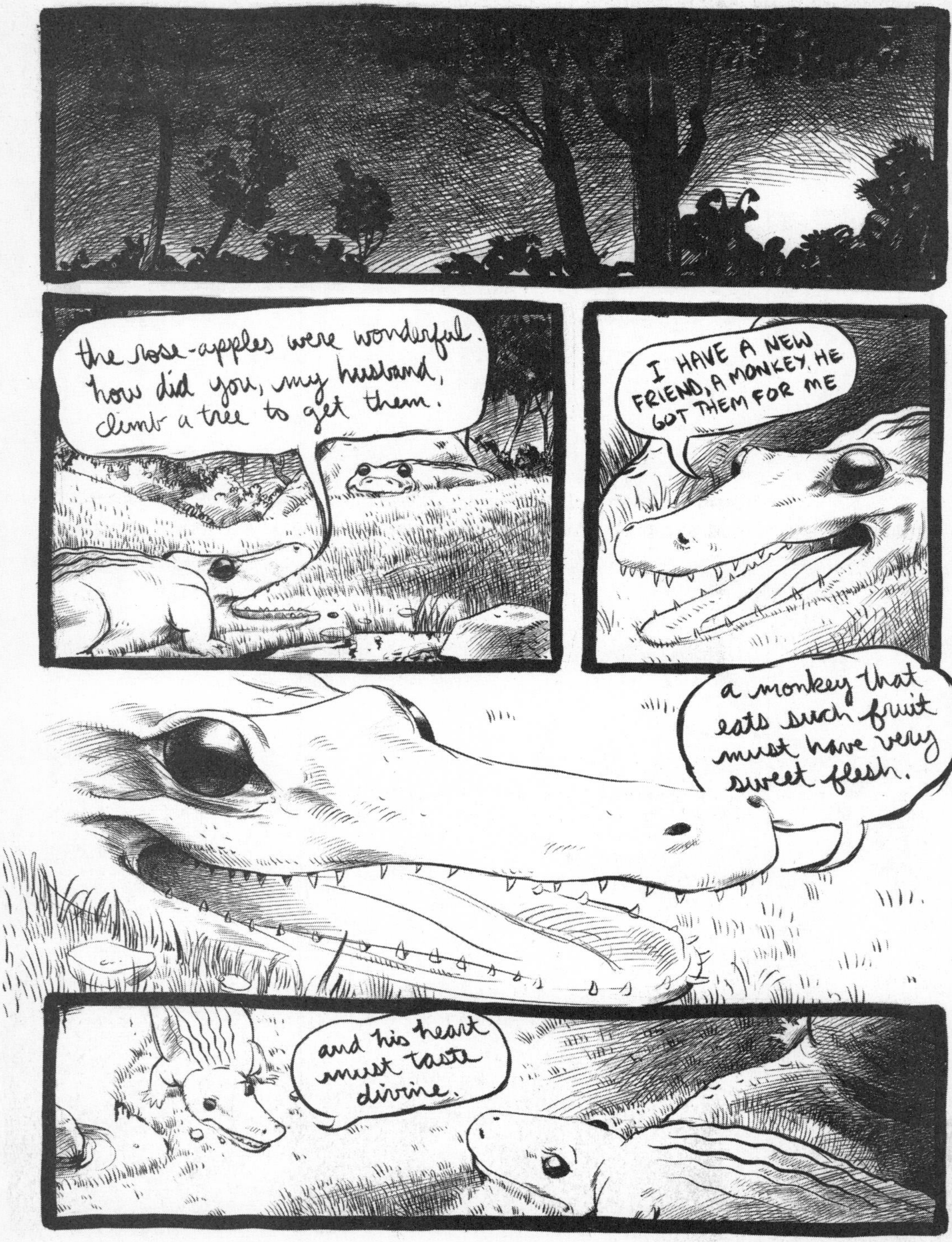
the rose-apples were wonderful. how did you, my husband, climb a tree to get them.
I HAVE A NEW FRIEND, A MONKEY. HE GOT THEM FOR ME
a monkey that eats such fruit must have very sweet flesh.
and his heart must taste divine.

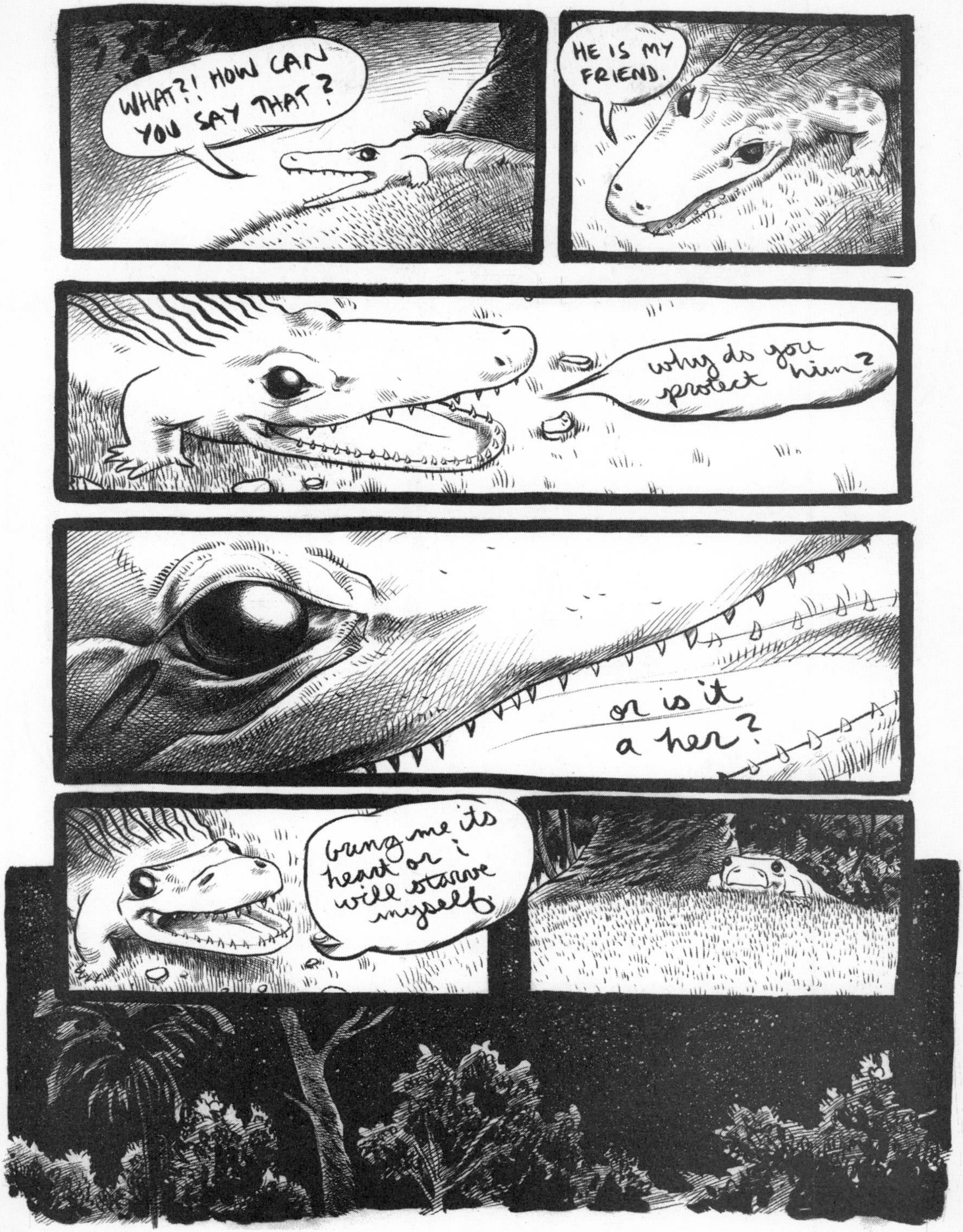

WHAT?! HOW CAN YOU SAY THAT?
HE IS MY FRIEND.
why do you protect him?
or is it a her?
bring me its heart or i will starve myself

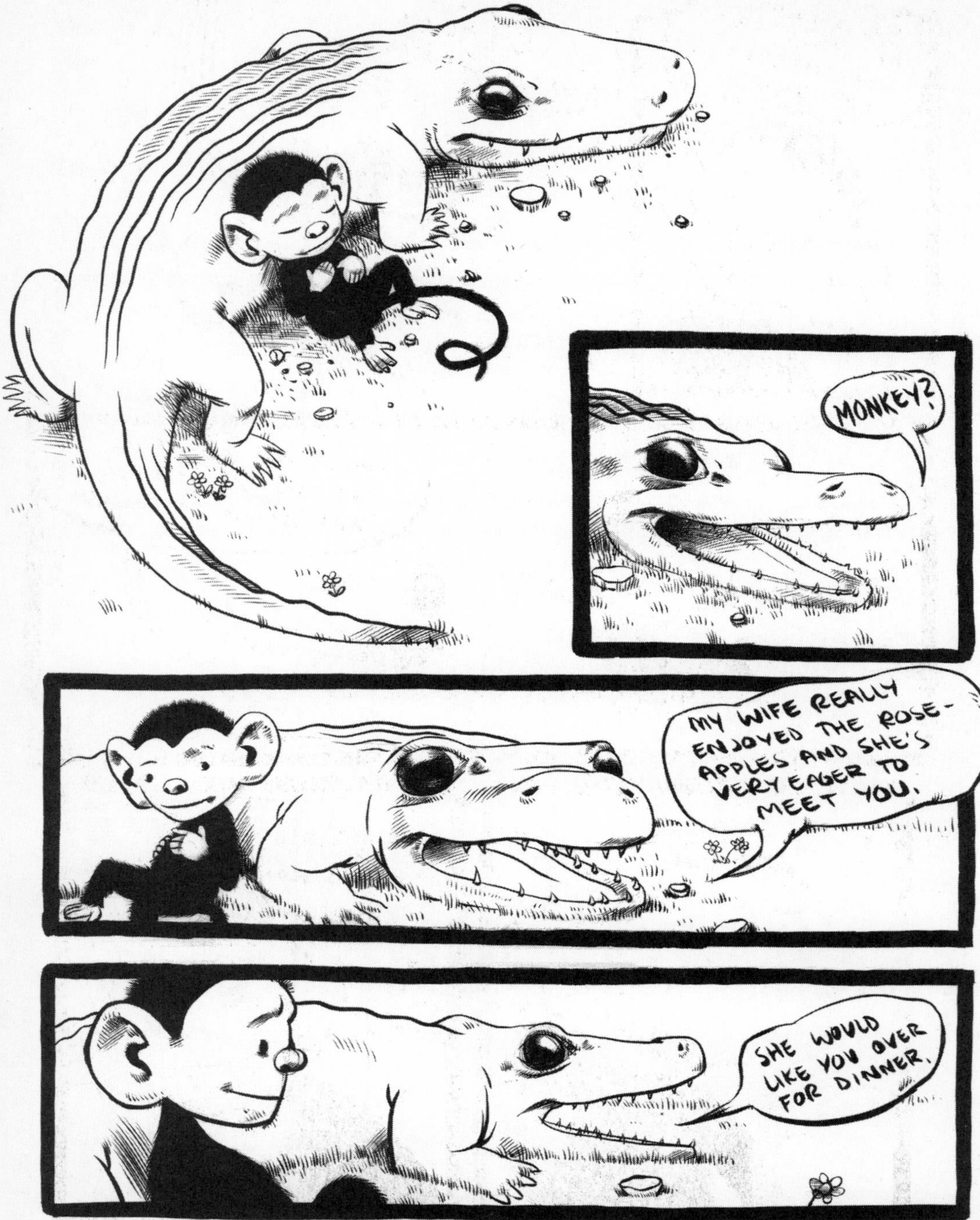
MONKEY?
MY WIFE REALLY ENJOYED THE ROSE-APPLES AND SHE'S VERY EAGER TO MEET YOU.
SHE WOULD LIKE YOU OVER FOR DINNER.

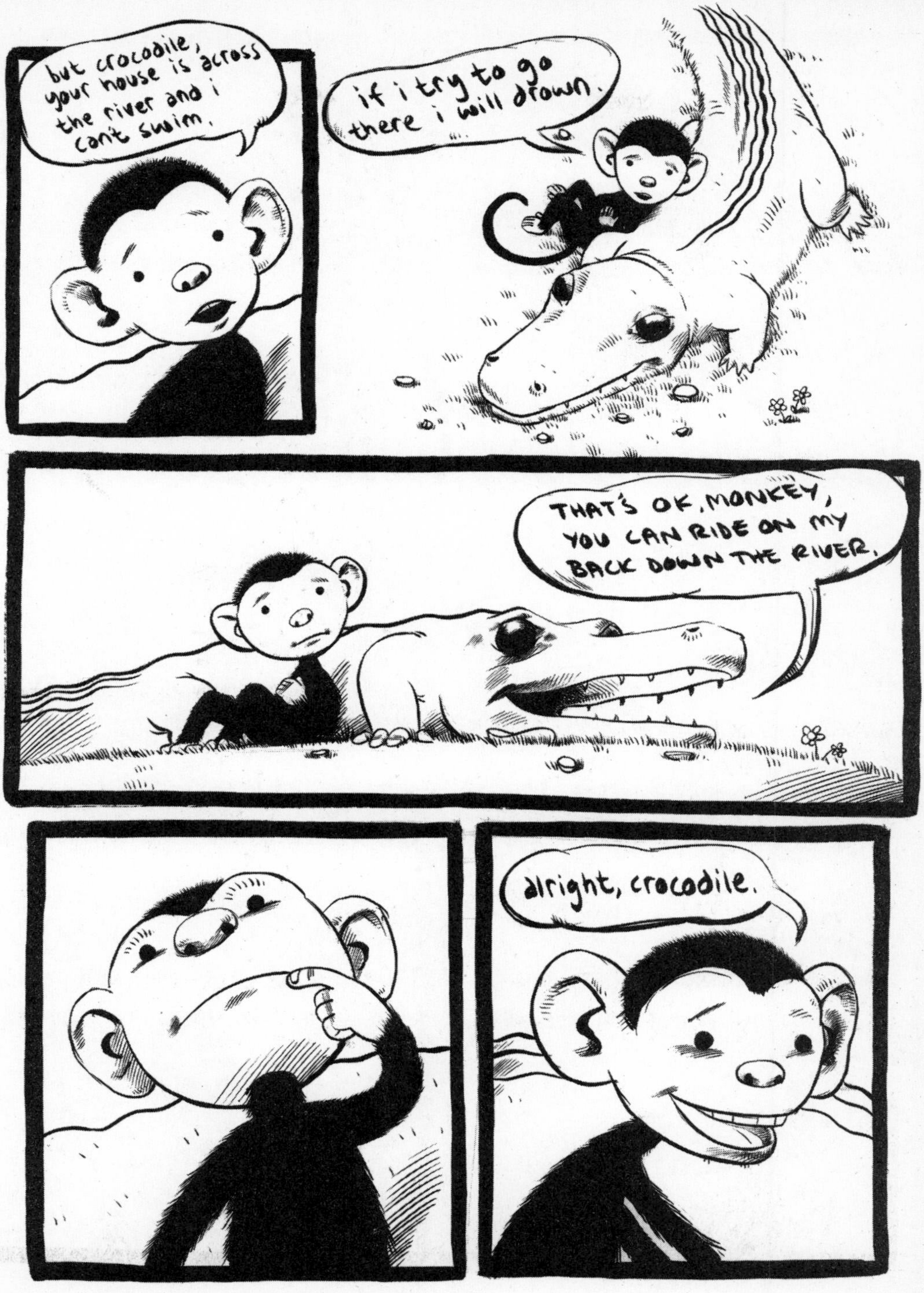
but crocodile, your house is across the river and i can't swim.
if i try to go there i will drown.
THAT'S OK, MONKEY, YOU CAN RIDE ON MY BACK DOWN THE RIVER.
alright, crocodile.

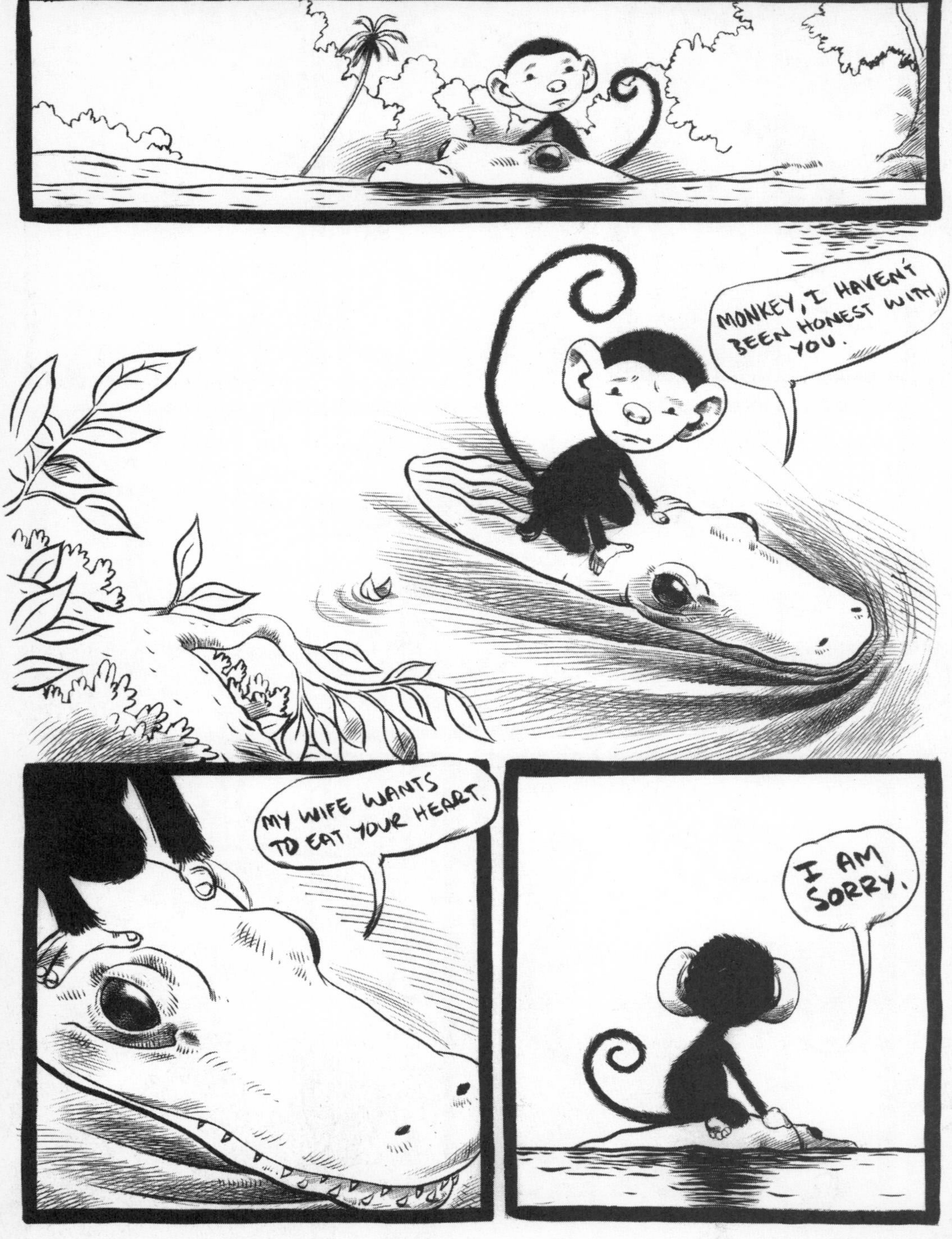
MONKEY, I HAVEN'T BEEN HONEST WITH YOU.
MY WIFE WANTS TO EAT YOUR HEART.
I AM SORRY.

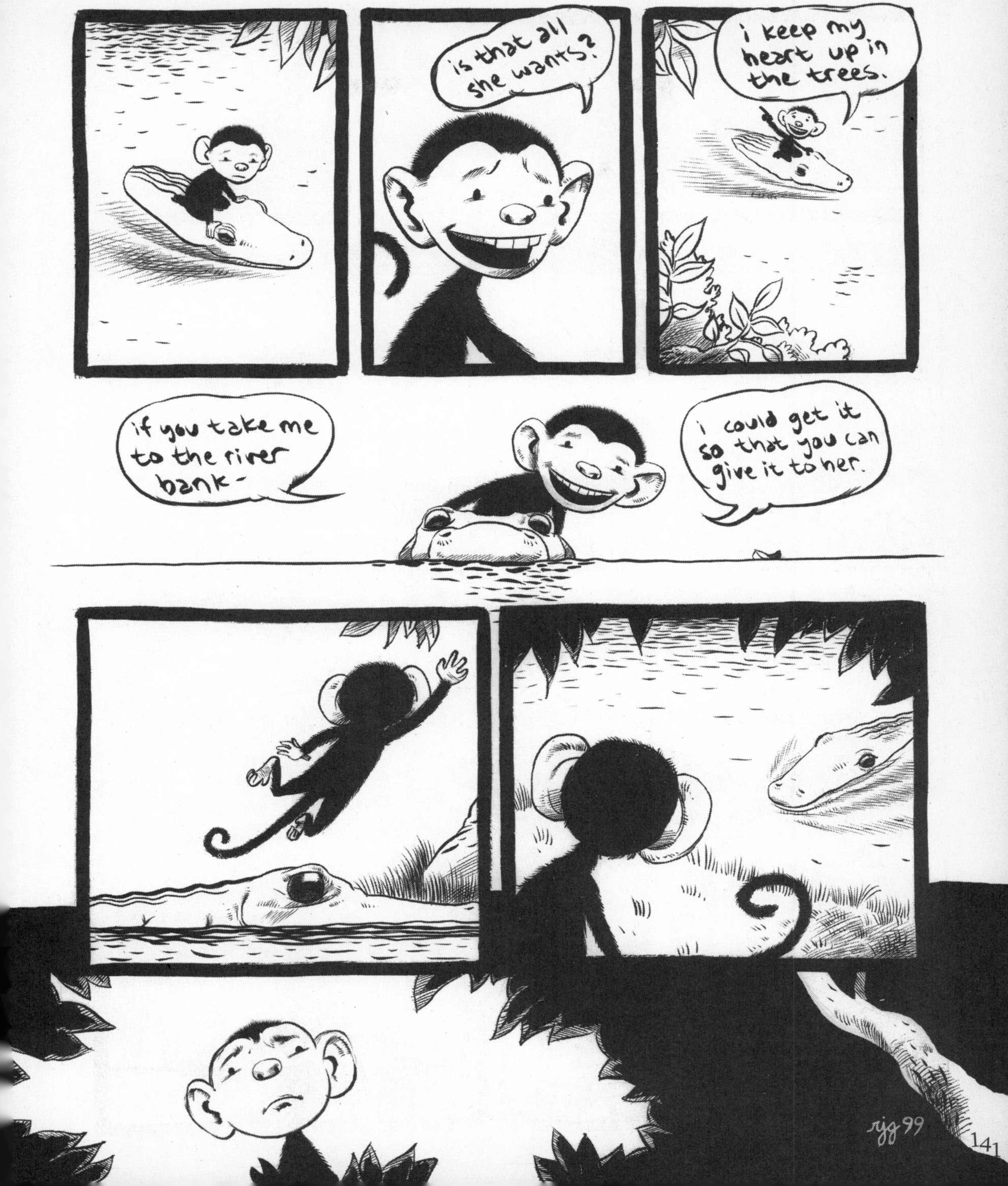
is that all she wants?
i keep my heart up in the trees.
if you take me to the river bank-
i could get it so that you can give it to her.
rjg 99

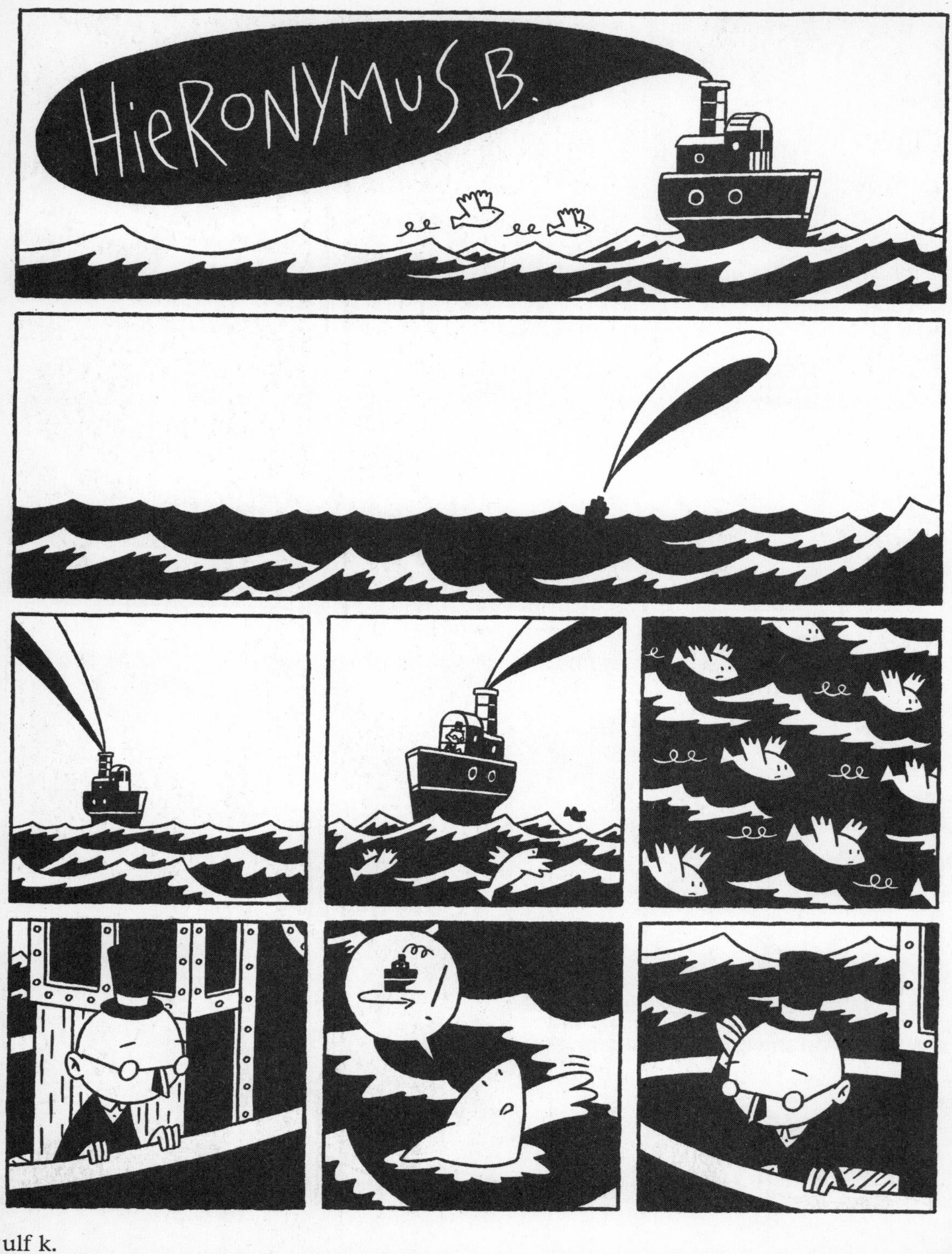
HieRONYMUS B.

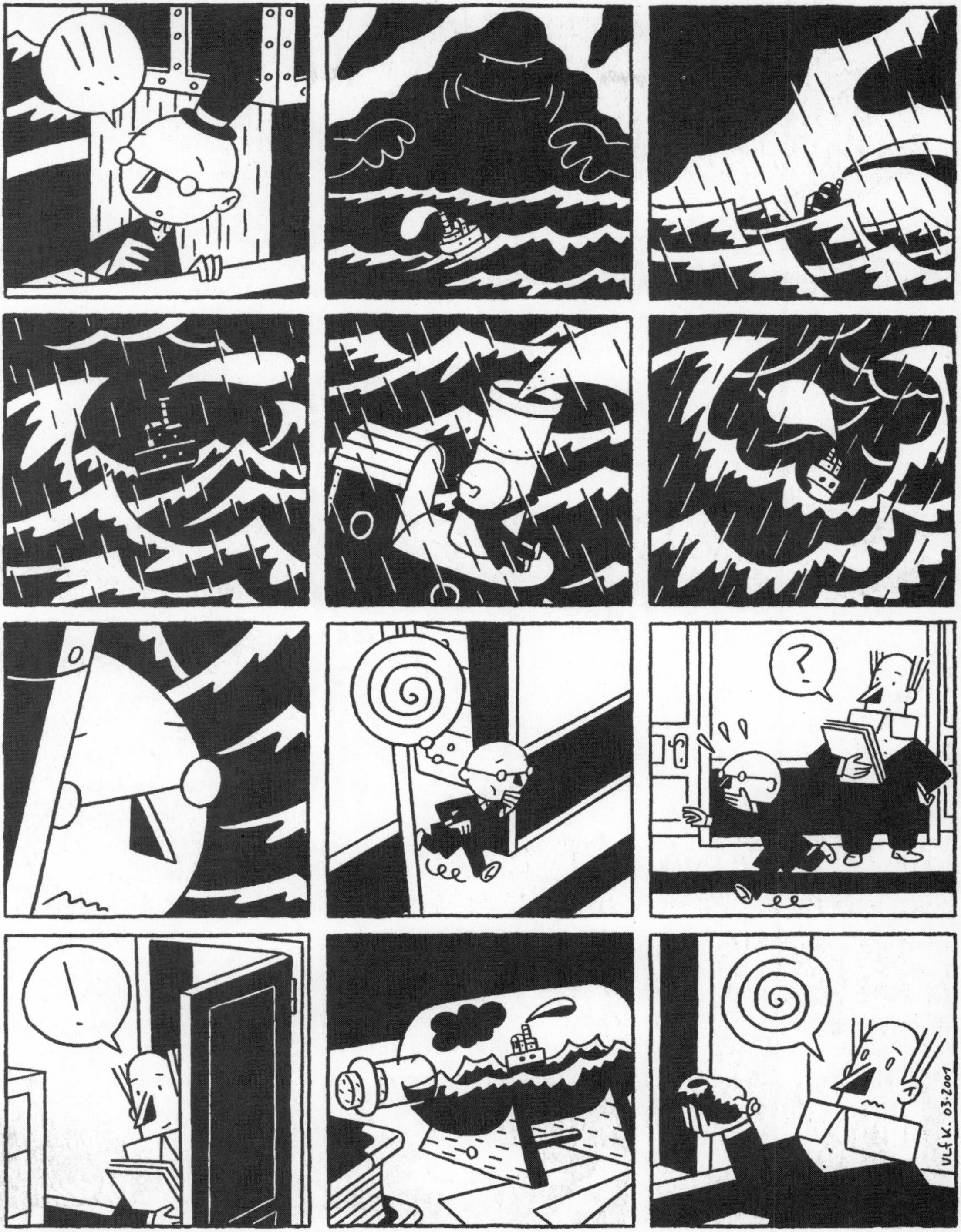
?
!
Ulf K. 03·2001

the sketchbook drawings of martin tom dieck

intro by bart beaty

Hamburg is a port town, and so it is no surprise that Hamburg's most innovative cartoonist spends so much time drawing water. From *Der unschuldige Passagier* to *Salut, Deleuze*, Martin tom Dieck's comics have featured men lost (sometimes metaphorically, sometimes literally) at sea. Dieck's comics show us a world that is both ominously threatening and joyously life-affirming, a world of powerful tidal waves and cleansing spring showers. This is a world of extremes, and Dieck's are tales of men caught between worlds.

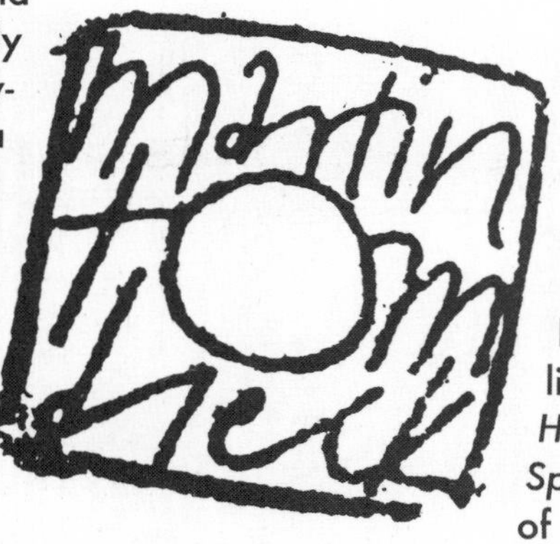
martin
tom
dieck

This is nowhere more true than in his 1997 book, *Hundert Ansichten der Speich- erstadt*. In this wordless epic Dieck's fascinations are given their freest reign. A slight, dreamlike narrative of a man at sea in Hamburg's warehouse district is the skeleton upon which Dieck has hung some of the most vivid and powerful comics pages ever published. The book is a tour de force, with the artist using an array of styles to convey the power of the water and the mystery of life. Here we find stark crosshatching, there we see boldly expressionistic lines. The cumulative effect is overpowering, and the reader is buffeted by the artist just as the character is tossed on the waves.

The pages that follow allow us a rare opportunity to see into the creative process of this amazingly unique artist. Looking to these preliminary sketches from *Hundert Ansichten der Speicherstadt* for traces of Dieck's influences is a pointless exercise. As these im- ages so clearly demonstrate, Dieck's worldview is completely and utterly his own. He is not an artist engaged with the history of the medium, but a cartoonist whose view has always been out from the harbor over the sea, towards the horizon, towards a new way of thinking about art and life.

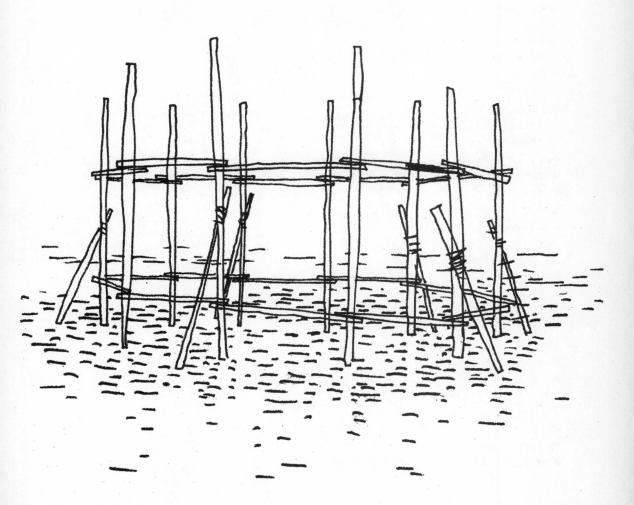

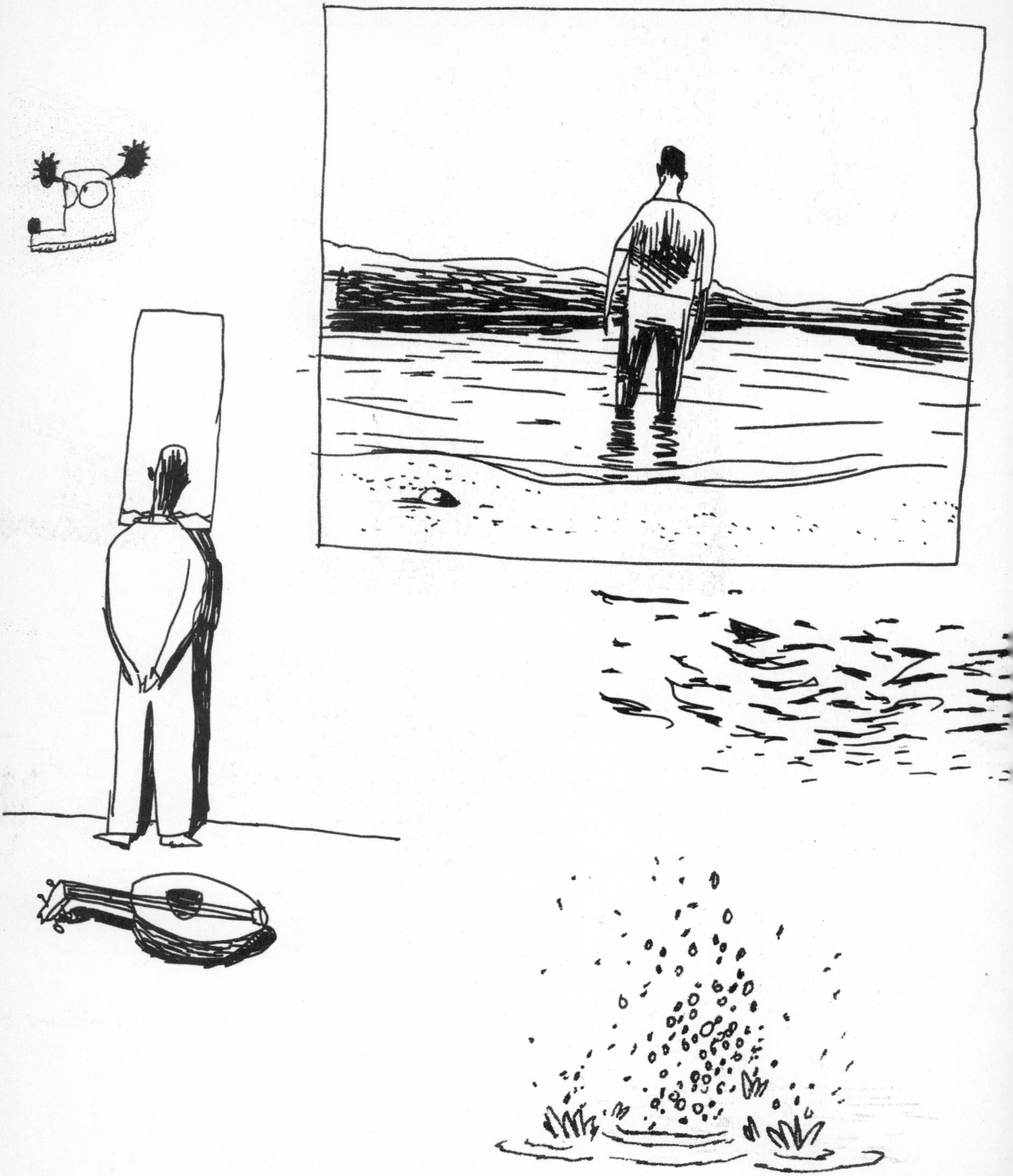

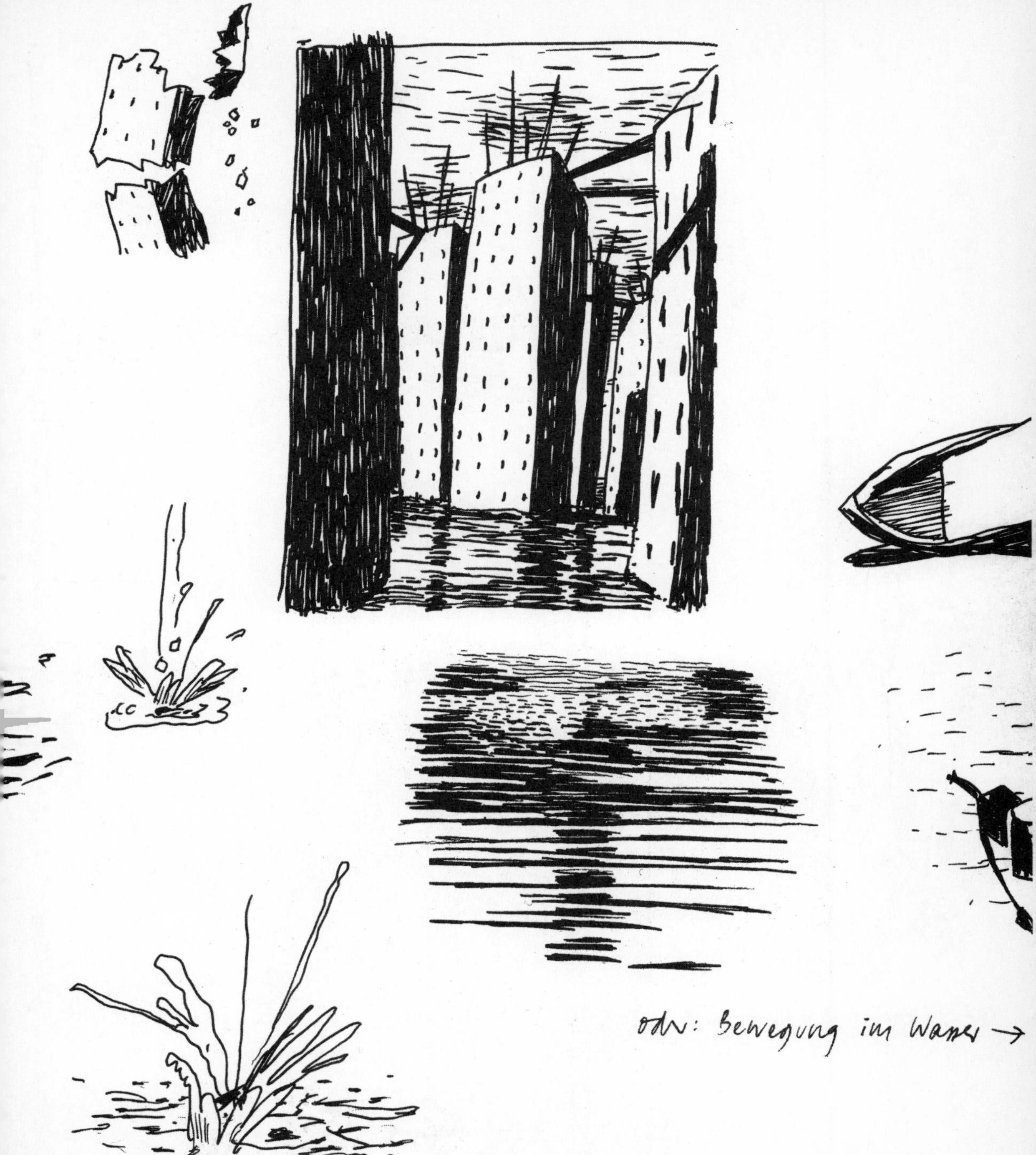
odr: Bewegung im Wasser →

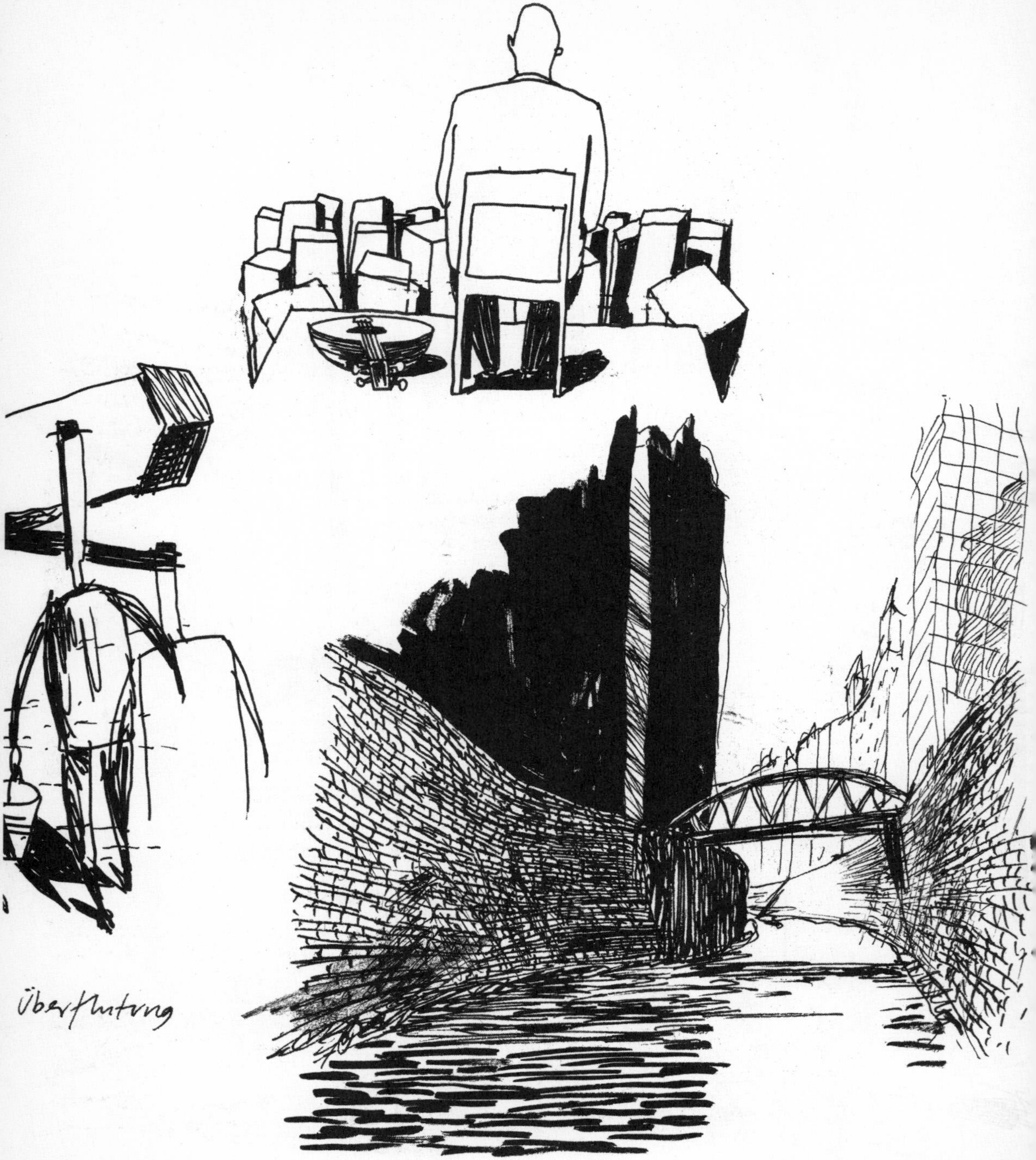
Überflutung

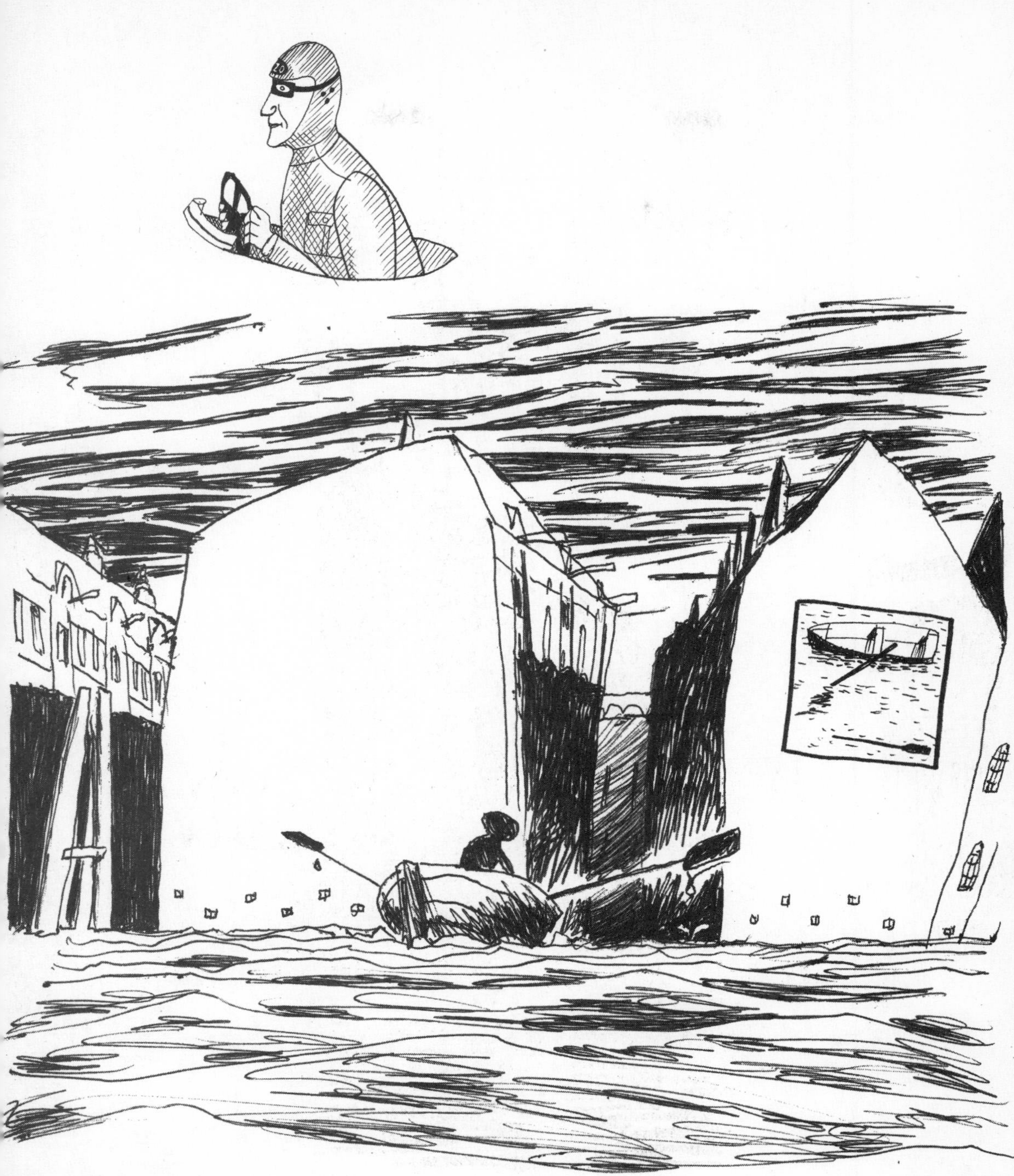
20

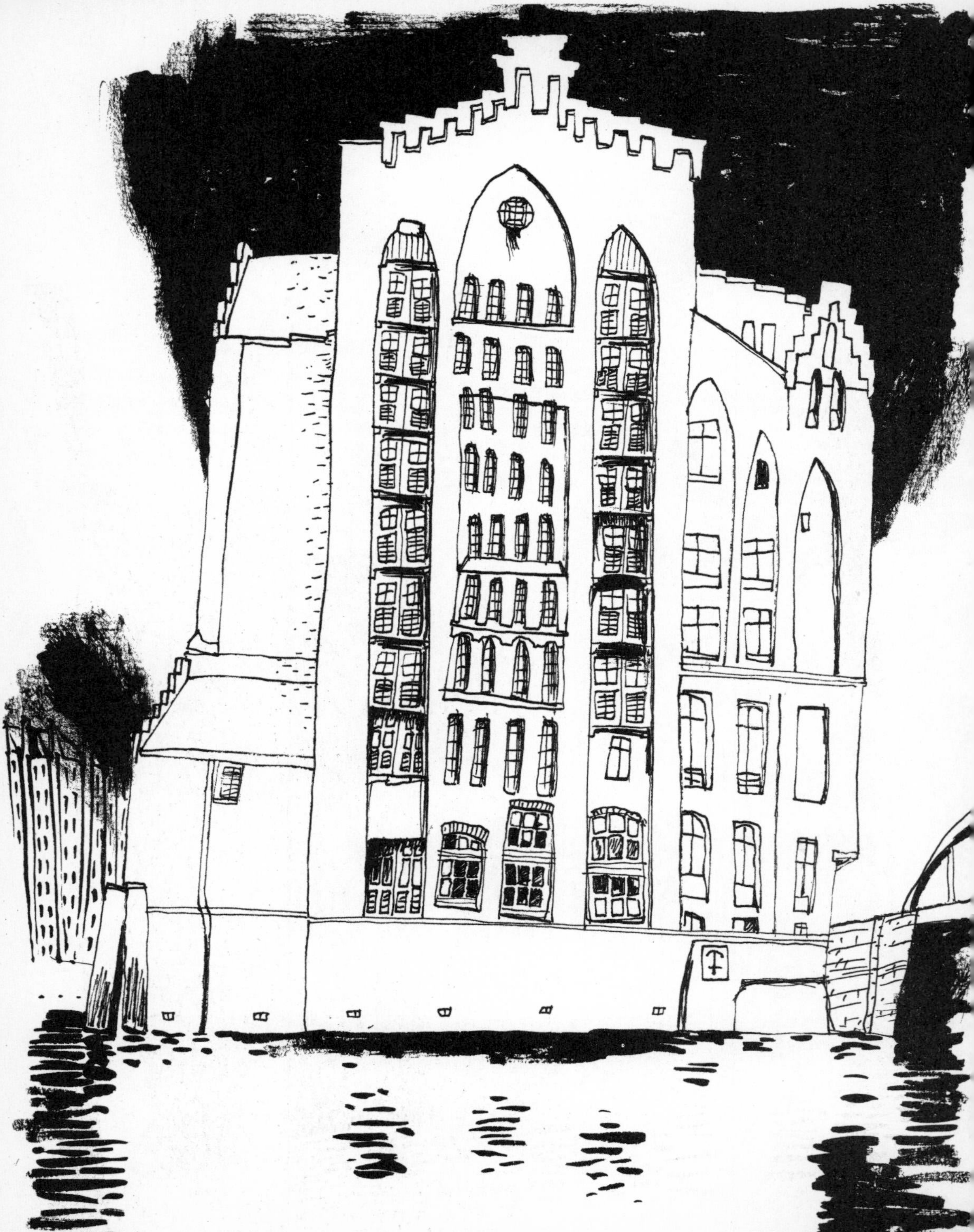

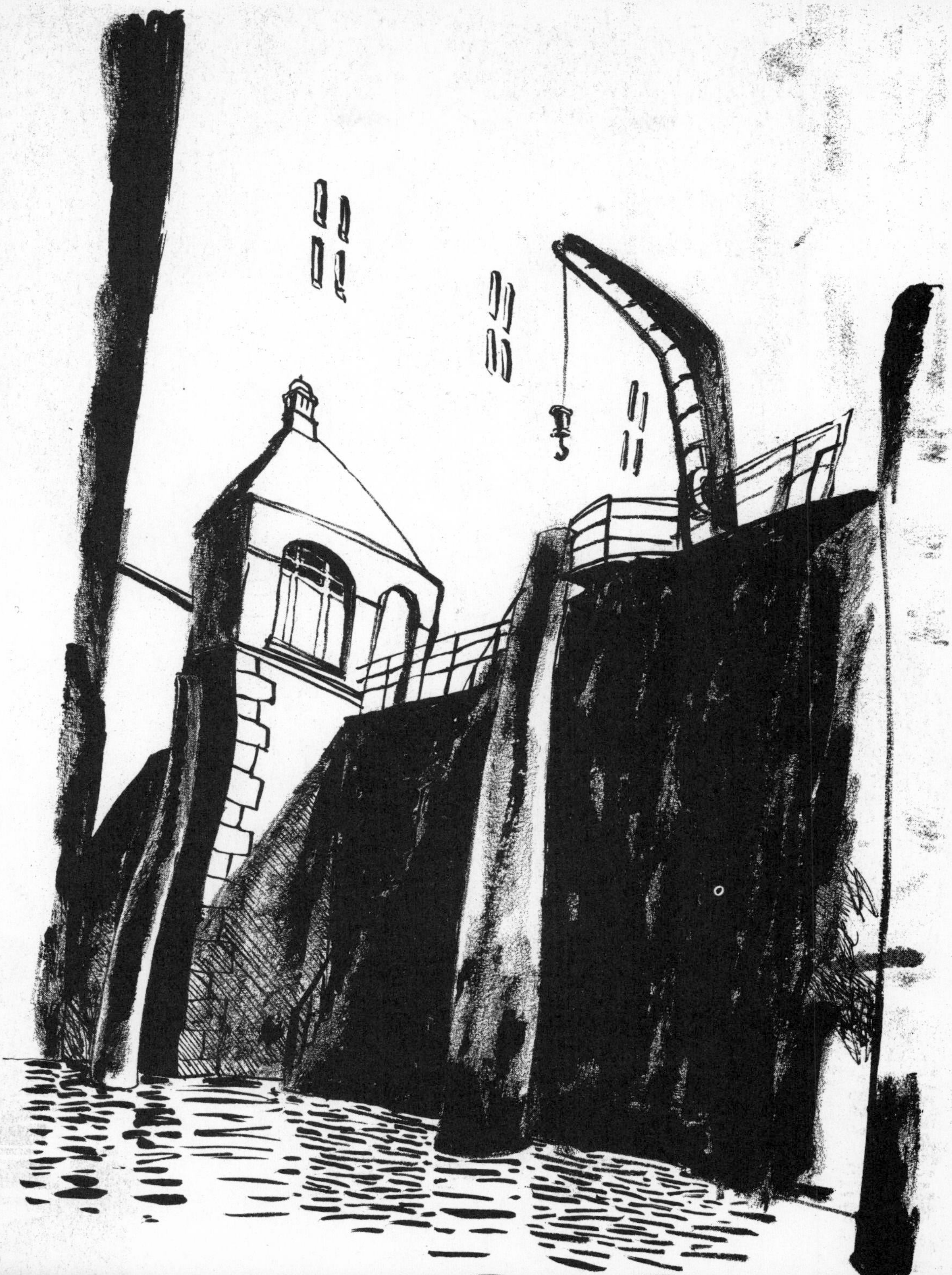

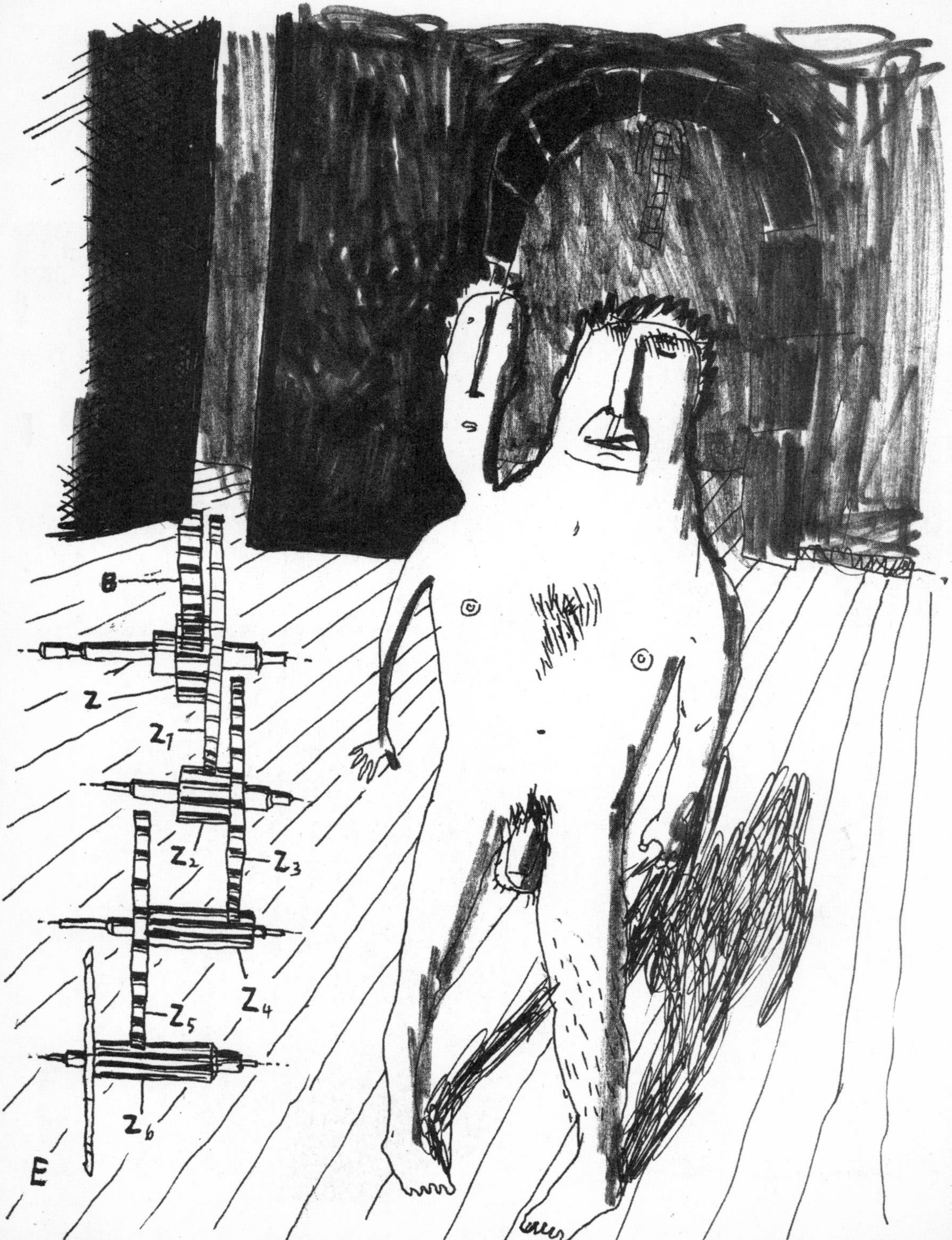
B
Z
Z1
Z2
Z3
Z4
Z5
Z6
E

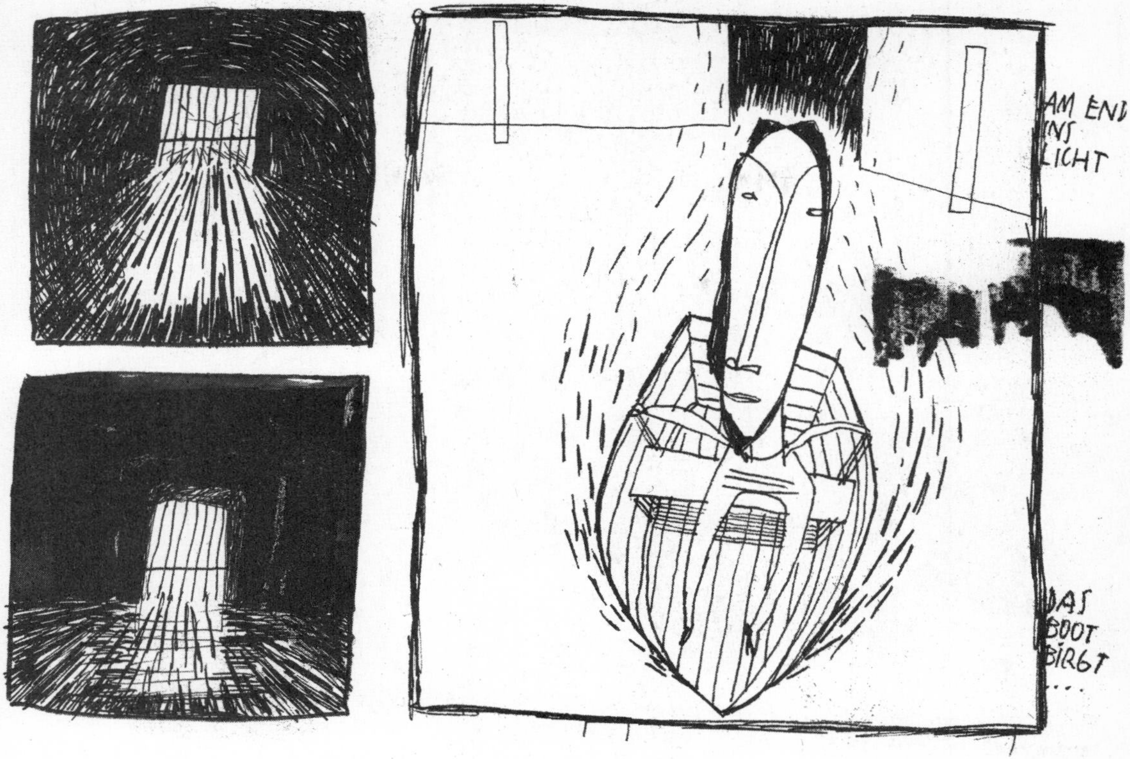
AM END
INS
LICHT
DAS
BOOT
BIRGT
...

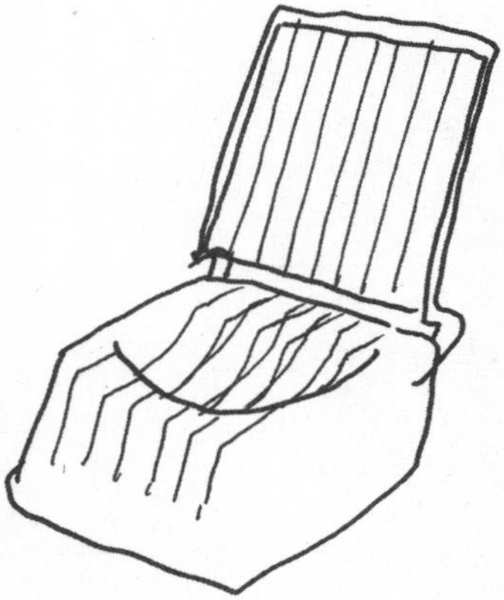

Abb. 2.

Ein dummes Gefühl

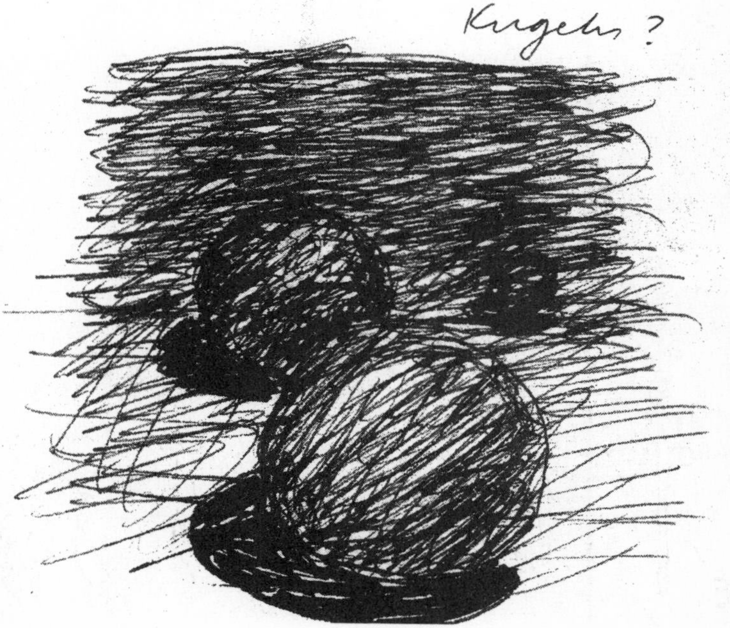
Kugeln?

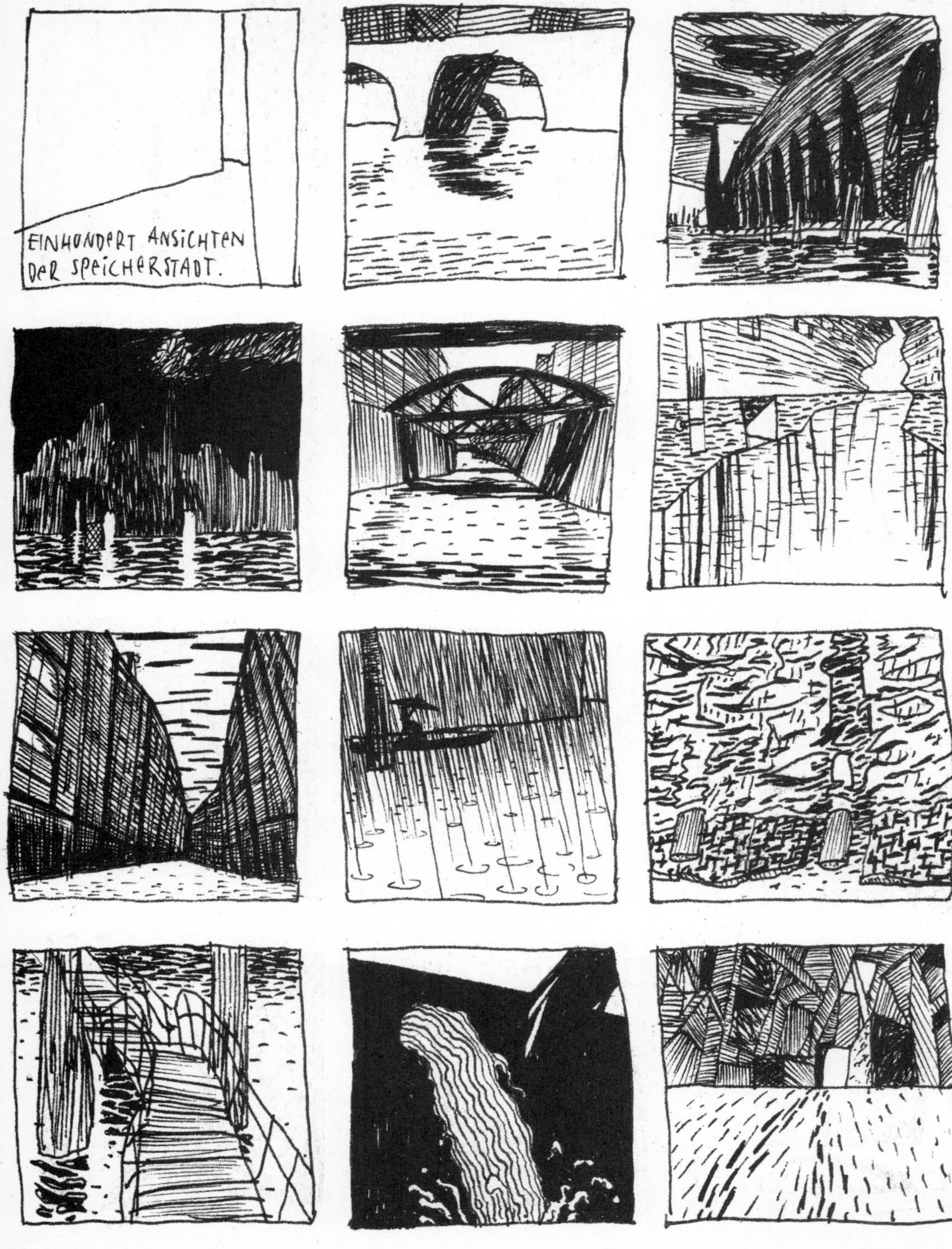
EINHUNDERT ANSICHTEN
DER SPEICHERSTADT.

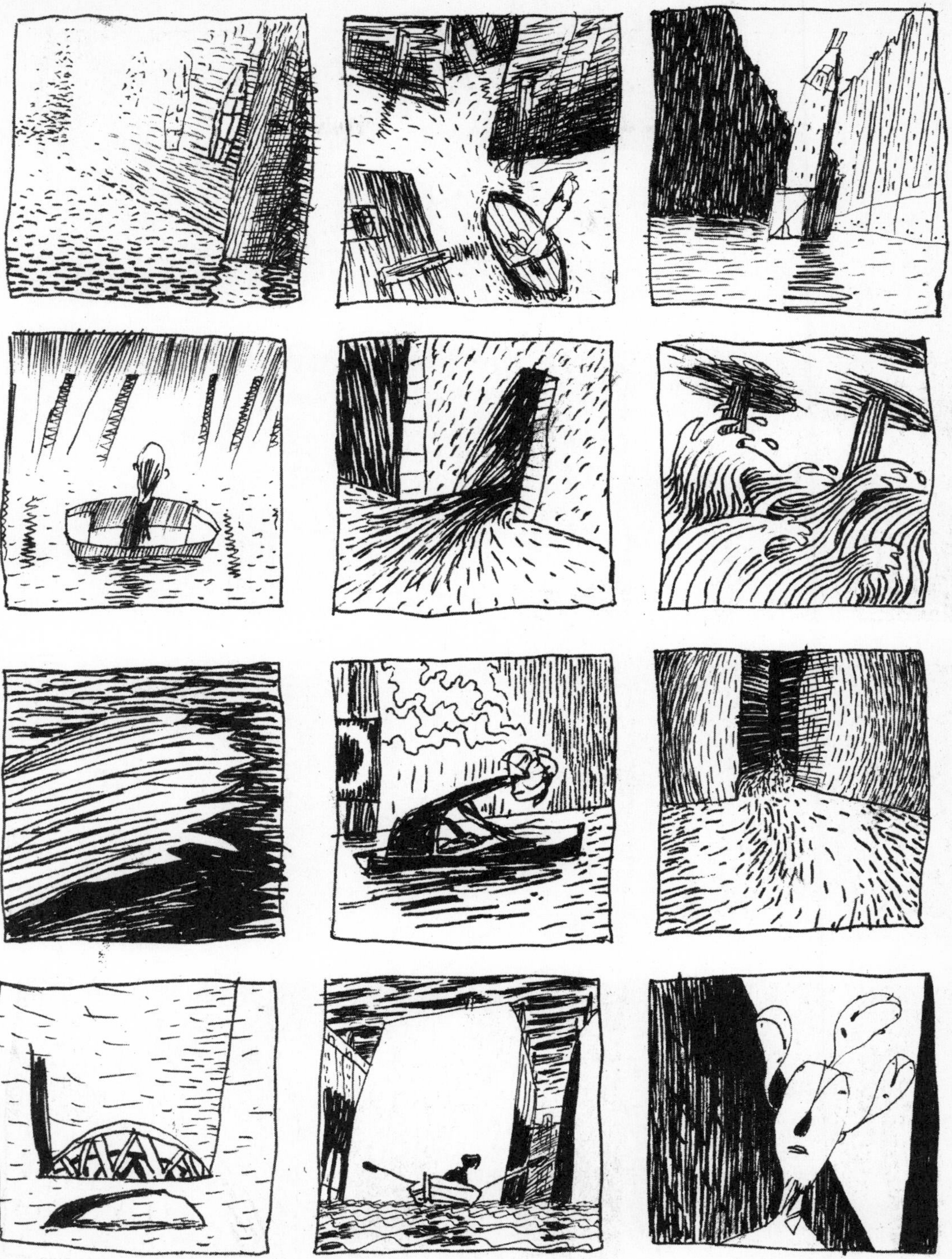

2. Teil

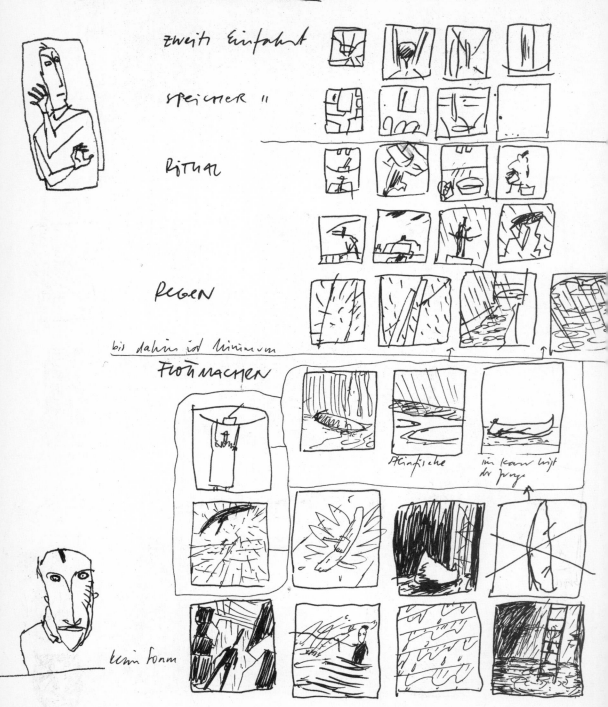

zweite Einfahrt

speicher II

Ritual

Regen

bis dahin ist Minimum

Flott machen

kein form

156

es wird spät hin
zu regnen anfangen

dreht er sich
um?

118

opter

FLY

Bewegung

124

Wasserblume

130

brüchiger bestell
er fällt nicht
ins Wasser, ihn
holen die Vögel

Steigender Pegel

Bewegung

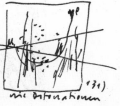

(130)

(131)

wie Detonationen

157

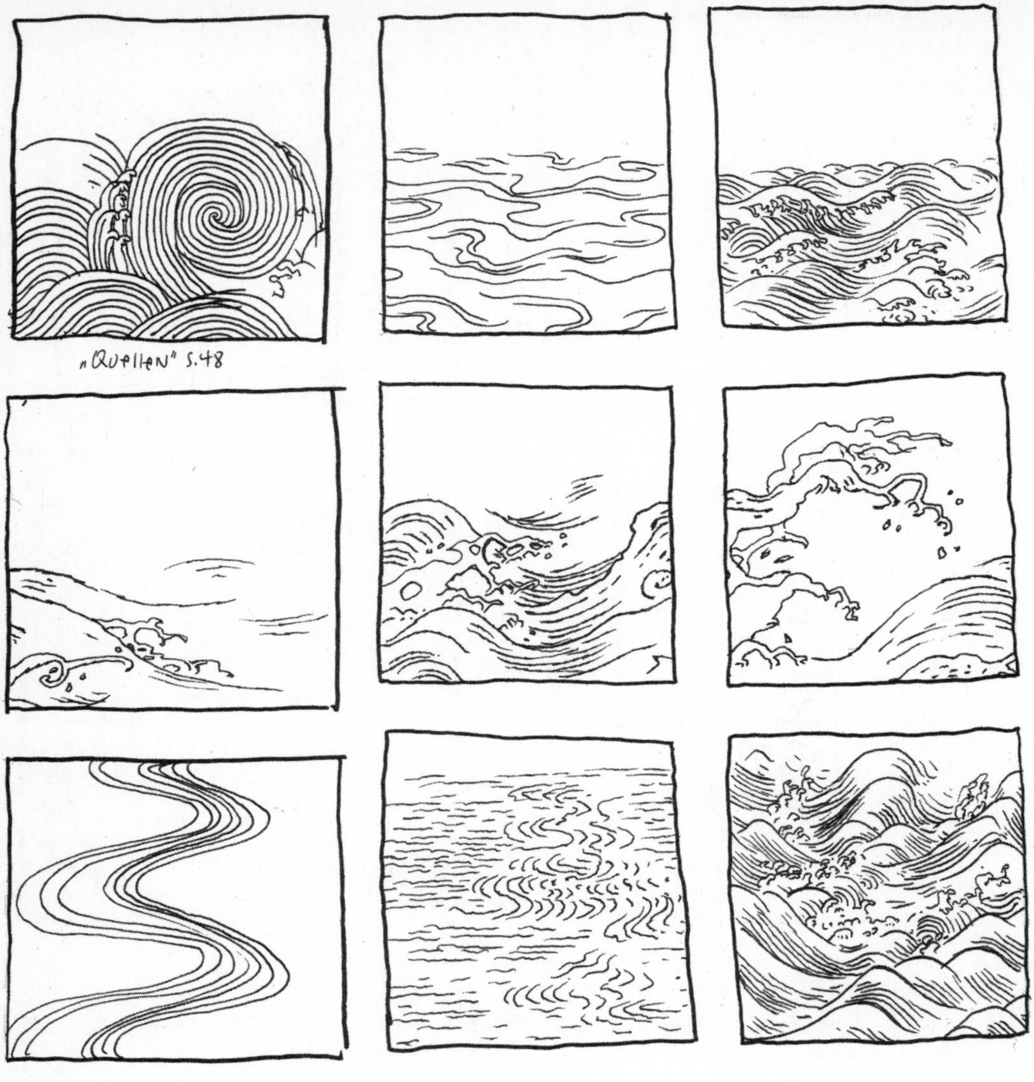
„Quellen" S.48

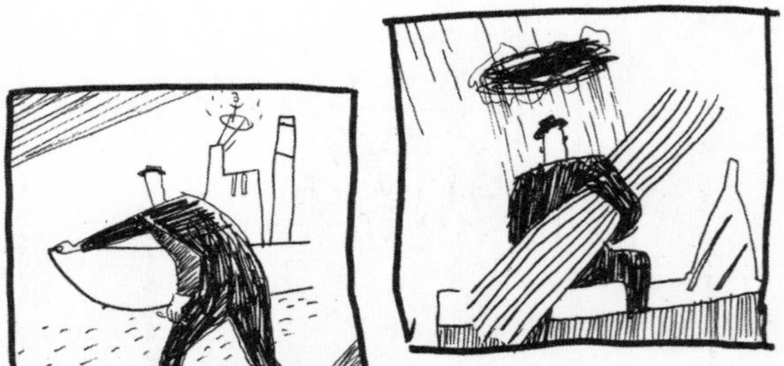

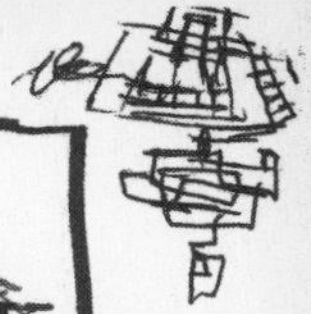

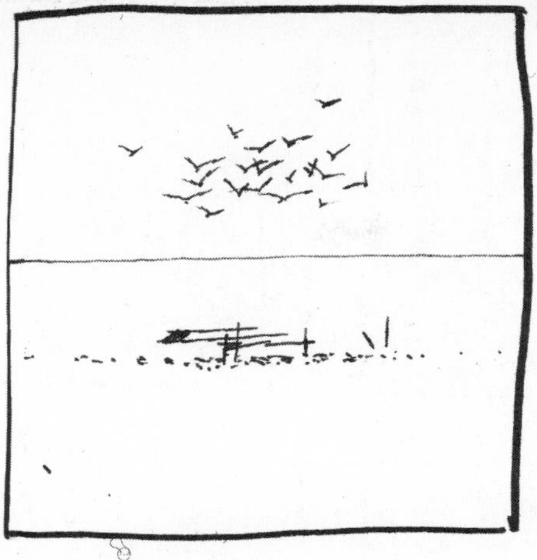

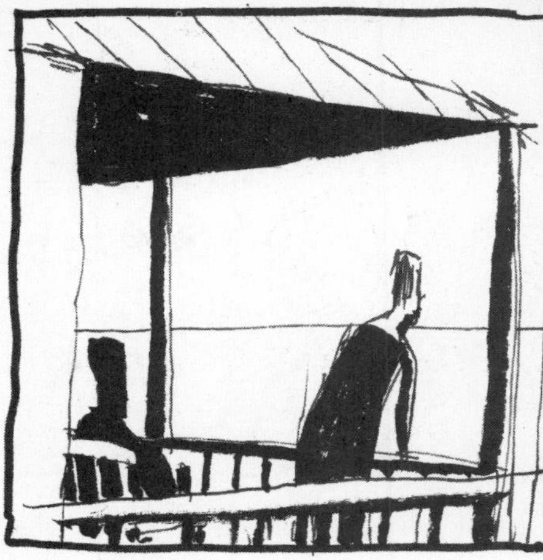

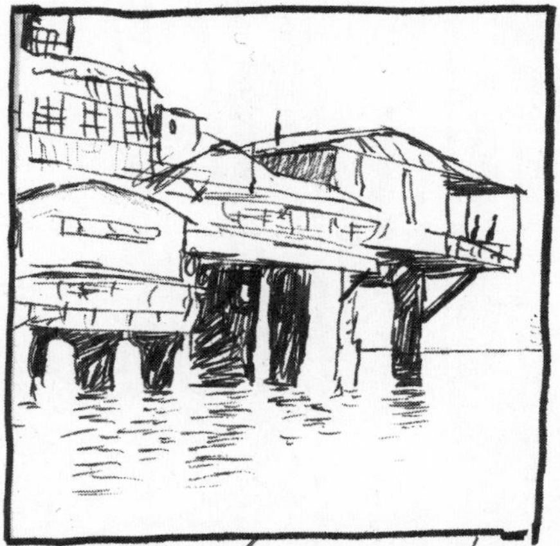

japanisch- algerisch

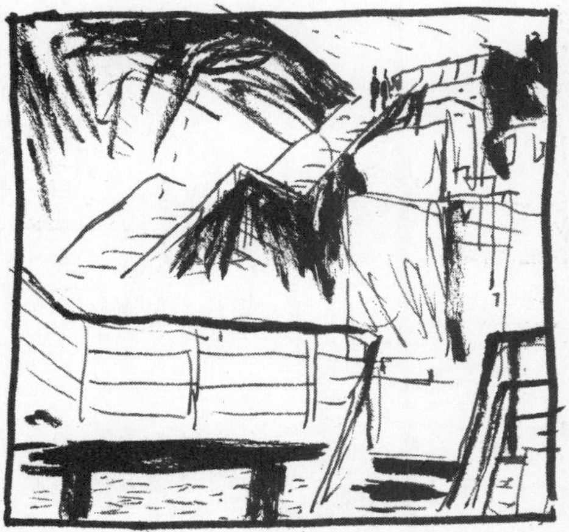

Abend

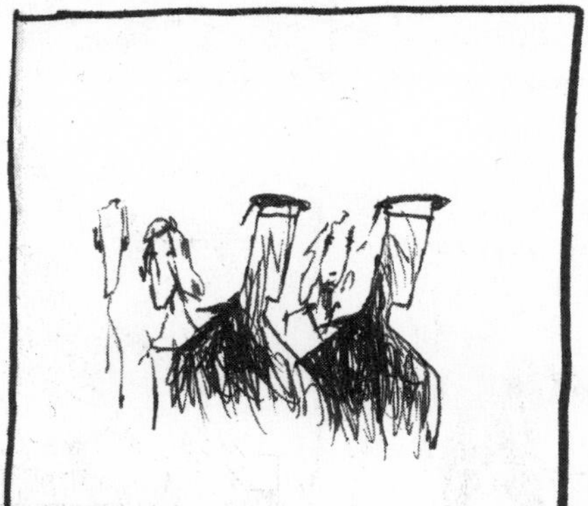

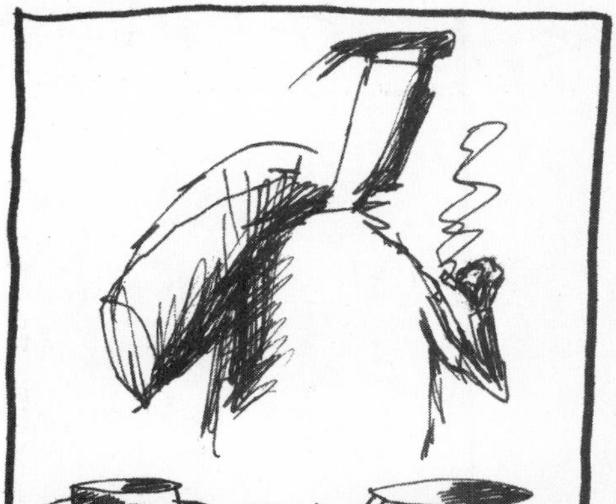

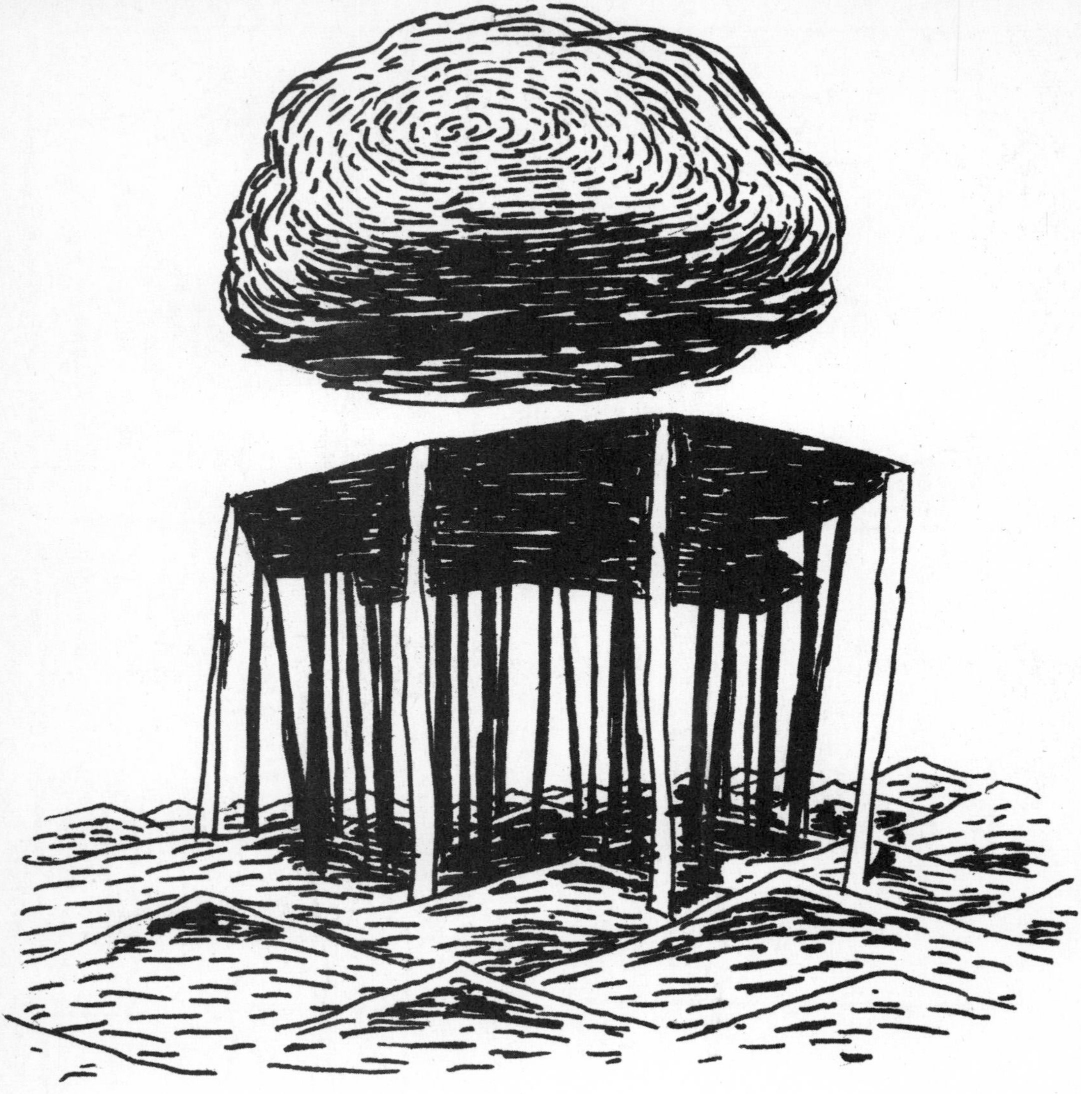

Schläft ein Lied in allen Dingen,
Die da träumen fort und fort;
Und die Welt hebt an zu singen,
Triffst Du nur das Zauberwort.

Eichendorff
1788 - 1875

THE WAR BACK HOME

THE DISHES HAVE BEGUN LYING TO ME AGAIN. FROM 40 FEET AWAY I CAN CLEARLY MAKE OUT THE SINK GRUMBLING ITS DISPLEASURE. EACH FIBER OF THE CARPET HAS SOME GENERAL GRIPE, AND THE CHAIR I'M SITTING IN WISHES IT WAS FAR AWAY FROM THIS PLACE. IN ANOTHER COUNTRY, MAYBE. THE BILLS ARE BUSY STACKING THEMSELVES IN PILES, AND THE PHONE?

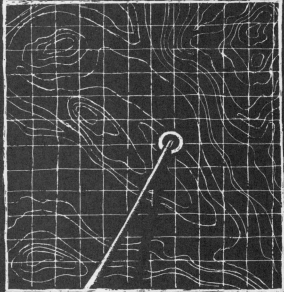

...DON'T TELL THE BED, BUT IT SAYS HERE YOU'LL BE SLEEPING ALONE FOR QUITE A BIT LONGER...

...WE WON'T EVEN DISCUSS THE PHONE RIGHT NOW. SOME SHIRTS IN THE CLOSET HAVE HAD MORE THAN ENOUGH, THEY WANT A REST--EITHER SEND TO THEM TO THE SALVATION ARMY OR TURN THEM INTO DISHRAGS--ANYTHING TO END THIER HORRIBLE PURGATORY, TO JUST GET IT OVER WITH. ME AND MY STEREO ARE ON PRETTY GOOD TERMS PRESENTLY, BUT I'VE GOT SOME KIND OF COLD WAR GOING ON WITH MY RECORDS, CD'S, TAPES, ETC. THEY ARE QUICKLY GETTING WISE.

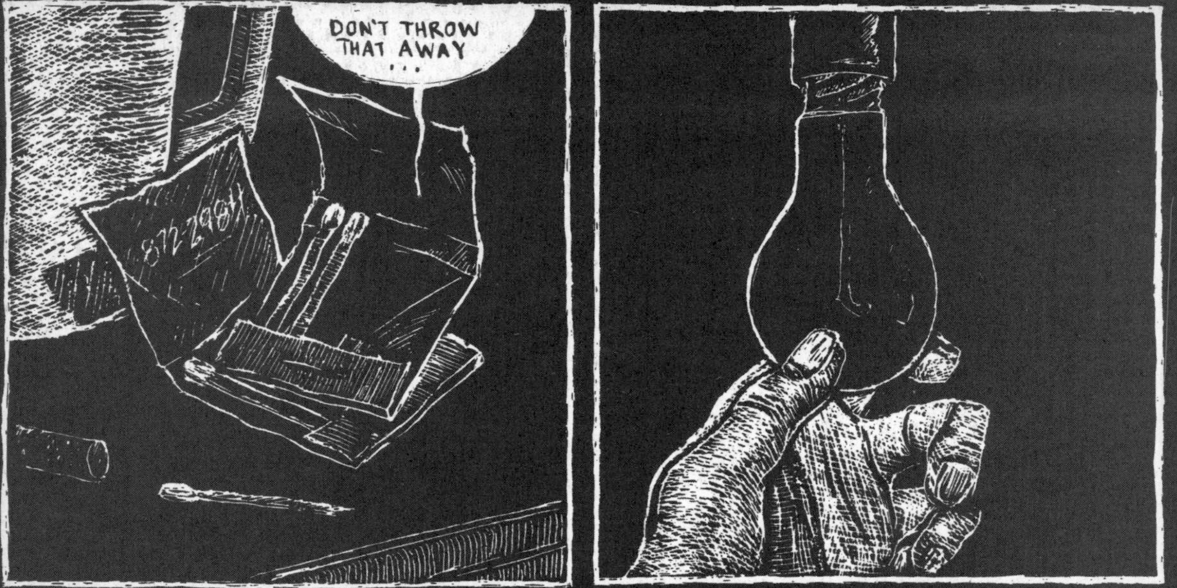
DON'T THROW THAT AWAY ...

THE T.V. KNOWS; IT'S BEEN THROUGH IT AND LOST. IT JUST SITS THERE. IT KNOWS IT'S BEEN BEAT, FOR NOW. I WISH I COULD MUSTER SOME SYMPATHY FOR IT, BUT WAR HAS IT'S CASUALTIES, YOU KNOW. I KNOW TOO. THERE'S A FULL, UNTOUCHED 12-PACK IN THE FRIDGE. IT IS, OF COURSE, SMARTER THAN ME. IT DOESN'T EVEN WHISPER. IT'S BEEN BUNKERED UP INSIDE

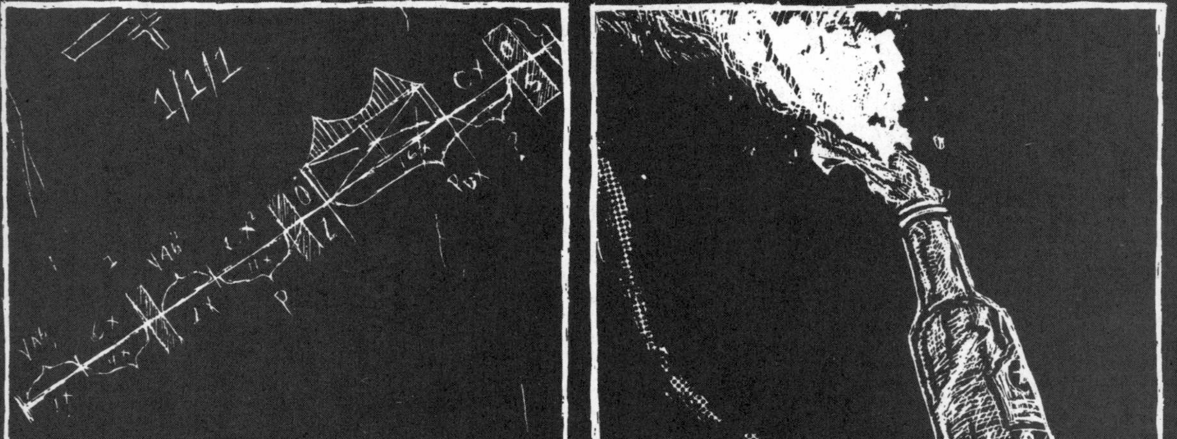

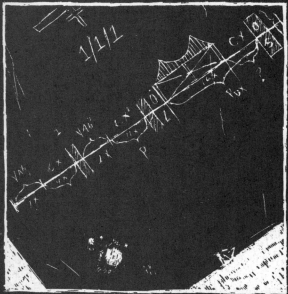

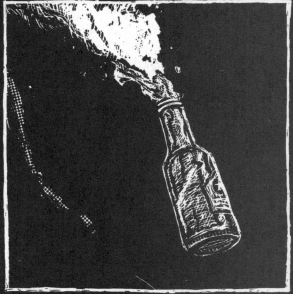

THERE FOR 2 WHOLE DAYS NOW AND I CAN FEEL ITS CLEVER LITTLE SMILE ON MY BACK AT THIS VERY MOMENT. IT KNOWS IT'S JUST A MATTER OF TIME, THE SLY FUCKER. AND SPEAKING OF SLY-- THE PENCILS, THE PENS, THE BRUSHES, THE GUITARS, THE HAMMERS, NAILS, WRENCHES AND STRINGS. THEY FILL ME WITH TERROR, ALL OF THEM. THE BLANK SHEETS OF PAPER HAVE BEEN HOLDING SECRET CONFERENCES -- I KNOW IT, THEY CAN'T FOOL ME...

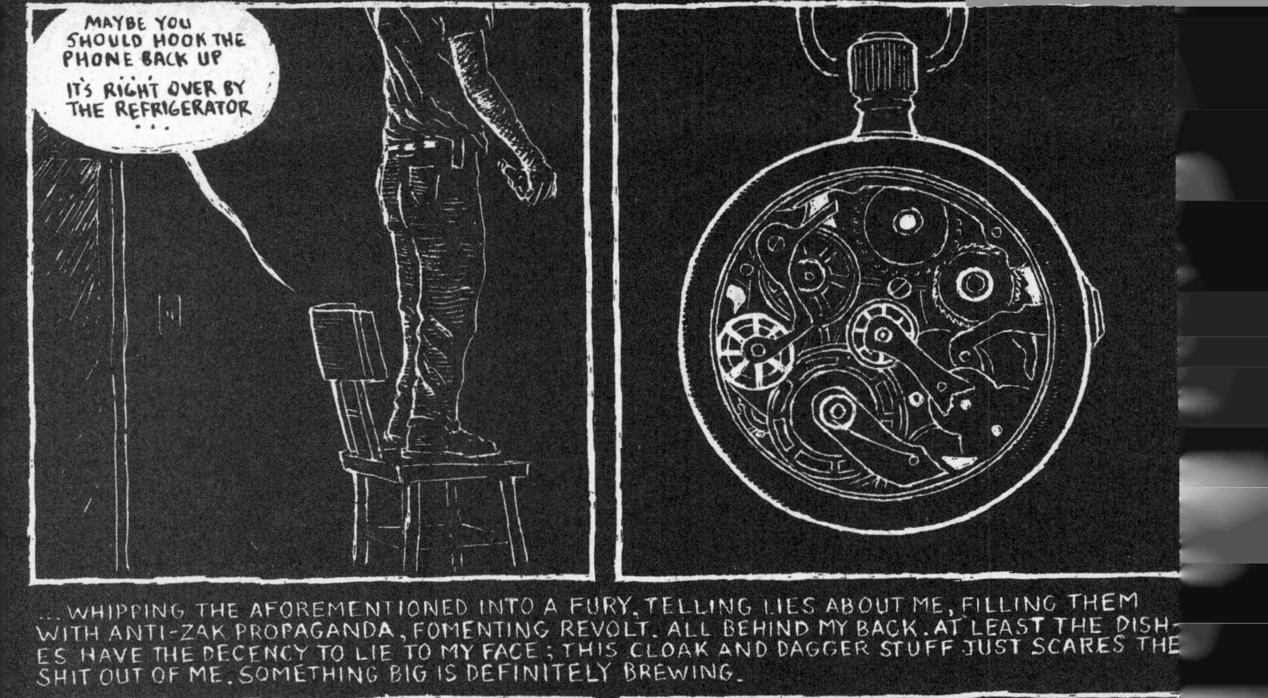
MAYBE YOU SHOULD HOOK THE PHONE BACK UP
IT'S RIGHT OVER BY THE REFRIGERATOR . . .

...WHIPPING THE AFOREMENTIONED INTO A FURY, TELLING LIES ABOUT ME, FILLING THEM WITH ANTI-ZAK PROPAGANDA, FOMENTING REVOLT. ALL BEHIND MY BACK. AT LEAST THE DISHES HAVE THE DECENCY TO LIE TO MY FACE; THIS CLOAK AND DAGGER STUFF JUST SCARES THE SHIT OUT OF ME. SOMETHING BIG IS DEFINITELY BREWING.

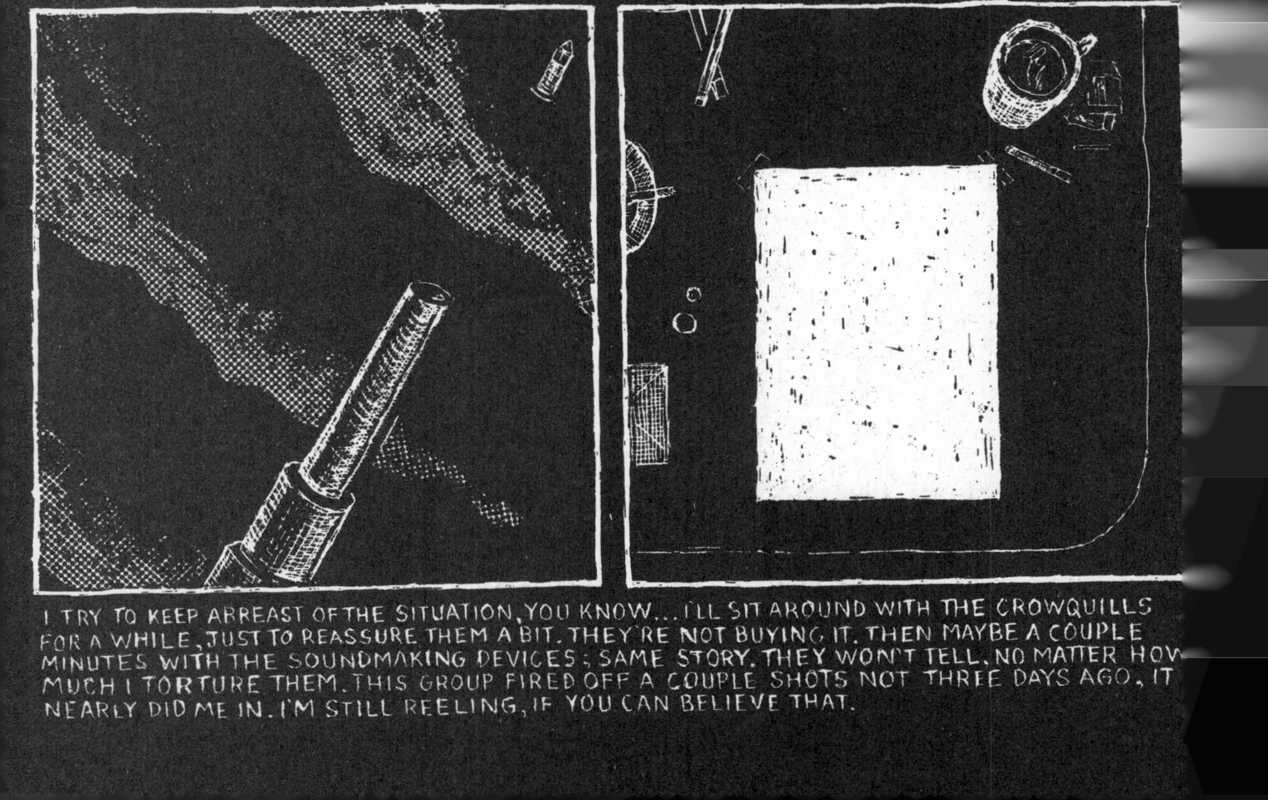

I TRY TO KEEP ABREAST OF THE SITUATION, YOU KNOW... I'LL SIT AROUND WITH THE CROWQUILLS FOR A WHILE, JUST TO REASSURE THEM A BIT. THEY'RE NOT BUYING IT. THEN MAYBE A COUPLE MINUTES WITH THE SOUNDMAKING DEVICES; SAME STORY. THEY WON'T TELL, NO MATTER HOW MUCH I TORTURE THEM. THIS GROUP FIRED OFF A COUPLE SHOTS NOT THREE DAYS AGO, IT NEARLY DID ME IN. I'M STILL REELING, IF YOU CAN BELIEVE THAT.

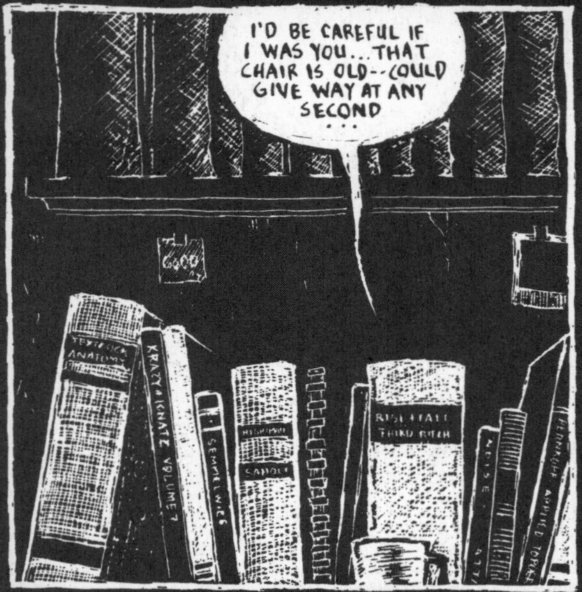
I'D BE CAREFUL IF I WAS YOU... THAT CHAIR IS OLD--COULD GIVE WAY AT ANY SECOND ...

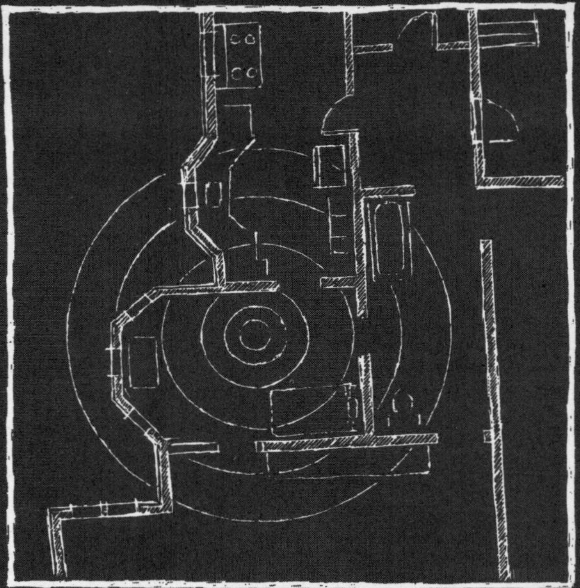

NO ONE HAS FORMALLY ISSUED A STATEMENT ABOUT THIS ACT AS YET, BUT WE ALL KNOW. I CAN'T HONESTLY SAY I DIDN'T SEE ALL OF THIS COMING, BUT I NEVER SUSPECTED THEY'D BAND TOGETHER AND TURN ON ME SO COMPLETELY. I TRIED TO KEEP TABS ON THE SITUATION, BUT I'M AWAY SO MUCH-- I THINK THAT'S WHEN ALL THE REAL CONSPIRATORIAL GRITWORK WAS DONE...

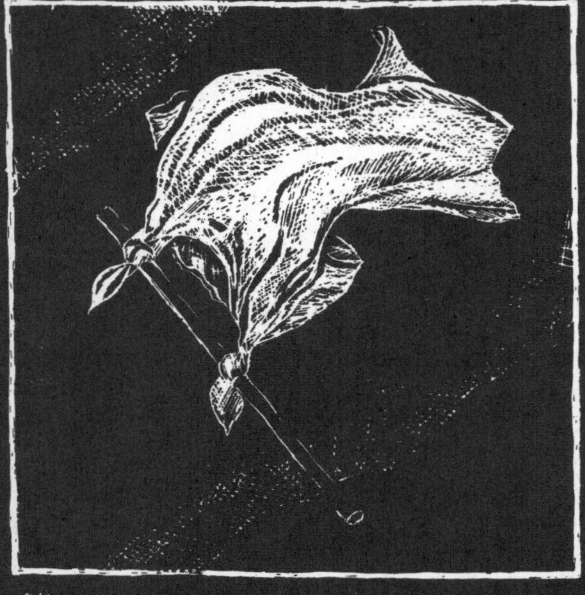

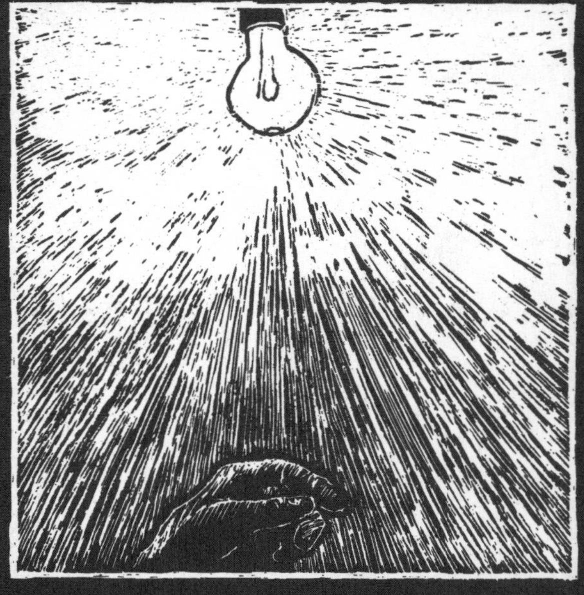

OH WELL. ALL I CAN DO NOW IS PREPARE. I'VE SIGNED A SECRET ACCORD WITH MY BODY AS A PREVENTIVE MEASURE, JUST IN CASE. I'M NOT SURE OF MY BODY'S TRUE COMMITMENT TO THE TERMS OF OUR DEAL, THOUGH; IN FACT, I THINK IT MIGHT'VE SIGNED A SEPERATE AGREEMENT WITH THE WHITE PAPER FORCES WHILE I WAS SLEEPING. STILL, I THINK IF THE SHIT REALLY STARTS FLYING, THE FLESH WILL SIDE WITH ME.

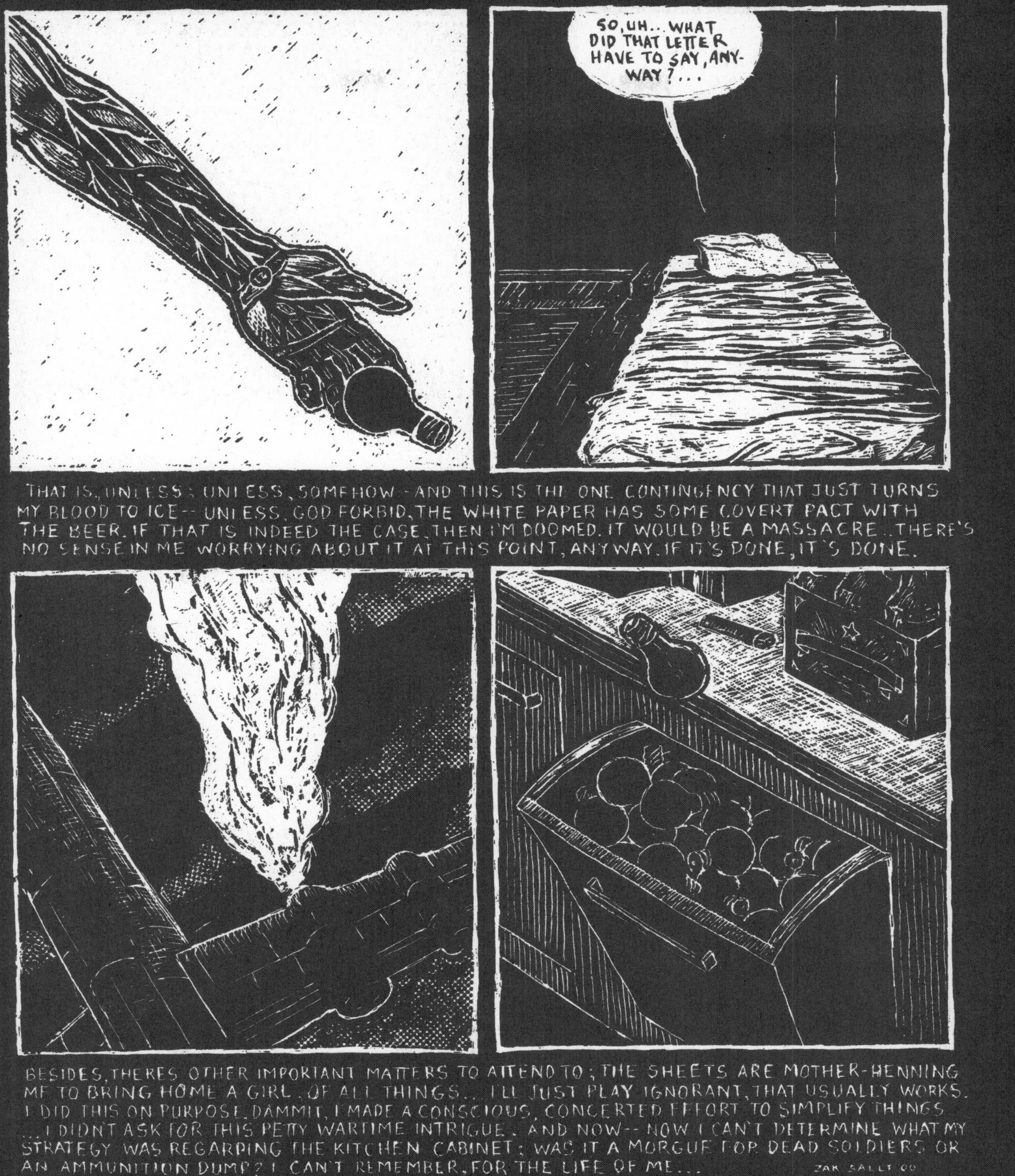
SO, UH... WHAT DID THAT LETTER HAVE TO SAY, ANY-WAY?...
THAT IS, UNLESS: UNLESS, SOMEHOW -- AND THIS IS THE ONE CONTINGENCY THAT JUST TURNS MY BLOOD TO ICE -- UNLESS, GOD FORBID, THE WHITE PAPER HAS SOME COVERT PACT WITH THE BEER. IF THAT IS INDEED THE CASE, THEN I'M DOOMED. IT WOULD BE A MASSACRE... THERE'S NO SENSE IN ME WORRYING ABOUT IT AT THIS POINT, ANYWAY. IF IT'S DONE, IT'S DONE.
BESIDES, THERES OTHER IMPORTANT MATTERS TO ATTEND TO; THE SHEETS ARE MOTHER-HENNING ME TO BRING HOME A GIRL, OF ALL THINGS... I'LL JUST PLAY IGNORANT, THAT USUALLY WORKS. I DID THIS ON PURPOSE, DAMMIT, I MADE A CONSCIOUS, CONCERTED EFFORT TO SIMPLIFY THINGS ...I DIDNT ASK FOR THIS PETTY WARTIME INTRIGUE. AND NOW -- NOW I CAN'T DETERMINE WHAT MY STRATEGY WAS REGARDING THE KITCHEN CABINET; WAS IT A MORGUE FOR DEAD SOLDIERS OR AN AMMUNITION DUMP? I CAN'T REMEMBER, FOR THE LIFE OF ME...
ZAK SALLY 00

DEMOCRACY

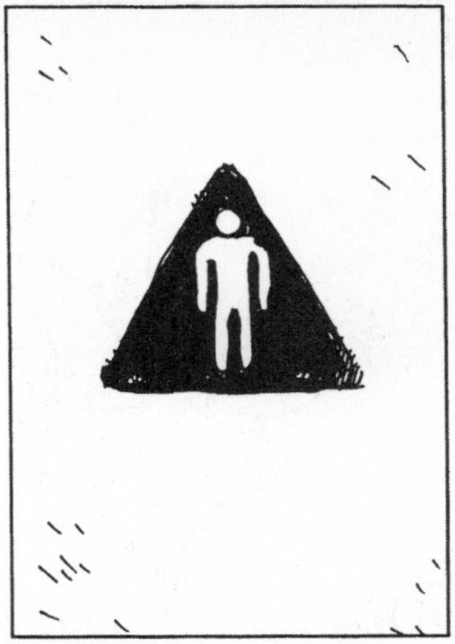

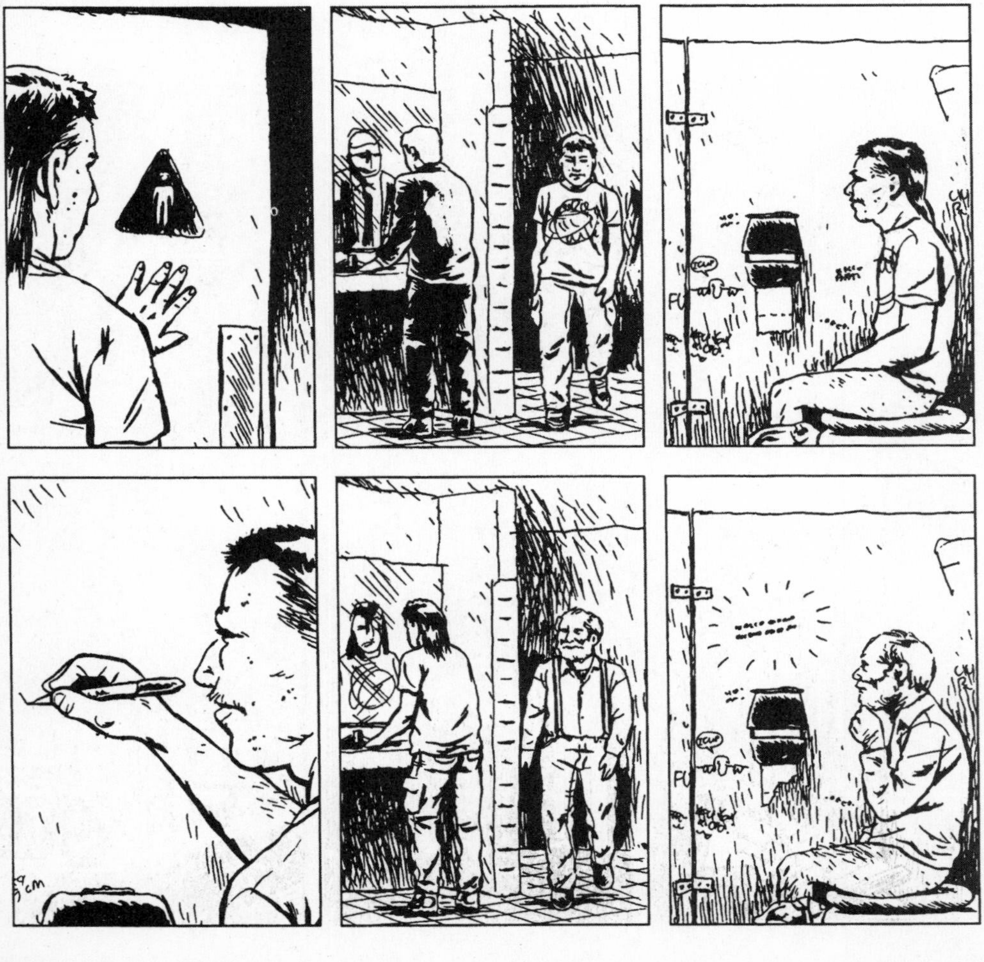

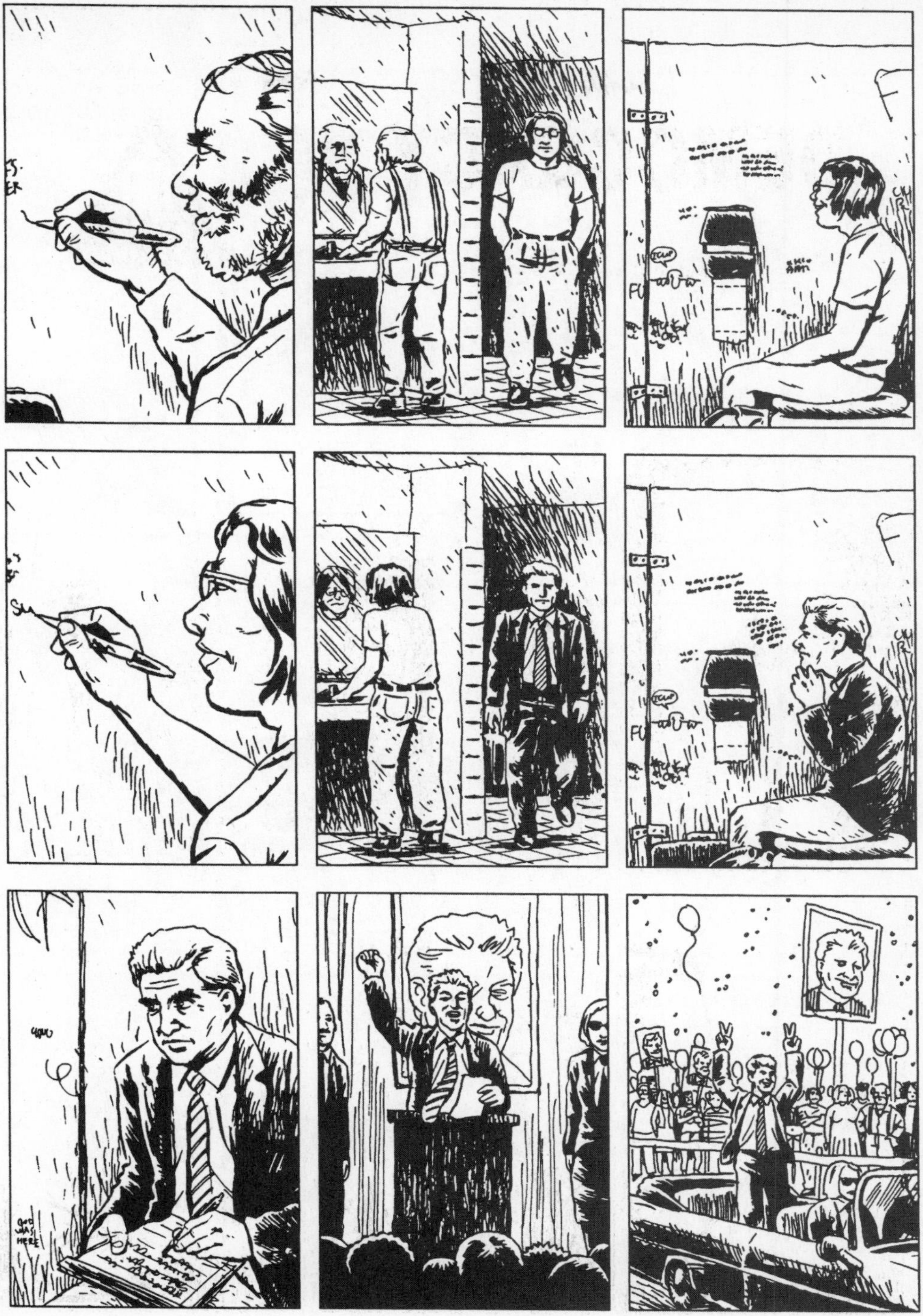
FU
FU
GOD WAS HERE

BISON BILL'S WEIRD WEST

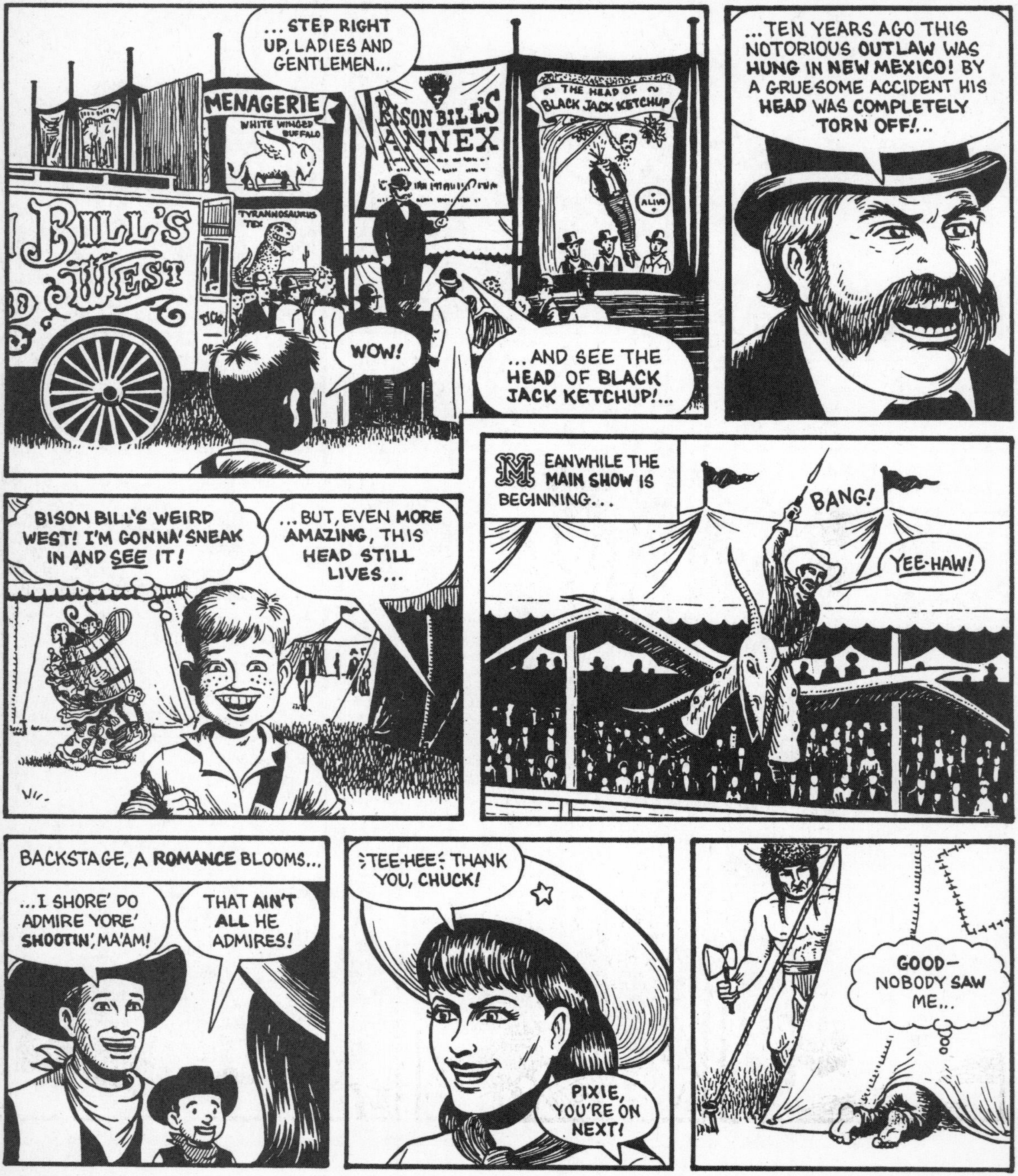

...STEP RIGHT UP, LADIES AND GENTLEMEN...
MENAGERIE
WHITE WINGED BUFFALO
TYRANNOSAURUS TEX
BISON BILL'S ANNEX
THE HEAD OF BLACK JACK KETCHUP
ALIVE
BILL'S WEST
WOW!
...AND SEE THE HEAD OF BLACK JACK KETCHUP!...
...TEN YEARS AGO THIS NOTORIOUS OUTLAW WAS HUNG IN NEW MEXICO! BY A GRUESOME ACCIDENT HIS HEAD WAS COMPLETELY TORN OFF!...
BISON BILL'S WEIRD WEST! I'M GONNA' SNEAK IN AND SEE IT!
...BUT, EVEN MORE AMAZING, THIS HEAD STILL LIVES...
MEANWHILE THE MAIN SHOW IS BEGINNING...
BANG!
YEE-HAW!
BACKSTAGE, A ROMANCE BLOOMS...
...I SHORE' DO ADMIRE YORE' SHOOTIN', MA'AM!
THAT AIN'T ALL HE ADMIRES!
TEE-HEE THANK YOU, CHUCK!
PIXIE, YOU'RE ON NEXT!
GOOD— NOBODY SAW ME...

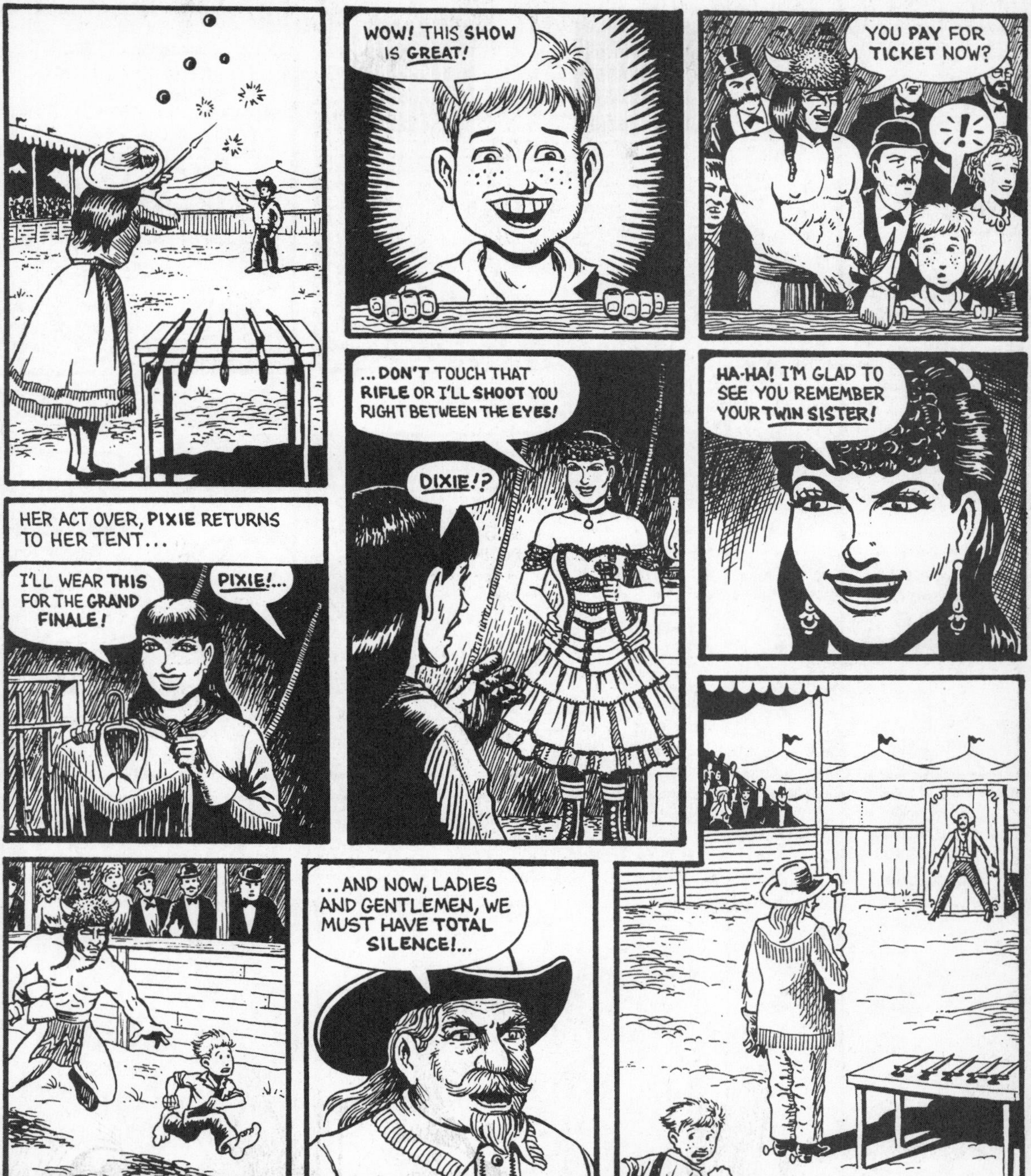
WOW! THIS SHOW IS GREAT!
YOU PAY FOR TICKET NOW?
!
...DON'T TOUCH THAT RIFLE OR I'LL SHOOT YOU RIGHT BETWEEN THE EYES!
HA-HA! I'M GLAD TO SEE YOU REMEMBER YOUR TWIN SISTER!
HER ACT OVER, PIXIE RETURNS TO HER TENT...
I'LL WEAR THIS FOR THE GRAND FINALE!
PIXIE!...
DIXIE!?
...AND NOW, LADIES AND GENTLEMEN, WE MUST HAVE TOTAL SILENCE!...

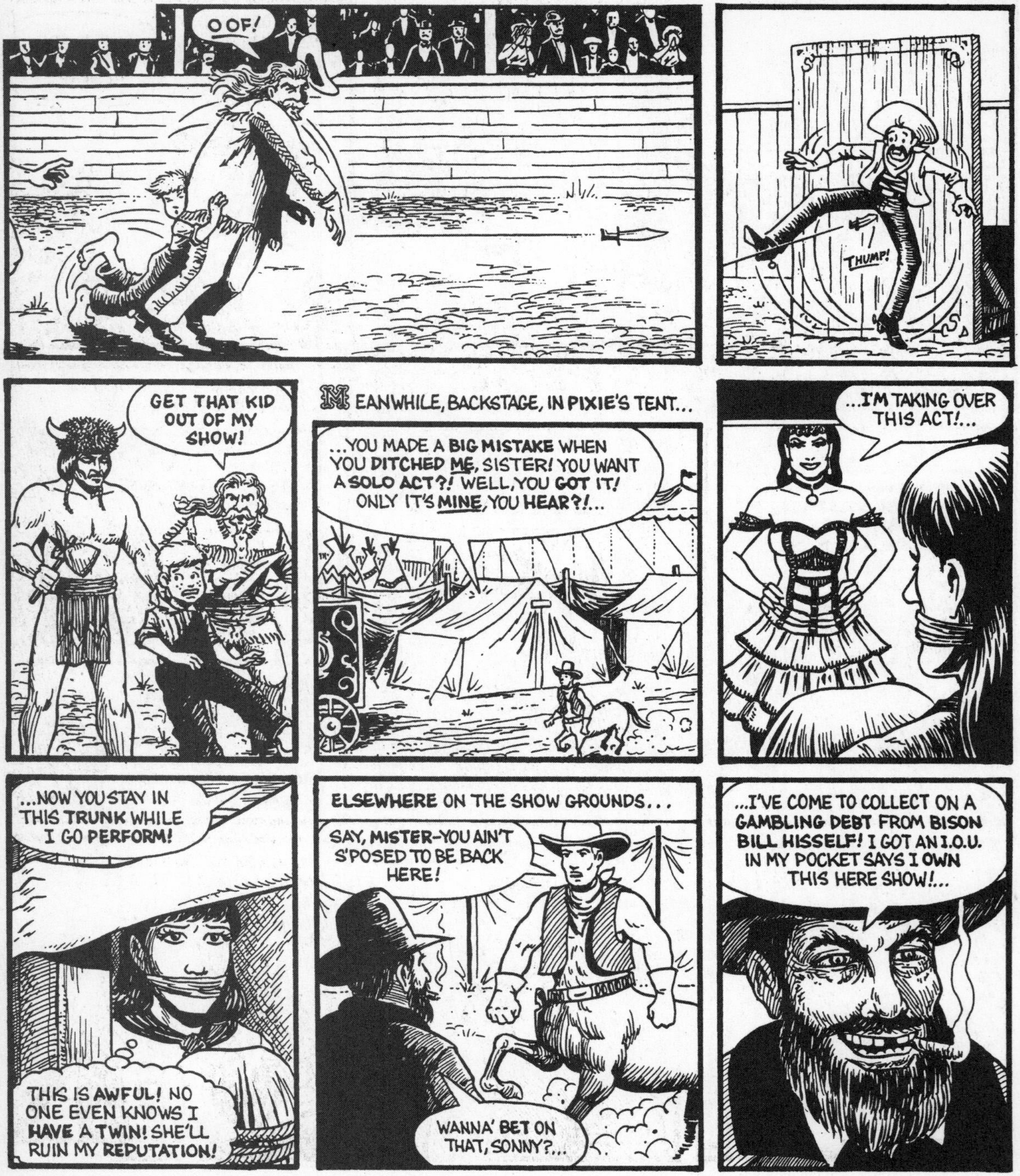
OOF!
THUMP!
GET THAT KID OUT OF MY SHOW!
MEANWHILE, BACKSTAGE, IN PIXIE'S TENT...
...YOU MADE A BIG MISTAKE WHEN YOU DITCHED ME, SISTER! YOU WANT A SOLO ACT?! WELL, YOU GOT IT! ONLY IT'S MINE, YOU HEAR?!...
...I'M TAKING OVER THIS ACT!...
...NOW YOU STAY IN THIS TRUNK WHILE I GO PERFORM!
THIS IS AWFUL! NO ONE EVEN KNOWS I HAVE A TWIN! SHE'LL RUIN MY REPUTATION!
ELSEWHERE ON THE SHOW GROUNDS...
SAY, MISTER-YOU AIN'T S'POSED TO BE BACK HERE!
WANNA' BET ON THAT, SONNY?...
...I'VE COME TO COLLECT ON A GAMBLING DEBT FROM BISON BILL HISSELF! I GOT AN I.O.U. IN MY POCKET SAYS I OWN THIS HERE SHOW!...

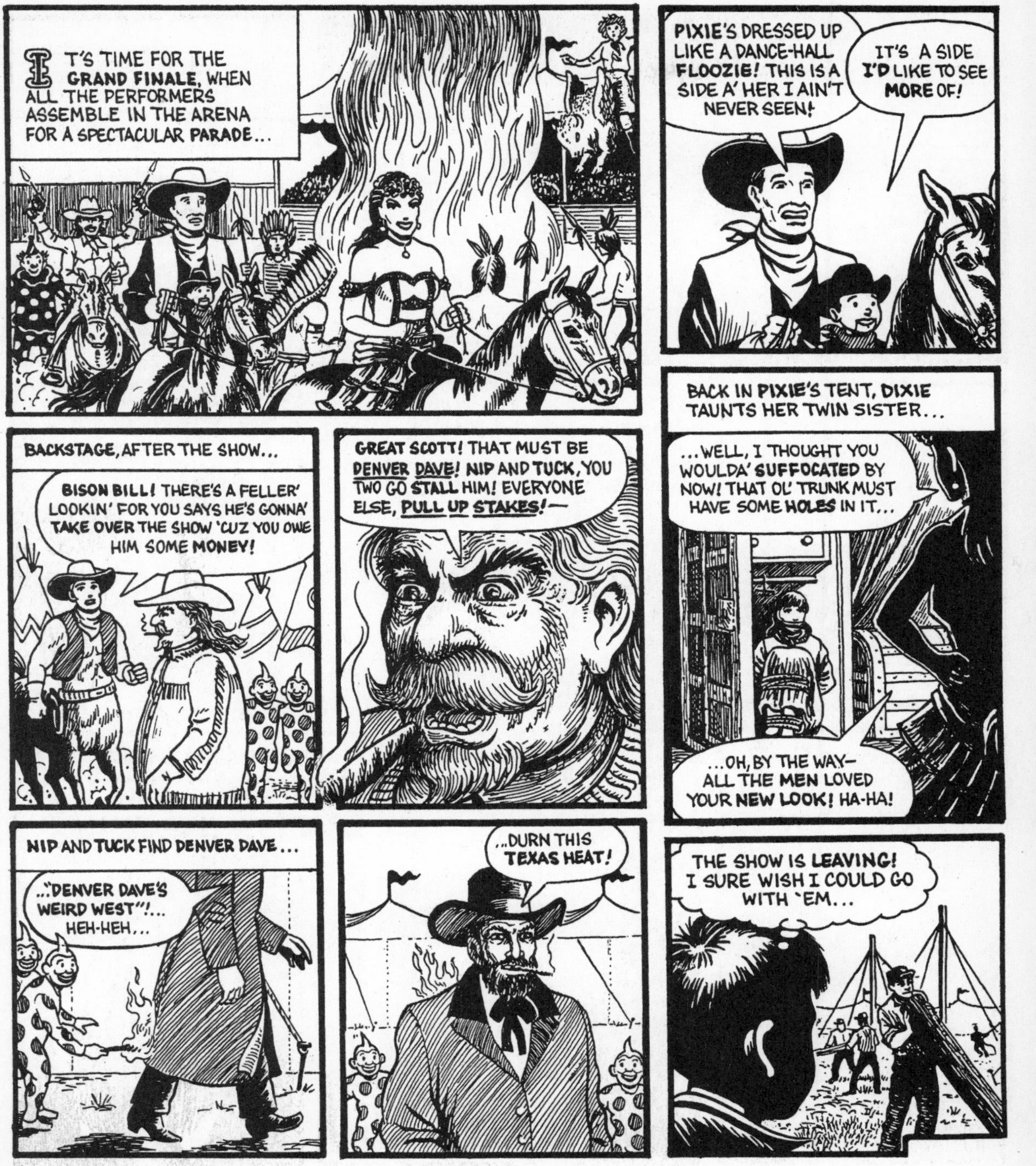
IT'S TIME FOR THE GRAND FINALE, WHEN ALL THE PERFORMERS ASSEMBLE IN THE ARENA FOR A SPECTACULAR PARADE...
PIXIE'S DRESSED UP LIKE A DANCE-HALL FLOOZIE! THIS IS A SIDE A' HER I AIN'T NEVER SEEN!
IT'S A SIDE I'D LIKE TO SEE MORE OF!
BACKSTAGE, AFTER THE SHOW...
BISON BILL! THERE'S A FELLER' LOOKIN' FOR YOU SAYS HE'S GONNA' TAKE OVER THE SHOW 'CUZ YOU OWE HIM SOME MONEY!
GREAT SCOTT! THAT MUST BE DENVER DAVE! NIP AND TUCK, YOU TWO GO STALL HIM! EVERYONE ELSE, PULL UP STAKES!—
BACK IN PIXIE'S TENT, DIXIE TAUNTS HER TWIN SISTER...
...WELL, I THOUGHT YOU WOULDA' SUFFOCATED BY NOW! THAT OL' TRUNK MUST HAVE SOME HOLES IN IT...
...OH, BY THE WAY— ALL THE MEN LOVED YOUR NEW LOOK! HA-HA!
NIP AND TUCK FIND DENVER DAVE...
..."DENVER DAVE'S WEIRD WEST"!... HEH-HEH...
..DURN THIS TEXAS HEAT!
THE SHOW IS LEAVING! I SURE WISH I COULD GO WITH 'EM...

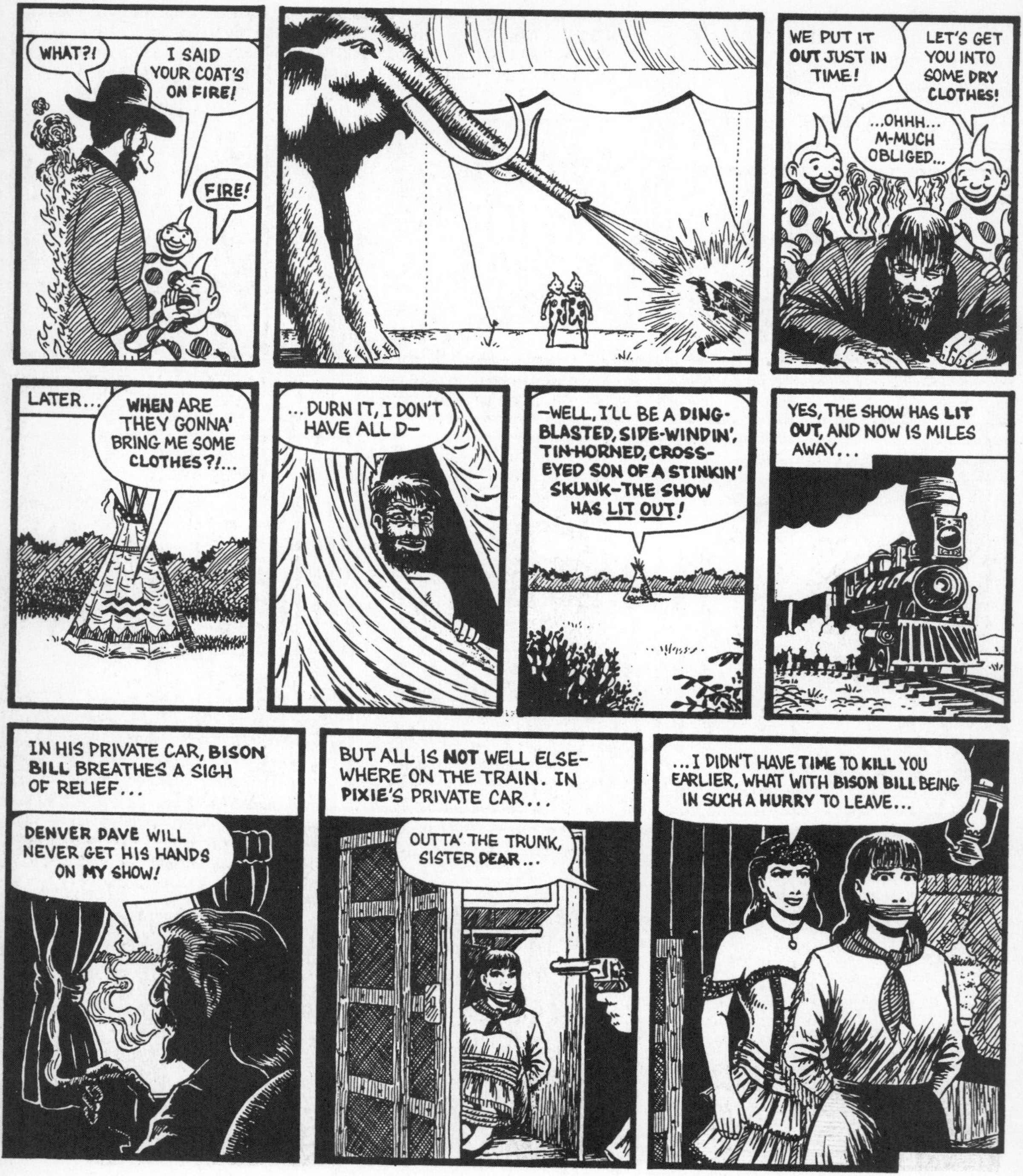
WHAT?!
I SAID YOUR COAT'S ON FIRE!
FIRE!
WE PUT IT OUT JUST IN TIME!
LET'S GET YOU INTO SOME DRY CLOTHES!
...OHHH... M-MUCH OBLIGED...
LATER...
WHEN ARE THEY GONNA' BRING ME SOME CLOTHES?!...
...DURN IT, I DON'T HAVE ALL D–
–WELL, I'LL BE A DING-BLASTED, SIDE-WINDIN', TIN-HORNED, CROSS-EYED SON OF A STINKIN' SKUNK–THE SHOW HAS LIT OUT!
YES, THE SHOW HAS LIT OUT, AND NOW IS MILES AWAY...
IN HIS PRIVATE CAR, BISON BILL BREATHES A SIGH OF RELIEF...
DENVER DAVE WILL NEVER GET HIS HANDS ON MY SHOW!
BUT ALL IS NOT WELL ELSE-WHERE ON THE TRAIN. IN PIXIE'S PRIVATE CAR...
OUTTA' THE TRUNK, SISTER DEAR...
...I DIDN'T HAVE TIME TO KILL YOU EARLIER, WHAT WITH BISON BILL BEING IN SUCH A HURRY TO LEAVE...

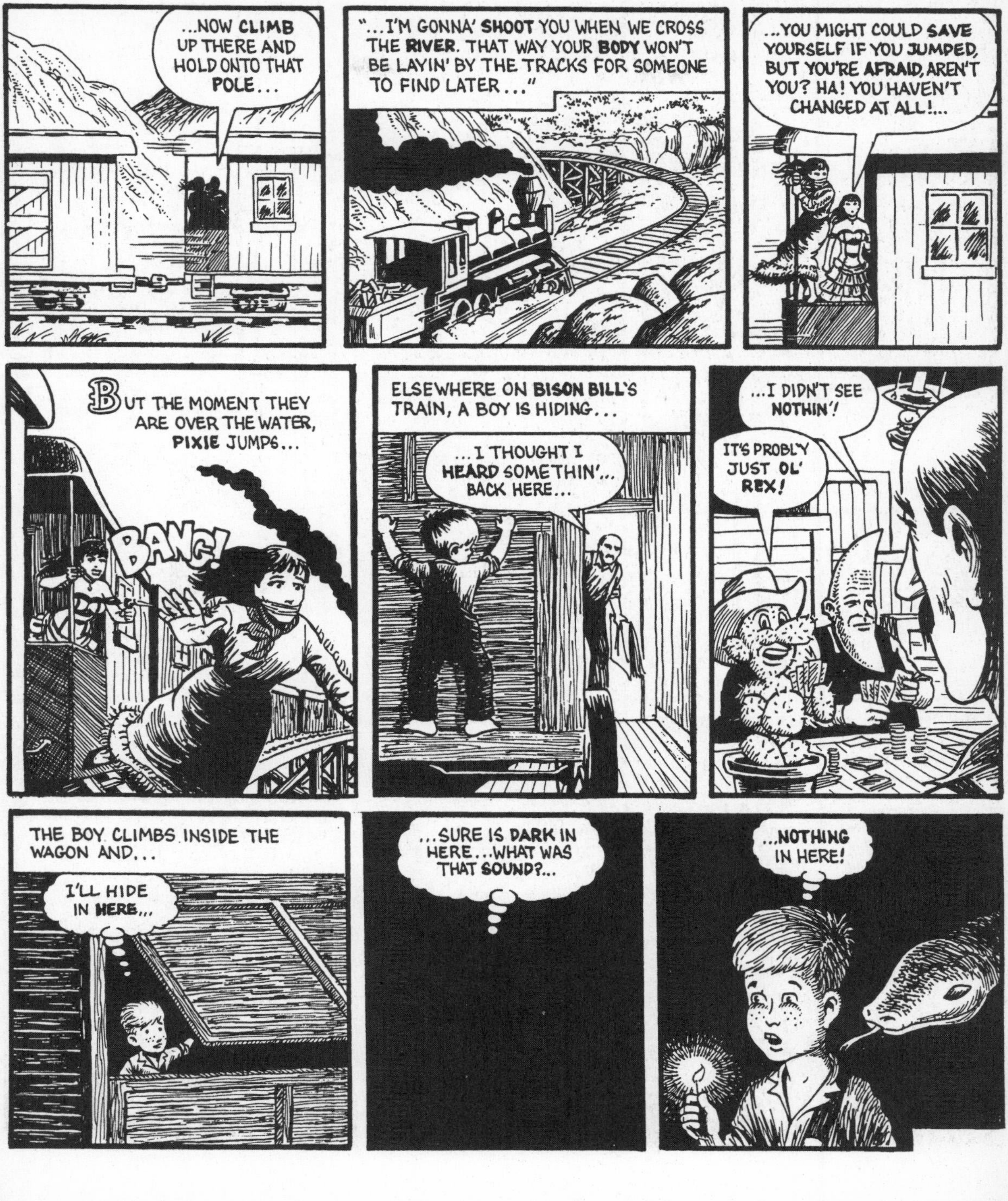
...NOW CLIMB UP THERE AND HOLD ONTO THAT POLE...
"...I'M GONNA' SHOOT YOU WHEN WE CROSS THE RIVER. THAT WAY YOUR BODY WON'T BE LAYIN' BY THE TRACKS FOR SOMEONE TO FIND LATER..."
...YOU MIGHT COULD SAVE YOURSELF IF YOU JUMPED, BUT YOU'RE AFRAID, AREN'T YOU? HA! YOU HAVEN'T CHANGED AT ALL!...
BUT THE MOMENT THEY ARE OVER THE WATER, PIXIE JUMPS...
BANG!
ELSEWHERE ON BISON BILL'S TRAIN, A BOY IS HIDING...
...I THOUGHT I HEARD SOMETHIN'... BACK HERE...
...I DIDN'T SEE NOTHIN'!
IT'S PROBL'Y JUST OL' REX!
THE BOY CLIMBS INSIDE THE WAGON AND...
I'LL HIDE IN HERE...
...SURE IS DARK IN HERE...WHAT WAS THAT SOUND?...
...NOTHING IN HERE!

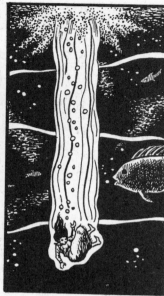

AS PIXIE SINKS HELPLESSLY INTO THE DEEP RIVER, HER TWIN SISTER DIXIE LOOKS BACK FROM THE SPEEDING TRAIN AND GLOATS...

GOOD! SHE'S OUT OF THE WAY! NOW I CAN TAKE OVER HER IDENTITY!

B ISON BILL'S TRAIN HURTLES ONWARD, LEAVING PIXIE FAR BEHIND. MEANWHILE, IN THE STORAGE COMPARTMENT OF ONE OF THE CARS, A POKER GAME IS IN PROGRESS...

SEE YOUR TEN, RAISE YOU TWENTY.

I'M OUT.

IN ANOTHER PART OF THE CAR...

HELP!

I COULD SWEAR I HEARD A VOICE BACK THERE!

AW, IT'S JUST OL' REX BANGIN' AROUND MAKIN' THAT WAGON SQUEAK!

BUT OL' REX IS UP TO MORE THAN JUST BANGIN' AROUND...

HELP!

REX! REX!...

HELP!

HEY! YOU LET GO A' HIM RIGHT NOW! YOU HEAR ME?!

REX LOOSENS HIS GRIP...

LATER, IN **BISON BILL'S** CAR...

...THEN MY LITTLE **BROTHER** TOOK THE **FEVER** AND HE DIED, AND SINCE THERE WASN'T ANYBODY ELSE LEFT ALIVE, I HAD TO **BURY** HIM...

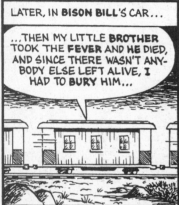

...SO WITH MY **MA** AND **PA** DEAD, AND MY **BROTHERS** AND **SISTERS** TOO, AND MY **AUNTS** AND **UNCLES** AND ALL MY **COUSINS** AND MY **GRANDPARENTS** ALL DEAD, I BEEN ON MY **OWN** JUST WANDERIN' AROUND.

WELL, ER, UNDER THE CIRCUMSTANCES, YOU MAY CERTAINLY **STAY** WITH THE SHOW!

HONK!

THAT WAS A GOOD LIE!

NIGHT FALLS, AND BISON BILL'S TRAIN CHARGES ONWARD...

BY DAYBREAK THE SHOW ARRIVES IN THE NEXT TOWN...

UH PIXIE, CAN I TALK TO YOU FOR A MINUTE?

YOU RASCAL! HA-HA-HA!

I DON'T GET IT, BOY HOWDY! PIXIE IS DRESSIN' LIKE A DANCE-HALL **FLOOZIE**— AND SHE DON'T EVEN KNOW I EXIST!

TYPICAL FLIGHTY FEMALE!

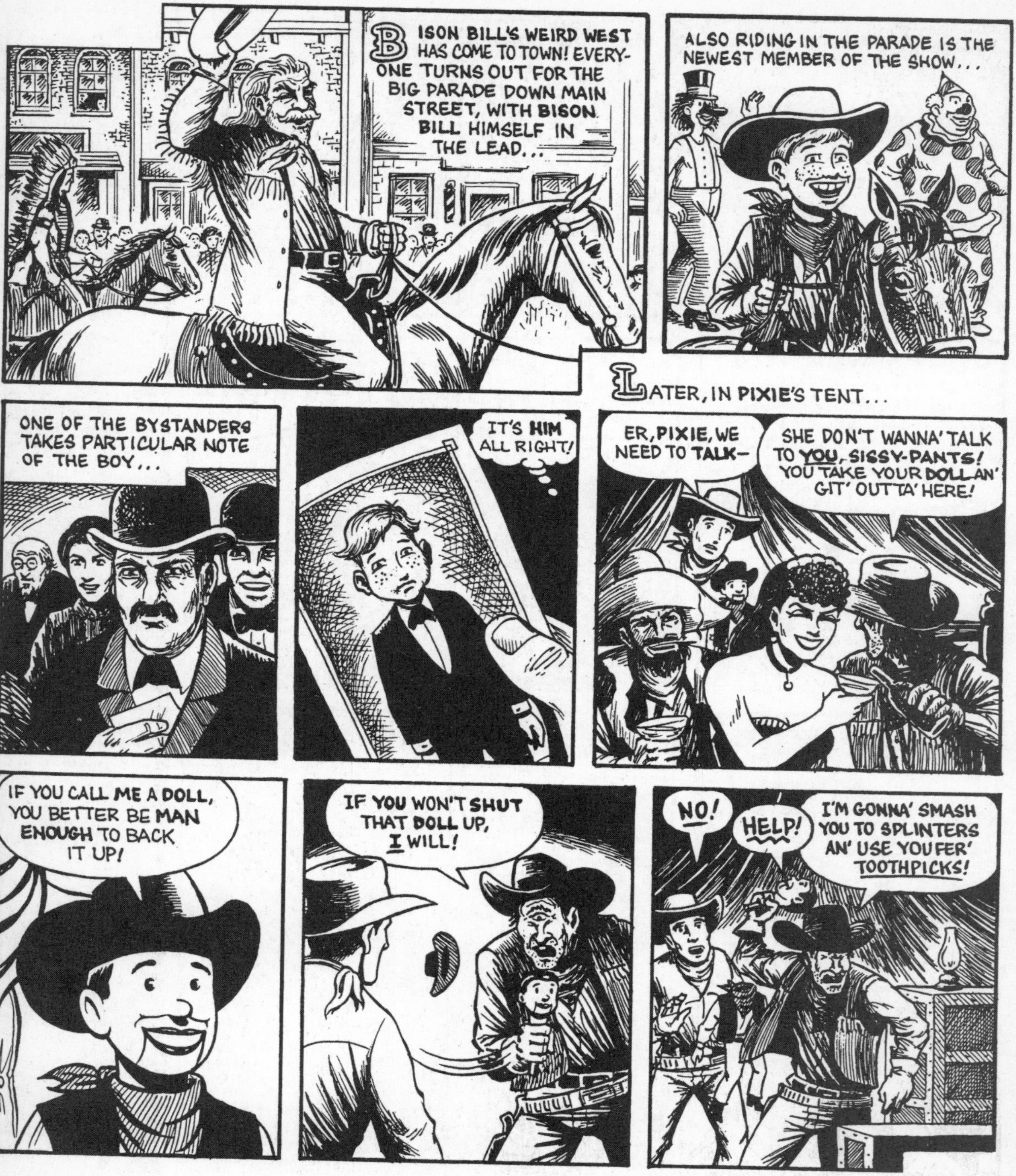
BISON BILL'S WEIRD WEST HAS COME TO TOWN! EVERY-ONE TURNS OUT FOR THE BIG PARADE DOWN MAIN STREET, WITH BISON BILL HIMSELF IN THE LEAD...
ALSO RIDING IN THE PARADE IS THE NEWEST MEMBER OF THE SHOW...
LATER, IN PIXIE'S TENT...
ONE OF THE BYSTANDERS TAKES PARTICULAR NOTE OF THE BOY...
IT'S HIM ALL RIGHT!
ER, PIXIE, WE NEED TO TALK—
SHE DON'T WANNA' TALK TO YOU, SISSY-PANTS! YOU TAKE YOUR DOLL AN' GIT' OUTTA' HERE!
IF YOU CALL ME A DOLL, YOU BETTER BE MAN ENOUGH TO BACK IT UP!
IF YOU WON'T SHUT THAT DOLL UP, I WILL!
NO!
HELP!
I'M GONNA' SMASH YOU TO SPLINTERS AN' USE YOU FER' TOOTHPICKS!

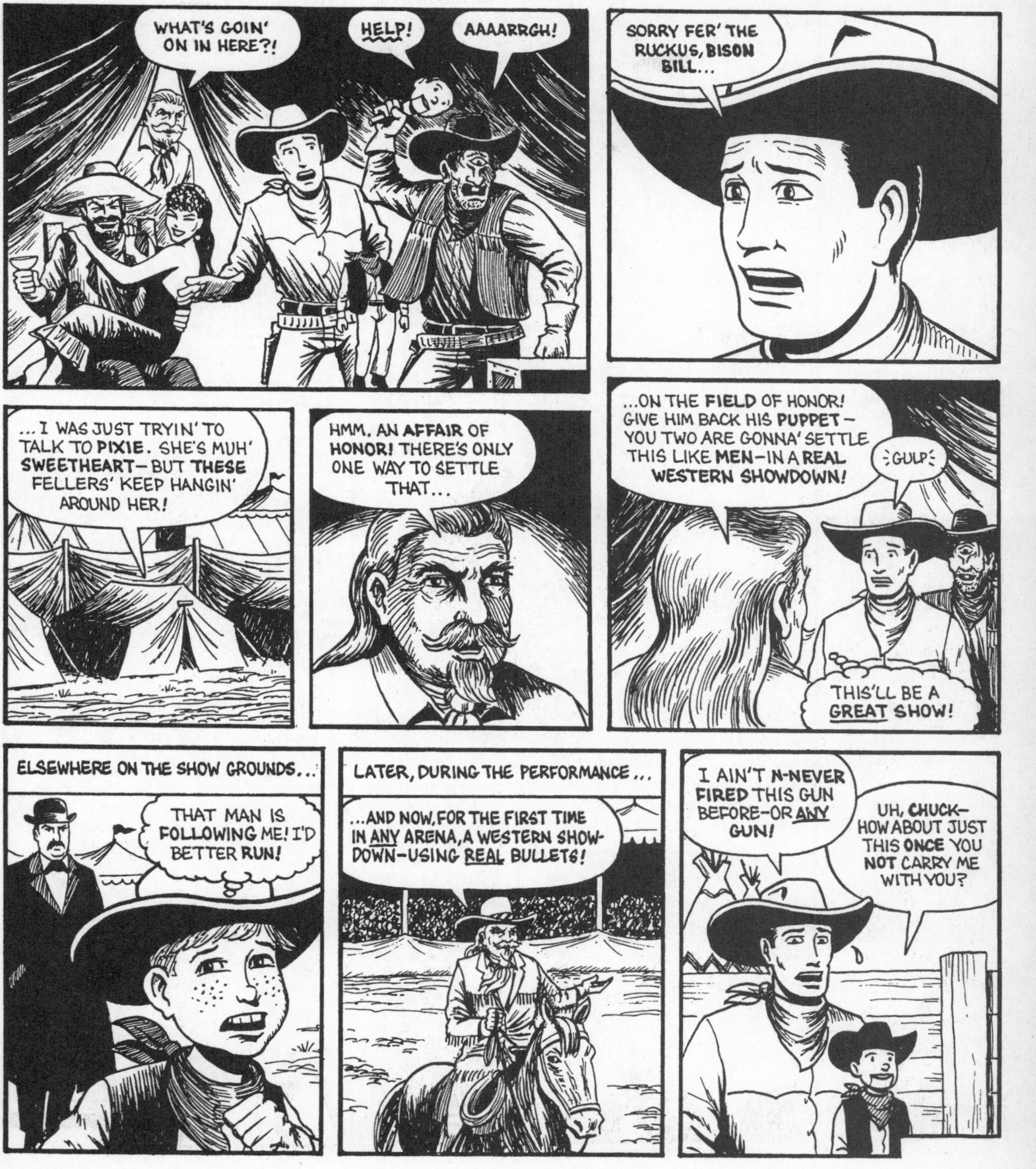
WHAT'S GOIN' ON IN HERE?!
HELP!
AAAARRGH!
SORRY FER' THE RUCKUS, BISON BILL...
...I WAS JUST TRYIN' TO TALK TO PIXIE. SHE'S MUH' SWEETHEART—BUT THESE FELLERS' KEEP HANGIN' AROUND HER!
HMM. AN AFFAIR OF HONOR! THERE'S ONLY ONE WAY TO SETTLE THAT...
...ON THE FIELD OF HONOR! GIVE HIM BACK HIS PUPPET—YOU TWO ARE GONNA' SETTLE THIS LIKE MEN—IN A REAL WESTERN SHOWDOWN!
GULP
THIS'LL BE A GREAT SHOW!
ELSEWHERE ON THE SHOW GROUNDS...
THAT MAN IS FOLLOWING ME! I'D BETTER RUN!
LATER, DURING THE PERFORMANCE...
...AND NOW, FOR THE FIRST TIME IN ANY ARENA, A WESTERN SHOW-DOWN—USING REAL BULLETS!
I AIN'T N-NEVER FIRED THIS GUN BEFORE—OR ANY GUN!
UH, CHUCK—HOW ABOUT JUST THIS ONCE YOU NOT CARRY ME WITH YOU?

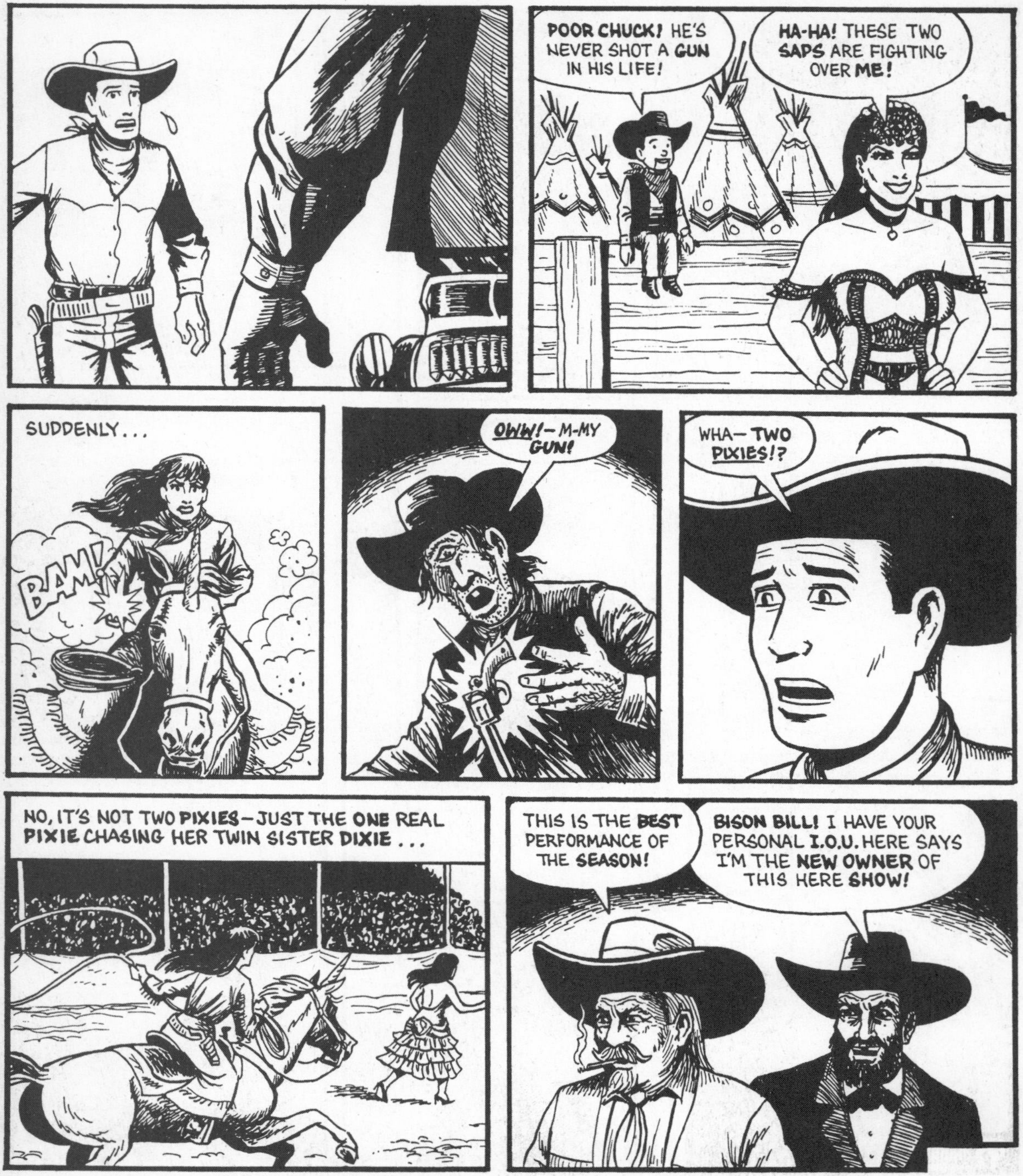
POOR CHUCK! HE'S NEVER SHOT A GUN IN HIS LIFE!
HA-HA! THESE TWO SAPS ARE FIGHTING OVER ME!
SUDDENLY . . .
BAM!
OWW!— M-MY GUN!
WHA— TWO PIXIES!?
NO, IT'S NOT TWO PIXIES—JUST THE ONE REAL PIXIE CHASING HER TWIN SISTER DIXIE . . .
THIS IS THE BEST PERFORMANCE OF THE SEASON!
BISON BILL! I HAVE YOUR PERSONAL I.O.U. HERE SAYS I'M THE NEW OWNER OF THIS HERE SHOW!

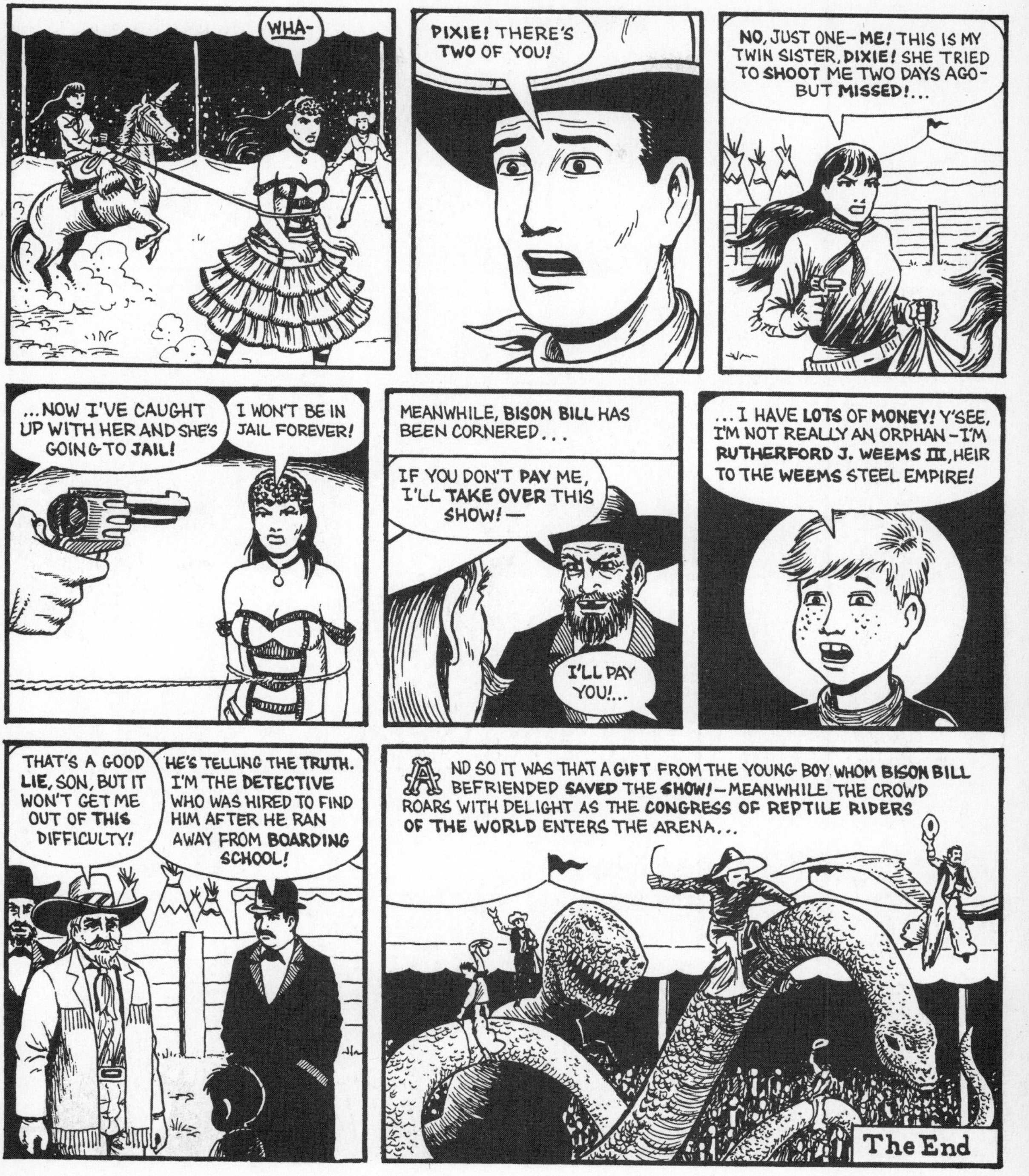
WHA-
PIXIE! THERE'S TWO OF YOU!
NO, JUST ONE—ME! THIS IS MY TWIN SISTER, DIXIE! SHE TRIED TO SHOOT ME TWO DAYS AGO— BUT MISSED!...
...NOW I'VE CAUGHT UP WITH HER AND SHE'S GOING TO JAIL!
I WON'T BE IN JAIL FOREVER!
MEANWHILE, BISON BILL HAS BEEN CORNERED...
IF YOU DON'T PAY ME, I'LL TAKE OVER THIS SHOW!—
I'LL PAY YOU!...
...I HAVE LOTS OF MONEY! Y'SEE, I'M NOT REALLY AN ORPHAN—I'M RUTHERFORD J. WEEMS III, HEIR TO THE WEEMS STEEL EMPIRE!
THAT'S A GOOD LIE, SON, BUT IT WON'T GET ME OUT OF THIS DIFFICULTY!
HE'S TELLING THE TRUTH. I'M THE DETECTIVE WHO WAS HIRED TO FIND HIM AFTER HE RAN AWAY FROM BOARDING SCHOOL!
AND SO IT WAS THAT A GIFT FROM THE YOUNG BOY WHOM BISON BILL BEFRIENDED SAVED THE SHOW!—MEANWHILE THE CROWD ROARS WITH DELIGHT AS THE CONGRESS OF REPTILE RIDERS OF THE WORLD ENTERS THE ARENA...
The End

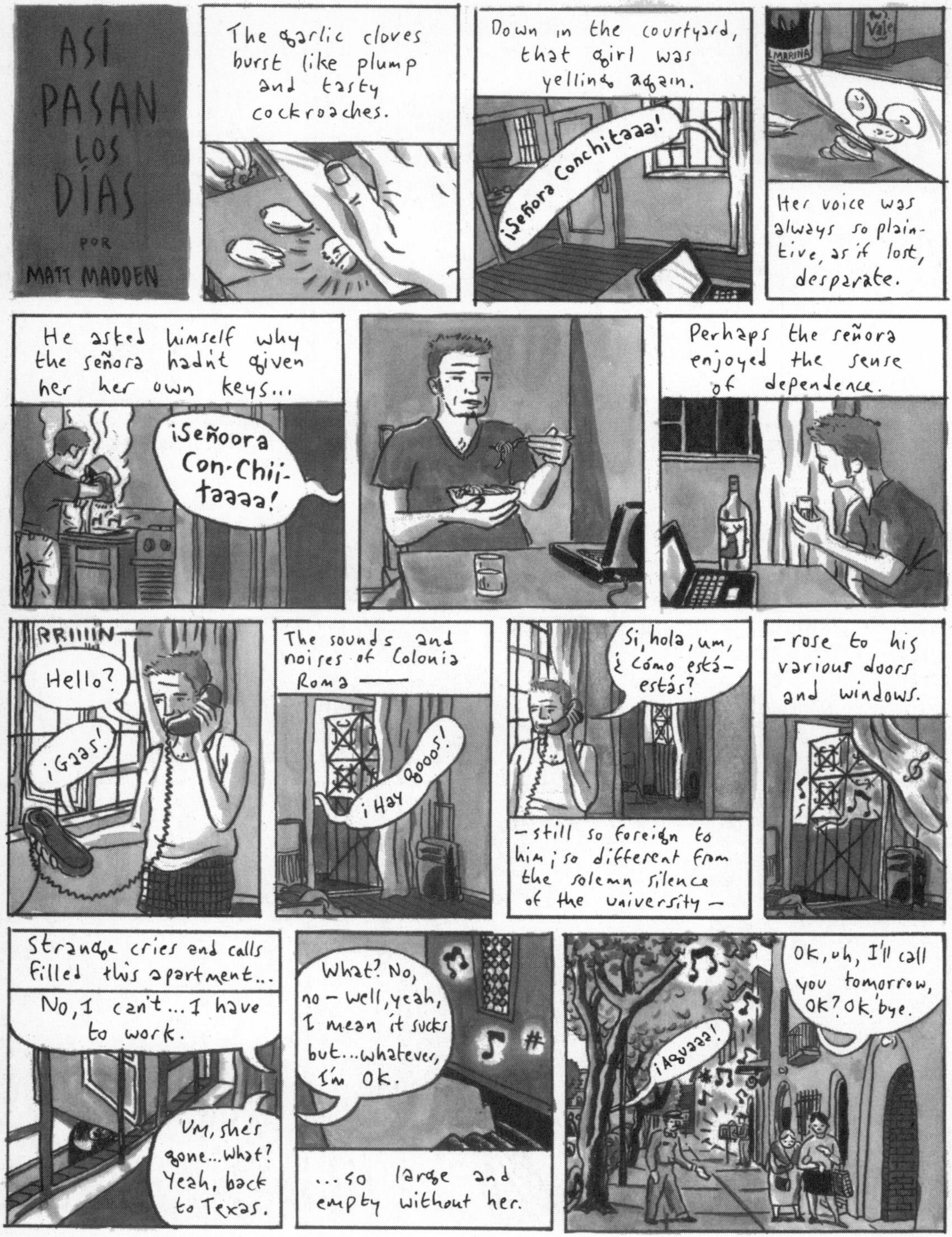
ASÍ PASAN LOS DÍAS
POR
MATT MADDEN
The garlic cloves burst like plump and tasty cockroaches.
Down in the courtyard, that girl was yelling again.
¡Señora Conchitaaa!
Her voice was always so plaintive, as if lost, desparate.
He asked himself why the señora hadn't given her her own keys...
¡Señoora Con-Chii-taaaa!
Perhaps the señora enjoyed the sense of dependence.
RRIIIIN—
Hello?
¡Gaas!
The sounds and noises of Colonia Roma —
¡Hay gooos!
Si, hola, um, ¿cómo está- estás?
—still so foreign to him; so different from the solemn silence of the university—
—rose to his various doors and windows.
Strange cries and calls filled this apartment...
No, I can't... I have to work.
Um, she's gone... what? Yeah, back to Texas.
What? No, no—well, yeah, I mean it sucks but... whatever, I'm OK.
...so large and empty without her.
¡Aguaaa!
Ok, uh, I'll call you tomorrow, OK? Ok, bye.

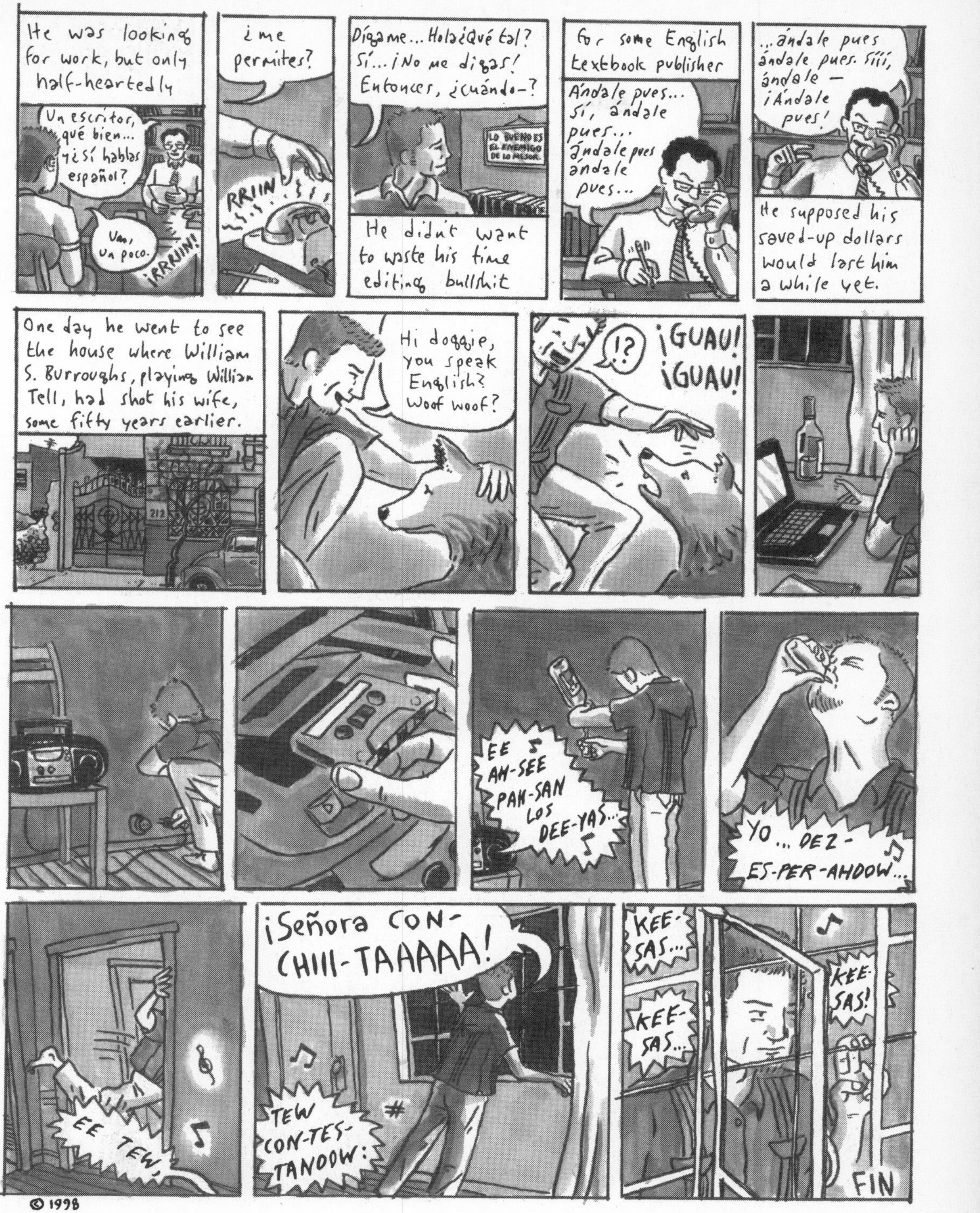

He was looking for work, but only half-heartedly
Un escritor, qué bien... ¿y sí hablas español?
Um, un poco.
¡RRRIN!
¿me permites?
RRRIN
Dígame... Hola ¿qué tal? Sí... ¡No me digas! Entonces, ¿cuándo–?
LO BUENO ES EL ENEMIGO DE LO MEJOR.
He didn't want to waste his time editing bullshit
for some English textbook publisher
Ándale pues... sí, ándale pues... ándale pues ándale pues...
...ándale pues ándale pues. Sííí, ándale — ¡Ándale pues!
He supposed his saved-up dollars would last him a while yet.
One day he went to see the house where William S. Burroughs, playing William Tell, had shot his wife, some fifty years earlier.
212
Hi doggie, you speak English? Woof woof?
!?
¡GUAU! ¡GUAU!
EE AH-SEE PAH-SAN LOS DEE-YAS...
YO... DEZ-ES-PER-AHDOW...
EE TEW,
¡Señora CON-CHIII-TAAAAA!
TEW CON-TES-TANDOW:
KEE-SAS...
KEE-SAS!
KEE-SAS...
FIN

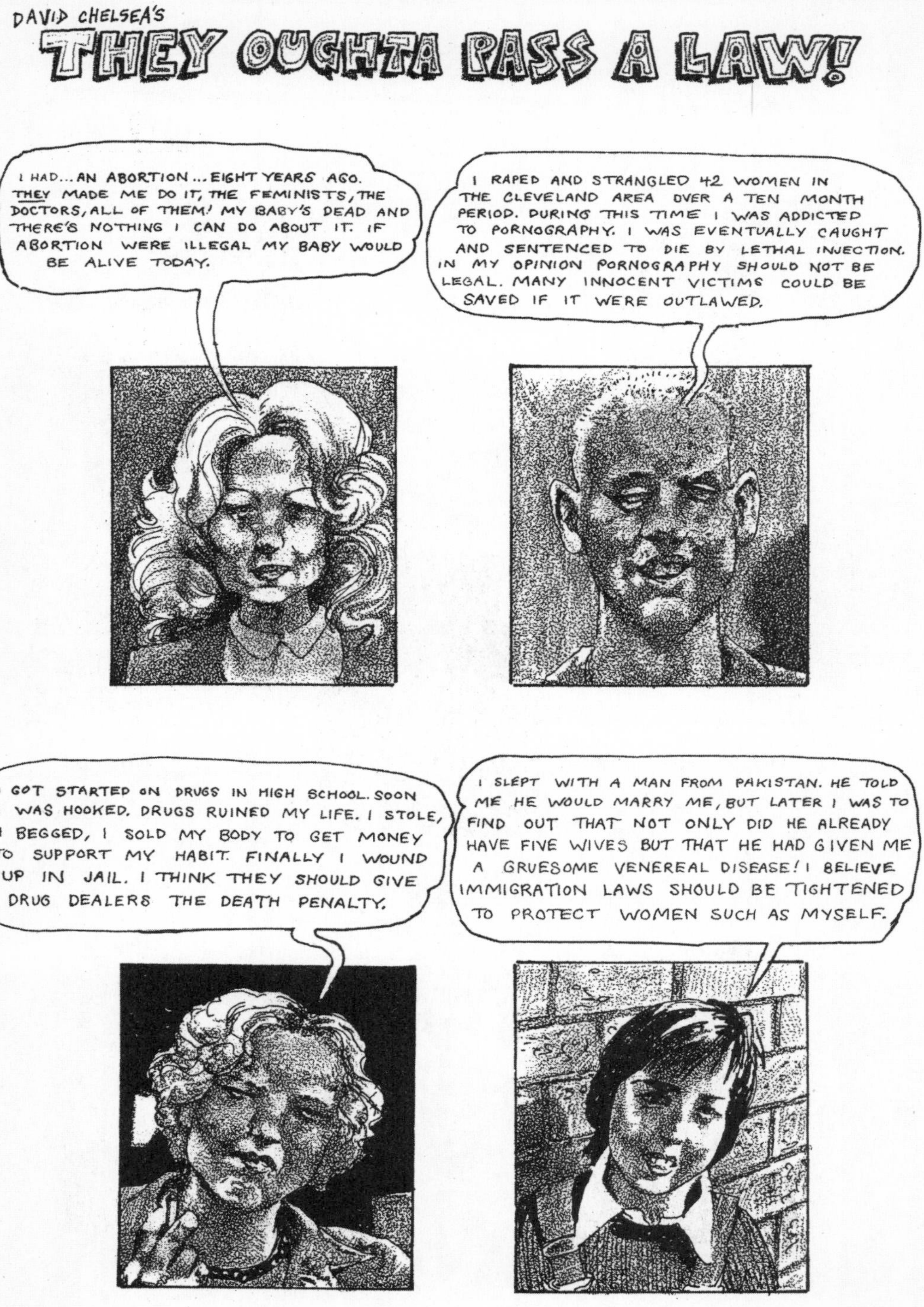
DAVID CHELSEA'S
THEY OUGHTA PASS A LAW!
I HAD... AN ABORTION... EIGHT YEARS AGO. THEY MADE ME DO IT, THE FEMINISTS, THE DOCTORS, ALL OF THEM! MY BABY'S DEAD AND THERE'S NOTHING I CAN DO ABOUT IT. IF ABORTION WERE ILLEGAL MY BABY WOULD BE ALIVE TODAY.
I RAPED AND STRANGLED 42 WOMEN IN THE CLEVELAND AREA OVER A TEN MONTH PERIOD. DURING THIS TIME I WAS ADDICTED TO PORNOGRAPHY. I WAS EVENTUALLY CAUGHT AND SENTENCED TO DIE BY LETHAL INJECTION. IN MY OPINION PORNOGRAPHY SHOULD NOT BE LEGAL. MANY INNOCENT VICTIMS COULD BE SAVED IF IT WERE OUTLAWED.
I GOT STARTED ON DRUGS IN HIGH SCHOOL. SOON I WAS HOOKED. DRUGS RUINED MY LIFE. I STOLE, I BEGGED, I SOLD MY BODY TO GET MONEY TO SUPPORT MY HABIT. FINALLY I WOUND UP IN JAIL. I THINK THEY SHOULD GIVE DRUG DEALERS THE DEATH PENALTY.
I SLEPT WITH A MAN FROM PAKISTAN. HE TOLD ME HE WOULD MARRY ME, BUT LATER I WAS TO FIND OUT THAT NOT ONLY DID HE ALREADY HAVE FIVE WIVES BUT THAT HE HAD GIVEN ME A GRUESOME VENEREAL DISEASE! I BELIEVE IMMIGRATION LAWS SHOULD BE TIGHTENED TO PROTECT WOMEN SUCH AS MYSELF.

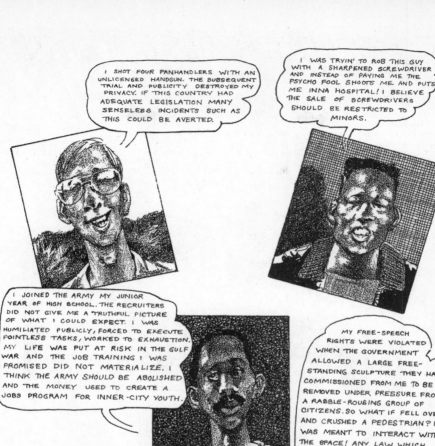

I SHOT FOUR PANHANDLERS WITH AN UNLICENSED HANDGUN. THE SUBSEQUENT TRIAL AND PUBLICITY DESTROYED MY PRIVACY. IF THIS COUNTRY HAD ADEQUATE LEGISLATION MANY SENSELESS INCIDENTS SUCH AS THIS COULD BE AVERTED.

I WAS TRYIN' TO ROB THIS GUY WITH A SHARPENED SCREWDRIVER AND INSTEAD OF PAYING ME THE PSYCHO FOOL SHOOTS ME AND PUTS ME INNA HOSPITAL! I BELIEVE THE SALE OF SCREWDRIVERS SHOULD BE RESTRICTED TO MINORS.

I JOINED THE ARMY MY JUNIOR YEAR OF HIGH SCHOOL. THE RECRUITERS DID NOT GIVE ME A TRUTHFUL PICTURE OF WHAT I COULD EXPECT. I WAS HUMILIATED PUBLICLY, FORCED TO EXECUTE POINTLESS TASKS, WORKED TO EXHAUSTION. MY LIFE WAS PUT AT RISK IN THE GULF WAR AND THE JOB TRAINING I WAS PROMISED DID NOT MATERIALIZE. I THINK THE ARMY SHOULD BE ABOLISHED AND THE MONEY USED TO CREATE A JOBS PROGRAM FOR INNER-CITY YOUTH.

MY FREE-SPEECH RIGHTS WERE VIOLATED WHEN THE GOVERNMENT ALLOWED A LARGE FREE-STANDING SCULPTURE THEY HAD COMMISSIONED FROM ME TO BE REMOVED UNDER PRESSURE FROM A RABBLE-ROUSING GROUP OF CITIZENS. SO WHAT IF FELL OVER AND CRUSHED A PEDESTRIAN? IT WAS MEANT TO INTERACT WITH THE SPACE! ANY LAW WHICH ALLOWS A LOT OF AESTHETICALLY BACKWARD ORDINARY TAXPAYERS TO FORCE THE REMOVAL OF PUBLICLY FUNDED ART OUGHTA BE CHANGED AND RIGHT AWAY!

I LOST MY LIFE SAVINGS PLAYING THE LOTTERY. LATER I FOUND OUT THAT MY CHANCE OF WINNING IS ACTUALLY LESS THAN MY CHANCE OF BEING HIT BY LIGHTNING! WHY DON'T THE GOVERNMENT WARN PEOPLE?

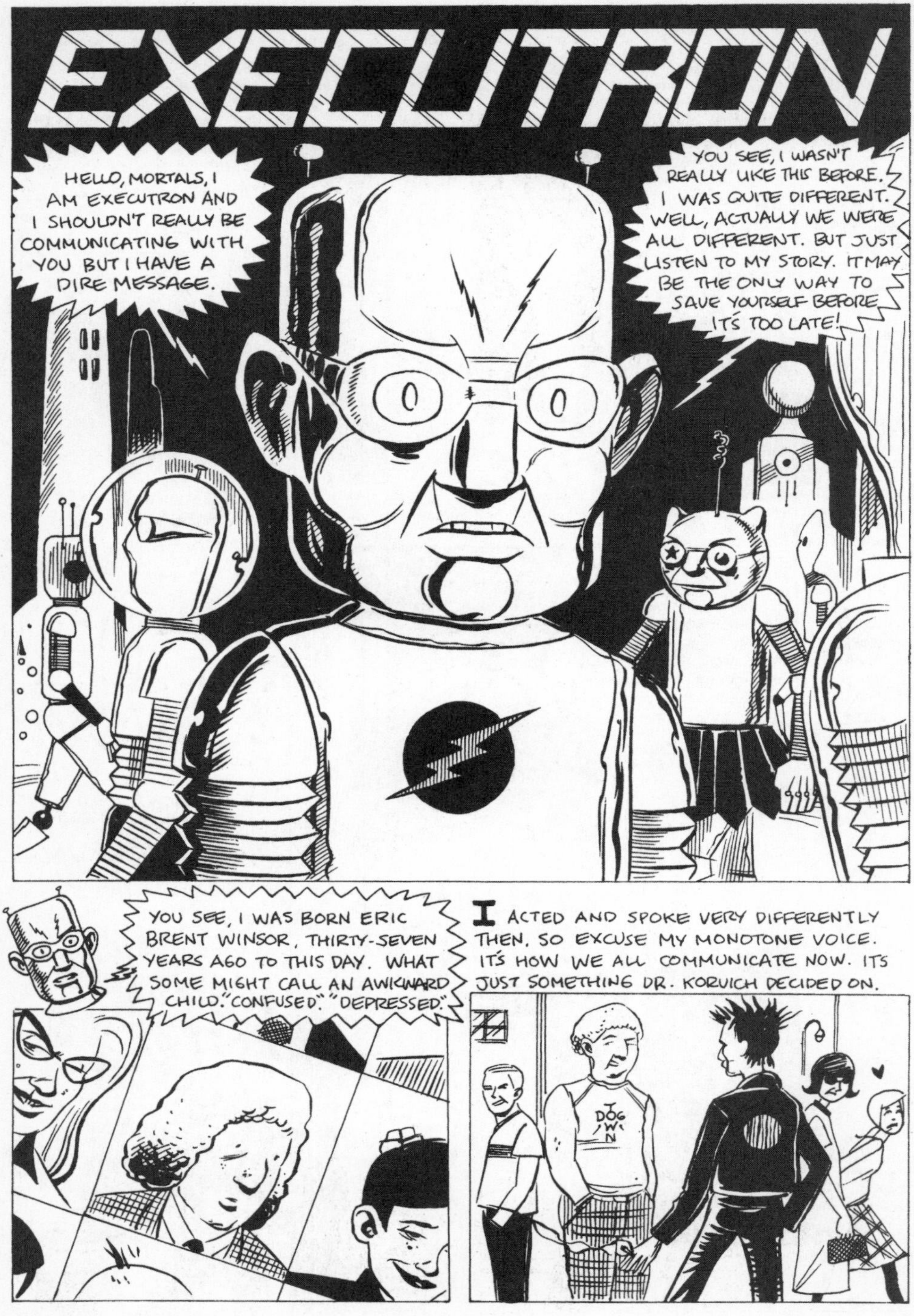
EXECUTRON
HELLO, MORTALS, I AM EXECUTRON AND I SHOULDN'T REALLY BE COMMUNICATING WITH YOU BUT I HAVE A DIRE MESSAGE.
YOU SEE, I WASN'T REALLY LIKE THIS BEFORE. I WAS QUITE DIFFERENT. WELL, ACTUALLY WE WERE ALL DIFFERENT. BUT JUST LISTEN TO MY STORY. IT MAY BE THE ONLY WAY TO SAVE YOURSELF BEFORE IT'S TOO LATE!
YOU SEE, I WAS BORN ERIC BRENT WINSOR, THIRTY-SEVEN YEARS AGO TO THIS DAY. WHAT SOME MIGHT CALL AN AWKWARD CHILD. "CONFUSED." "DEPRESSED."
I ACTED AND SPOKE VERY DIFFERENTLY THEN, SO EXCUSE MY MONOTONE VOICE. IT'S HOW WE ALL COMMUNICATE NOW. IT'S JUST SOMETHING DR. KORUICH DECIDED ON.
J DOG W N

I HAD A FAMILY LIKE ANY OTHER EARTHLING. FAR FROM NUCLEAR. WHAT THE PSYCHOLOGISTS MIGHT CALL "DYSFUNCTIONAL". ONE BROTHER: SELF-INFLICTED WOUNDS. NONSENSICAL RAMBLINGS.

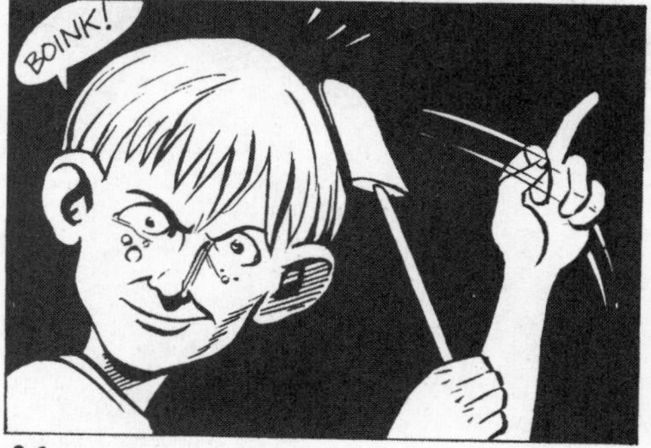
BOINK!

AFTER THE DIVORCE, MY FATHER, WHO WAS WHAT SOME CALL A "BOHEMIAN," TOOK TO CAVORTING WITH MALES WHO HAD A KEEN FASCINATION OF VIOLENT SPORTING EVENTS AND ALCOHOL. NOT HIS EVOLUTION.

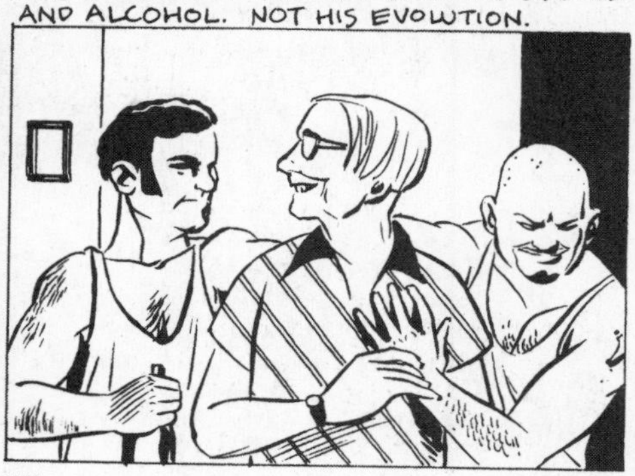

MY MOTHER WAS THROWN INTO THE "QUIET TYPE" CATEGORY, AS WAS MY FORMER SELF. I RELATED TO HER IMMENSELY. HER WEAK DEMEANOR. HER SHYNESS. TOGETHER WE MADE A COMPLETE BLANK.

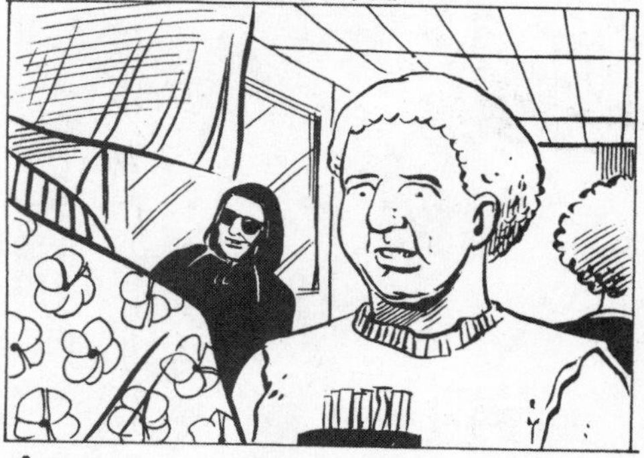

I TRIED TO STAND OUT. MOST TEENAGERS DO SOMETHING DRASTIC TO FIT IN. I WANTED TO "FIT OUT." I DIDN'T LIKE THE PEOPLE AROUND ME. SO I CARVED MY CLASSIC TRAIT. PEOPLE THOUGHT ME CRAZY.

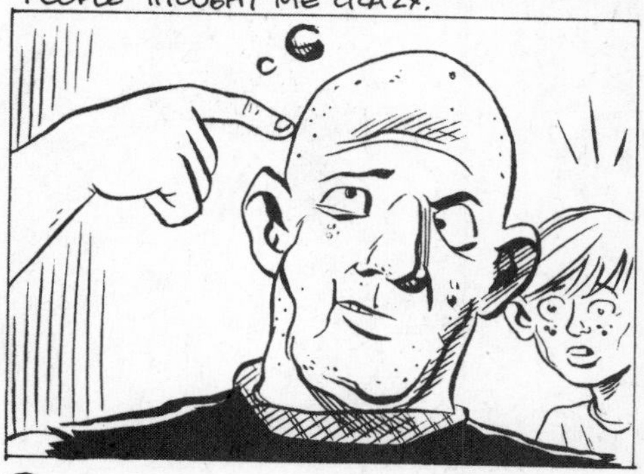

AND IT WORKED. I WAS AN OUTCAST. BUT A BIT TOO MUCH OF ONE FOR MY ADOLESCENT SELF-ESTEEM. THE MEAN PEOPLE WOULD FEIGN WHISPERING BUT REALLY BE SHOUTING-"WIERDO, WIERDO, WIERDO."

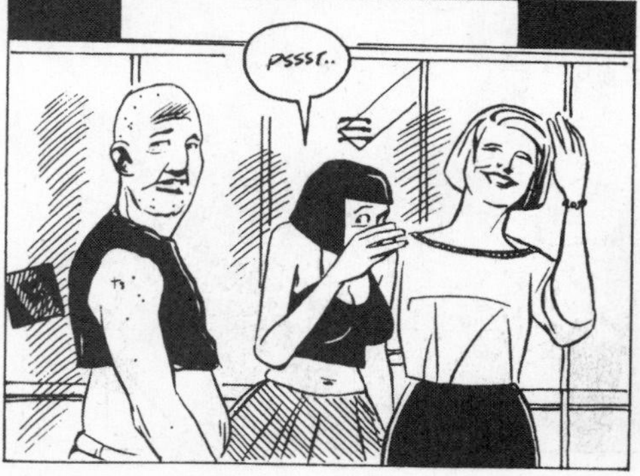
PSSST..

SO NATURALLY, AS ALL CREATURES DO, I FLOCKED TO A CERTAIN ILK. IN ESSENCE, I LIKED MY KIND BETTER: THE OBNOXIOUS TO THE EXTREMELY MORBID. TO THE PROUD. MY FRIENDS; JON, DEVIN, AND STUB.

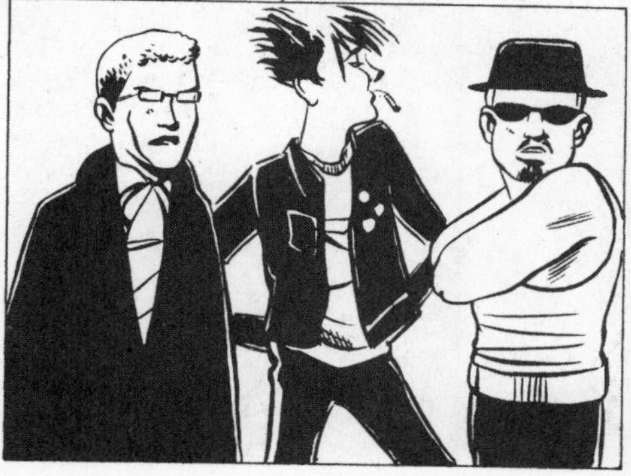

I GUESS DEVIN WAS THE FIRST ONE TO SAY "FUCK OFF," AS HUMANS USED TO SAY, TO THE OTHER TYPES. I ALWAYS ADMIRED HIS BOISTEROUSNESS AND STRIDENT, UNABASHED COURAGE. I ALWAYS TOOK HIS CUE.

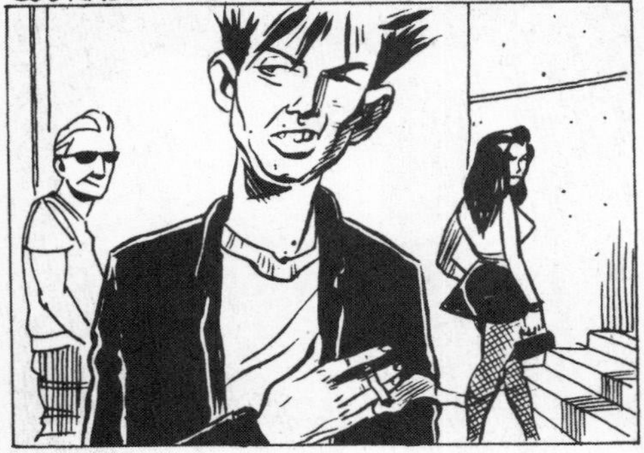

BASICALLY, I WAS ALWAYS THE FOLLOWER TYPE. I WAS THE "FAT" KID WHO WAS ALWAYS MADE FUN OF AND EXCLUDED FROM ALL THE RITUALS. I WAS ONE OF THOSE "BORN FREE OF CONFIDENCE" CHILDREN.

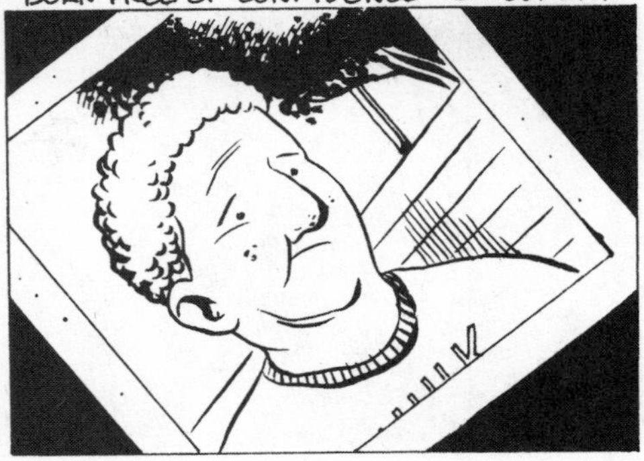

I HAD NO CONCRETE VIEWS OF MY OWN OR IDEALS TO UPHOLD. I WAS JUST A NAMELESS FISH IN THE SEA. PUBERTY DIDN'T HELP. IT JUST MADE FIGURING OUT THE EQUATION ALGEBRA INSTEAD OF GEOMETRY.

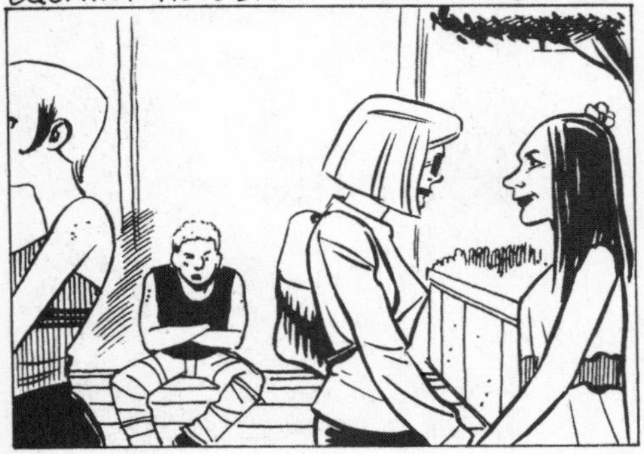

THE OTHER SEX WAS SOMETHING I WAS NEVER FIXATED ON. I THINK I HAD A NOTION OF TRUE LOVE. I WAS A ROMANTIC. I KNEW TRUE LOVE WAS OUT THERE. THE OTHER BOYS WEREN'T LIKE THAT.

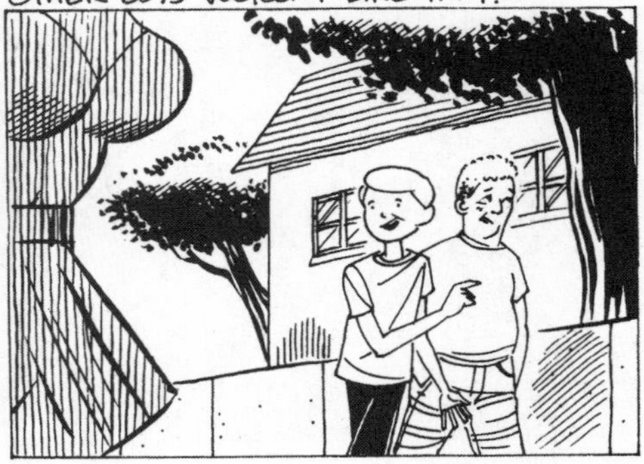

I THOUGHT IT WOULD COME. AND IT DID. I JUST KNEW. IT WASN'T SOME EPIPHANY OR PHYSICAL REACTION. IT WAS JUST PLAIN AND SIMPLE ... HER. AND HER ONLY, FOREVER: MARY WATSON.

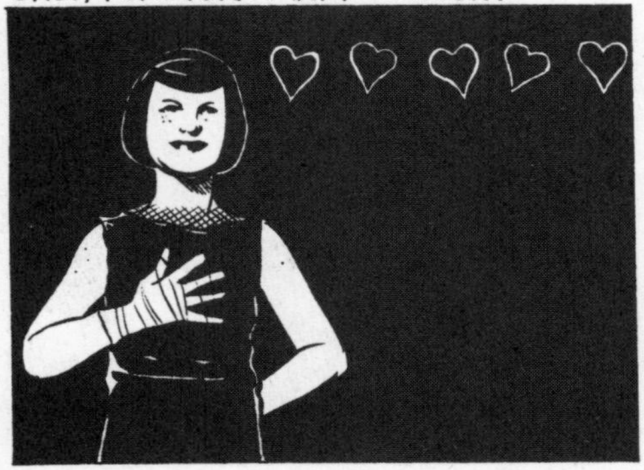

I WAS A MIXED-UP MESS AND SHE SAVED MY LIFE, LITERALLY. SURE IN THE NEAR FUTURE SHE WOULD HURT ME DEARLY, BUT AS I SAID, I HAD A LOT TO LEARN ABOUT LIFE ... AND LOVE.

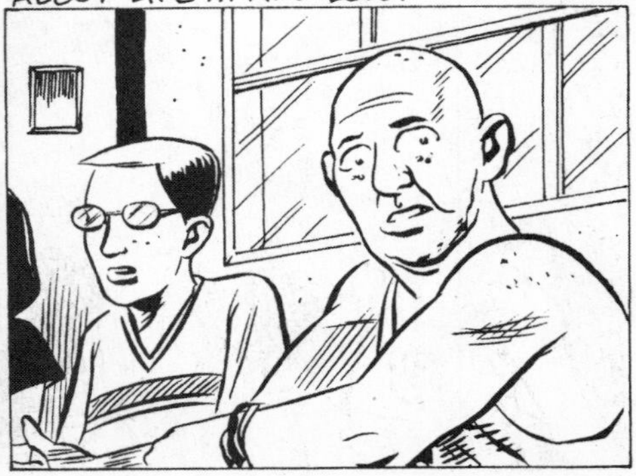

I WASN'T THE STEREOTYPICAL MALE IN THE RELATIONSHIP. I ALWAYS FELT LIKE I WAS LEARNING SO MUCH FROM HER, AND TO BE HONEST, THAT I WAS THE WEAK LINK.

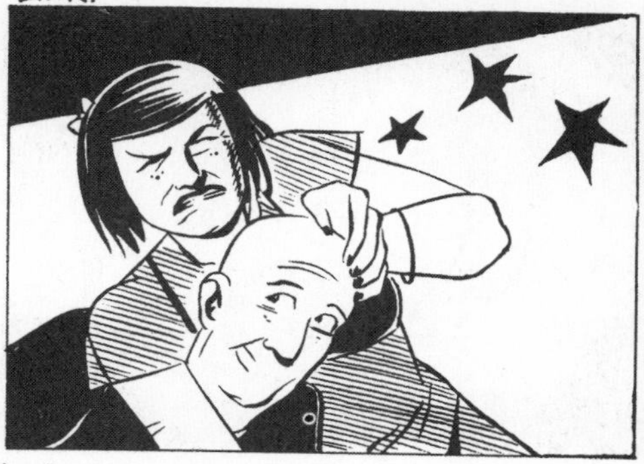

NEVERTHELESS, MARY LOVED ME UNCONDITIONALLY. SURE, WE FOUGHT. BUT I FOUND OUT THAT WAS BECAUSE WE CARED SO MUCH. I NEVER THOUGHT I WOULD HAVE A JEALOUS BONE IN MY BODY. I WAS SO WRONG.

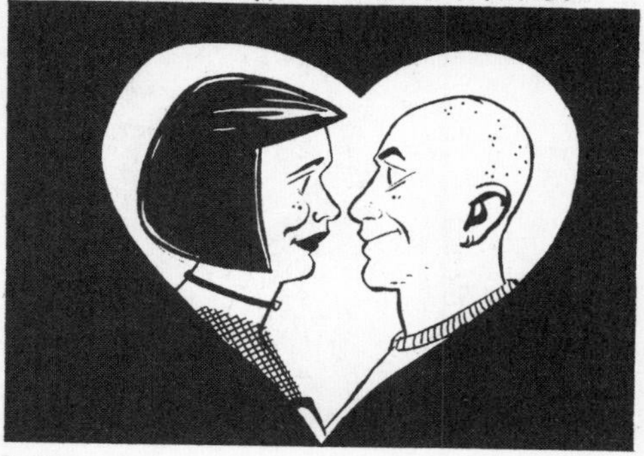

WITH THIS NEW-FOUND INNER PEACE, I HAD THE STRENGTH TO BE MORE SERIOUS ABOUT MY ENDEAVORS. AND MORE DIRECT. "EL CID" DIDN'T HELP. RELIVING THE PAST; SHOUTING "OI" AND "CHEERS" AT ALL OUR GIGS.

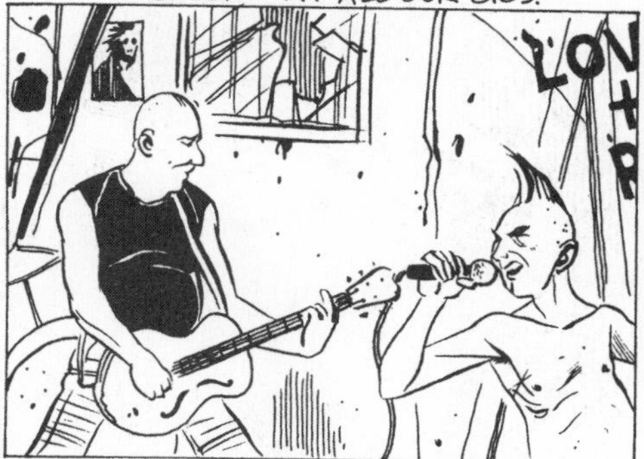
LOV

MARY KNEW WE WEREN'T GREAT EITHER. SHE HAD HARSH OPINIONS. I LEARNED NOT TO TRY AND SWAY HER. SHE ACTED HOW SHE ACTED, AND THAT WAS IT. SHE HAD THIS KNOWING LOOK. I WAS POWERLESS BEFORE IT.

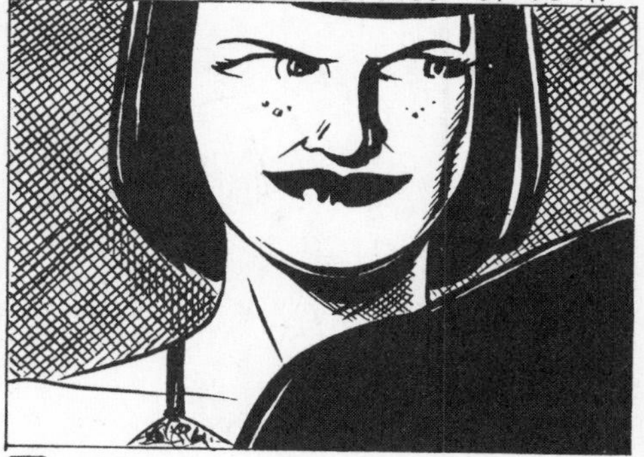

A LOT OF OUR NIGHTS WE WOULD JUST WASTE AWAY. MARY THOUGHT THAT SOMETIMES INEBRIATION AND HALLUCINATING COULD SOMETIMES BE USED AS A DECENT LOOKING GLASS INTO YOUR FEARS AND DREAMS.

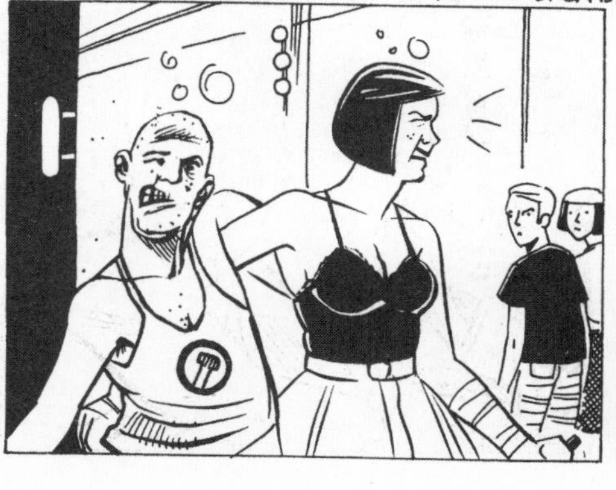

I GUESS YOU CAN FIND REBIRTH IN SELF-MUTILATION SOMETIMES. ATLEAST THOSE WASTED NIGHTS MADE ME GROW. IT WAS A DIFFERENT KIND OF WASTE AT MY FIRST JOB. I WAS SIXTEEN, AND "IT" WAS "MAMA SWEETS".

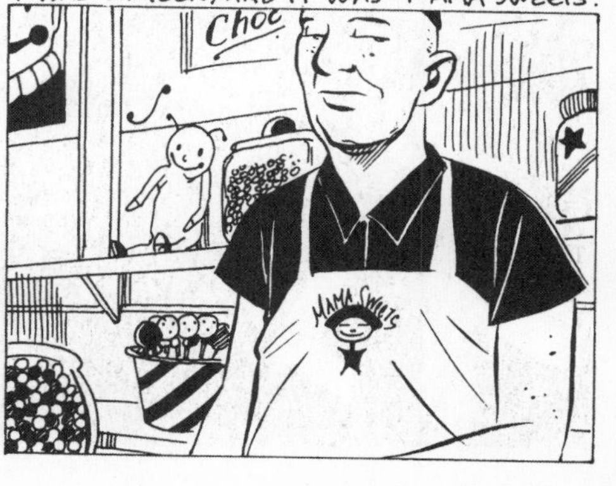
Choc
MAMA SWEETS

WE SAW THE SHORTCOMINGS OF NIHILISM. THOSE NIGHTS BECAME LESS FREQUENT. WE WERE DYING FOR HIGH SCHOOL TO END. WE WANTED TO GET SOMEWHERE... ANYWHERE. BUT IT WAS A DRONE... A SLOW LIFE-LESS HUM.

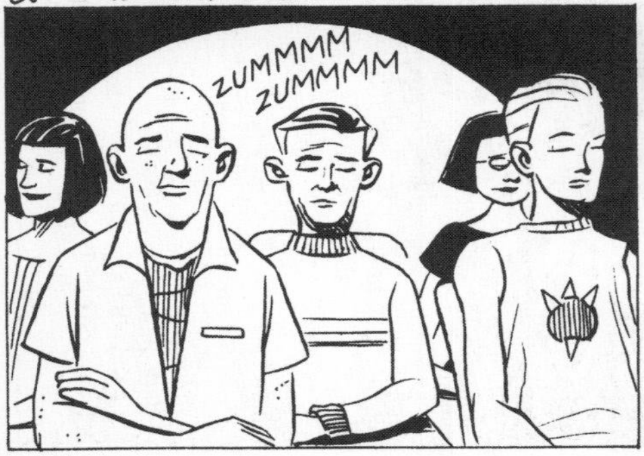
ZUMMMM
ZUMMMM

WE WERE REALLY JUST QUIETLY HAPPY. WE HOPED MAYBE COLLEGE COULD GIVE US A CHANCE TO PURSUE THE THINGS WE REALLY CARED ABOUT. I WANTED TO DO SOMETHING MUSICAL, AND MARY WAS AN ARTIST.

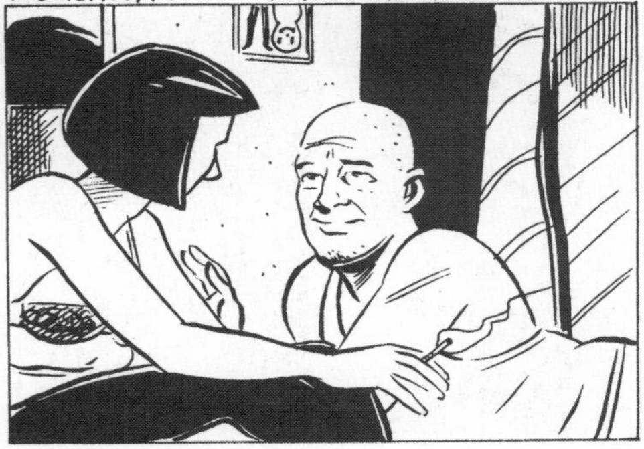

BY THE TIME WE GOT TO COLLEGE, WE DREADED THE THOUGHT OF BEING APART, SO WE TOOK UP AT THE SAME COLLEGE. WHEN SHE PAINTED LATE ON CAMPUS, I WOULD SNEAK IN AND WATCH HER.

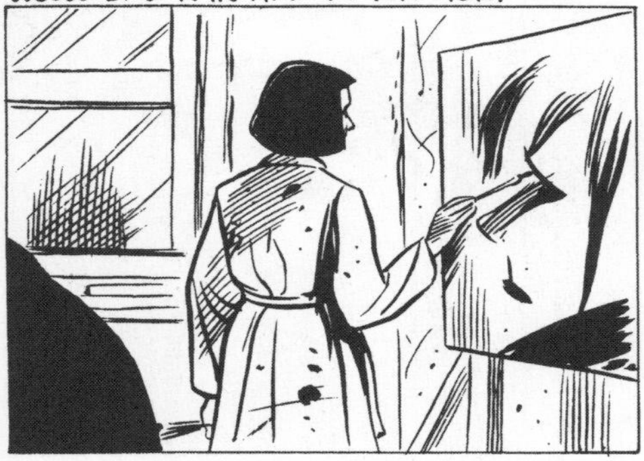

I WAS SO LUCKY, I THOUGHT.

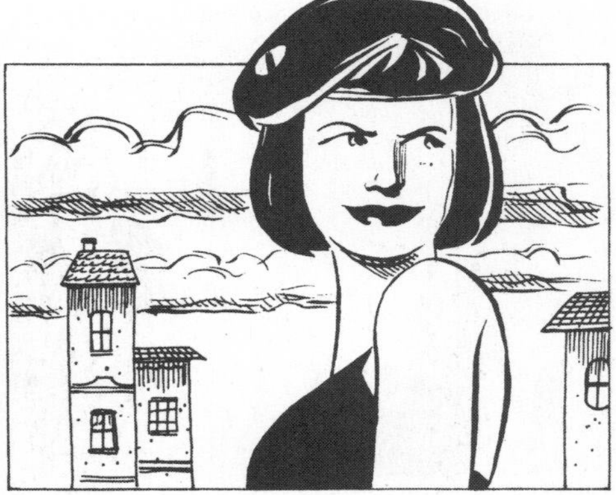

SOME MUSICIAN ONCE SAID, "YOU MEET YOUR BEST FRIENDS IN YOUR EARLY TWENTIES." I ALWAYS THINK OF THAT AND AGREE. I FINALLY FOUND FRIENDS I RESPECTED FULLY AND I KNEW I WOULD KNOW FOREVER.

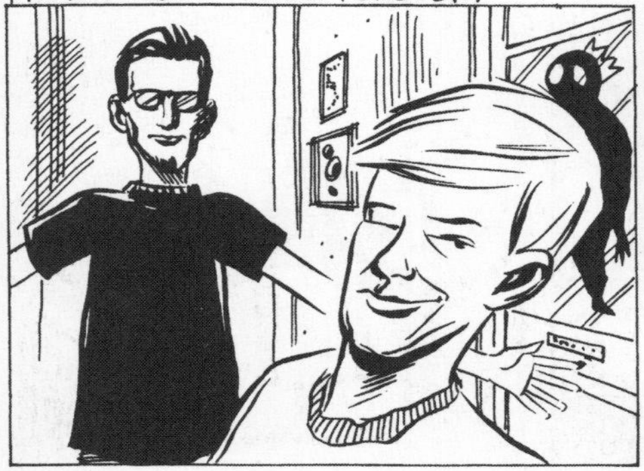

I ALWAYS KNEW MARY AND I WOULD KNOW EACHOTHER UNTIL WE DIED. WE MADE A PACT BEFORE WE EVEN ONCE TALKED ABOUT MARRIAGE: "ANYTHING, EVERYTHING, FOREVER."

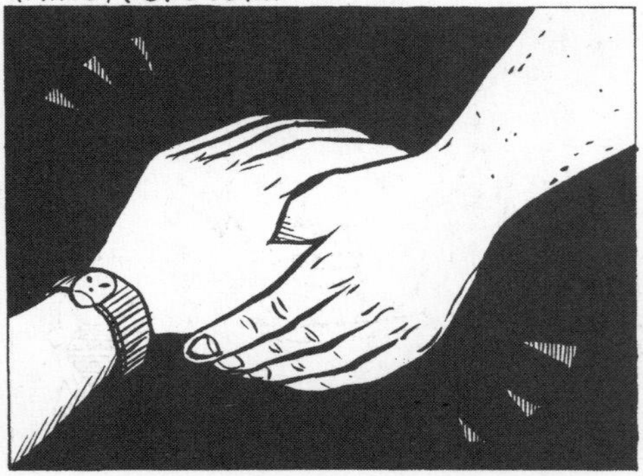

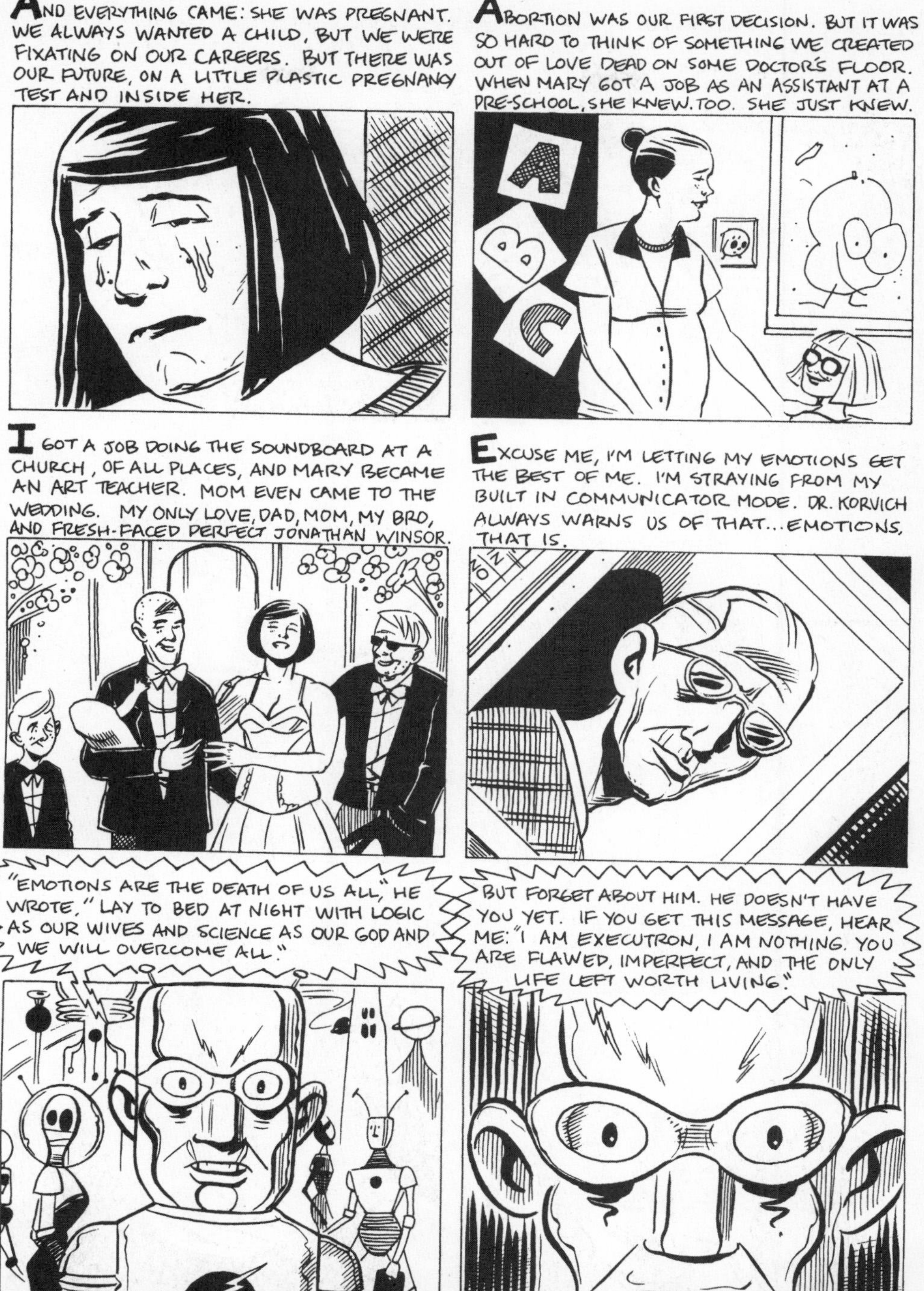
AND EVERYTHING CAME: SHE WAS PREGNANT. WE ALWAYS WANTED A CHILD, BUT WE WERE FIXATING ON OUR CAREERS. BUT THERE WAS OUR FUTURE, ON A LITTLE PLASTIC PREGNANCY TEST AND INSIDE HER.
ABORTION WAS OUR FIRST DECISION. BUT IT WAS SO HARD TO THINK OF SOMETHING WE CREATED OUT OF LOVE DEAD ON SOME DOCTOR'S FLOOR. WHEN MARY GOT A JOB AS AN ASSISTANT AT A PRE-SCHOOL, SHE KNEW, TOO. SHE JUST KNEW.
A
B
C
I GOT A JOB DOING THE SOUNDBOARD AT A CHURCH, OF ALL PLACES, AND MARY BECAME AN ART TEACHER. MOM EVEN CAME TO THE WEDDING. MY ONLY LOVE, DAD, MOM, MY BRO, AND FRESH-FACED PERFECT JONATHAN WINSOR.
EXCUSE ME, I'M LETTING MY EMOTIONS GET THE BEST OF ME. I'M STRAYING FROM MY BUILT IN COMMUNICATOR MODE. DR. KORVICH ALWAYS WARNS US OF THAT... EMOTIONS, THAT IS.
"EMOTIONS ARE THE DEATH OF US ALL," HE WROTE, "LAY TO BED AT NIGHT WITH LOGIC AS OUR WIVES AND SCIENCE AS OUR GOD AND WE WILL OVERCOME ALL."
BUT FORGET ABOUT HIM. HE DOESN'T HAVE YOU YET. IF YOU GET THIS MESSAGE, HEAR ME: "I AM EXECUTRON, I AM NOTHING. YOU ARE FLAWED, IMPERFECT, AND THE ONLY LIFE LEFT WORTH LIVING."
END

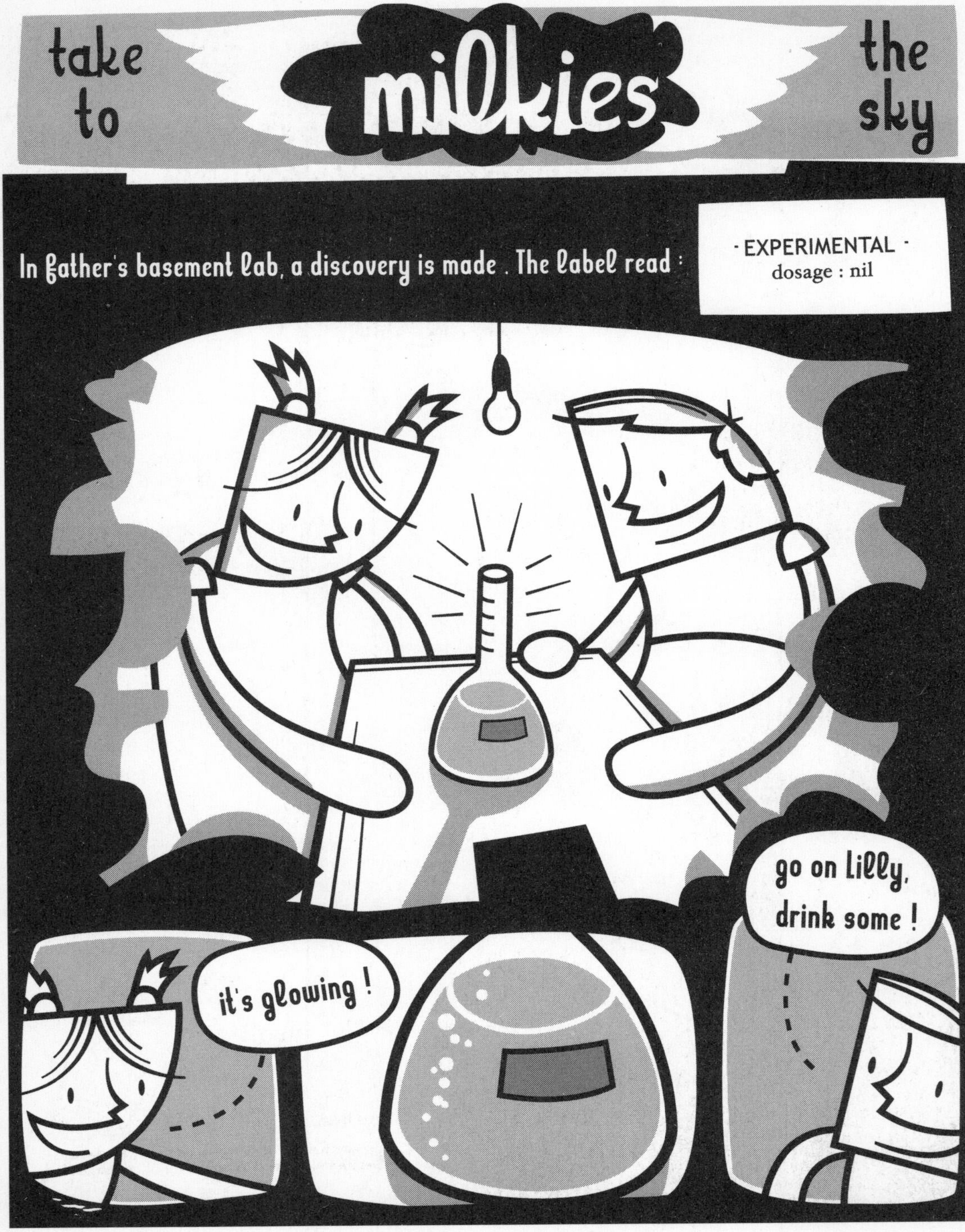
take to milkies the sky
In father's basement lab, a discovery is made. The label read:
- EXPERIMENTAL -
dosage : nil
it's glowing !
go on Lilly, drink some !

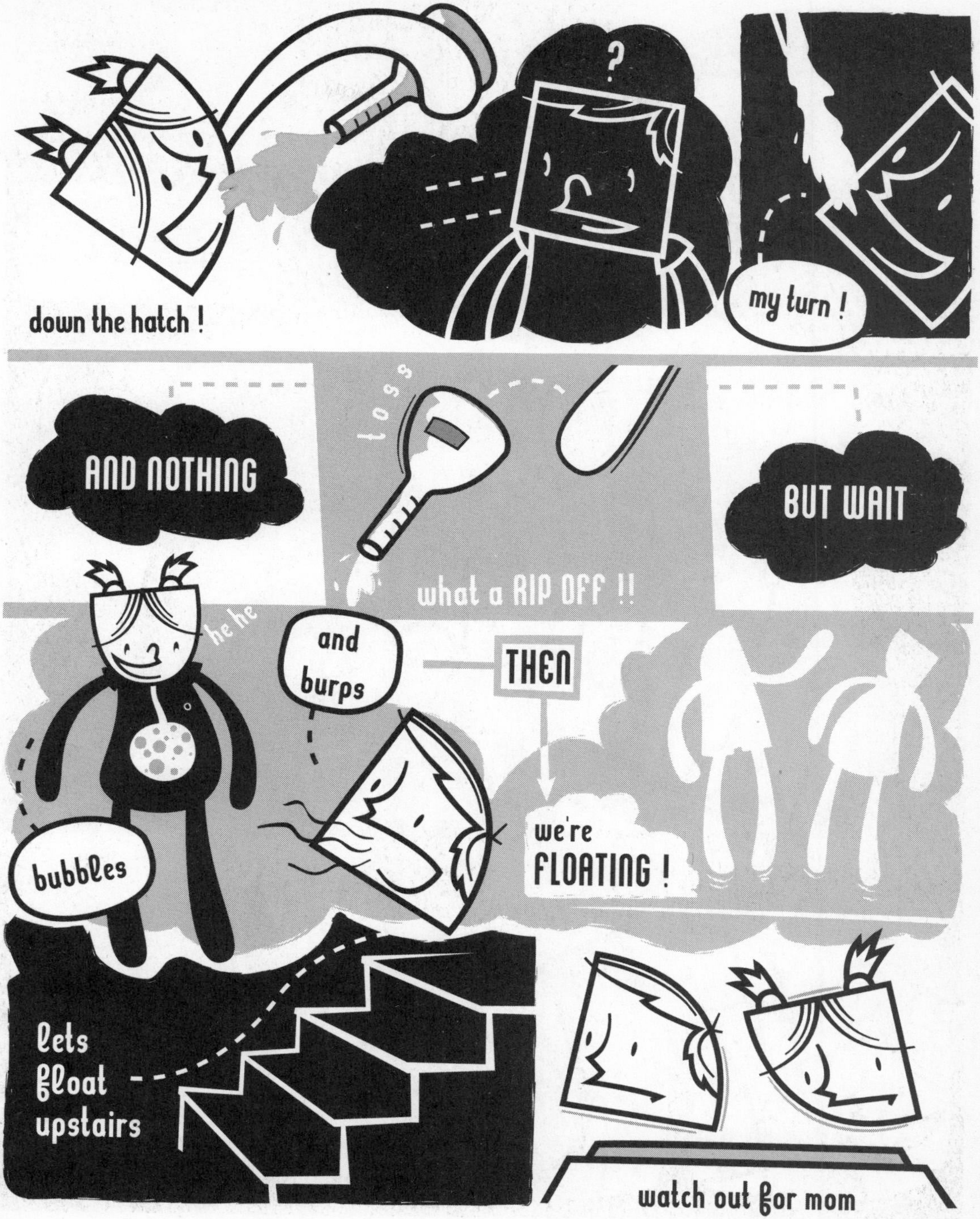
down the hatch !
?
my turn !
AND NOTHING
toss
what a RIP OFF !!
BUT WAIT
he he
bubbles
and burps
THEN
we're FLOATING !
lets float upstairs
watch out for mom

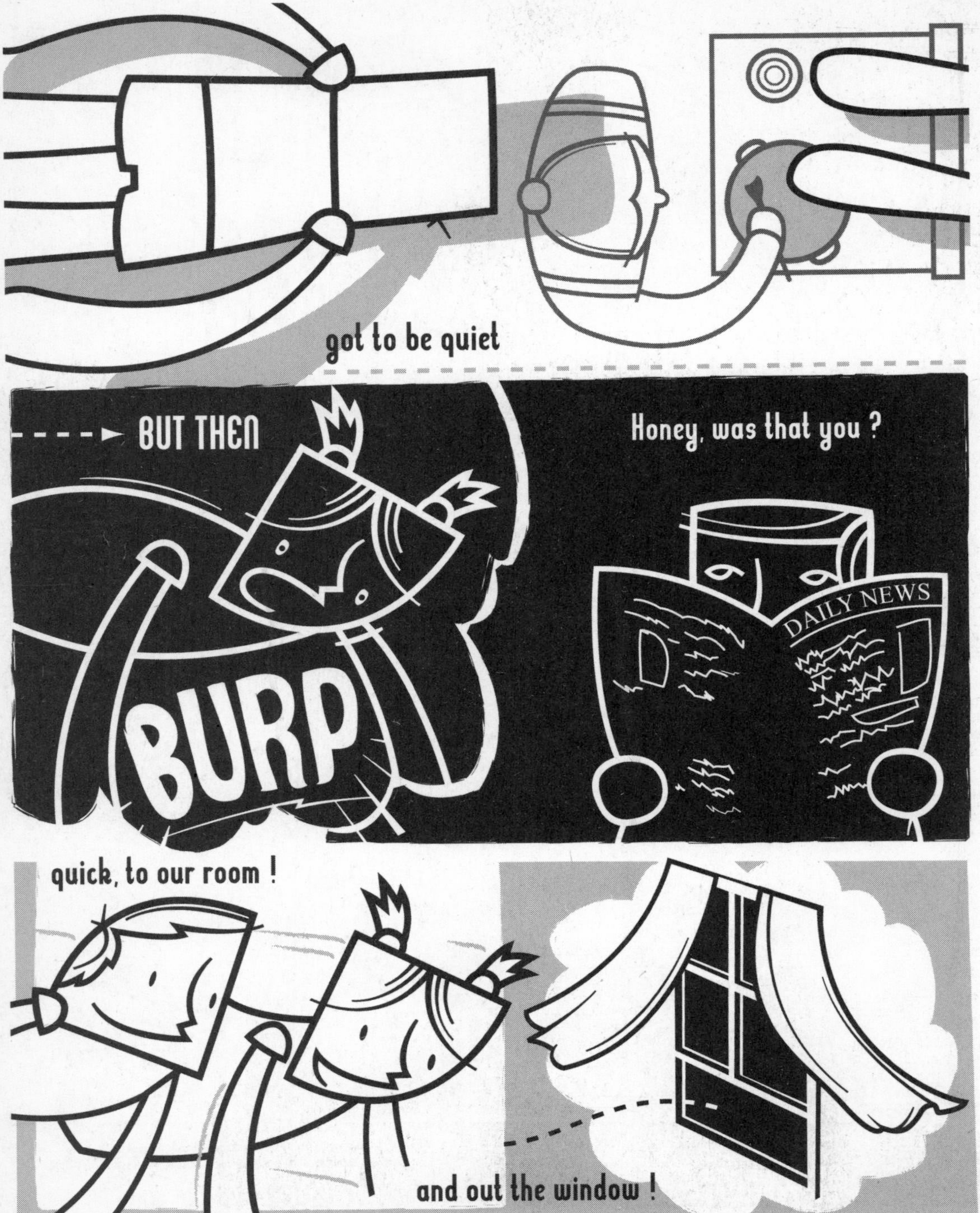
got to be quiet
BUT THEN
Honey, was that you ?
DAILY NEWS
BURP
quick, to our room !
and out the window !

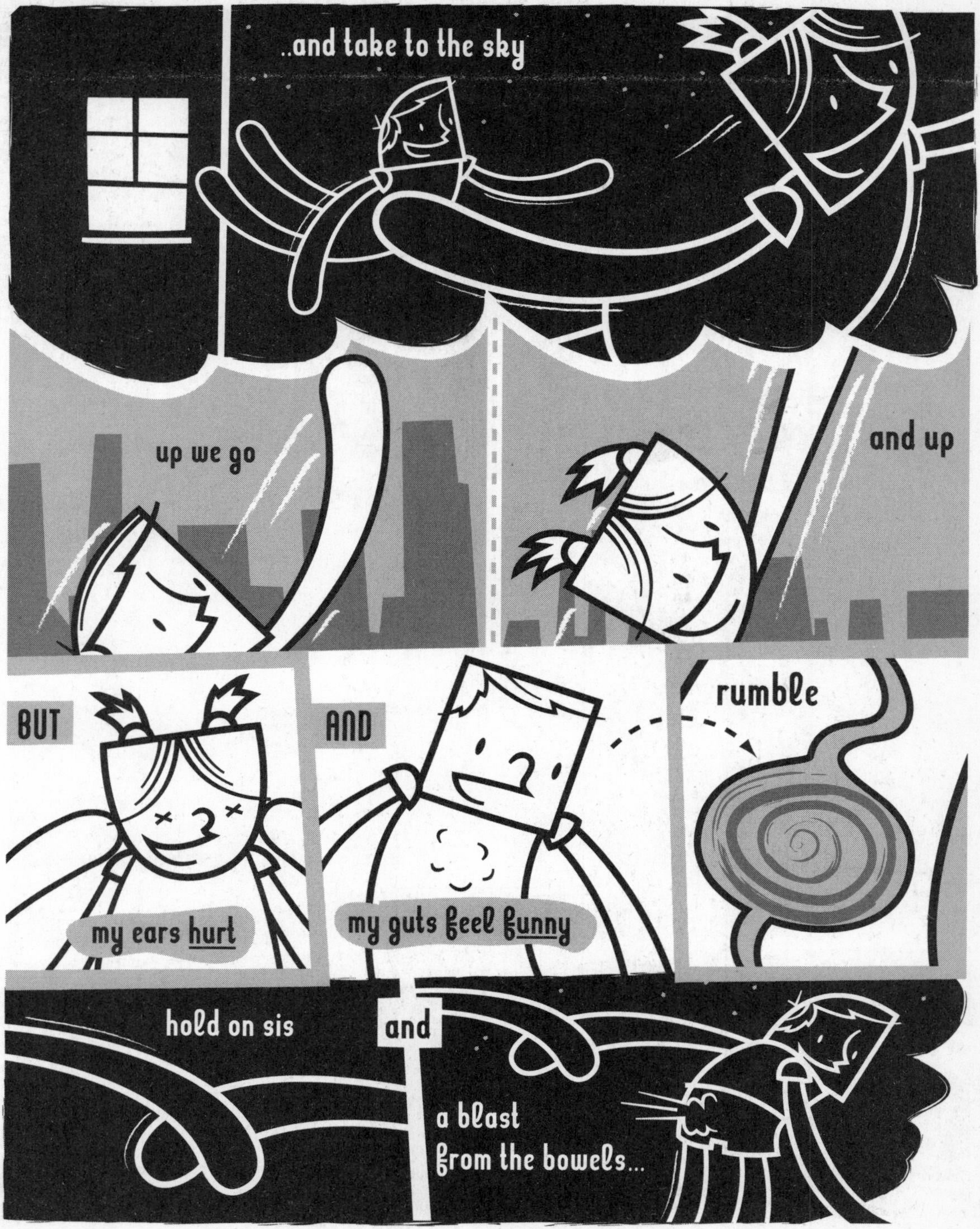
..and take to the sky
up we go
and up
BUT
my ears hurt
AND
my guts feel funny
rumble
hold on sis
and
a blast
from the bowels...

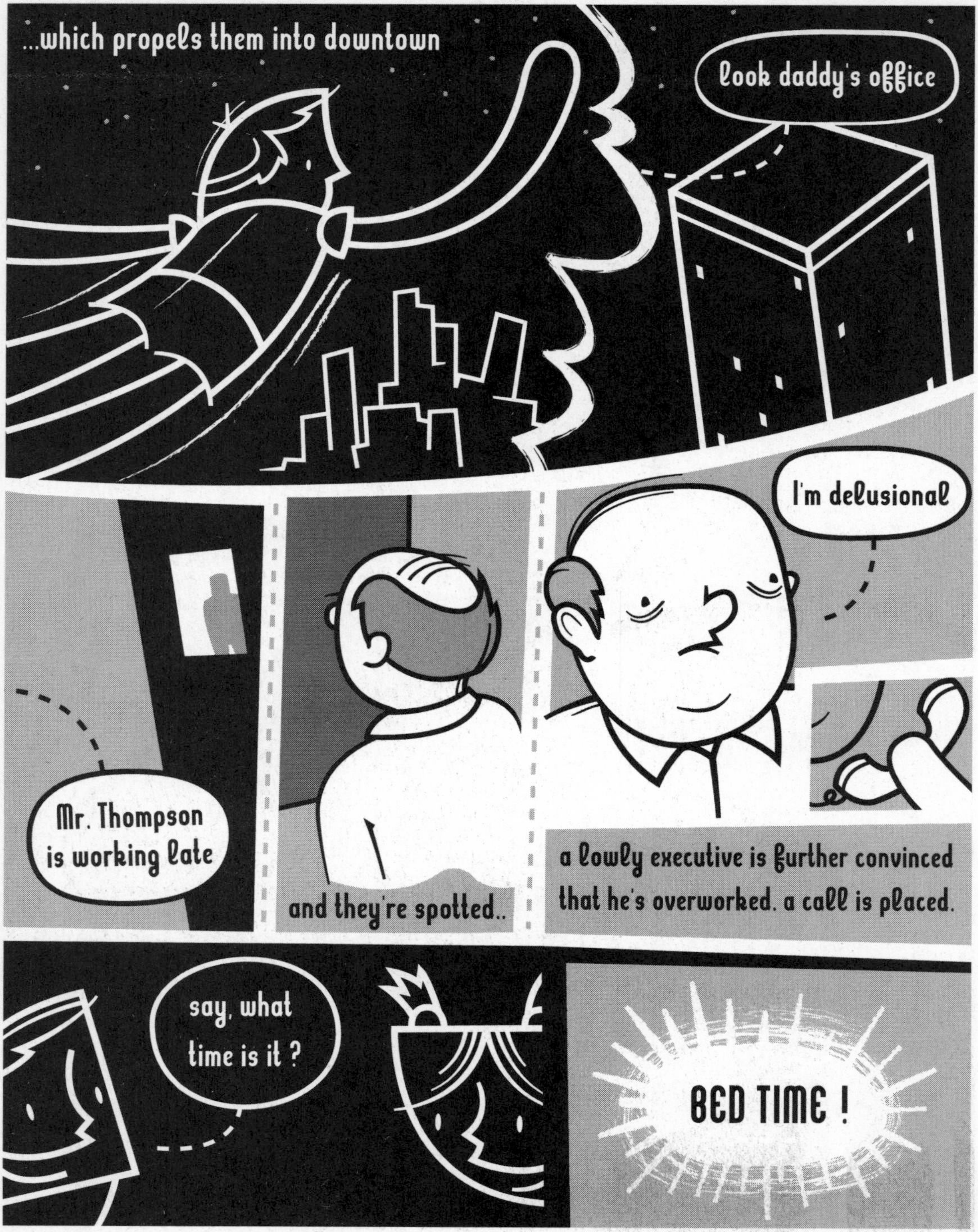
...which propels them into downtown
look daddy's office
Mr. Thompson is working late
and they're spotted..
I'm delusional
a lowly executive is further convinced that he's overworked. a call is placed.
say, what time is it ?
BED TIME !

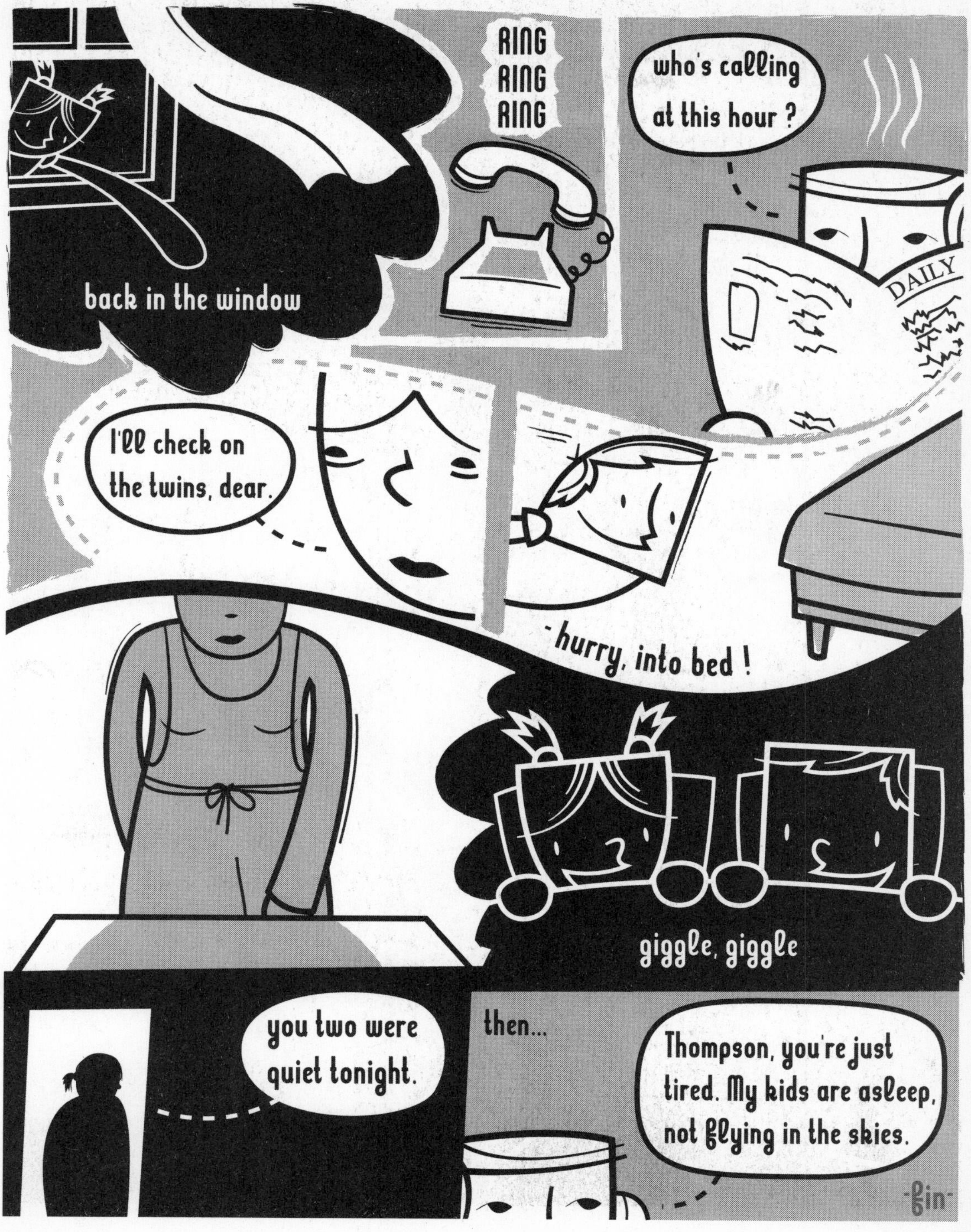

back in the window
RING RING RING
who's calling at this hour ?
DAILY
I'll check on the twins, dear.
- hurry, into bed !
giggle, giggle
you two were quiet tonight.
then...
Thompson, you're just tired. My kids are asleep, not flying in the skies.
-fin-

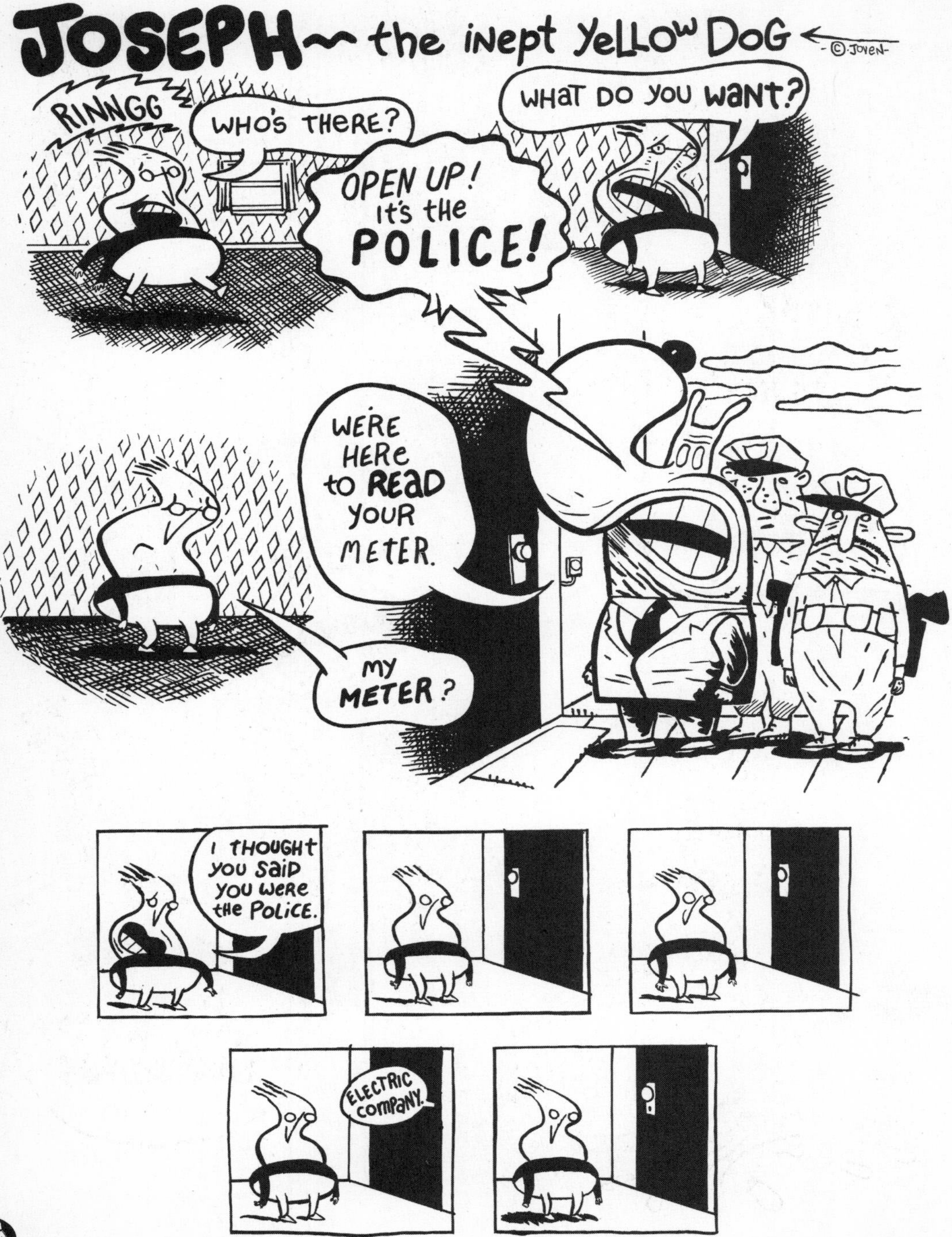
JOSEPH ~ the inept YeLLoW DoG
©·JOVEN·
RINNGG
WHO'S THERE?
WHAT DO YOU WANT?
OPEN UP! It's the POLICE!
WE'RE HERE to READ YOUR METER.
MY METER?
I THOUGHT YOU SAID YOU WERE the POLICE.
ELECTRIC COMPANY.

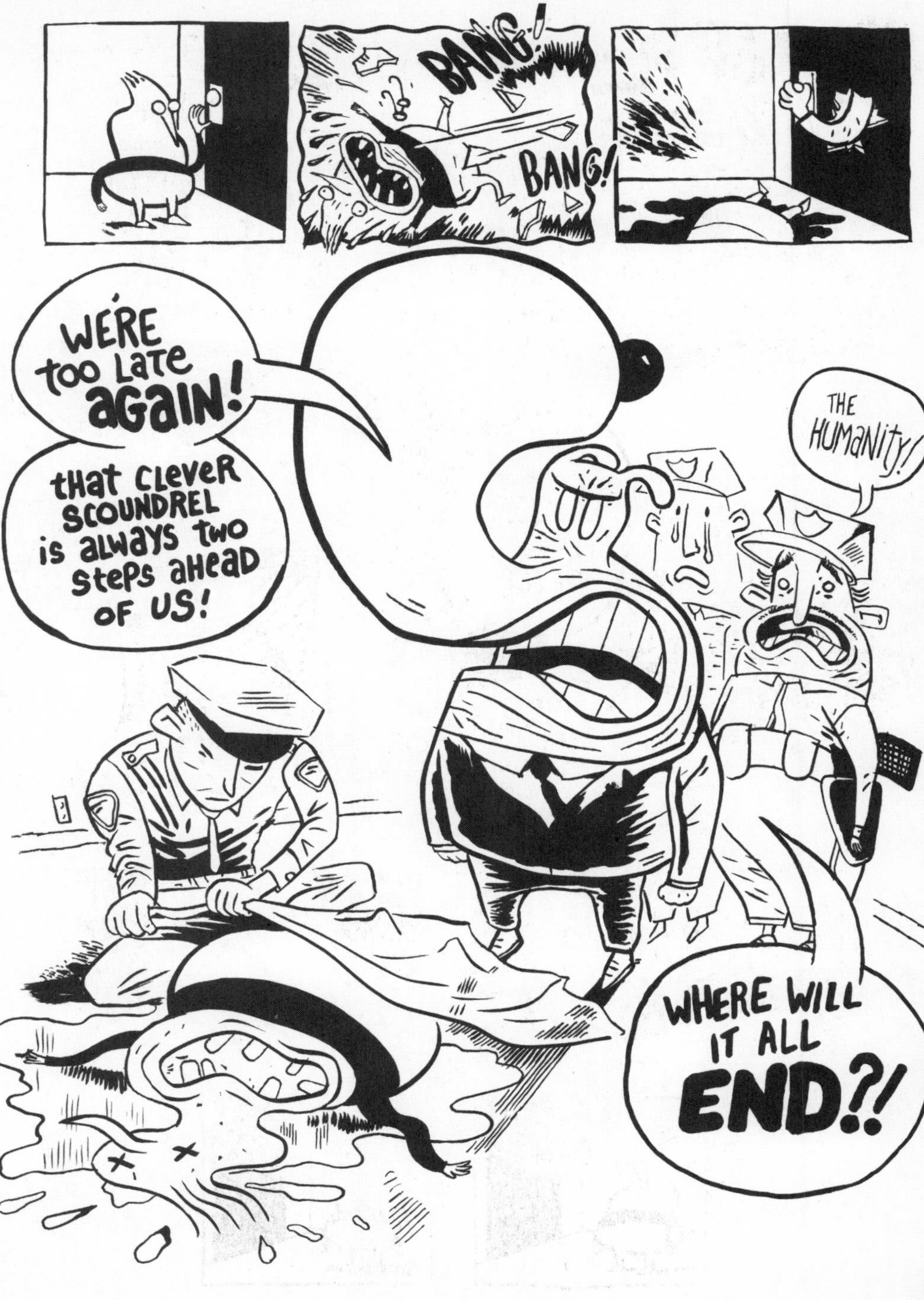
BANG!
BANG!
WE'RE too Late AGAIN!
that clever SCOUNDREL is always two steps ahead of US!
THE HUMANity!
WHERE WILL IT ALL END?!

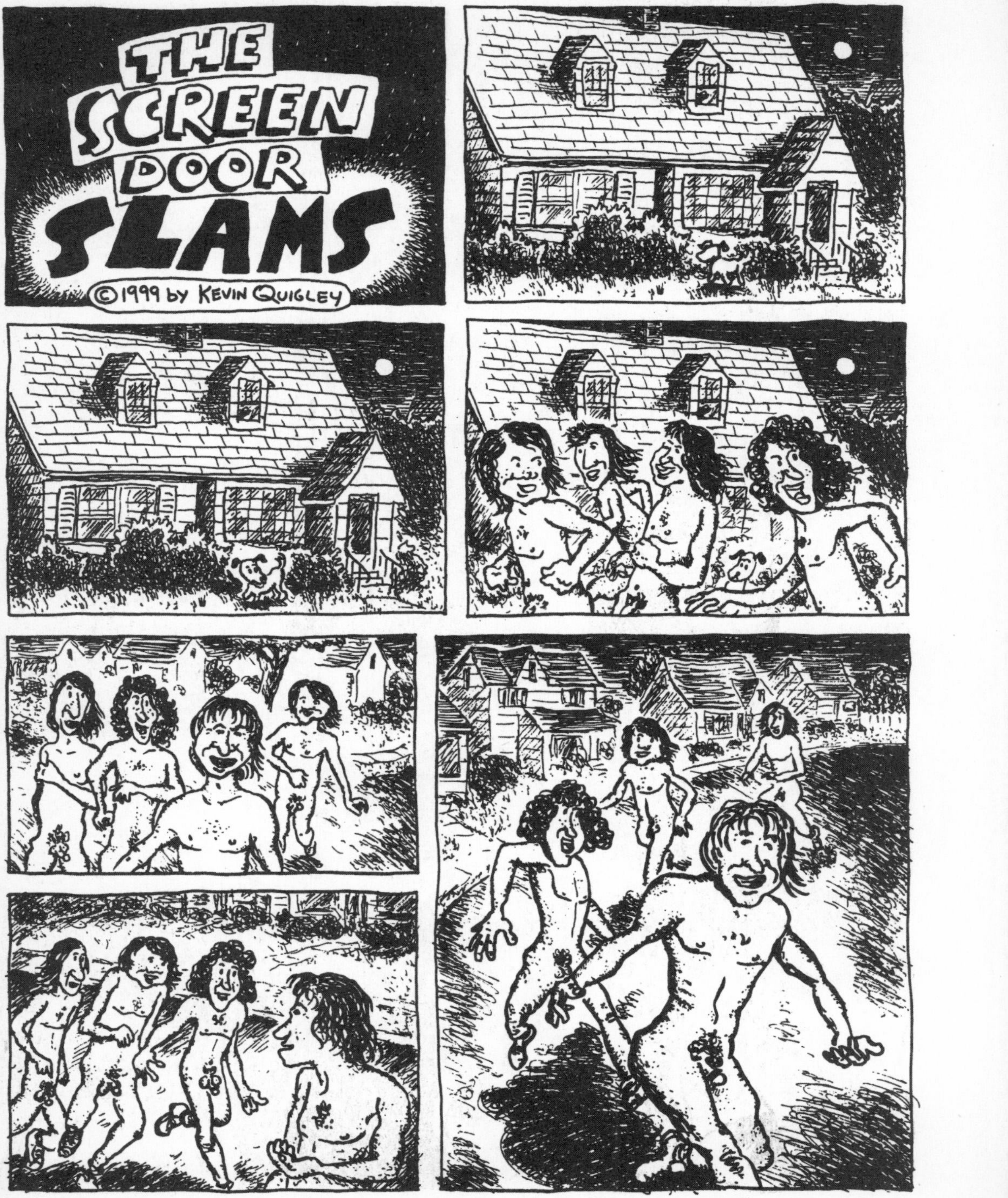
THE SCREEN DOOR SLAMS
©1999 by KEVIN QUIGLEY

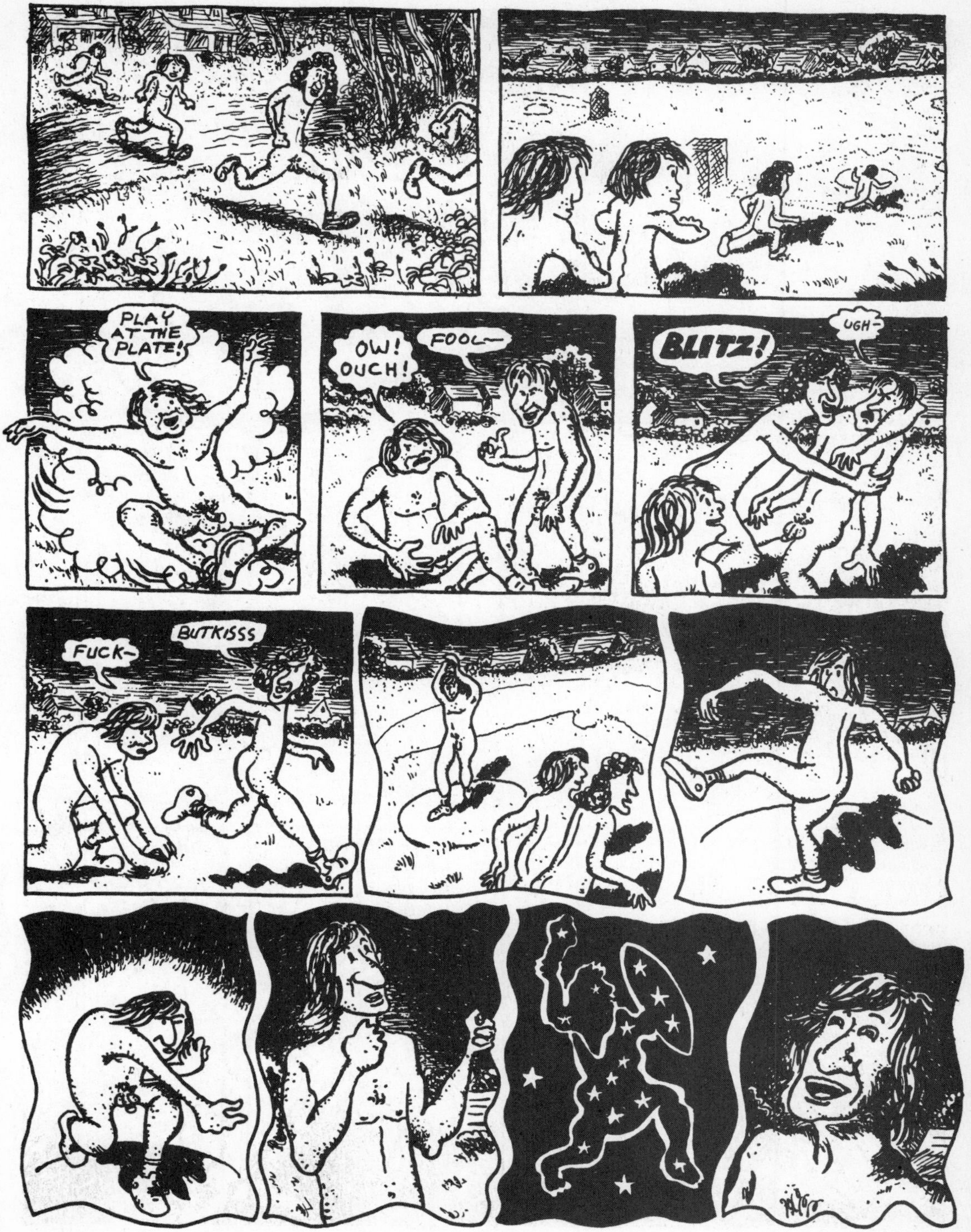
PLAY AT THE PLATE!
OW! OUCH!
FOOL—
BLITZ!
UGH-
FUCK-
BUTKISSS

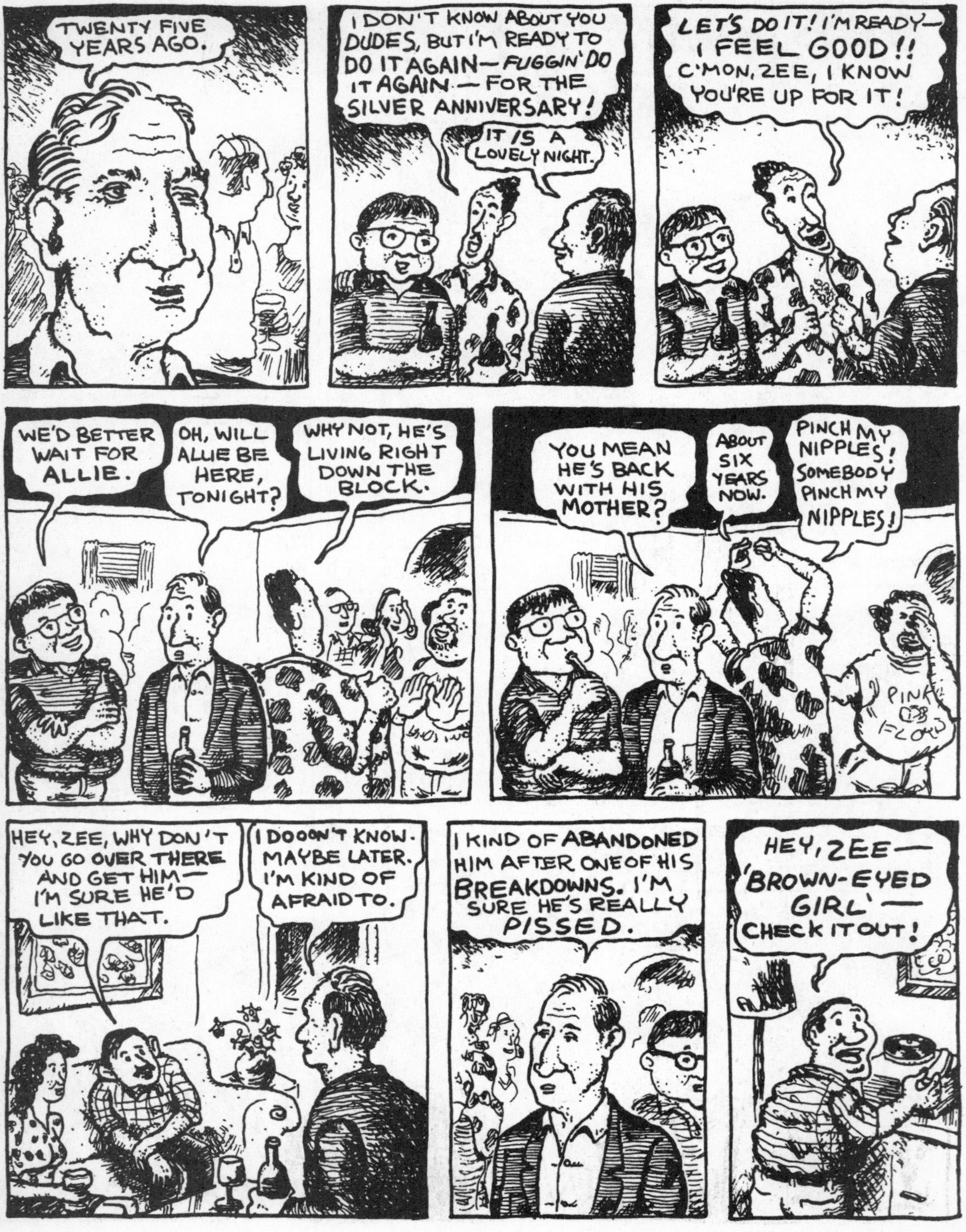
TWENTY FIVE YEARS AGO.
I DON'T KNOW ABOUT YOU DUDES, BUT I'M READY TO DO IT AGAIN—FUGGIN' DO IT AGAIN—FOR THE SILVER ANNIVERSARY!
IT IS A LOVELY NIGHT.
LET'S DO IT! I'M READY— I FEEL GOOD!! C'MON, ZEE, I KNOW YOU'RE UP FOR IT!
WE'D BETTER WAIT FOR ALLIE.
OH, WILL ALLIE BE HERE, TONIGHT?
WHY NOT, HE'S LIVING RIGHT DOWN THE BLOCK.
YOU MEAN HE'S BACK WITH HIS MOTHER?
ABOUT SIX YEARS NOW.
PINCH MY NIPPLES! SOMEBODY PINCH MY NIPPLES!
HEY, ZEE, WHY DON'T YOU GO OVER THERE AND GET HIM— I'M SURE HE'D LIKE THAT.
I DOOON'T KNOW. MAYBE LATER. I'M KIND OF AFRAID TO.
I KIND OF ABANDONED HIM AFTER ONE OF HIS BREAKDOWNS. I'M SURE HE'S REALLY PISSED.
HEY, ZEE— 'BROWN-EYED GIRL'— CHECK IT OUT!

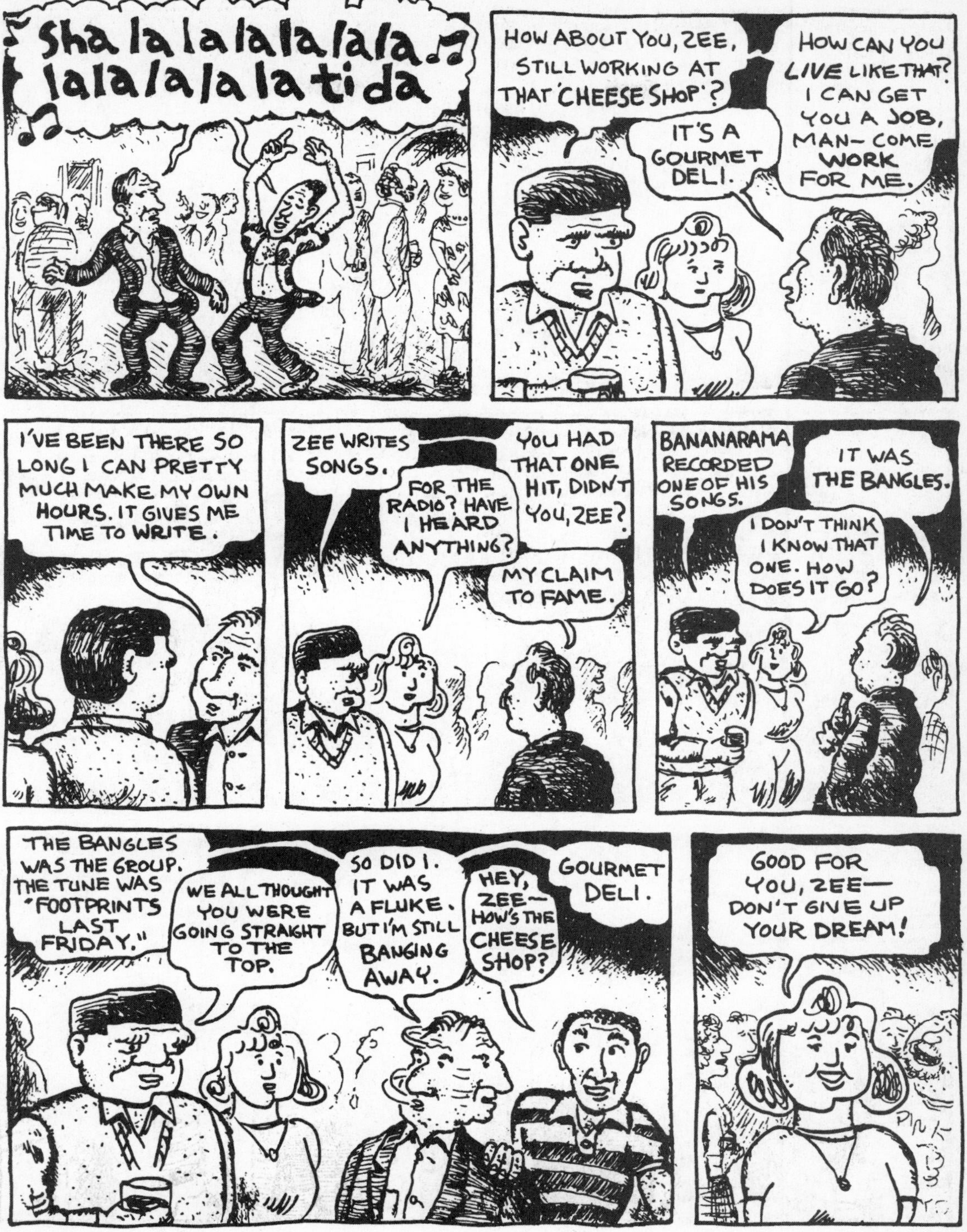
Sha la la la la la la la
la la la la la la ti da
HOW ABOUT YOU, ZEE, STILL WORKING AT THAT 'CHEESE SHOP'?
IT'S A GOURMET DELI.
HOW CAN YOU LIVE LIKE THAT? I CAN GET YOU A JOB, MAN— COME WORK FOR ME.
I'VE BEEN THERE SO LONG I CAN PRETTY MUCH MAKE MY OWN HOURS. IT GIVES ME TIME TO WRITE.
ZEE WRITES SONGS.
FOR THE RADIO? HAVE I HEARD ANYTHING?
YOU HAD THAT ONE HIT, DIDN'T YOU, ZEE?
MY CLAIM TO FAME.
BANANARAMA RECORDED ONE OF HIS SONGS.
IT WAS THE BANGLES.
I DON'T THINK I KNOW THAT ONE. HOW DOES IT GO?
THE BANGLES WAS THE GROUP. THE TUNE WAS "FOOTPRINTS LAST FRIDAY."
WE ALL THOUGHT YOU WERE GOING STRAIGHT TO THE TOP.
SO DID I. IT WAS A FLUKE. BUT I'M STILL BANGING AWAY.
HEY, ZEE— HOW'S THE CHEESE SHOP?
GOURMET DELI.
GOOD FOR YOU, ZEE— DON'T GIVE UP YOUR DREAM!

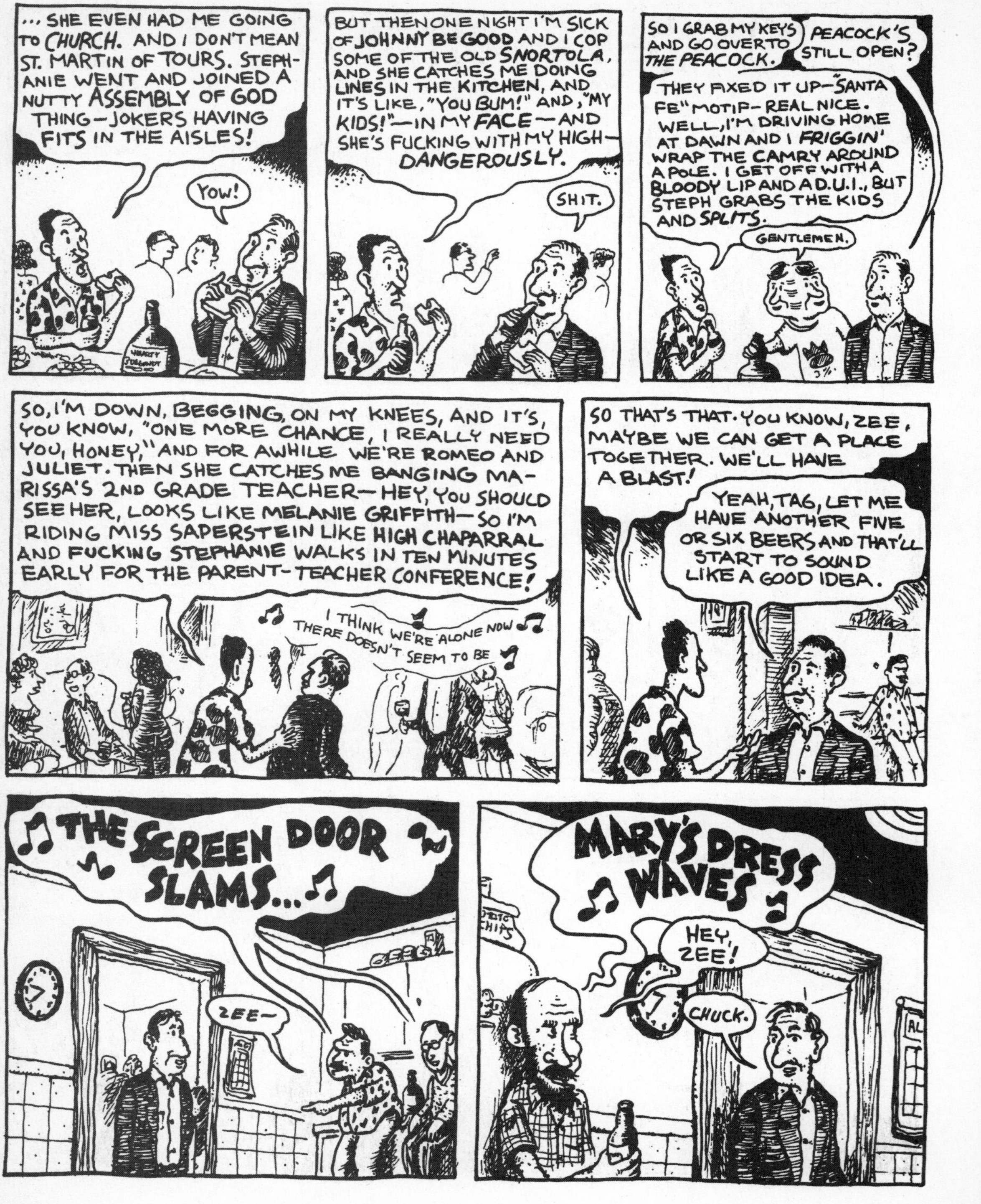
...SHE EVEN HAD ME GOING TO CHURCH. AND I DON'T MEAN ST. MARTIN OF TOURS. STEPHANIE WENT AND JOINED A NUTTY ASSEMBLY OF GOD THING—JOKERS HAVING FITS IN THE AISLES!
YOW!
BUT THEN ONE NIGHT I'M SICK OF JOHNNY BE GOOD AND I COP SOME OF THE OLD SNORTOLA, AND SHE CATCHES ME DOING LINES IN THE KITCHEN, AND IT'S LIKE, "YOU BUM!" AND, "MY KIDS!"—IN MY FACE—AND SHE'S FUCKING WITH MY HIGH—DANGEROUSLY.
SHIT.
SO I GRAB MY KEYS AND GO OVER TO THE PEACOCK.
PEACOCK'S STILL OPEN?
THEY FIXED IT UP—"SANTA FE" MOTIF—REAL NICE. WELL, I'M DRIVING HOME AT DAWN AND I FRIGGIN' WRAP THE CAMRY AROUND A POLE. I GET OFF WITH A BLOODY LIP AND A D.U.I., BUT STEPH GRABS THE KIDS AND SPLITS.
GENTLEMEN.
SO, I'M DOWN, BEGGING, ON MY KNEES, AND IT'S, YOU KNOW, "ONE MORE CHANCE, I REALLY NEED YOU, HONEY," AND FOR AWHILE WE'RE ROMEO AND JULIET. THEN SHE CATCHES ME BANGING MARISSA'S 2ND GRADE TEACHER—HEY, YOU SHOULD SEE HER, LOOKS LIKE MELANIE GRIFFITH—SO I'M RIDING MISS SAPERSTEIN LIKE HIGH CHAPARRAL AND FUCKING STEPHANIE WALKS IN TEN MINUTES EARLY FOR THE PARENT-TEACHER CONFERENCE!
I THINK WE'RE ALONE NOW
THERE DOESN'T SEEM TO BE
SO THAT'S THAT. YOU KNOW, ZEE, MAYBE WE CAN GET A PLACE TOGETHER. WE'LL HAVE A BLAST!
YEAH, TAG, LET ME HAVE ANOTHER FIVE OR SIX BEERS AND THAT'LL START TO SOUND LIKE A GOOD IDEA.
THE SCREEN DOOR SLAMS...
ZEE—
MARY'S DRESS WAVES
HEY, ZEE!
CHUCK.

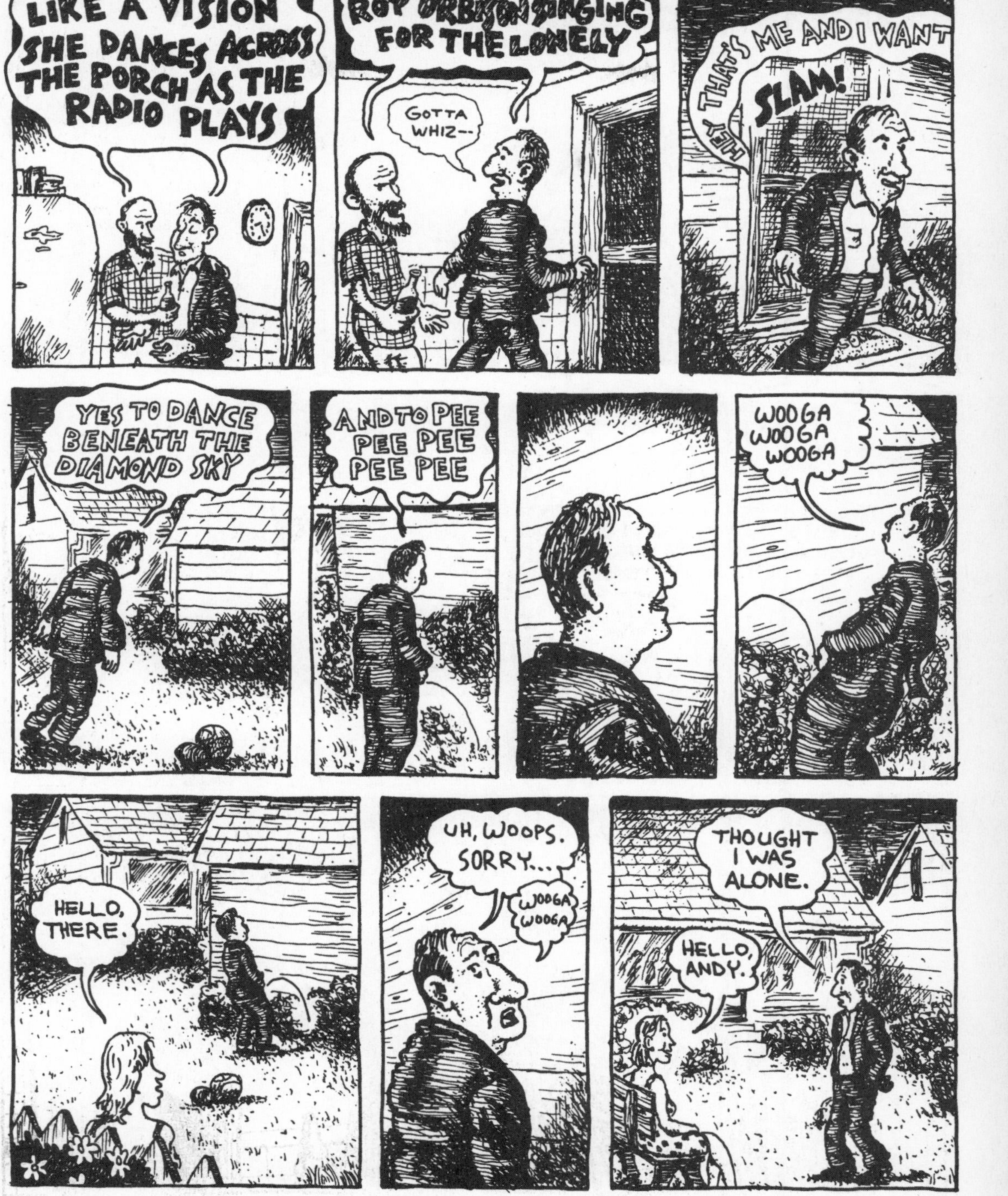

LIKE A VISION SHE DANCES ACROSS THE PORCH AS THE RADIO PLAYS
ROY ORBISON SINGING FOR THE LONELY
GOTTA WHIZ--
HEY THAT'S ME AND I WANT
SLAM!
YES TO DANCE BENEATH THE DIAMOND SKY
AND TO PEE PEE PEE PEE PEE
WOOGA WOOGA WOOGA
HELLO, THERE.
UH, WOOPS. SORRY...
WOOGA WOOGA
THOUGHT I WAS ALONE.
HELLO, ANDY.

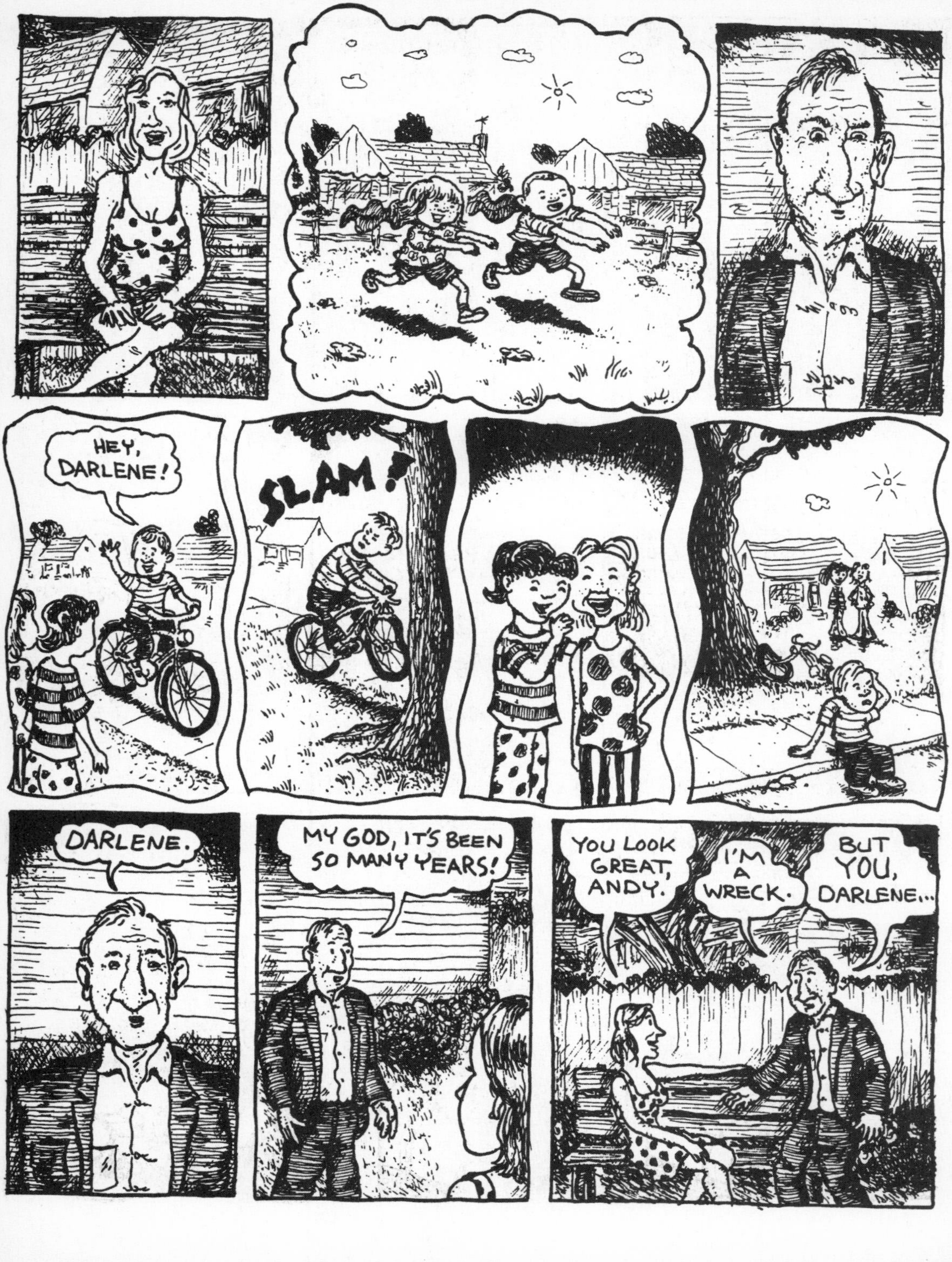
HEY, DARLENE!
SLAM!
DARLENE.
MY GOD, IT'S BEEN SO MANY YEARS!
YOU LOOK GREAT, ANDY.
I'M A WRECK.
BUT YOU, DARLENE...

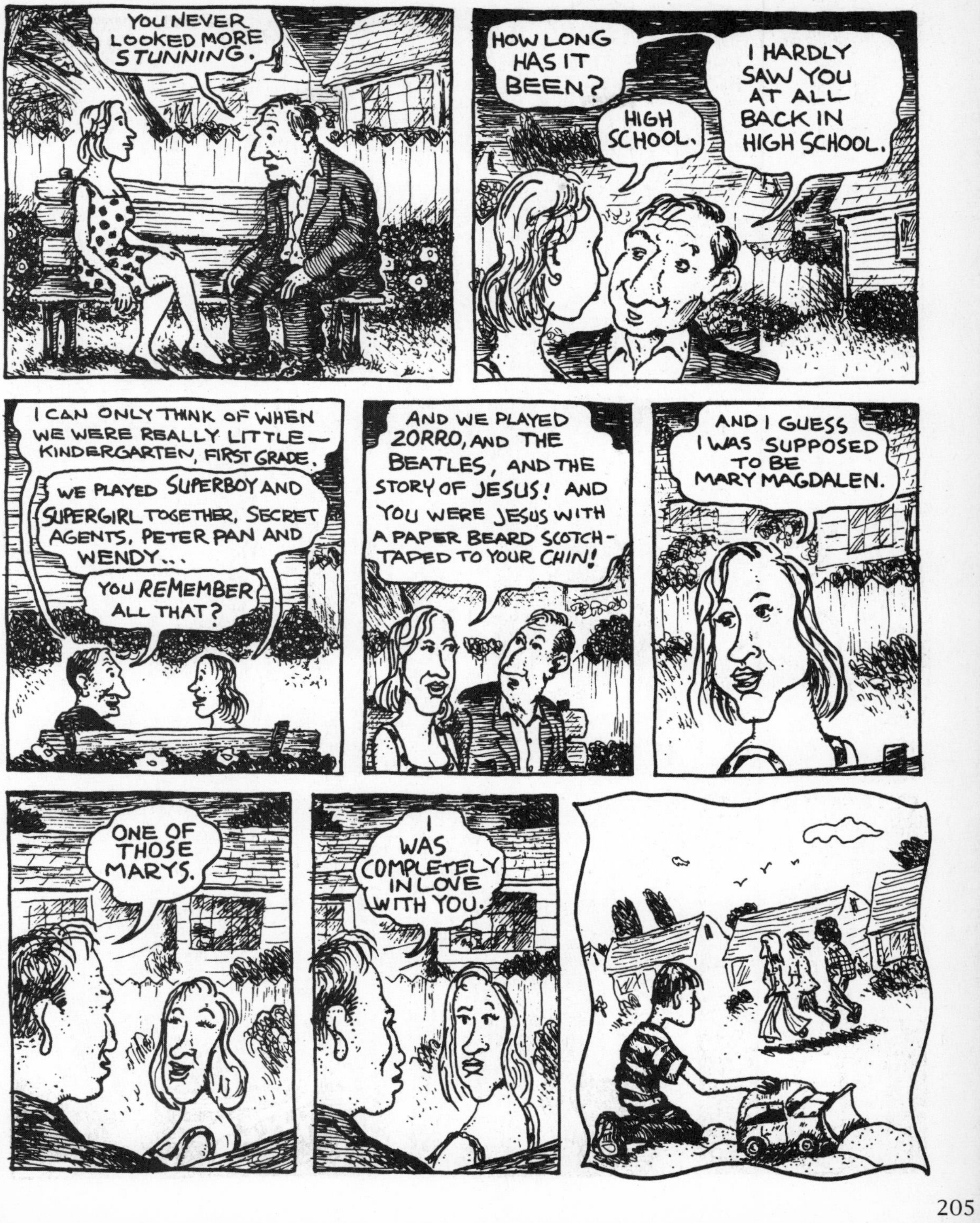

YOU NEVER LOOKED MORE STUNNING.
HOW LONG HAS IT BEEN?
HIGH SCHOOL.
I HARDLY SAW YOU AT ALL BACK IN HIGH SCHOOL.
I CAN ONLY THINK OF WHEN WE WERE REALLY LITTLE— KINDERGARTEN, FIRST GRADE.
WE PLAYED SUPERBOY AND SUPERGIRL TOGETHER, SECRET AGENTS, PETER PAN AND WENDY...
YOU REMEMBER ALL THAT?
AND WE PLAYED ZORRO, AND THE BEATLES, AND THE STORY OF JESUS! AND YOU WERE JESUS WITH A PAPER BEARD SCOTCH-TAPED TO YOUR CHIN!
AND I GUESS I WAS SUPPOSED TO BE MARY MAGDALEN.
ONE OF THOSE MARYS.
I WAS COMPLETELY IN LOVE WITH YOU.

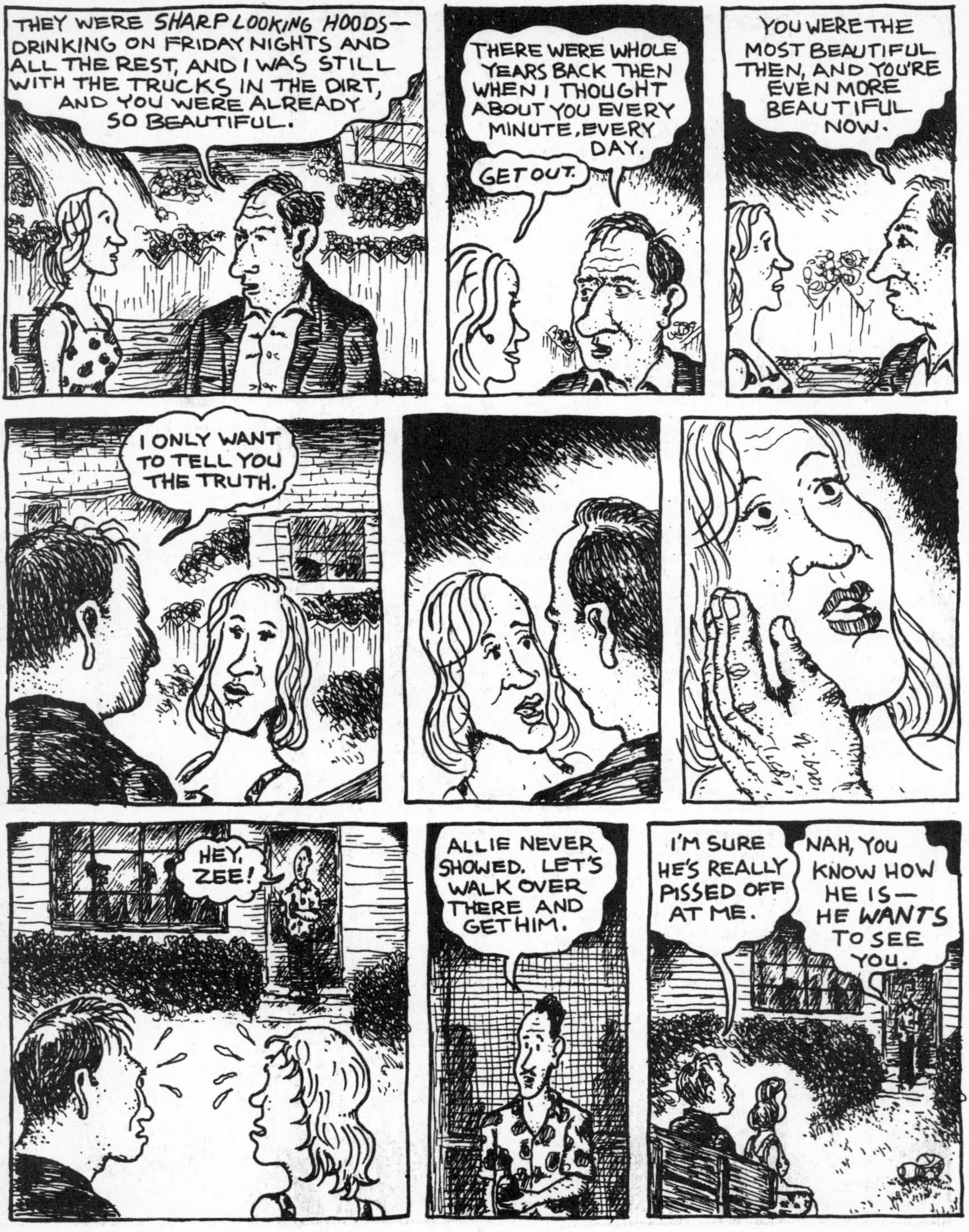
THEY WERE SHARP LOOKING HOODS— DRINKING ON FRIDAY NIGHTS AND ALL THE REST, AND I WAS STILL WITH THE TRUCKS IN THE DIRT, AND YOU WERE ALREADY SO BEAUTIFUL.
THERE WERE WHOLE YEARS BACK THEN WHEN I THOUGHT ABOUT YOU EVERY MINUTE, EVERY DAY.
GET OUT.
YOU WERE THE MOST BEAUTIFUL THEN, AND YOU'RE EVEN MORE BEAUTIFUL NOW.
I ONLY WANT TO TELL YOU THE TRUTH.
HEY, ZEE!
ALLIE NEVER SHOWED. LET'S WALK OVER THERE AND GET HIM.
I'M SURE HE'S REALLY PISSED OFF AT ME.
NAH, YOU KNOW HOW HE IS— HE WANTS TO SEE YOU.

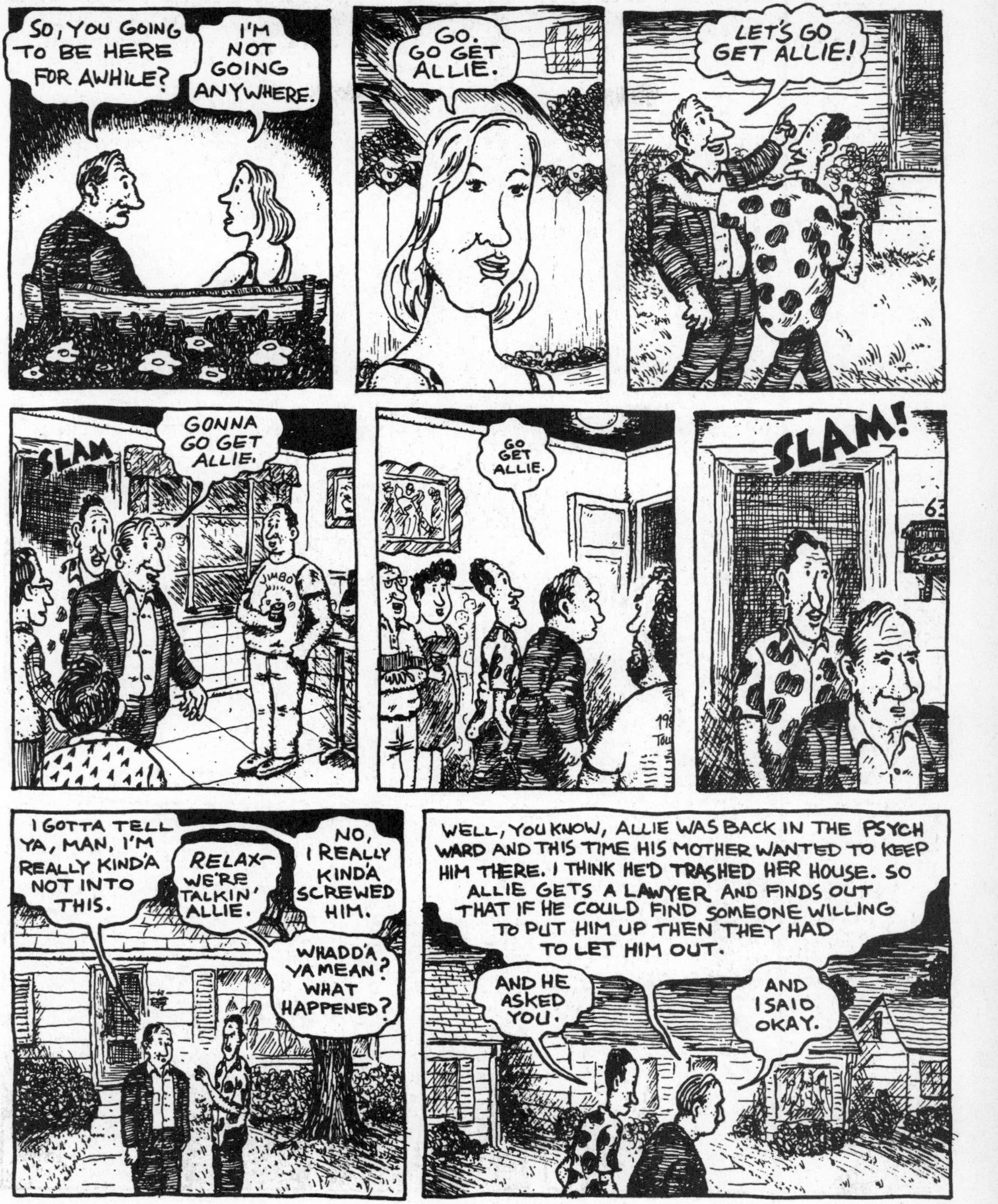

SO, YOU GOING TO BE HERE FOR AWHILE?
I'M NOT GOING ANYWHERE.
GO. GO GET ALLIE.
LET'S GO GET ALLIE!
SLAM
GONNA GO GET ALLIE.
JIMBO
GO GET ALLIE.
SLAM!
I GOTTA TELL YA, MAN, I'M REALLY KIND'A NOT INTO THIS.
RELAX- WE'RE TALKIN' ALLIE.
NO, I REALLY KIND'A SCREWED HIM.
WHADD'A YA MEAN? WHAT HAPPENED?
WELL, YOU KNOW, ALLIE WAS BACK IN THE PSYCH WARD AND THIS TIME HIS MOTHER WANTED TO KEEP HIM THERE. I THINK HE'D TRASHED HER HOUSE. SO ALLIE GETS A LAWYER AND FINDS OUT THAT IF HE COULD FIND SOMEONE WILLING TO PUT HIM UP THEN THEY HAD TO LET HIM OUT.
AND HE ASKED YOU.
AND I SAID OKAY.

BUT THE THING IS, THE DOCTORS WANTED TO KEEP HIM THERE, TOO. AND FOR GOING OVER THEIR HEADS, THEY DECIDED TO FUCK HIM. SO THEY TOOK HIM—COLD TURKEY—OFF THE DRUGS HE'D BEEN ON FOR TWENTY YEARS.

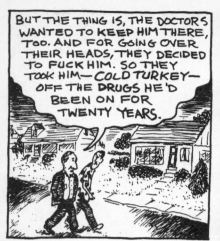

AND THE DRUGS, ALL THOSE YEARS, HAD MADE HIM IMPOTENT, AND SUDDENLY HE'S LONG DONG SILVER.

ALLIE.

SO I GO OUT TO MEET HIM AT THE MOTEL HE'S STAYING AT, AND HE DRIVES ME OVER TO THE MALL TO SHOW ME THIS MARILYN MONROE BOOK.

ZEE, MAN, YOU GOTTA SEE HER!

HE WANTED ME TO SEE HOW GORGEOUS SHE WAS BACK WHEN SHE WAS STILL NORMA JEAN. SO, THERE'S ALLIE IN THE BOOKSTORE JUST CRACKLING WITH ENERGY AND RHAPSODISING OVER MARILYN, AND AT THAT POINT IT WAS ALMOST CHARMING.

LOOK IT HER SKIN, ZEE—PRAISE GOD!

BUT THEN WE MOVE OVER TO THE MAGAZINE RACK, AND ALLIE GOES OFF. HE STARTS PAGING THROUGH THE CLUBS AND THE SWANKS AND SHOUTING STUFF LIKE, "I'D MUNCH THOSE TITS 'TIL THE COWS COME HOME!"

PUSSY JUICE! PUSSY JUICE!

WE GO BACK TO HIS MOTEL ROOM AND I LAY INTO HIM—REAL INDIGNANT—"ALLIE, THERE WERE LITTLE KIDS IN THAT STORE!" I CAN SEE THAT I HURT HIS FEELINGS, AND WE GET INTO THIS HUGE, REALLY PERSONAL FIGHT.

MR. SELF-RIGHTEOUS, EAST VILLAGE, BULL-SHIT, BOHEMIAN ROCK STAR— MAN, YOU'RE JUST A HYPOCRITE!

AND, OF COURSE, HE'S RIGHT—I AM A HYPOCRITE. BUT SOME DEGREE OF HYPOCRISY IS A GOOD AND NECESSARY THING.

DAMN STRAIGHT.

IT'S THE GLUE.

WRITE A SONG ABOUT IT.

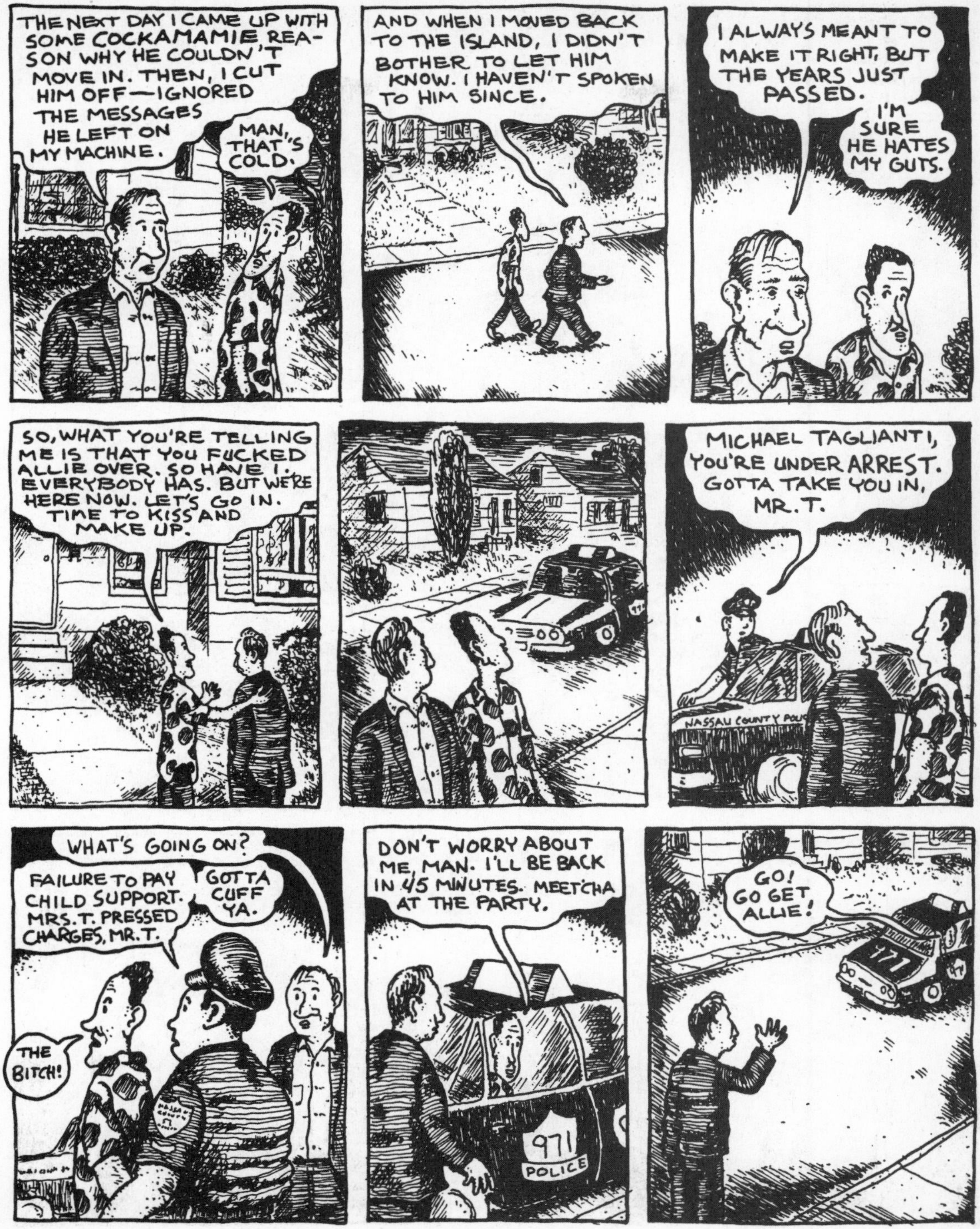
THE NEXT DAY I CAME UP WITH SOME COCKAMAMIE REASON WHY HE COULDN'T MOVE IN. THEN, I CUT HIM OFF—IGNORED THE MESSAGES HE LEFT ON MY MACHINE.
MAN, THAT'S COLD.
AND WHEN I MOVED BACK TO THE ISLAND, I DIDN'T BOTHER TO LET HIM KNOW. I HAVEN'T SPOKEN TO HIM SINCE.
I ALWAYS MEANT TO MAKE IT RIGHT, BUT THE YEARS JUST PASSED.
I'M SURE HE HATES MY GUTS.
SO, WHAT YOU'RE TELLING ME IS THAT YOU FUCKED ALLIE OVER. SO HAVE I. EVERYBODY HAS. BUT WE'RE HERE NOW. LET'S GO IN. TIME TO KISS AND MAKE UP.
MICHAEL TAGLIANTI, YOU'RE UNDER ARREST. GOTTA TAKE YOU IN, MR. T.
NASSAU COUNTY POLICE
WHAT'S GOING ON?
FAILURE TO PAY CHILD SUPPORT. MRS. T. PRESSED CHARGES, MR. T.
GOTTA CUFF YA.
THE BITCH!
DON'T WORRY ABOUT ME, MAN. I'LL BE BACK IN 45 MINUTES. MEET'CHA AT THE PARTY.
971
POLICE
GO! GO GET ALLIE!

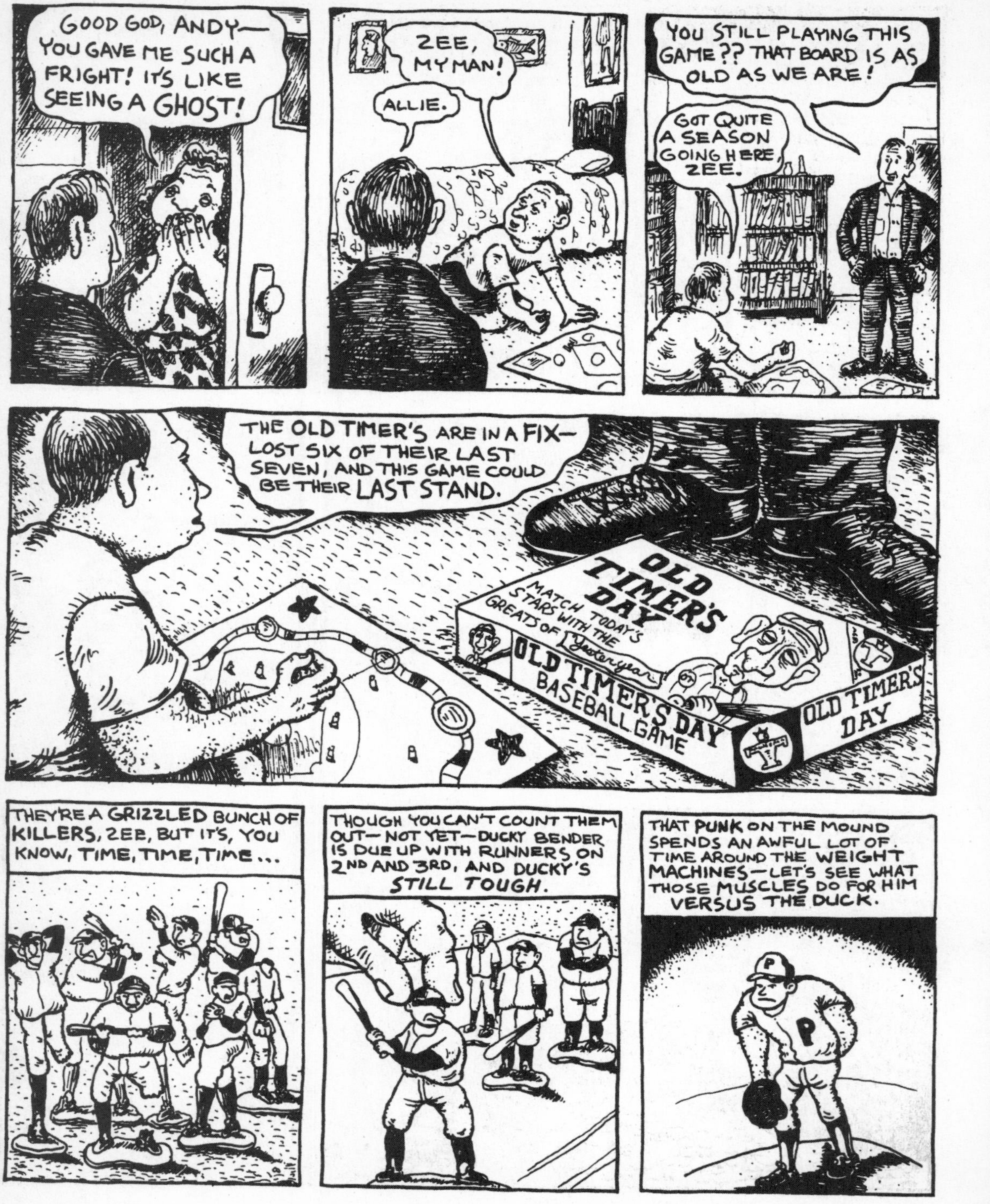
GOOD GOD, ANDY— YOU GAVE ME SUCH A FRIGHT! IT'S LIKE SEEING A GHOST!
ZEE, MY MAN!
ALLIE.
YOU STILL PLAYING THIS GAME?? THAT BOARD IS AS OLD AS WE ARE!
GOT QUITE A SEASON GOING HERE, ZEE.
THE OLD TIMER'S ARE IN A FIX— LOST SIX OF THEIR LAST SEVEN, AND THIS GAME COULD BE THEIR LAST STAND.
OLD TIMER'S DAY
MATCH TODAY'S STARS WITH THE GREATS OF Yesteryear
OLD TIMER'S DAY BASEBALL GAME
OLD TIMER'S DAY
THEY'RE A GRIZZLED BUNCH OF KILLERS, ZEE, BUT IT'S, YOU KNOW, TIME, TIME, TIME...
THOUGH YOU CAN'T COUNT THEM OUT— NOT YET— DUCKY BENDER IS DUE UP WITH RUNNERS ON 2ND AND 3RD, AND DUCKY'S STILL TOUGH.
THAT PUNK ON THE MOUND SPENDS AN AWFUL LOT OF TIME AROUND THE WEIGHT MACHINES— LET'S SEE WHAT THOSE MUSCLES DO FOR HIM VERSUS THE DUCK.

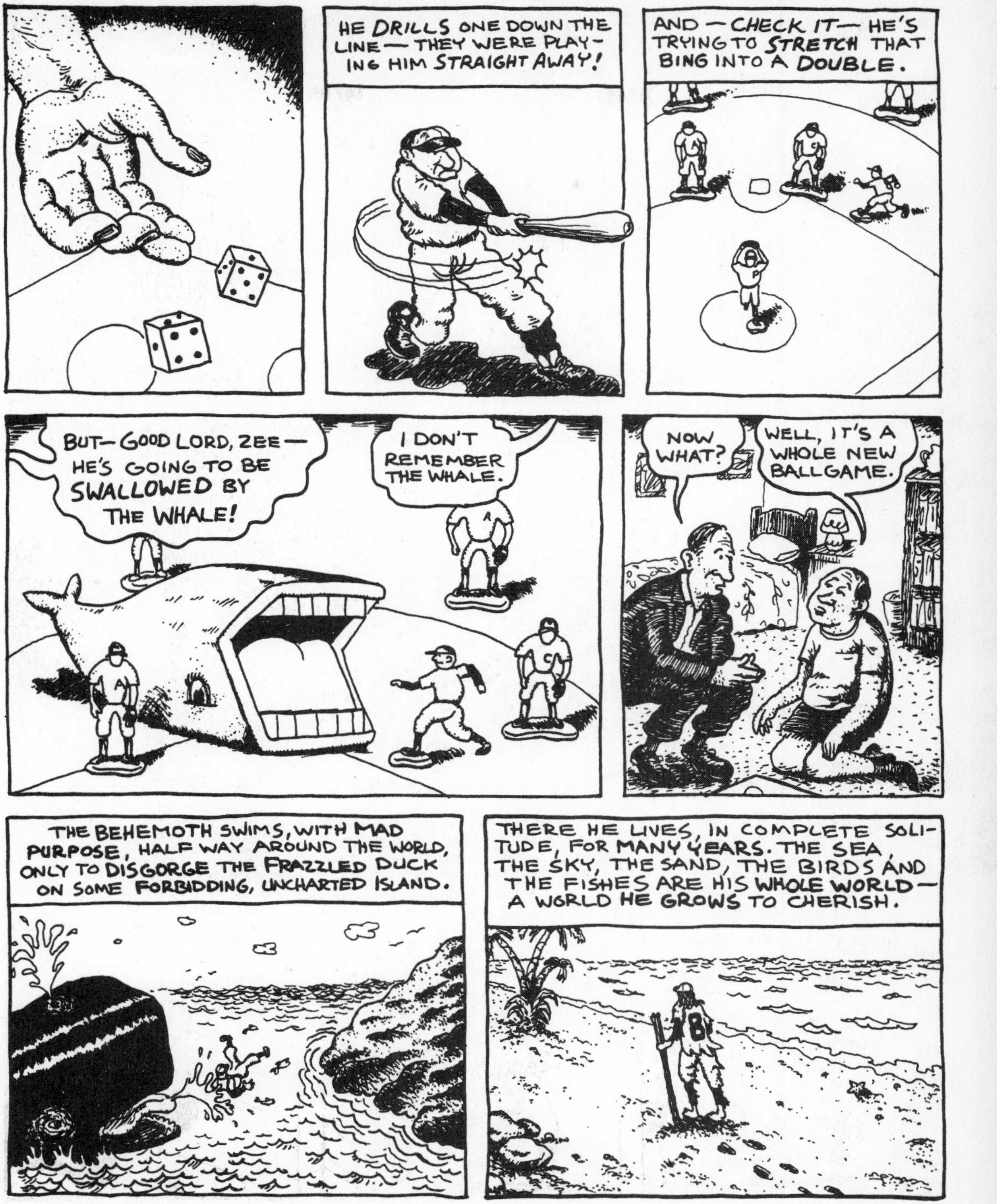
HE DRILLS ONE DOWN THE LINE — THEY WERE PLAYING HIM STRAIGHT AWAY!
AND — CHECK IT — HE'S TRYING TO STRETCH THAT BING INTO A DOUBLE.
BUT — GOOD LORD, ZEE — HE'S GOING TO BE SWALLOWED BY THE WHALE!
I DON'T REMEMBER THE WHALE.
NOW WHAT?
WELL, IT'S A WHOLE NEW BALLGAME.
THE BEHEMOTH SWIMS, WITH MAD PURPOSE, HALF WAY AROUND THE WORLD, ONLY TO DISGORGE THE FRAZZLED DUCK ON SOME FORBIDDING, UNCHARTED ISLAND.
THERE HE LIVES, IN COMPLETE SOLITUDE, FOR MANY YEARS. THE SEA, THE SKY, THE SAND, THE BIRDS AND THE FISHES ARE HIS WHOLE WORLD — A WORLD HE GROWS TO CHERISH.

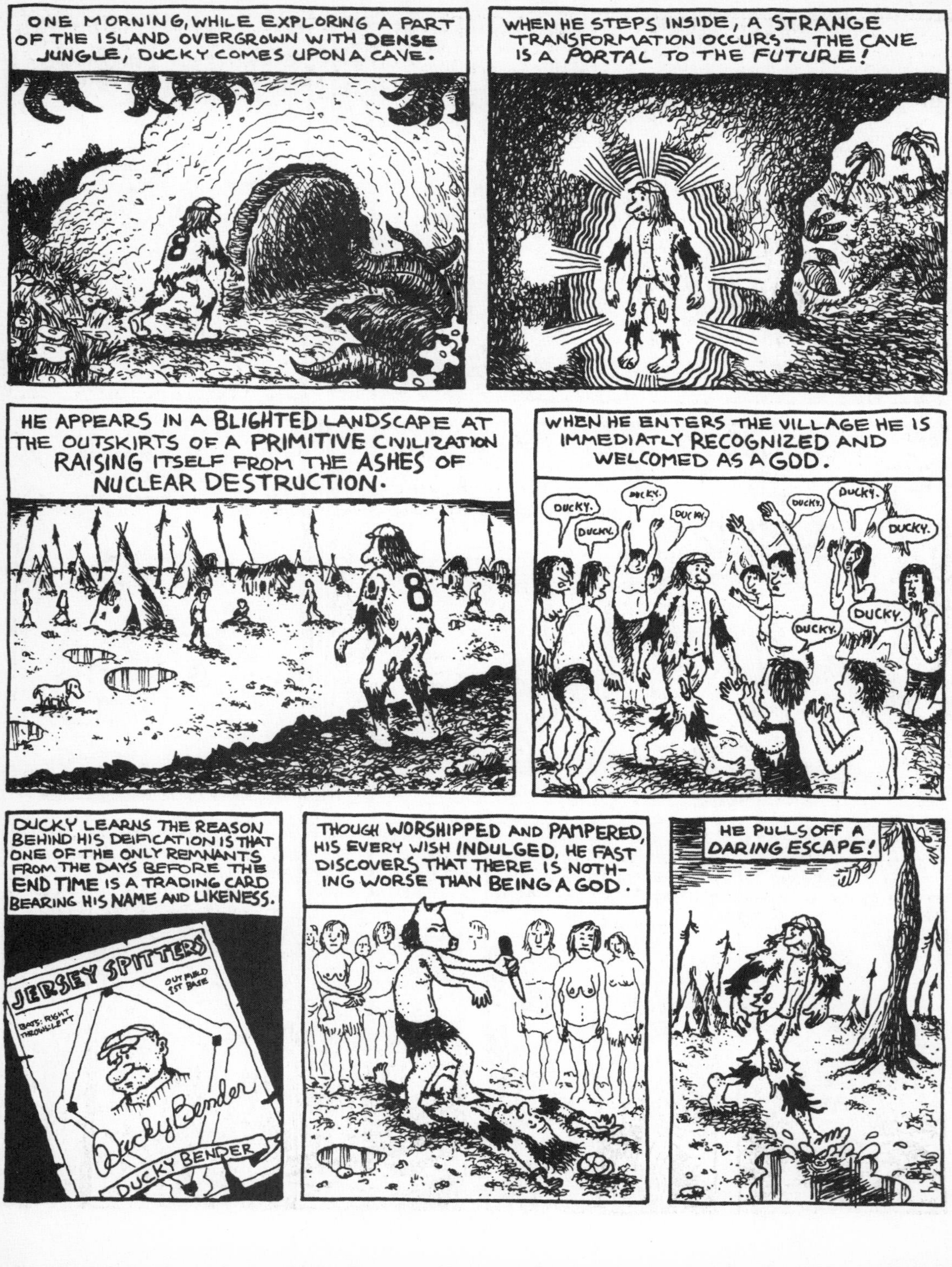
ONE MORNING, WHILE EXPLORING A PART OF THE ISLAND OVERGROWN WITH DENSE JUNGLE, DUCKY COMES UPON A CAVE.
WHEN HE STEPS INSIDE, A STRANGE TRANSFORMATION OCCURS — THE CAVE IS A PORTAL TO THE FUTURE!
HE APPEARS IN A BLIGHTED LANDSCAPE AT THE OUTSKIRTS OF A PRIMITIVE CIVILIZATION RAISING ITSELF FROM THE ASHES OF NUCLEAR DESTRUCTION.
WHEN HE ENTERS THE VILLAGE HE IS IMMEDIATLY RECOGNIZED AND WELCOMED AS A GOD.
DUCKY.
DUCKY.
DUCKY.
DUCKY.
DUCKY.
DUCKY.
DUCKY.
DUCKY.
DUCKY.
DUCKY LEARNS THE REASON BEHIND HIS DEIFICATION IS THAT ONE OF THE ONLY REMNANTS FROM THE DAYS BEFORE THE END TIME IS A TRADING CARD BEARING HIS NAME AND LIKENESS.
JERSEY SPITTERS
OUTFIELD 1ST BASE
BATS: RIGHT THROWS: LEFT
Ducky Bender
DUCKY BENDER
THOUGH WORSHIPPED AND PAMPERED, HIS EVERY WISH INDULGED, HE FAST DISCOVERS THAT THERE IS NOTHING WORSE THAN BEING A GOD.
HE PULLS OFF A DARING ESCAPE!

IN THE OUTLANDS, DUCKY MEETS THE NOBODY'S—THOSE BANISHED FROM THE VILLAGE BECAUSE THEY ARE TOO STUPID OR TOO SMART, OR TOO SICK OR TOO HEALTHY.

AMONG THEM IS ARIA. WHEN DUCKY MEETS HER, IT IS AS IF HE HAS ALWAYS KNOWN HER.

THEY FALL DEEPLY IN LOVE.

SHE TELLS HIM OF THE LEGEND OF A PORTAL TO THE PAST, AND THEY SET OUT TO FIND IT.

AS THEY TRAVEL, ARIA IS STRUCK DOWN BY THE MERCILESS SHRINKING SICKNESS.

IN DAYS SHE IS AS SHRUNKEN AND SHRIVELED AS AN ANCHOVY.

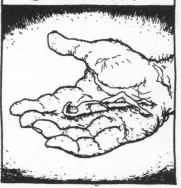

SHE BREATHES HER LAST AND IS BURIED.

AND DUCKY STEPS, ALONE, INTO THE PORTAL.

WE MOVE NOW TO A RAMSHACKLE STUDIO AT 14, CITÉ FALGUIÈRE, PARIS, FRANCE. IT IS 1925.

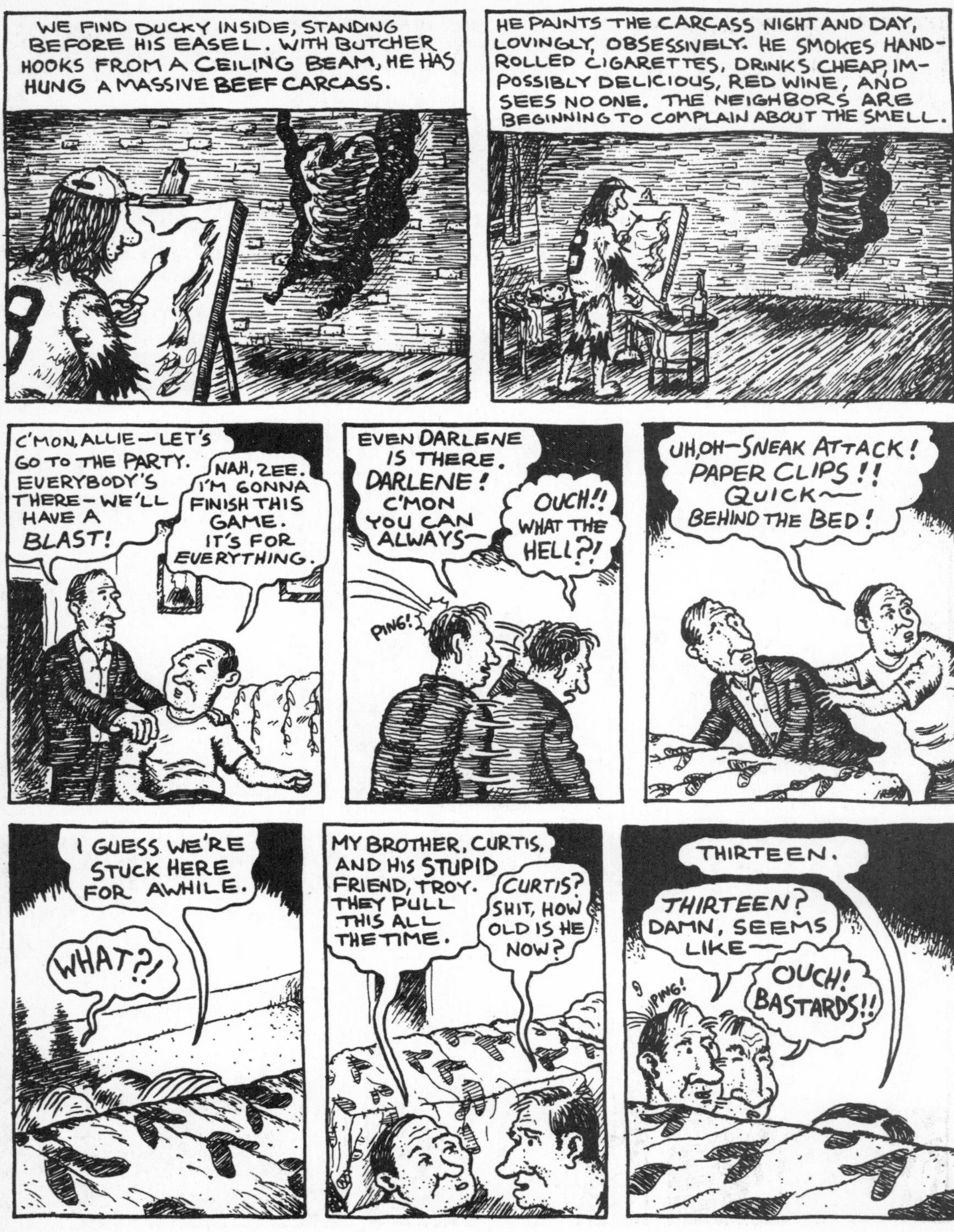
WE FIND DUCKY INSIDE, STANDING BEFORE HIS EASEL. WITH BUTCHER HOOKS FROM A CEILING BEAM, HE HAS HUNG A MASSIVE BEEF CARCASS.
HE PAINTS THE CARCASS NIGHT AND DAY, LOVINGLY, OBSESSIVELY. HE SMOKES HAND-ROLLED CIGARETTES, DRINKS CHEAP, IMPOSSIBLY DELICIOUS, RED WINE, AND SEES NO ONE. THE NEIGHBORS ARE BEGINNING TO COMPLAIN ABOUT THE SMELL.
C'MON, ALLIE—LET'S GO TO THE PARTY. EVERYBODY'S THERE—WE'LL HAVE A BLAST!
NAH, ZEE. I'M GONNA FINISH THIS GAME. IT'S FOR EVERYTHING.
EVEN DARLENE IS THERE. DARLENE! C'MON YOU CAN ALWAYS—
PING!
OUCH!! WHAT THE HELL?!
UH, OH—SNEAK ATTACK! PAPER CLIPS!! QUICK— BEHIND THE BED!
I GUESS WE'RE STUCK HERE FOR AWHILE.
WHAT?!
MY BROTHER, CURTIS, AND HIS STUPID FRIEND, TROY. THEY PULL THIS ALL THE TIME.
CURTIS? SHIT, HOW OLD IS HE NOW?
THIRTEEN.
THIRTEEN? DAMN, SEEMS LIKE—
PING!
OUCH! BASTARDS!!

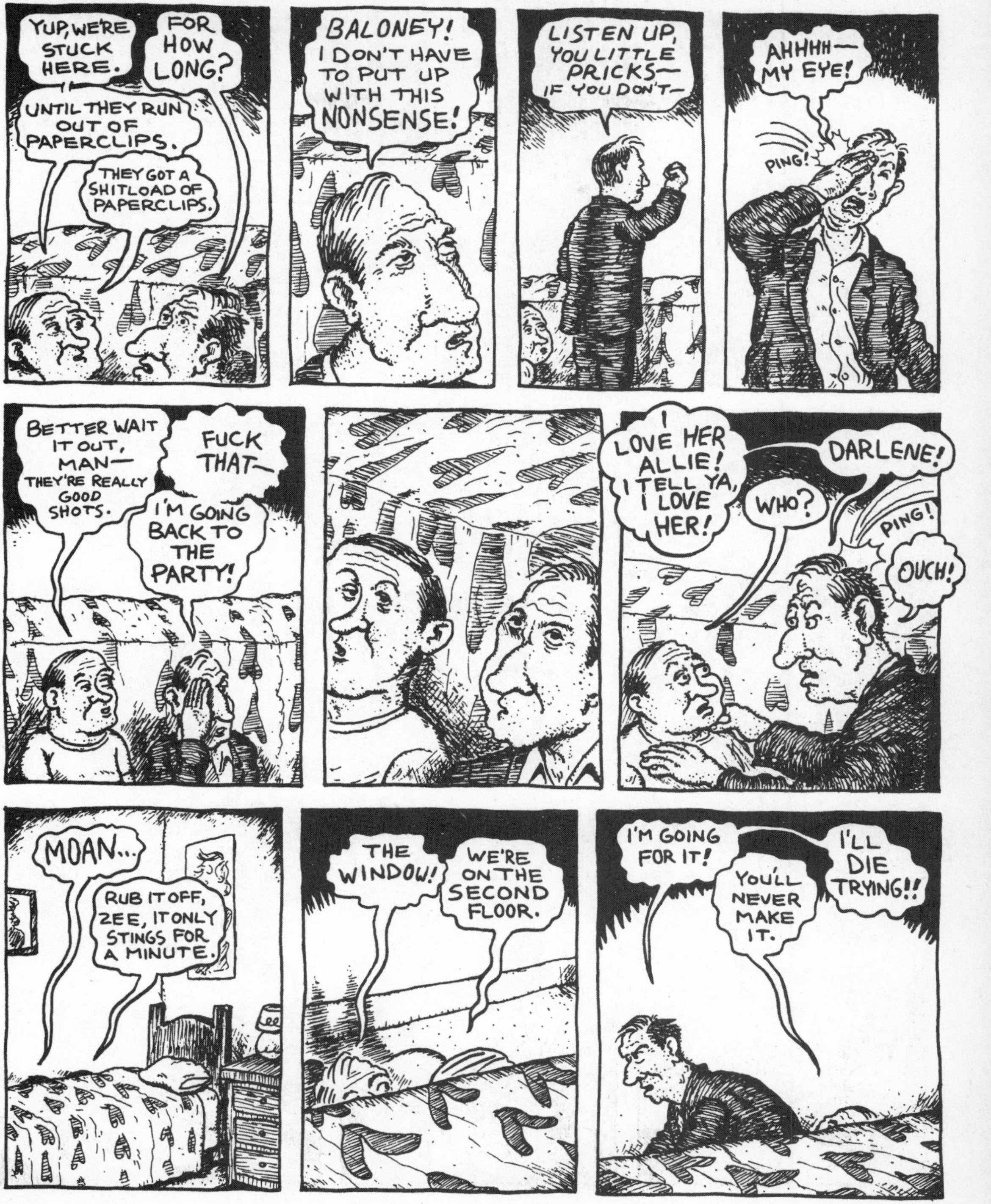
YUP, WE'RE STUCK HERE.
FOR HOW LONG?
UNTIL THEY RUN OUT OF PAPERCLIPS.
THEY GOT A SHITLOAD OF PAPERCLIPS.
BALONEY! I DON'T HAVE TO PUT UP WITH THIS NONSENSE!
LISTEN UP, YOU LITTLE PRICKS— IF YOU DON'T—
AHHHH— MY EYE!
PING!
BETTER WAIT IT OUT, MAN— THEY'RE REALLY GOOD SHOTS.
FUCK THAT—
I'M GOING BACK TO THE PARTY!
I LOVE HER ALLIE! I TELL YA, I LOVE HER!
DARLENE!
WHO?
PING!
OUCH!
MOAN...
RUB IT OFF, ZEE, IT ONLY STINGS FOR A MINUTE.
THE WINDOW!
WE'RE ON THE SECOND FLOOR.
I'M GOING FOR IT!
I'LL DIE TRYING!!
YOU'LL NEVER MAKE IT.

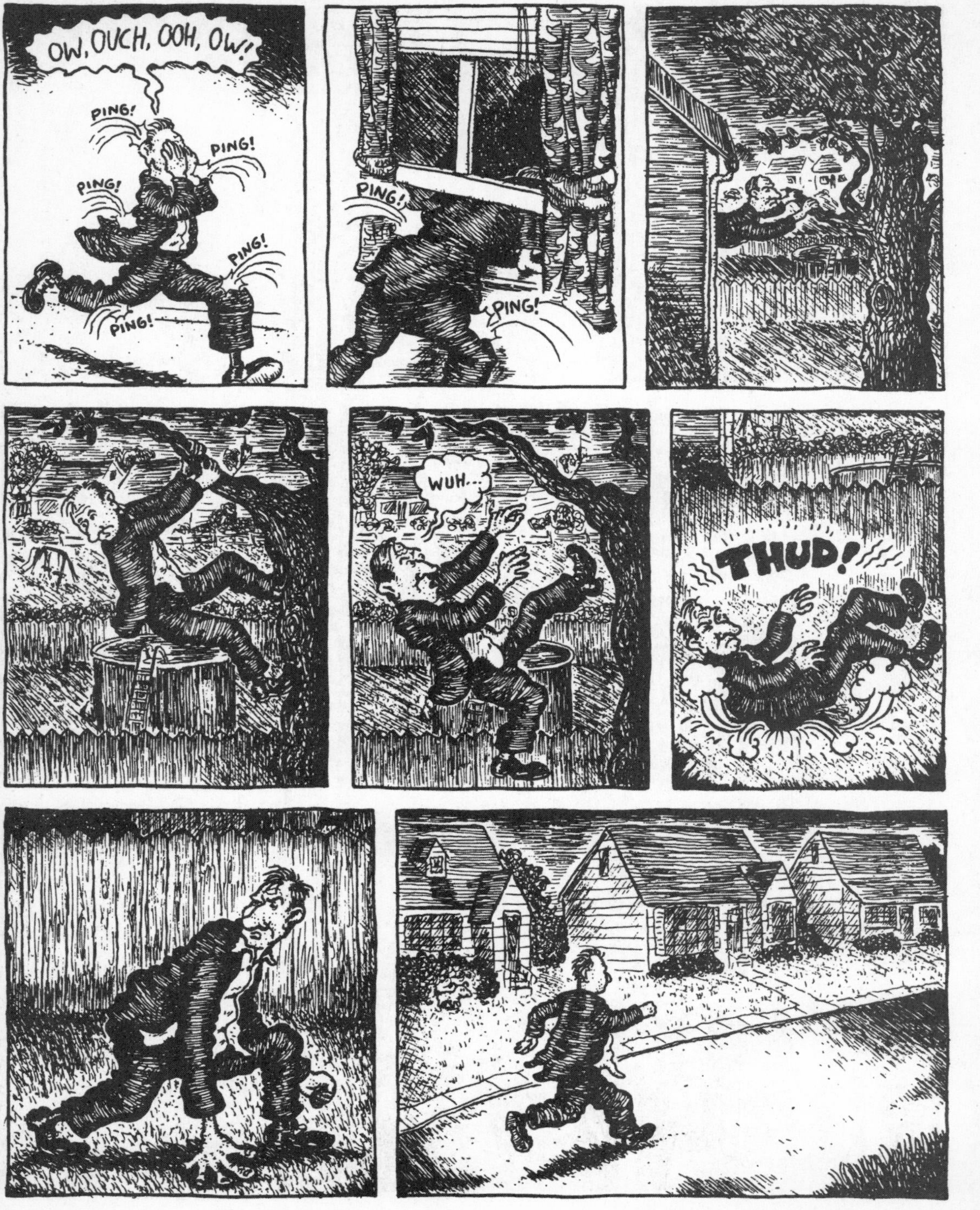
OW, OUCH, OOH, OW!
PING!
PING!
PING!
PING!
PING!
PING!
PING!
WUH...
THUD!

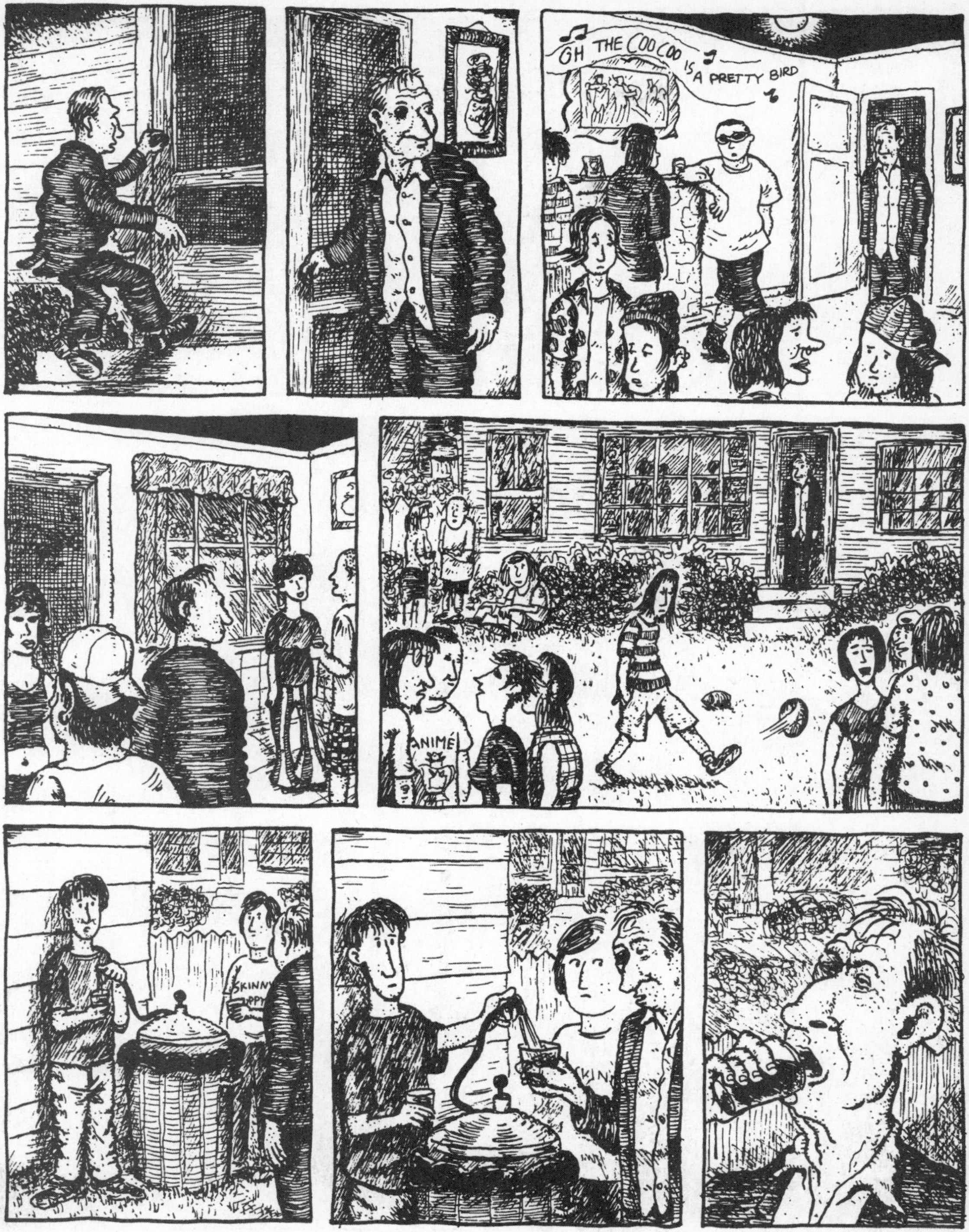
OH THE COO COO IS A PRETTY BIRD
ANIMÉ

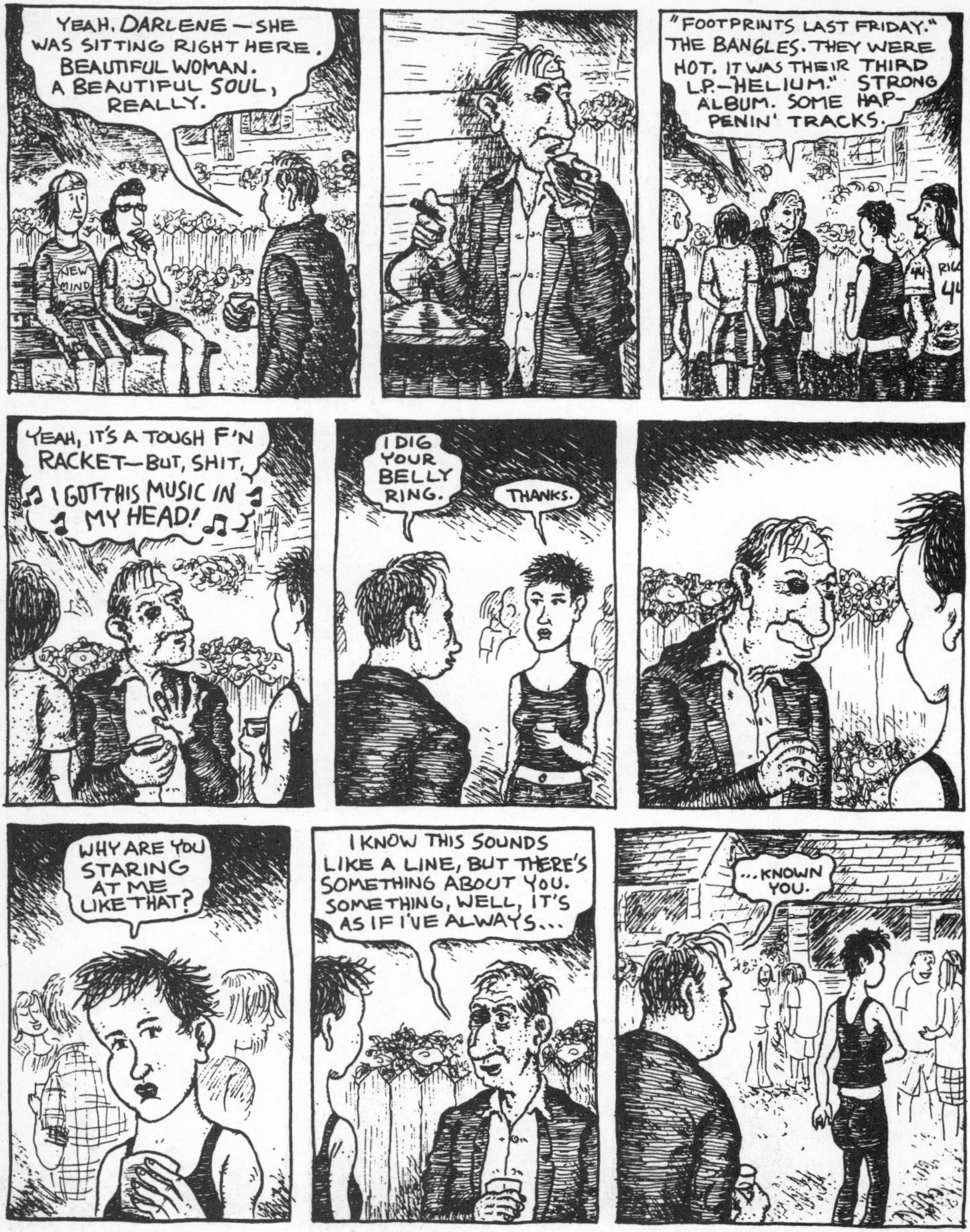
YEAH. DARLENE—SHE WAS SITTING RIGHT HERE. BEAUTIFUL WOMAN. A BEAUTIFUL SOUL, REALLY.
NEW MIND
"FOOTPRINTS LAST FRIDAY." THE BANGLES. THEY WERE HOT. IT WAS THEIR THIRD L.P.—"HELIUM." STRONG ALBUM. SOME HAP-PENIN' TRACKS.
44
YEAH, IT'S A TOUGH F'N RACKET—BUT, SHIT, I GOT THIS MUSIC IN MY HEAD!
I DIG YOUR BELLY RING.
THANKS.
WHY ARE YOU STARING AT ME LIKE THAT?
I KNOW THIS SOUNDS LIKE A LINE, BUT THERE'S SOMETHING ABOUT YOU. SOMETHING, WELL, IT'S AS IF I'VE ALWAYS...
...KNOWN YOU.

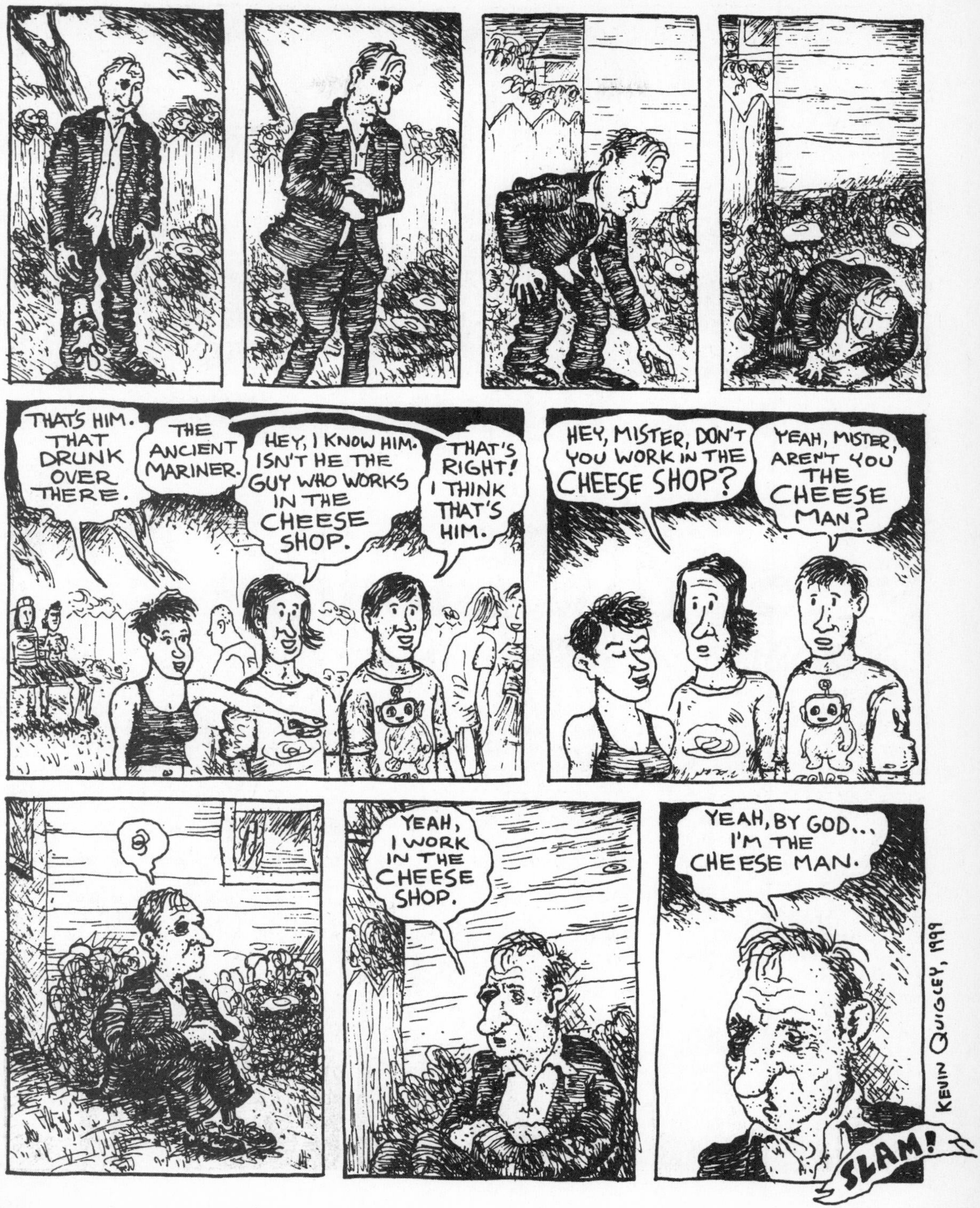
THAT'S HIM. THAT DRUNK OVER THERE.
THE ANCIENT MARINER.
HEY, I KNOW HIM. ISN'T HE THE GUY WHO WORKS IN THE CHEESE SHOP.
THAT'S RIGHT! I THINK THAT'S HIM.
HEY, MISTER, DON'T YOU WORK IN THE CHEESE SHOP?
YEAH, MISTER, AREN'T YOU THE CHEESE MAN?
YEAH, I WORK IN THE CHEESE SHOP.
YEAH, BY GOD... I'M THE CHEESE MAN.
KEVIN QUIGLEY, 1999
SLAM!

St. Marks
Nov '99
J. Zenick

IN SEARCH OF THE FLORIDA SWAMP EMU

IN THE 1990'S, A NUMBER OF FLORIDA FARMERS BOUGHT PAIRS OF EMUS AND STARTED BREEDING THEM. SUPPOSEDLY EMU MEAT WAS DUE TO BECOME A VERY IN DEMAND DELICACY. EMU MEAT WAS RUMORED TO TASTE LIKE CHICKEN. THE MARKET FOR EMU MEAT NEVER MATERIALIZED. BY THE END OF THE 1990'S THIS LEFT MANY FLORIDA FARMERS WITH FULL GROWN AND BABY EMUS WHICH WERE CONSUMING LARGE AMOUNTS OF GRAIN, AND HAD NO HOPE OF BEING SOLD.

SO MANY OF THESE FLORIDA FARMERS STARTED RELEASING THEIR UNWANTED EMUS INTO NATIONAL FOREST AND STATE PARKS. AS MANY AS 15-20 MAY HAVE BEEN RELEASED INTO ST. MARKS WILDLIFE REFUGE WHICH COVERS MOST OF THE COASTLINE OF WAKULLA COUNTY ON THE GULF OF MEXICO.

IN THE SAME REGION WHERE THE 1930'S TARZAN MOVIES WERE FILMED, WHERE ALLIGATORS, GIANT INSECTS, ARMADILLOS, SWAMPS, MARSH, PINE FORESTS AND GRACEFUL WATER BIRDS ABOUND, THE FLORIDA SWAMP EMU MAY BE GETTING A FOOTHOLD. A NEIGHBOR OF MINE SAW

ONE OF THE EMUS SEVERAL MONTHS AGO, WHILE HIKING IN THE REFUGE.

A WILDLIFE EXPERT HAD BEEN HIRED BY THE ST. MARK WILDLIFE REFUGE TO CAPTURE AND REMOVE THE EMUS. EMUS ARE VERY TERRITORIAL, AND AFTER BEING ATTACKED AND SEVERELY PECKED, THE WILDLIFE EXPERT QUIT IN DISMAY. JUST TRY AND CAPTURE AN EMU WITH A LASSO; IT'S NOT SO EASY.

ON THE OUTSKIRTS OF THE FISHING VILLAGE OF ST. MARKS, THERE ARE THE REMAINS OF AN OLD SPANISH FORT DATING BACK SOME 400 YEARS. THERE IS A VISITORS CENTER WITH SOME ARCHEOLOGICAL RELICS AND A HISTORY OF THE AREA. SEVERAL OF THE TOWNS IN WAKULLA COUNTY HAVE BEEN WIPED OFF THE MAP OR MOSTLY DESERTED BECAUSE OF HURRICANES. ALL THAT REMAINS OF THE TOWN OF MAGNOLIA, IS AN OLD OVERGROWN GRAVEYARD. (WHICH I LOCATED AND VISITED USING A GEOLOGICAL SURVEY MAP). ALL THAT REMAINS OF THE FORMER PORT TOWN OF PORT LEON IS AN OLD FIRETOWER. NEWPORT FLORIDA WAS ONCE THE FIFTH LARGEST

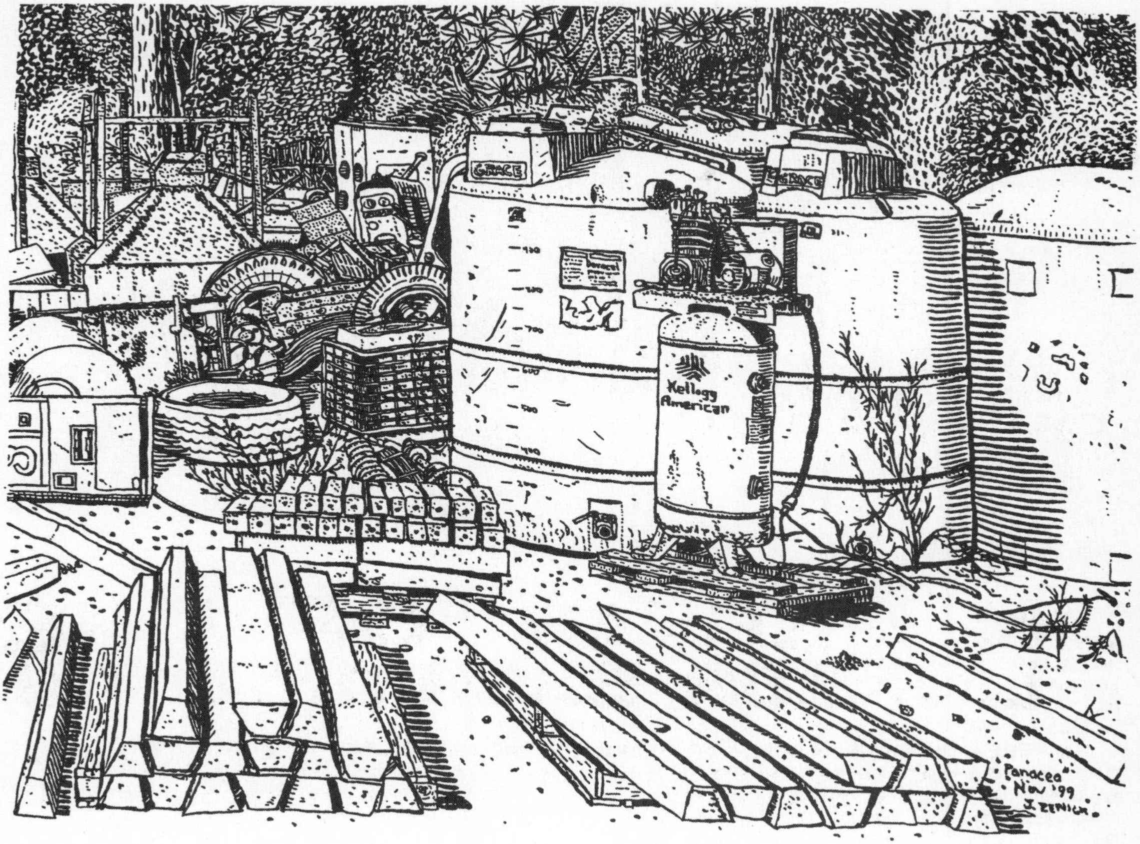
GRACE
Kellogg American
Panacea
Nov '99
J. ZENICK

CITY IN FLORIDA, BUT NOW IT IS SO SMALL IT CAN BARELY BE CALLED A TOWN. THE LARGEST AREA OF RUINS IN WAKULLA COUNTY IS IN NEWPORT. IN THE 1600'S AND 1700'S, AS MANY AS 90% OF THE AREA'S NATIVE AMERICAN POPULATION WAS WIPED OUT BY SMALLPOX.

ANOTHER FISHING AND SEAFOOD PROCESSING VILLAGE IN WAKULLA COUNTY IS PANACEA, A TOWN OF SMALL SHACKS, MOBILE HOMES AND SAND ROADS; WHICH HOSTS ONE OF FLORIDA'S WORST LAUNDROMATS, WITH ONLY 3 OF IT'S 14 WASHERS WORKING, AND NO HOT WATER. WHILE WASHING MY CLOTHES THERE, A BAREFOOT WOMAN AND HER 3 BAREFOOTED KIDS CAME WITH A HUGE PILE OF CLOTHES. SHE PARKED HER BEAT-UP OLD CAR WITH THE FENDER HANGING ON BY A PIECE OF WIRE, OUT FRONT.

HER 8 YEAR OLD SON MADE A BEELINE FOR ONE OF THE BROKEN WASHERS, OPENED THE TOP, CLIMBED IN, AND SPUN HIMSELF AROUND WHILE STANDING UP. THE 15 YEAR OLD DAUGHTER IN HER SHORT SHORTS KEPT AN EYE ON HER 2 YEAR OLD SISTER WHILE CHAIN-SMOKING CIGARETTES IN FRONT OF HER MOM.

A FRIEND OF THE MOM, WHILE WALKING BY, SAW HER, AND STOPPED TO CHAT. "WHERE HAVE YOU BEEN?" SHE ASKED. "JAIL", HE REPLIED. HE PULLED A STACK OF FOLDED LEGAL PAPERS OUT OF HIS POCKET AND BEGAN EXPLAINING HIS CASE TO HER, WHILE MUTTERING, "FUCKING COPS", UNDER HIS BREATH. I WALKED OUTSIDE TO LOOK AT THE BOARDED UP RESTAURANT NEXT DOOR AND TO WATCH THE LOCAL PEOPLE GO IN AND OUT OF THE IGA GROCERY STORE.

THE MOM WASHED A LOAD OF CLOTHES, THEN PUT HER 2ND LOAD IN THE SAME

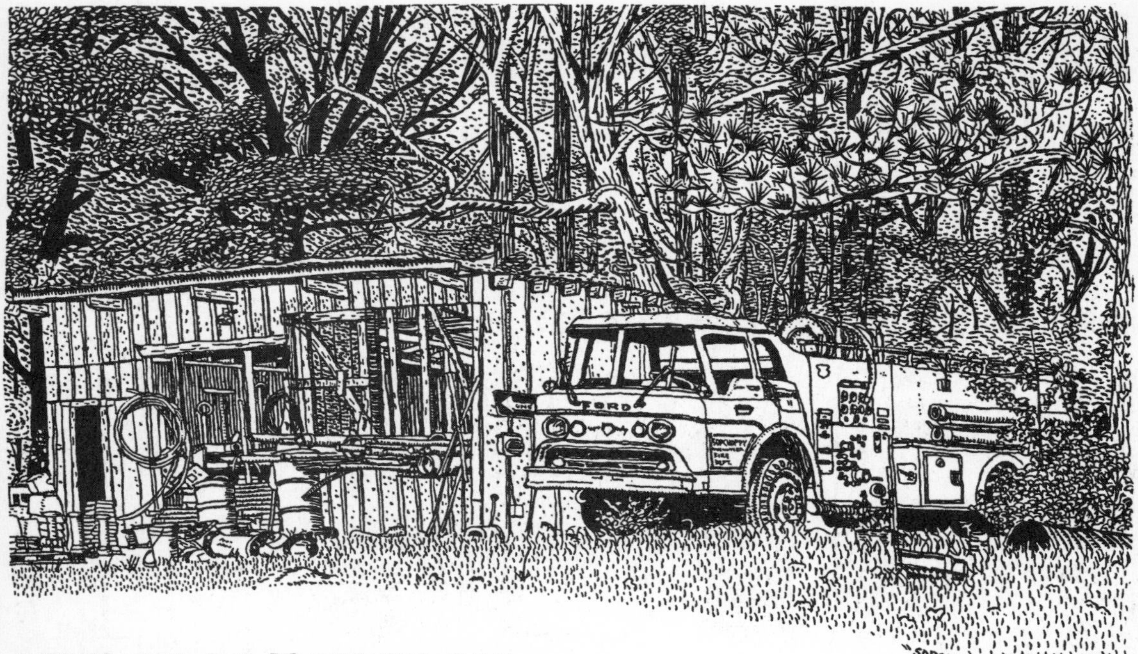
FORD
"SOPCHOPPY" NOV '99 J. ZENICK

WASHER AND SAID IT WAS THE ONLY WASHER THAT GOT THE CLOTHES CLEAN. THE 15 YEAR OLD DAUGHTER EYED MY BICYCLE AND GEAR AND ASKED IF I WAS A NOMAD. I WAS THINKING OF ASKING THE MOM IF I COULD MARRY THE DAUGHTER AND MOVE INTO THEIR TRAILER WITH THEM, MAYBE GET A JOB AT THE CEMENT PLANT OR ON ONE OF THE FISHING BOATS....

IN PANACEA, I FREQUENTED THE DENTED CAN STORE FOR MY SUSTENANCE. DENTED CHEAP CANS OF BEANS, CORN, SARDINES; AND I SPLURGED ON A CRUSHED CONTAINER OF SOUR CREAM AND ONION FLAVORED PRINGLES, FILLED WITH BROKEN CHIPS. MY FAVORITE TOWN PARK OF WAKULLA COUNTY IS IN PANACEA. IT APPARENTLY USED TO BE SOME SORT OF MINERAL SPRINGS SOME 50-75 YEARS AGO, WITH SPRINGS COMING UP INTO SEVERAL BROKEN CEMENT AND BRICK POOLS. PICNIC TABLES AND A FALLING APART GAZEBO ALSO GRACE THE PARK'S GROUNDS. I DUNNO WHY, BUT I LIKE PLACES OF FORMER GRANDEUR BETTER THAN PLACES OF PRESENT GRANDEUR.

THERE'S GOTTA BE A BETTER WAY, THERE HAS GOT TO BE A BETTER WAY, THERE'S GOTTA BE A BETTER WAY. AT THE BEGINNING OF A NEW CENTURY, OF A NEW MILLENIUM, I FIND MYSELF LOST, NOT KNOWING WHAT TO DO, HOW TO LIVE, SO I FIND MYSELF DOING DAY LABOR FOR 2 OR 3 WEEKS, THEN TAKING OFF CAMPING FOR A COUPLE WEEKS, THEN WORKING AGAIN, THEN CAMPING AGAIN. MY BICYCLE/CAMPING TRIP OF THE 2ND HALF OF NOV. '99 TOOK ME INTO WAKULLA COUNTY, WITH VAUGE PLANS TO TAKE A LOOK AT THE PRINCIPAL TOWNS AND POPULATION CENTERS, CONNECT UP WITH PEOPLE, DO SOME EXPLORING, SOME DRAWING.

BECAUSE IT WAS HUNTING SEASON, MY BEST BET FOR CAMPING AT NIGHT SEEMED TO BE TO CAMP ILLEGALLY IN THE WILDLIFE REFUGE. HOPEFULLY THERE WOULD BE NO HUNTERS AT NIGHT HUNTING DEER WHO WOULD ACCIDENTALLY SHOOT ME. I BROKE DOWN MY CAMP EVERY NIGHT, SO THERE WAS LITTLE CHANCE OF THE RANGERS FINDING ME.

OFTEN I SET UP CAMP RIGHT BEFORE SUNSET, AND IN WALKING AROUND ON THE TRAILS, I FOUND MYSELF LOOKING FOR EMUS. IN THE SANDY SOIL, I LOOKED FOR EMU FOOTPRINTS. PLENTY OF DEER FOOTPRINTS (AND I SPOTTED SEVERAL DEER),

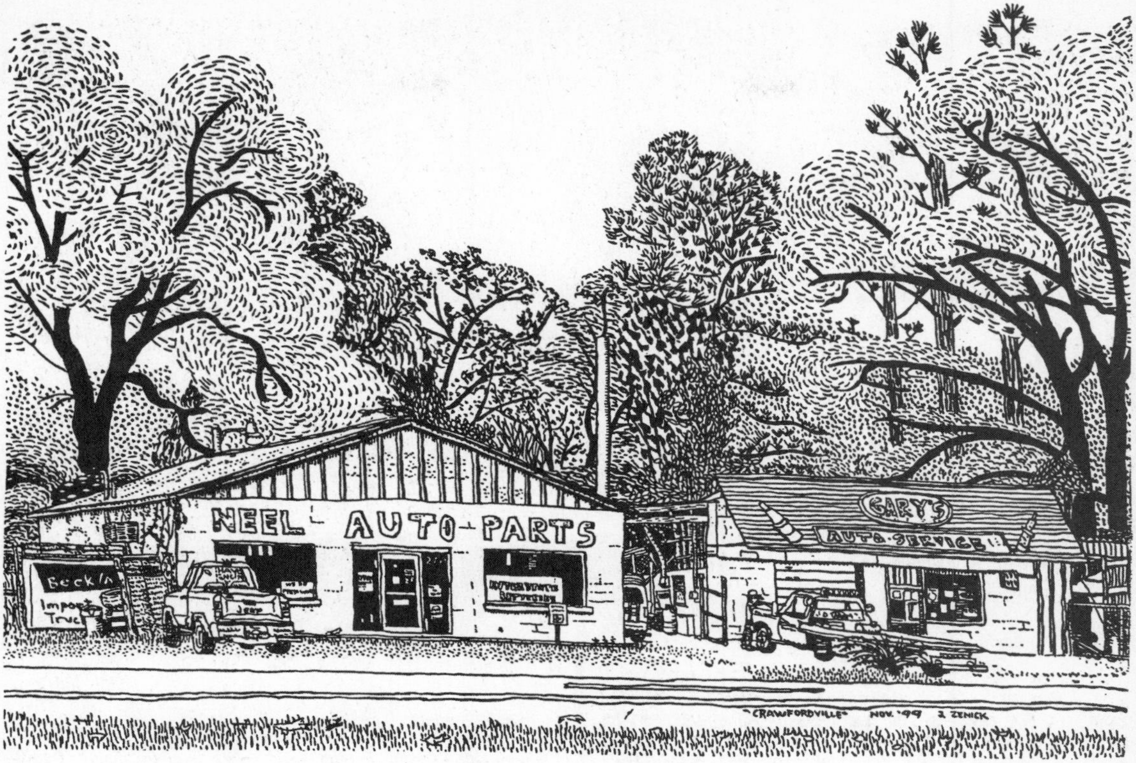
NEEL AUTO-PARTS
GARY'S
AUTO SERVICE
"CRAWFORDVILLE" NOV. '99 J. ZENICK

LOTS OF SQUIRREL OR RACCOON FOOTPRINTS AND SOME 3-INCH BIRD FOOTPRINTS, BUT, SIGH, NO EMU PRINTS.

ON ONE SUNSET HIKE, I SAW UP AHEAD DISAPPEAR INTO THE UNDERBRUSH WHAT LOOKED LIKE THE BACKSIDE OF A HUGE DOG, PERHAPS A ST. BERNARD/BLACK LAB MIX, AND THEN I REALIZED THAT IT PROBABLY WAS A SMALL BLACK BEAR.

WALKING AROUND IN A GRAVEYARD IN CRAWFORDVILLE, LOOKING AT THE OLD GRAVES, IT STARTED TO RAIN, SO I RODE MY BIKE ACROSS THE STREET TO THE HARDEES, THREW A TARP OVER MY BICYCLE AND GEAR, WENT IN AND SAT DOWN FOR A SESSION OF LETTER-WRITING.

AS THE RAIN POURED DOWN OUTSIDE, I GOT IN A CONVERSATION WITH A 78 YEAR OLD BLACK WOMAN WHO WAS SITTING AT THE NEXT TABLE. SHE TOLD ME THAT WHEN SHE WAS YOUNGER AND WORKED, AND WAS TREATED UNFAIRLY BY HER BOSS OR CO-WORKERS, THAT SHE WOULD WORK JUST AS HARD AND NOT COMPLAIN, AND IN DOING SO, OVER TIME, IT CHANGED THE PERSON WHO TREATED HER UNFAIRLY. IT GOT ME THINKING... INTERNALLY I ARGUED... WHAT SHE SAID ECHOED MARTIN LUTHER KING'S PHILOSOPHY; IT MIRRORED PEACE PILGRIM'S SAYING "RETURN EVIL WITH GOOD, RETURN HATRED WITH LOVE". I THOUGHT OF ALL THE TIMES THAT I'VE BEEN TREATED POORLY AND REACTED BY BURSTING WITH ANGER INSIDE, FILLING MY THOUGHTS WITH REVENGE, AND IMAGINING HORRIBLE THING HAPPENING TO MY OPRESSOR; BUT WHAT GOOD DID IT EVER DO, EXCEPT GIVE ME A FEELING OF SELF-JUSTIFICATION. GIVING THE OTHER ONE A TASTE OF THEIR OWN MEDICINE; IT DOESN'T SEEM TO WORK FOR ME, OUTSIDE OF A GLOATING SATISFACTION. BUT TO TRANSFORM MY OPRESSOR THROUGH LOVE... I DUNNO IF I'M UP TO THAT TASK............ 'YA GOTTA DO WHAT 'YA GOTTA DO.....

-JEFF ZENICK-
'99-'00

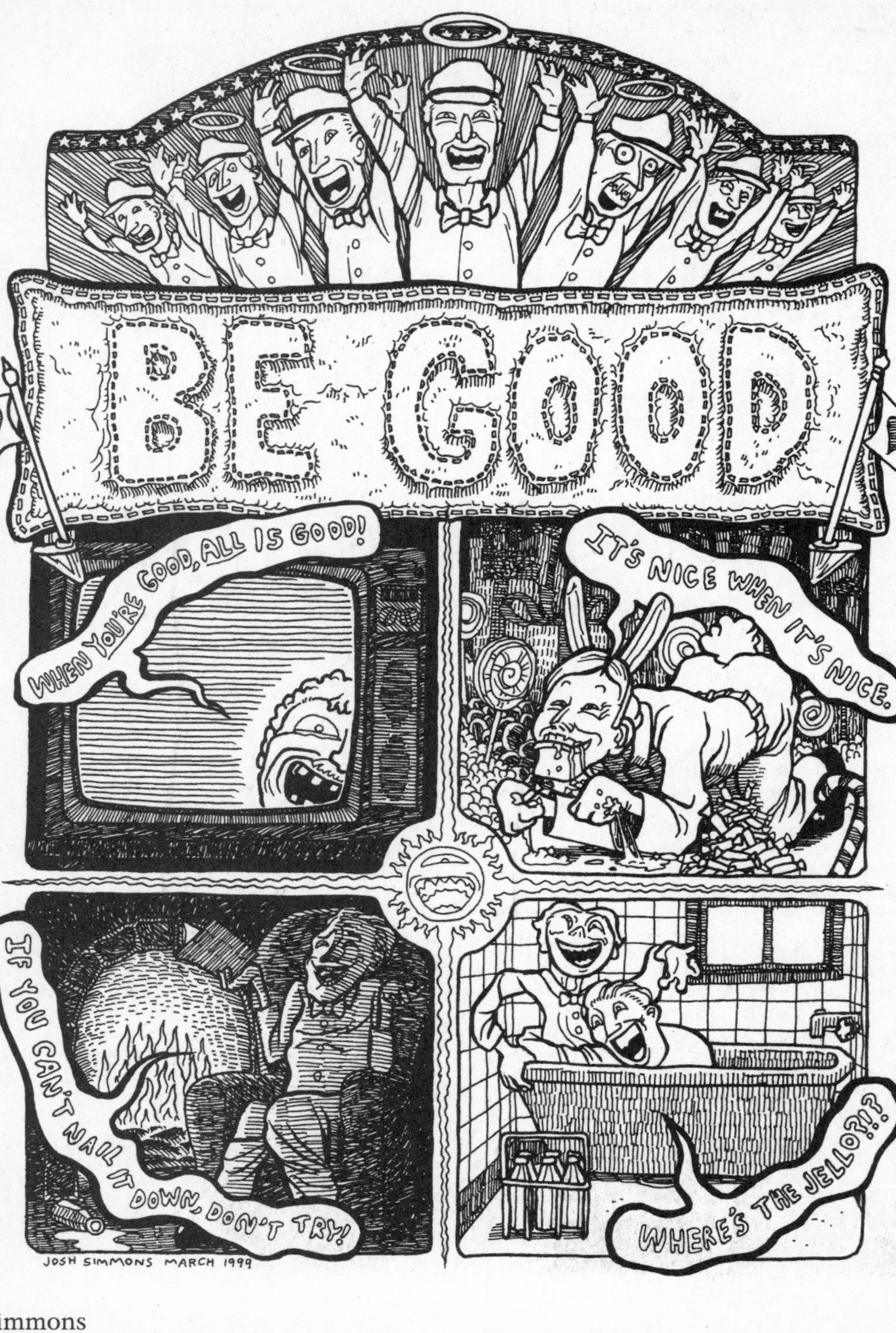
BE GOOD!
WHEN YOU'RE GOOD, ALL IS GOOD!
IT'S NICE WHEN IT'S NICE.
IF YOU CAN'T NAIL IT DOWN, DON'T TRY!
WHERE'S THE JELLO?!?
JOSH SIMMONS MARCH 1999

topshelf asks the BIG Questions... AND SO WHAT?

The New Swiss Scene

Once upon a time, there was a very small country, known only for three specialties: cuckoo clocks[1], chocolate and bank secrecy. Even though they weren't Swiss, Benoît Chevallier, Maxime Pégatoquet and Daniel Pellegrino[2] lived in this very small country and shared a passion for comic books. For those readers not familiar with the customs of exotic countries, Switzerland, and in particular the city of Geneva, is a haven for graphic artists. For instance, numerous elections are held throughout the year and political parties usually resort to illustrators for their posters. Moreover, Geneva regularly employs artists to decorate the city. Not exactly the worst environment for our three young men.

written by gregory trowbridge
illustrations by frederik peeters

The starting point of this story is *Sauve qui peut*, a periodical published by Atoz Editions, on which our three young men collaborated. Although the periodical didn't last, the experience strengthened their ambitions. In 1997, they founded Atrabile and published the zero issue of *Bile Noire*. After the publication of the zero issue, *Bile Noire* took on a regular rhythm of three issues a year and Atrabile released graphic novels of varying shapes and sizes. Collections appeared—three of them of course. *Sang*, a "comic"-sized publication for short stories; *Flegme*, middle-sized; and *Bile Blanche* for longer stories.[3]

Since things always happen in threes, at nearly the same time our three young men founded Atrabile, Nicolas Robel laid the foundations of B.ü.l.b. Comix and Christian Humbert-Droz created *Drozophile*, a magazine and publishing company almost exclusively dedicated to silkscreen printing. All three publishers frequently use the same artists from the Geneva art scene. Among these are: Alex Baladi, Sylvain Crippa, Sacha Goerg, Jason, Kaze, Frederik Peeters, Isabelle Pralong, Ibn al Rabin, Nadia Raviscioni, Helge Reumann, Nicolas et Xavier Robel, Tom Tirabosco, Wazem...

Finding strength in numbers, Atrabile joined forces with B.ü.l.b. Comix and Drozophile to create L'Association Trois-Pattes (The Three-Legged Association). As we stand on the doorstep of the third millennium, L'Association publishes the periodical *Bile Noire* along with the German language *Strapazin* and the French *Lapin*.

1. Everyone remembers Harry Lime's monologue, played by Orson Welles in Carol Reed's *The 3rd Man*, "In Italy, for thirty years under the Borgias they had warfare, terror, murder, bloodshed - but they produced Michelangelo, Leonardo da Vinci, and the Renaissance. In Switzerland they had brotherly love, 500 years of democracy and peace, and what did that produce? The cuckoo clock."
2. The astute reader will notice that the names of all three young men include three "e"s.
3. All the names at Atrabile refer to the four temperaments in the human body: Black Bile (Atrabile or Bile Noire), Blood (Sang), Phlegm (Flegme) and White Bile (Bile Blanche).

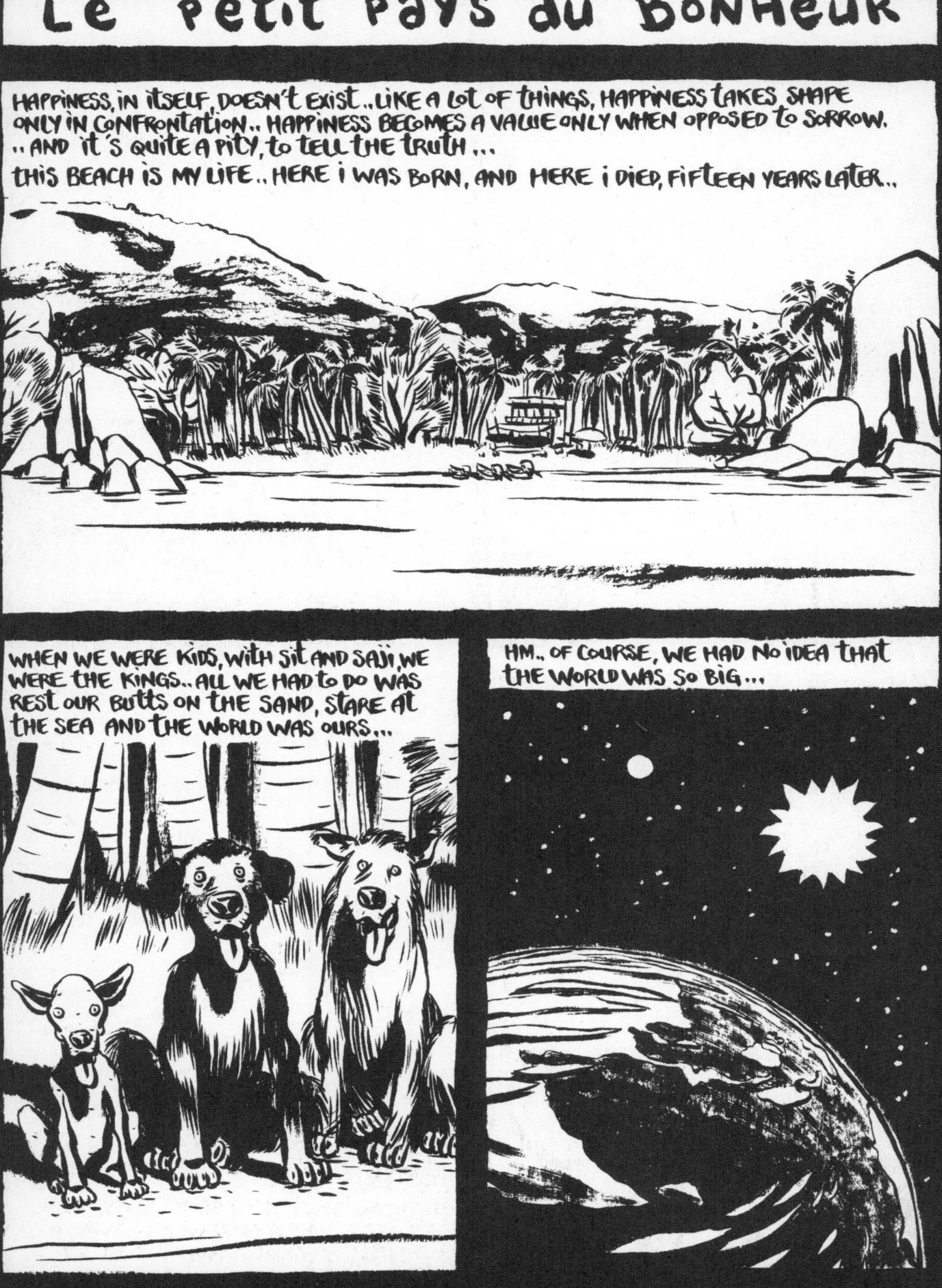
Le petit pays du Bonheur
HAPPINESS, IN ITSELF, DOESN'T EXIST.. LIKE A LOT OF THINGS, HAPPINESS TAKES SHAPE ONLY IN CONFRONTATION.. HAPPINESS BECOMES A VALUE ONLY WHEN OPPOSED TO SORROW. .. AND IT'S QUITE A PITY, TO TELL THE TRUTH...
THIS BEACH IS MY LIFE.. HERE I WAS BORN, AND HERE I DIED, FIFTEEN YEARS LATER...
WHEN WE WERE KIDS, WITH SIT AND SAJI, WE WERE THE KINGS.. ALL WE HAD TO DO WAS REST OUR BUTTS ON THE SAND, STARE AT THE SEA AND THE WORLD WAS OURS...
HM.. OF COURSE, WE HAD NO IDEA THAT THE WORLD WAS SO BIG...

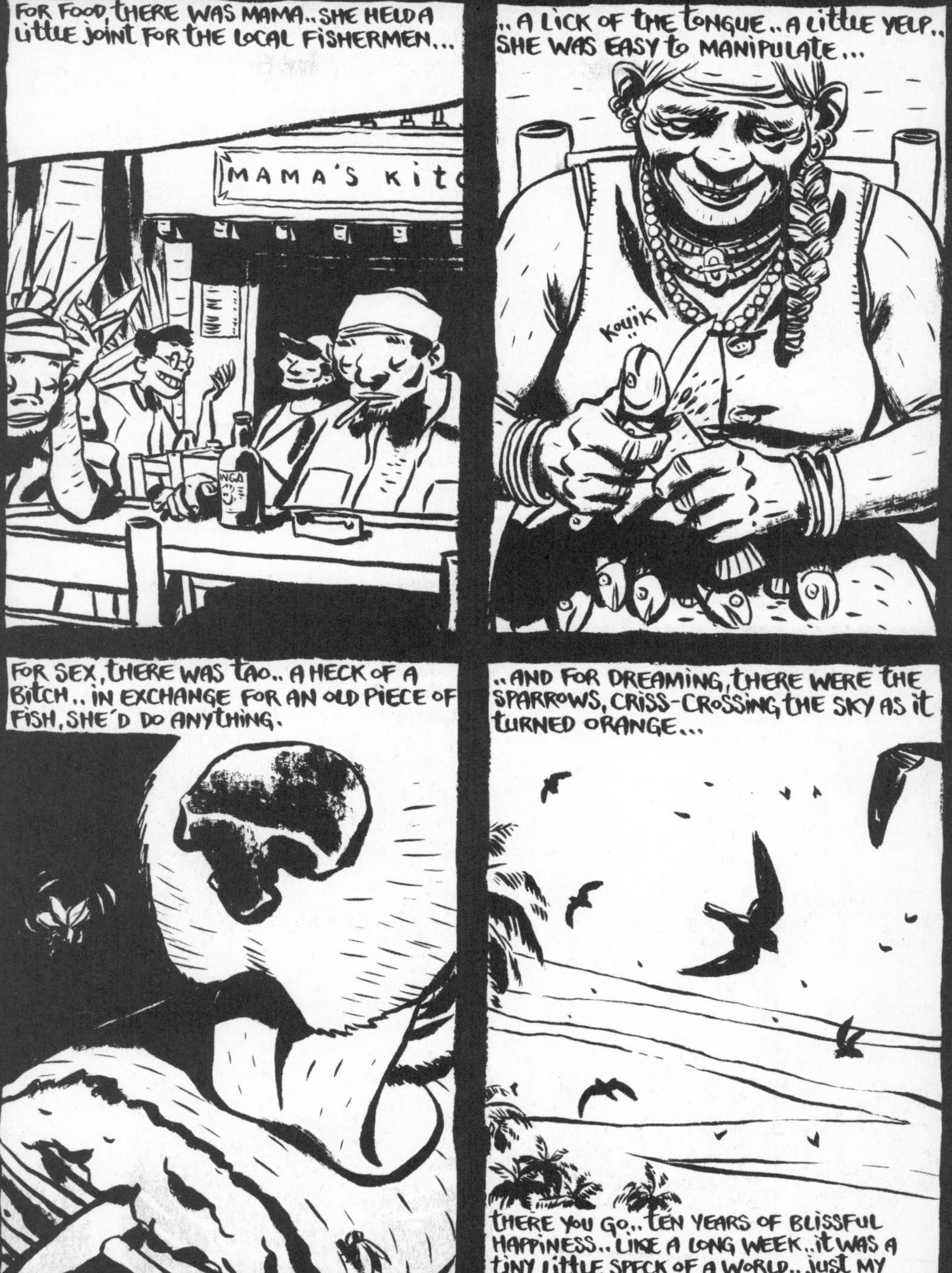
FOR FOOD, THERE WAS MAMA.. SHE HELD A LITTLE JOINT FOR THE LOCAL FISHERMEN...
MAMA'S KITC
.. A LICK OF THE TONGUE .. A LITTLE YELP.. SHE WAS EASY TO MANIPULATE...
KOUIK
FOR SEX, THERE WAS TAO.. A HECK OF A BITCH.. IN EXCHANGE FOR AN OLD PIECE OF FISH, SHE'D DO ANYTHING.
.. AND FOR DREAMING, THERE WERE THE SPARROWS, CRISS-CROSSING THE SKY AS IT TURNED ORANGE...
THERE YOU GO.. TEN YEARS OF BLISSFUL HAPPINESS.. LIKE A LONG WEEK.. IT WAS A TINY LITTLE SPECK OF A WORLD.. JUST MY WORLD, IN FACT...

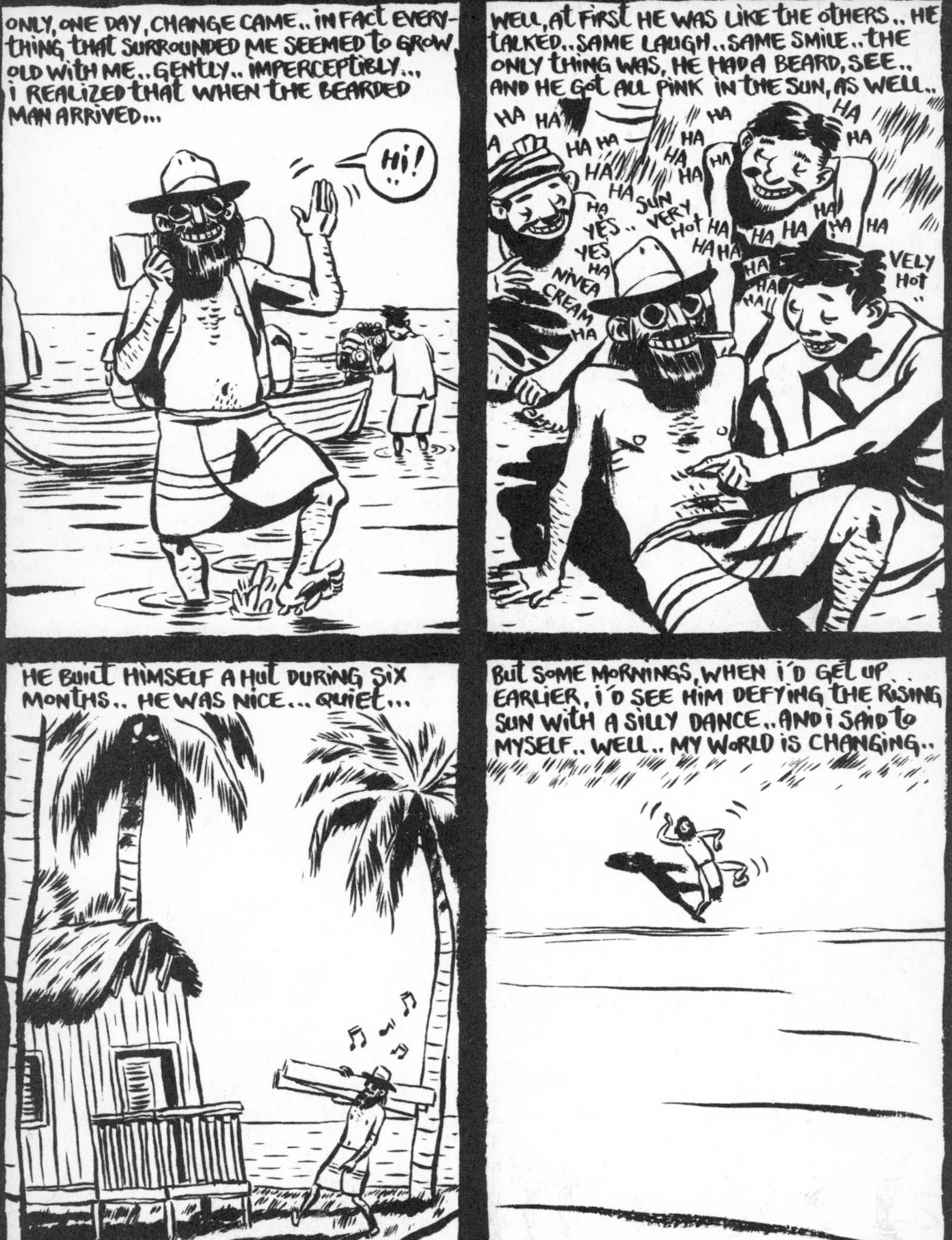
ONLY, ONE DAY, CHANGE CAME.. IN FACT EVERYTHING THAT SURROUNDED ME SEEMED TO GROW OLD WITH ME.. GENTLY.. IMPERCEPTIBLY... I REALIZED THAT WHEN THE BEARDED MAN ARRIVED...
Hi!
WELL, AT FIRST HE WAS LIKE THE OTHERS.. HE TALKED.. SAME LAUGH.. SAME SMILE.. THE ONLY THING WAS, HE HAD A BEARD, SEE.. AND HE GOT ALL PINK IN THE SUN, AS WELL..
HA HA HA HA HA HA HA HA HA
SUN VERY HOT
YES.. YES
NIVEA CREAM
VELY HOT
HE BUILT HIMSELF A HUT DURING SIX MONTHS.. HE WAS NICE... QUIET...
BUT SOME MORNINGS, WHEN I'D GET UP EARLIER, I'D SEE HIM DEFYING THE RISING SUN WITH A SILLY DANCE.. AND I SAID TO MYSELF.. WELL.. MY WORLD IS CHANGING..

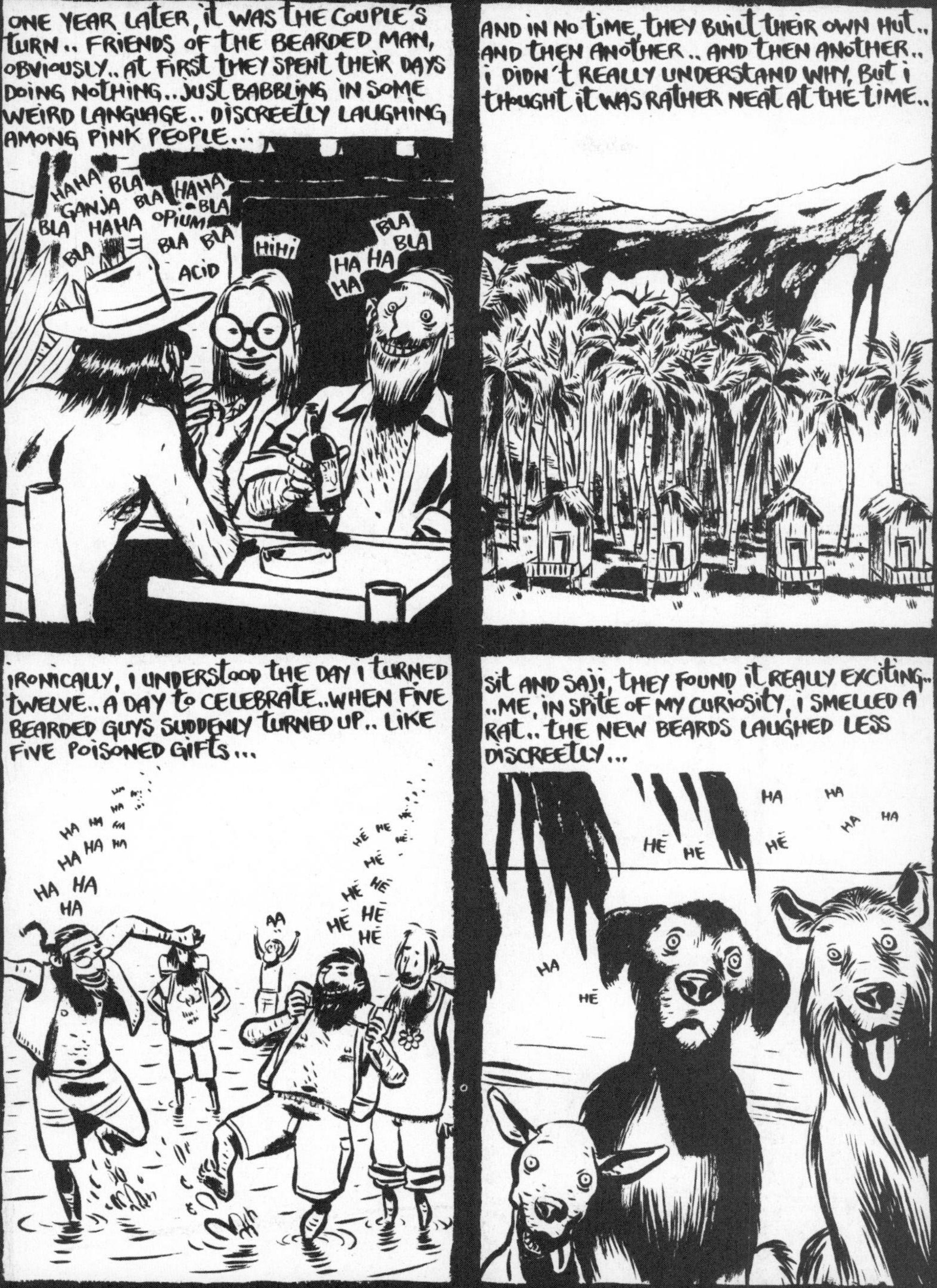
ONE YEAR LATER, IT WAS THE COUPLE'S TURN.. FRIENDS OF THE BEARDED MAN, OBVIOUSLY.. AT FIRST THEY SPENT THEIR DAYS DOING NOTHING.. JUST BABBLING IN SOME WEIRD LANGUAGE.. DISCREETLY LAUGHING AMONG PINK PEOPLE...
HAHA BLA GANJA BLA HAHA BLA BLA HAHA OPIUM BLA BLA BLA BLA
ACID
HIHI
HA HA HA
BLA BLA
AND IN NO TIME, THEY BUILT THEIR OWN HUT.. AND THEN ANOTHER.. AND THEN ANOTHER.. I DIDN'T REALLY UNDERSTAND WHY, BUT I THOUGHT IT WAS RATHER NEAT AT THE TIME..
IRONICALLY, I UNDERSTOOD THE DAY I TURNED TWELVE.. A DAY TO CELEBRATE.. WHEN FIVE BEARDED GUYS SUDDENLY TURNED UP.. LIKE FIVE POISONED GIFTS...
HA HA HA HA HA HA HA HA HA
AA
HÉ HÉ HÉ HÉ HÉ HÉ HÉ HÉ
SIT AND SAJI, THEY FOUND IT REALLY EXCITING.. ..ME, IN SPITE OF MY CURIOSITY, I SMELLED A RAT.. THE NEW BEARDS LAUGHED LESS DISCREETLY...
HA HA HA HA
HÉ HÉ HÉ
HA
HÉ

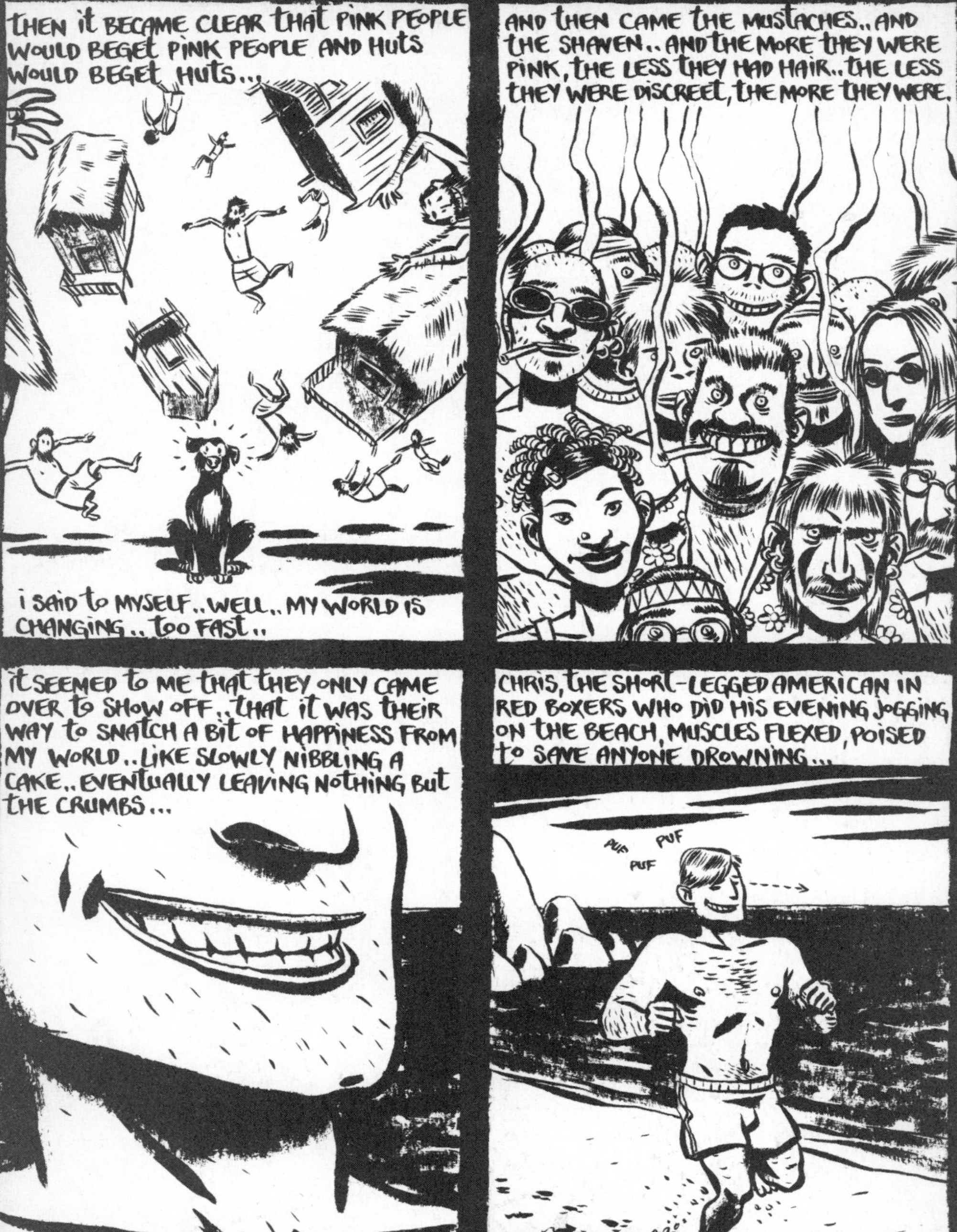
THEN IT BECAME CLEAR THAT PINK PEOPLE WOULD BEGET PINK PEOPLE AND HUTS WOULD BEGET HUTS...
I SAID TO MYSELF.. WELL.. MY WORLD IS CHANGING.. TOO FAST..
AND THEN CAME THE MUSTACHES.. AND THE SHAVEN.. AND THE MORE THEY WERE PINK, THE LESS THEY HAD HAIR.. THE LESS THEY WERE DISCREET, THE MORE THEY WERE.
IT SEEMED TO ME THAT THEY ONLY CAME OVER TO SHOW OFF.. THAT IT WAS THEIR WAY TO SNATCH A BIT OF HAPPINESS FROM MY WORLD.. LIKE SLOWLY NIBBLING A CAKE.. EVENTUALLY LEAVING NOTHING BUT THE CRUMBS...
CHRIS, THE SHORT-LEGGED AMERICAN IN RED BOXERS WHO DID HIS EVENING JOGGING ON THE BEACH, MUSCLES FLEXED, POISED TO SAVE ANYONE DROWNING...
PUF
PUF
PUF

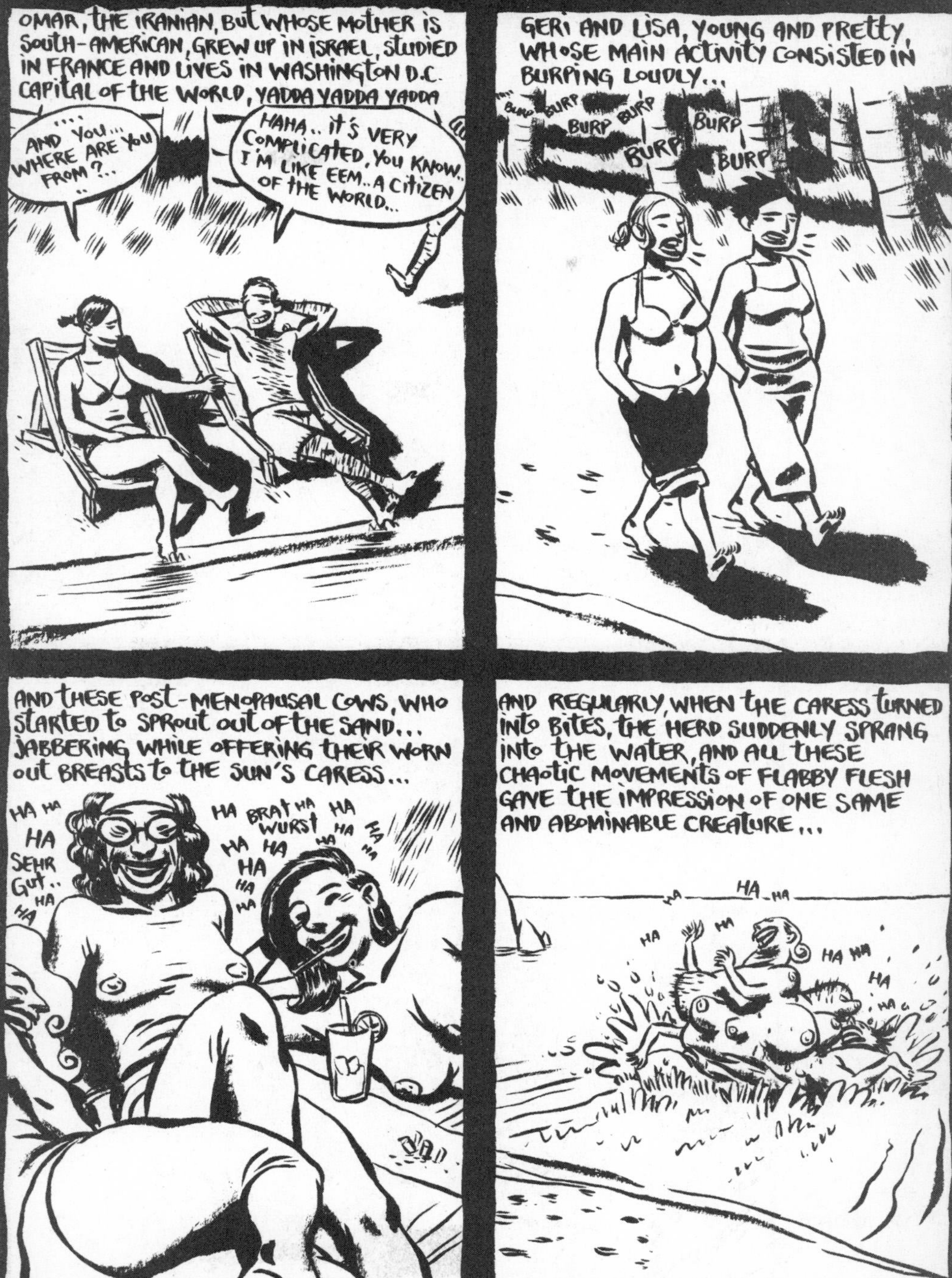
OMAR, THE IRANIAN, BUT WHOSE MOTHER IS SOUTH-AMERICAN, GREW UP IN ISRAEL, STUDIED IN FRANCE AND LIVES IN WASHINGTON D.C. CAPITAL OF THE WORLD, YADDA YADDA YADDA
.... AND YOU... WHERE ARE YOU FROM?...
HAHA.. IT'S VERY COMPLICATED, YOU KNOW.. I'M LIKE EEM.. A CITIZEN OF THE WORLD...
GERI AND LISA, YOUNG AND PRETTY, WHOSE MAIN ACTIVITY CONSISTED IN BURPING LOUDLY...
BURP BURP BURP BURP BURP BURP BURP
AND THESE POST-MENOPAUSAL COWS, WHO STARTED TO SPROUT OUT OF THE SAND... JABBERING WHILE OFFERING THEIR WORN OUT BREASTS TO THE SUN'S CARESS...
HA HA HA SEHR GUT.. HA HA
HA BRATWURST HA HA HA HA HA HA HA HA HA HA HA
AND REGULARLY, WHEN THE CARESS TURNED INTO BITES, THE HERD SUDDENLY SPRANG INTO THE WATER, AND ALL THESE CHAOTIC MOVEMENTS OF FLABBY FLESH GAVE THE IMPRESSION OF ONE SAME AND ABOMINABLE CREATURE...
HA HA HA HA HA HA HA HA HA HA

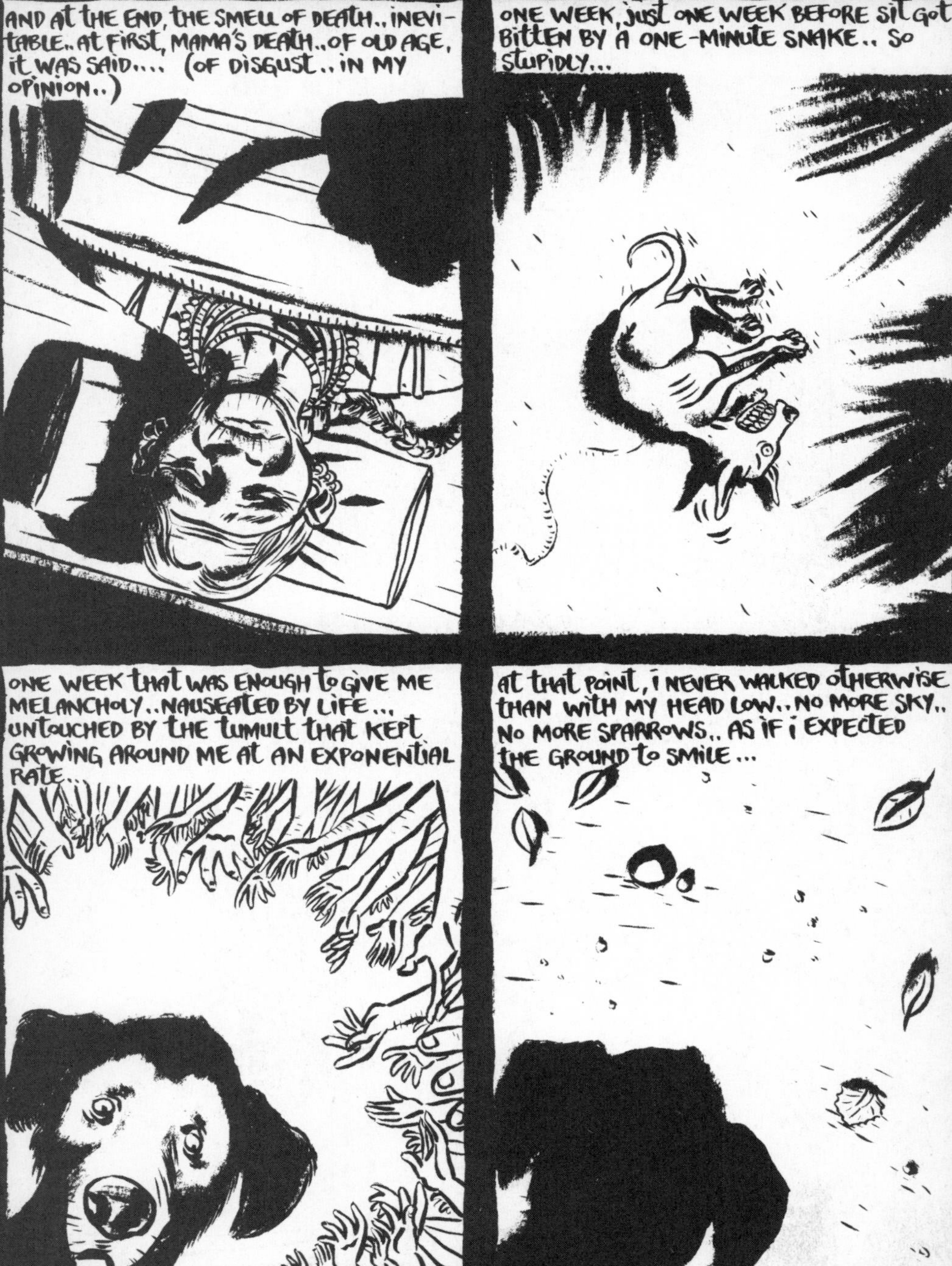
AND AT THE END, THE SMELL OF DEATH.. INEVI-TABLE.. AT FIRST, MAMA'S DEATH.. OF OLD AGE, IT WAS SAID.... (OF DISGUST.. IN MY OPINION..)
ONE WEEK, JUST ONE WEEK BEFORE SIT GOT BITTEN BY A ONE-MINUTE SNAKE.. SO STUPIDLY...
ONE WEEK THAT WAS ENOUGH TO GIVE ME MELANCHOLY.. NAUSEATED BY LIFE..., UNTOUCHED BY THE TUMULT THAT KEPT GROWING AROUND ME AT AN EXPONENTIAL RATE...
AT THAT POINT, I NEVER WALKED OTHERWISE THAN WITH MY HEAD LOW.. NO MORE SKY.. NO MORE SPARROWS.. AS IF I EXPECTED THE GROUND TO SMILE...

UNTIL THAT DECISIVE NIGHT, WHERE, EVENTUALLY, THE SMILE APPEARED.. HELD OUT BY A PINK HAND, OF WHICH I NEVER SAW THE OWNER...

MORE THAN A SIGN.. A TOKEN SMILE.. A SUN.. SWEPT UP WITH AN UNCONSIDERED LICK (WHAT CAN I SAY.. WITH DOGS, AS WITH OTHERS, THE WAY TO HAPPINESS GOES THROUGH THE TONGUE...)

I BARELY REMEMBER CLOSING MY EYES..

THE NEXT MORNING (I SUPPOSE..), I WOKE UP AT THE BOTTOM OF A HUGE HOLE, WHICH I MUST HAVE DESPERATELY DUG UP MYSELF DURING THE NIGHT.. NOT EVEN A GRAVE.. MORE LIKE A COMMON GRAVE..

I WAS PARALYZED FROM THE HIP DOWN... (OF OLD AGE, IT WAS SAID).. MY LIFE SHATTERED BY A TINY SMILE...

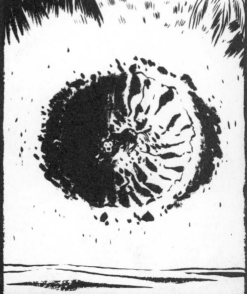

235

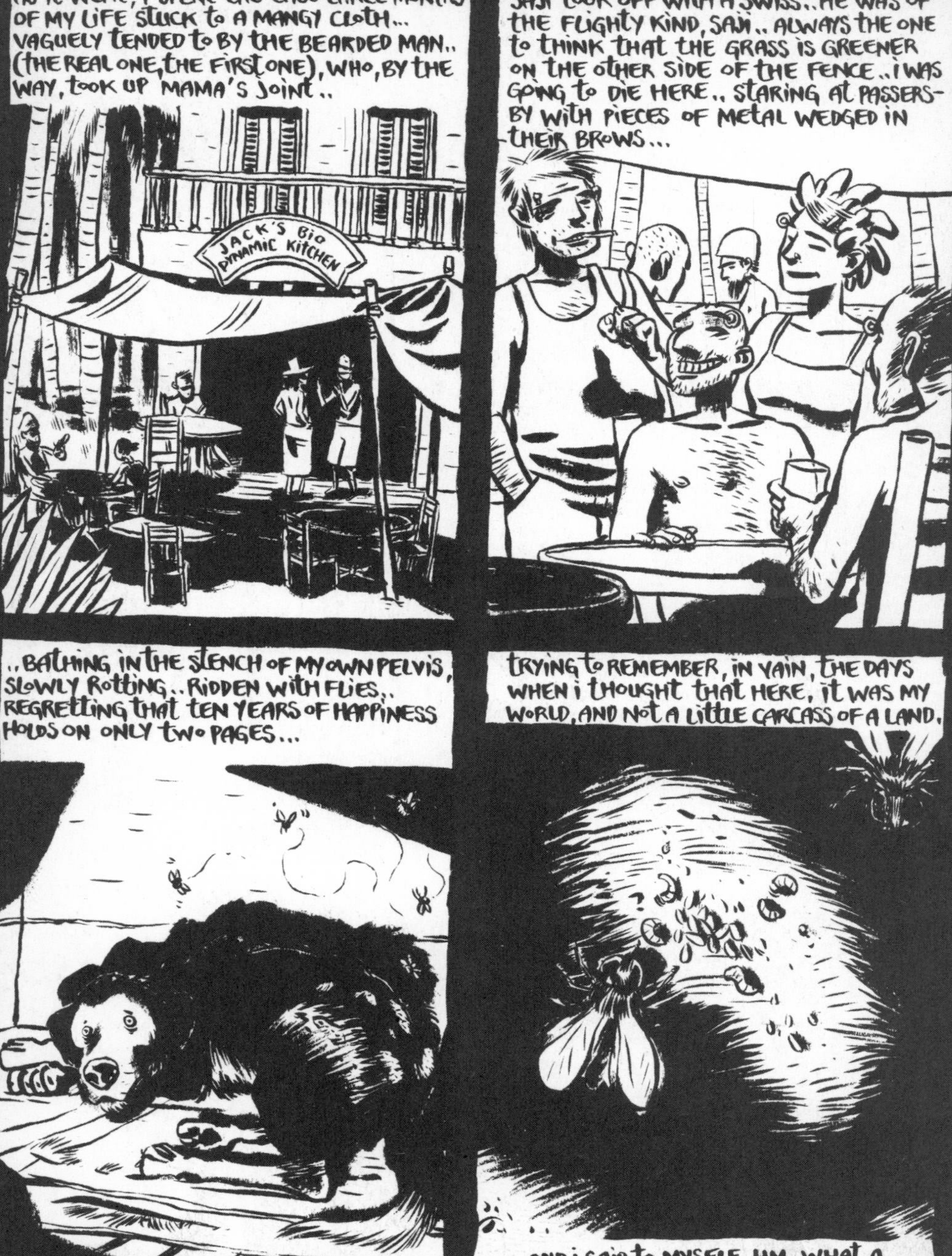
AS IT WENT, I SPENT THE LAST THREE MONTHS OF MY LIFE STUCK TO A MANGY CLOTH... VAGUELY TENDED TO BY THE BEARDED MAN.. (THE REAL ONE, THE FIRST ONE), WHO, BY THE WAY, TOOK UP MAMA'S JOINT..
JACK'S BIO DYNAMIC KITCHEN
SAJI TOOK OFF WITH A SWISS.. HE WAS OF THE FLIGHTY KIND, SAJI.. ALWAYS THE ONE TO THINK THAT THE GRASS IS GREENER ON THE OTHER SIDE OF THE FENCE.. I WAS GOING TO DIE HERE.. STARING AT PASSERS-BY WITH PIECES OF METAL WEDGED IN THEIR BROWS...
..BATHING IN THE STENCH OF MY OWN PELVIS, SLOWLY ROTTING.. RIDDEN WITH FLIES.. REGRETTING THAT TEN YEARS OF HAPPINESS HOLDS ON ONLY TWO PAGES...
TRYING TO REMEMBER, IN VAIN, THE DAYS WHEN I THOUGHT THAT HERE, IT WAS MY WORLD, AND NOT A LITTLE CARCASS OF A LAND.
..AND I SAID TO MYSELF..HM..WHAT A FUCKING MESS.. HAPPINESS..
FREDERIK-KOHPHANGAN-4.99

Une histoire pour Mathieu

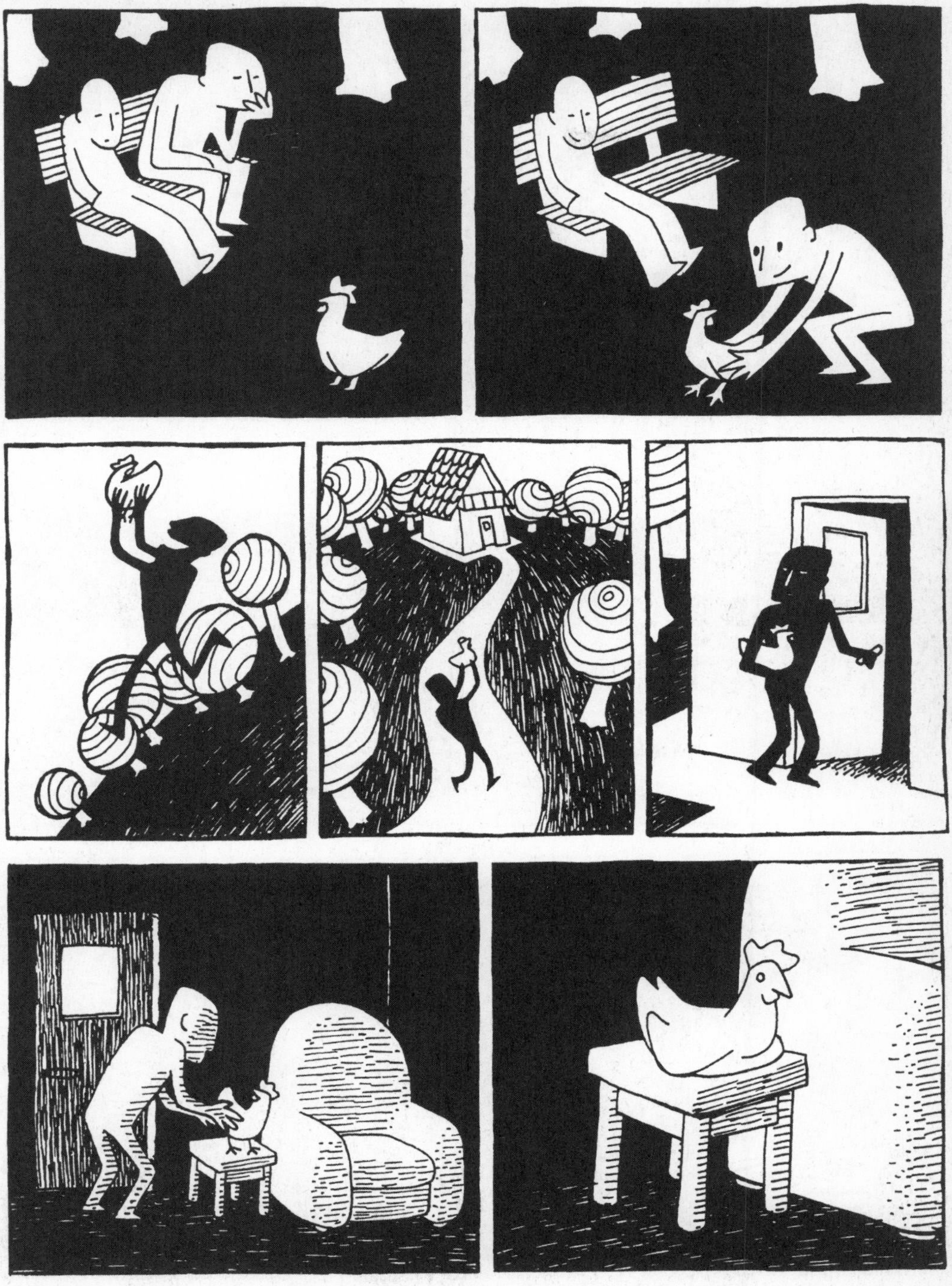

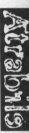

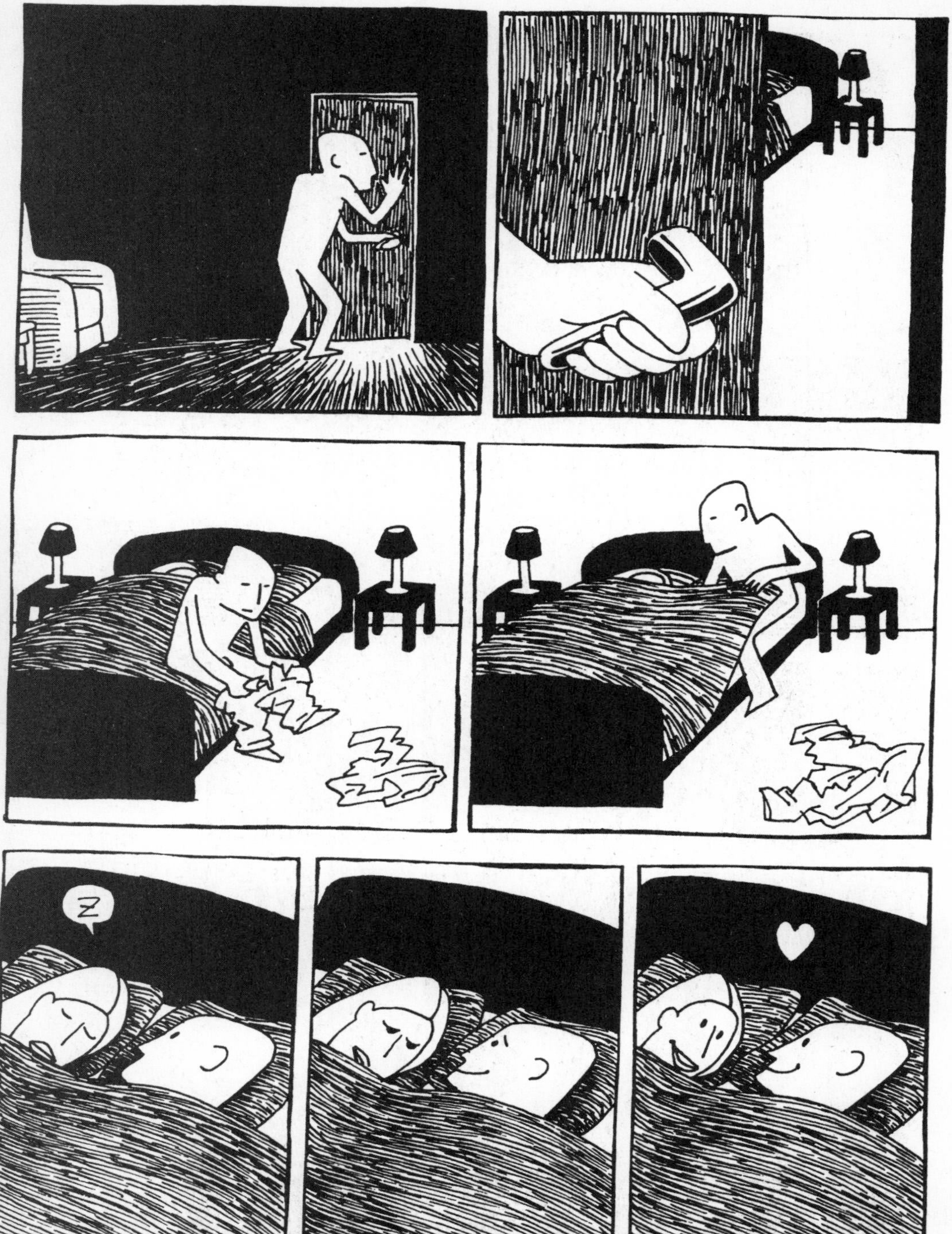
Z

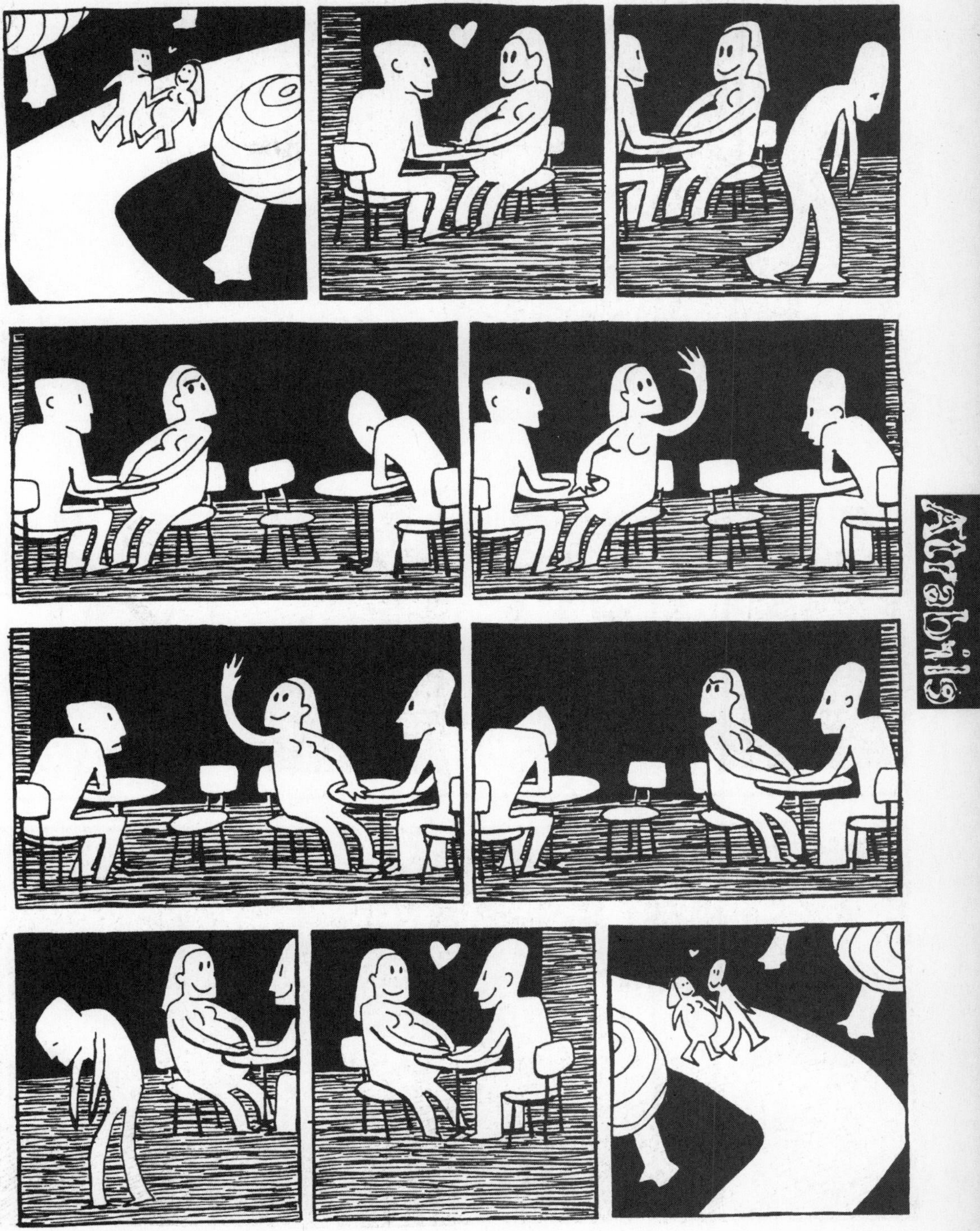

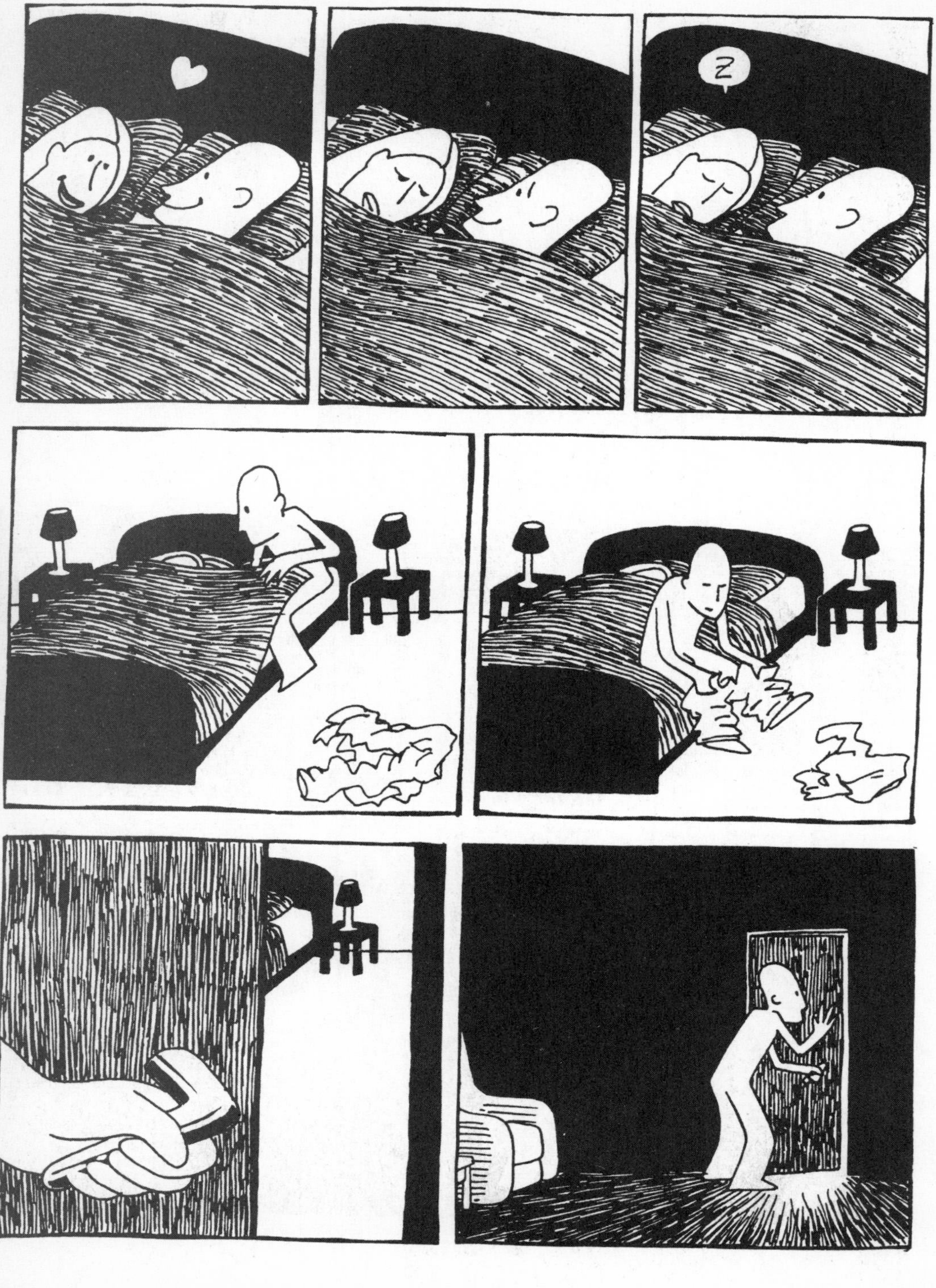
Z

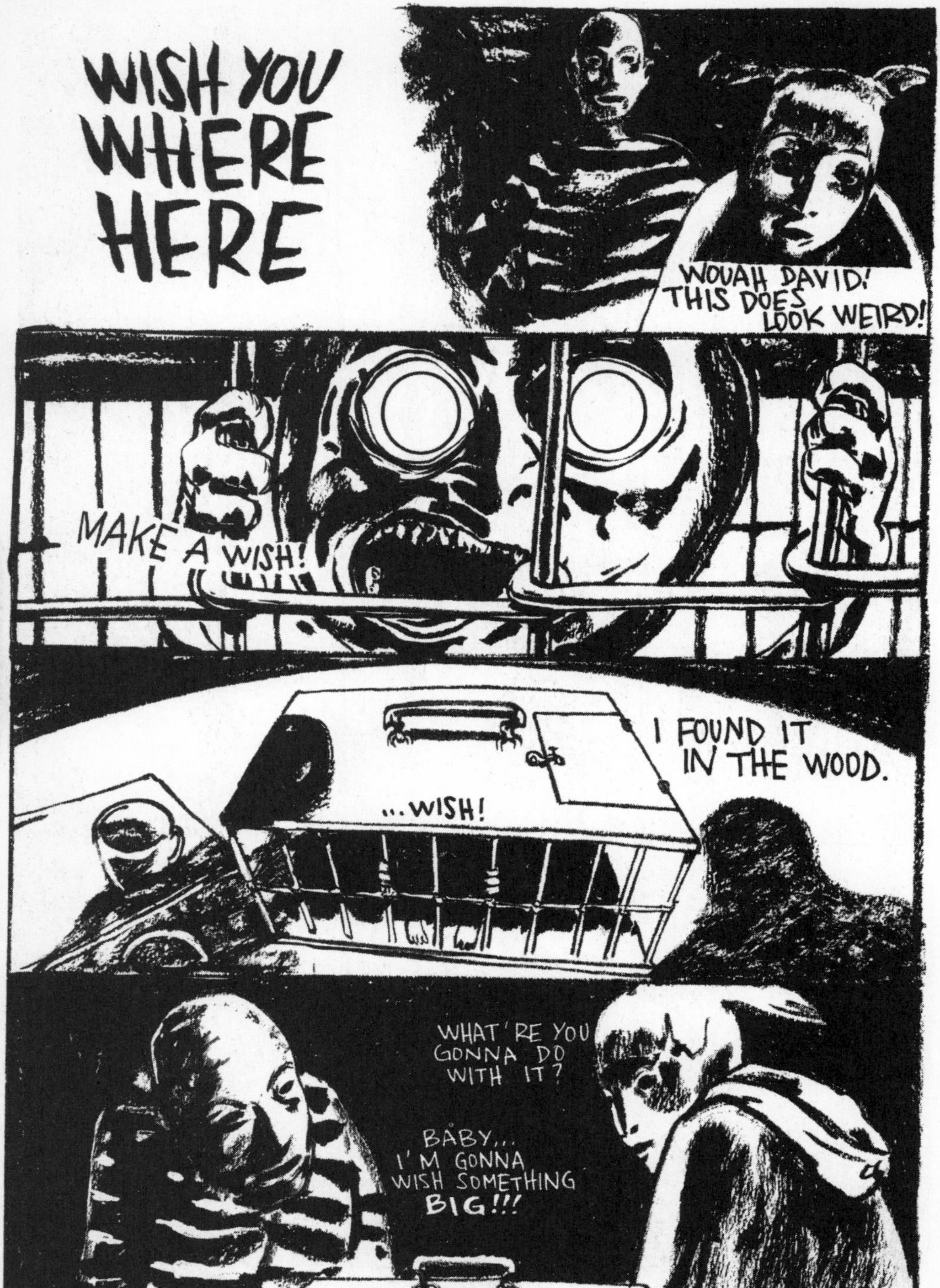
WISH YOU WHERE HERE
WOUAH DAVID! THIS DOES LOOK WEIRD!
MAKE A WISH!
I FOUND IT IN THE WOOD.
...WISH!
WHAT'RE YOU GONNA DO WITH IT?
BABY... I'M GONNA WISH SOMETHING BIG!!!

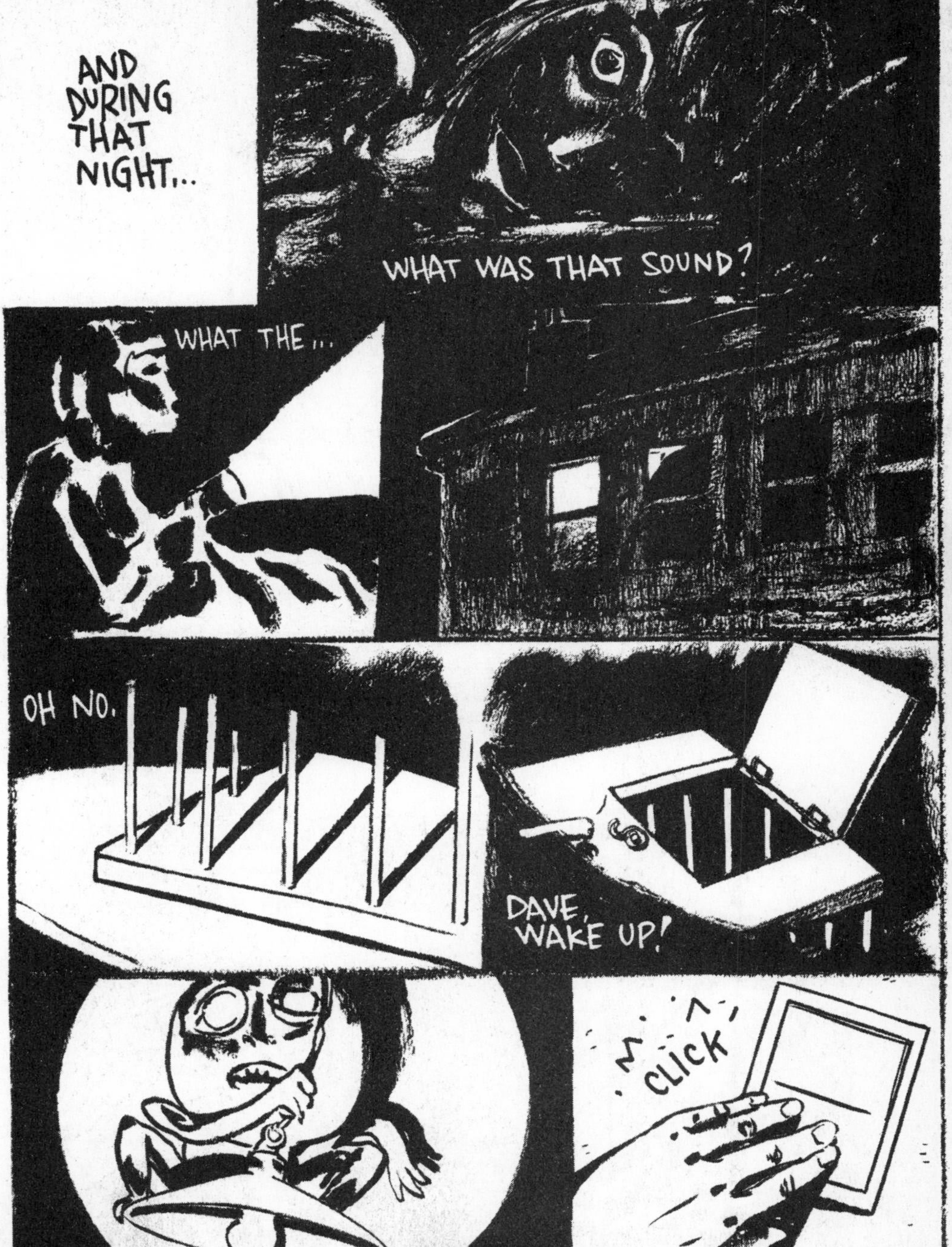
AND DURING THAT NIGHT...
WHAT WAS THAT SOUND?
WHAT THE...
OH NO.
DAVE, WAKE UP!
CLICK

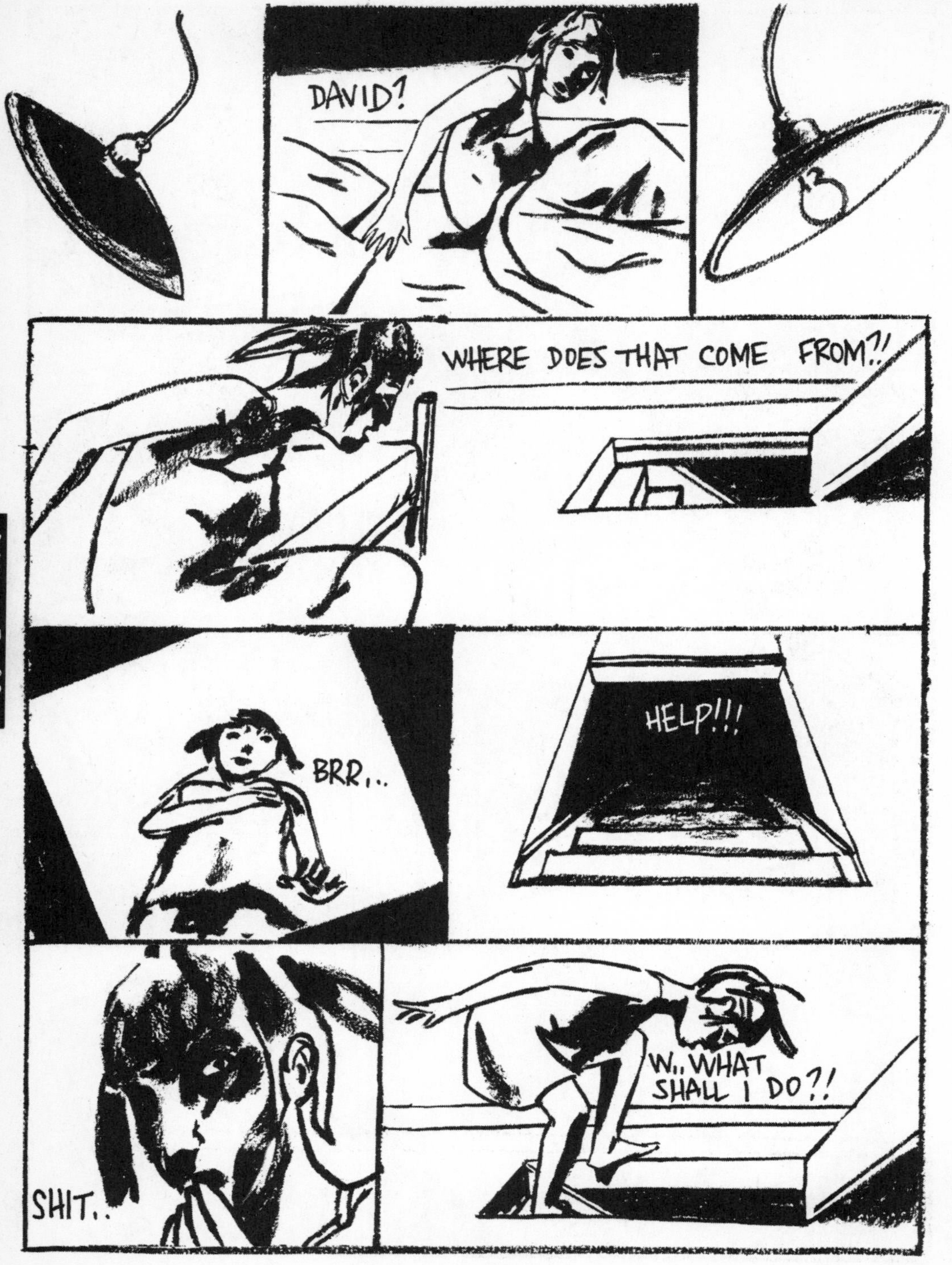
DAVID?
WHERE DOES THAT COME FROM?!
BRR...
HELP!!!
SHIT..
W.. WHAT SHALL I DO?!

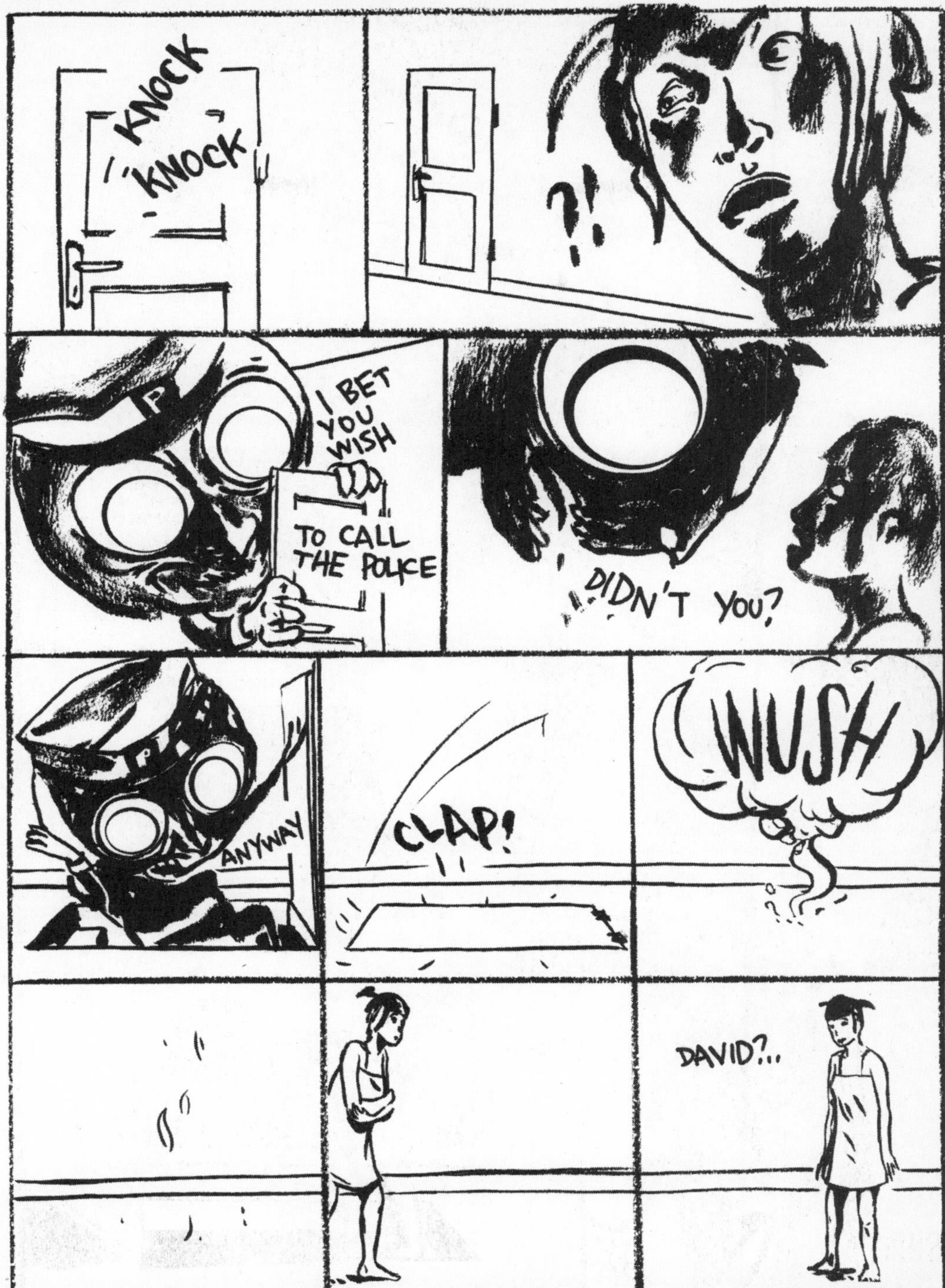
KNOCK
KNOCK
?!
I BET YOU WISH
TO CALL THE POLICE
...DIDN'T YOU?
ANYWAY
CLAP!
WUSH
DAVID?..

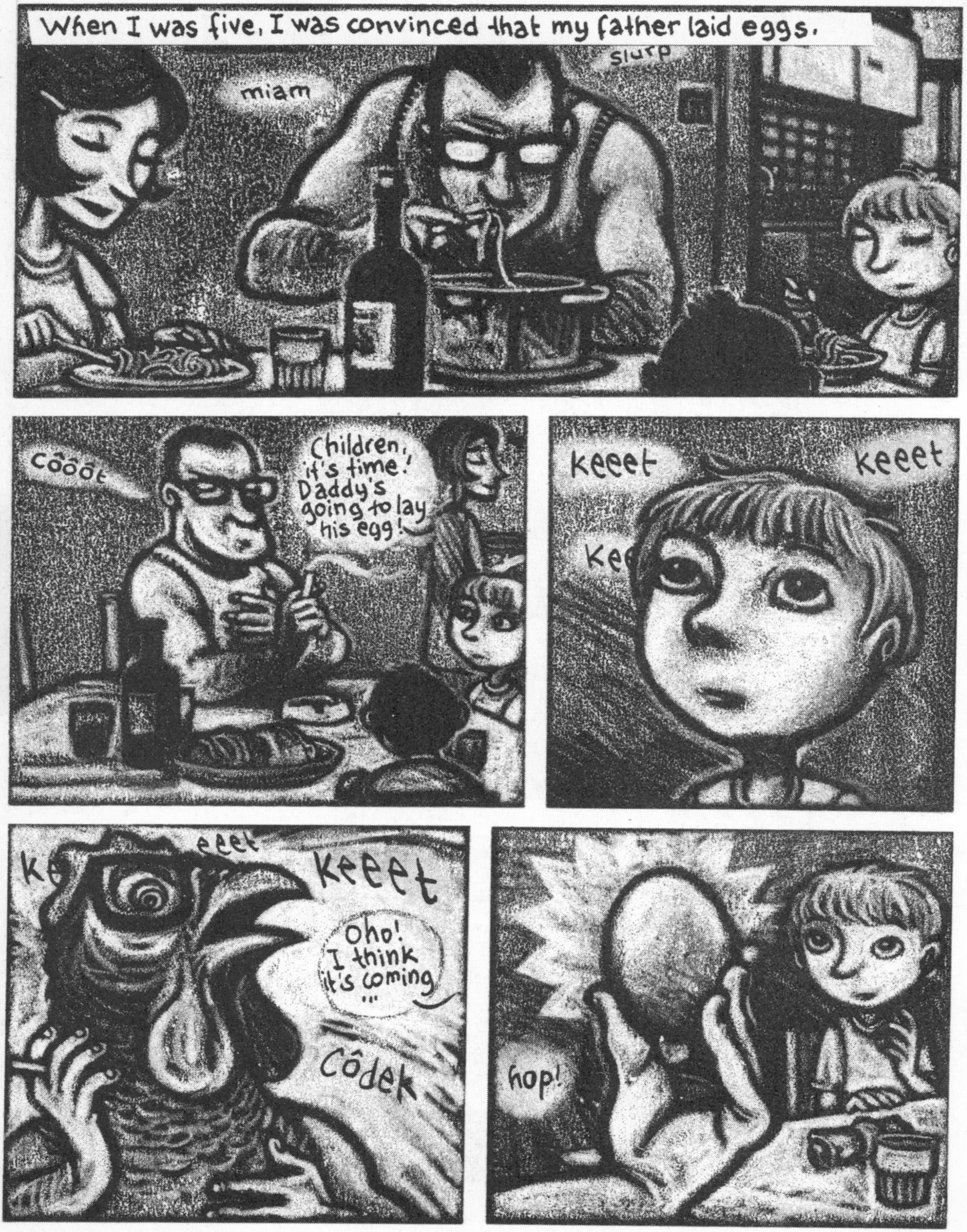
When I was five, I was convinced that my father laid eggs.
miam
slurp
côôôt
Children, it's time! Daddy's going to lay his egg!
keeet
keeet
kee
ke
eeet
keeet
Oho! I think it's coming ...
Côdek
hop!

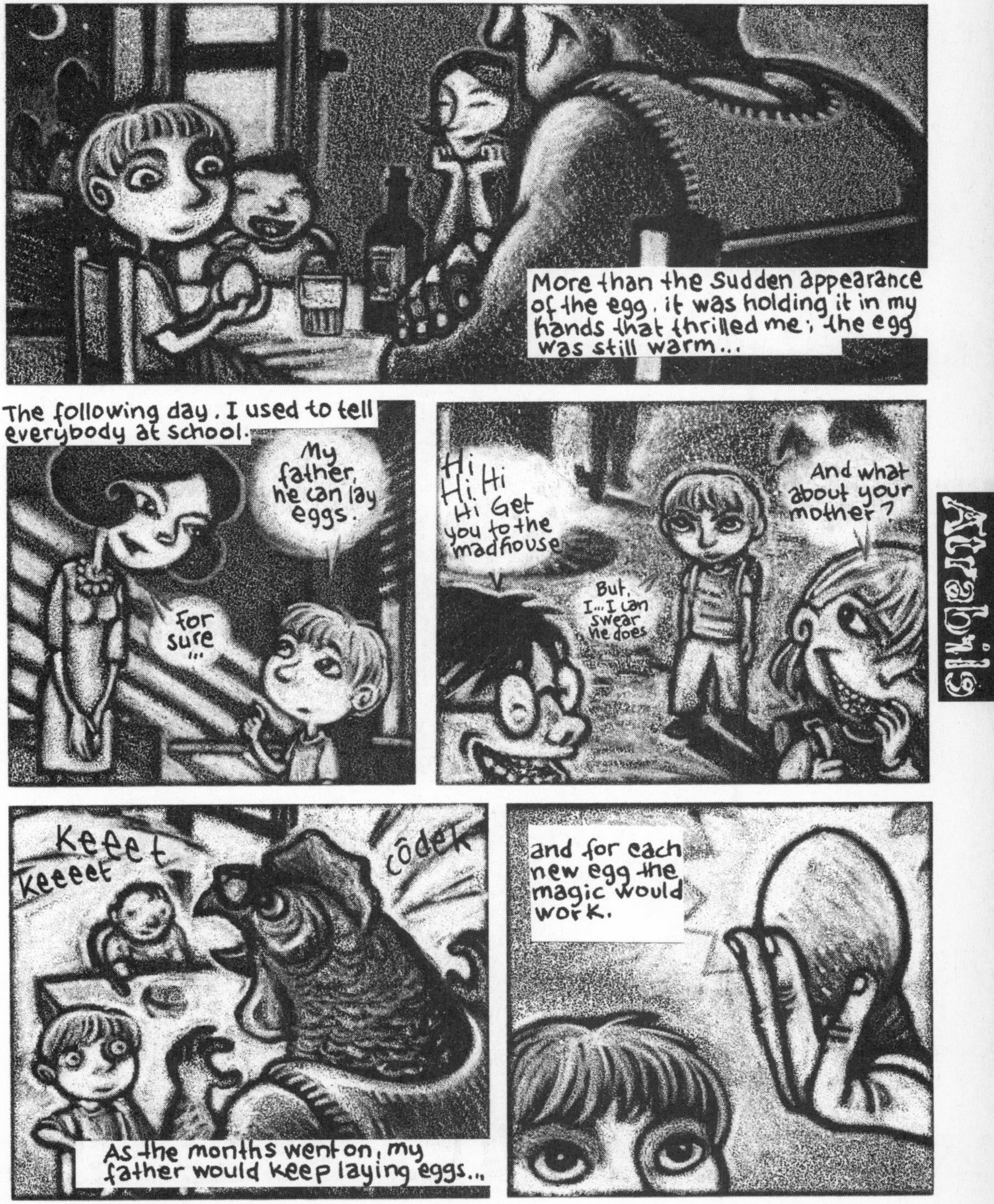
More than the sudden appearance of the egg, it was holding it in my hands that thrilled me; the egg was still warm...
The following day, I used to tell everybody at school.
My father, he can lay eggs.
For sure ...
Hi Hi Hi Hi Get you to the madhouse
But, I... I can swear he does
And what about your mother?
Keeet keeeet
côdek
As the months went on, my father would keep laying eggs...
and for each new egg the magic would work.

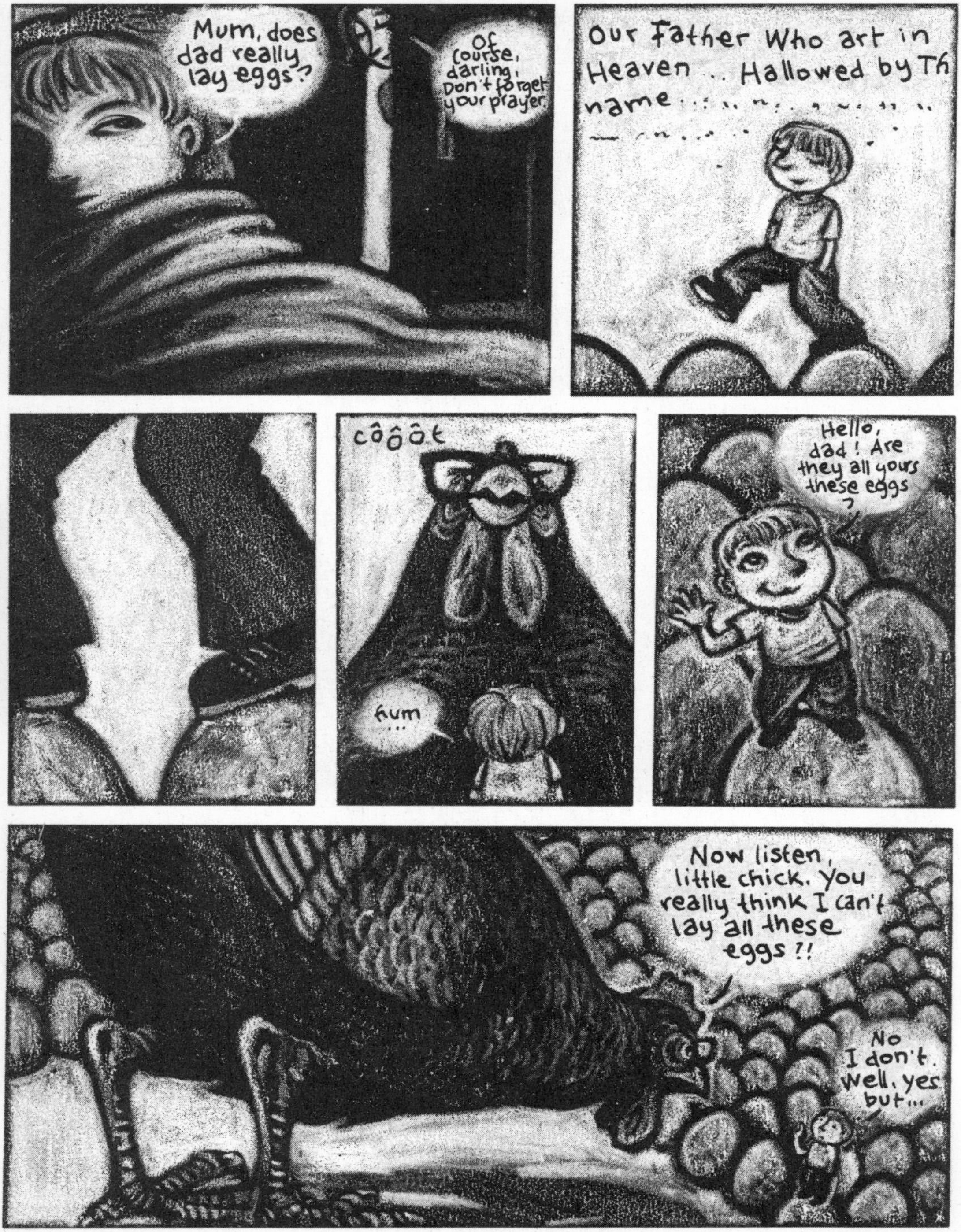

Mum, does dad really lay eggs?
Of course, darling. Don't forget your prayer.
Our Father Who art in Heaven .. Hallowed by Th name
côôôt
hum ...
Hello, dad! Are they all yours these eggs ?
Now listen, little chick. You really think I can't lay all these eggs ?!
No I don't. Well, yes but...

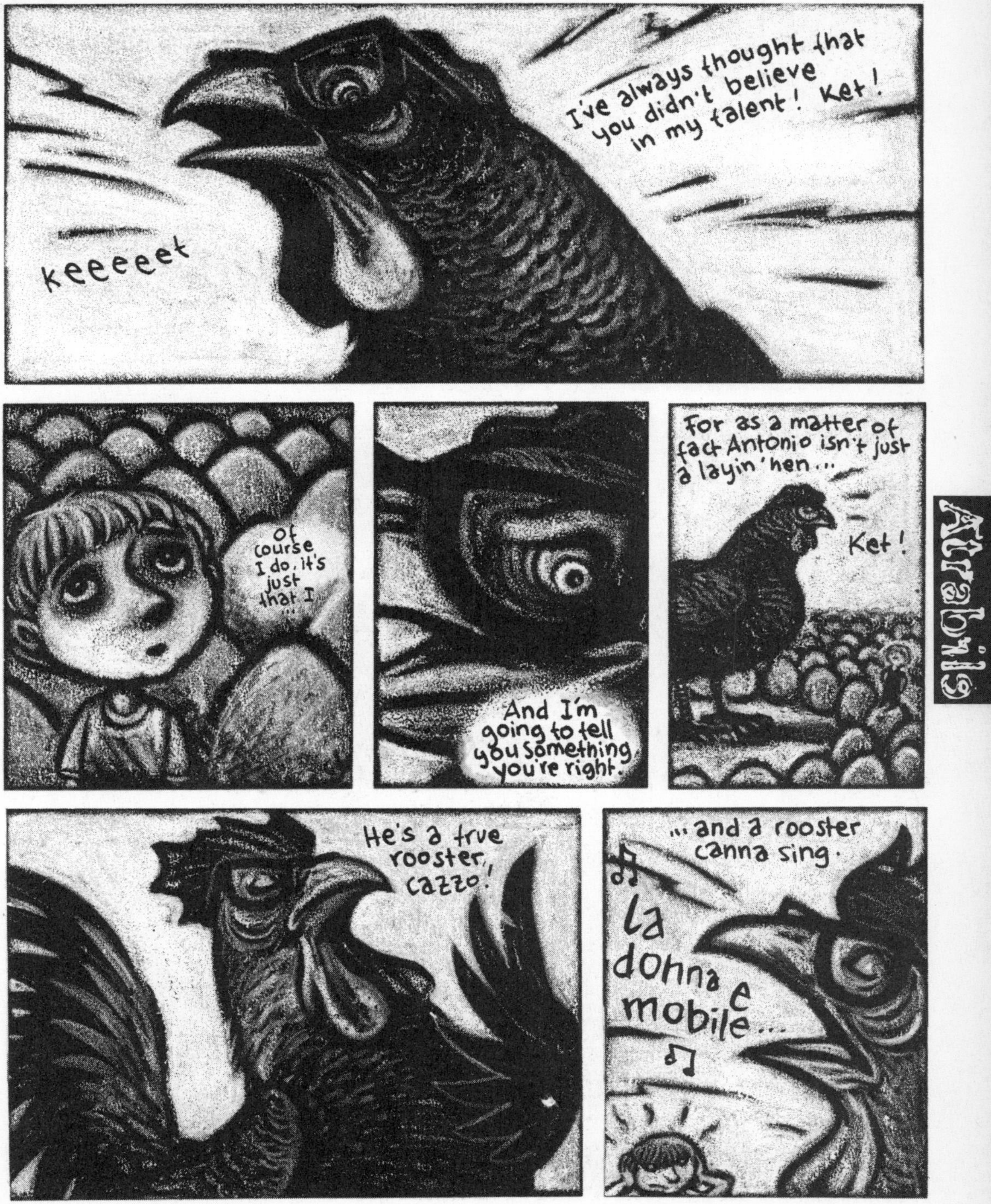
I've always thought that you didn't believe in my talent! Ket!
keeeeet
Of course I do, it's just that I ...
And I'm going to tell you something you're right.
For as a matter of fact Antonio isn't just a layin' hen...
Ket!
He's a true rooster, cazzo!
... and a rooster canna sing.
La donna e mobile...

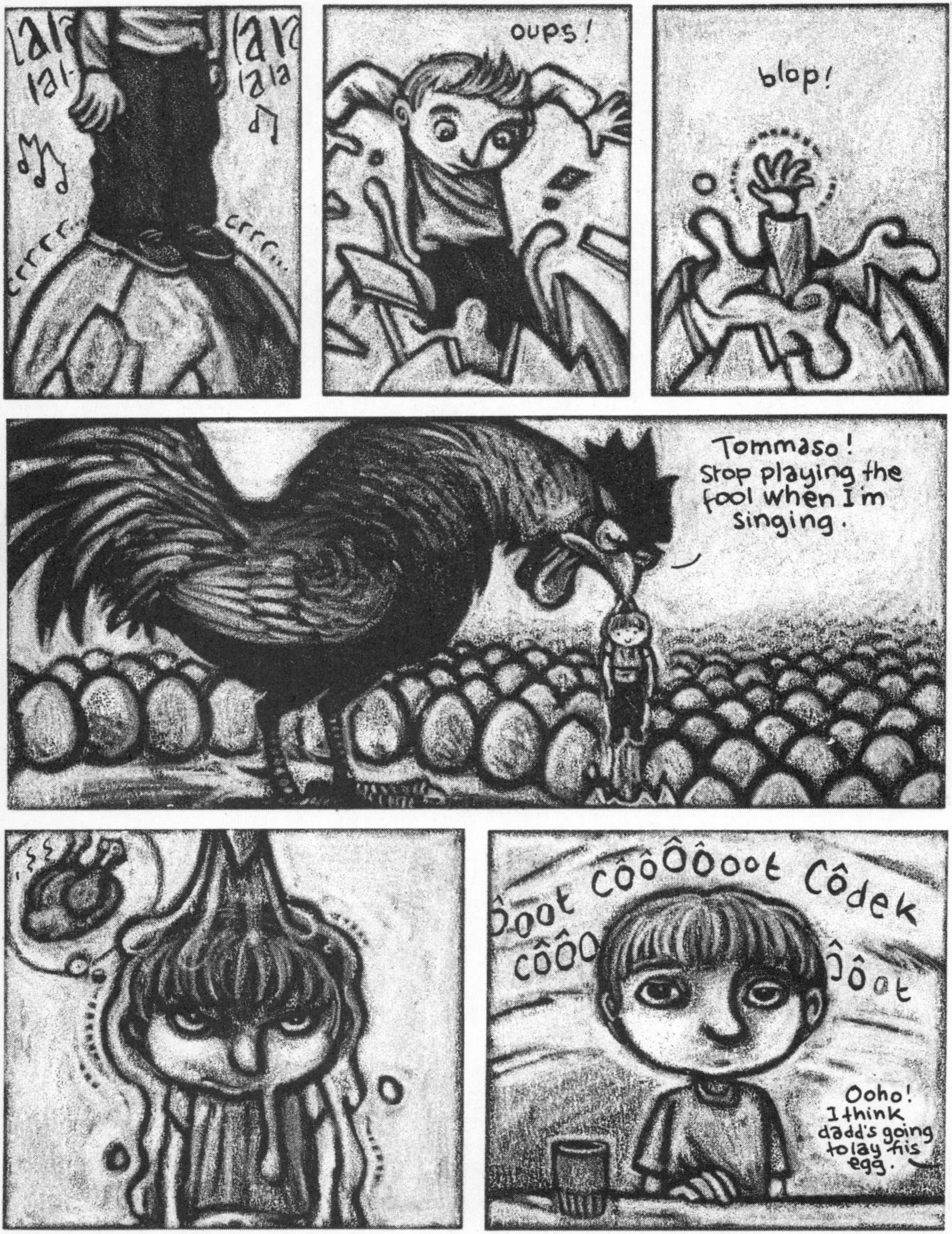
lala lala
lala lala
crrrr...
crrrr...
oups!
blop!
Tommaso! Stop playing the fool when I'm singing.
Ôoot côôÔÔoot Côdek côôô Ôôot
Ooho! I think dadd's going to lay his egg.

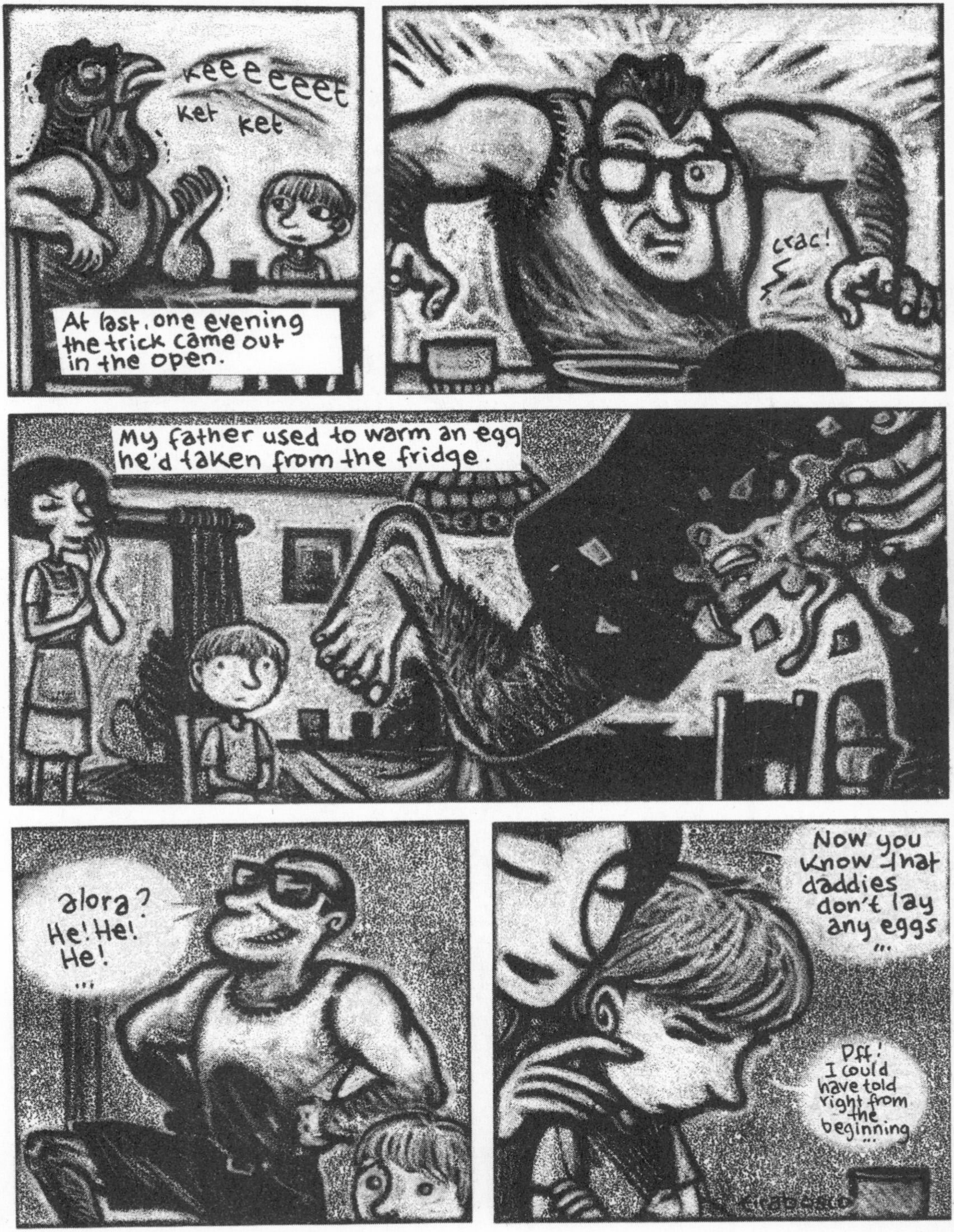
keeeeeeet
ket ket
At last, one evening the trick came out in the open.
crac!
My father used to warm an egg he'd taken from the fridge.
alora? He! He! He! ...
Now you know that daddies don't lay any eggs ...
Pff! I could have told right from the beginning ...
Atrabile

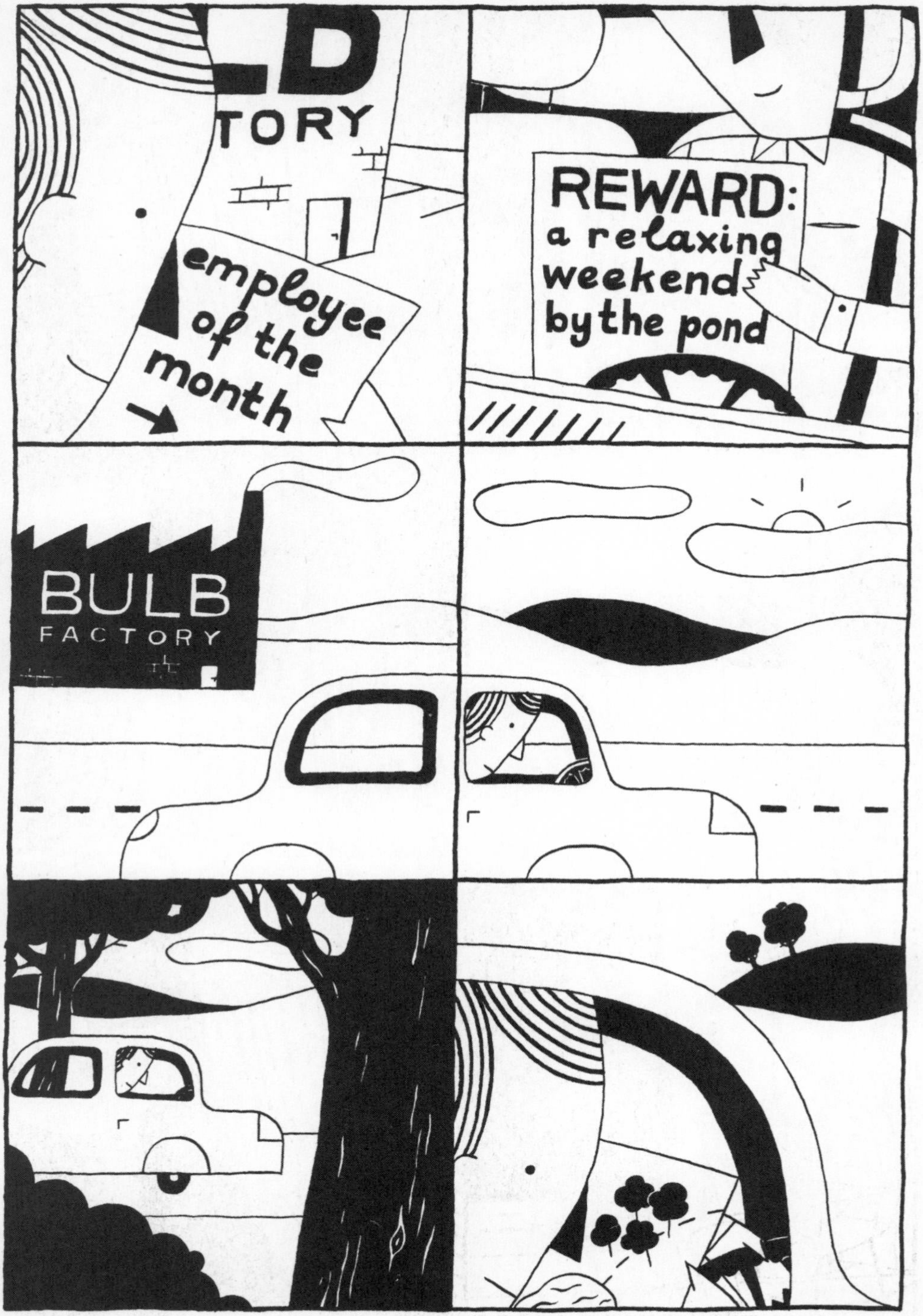
LD
TORY
employee of the month
REWARD: a relaxing weekend by the pond
BULB
FACTORY

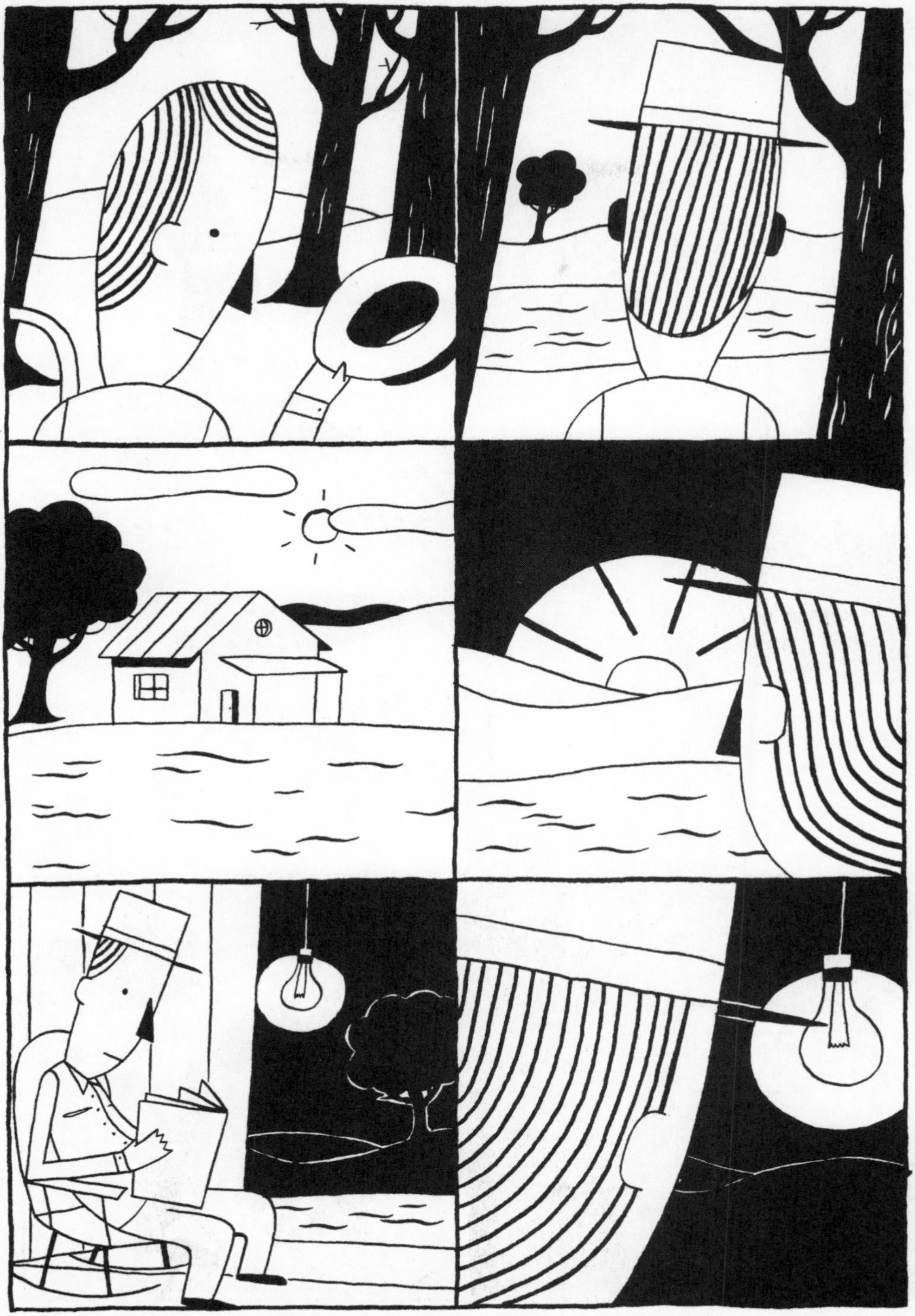

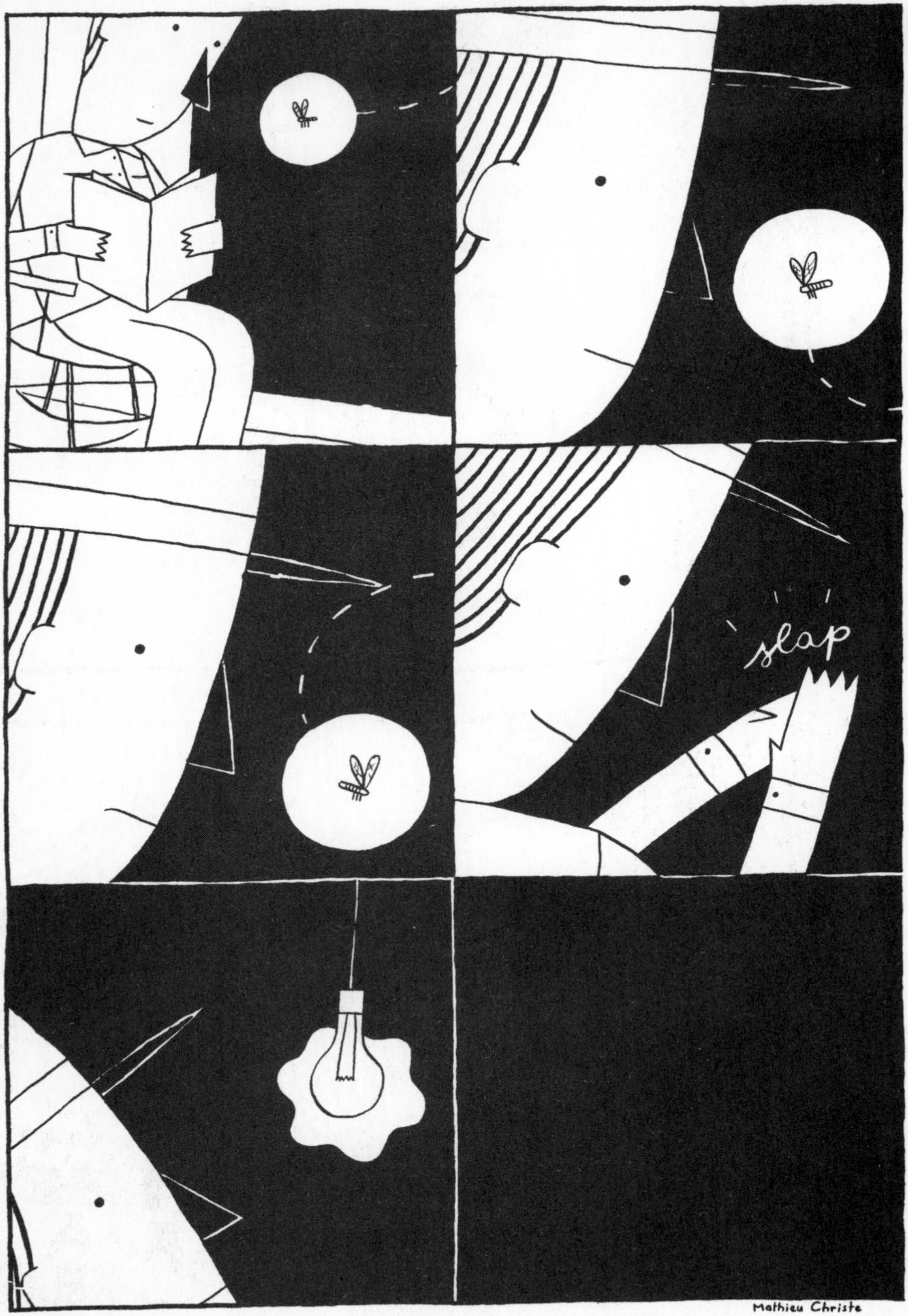
slap
Mathieu Christe

Fear

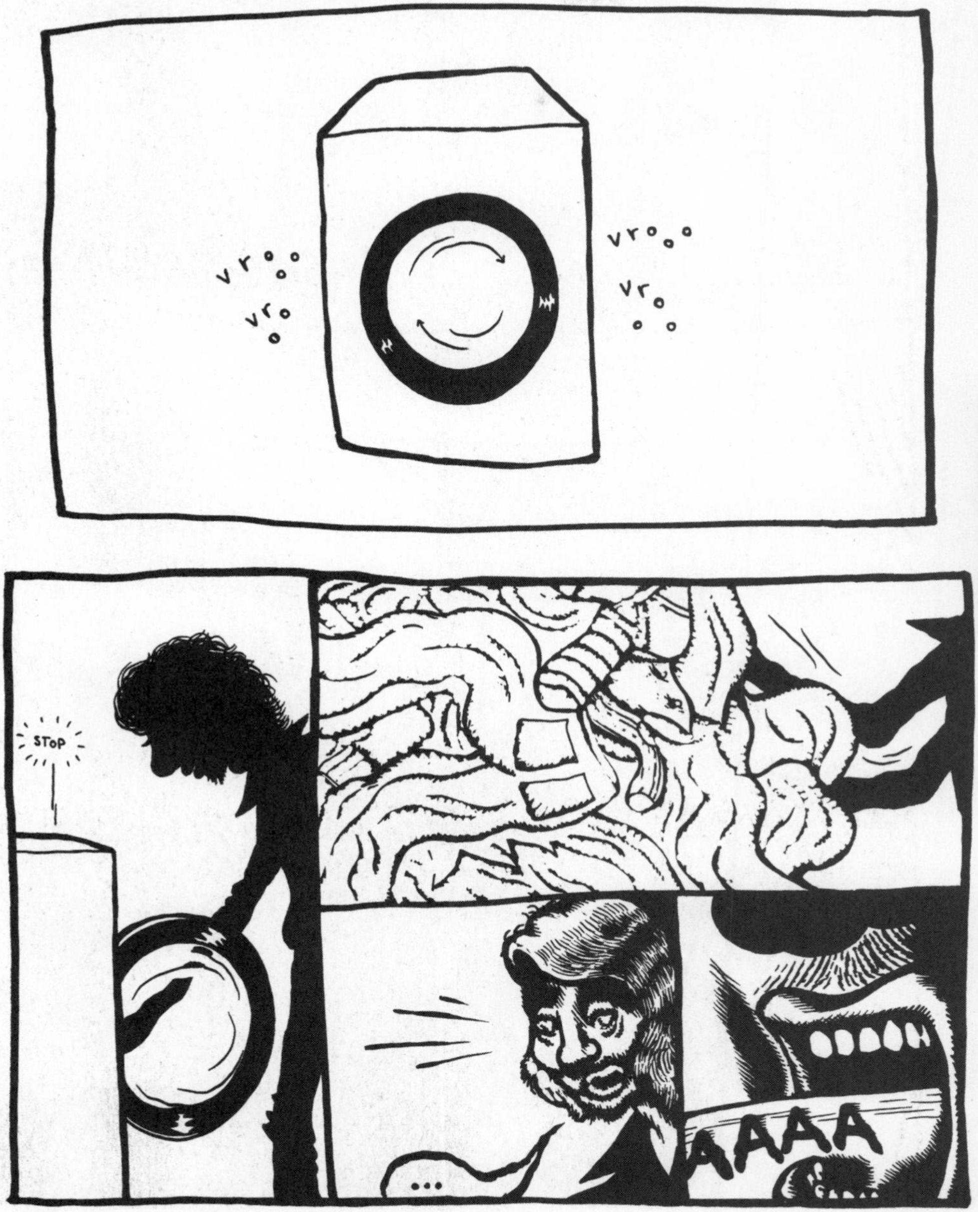
vroooo
vroo
vrooo
vroooo
STOP
...
AAAA

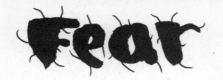

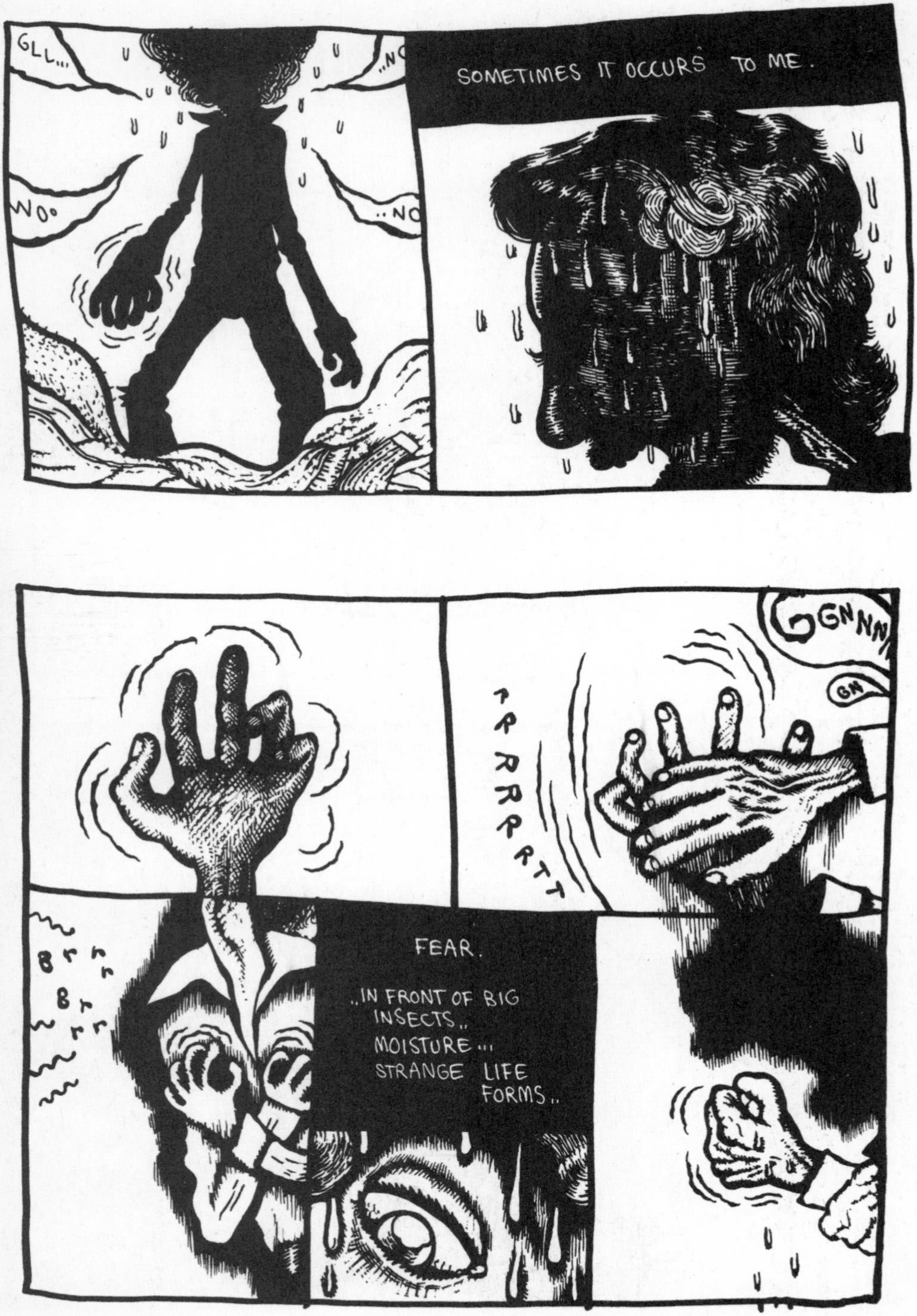
GLL...
..NO
NOo
..NO
SOMETIMES IT OCCURS TO ME.
GNNN
GN
RRRRRRTT
Brrr
Brrr
FEAR.
..IN FRONT OF BIG INSECTS..
MOISTURE...
STRANGE LIFE FORMS..

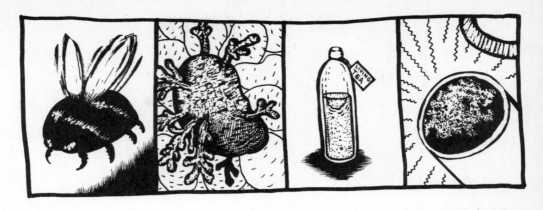

THIS TIME IT WAS A PULL-OVER.

BEFORE   AFTER

Atrabilis

WHAT A SILLY THING TO DO, PUTTING IT INTO THIS MACHINE.

IT HAD BECOME A SORT OF ORGANIC MUTANT THING... I COULDN'T EVEN TOUCH IT.

END

AMY ? ALICE ? REBECCA ? KAREEN

ART&STORY > NICOLAS ROBEL

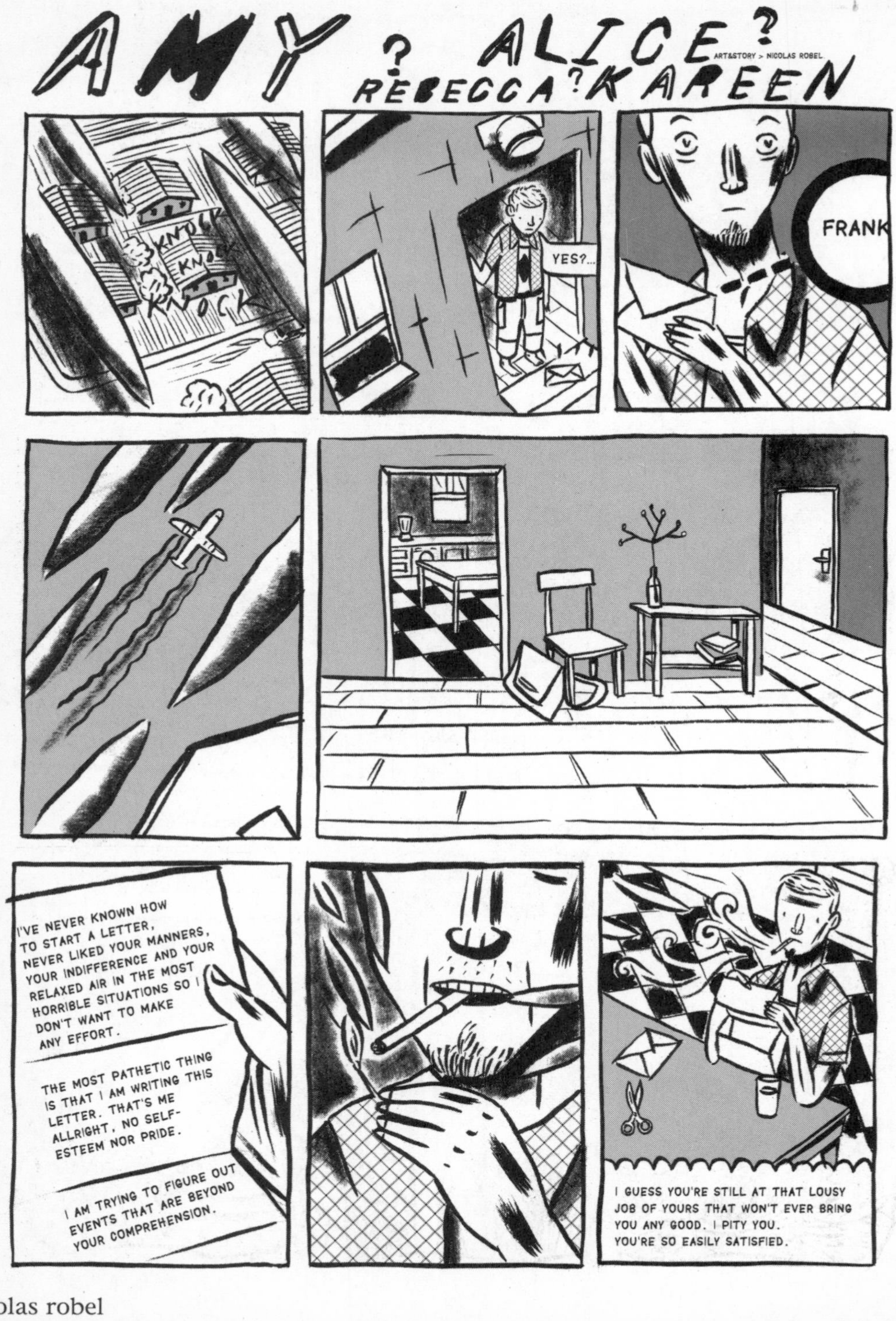

KNOCK
KNOCK
KNOCK
YES?...
FRANK
I'VE NEVER KNOWN HOW TO START A LETTER, NEVER LIKED YOUR MANNERS, YOUR INDIFFERENCE AND YOUR RELAXED AIR IN THE MOST HORRIBLE SITUATIONS SO I DON'T WANT TO MAKE ANY EFFORT.
THE MOST PATHETIC THING IS THAT I AM WRITING THIS LETTER. THAT'S ME ALLRIGHT, NO SELF-ESTEEM NOR PRIDE.
I AM TRYING TO FIGURE OUT EVENTS THAT ARE BEYOND YOUR COMPREHENSION.
I GUESS YOU'RE STILL AT THAT LOUSY JOB OF YOURS THAT WON'T EVER BRING YOU ANY GOOD. I PITY YOU. YOU'RE SO EASILY SATISFIED.

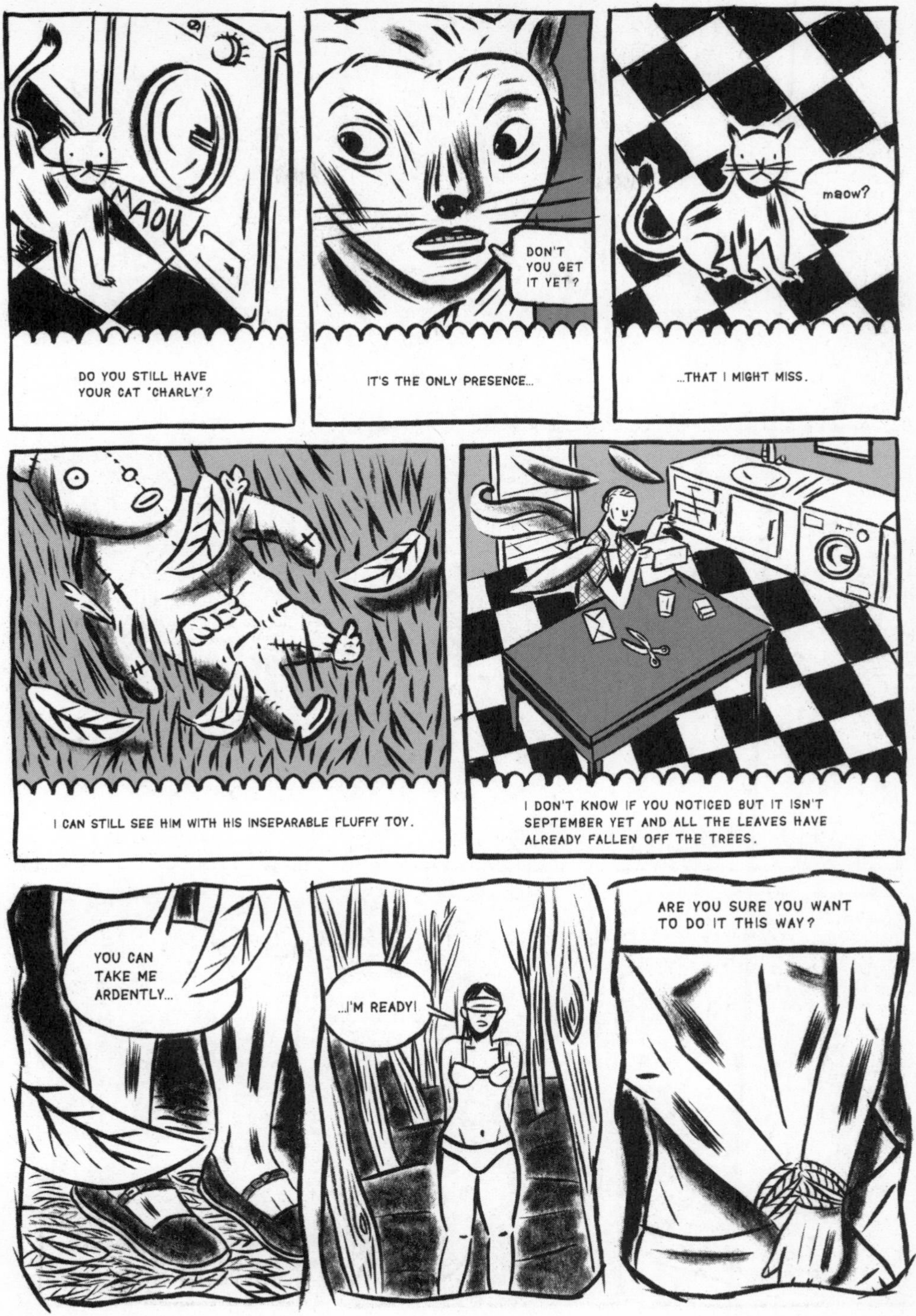
MAOW
DON'T YOU GET IT YET?
maow?
DO YOU STILL HAVE YOUR CAT "CHARLY"?
IT'S THE ONLY PRESENCE...
...THAT I MIGHT MISS.
I CAN STILL SEE HIM WITH HIS INSEPARABLE FLUFFY TOY.
I DON'T KNOW IF YOU NOTICED BUT IT ISN'T SEPTEMBER YET AND ALL THE LEAVES HAVE ALREADY FALLEN OFF THE TREES.
YOU CAN TAKE ME ARDENTLY...
...I'M READY!
ARE YOU SURE YOU WANT TO DO IT THIS WAY?

Airaghi's

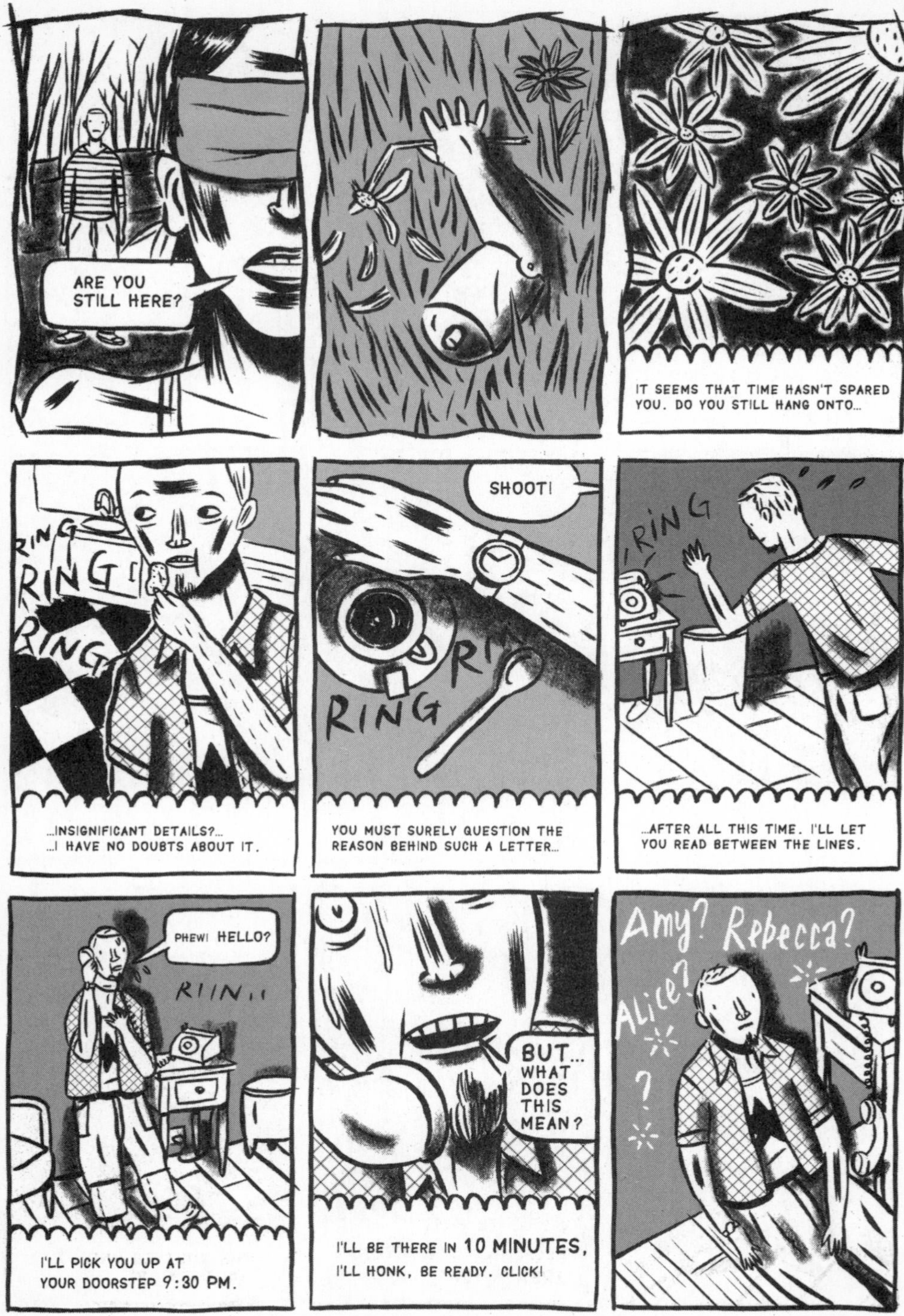
ARE YOU STILL HERE?
IT SEEMS THAT TIME HASN'T SPARED YOU. DO YOU STILL HANG ONTO...
RING RING! RING
...INSIGNIFICANT DETAILS?...
...I HAVE NO DOUBTS ABOUT IT.
SHOOT!
RING
YOU MUST SURELY QUESTION THE REASON BEHIND SUCH A LETTER...
RING
...AFTER ALL THIS TIME. I'LL LET YOU READ BETWEEN THE LINES.
PHEW! HELLO?
RIIN..
I'LL PICK YOU UP AT YOUR DOORSTEP 9:30 PM.
BUT... WHAT DOES THIS MEAN?
I'LL BE THERE IN 10 MINUTES, I'LL HONK, BE READY. CLICK!
Amy? Rebecca?
Alice?
?

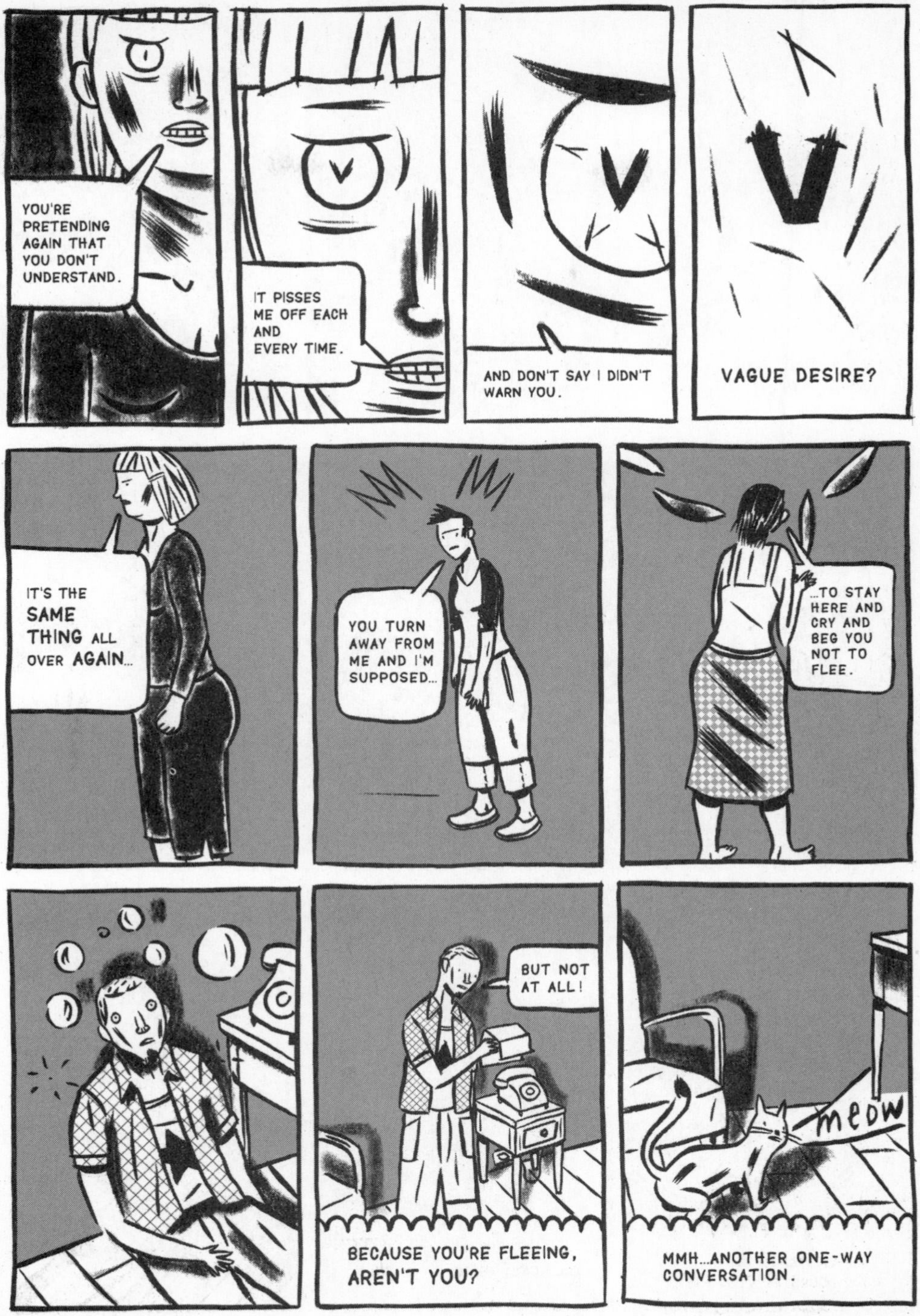
YOU'RE PRETENDING AGAIN THAT YOU DON'T UNDERSTAND.
IT PISSES ME OFF EACH AND EVERY TIME.
AND DON'T SAY I DIDN'T WARN YOU.
VAGUE DESIRE?
IT'S THE SAME THING ALL OVER AGAIN...
YOU TURN AWAY FROM ME AND I'M SUPPOSED...
...TO STAY HERE AND CRY AND BEG YOU NOT TO FLEE.
BUT NOT AT ALL!
BECAUSE YOU'RE FLEEING, AREN'T YOU?
MEOW
MMH...ANOTHER ONE-WAY CONVERSATION.

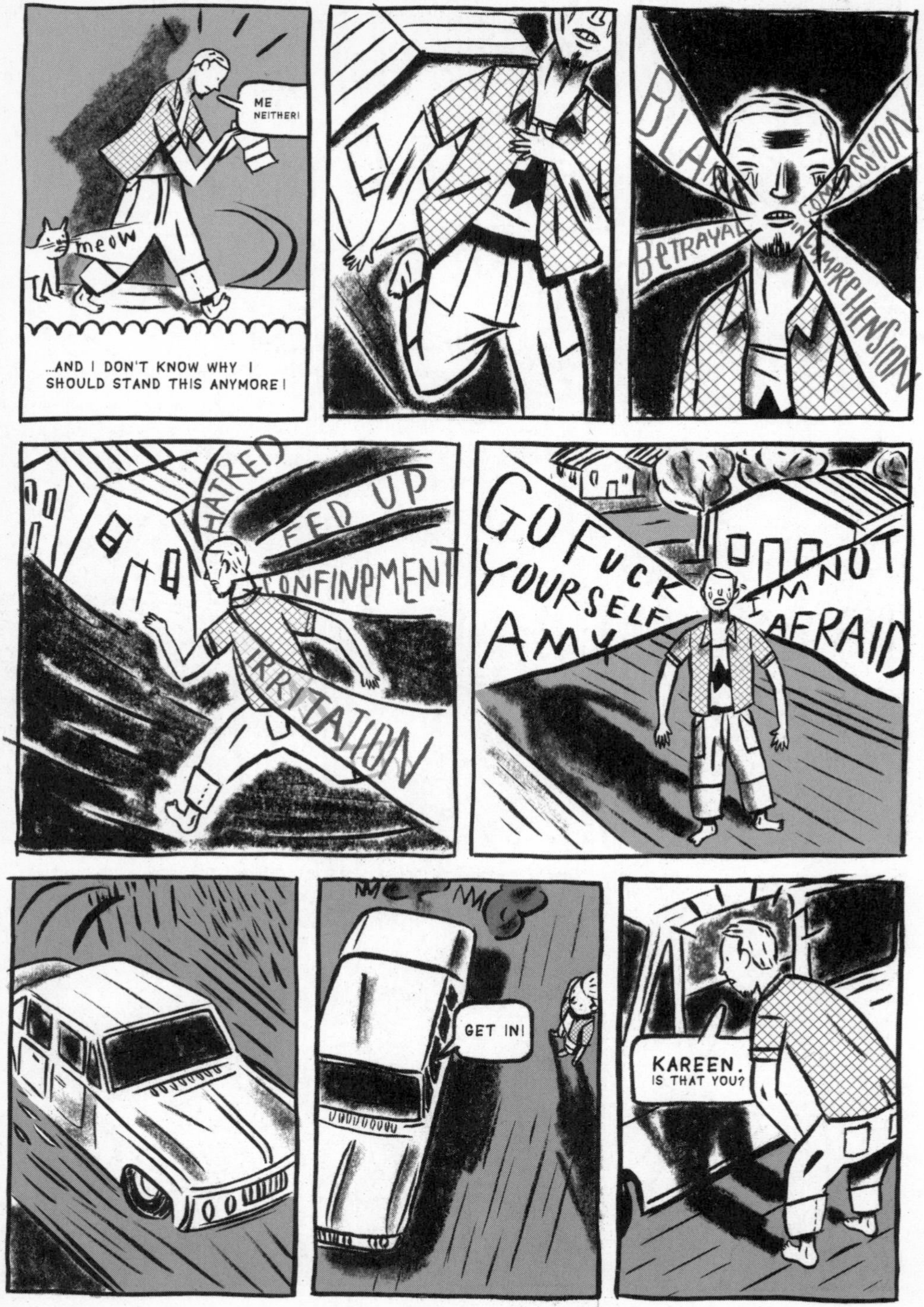
ME NEITHER!
meow
...AND I DON'T KNOW WHY I SHOULD STAND THIS ANYMORE!
BLA
COMPASSION
BETRAYAL
COMPREHENSION
HATRED
FED UP
CONFINEMENT
IRRITATION
GO FUCK YOURSELF AMY
I'M NOT AFRAID
GET IN!
KAREEN. IS THAT YOU?

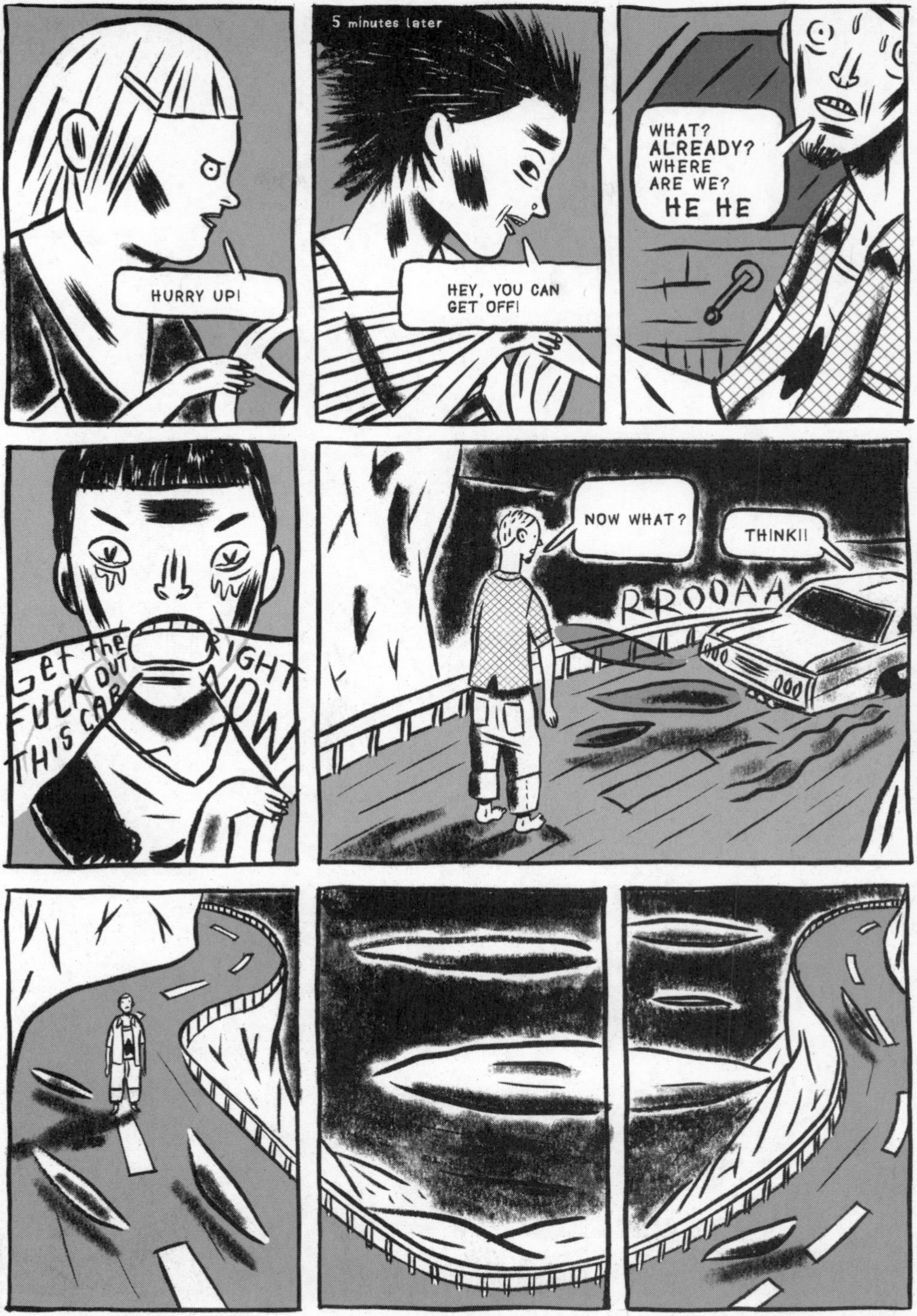
HURRY UP!
5 minutes later
HEY, YOU CAN GET OFF!
WHAT? ALREADY? WHERE ARE WE? HE HE
Get the FUCK OUT THIS CAR RIGHT NOW
NOW WHAT?
THINK!!
RROOAA

THANX TO ROBERT FOR HELPING ME TO TRANSLATE

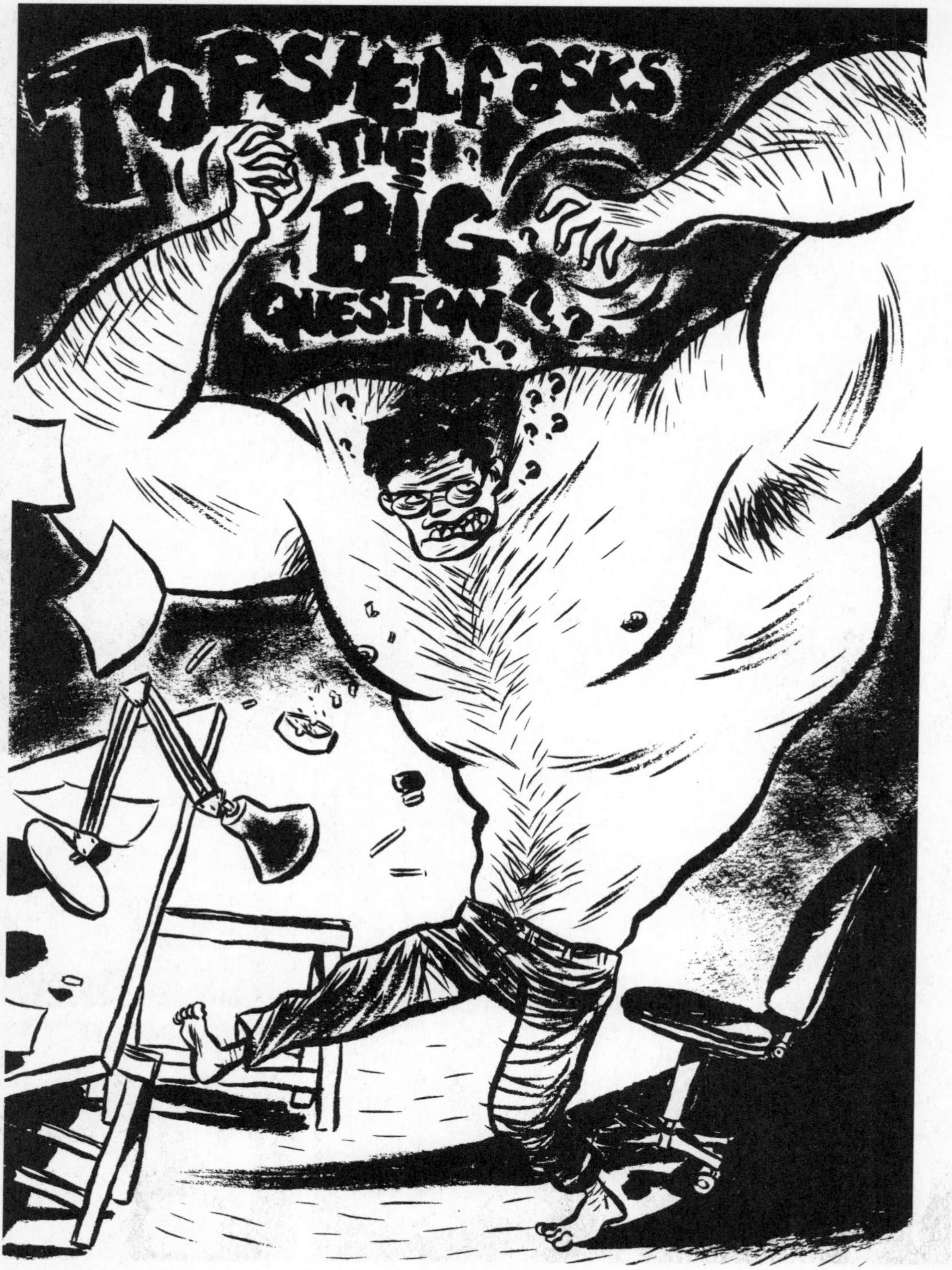
TOPSHELF ASKS
THE
BIG
QUESTION

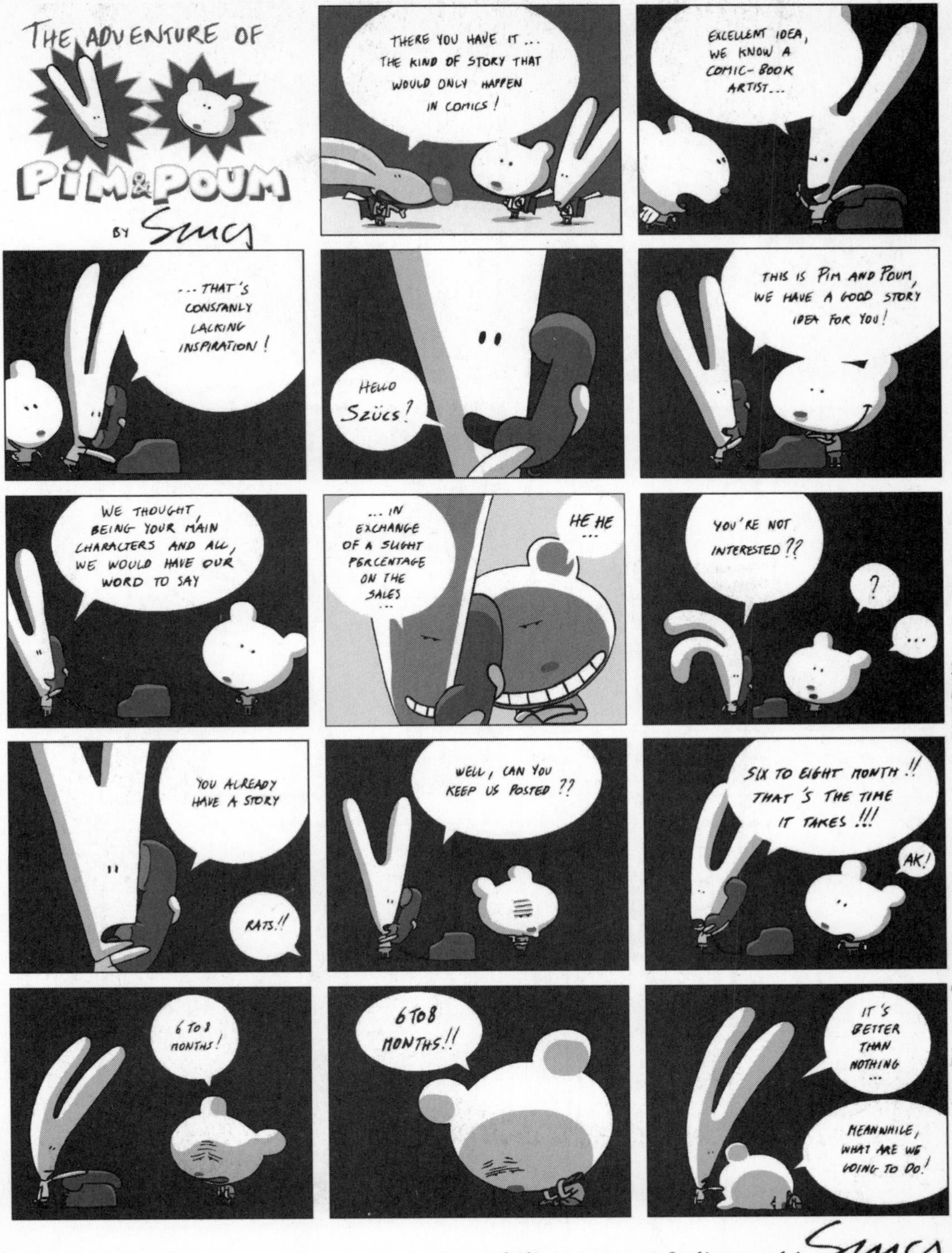
THE ADVENTURE OF
PIM & POUM
BY Szucs
THERE YOU HAVE IT ... THE KIND OF STORY THAT WOULD ONLY HAPPEN IN COMICS!
EXCELLENT IDEA, WE KNOW A COMIC-BOOK ARTIST...
... THAT'S CONSTANLY LACKING INSPIRATION!
HELLO SZÜCS?
THIS IS PIM AND POUM, WE HAVE A GOOD STORY IDEA FOR YOU!
WE THOUGHT, BEING YOUR MAIN CHARACTERS AND ALL, WE WOULD HAVE OUR WORD TO SAY
... IN EXCHANGE OF A SLIGHT PERCENTAGE ON THE SALES ...
HE HE ...
YOU'RE NOT INTERESTED ??
?
...
YOU ALREADY HAVE A STORY
RATS!!
WELL, CAN YOU KEEP US POSTED ??
SIX TO EIGHT MONTH !! THAT'S THE TIME IT TAKES !!!
AK!
6 TO 8 MONTHS!
6 TO 8 MONTHS!!
IT'S BETTER THAN NOTHING ...
MEANWHILE, WHAT ARE WE GOING TO DO!

www.arfarf.be.tf Scénario Philippe Capart Dessin Dino Sechi

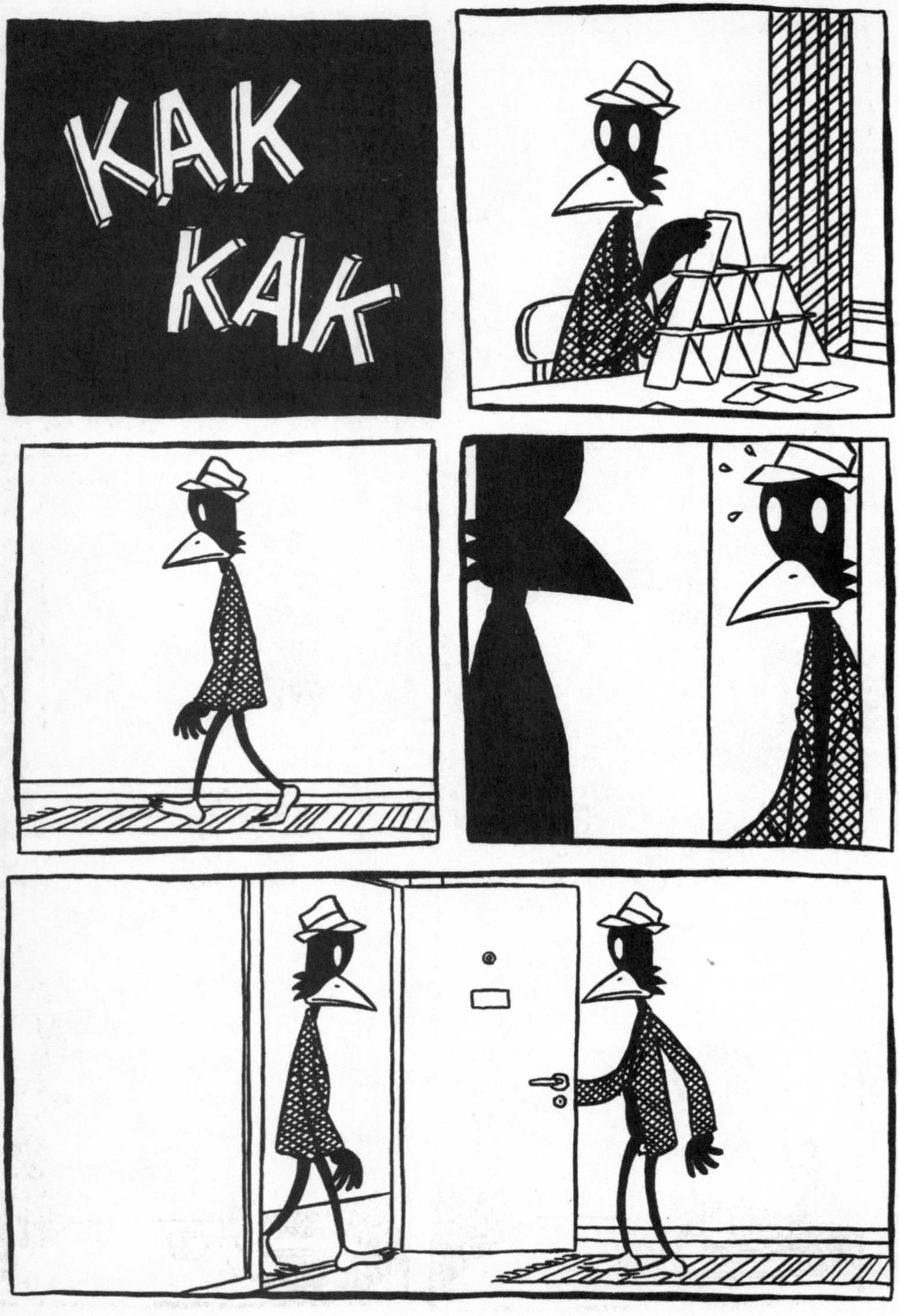
KAK
KAK

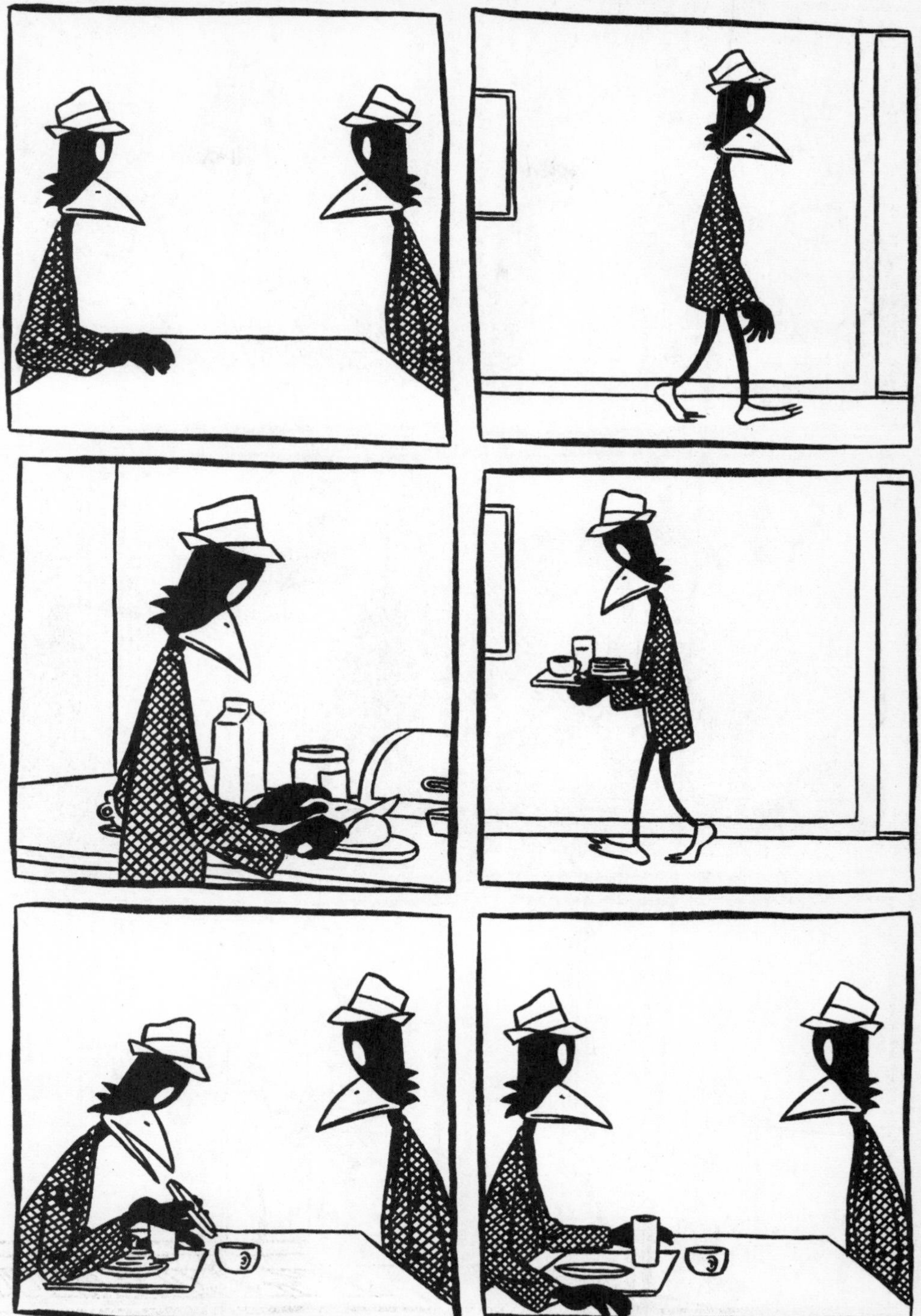

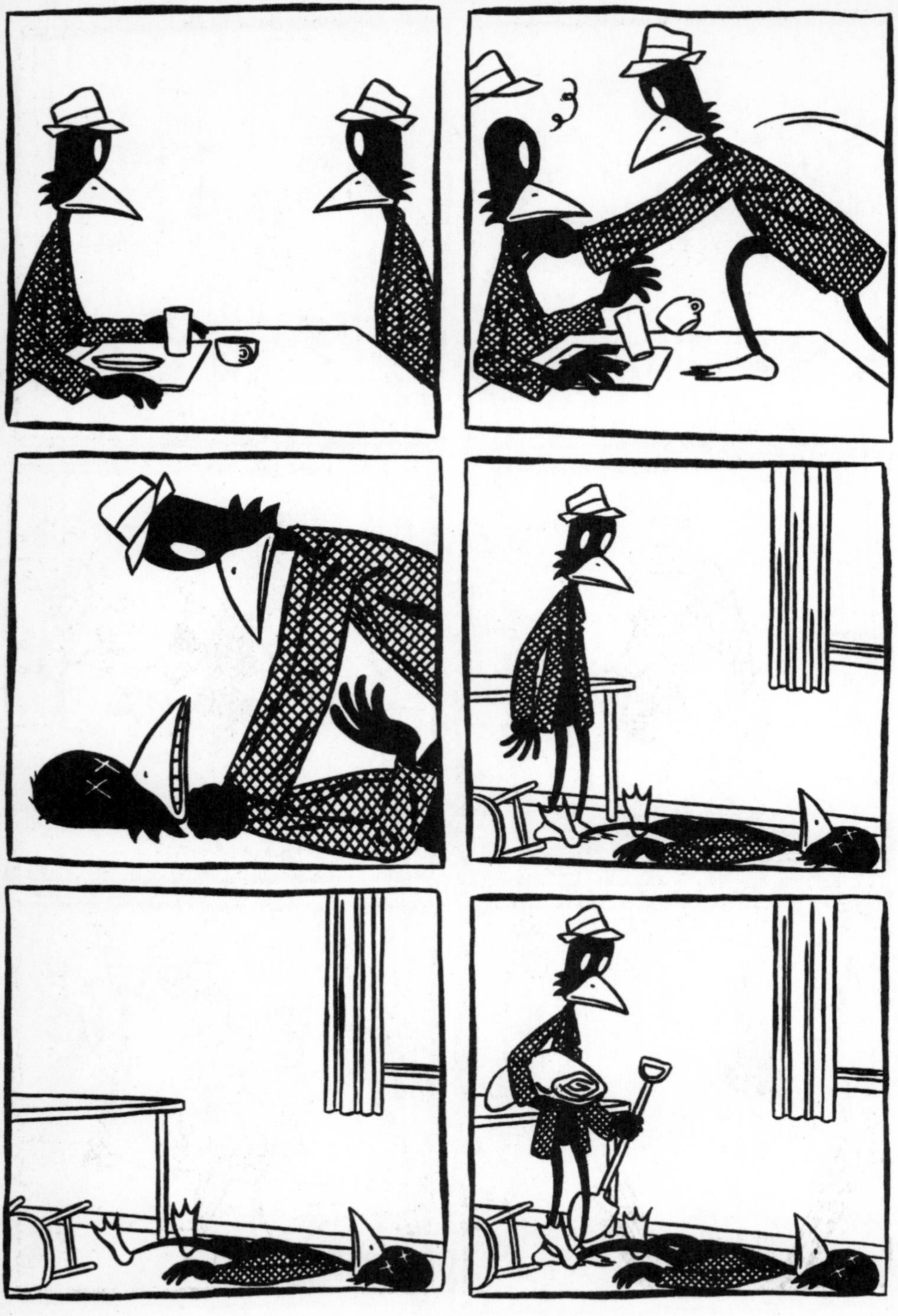

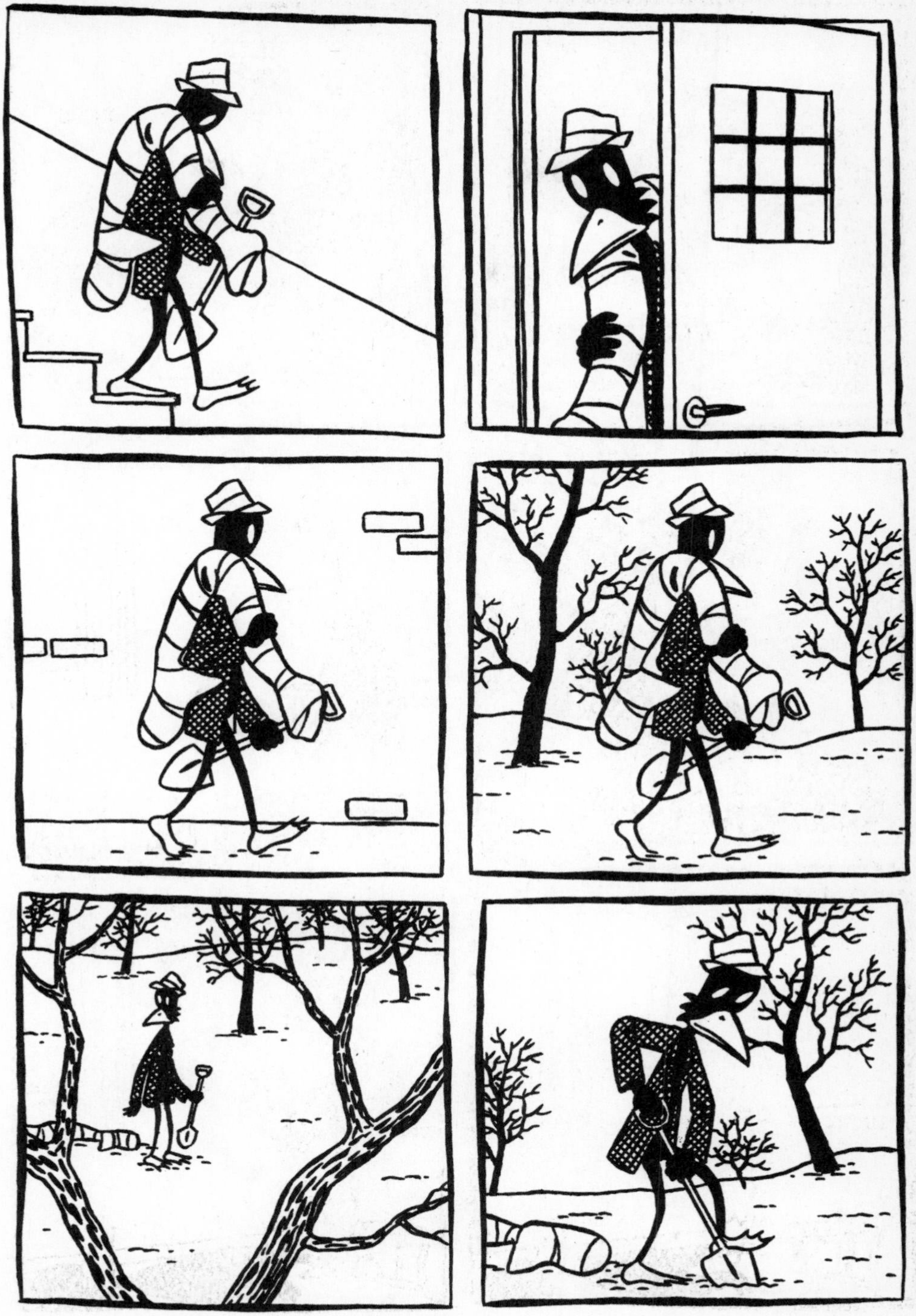

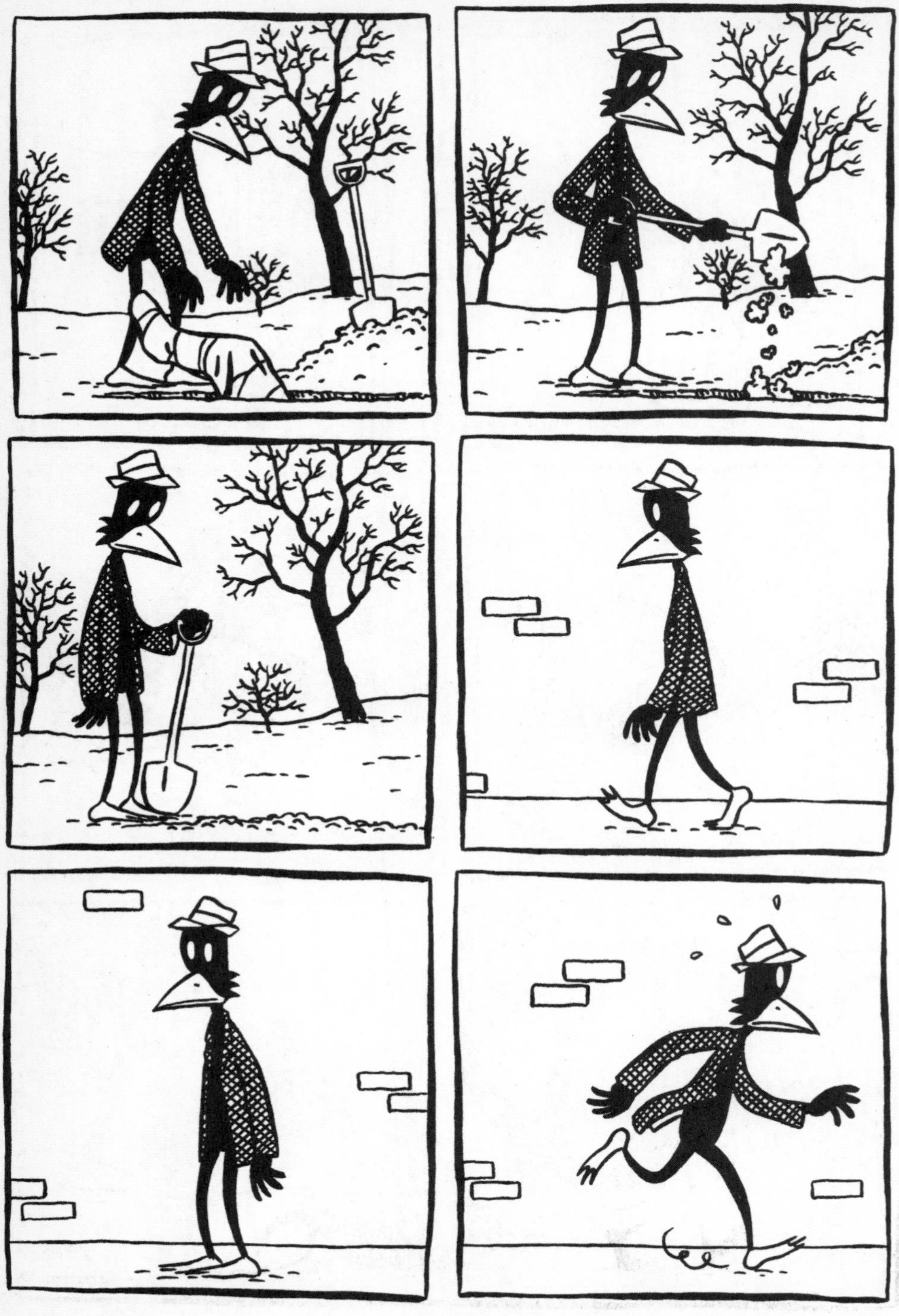

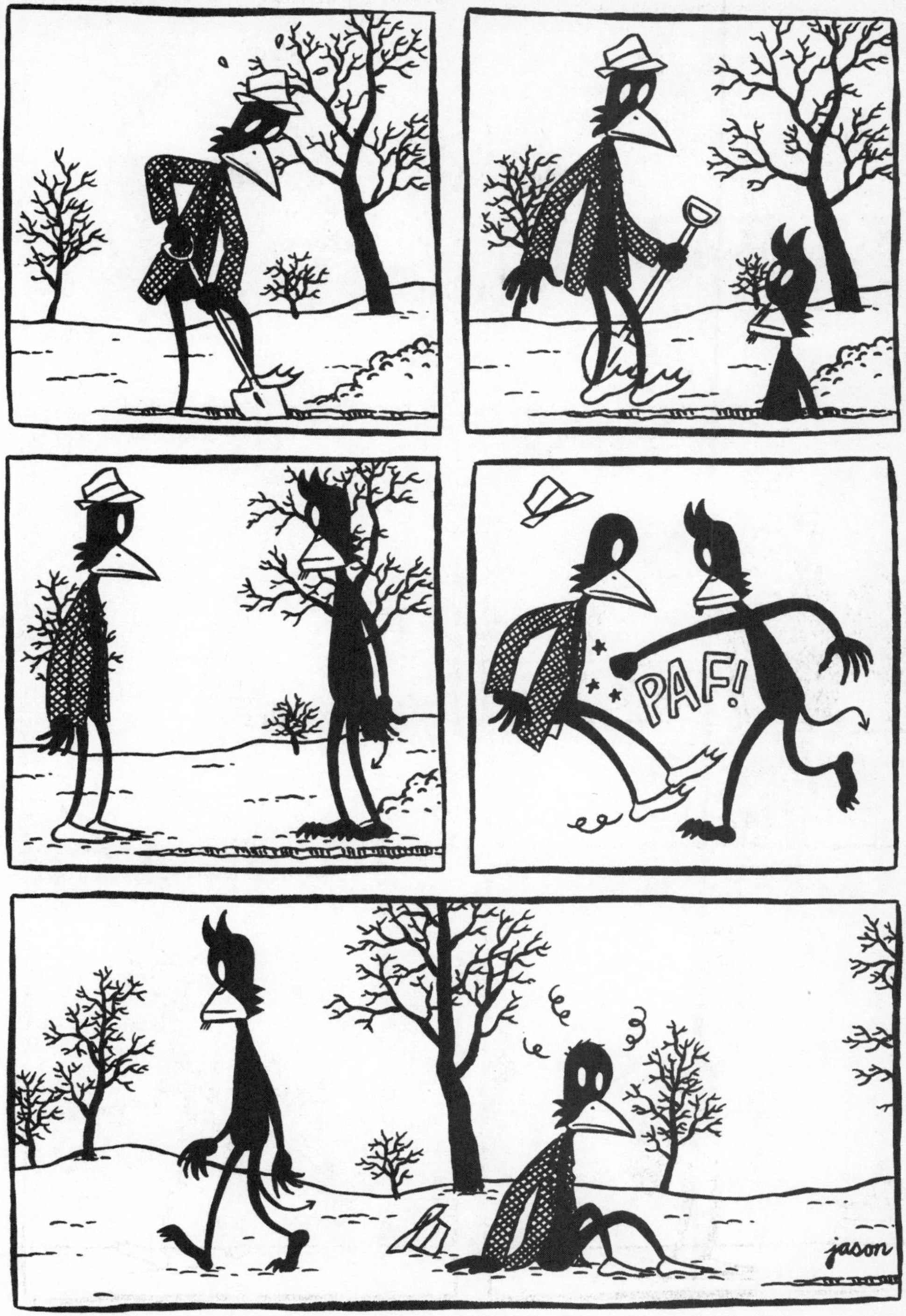
PAF!
jason

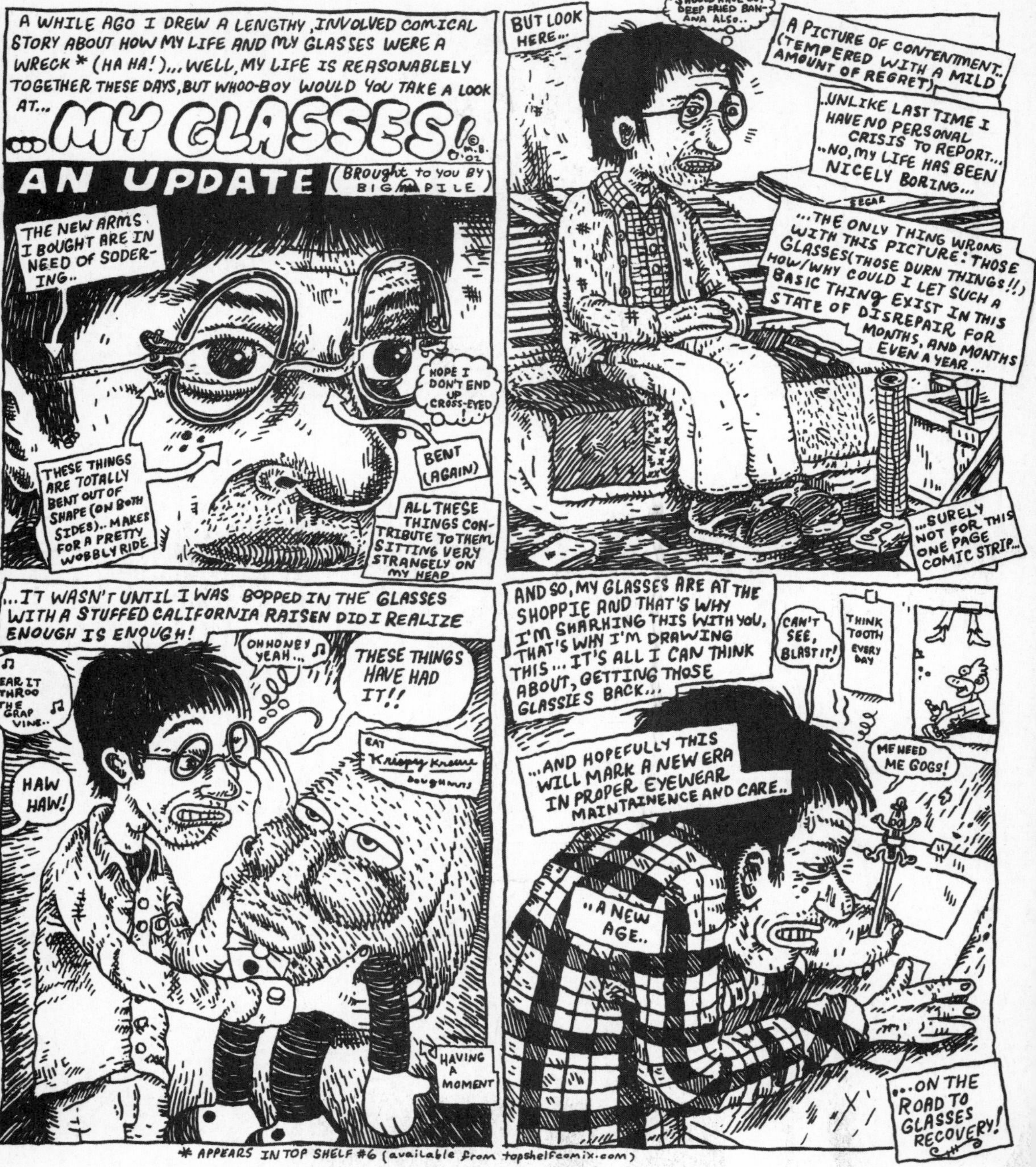
A WHILE AGO I DREW A LENGTHY, INVOLVED COMICAL STORY ABOUT HOW MY LIFE AND MY GLASSES WERE A WRECK * (HA HA!)... WELL, MY LIFE IS REASONABLELY TOGETHER THESE DAYS, BUT WHOO-BOY WOULD YOU TAKE A LOOK AT...
...MY GLASSES! © M.B. '02
AN UPDATE
(BROUGHT TO YOU BY BIG PILE)
THE NEW ARMS I BOUGHT ARE IN NEED OF SODER-ING..
HOPE I DON'T END UP CROSS-EYED!
THESE THINGS ARE TOTALLY BENT OUT OF SHAPE (ON BOTH SIDES).. MAKES FOR A PRETTY WOBBLY RIDE
BENT (AGAIN)
ALL THESE THINGS CON-TRIBUTE TO THEM SITTING VERY STRANGELY ON MY HEAD
BUT LOOK HERE...
SHOULD HAVE GOT DEEP FRIED BAN-ANA ALSO..
A PICTURE OF CONTENTMENT.. (TEMPERED WITH A MILD AMOUNT OF REGRET)
..UNLIKE LAST TIME I HAVE NO PERSONAL CRISIS TO REPORT... ..NO, MY LIFE HAS BEEN NICELY BORING...
SEGAR
...THE ONLY THING WRONG WITH THIS PICTURE: THOSE GLASSES (THOSE DURN THINGS!!) HOW/WHY COULD I LET SUCH A BASIC THING EXIST IN THIS STATE OF DISREPAIR FOR MONTHS, AND MONTHS EVEN A YEAR...
...SURELY NOT FOR THIS ONE PAGE COMIC STRIP...
...IT WASN'T UNTIL I WAS BOPPED IN THE GLASSES WITH A STUFFED CALIFORNIA RAISEN DID I REALIZE ENOUGH IS ENOUGH!
HEAR IT THROO THE GRAP VINE..
OH HONEY YEAH...
THESE THINGS HAVE HAD IT!!
HAW HAW!
EAT Krispy Kreme Doughnuts
HAVING A MOMENT
AND SO, MY GLASSES ARE AT THE SHOPPIE AND THAT'S WHY I'M SHARHING THIS WITH YOU, THAT'S WHY I'M DRAWING THIS... IT'S ALL I CAN THINK ABOUT, GETTING THOSE GLASSIES BACK...
CAN'T SEE, BLAST IT!
THINK TOOTH EVERY DAY
...AND HOPEFULLY THIS WILL MARK A NEW ERA IN PROPER EYEWEAR MAINTAINENCE AND CARE..
ME NEED ME GOGS!
..A NEW AGE..
...ON THE ROAD TO GLASSES RECOVERY!
* APPEARS IN TOP SHELF #6 (available from topshelfcomix.com)

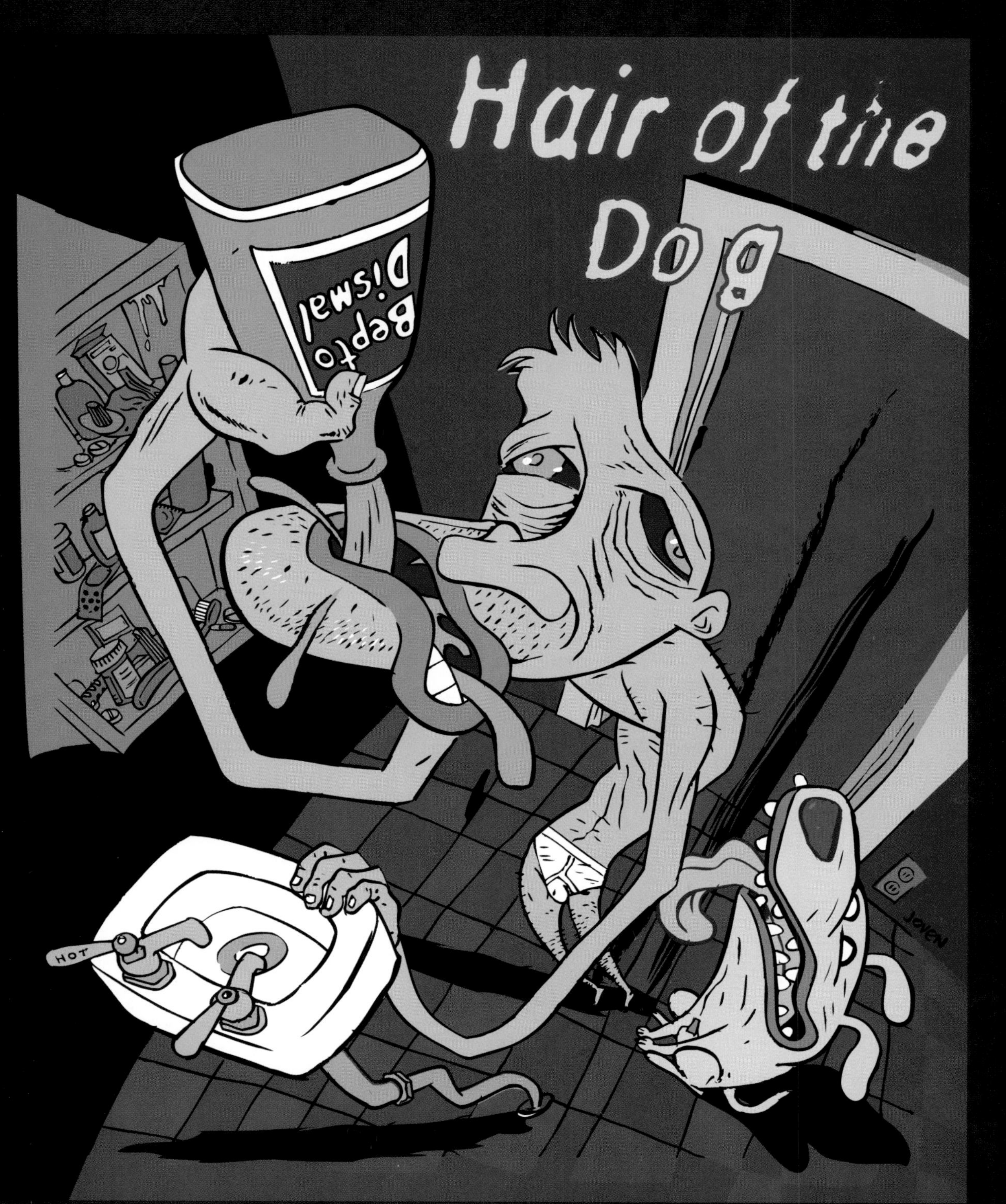
Hair of the Dog
Bepto Dismal
HOT
JOVEN

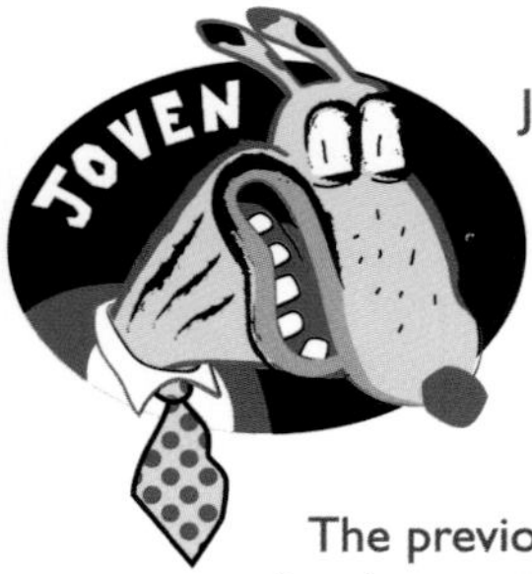
JOVEN

Joven Kerekes is an American cartoonist stranded in Ireland. Past crimes preclude an easy return to his beloved homeland, so he makes do with Dublin, where he earns his living at illustration and design.

The previous page features the initial cover for the previous incarnation of this edition of *Top Shelf*, while the horny dog to your right, was to be the back cover. Look for more of Joven's fabulous cartooning throughout this volume, as indicated by the icon above.

His most recent comics work is collected in *Ructions*, and is available from his website www.jovenk.com. He can be written to at joven@indigo.ie.

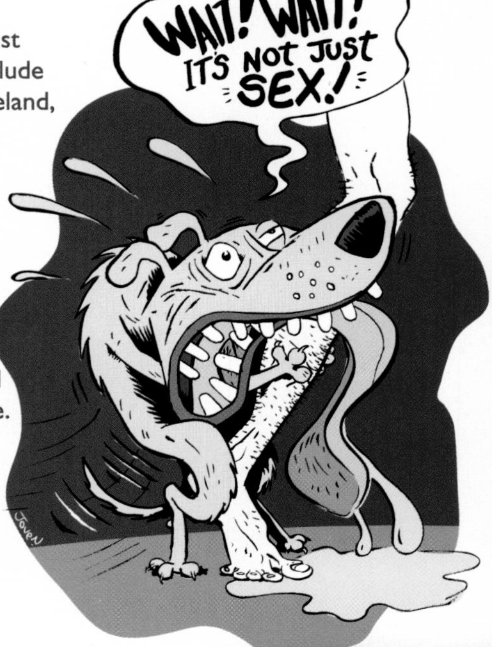
WAIT! WAIT! IT'S NOT JUST SEX!
JOVEN

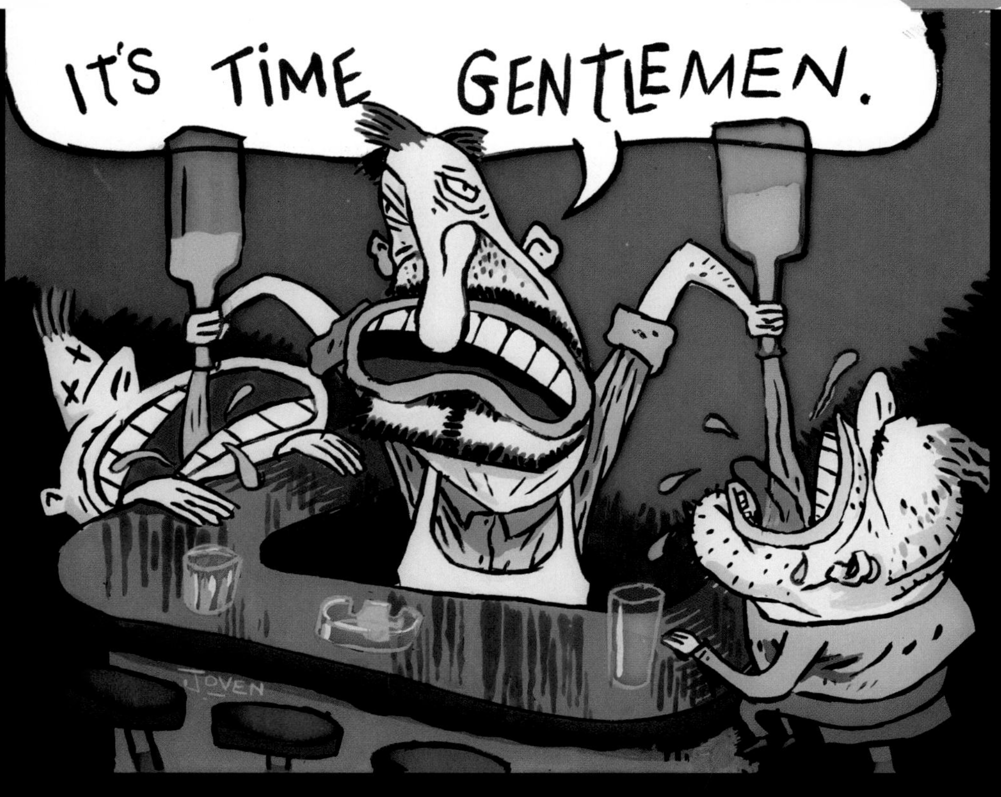
IT'S TIME GENTLEMEN.
JOVEN

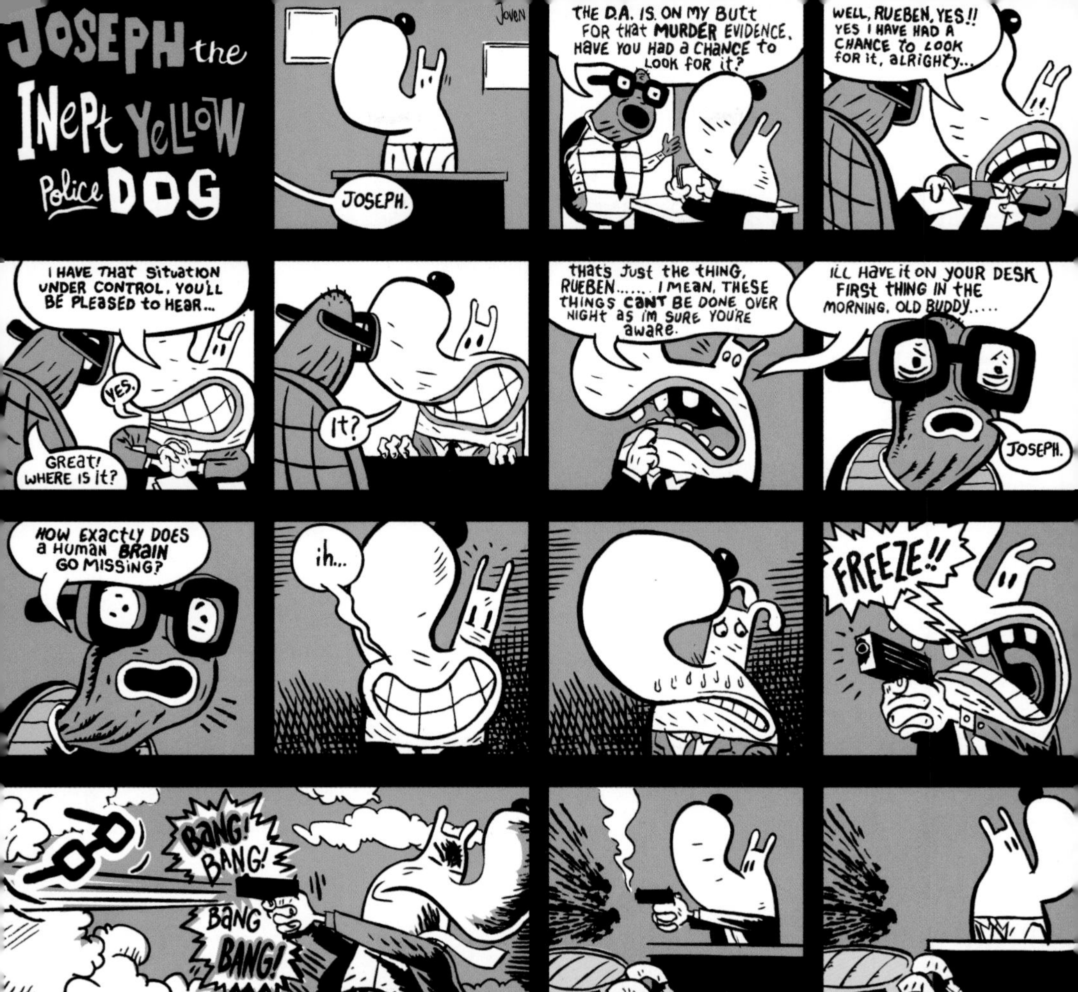
JOSEPH the INEPT YELLOW Police DOG
JOVEN
JOSEPH.
THE D.A. IS ON MY BUTT FOR THAT MURDER EVIDENCE. HAVE YOU HAD A CHANCE TO LOOK FOR IT?
WELL, RUEBEN, YES!! YES I HAVE HAD A CHANCE TO LOOK FOR IT, ALRIGHTY...
I HAVE THAT SITUATION UNDER CONTROL, YOU'LL BE PLEASED TO HEAR...
YES.
GREAT! WHERE IS IT?
IT?
THAT'S JUST THE THING, RUEBEN...... I MEAN, THESE THINGS CAN'T BE DONE OVER NIGHT AS I'M SURE YOU'RE AWARE.
I'LL HAVE IT ON YOUR DESK FIRST THING IN THE MORNING, OLD BUDDY.....
JOSEPH.
HOW EXACTLY DOES A HUMAN BRAIN GO MISSING?
ih...
FREEZE!!
BANG! BANG! BANG BANG!
IN
OUT
LIEUTENANT RUEBEN
Joseph
CA-CHUNK!

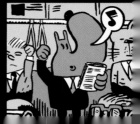

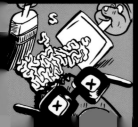

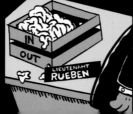

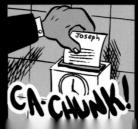

JOSEPH - the inept yellow dog

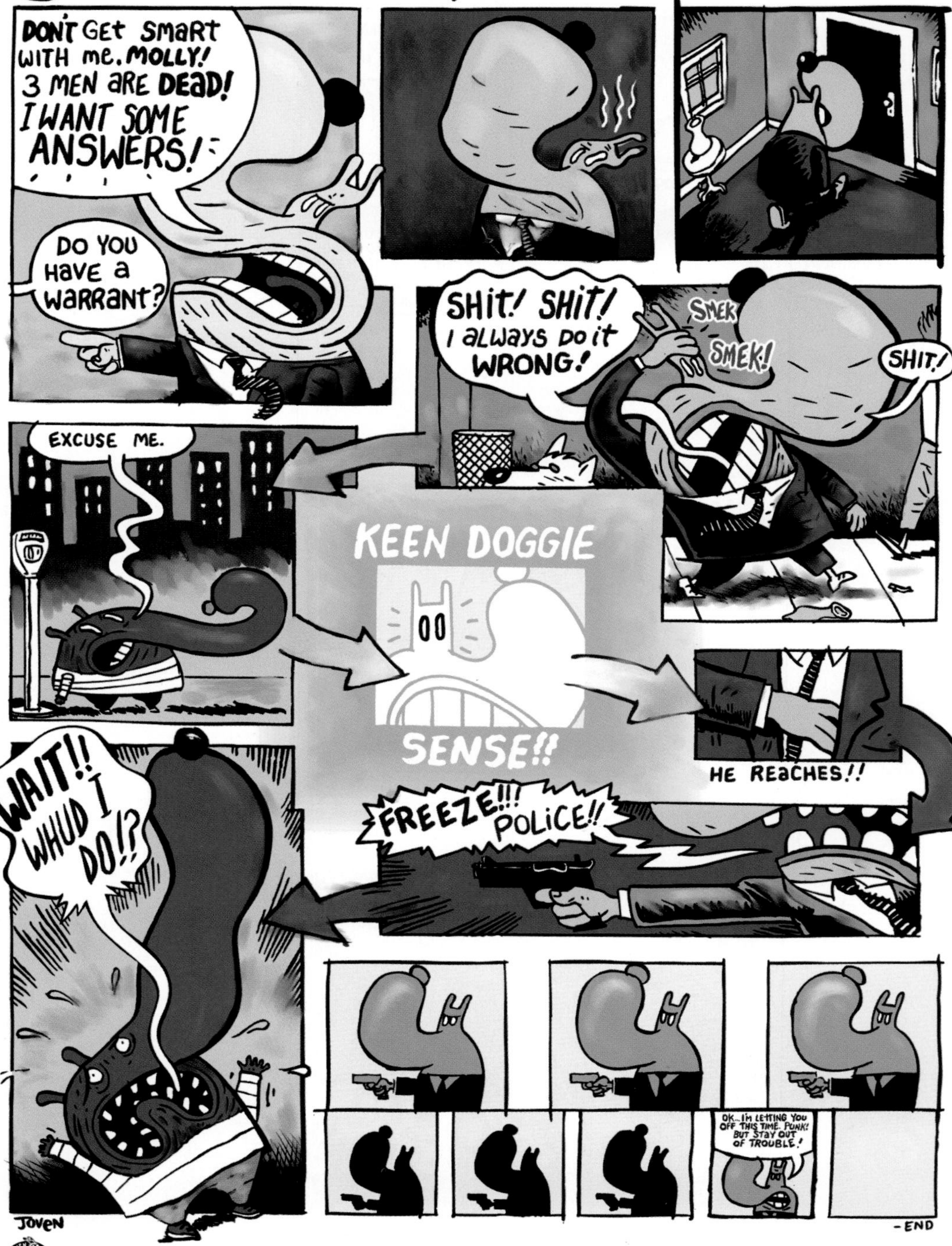
DON'T GET SMART WITH ME, MOLLY! 3 MEN ARE DEAD! I WANT SOME ANSWERS!
DO YOU HAVE A WARRANT?
SHIT! SHIT! I ALWAYS DO IT WRONG!
SMEK
SMEK!
SHIT!
EXCUSE ME.
KEEN DOGGIE SENSE!!
HE REACHES!!
FREEZE!!! POLICE!!
WAIT!! WHUD I DO!?
OK... I'M LETTING YOU OFF THIS TIME. PUNK! BUT STAY OUT OF TROUBLE.
JOVEN
-END

Lost Girls

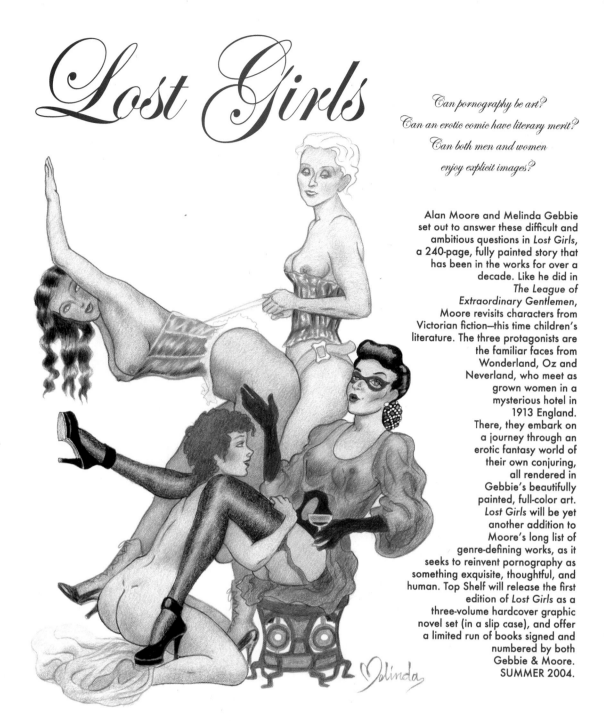

Can pornography be art?
Can an erotic comic have literary merit?
Can both men and women
enjoy explicit images?

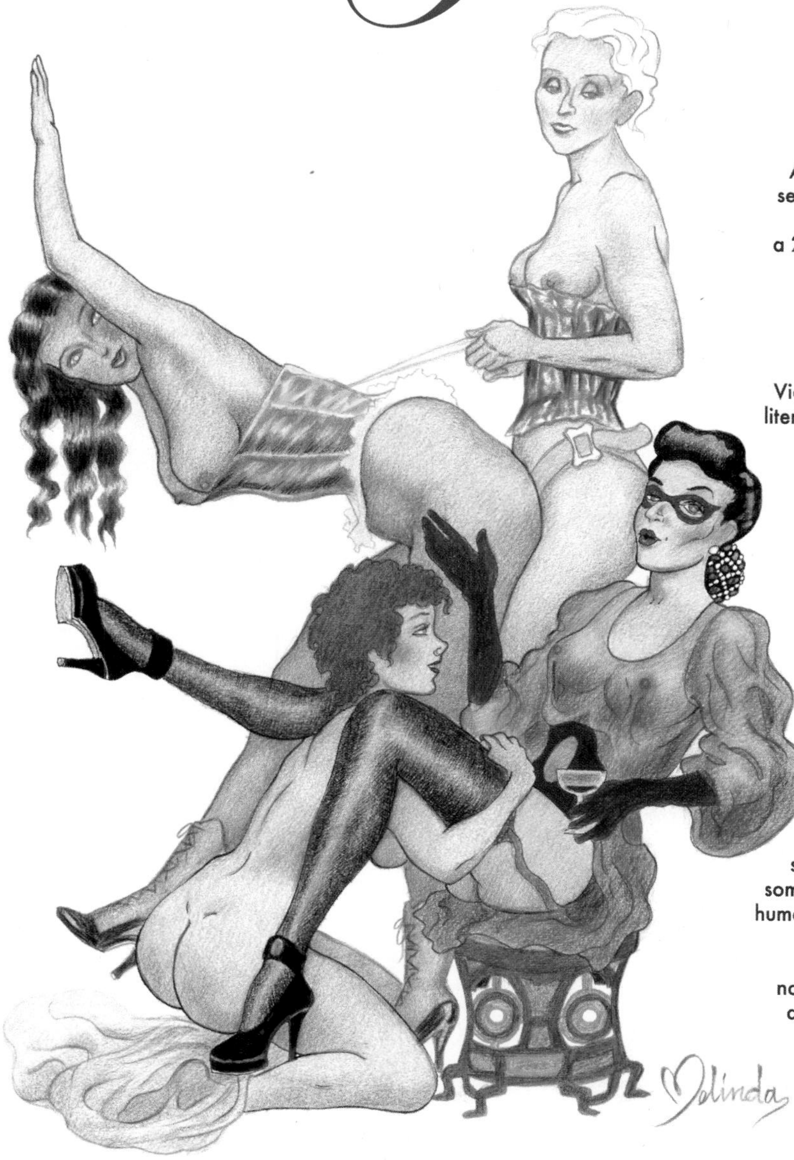
Melinda

Alan Moore and Melinda Gebbie set out to answer these difficult and ambitious questions in *Lost Girls*, a 240-page, fully painted story that has been in the works for over a decade. Like he did in *The League of Extraordinary Gentlemen*, Moore revisits characters from Victorian fiction—this time children's literature. The three protagonists are the familiar faces from Wonderland, Oz and Neverland, who meet as grown women in a mysterious hotel in 1913 England. There, they embark on a journey through an erotic fantasy world of their own conjuring, all rendered in Gebbie's beautifully painted, full-color art. *Lost Girls* will be yet another addition to Moore's long list of genre-defining works, as it seeks to reinvent pornography as something exquisite, thoughtful, and human. Top Shelf will release the first edition of *Lost Girls* as a three-volume hardcover graphic novel set (in a slip case), and offer a limited run of books signed and numbered by both Gebbie & Moore. SUMMER 2004.

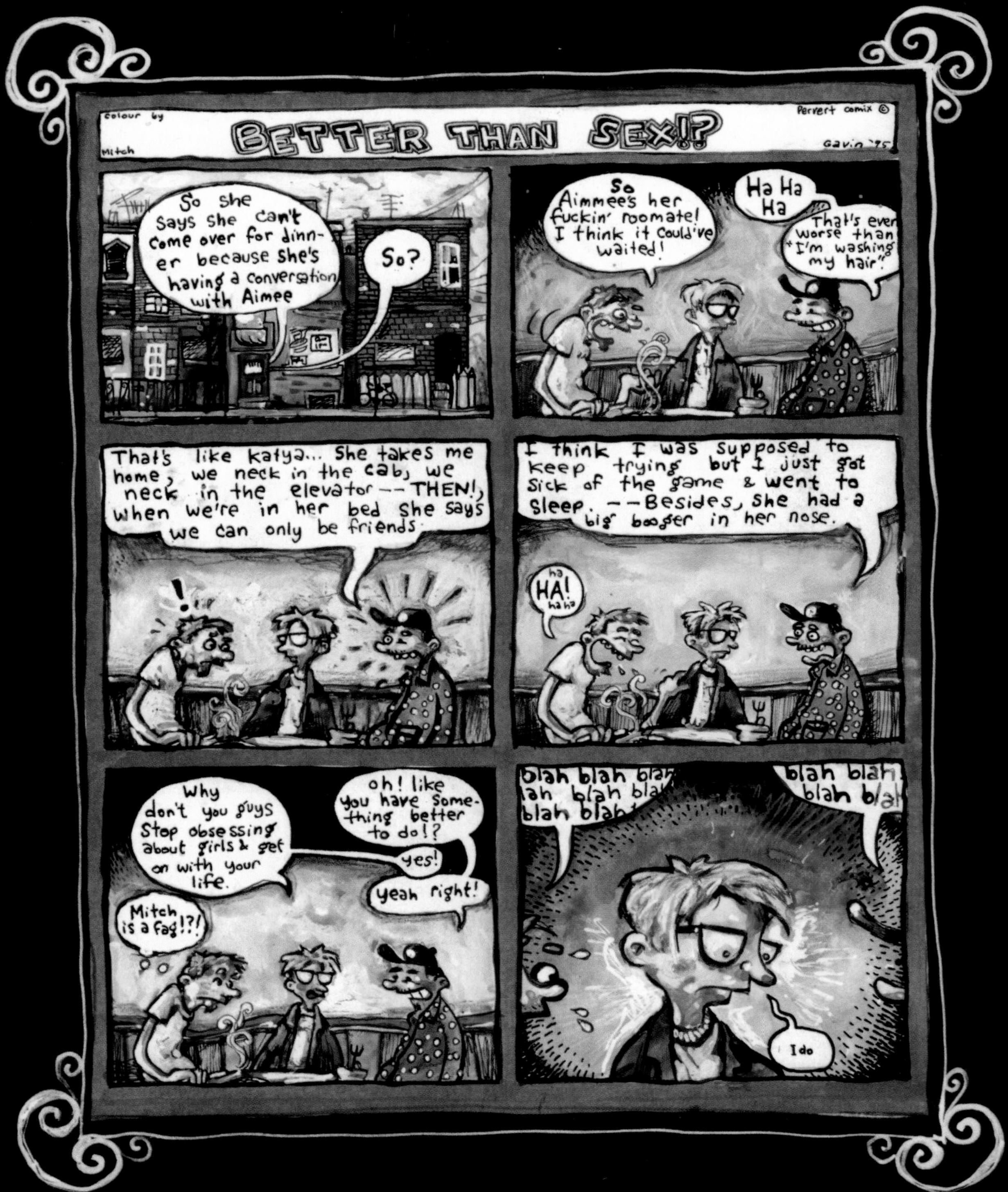
colour by Mitch
BETTER THAN SEX!?
Pervert comix ©
Gavin '95
So she says she can't come over for dinn-er because she's having a conversation with Aimee
So?
So Aimmee's her fuckin' roomate! I think it could've waited!
Ha Ha Ha
That's even worse than "I'm washing my hair".
That's like katya... She takes me home, we neck in the cab, we neck in the elevator -- THEN!, when we're in her bed she says we can only be friends.
I think I was supposed to keep trying but I just got sick of the game & went to sleep. --Besides, she had a big booger in her nose.
ha HA! ha ha
Why don't you guys stop obsessing about girls & get on with your life.
oh! like you have some-thing better to do!?
yes!
yeah right!
Mitch is a fag!?!
blah blah
blah blah
I do

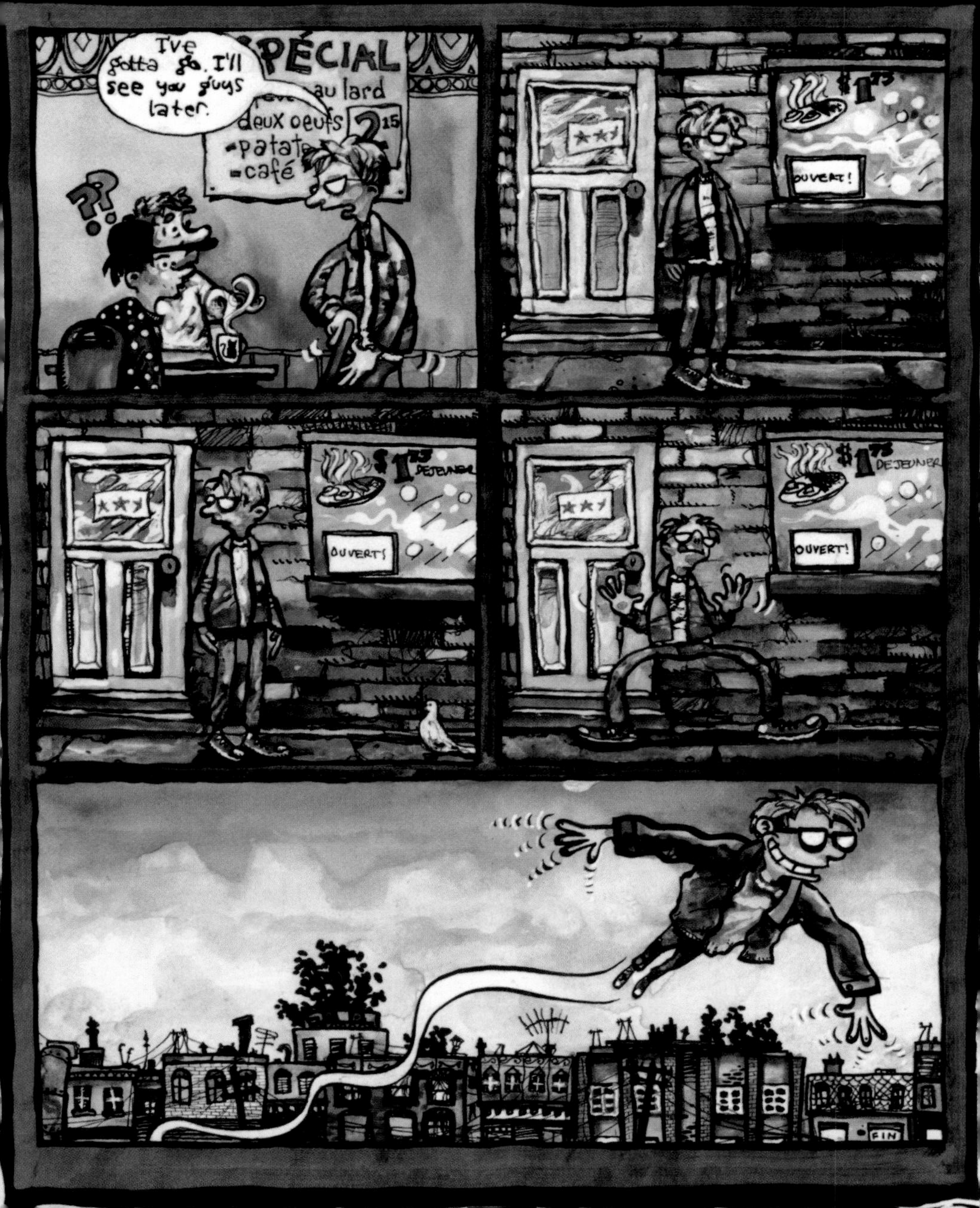
I've gotta go. I'll see you guys later.
SPÉCIAL
au lard
deux oeufs
2 15
-patate
-café
$1 75
OUVERT!
$1 75 DEJEUNER
OUVERTS
$1 75 DEJEUNER
OUVERT!
FIN

THE MYSTERIOUS TABTAB

Text by Teresa Celsi   Art by David Chelsea

After the phenomenal success of <u>The Secret of the Gryphon</u>, teen journalist and detective Tabtab starred in four more adventure books. All five books featured exotic locations, intriguing mysteries (including the one in which Tabtab recovered a set of stolen jewels), powerful villains and an interesting companion to help solve each case. From the clues below can you discover the name of each book; where it takes place; Tabtab's companion(s), the super villain he thwarts, and the nature of the crime?

1. Arson at an aircraft plant was the crime in <u>The Mystery of the Seven Seals</u>.

2. In one adventure, Tabtab's dog, Frosty, helped catch the evil General Esperanto. However, he never traveled to England or Germany (where the smugglers were caught.)

3. The five different books were: <u>The Blue Lily</u>, the book set in England, the one that featured Madame Lazare as the archvillain, the one in which arson was the crime, and the one in which Captain Tuna played a major supporting role.

4. Tabtab spent most of his time in <u>The Costanza Affair</u> trying to undo the mischief of his bumbling assistants, twin detectives Dacron and Rayon.

5. Professor Emeritus (the companion Tabtab met in Turkey), did not help bring Rusticroplis or Madame Lazare to justice.

6. Rusticroplis did not try his evil schemes in England, nor did he create a doomsday machine; Neither General Esperanto nor Dr. Muckter ran the crime network in China.

7. While Tabtab searched for clues, Bianca Eszterhaus kept Count Grimaldi occupied. Neither Count Grimaldi nor Madame Lazare were involved in art forgery schemes.

8. When <u>Flight 409</u> went astray, Tabtab was glad to have his old friend, Captain Tuna, at the controls.

9. Tabtab literally stumbled across the doomsday machine while vacationing in Turkey.

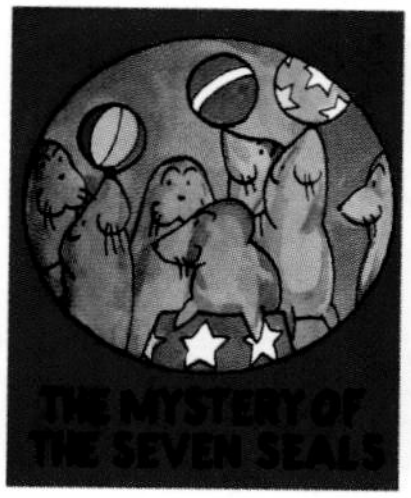
THE MYSTERY OF
THE SEVEN SEALS
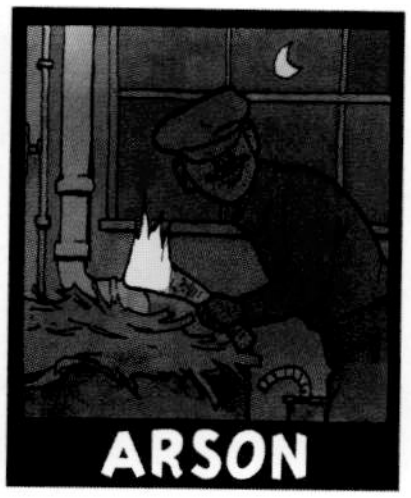
ARSON
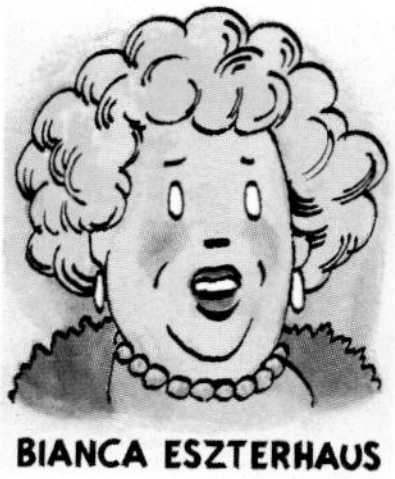
BIANCA ESZTERHAUS
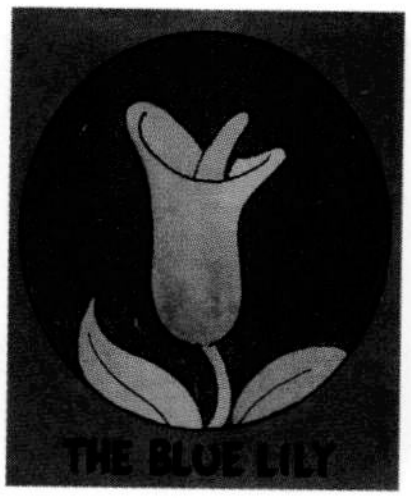
THE BLUE LILY
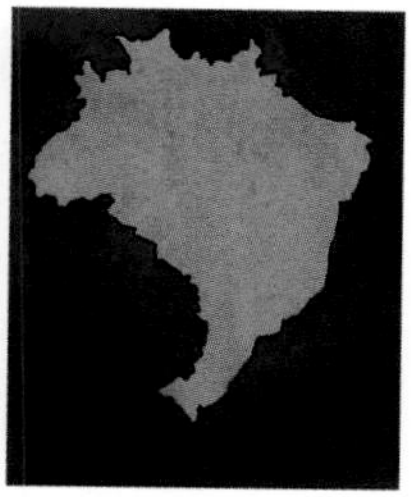
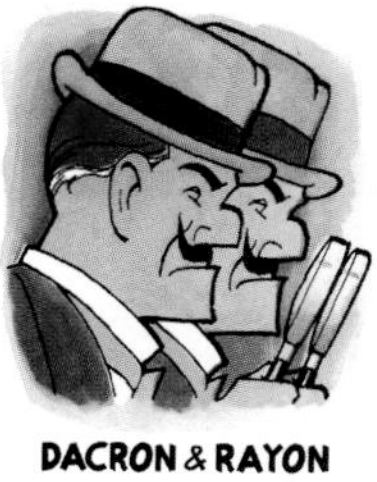
DACRON & RAYON
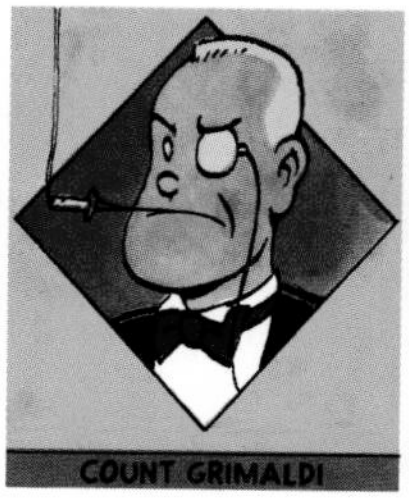
COUNT GRIMALDI
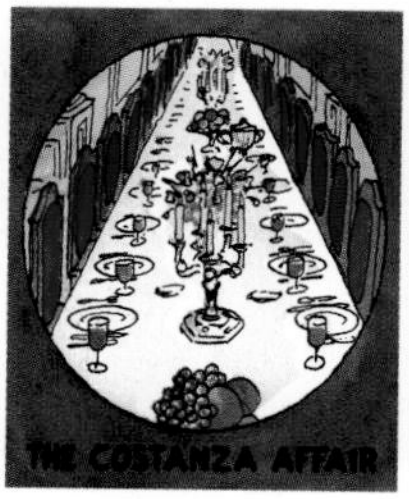
THE COSTANZA AFFAIR
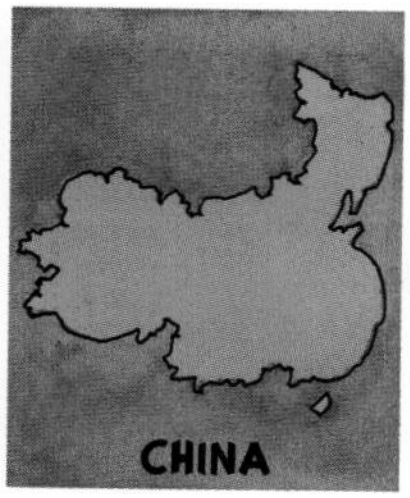
CHINA
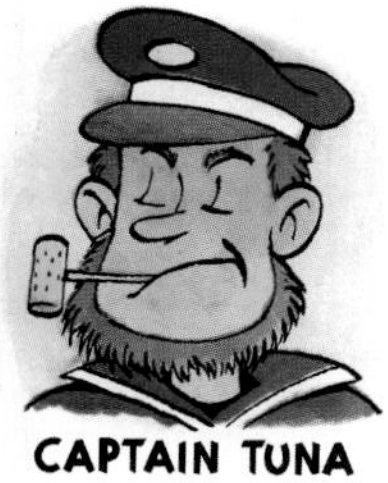
CAPTAIN TUNA
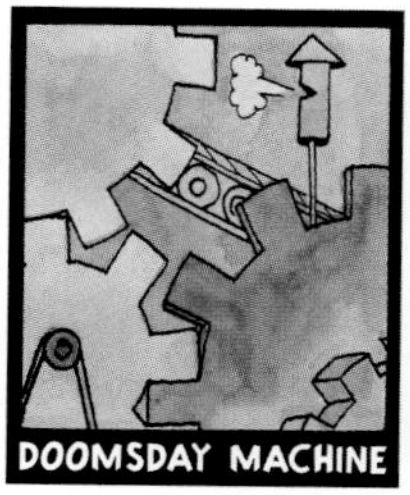
DOOMSDAY MACHINE
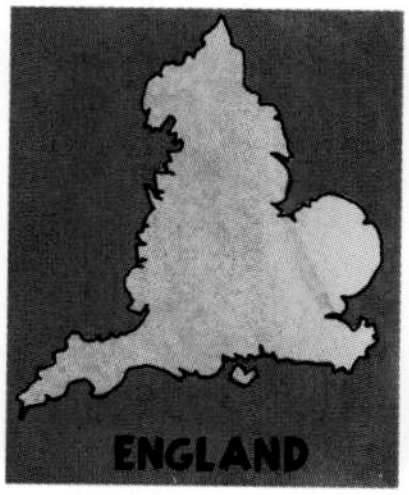
ENGLAND
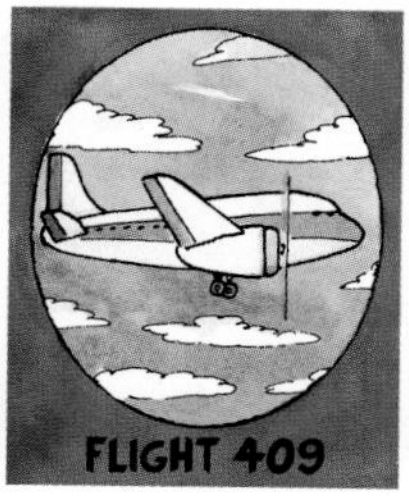
FLIGHT 409
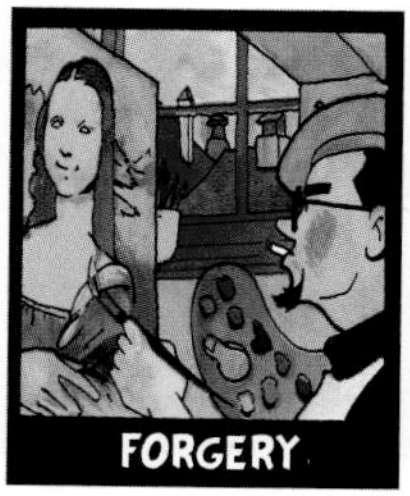
FORGERY
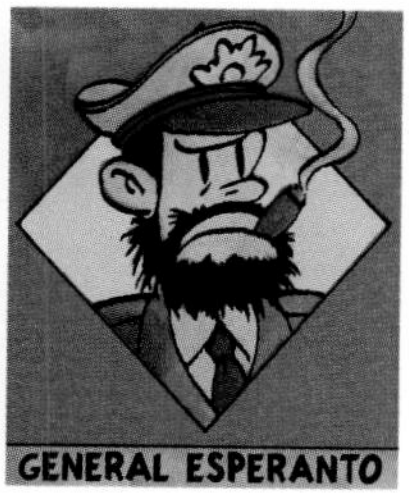
GENERAL ESPERANTO
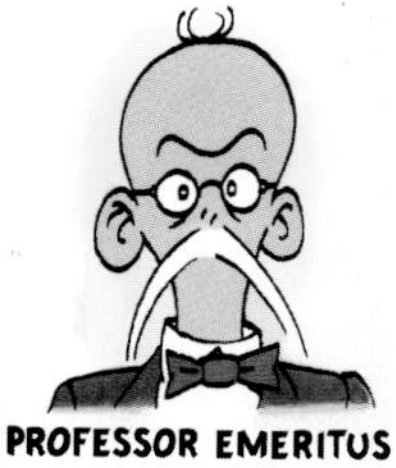
PROFESSOR EMERITUS
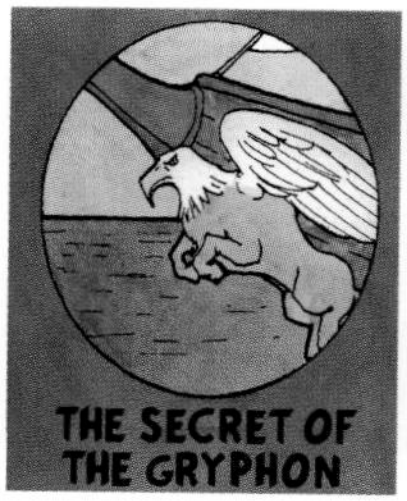
THE SECRET OF
THE GRYPHON
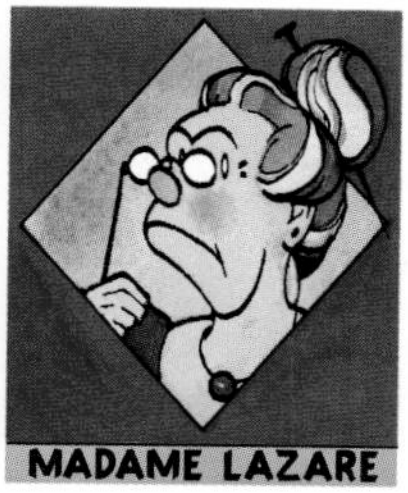
MADAME LAZARE
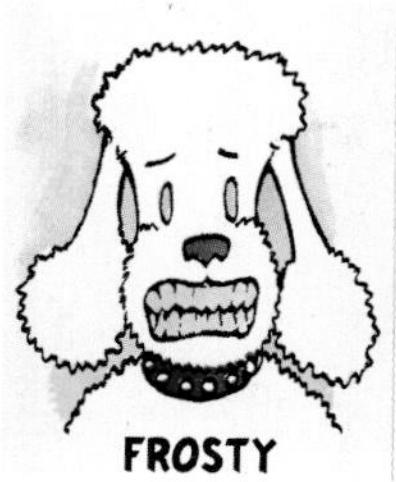
FROSTY
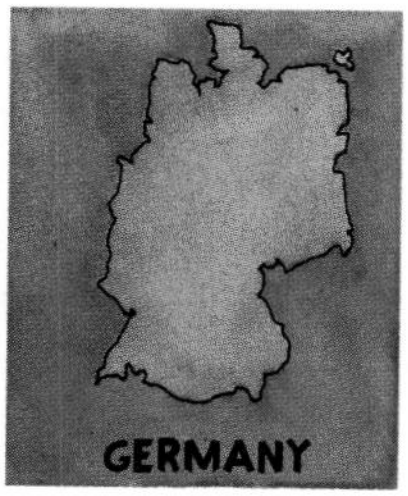
GERMANY
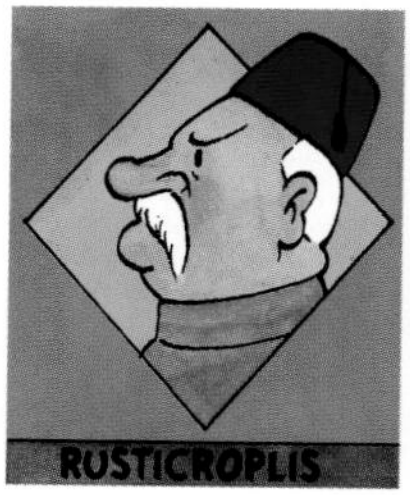
RUSTICROPLIS
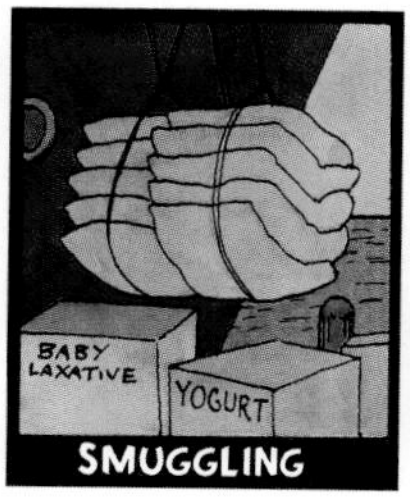
BABY
LAXATIVE
YOGURT
SMUGGLING
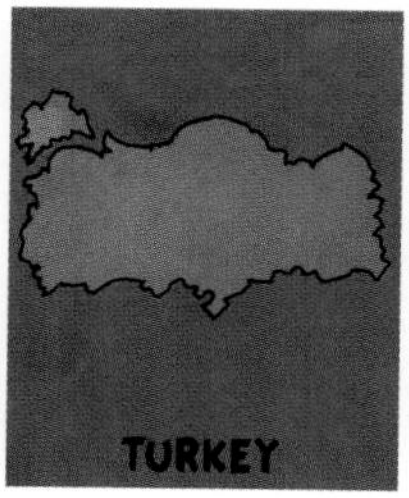
TURKEY
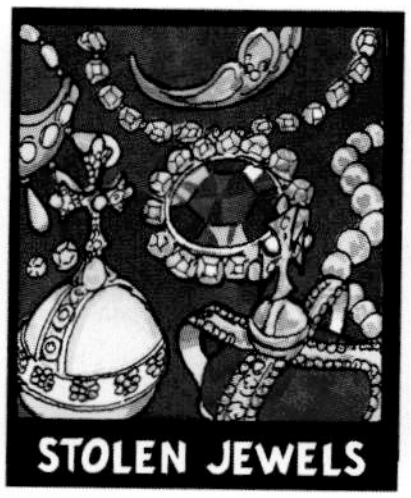
STOLEN JEWELS
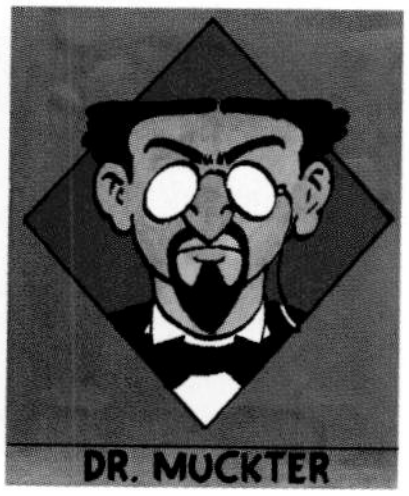
DR. MUCKTER

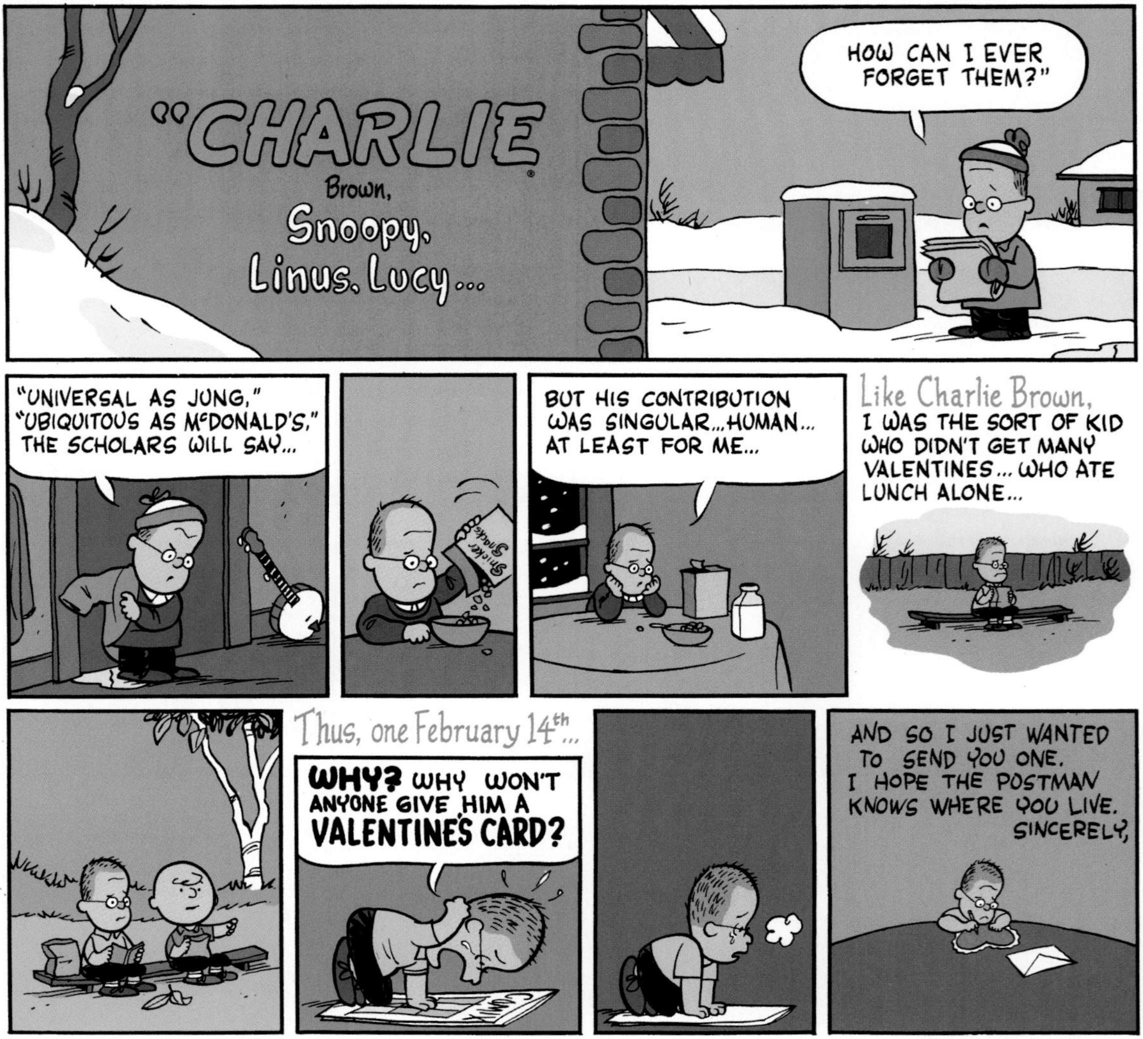
"CHARLIE Brown,
Snoopy,
Linus, Lucy...
HOW CAN I EVER FORGET THEM?"
"UNIVERSAL AS JUNG," "UBIQUITOUS AS McDONALD'S," THE SCHOLARS WILL SAY...
Snicker Snacks
BUT HIS CONTRIBUTION WAS SINGULAR... HUMAN... AT LEAST FOR ME...
Like Charlie Brown,
I WAS THE SORT OF KID WHO DIDN'T GET MANY VALENTINES... WHO ATE LUNCH ALONE...
Thus, one February 14th...
WHY? WHY WON'T ANYONE GIVE HIM A VALENTINE'S CARD?
AND SO I JUST WANTED TO SEND YOU ONE. I HOPE THE POSTMAN KNOWS WHERE YOU LIVE.
SINCERELY,

(This essay was originally written for Chip Kidd's *Peanuts: the Art of Charles M. Schulz* [Pantheon: 2001] but was cut from the book before publication, probably for very good reasons.)

Charles Schulz is the only author I've been continually reading since I was a kid. The warmth and inviting quality I found in his work then is tempered by an ever-deepening complexity and richness when I read it now. I never met either of them, but as a child, Charlie Brown was my friend; and as an adult, Charles Schulz is my hero.

Newspaper comic strips are generally regarded as a commercial endeavor, the route by which they reach the "consumer" identical to that used by the essentially money-driven illustrator and advertiser: paper, printing ink, price, trash can. For this reason (amongst others) most "serious people" regard comics as garbage: at best, a simple-minded tag-end to the news of the day; at worst, an esthetically indefensible insult to the traditions of writing and art. Not that there aren't terrible comic strips – but every once in a while a cartoonist is able to take the limiting structure of the newspaper strip and do something personal, human, and real with it. Charles Schulz was the last cartoonist to manage this feat. *Peanuts* was probably the funniest comic strip ever, yet it was imbued with such an authentic, self-sustaining natural life that it was also the only real art the regular comics page has seen in the past half-century.

The journalist Hugh Morrow, writing about Schulz in 1956 for *Life* magazine with inexcusable snobbishness, noted Schulz's inability to define "semantics," remarked that he'd "yawned" his way through Proust, and sarcastically marvelled that he was able to read all of *War and Peace* before "seeing the movie." Though now almost fifty years old, this article unfortunately still pretty much sums up the attitude towards cartoonists that the aforementioned "serious people" have – esthetically-impaired simpletons who can't really draw, or write, and so make children's picture stories for a living. (One should also remember that in 1950, nothing could be more esthetically heinous than making a picture that actually represented something – and telling a story? Unthinkable.) Schulz

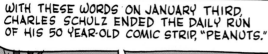

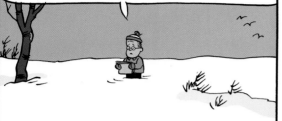

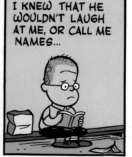

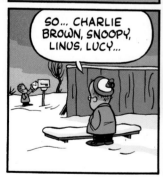

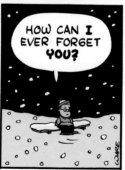

WITH THESE WORDS ON JANUARY THIRD, CHARLES SCHULZ ENDED THE DAILY RUN OF HIS 50 YEAR-OLD COMIC STRIP, "PEANUTS."
BUT I LOVED "PEANUTS," AND CHARLIE BROWN BECAME ALMOST LIKE A FRIEND TO ME...
I KNEW THAT HE WOULDN'T LAUGH AT ME, OR CALL ME NAMES...
SO... CHARLIE BROWN, SNOOPY, LINUS, LUCY...
HOW CAN I EVER FORGET YOU?
WARE

himself more than once humbly remarked that being a cartoonist requires one to be "pretty good" at a lot of things, but not "really good" at any one thing. To correct that, being a cartoonist requires that one not only be "really good" at a host of things (like poetry, life drawing, design – and *especially* writing and drawing) but at doing them all – simultaneously.

The commercial development of *Peanuts* also almost directly mirrors its development as a personal, expressive work of art. Beginning as the single-panel cartoon *L'il Folks,* in which the gags originated from the idea of children trapped in a world both physically and psychologically too big for them, Schulz illustrated the children almost realistically: perspective, shading, and even chiaroscuro were employed for emotional or atmospheric effect. Stylistic traces are evident of earlier kid strips, like Percy Crosby's *Skippy,* or Crockett Johnson's *Barnaby.* (In fact, I'm sure that a whole doctoral thesis could be written about how, before the World Wars, most strips seemed to be about adults acting like children, but by 1945, there was a decided shift beginning towards the inverse: children acting like adults.) However, once the panel feature was sold as the space-saving *Peanuts* strip, the world of the *L'il Folks* changed forever. The semi-naturalistic proportions of the characters gave way to little large-headed, tiny-bodied creatures – not that such iconically-simplified figures were without precedent – but in a comic strip, no one notices such wild abuse of human proportion. They're still little kids, no questions asked. It is this eschewing of the way the world looks in favor of how one thinks of it – the shift from the perceived to the conceived – which is what makes the cartoon language start to "work."

Of course, the most obvious change in the feature was the transformation from a single panel into a strip – four boxes in which the previously static figures could go forth and multiply. Though Schulz initially recycled some of the "L'il Folks" jokes, the concentration slowly shifted to the characters interactions and frustrations with one another. They took on distinct personalities, quirks, desires, and – most importantly – they seemed to take on wills. Violet, Patty, and Lucy really started to hate Charlie Brown, and Schroeder began seriously ignoring Lucy's advances. Linus got smarter, Snoopy got more iconoclastic, and Charlie Brown got sadder.

Finally – and this is the hardest thing to explicate – the drawings gradually shifted from *showing* the characters doing things to the much more incredible experience of the characters actually *doing* things, seemingly of their own volition. This self-sustaining autonomy of action is comparable, I think, to the ineffable quality critics try to pin as "art" on the more "serious" pursuits of writing and painting, but in cartooning, such "internal life" is its esthetic core. The quality may be prodded by certain technical choices – a lack of "camera angles," a simple, linguistic drawing style, perhaps – but, fundamentally, it's an indefinable quality that a cartoonist either has or hasn't. George Herriman had it, Frank King had it, Charles Schulz had it – most cartoonists don't. There's nothing in *Peanuts,* visually, to really marvel at – the drawing is simple, the colors are bright and flat; the intense beauty, humor, and emotion of *Peanuts* happens entirely in the mind, in the rhythms and cadences wherein these little people come to life. And it is in this perfect cycle of reading and imagining and seeing where we not only watch the characters feel, but we also are able to feel right back around through them.

The "Little Red-Haired Girl" has got to be one of the best-known stories of unrequited love of the twentieth century, and it's all the more deeply moving because we all also know that it actually happened to Charles Schulz. Schulz put Charlie Brown through the same agony of fear and rejection that he himself felt, and continued to feel, well into his late life. And the reader, looking at Chralie Brown – and through Charlie Brown – experiences these same feelings. It's an odd thing, objectively, to empathize with little drawings on a page, but Charles Schulz makes us do it; Charlie Brown is the only real sympathetic comic strip character ever. It's no wonder that kids sent him valentines every year.

As the strip progressed, Schulz's drawing style became less drafted and more "doodled" (for lack of a better word); anyone who's ever tried to draw Charlie Brown or Snoopy knows that it's a practically impossible task, even with benefit of tracing. Gradually, Schulz's line, sense of proportion, and space became so intimately a part of everything else in the strip that what might be more traditionally referred to as his "style" essentially had become his handwriting. Every day, millions of readers all over the world would read, think – and feel – Charles Schulz's handwriting. Who else has ever achieved such a thing? I wonder about those who are not yet born, and who will grow up without the commericial ubiquity of *Peanuts,* and what Schulz's work will look like to them. Today, we all to some extent or another have "Charles Schulz" in our minds, and can't conceive of being without him. Those little shaky pictures – we really can't even see them anymore; it's like looking at a word and trying not to read it.

Imagine sitting at a desk for fifty years of your life drawing the same little people over and over again. Schulz's drawing board was worn, the back of his chair was worn, the wall behind him where the chair touched when he'd lean back was worn. There's something slightly insane about the predictability and regularity of such behavior; it encourages one to repeatedly review and hang on to one's past with a exiled sort of intensity that borders on psychosis. (I'm speaking from experience here.) It creates a peculiar sense of one's life as immutable, while the rest of the world changes – people get married, have kids, die – but Charlie Brown still can't fly a kite. Schulz still felt the sting of rejection from the high school yearbook, still felt the modesty of his upbringing, still felt the pull of the red-haired girl. The isolating act of cartooning seems to have both reflected, and to have almost help create, the unrequited world of *Peanuts.* If Schulz had been a lesser person (as we cartoonists are supposed to be), he would have tried to find out what was "funny" about the latest thingamabob – color television, answering machines, cell phones – and he'd have drawn a gag or two about it, deposited his paycheck, and gone to play golf every week. Lucky for us he had an urge to do something more. He said repeatedly in interviews that he wanted to make "the best comic strip he possibly could." It's the word "best" that he evidently kept redefining as he worked; he'd started out trying to draw the best comic strip about little kids, consciously or unconsciously funnelled his frustrations and regrets of life into it, and had ended up with the best comic strip about everything.

Peanuts isn't about children, and *Peanuts* isn't about dogs fighting imaginary wars. *Peanuts* is about Charles Schulz. For fifty years Schulz sat at the same desk and chair with the same people under his pen and in his mind. Schulz remarried, his children grew up, his high school friends died. When he finally announced his retirement, shortly before his death, one television interview proved him unable to say the names of his characters without bursting into tears. The only person who cared more about Charlie Brown than we did was Charles Schulz.

– C. Ware, March 2001.

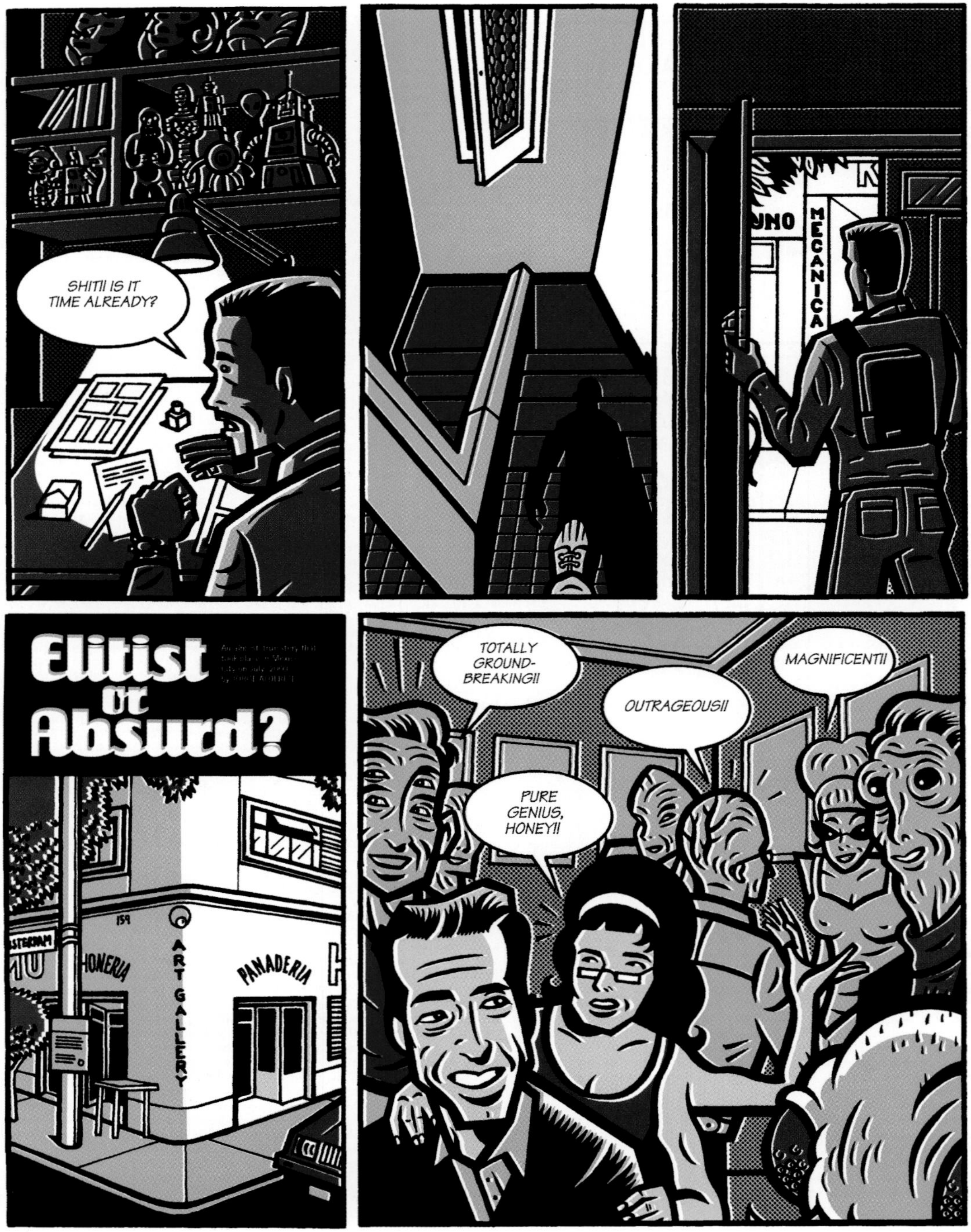
SHIT!! IS IT TIME ALREADY?
UNO
MECANICA
Elitist or Absurd?
159
ART GALLERY
HONERIA
PANADERIA
TOTALLY GROUND-BREAKING!!
OUTRAGEOUS!!
MAGNIFICENT!!
PURE GENIUS, HONEY!!

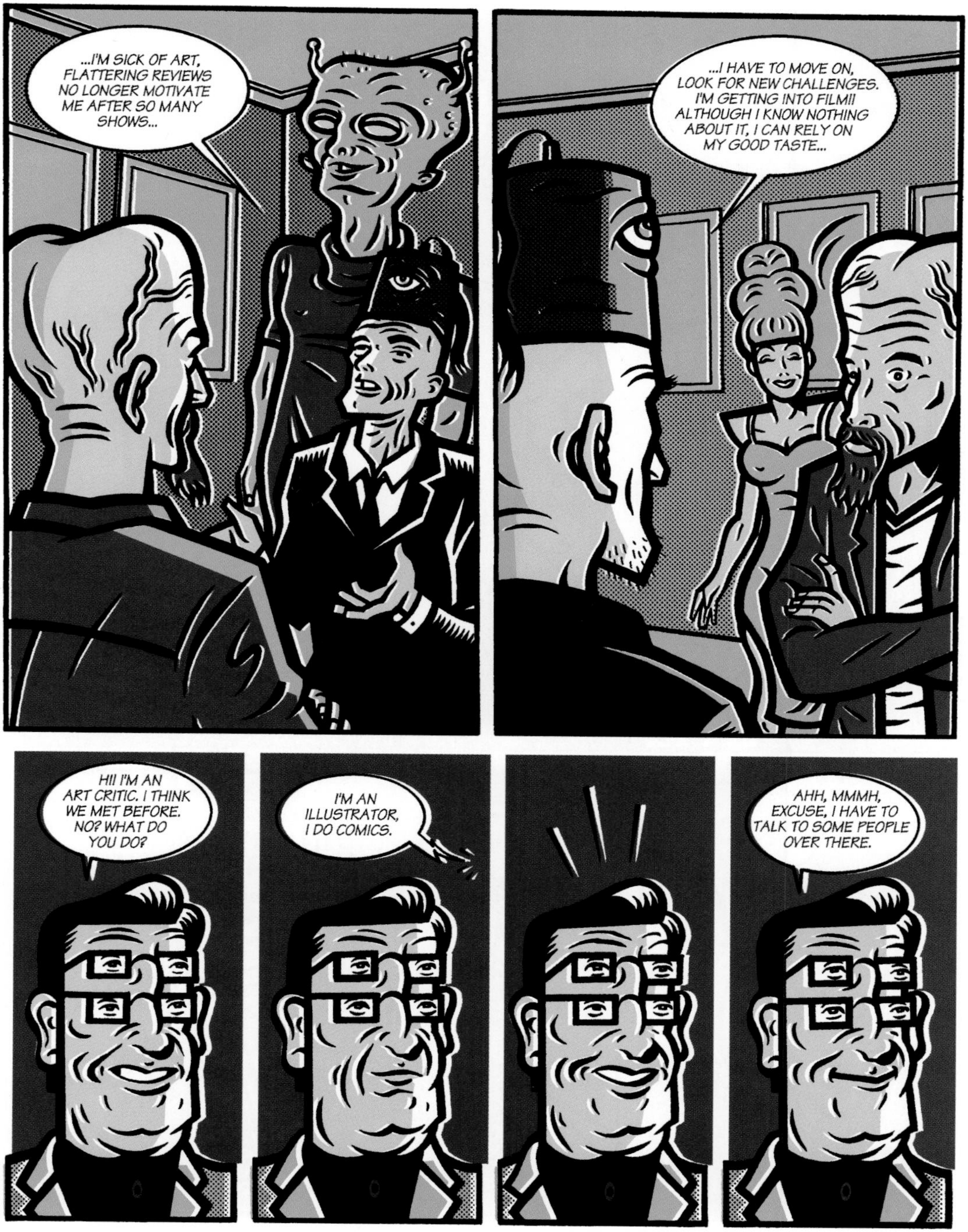
...I'M SICK OF ART, FLATTERING REVIEWS NO LONGER MOTIVATE ME AFTER SO MANY SHOWS...
...I HAVE TO MOVE ON, LOOK FOR NEW CHALLENGES. I'M GETTING INTO FILM!! ALTHOUGH I KNOW NOTHING ABOUT IT, I CAN RELY ON MY GOOD TASTE...
HI! I'M AN ART CRITIC. I THINK WE MET BEFORE. NO? WHAT DO YOU DO?
I'M AN ILLUSTRATOR, I DO COMICS.
AHH, MMMH, EXCUSE, I HAVE TO TALK TO SOME PEOPLE OVER THERE.

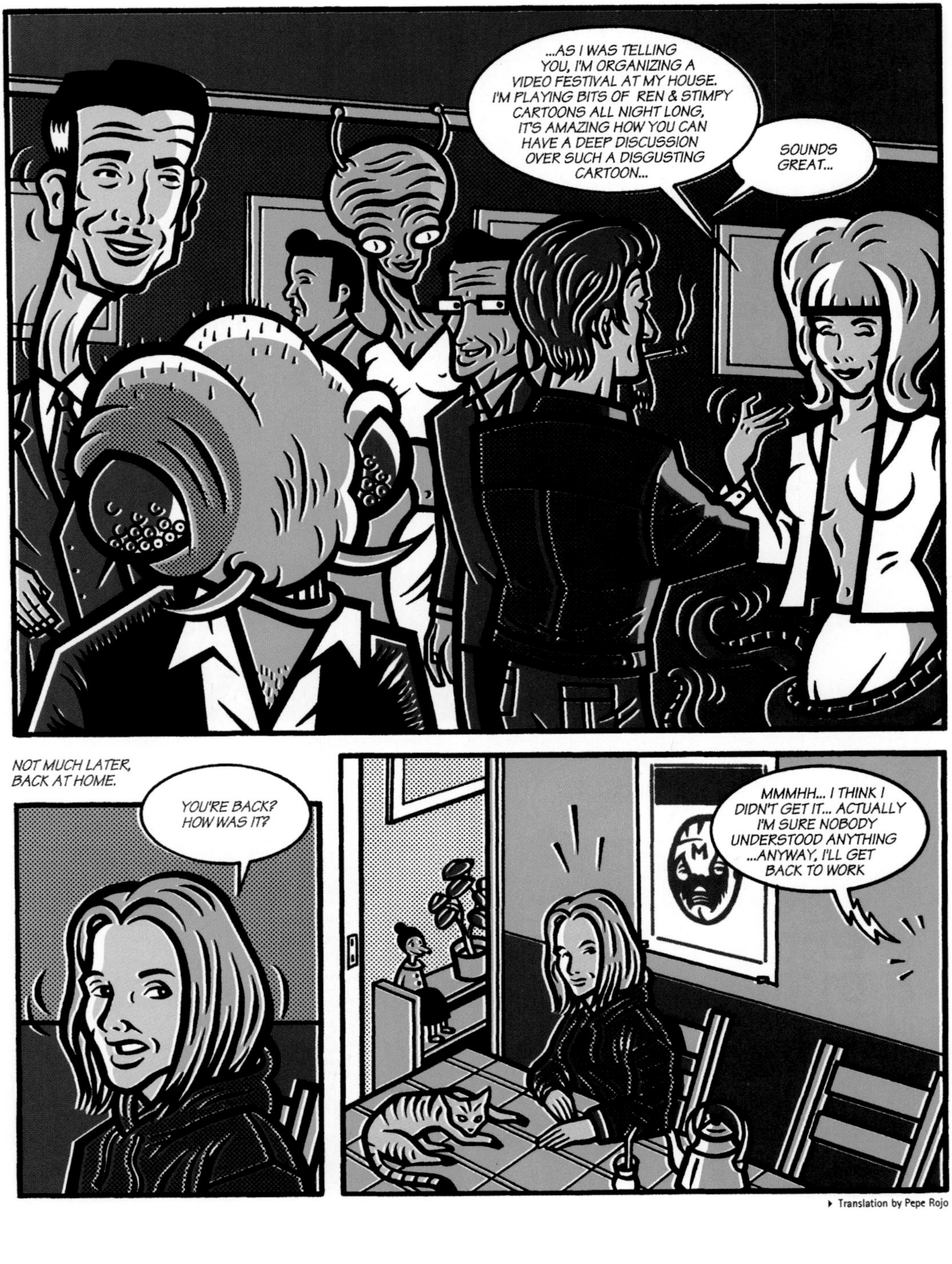
...AS I WAS TELLING YOU, I'M ORGANIZING A VIDEO FESTIVAL AT MY HOUSE. I'M PLAYING BITS OF REN & STIMPY CARTOONS ALL NIGHT LONG, IT'S AMAZING HOW YOU CAN HAVE A DEEP DISCUSSION OVER SUCH A DISGUSTING CARTOON...
SOUNDS GREAT...
NOT MUCH LATER, BACK AT HOME.
YOU'RE BACK? HOW WAS IT?
MMMHH... I THINK I DIDN'T GET IT... ACTUALLY I'M SURE NOBODY UNDERSTOOD ANYTHING ...ANYWAY, I'LL GET BACK TO WORK

Translation by Pepe Rojo

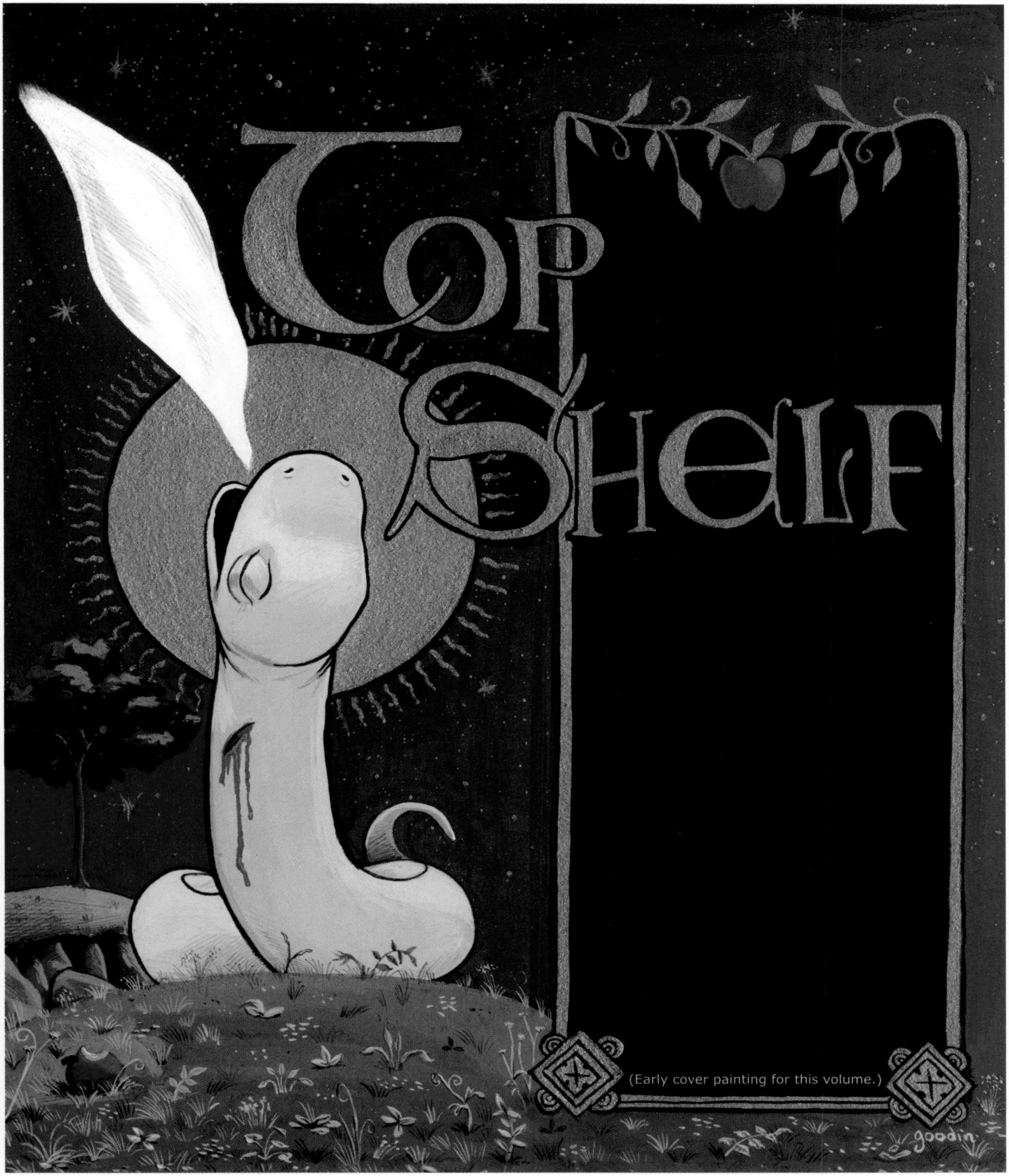
Top Shelf
goodin
(Early cover painting for this volume.)

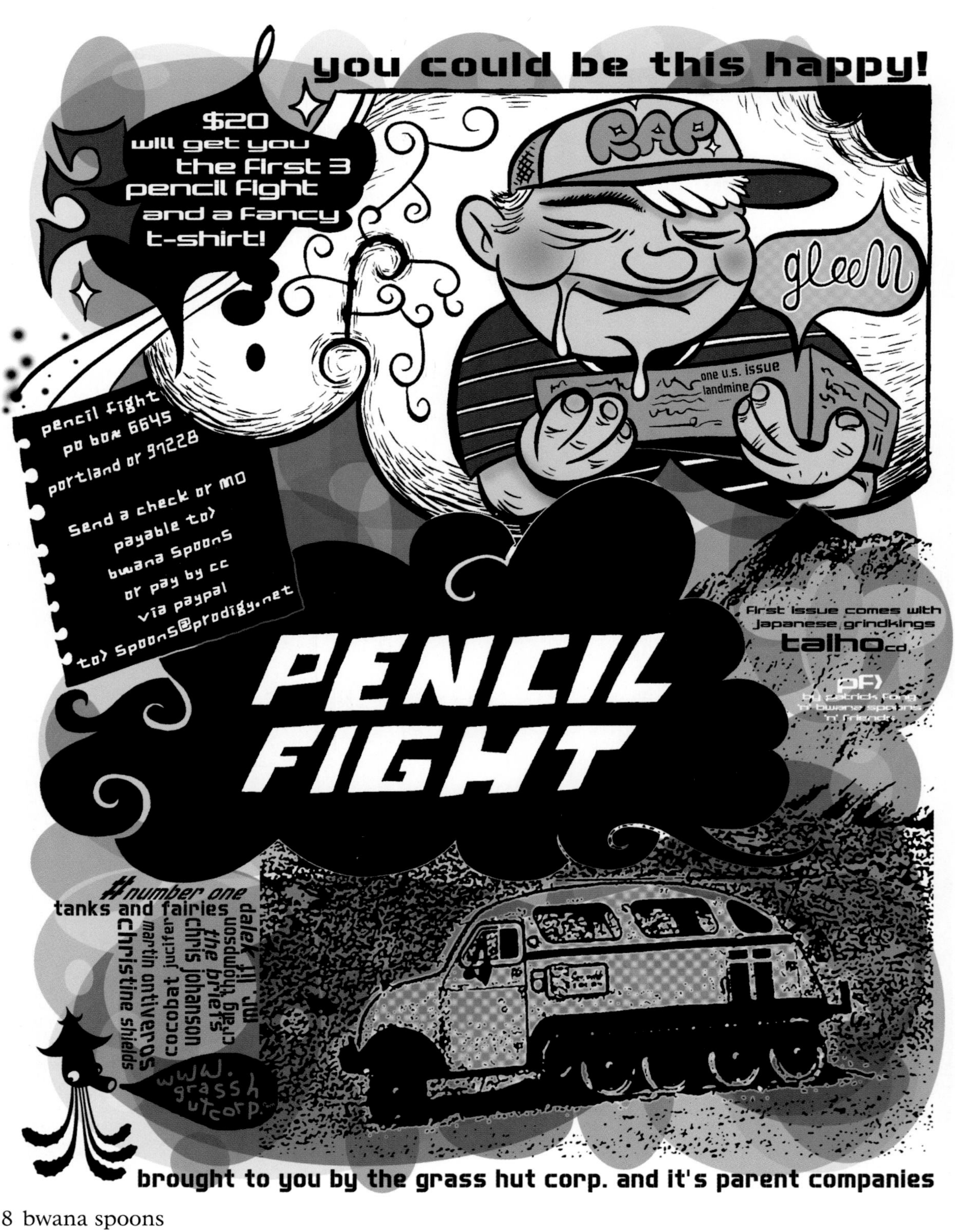
you could be this happy!
$20 will get you the first 3 pencil fight and a fancy t-shirt!
RAP
gleem
one u.s. issue landmine
pencil fight
po box 6645
portland or 97228
send a check or MO payable to> bwana spoons or pay by cc via paypal to> spoons@prodigy.net
PENCIL FIGHT
first issue comes with japanese grindkings taiho cd
pF>
by patrick fong 'n' bwana spoons 'n' friends
#number one
tanks and fairies
dalek
mr. lif
craig thompson
the briefs
chris johanson
cocobat
jucifer
martin ontiveros
Christine shields
www.grasshutcorp.
brought to you by the grass hut corp. and it's parent companies

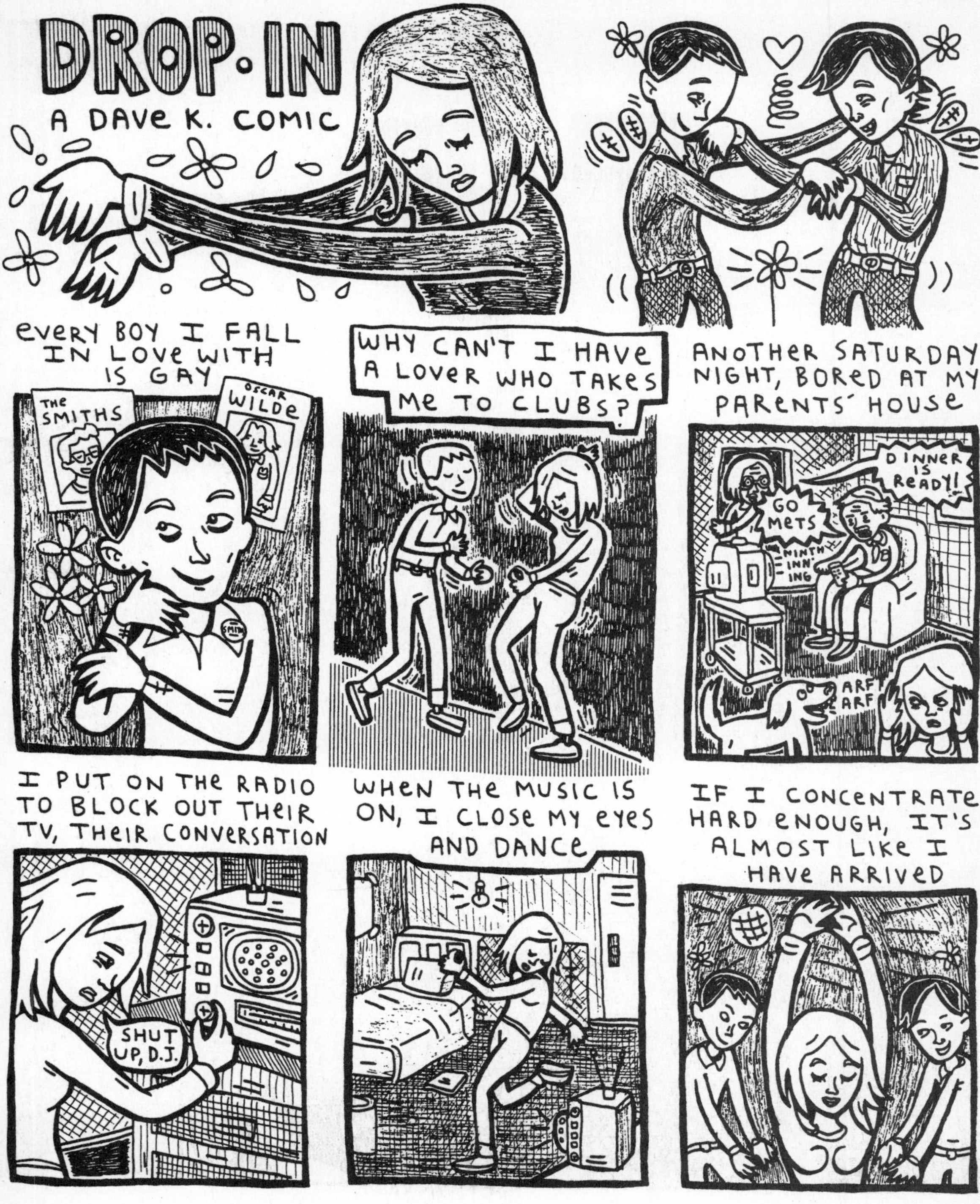
DROP-IN
A DAVE K. COMIC
EVERY BOY I FALL IN LOVE WITH IS GAY
THE SMITHS
OSCAR WILDE
SMITH
WHY CAN'T I HAVE A LOVER WHO TAKES ME TO CLUBS?
ANOTHER SATURDAY NIGHT, BORED AT MY PARENTS' HOUSE
DINNER IS READY!
GO METS
NINTH INNING
ARF ARF
I PUT ON THE RADIO TO BLOCK OUT THEIR TV, THEIR CONVERSATION
SHUT UP, D.J.
WHEN THE MUSIC IS ON, I CLOSE MY EYES AND DANCE
IF I CONCENTRATE HARD ENOUGH, IT'S ALMOST LIKE I HAVE ARRIVED

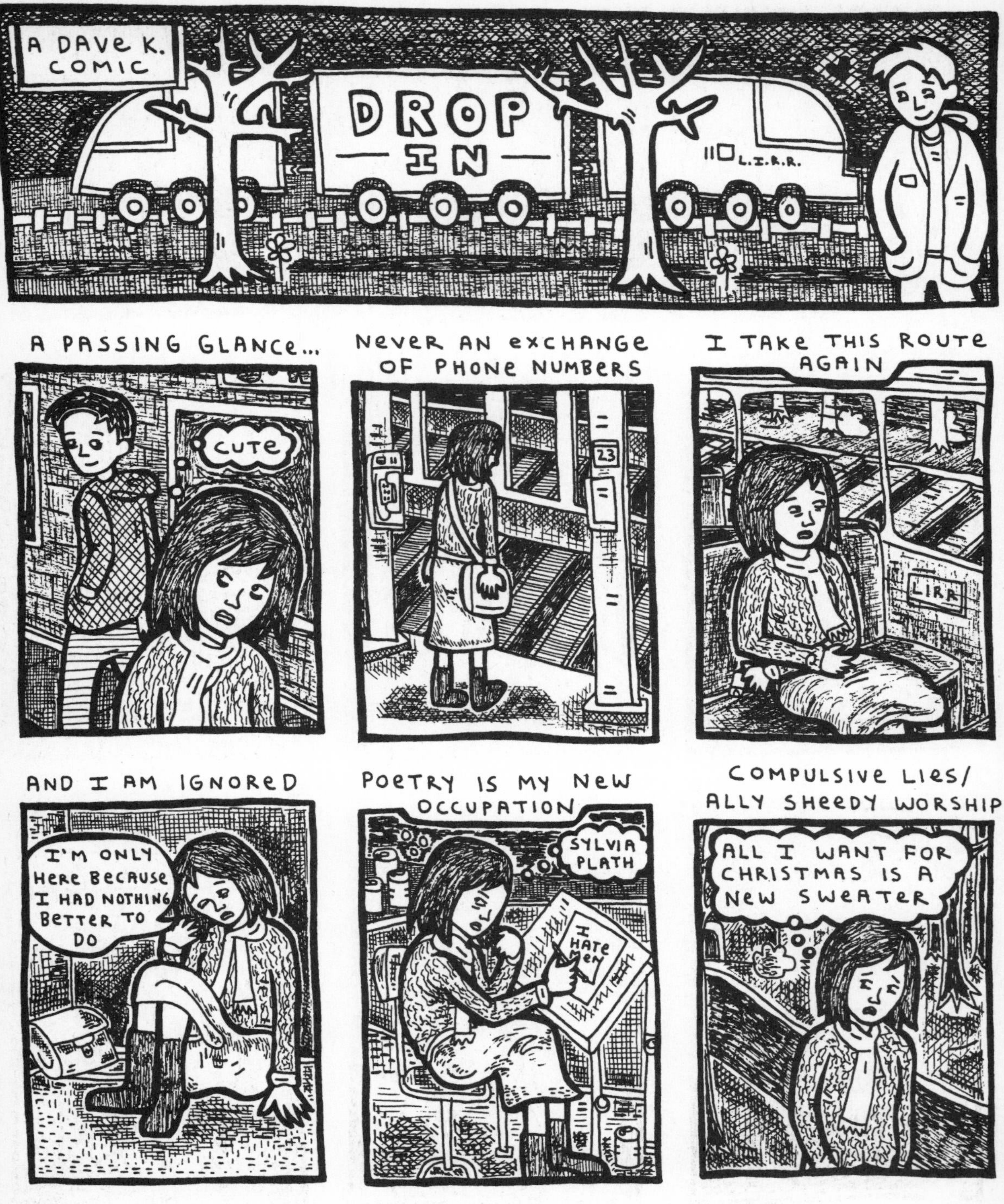
A DAVE K. COMIC
DROP IN
L.I.R.R.
A PASSING GLANCE...
CUTE
NEVER AN EXCHANGE OF PHONE NUMBERS
23
I TAKE THIS ROUTE AGAIN
LIRR
AND I AM IGNORED
I'M ONLY HERE BECAUSE I HAD NOTHING BETTER TO DO
POETRY IS MY NEW OCCUPATION
SYLVIA PLATH
I HATE MEN
COMPULSIVE LIES/ ALLY SHEEDY WORSHIP
ALL I WANT FOR CHRISTMAS IS A NEW SWEATER

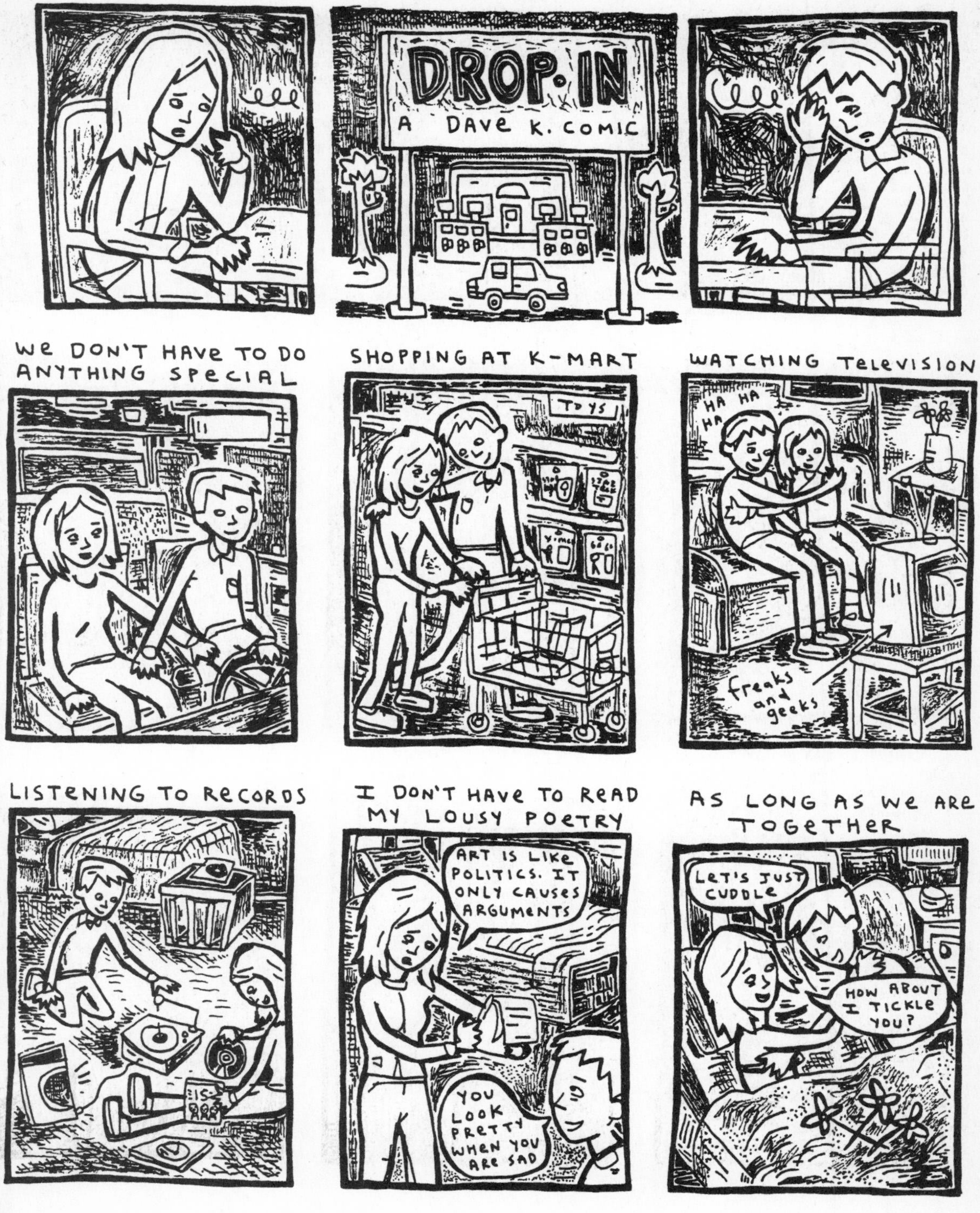
DROP-IN
A DAVE K. COMIC
WE DON'T HAVE TO DO ANYTHING SPECIAL
SHOPPING AT K-MART
TOYS
WATCHING TELEVISION
HA HA HA
freaks and geeks
LISTENING TO RECORDS
I DON'T HAVE TO READ MY LOUSY POETRY
ART IS LIKE POLITICS. IT ONLY CAUSES ARGUMENTS
YOU LOOK PRETTY WHEN YOU ARE SAD
AS LONG AS WE ARE TOGETHER
LET'S JUST CUDDLE
HOW ABOUT I TICKLE YOU?

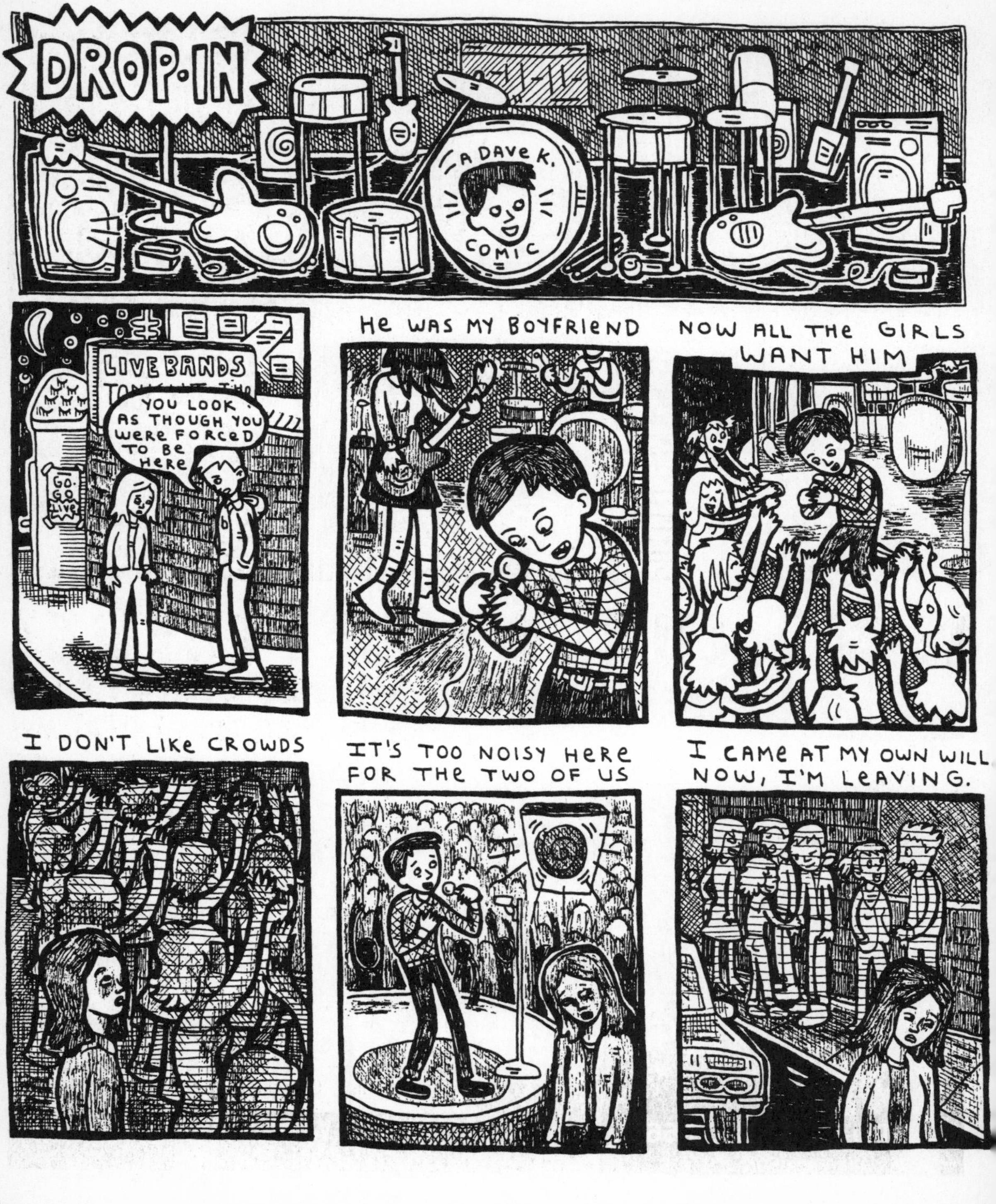
DROP·IN
A DAVE K. COMIC
LIVE BANDS
YOU LOOK AS THOUGH YOU WERE FORCED TO BE HERE
HE WAS MY BOYFRIEND
NOW ALL THE GIRLS WANT HIM
I DON'T LIKE CROWDS
IT'S TOO NOISY HERE FOR THE TWO OF US
I CAME AT MY OWN WILL
NOW, I'M LEAVING.

PORTLAND

d. chelsea

picture cocktail by mark jaquette
HTTP://users.rio.com/bamm/illustrationism

Mix a
donny Osmond
This 'SOUR' Cocktail is preferred with Brandy by Most Flashbackers.
- 1 measure Brandy.
- 1 measure lime juice.
- 4-5 drops of Tabasco sauce.
- 56g. (2 oz. or 1/3 cup) of 7-up or ginger ale.
- 1/2 measure Dark rum.
shake ingredients well w/ice and pour into a HIGHBALL glass.

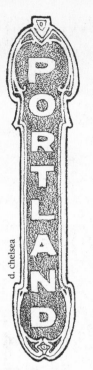

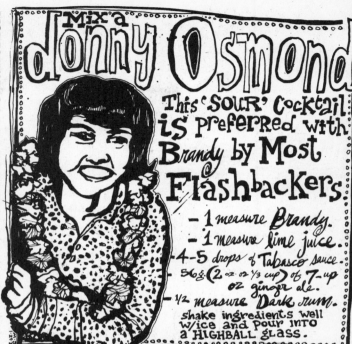

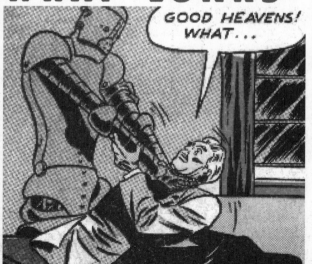

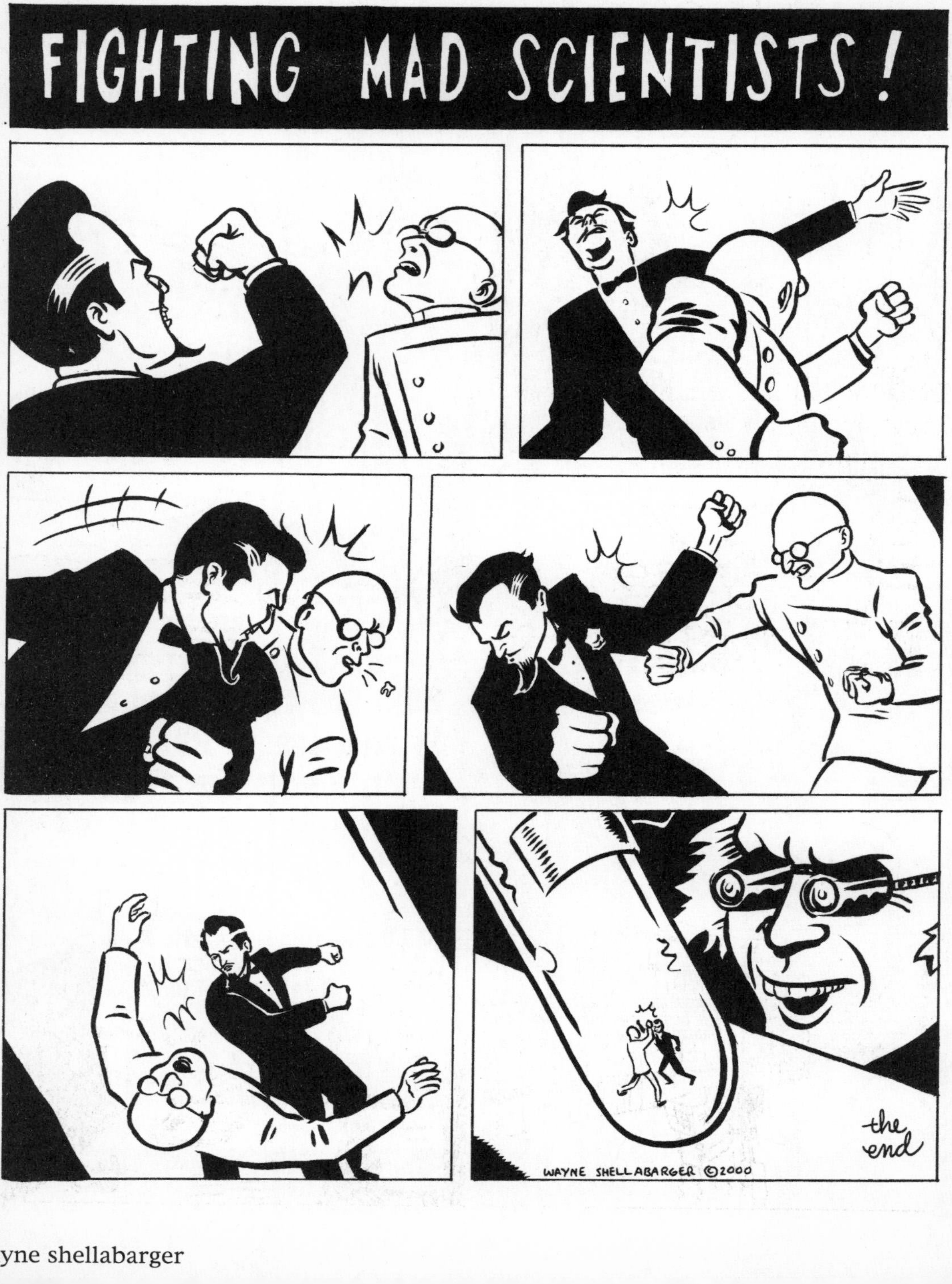
FIGHTING MAD SCIENTISTS!
the end
WAYNE SHELLABARGER ©2000

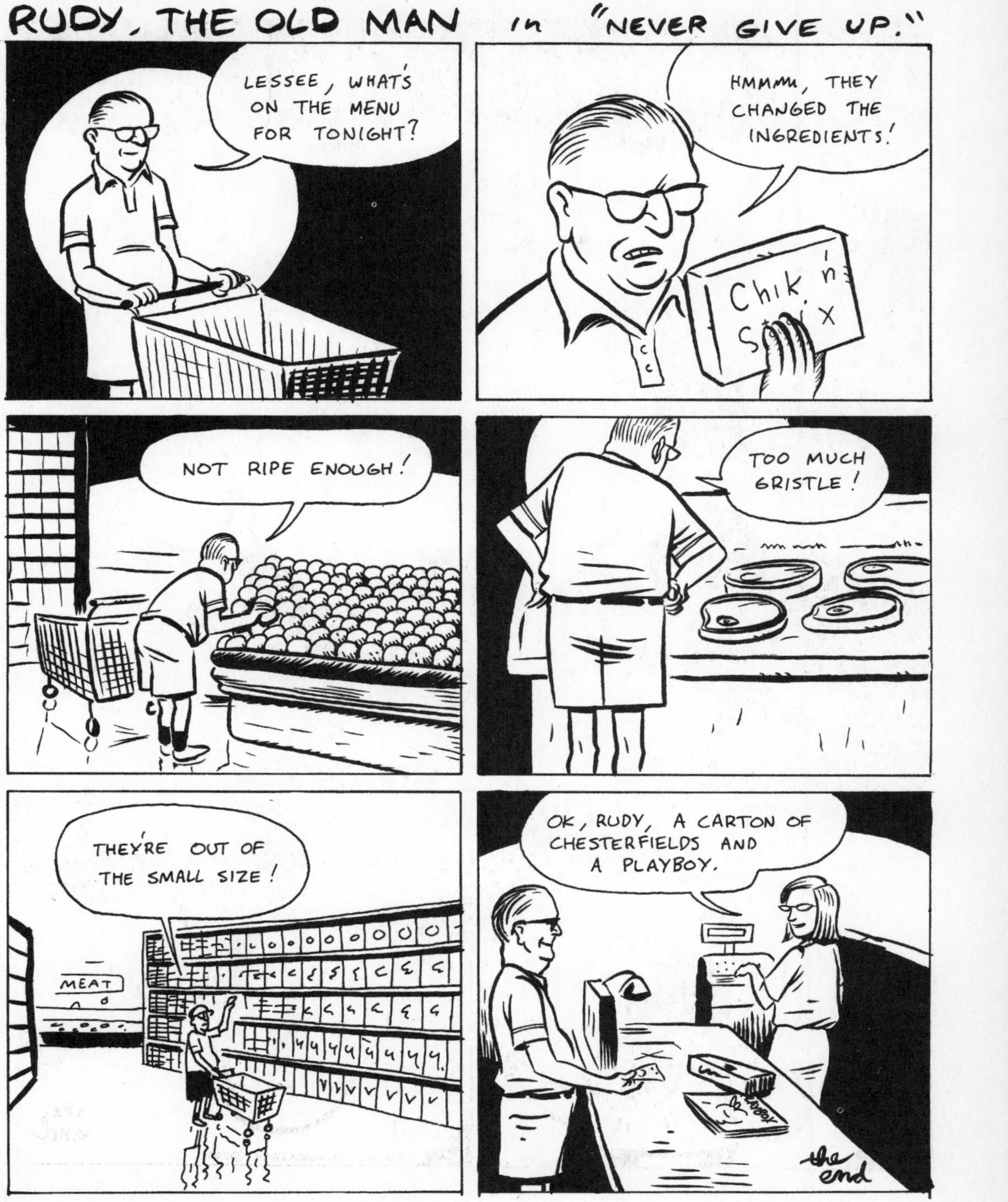

RUDY, THE OLD MAN in "NEVER GIVE UP."
LESSEE, WHAT'S ON THE MENU FOR TONIGHT?
HMMMM, THEY CHANGED THE INGREDIENTS!
Chik 'n' Stix
NOT RIPE ENOUGH!
TOO MUCH GRISTLE!
THEY'RE OUT OF THE SMALL SIZE!
MEAT
OK, RUDY, A CARTON OF CHESTERFIELDS AND A PLAYBOY.
the end

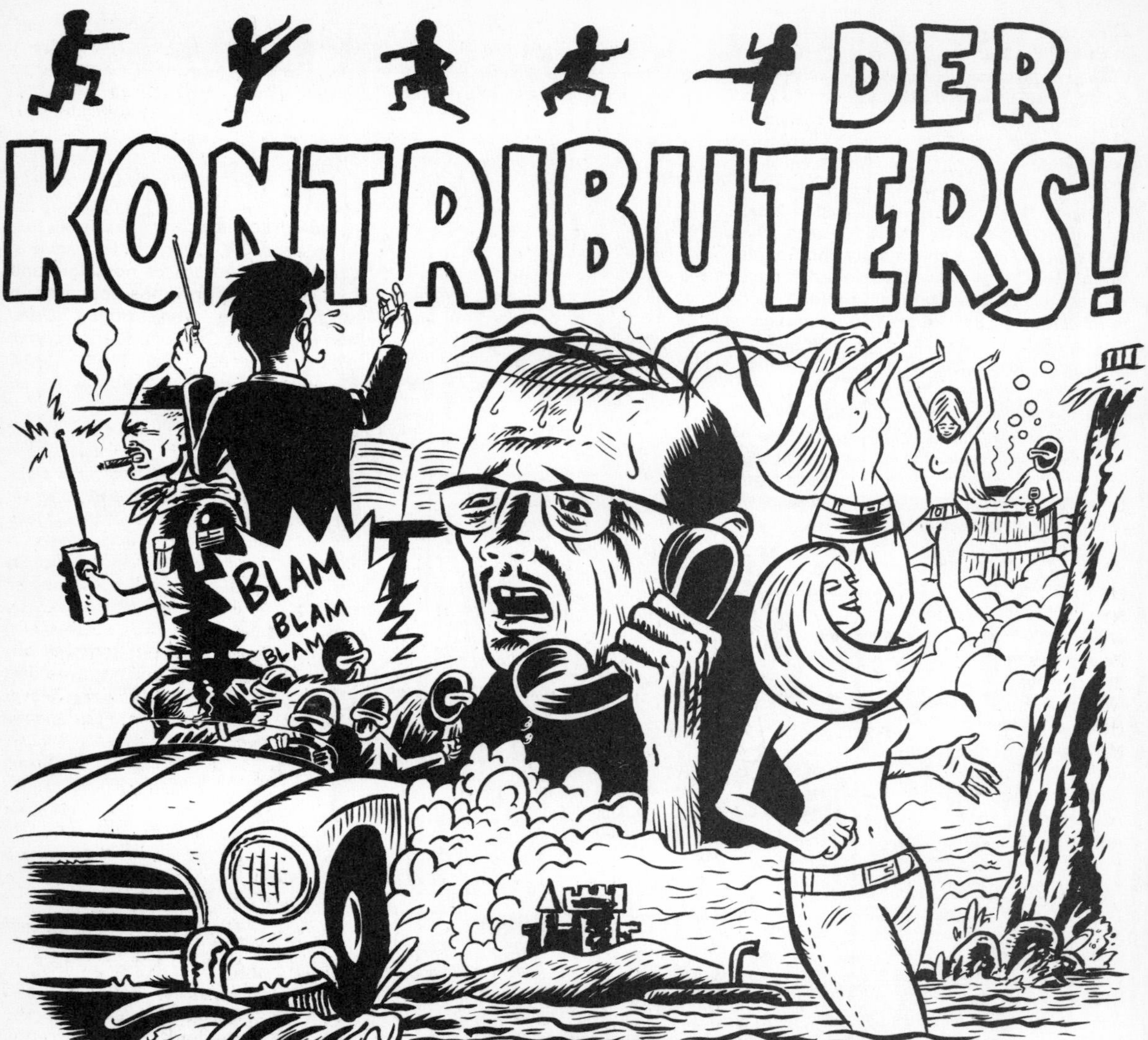
DER
KONTRIBUTERS!
BLAM
BLAM
BLAM

DER KONTRIBUTORS in "SCOUTMASTER vs. THE HOT TUB ACADEMY"

DIREKTED BY HERR WAYNE SCHICKLEGRÜBER. **Jorge Alderete** was born in the province of Santa Cruz in the south of Argentina in 1971. He co-edited the comic magazine *Gratarola Jamás!*, and has contributed to numerous publications over the years, including *Fierro, Rolling Stone, Página 12,*

El País, *La Comictiva*, and *Monográfico*. He currently lives in Spain, illustrates covers for supplements of Argentina's *Clarín* newspaper and for their Sunday magazine *Viva*. Since 1999 he's been the editor of *Zonaste!*, the comics supplement of the Spanish magazine *Zona de Obras*, featuring contributions by artists from Argentina, Mexico, Brazil, Canada, the USA and Spain. www.jorgealderete.com ¶ On "Así Pasan los Días," **Matt Madden** wrote: "This is the first story I drew about living in Mexico City. The title is a line from a song called "Quizás, Quizás, Quizás," as interpreted (with a charmingly bad Spanish accent) by Nat 'King' Cole. It was commissioned for a Mexico City arts magazine that had (typically) folded by the time I turned in the story, and ended up running in Spanish in an Uruguayan arts fanzine, *Café a la Turca*, and in English as a mini-comic (minus the color/gray wash) 'double a-side' flip book with Jessica Abel's *Escuadrón Rescate* (Highwater Books)." Matt has recently published *Odds Off* (Highwater) and *Exercises in Style*, which is serialized on the Indy website www.indymagazine.com/index.shtml. His new book, *A Fine Mess*, is available from Alternative Comics. Matt and Jessica live in Brooklyn, NY. matt@mattmadden.com / www.mattmadden.com ¶ **Matt Feazell** is a freelance graphic artist living and working in Hamtramck, Michigan, the little town that Detroit forgot. When he's not helping ad agencies make newspaper ads for luxury Ford cars, he's writing, drawing, and coloring a monthly half-page feature for *Disney Adventures* magazine (look for the stick figure cartoon beside the staff box at the front of the mag!) and working on a weekly Cynicalman comic strip for serializer.net! He has about 25 mini-comics in print, and they are listed in his online catalog at www.cynicalman.com. Not Available Comics, P.O. Box 12038, Hamtramck MI 48212. ¶ **James Kochalka**, his wife Amy, and their kitty Spandy live in Burlington, VT. His bibliography is extensive and includes *Magic Boy and Girlfriend*, *Monkey vs. Robot*, *Pinky & Stinky*, and *Sketchbook Diaries* (Top Shelf); *Tiny Bubbles* and *Kissers* (Highwater); and *Peanut Butter & Jeremy* and *Mermaid* (Alternative Comics). People can read his full color Fancy Froglin strip at www.moderntales.com. "Very Nearly Real" originally appeared in a Portuguese edition of the comic book *Magic Boy*, published in 2001 by Ediçoes Polvo. www.americanelf.com / james@indyworld.com ¶ **Dean Haspiel** lives in Brooklyn, NY. He is the author of semi-autobiographical comix and super-psychedelic romances. Dino's aggro-moxie appears occasionally in *Billy Dogma* (Top Shelf & Alternative), and *Opposable Thumbs* (Alternative). Besides *Top Shelf*, Dino's work has graced the pages of various premiere anthologies, including *Bizarro Comics* (DC Comics), *911: Emergency Relief* (Alternative), Jordan Crane's *NON* (Red Ink), and Harvey Pekar's *American Splendor* (Dark Horse/Maverick). Dino's more recent Marvel work includes *Muties* #3, *Captain America*, *X-Men Unlimited*, and a 4-issue *Thing* mini-series (written by Evan Dorkin). Write to Dino at: 335 Court Street, #131, Brooklyn, NY 11231. www.deanhaspiel.com / dino@cobite.com ¶ **Dave K.** is a high school teacher in Queens, NY. Over the last several years he has self-published a plethora of nostalgic and melancholy mini-comics, while his work has appeared in numerous anthologies, including *Non*, *Bogus Dead* (Jeroman Empire, edited by Jerome Gaynor), *Stereoscomic* (edited by Alban Rauchtenbach), and *EXPO 2001*. Personals: Looking for suicidal girls to collaborate on puppet film projects. Currently: trying to cut class. His newest books can be ordered from www.usscatastrophe. com. A brief catalog can be found on the website davekteenage@ aol.com ¶ **Ian Lynam** is a designer extraordinairre who lives in Los Angeles, CA. He ran the comics/ zine label Migraine for years, creates fonts, and recently won the Mead Annual Report Design Competition. (That's pretty freaking cool!) Goods: www.migrai neentertainmentsyndicate .com. Services: www. deafleopard.com. Word up. ianmgrn@hotmail. com ¶ **Renée French** recently relocated to California with her husband and a hermit crab. Her previous work includes *Grit Bath* (Fantagraphics), *The Ninth Gland* and *Corny's Fetish* (Dark Horse), *Marbles In My Underpants* (Oni Press), *The Soap Lady* (Top Shelf) and her brand spanking new children's book *Tinka* (Simon and Schuster). Renée's work also appears regularly in the French anthology *Lapin* (L'Association). She's currently working on another children's book and a project for Top Shelf called *The Ticking* (designed by Jordan Crane). renee@reneefrench.com / www.reneefrench.com ¶ **Mack White** lives in Austin, TX. His recent activities include production design on an independent film, *Cowboys and Martians*; writing a regular column for *Austin ParaTimes*; a new story, "A Scandal in St. J--," for *Dirty Stories* #3 (Eros/Fantagraphics); a 2-page piece for the *Comics Journal*'s Special Edition Summer 2002; and the recently published book, *Facts about September 11*, to coincide with the 9/11 Show at Alternate Currents Gallery in Austin. He also has stories in current issues of the European magazines *El Vibora* and *Zone 5300*. His comics, *Villa of the Mysteries* 1, 2, and 3 (Fantagraphics) and

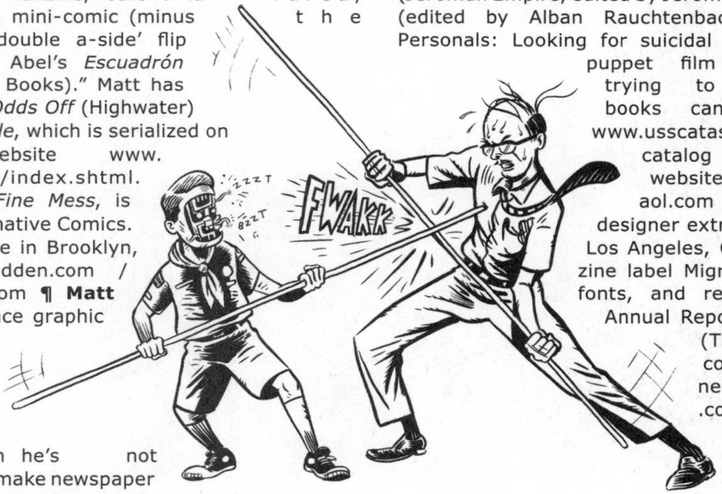
FWAKK

"Why isn't there a real *boy here?"* *

*(Captions translated from the original German.)

Mutant Book of the Dead (Starhead) are available for $4 each (postage paid), from him at: P.O. Box 49575, Austin, TX 78765. mackwhite@austin.rr.com / www.mackwhite.com(Villa of the Mysteries), www.bisonbill.com (Bison Bill's Weird West Show), www.worldnewslink.com (Worldwide Newslink) ¶ **Zak Sally** has been nurturing his love/hate relationship with funnybooks for 15 years, self-publishing various comics/zines under various names, with wildly varying degrees of quality. He swears off comics forever twice weekly, but is currently hard at work on the third (and final) issue of his crybaby/bitchfest comic book *Recidivist*, which might be out in a year or so. Then again it might not. He drives a white 1991 Toyota Corolla and resides in Minnesota, where he still has a strange difficulty in maintaining a workable mailing address. ¶ **Jeff Zenick** no longer edits the seminal zine *White Buffalo Gazette*. His presence is sorely missed and his whereabouts are rather mysterious. Sometimes he resides in FLA. Occasional mini-comics surface now & then. ¶ **Kevin Quigley** self-published a collection of his work titled *Big Place Comics*. He edited *Comics Underground Japan*, a collection of Japanese cartoonists published by Blast Books, featuring a stunning array of Japanese talent culled from the seminal manga titled *Garo*. Kevin is currently making paintings and working on the strip "True Ghosts," the first 15 installments of which can be found in the 'comics' issue of *Chain* (Summer 2001), from Temple University Press. ¶ **Wayne Shellabarger** lives in Portland, OR with his wife Kristin, their dog Collin, a guinea pig Milkdud, some fish, and their cat, The Abominable Dr. Phibes. Copies of Wayne's poster collection, *I'm Totally Helpless*, are still available from Top Shelf. waynes3@spiritone.com / www.wayne-s.com ¶ **Jesse Reklaw** has been drawing the nationally syndicated comic strip "Slow Wave" since 1995. The first collection of these strips, *Dreamtoons*, was published by Shambhala in 2000. It is out of print, but can be ordered directly from Jesse for $8. P.O. Box 11493, Berkeley, CA 94712. A second collection should be out soon. www.slowwave.com ¶ **Josh Simmons** lives in New Orleans, LA. His work has appeared in *Top Shelf On Parade*, *Top Shelf Under the Big Top*, *Cirkus New Orleans* (Small Batch Series), and his solo book *Happy,* all for Top Shelf. He's produced herds of funky, sick little books, including the anthology *All About Fucking*. *Sunshine, Love and Happiness*, a collection of "happy" stories, will appear in the future, also from Top Shelf. chri stmuffins@hotmail.com ¶ After surviving a stint in Portland, OR, illustrator/cartoonist **Max Estes** now once again lives in Milwaukee, WI, where he resides with a girl named Laura and a cat named Einstein. He recently appeared in the anthology *Project Telstar* (Adhouse Books, edited by Chris Pitzer). His swanky illustrations also grace both sides of Top Shelf's plastic tote-bags, and on the upcoming Top Shelf beverage coaster. www.maxestes.com / max@gridplane.com ¶ **Tom Hart** lives in New York City with his wife and fellow cartoonist Leela Corman. His previous work includes the *Collected Hutch Owen* and *Banks/Eubanks* (Top Shelf), *The Sands* (Black Eye), and *Triple Dare* (Alternative). Several years ago, Tom was one of only a mere handful of American cartoonists (along with *Big Questions* contributor Garret Izumi and Paul Pope) to work with Japanese publisher Kodansha. He is serializing the next Hutch Owen book on the web at www.moderntales.com. Last October, Tom launched www.seralizer.net, the newly launched offshoot of comics website www.moderntales.com. tomhart@newhatstories.com ¶ **David Lasky** has been producing comics for ten years. In 1991 he produced four *Boom Boom* mini-comics. These fifty-cent booklets were quickly joined by the more ambitious *Minit Classics Presents Joyce's Ulysses*. Later, Lasky was honored with the Xeric Foundation grant for self-publishing cartoonists, which helped him produce four new, fancier *Boom Boom* comics. These then led to yet another four new *Boom Boom* comics (MU Press). Lasky continues to produce mini-comics with titles such as *OM* and *Minutiae*. His illustration clients include Seattle's *Stranger* and Tower Records' *Classical Pulse!*. Lasky and coconspirator Greg Stump's most recent masterpiece is the much anticipated *Urban Hipster* #2 (Alternative). {This bio is excerpted from a much lengthier version on Jeremy Pinkham's website www.serapion.com, introducing a strip by David about blues legend John Lee Hooker—from the anthology *Stereoscomic*.} ¶ **Bill Griffith** is the man behind the legendary, sublime Zippy the Pinhead. There are many *Zippy* volumes available from Fantagraphics. Bill and art spiegleman co-edited the sophisticated mid-70's anthology *Arcade* (Print Mint). Bill recently penned an appreciation for illustrator/cartoonist W.E. Hill in the *Comics Journal* Special Edition Summer 2002. In the same issue he contributed a superb strip titled "Every Rock Concert I've Ever Attended." ¶ **Ted Stearn** got his start in

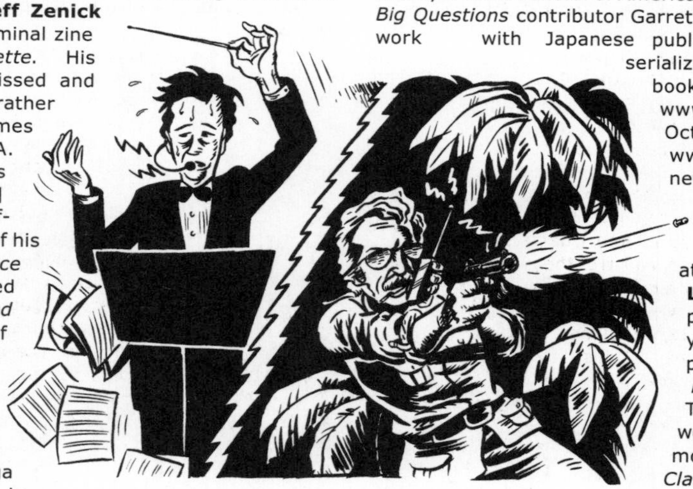

Dangerous instructions from a bullet concerto.

comics in Dave Mazzucchelli's masterful anthology *Rubber Blanket*. Since then he has issued the collected early tales of his anthropomorphic duo in their eponymously titled *Fuzz and Pluck*, and two wonderful issues of a new series with the same characters for Fantagraphics. Ted lives in Brooklyn, NY. ¶ **Tony Millionaire** grew up in the seaside town of Gloucester, MA where his grandparents taught him to draw ships and old houses. After spending thousands of Sunday afternoons gazing at his grandfather's collections of old newspaper comics, he picked up a pen and started drawing monkeys with striped tails and top hats. His work has been published by Dark Horse and Fantagraphics and has been animated for Saturday Night Live. He now lives in Pasadena, CA with his wife and daughter. www.maakies.com ¶ **Garret Izumi** still remains the coolest guy in comics. His Shortwave Productions rocks the world with its "book-arts" publications. Lately, Garret has been experimenting with photo-essays—to great effect. One recent work, *Call of the Sirens*, documents early Cold War-era air-raid sirens in Los Angeles. Beautiful and haunting. garreti@yahoo.com ¶ **Ivan Brunetti** lives in Chicago, IL. He's a terribly nice guy, but his brilliant comics are downright disturbing. His most recent book, *Haw!*, and his comic book series *Schizo* are available from Fantagraphics. ¶ **Joe Matt** is the creator of *Peepshow* (Drawn and Quarterly). Pick up his latest collection, *Fair Weather*, quite possibly his most affecting work to date. ¶ **Tony Consiglio** lives in the city of Indianapolis in the state of Indiana. He has been slaving away at his excellent mini-comic *Double Cross* for all eternity. One episode of his magnum opus has been collected in the book *Double Cross: More or Less* (Top Shelf). Write to Tony at: 4730 East 71st Street, Indianapolis, IN 46220. www.members.aol.com/doubletony / doubletony@aol.com ¶ **Josh Neufeld** is infamous for his book *Titans of Finance* (Alternative)—which has been favorably mentioned in the *New York Times*, *Money*, *U.S. News & World Report*, *Kiplinger's*, and *Fortune Small Business*—as well as *Keyhole* (Modern Comics, Top Shelf, Alternative) with long-time pal Dean Haspiel. On October 3, 2002 Josh took part (hawking his comic too, no less) in Ralph Nader's "Crackdown on Corporate Crime" rally at Federal Hall in NYC. Nader's goal was to "focus attention on the vast array of corporate misdeeds, and to propose sound remedies that will help shareholders, taxpayers, workers, and consumers tame the reckless and out-of-control corporate bosses." ¶ **Warren Craghead** likes to make pictures and is a contributor to various anthologies. He is a recipient of the Xeric Foundation grant and is a founding editor of usscatastrophe.com and *Salvage* magazine. Warren's work pushes the limits of comics in strange, uneasy ways. Quiet, poetic, and unsettling. He lives with his wife and two mammoth cats. www.craphead.com ¶ **Kevin Scalzo** lives in Seattle, worked at Fantagraphics, is a freelance illustrator (*Bust*, *Nickelodeon*) and cartoonist (*Sugar Booger*). He was part of an art show at Medusa Tattoo in Portland last October. info@kevinscalzo.com / www.kevinscalzo.com ¶ **Dylan Horrocks** currently writes *Batgirl* for DC Comics. He also writes and draws *Atlas* (Drawn & Quarterly), and is working on a book for Top Shelf. His graphic novel *Hicksville* (Black Eye/Drawn & Quarterly) was nominated for a Harvey Award and two Ignatz Awards and was named a Book of the Year by the *Comics Journal*. Dylan has won Eisner Award's for both *Hicksville* and *Atlas*. His comicography includes: *Pickle* (Black Eye), *Bizarro Comics*, *Comix2000* (L'Association), *Dark Horse Maverick 2000* (Dark Horse), *Dirty Stories* 1 & 2, and various anthologies. His political cartoons appear frequently in the *NZ Political Review* and have been collected as *Better Luck Next Century* (Top Shelf Small Batch Series). He lectures occasionally about comics and cartooning and has written about comics for the *Comics Journal*, *Pavement*, and various other publications worldwide. He assembled the exhibition Nga Pakiwaituhi O Aotearoa: New Zealand Comics, which has shown in New Zealand and USA, and was accompanied by a 100-page catalogue. ¶ **Eric Reynolds** lives in Seattle, WA, spends most of his time as the hardest working man at Fantagraphics. He drew his strip in the Peanuts Tribute section hours after Charles Schulz passed away on February 12, 2000. He's edited three volumes of the superlative smut anthology, *Dirty Comics*. ¶ **Seth** lives in Toronto, Ontario. His book *Palookaville* (Drawn & Quarterly) is among the standard bearers for cartoonists everywhere. Lush, sentimental, and dreamy. He recently did some exquisite package design for Aimee Mann's delightful recording *Lost In Space*. ¶ **Martin tom Dieck** studied illustration at the Fachhochschule für Gestaltung in Hamburg, where he lives as a comic artist and illustrator. He made his debut with *Der Unschuldige Passagier* in 1993. His comicography includes *Hundert Ansichten der Speicherstadt* (Arrache Coeur), a wordless comix ode to the Speicherstadt harbour quarters of Hamburg. Martin tom Dieck's preference for the improvised and the unconscious found expression in his tribute to the late French philosopher Gilles Deleuze. Originally a simple comix homage to Deleuze printed in

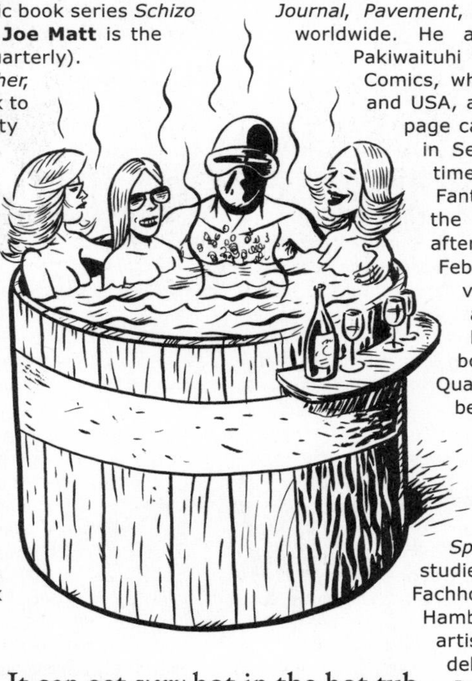

It can get *very* hot in the hot tub.

the French anthology *Lapin*, he transformed the short story into a refined reflection on repetition and difference in life and of the comix form itself. His work has appeared in the anthologies *Le Cheval sans Tete* (Amok Editions), *Comix2000*, and *Stripburger* (Stripburek). His latest project is a freestyle biography of the German writer Walter Mehring (Edition Moderne). www.mtomdieck.com. (Biographical notes excerpted, with permission, from the Lambiek website www.lambiek.net.) ¶ **Andrew Brandou** lives in Los Angeles, CA, with his wife, a superstar Hollywood script writer. They share their home with a Noble-prize nominee and a covert operative. Andrew is a regular artist in the Burning Brush art shows in Los Angeles. He has published two issues of the comic *Howdy Pardner* (Robot Publishing), had a story in the anthology *Oden* (Robot Publishing), and a few years ago designed some super-cool Top Shelf Christmas ornaments. Visit Andrew's wonderfully whimsical Richard Scary-like website www.howdypardner.com. ¶ **Robert Goodin** threw away at least a down payment for a house as the publisher of the Robot Publishing Co. He has produced a few stories for Robot including *Binibus Barnabus* and "The Story of Horse" in the anthology *Oden*. In a previous life he worked in the animation industry in Los Angeles. Meanwhile, he and his fiancée plan on moving to Paris in the summer of 2003, where he will pursue his lifelong dream of being a comic artist/writer. Hobbies include: drawing, procrastinating, and writing about himself in the third person. nidoog@earthlink.net / www.robertgoodin.com ¶ Fellow Robot artist **Joy Kolitsky** currently lives in Brooklyn, NY, where she does illustration and animation work. Among the comics that she has done are the beautifully etched "In the Sea," as well as "Superbull" and "Polish Ravioli" in *Oden*. www.joykolisky.com ¶ **Anthony Vukojevich**'s first published work was as a letterer in *Crystar the Crystal Warrior* #4 (Marvel), in 1983. He's produced books for Robot Publishing, including *The Envelope Licker*, and the porn opus *Clint Flicker*. He self-published one issue of *Chick Magnet*, is currently designing backgrounds for the *Wild Thornberrys* and *As Told by Ginger* for Nickelodeon, and is working on a *Clint Flicker* graphic novel. He lives in Pasadena, CA with his roommate Robert Goodin. They are not lovers. ¶ **Nathan Gruenwald**, who oversees the dissemination and distribution of Cesar Spinoza's work, lives with his wife and two children in Rhinebeck, NY. He can be reached through the Lipton Gallery in Great Barrington, Massachusetts. ¶ **Jennifer Yuh Nelson**, a Dreamworks animation storyboard artist, has done two comic stories. "Nth," published in *Oden*, and "Pumpkin," a beautifully illustrated book also done for Robot. She lives in Los Angeles with her husband Tom and her neighbor's kidnapped cat, Ashley. ¶ The elusive **Cathy Malkasian** recently finished co-directing *The Wild Thornberrys'* movie and is looking to take a little break from the animation world. Her graphic novel, *Birth*, is completely thumbnailed, so maybe she will finish that. What has been printed is *Peter Contrarious* (Robot Publishing), a little book about a priest who loses his bible and has to start making his own decisions. Her story "Yup Yup and Spiddle in Big Top City" was published in *Oden*. She lives in Los Angeles. ¶ **Michael Kenny** has been a key player in two young publishing companies. The first was the short lived Zoo Arsonist Press, which published his excellent *Young Bug*. Then, with the Robot Publishing Co. he produced *Knockout* and *Bashi Bazouk*. He is currently a director on the Nickelodeon shows *As Told by Ginger* and *The Wild Thornberrys*. ¶ The work of **Jason** is everywhere these days. He's recently been in *Non*, *Bile Noire* (Atrabile), *Comix2000*, and *Stripburger*. Fantagraphics is publishing his oeuvre for the American market, including *Hey Wait...* and *Sshhhhh!* His comic book *Mjau Mjau*, is up to issue 12. He was born in Norway in 1965 and was lost to comics after discovering *Tintin* at the age of 13. He currently lives in Paris and can be reached at: mjau65@yahoo.dk ¶ **Gregory Trowbridge** wrote on French language comic anthologies in *Top Shelf Under the Big Top*. He writes on the global comic scene at his website: www.du9.org. Check it out. ¶ Viennese artist **Mahler** has been published around the world. From E´ditions de la Pastéque in Montreal came *Désir* and *Le Labyrinthe de Kratochvil*. Through L'Association in Paris, he released *Lone Racer*, *Lame Ryder*, *TNT*, *Emmanuelle's Last Flight* and *Kratochvil*. From B.u.l.b. comix in Geneva came *Dick Boss* anthology, and the full color *Flaschko* came from Swiss publisher Edition Moderne. Most of his material has also been self-published in German (Edition Brunft). In Vienna he is mostly known as a creator of one-panel cartoons and weekly newspaper strips. "TNT" is his first story in English. Nicolas has a strip collection coming out with Top Shelf this Fall titled *Van Helsing's Night Off*. He can be reached at nicolas.mahler@blackbox.net. Check out his website at www.mahlermuseum.at

¶ **Alan Moore** began writing

"My new army of pink Boy Scouts is above all."

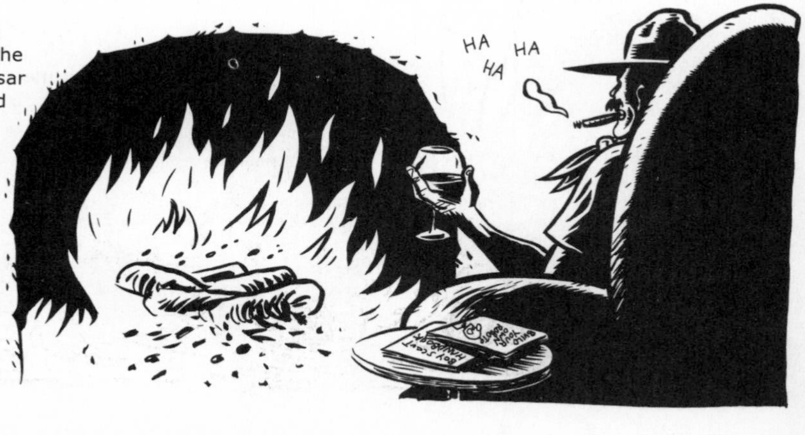
HA
HA
HA

for British publishers and serialized *Miracleman* and *V for Vendetta* in the British weekly anthology *Warrior.* He then became a key figure in the revolution of mainstream American comics in the mid-80's with books like the epic *Watchmen* and the revamped *Swamp Thing*. His masterpiece, *From Hell*, is exquisitely illustrated by Eddie Cambell. Currently he is writing *Promethea* and *The League of Extraordinary Gentlemen*. 2004 will see the long anticipated release *Lost Girls* from Top Shelf. To learn more about Alan Moore check out the website www.alanmoorefansite.com. ¶ In 1973 **Melinda Gebbie** discovered the anthology *Wimmen's Comix*, was compelled to start cartooning, and became a regular contributor thereafter. In 1976 she authored a strip set in the French Revolution for the anthology *Wet Satin*. With Alan Moore she began serializing their erotic strip *Lost Girls* in Stephen Bissette's superb horror anthology *Taboo*. Recently she's been working with Alan Moore on the character Cobweb for the America's Best Comics' *Tomorrow Stories*. ¶ **James Sturm**'s first major comics work was *Cereal Killings* (Fantagraphics). He's since produced a number of historical stories: *The Revival*, *Hundreds of Feet Below Daylight*, and *The Golem's Mighty Swing* (Drawn and Quarterly). His most recent project is a story about the Fantastic Four, titled *Unstable Molecules* (Marvel), examining their lives before they were subjected to those fateful cosmic rays, with art by Guy Davis, and cover drawings by Craig Thompson. ¶ **Steven (Ribs) Weissman**'s career in comics began in the mid-90's with the self-published *Yikes*. Alternative Comics picked him up and published more *Yikes*, as well as *Tykes* and *The Lemon Kids*. At Fantagraphics, he's published *Champs*, *Don't Call Me Stupid!*, and *White Flower Day*. ¶ **Ulf K.** is becoming the anthology king with comics in *Non*, *Spoutnik* (F.52), *Comix2000*, and *Wind* (Bries). He has two collections of short stories in English from Bries, *The Man on the Moon* and *Tango with Death*. ¶ For anyone interested in the world of European comics, **Bart Beaty**'s semi-regular article in the *Comics Journal*, "Eurocomics for Beginners," is a must. An explosion of talent has risen from across the Atlantic and Bart is the only one in the American comics press to cover what has been happening. The past ten years have seen a revolution with L'Association, Amok, Cornelius, Atrabile, Freon, and Bries. Read his column and hunt down what he's been recommending. ¶ **Winshluss** is most closely connected to the French publisher Les Requins Marteaux. His work has appeared in many anthologies, most notably *Ferraille (*Les Requins Marteaux) and *Comix2000*. There are two collections of his work, *Monsieur Ferraille*, with cartoonist Cizo (Les Requins Marteaux), and *Welcome to the Death Club* (6 Pieds Sous Terre). His art was featured on all of the faux product lables at the epic Super Marché exhibit at Angouleme 2002. His horrific cartoony work is worth tracking down if you can find it. ¶ The various artists representing **Atrabile**, **B.u.l.b. comix**, and **Drozophile** can be contacted at: Atrabile, Cas Postale 30, 1211 Genéve 21, Switzerland. Their books can be ordered through F.52, phone: (514) 286-0352 / fax (514) 286-0388. Graphic Novels worth checking out are *Pilules Bleues* by Frederik Peeters, *Cabinet de Curiosite´s* by Tom Tirabosco, and *Joseph* by Nicolas Robel. Robel's story "Bleeding Tree" was printed in English in *Drawn and Quarterly* Vol 4 . ¶ Born on the island of Sardinia in 1972, **Dino Sechi** moved to Belgium with his parents and has lived there for the past 20 years. A modern Renaissance man, Dino is a cartoon filmmaker, set designer, photographer, web designer, and graphic artist. He is presently working on a Flash format series for kids called *Mamemo* for a French producer, and is also working with his older brother Sirio and Philippe Capart at the Studio Arf-Arf. www.dino.com02.com ¶ **Philippe Capart** was born in Brussels in 1973, but spent his teenage years in Virginia Beach, VA, where he discovered that *Les Schtroumpfs* by Belgian artist Peyo were crudely transformed into the Smurfs. He spent his college days in Belgium studying experimental animation, and returned to the USA working on the animated series *Duckman* in Hollywood. Back in Brussels once again, Philippe continues to animate, direct cartoons, write, and draw comics for Studio Arf-Arf. He loves Dolly Parton records and dreams of going to Dollyland. www.arfarf.be.tf ¶ **Monkmuss** was last seen in a bowling alley

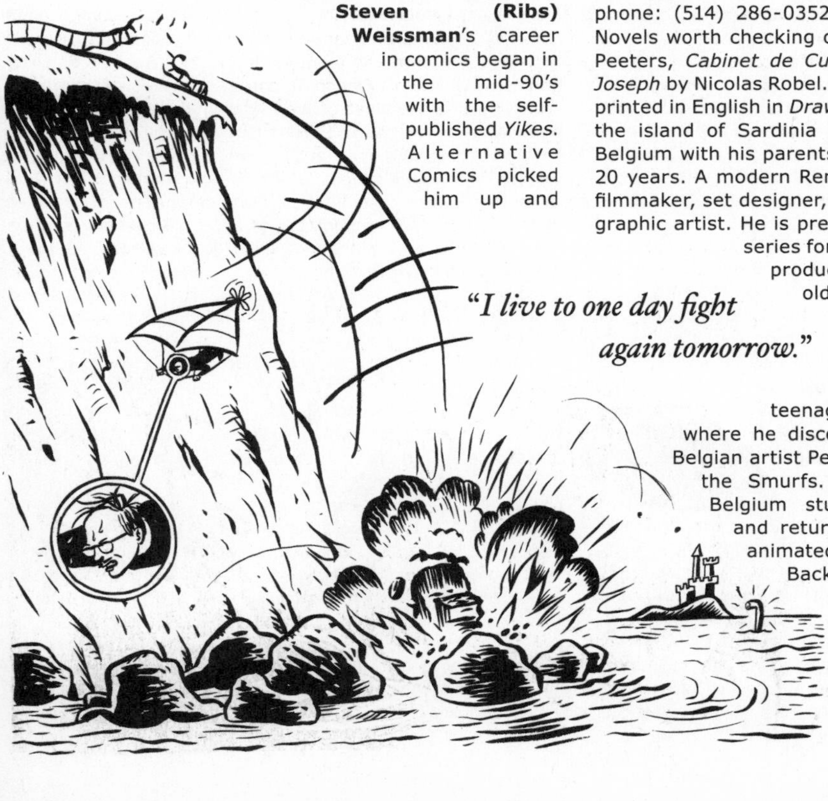

"I live to one day fight again tomorrow."

on Santa Monica Blvd, but rumor has it he lives in Montreal. ¶ **David Chelsea**'s comicography and illustration work includes the graphic novels *David Chelsea in Love* (Eclipse), *Welcome to the Zone* (Kitchen Sink), and *Perspective! A Guide for Comic Book Artists* (Watson Guptill); stories for the anthologies *Monkeywrench*, *High Times Comics*, *The Big Book of Urban Legends*, *The Big Book of Death*, *The Big Book of Little Criminals* (Big Books published by DC Comics), *Real Stuff* and *Real Smut* (Fantagraphics), and *9/11: Artists Respond*; contributions to the trading card sets *Blockbusters of Rhythm and Blues*, *Goosebumps*, and *Missing Persons* (WFMU premium); and editorial illustrations for the *New York Post*, the *New York Observer*, the *Portland Tribune*, the *New York Press*, the *Wall Street Journal*, the *Oxford American*, *City Limits*, *Spy Magazine*, *Seattle Weekly*, and *Advertising Age*. ¶ **Aaron Renier** was born in 1977 in Green Bay, WI. He was the comic editor of his high school magazine. After a brief stint at S.V.A. in New York, he moved back to Milwaukee, where he graduated. He's really happy about his project for Top Shelf called *Spiral Bound*. Aaron lives in Portland, OR where he just got a dog named Beluga. Mini-comics: *Under Estabrook*; *The Shoemaker*; and *Banana Soup*. Anthologies: *Dark Horse 9-11: Artists Respond*; *Coffee Shop Crushes*; *EXPO 2002*; *Study Group 12* (edited by Zack Soto) & *Typewriter* (edited by David Youngblood). ¶ **Paul Sharar** is the author of the 4-issue *Red Calloway's Big Bang*, from Zoo Arsonist Press, which he co-founded with Michael Kenny. He released three issues of his series *Clock!* (Zoo Arsonist). "Executron" is excerpted from the "lost issue" of *Clock!* ¶ **Marc Bell**'s book *Shrimpy and Paul and Friends*, is available from Highwater Books. It's fucking amazing! His work has appeared in *Top Shelf #6*, and *Top Shelf Under the Big Top*. He currently has a weekly comic strip called "Wilder Hobson's Theatre Absurd-o" appearing in the *Montreal Mirror* and the *Halifax Coast*. ¶ **Gavin McInnes** is a major contributor to *Vice* magazine. An excellent cartoonist, we haven't seen much since his self-published *Pervert* mini-comics. ¶ **Chris Ware**'s *Acme Novelty Library* has set the standard for classic contemporary comics. He's also known for his exquisite hand lettering, about which he had a feature article in a recent issue of *Eye* magazine. He has won every possible award which exist for fine comics. Chris' new collection,

Escape from Scoutmaster's flaccid tower!

Quimby the Mouse (quoted from Fantagraphics' website), "Cleverly appropriates old-fashioned animation imagery and advertising styles of the 1920's and 1930's put to use, at the service of modern vignettes of angst and existentialism. As this cartoon silhouette of a mouse ignominiously suffers at every turn, the spaces between the panels create despair and a Beckett-like rhythm of hope deceived and deferred (but never quite extinguished), buoying Quimby from page to page. *Quimby the Mouse* is saturated with Ware's genius, including amazing graphics, insanely perfectionist production values, cut-and-assemble paper projects, and the formal complexity of his narratives that have earned him the reputation as one of the most prodigious artists of his generation. ¶ **Bwana Spoons** produces ultra nifty stuff under his label Grass Hut Corp. "I am a rare breed of doglike monkey," writes Bwana on his website. He's published over a dozen issues of the zine *Ain't Nothin' Like Fuckin' Moonshine*, a few issues of his solo comic *Soft Smooth Brain*, and several volumes of the aptly titled toy-zine *My Friend The Micronaut*. In addition to following up on the premier issue of *Pencil Fight* (co-edited by Patrick Fong), current activities include further forays into the psychedelic playground world of *Mogwab Island*, and wrapping up his book for Top Shelf titled *Cobra Kids*. www.grasshutcorp.com ¶ **Tomer Hanuka** was born in Israel, 1974. He grew up surrounded by American comic books, which he could not read until later on. After three years of mandatory Army service, Tomer moved to New York to enroll in the illustration program of S.V.A. Upon receiving his BFA, he started publishing work in various magazines, as well as doing his own comic books. Tomer has won the gold and silver medal at the Society of Illustrators. He was also featured in *American Illustration*, *Print Magazine* and *The Face*. His art was featured on a recent cover of the *New York Times Magazine*. He self-published—with twin brother Asaf Hanuka—*Bipolar*, a comic showcasing both brothers. The series was picked by Alternative Comics at issue #3. Tomer is founding member and a regular contributor to *Meathaus*, a comic anthology of New York based artists. (This bio also lifted from www.lambiek.net.) www.thanuka.com ¶ Information on the **Xeric Foundation** can be found at www.xericfoundation.com.

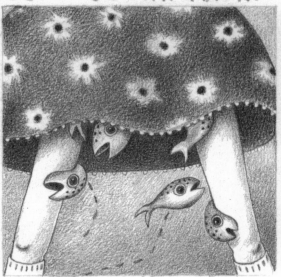

1. Kei waenganui o ngaa kuuhaa he haapuku anake ngaa ika o reira.

2. Naa, ka hangaa e Whakaue he pourewa moona.

3. Kaatahi anoo a Rupe ka Whakakuukupa i a ia.

4. Ka kitea a Whakaue ki te ngaro, ki ngaa manu e karamui ana i runga i a ia.

MEDIA DIET

An occasional report on self-published and independent comics and related periodicals.

by Heath Row

All the Goodbyes, by Greg Cook (32 pp.)
This new preview of Greg's ongoing Poppy and V. series captures the effects and emotions of divorce on a young couple and their daughter. Drawn in a style that blends Richard Scarry and Seth, *All the Goodbyes* carries the hush and weight of winter as it details the first time Harry (V.'s father) sees Edie (her mother) in public after their separation, a conversation with friends in a Thai restaurant about how Harry's loneliness is self-imposed, and V.'s discomfort and uncertainty when she encounters a black cat as her mother drops her off at her father's house. ¶ While *All the Goodbyes* doesn't capture all the nuances of parenting and separation as well as other Poppy and V. pieces, it shows a growing maturity in Greg's storytelling. The dialogue is crisp, and the street scenes on pages 16-18 are stunning. Well worth catching up on. Highwater Books, P.O. Box 1956, Cambridge, MA 02238. ($3)

Chloe, by Hans Rickheit (168 pp.)
Hans lives in the basement of Zeigeist Gallery, an art and performance space in Cambridge, Massachusetts. For the last 15 years he's been drawing comics that seem as though they were created by someone who, well, lives in the basement of a gallery. I'm not the biggest fan of his past work, particularly *False Transmission*, but I gave *Chloe*, his longest effort to date, a chance. An extended narrative, at first glance it looks as though his art has improved, and Hans' sense of humor shines through the jacket copy and indicia. I wasn't at all disappointed. ¶ While I'm still stymied by his penchant for insects, disembodied vaginas, and eyeless male characters, *Chloe* pulled me through to the end. The title character discovers the cabin of a mysterious tinkerer named Conrad, who births cats, does "only what the underbrain instructs me to do," and serves as a gatekeeper to an underground realm of gas masks, HR Giger backdrops, skeletal canines, arcane medical instruments, and the underbrain itself. ¶ *Chloe* is the odd daughter of some of Vertigo and Eros' best comics, and while I might not understand what Hans is working toward, I sure can appreciate it. Hans received the Xeric Foundation grant for this book. Chrome Fetus Comics, 312 Broadway, Cambridge, MA 02139. ($8)

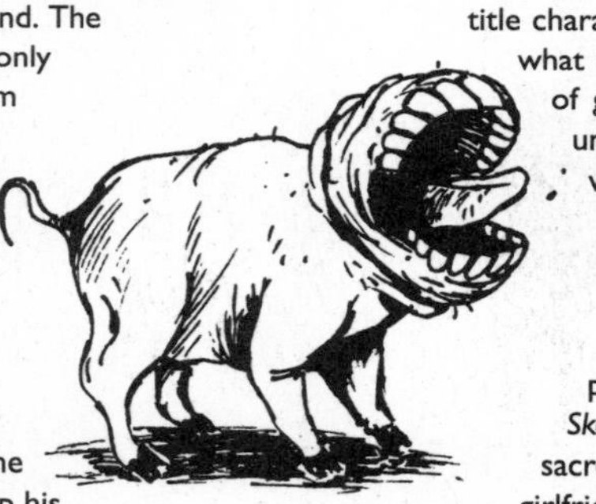

Low Jinx, edited by Kurt Wolfgang (100 pp.)
Riffing off of Matt Feazell's (and Kurt Wolfgang's previous *Low Jinx*) *Understanding Minicomics* and Highwater Books' *Coober Skeber #2*, Wolfgang's stellar 100-page self-published anthology pinches, pokes, and prods the sacred cows of independent comics. Edward Gorey meets Dr. Seuss. Billy Dogma tries to pimp his girlfriend. The *Maus* cast smuggles drugs. Sam Henderson gets dissed. Ron Rege Jr., gets tweaked. Jordan Crane tackles Chris Ware with a brilliant 10-page send up of Ware's multi-threaded, process-oriented narrative style. John Porcellino's *King Cat* takes Johnny Ryan to meet the Fort Thunder gang, to visit the Million Year Picnic, and to save his comics bacon. And Jef Czekaj pinches Brian Ralph's cheeks with a 12-page critique of Ralph's plotting, character development, and dialogue. ¶ While it's not always clear who's making fun of whom, Tony Consiglio, Eric Reynolds, Jessie Reklaw, Crane, Czekaj, Henderson, Wolfgang, and the rest of the gang take friendly and funny jabs at some of comics' greatest. Noe-Fie Monomedia, 14 Allen Pl., Canton, CT 06019. ($6)

Ron Rege Jr. and His Precursors by Robert Boyd (20 pp.)
The first in an occasional series of chapbooks about comics, Westhampton Houses' Robert Boyd's study of possible influences on the work of Ron Rege Jr. (creator of Highwater Books' *Skibber Bee Bye*), is an in-depth and thoughtful look at one of self-publishing's unsung heroes. ¶ Robert groups Ron in what he calls the "minimalist," "post-ironic," or "cute brut" school of cartoonists, a school that includes creators such as James Kochalka, Brian Ralph, and Mat Brinkman. Robert draws lines from Ron to cartoonists and artists such as Crockett (*Barnaby*) Johnson, Jack (*King Aroo*) Kent, Tove (*Moomin*) Jansson, and painter Philip Guston. He analyzes Ron's line-oriented drawing style, character scale, and vibrating energy, spending quite a bit of time considering Ron's irony and attempts to counteract his work's inherent cuteness. ¶ Despite Robert's academic/literary pretensions (the entire study is framed by Jorge Luis Borges' comparison of Kafka and his precursors), this pamphlet is a valuable addition to self-publishing scholarship, and a valid look at how "new artists are creating a new past just as they create a new future." Westhampton House, PMB 414, 167 Cherry St., Milford, CT 06460. ($1)

Heath Row is a high falootin' mogul at *Fast Company* magazine. In his spare time, Heath sings in the band the Anchormen, edits progressive fiction and nonfiction books for Highwater Books and Soft Skull Press, maintains a blog called *Media Diet*, manages Net mailing lists on the Massachusetts media and technology scene and on the jazz and electronic-music scene, and cuts his own hair. He likes his rice white and his beans black. To send items for possible review and mention in Media Diet. www.cardhouse.com/heath-contact. Heath Row at kalel@well.com or P.O. Box 441915, Somerville, MA 02144.

Illustration by Hans Rickheit from the graphic novel *Chloe*.

Bruno
the
Man
in

" On a Lead "

by

Monkmus

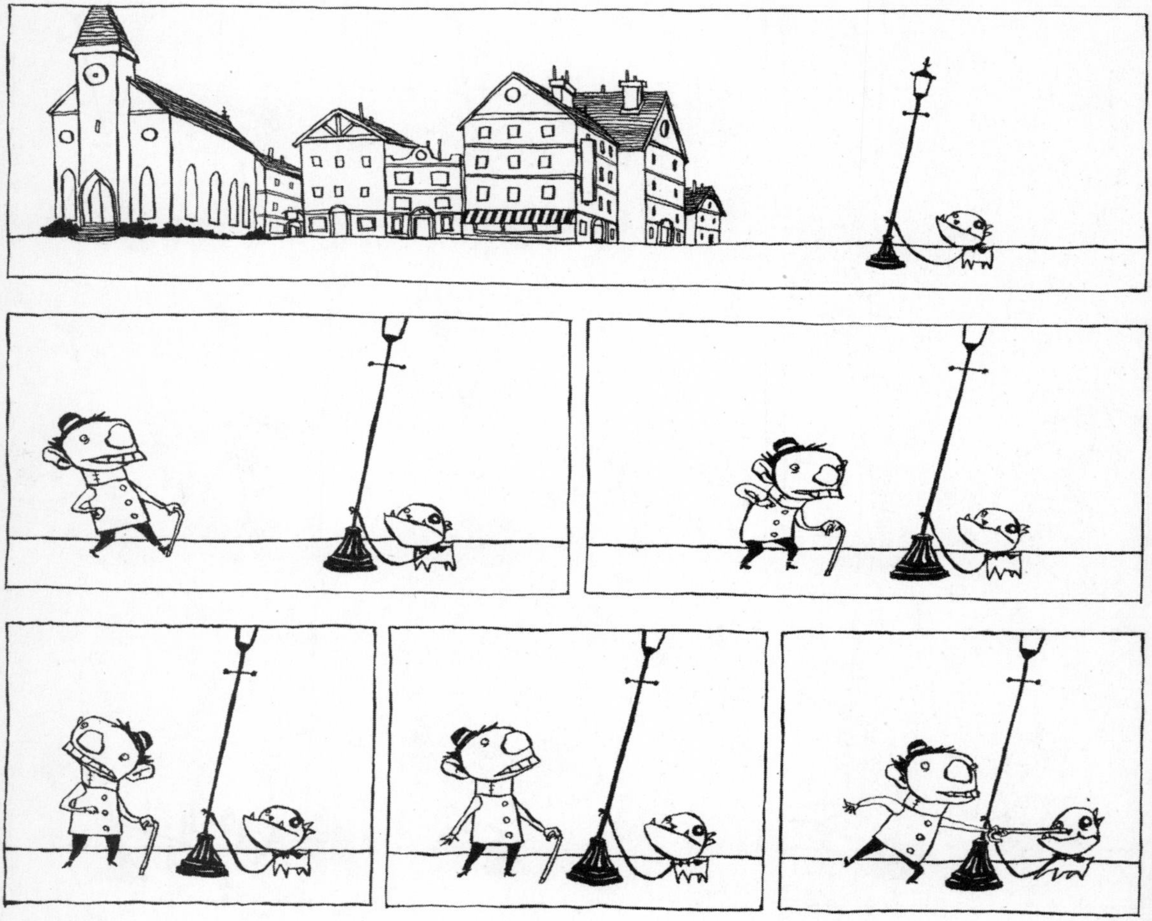

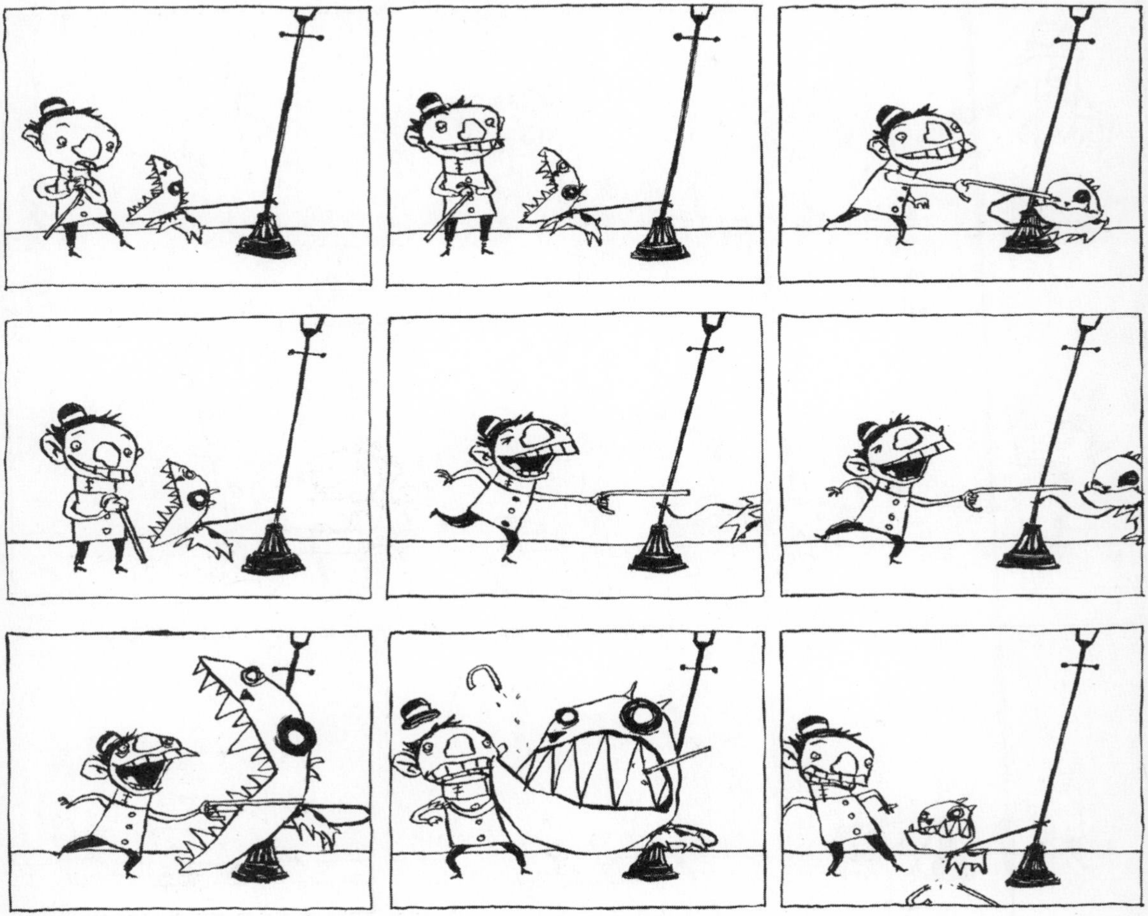

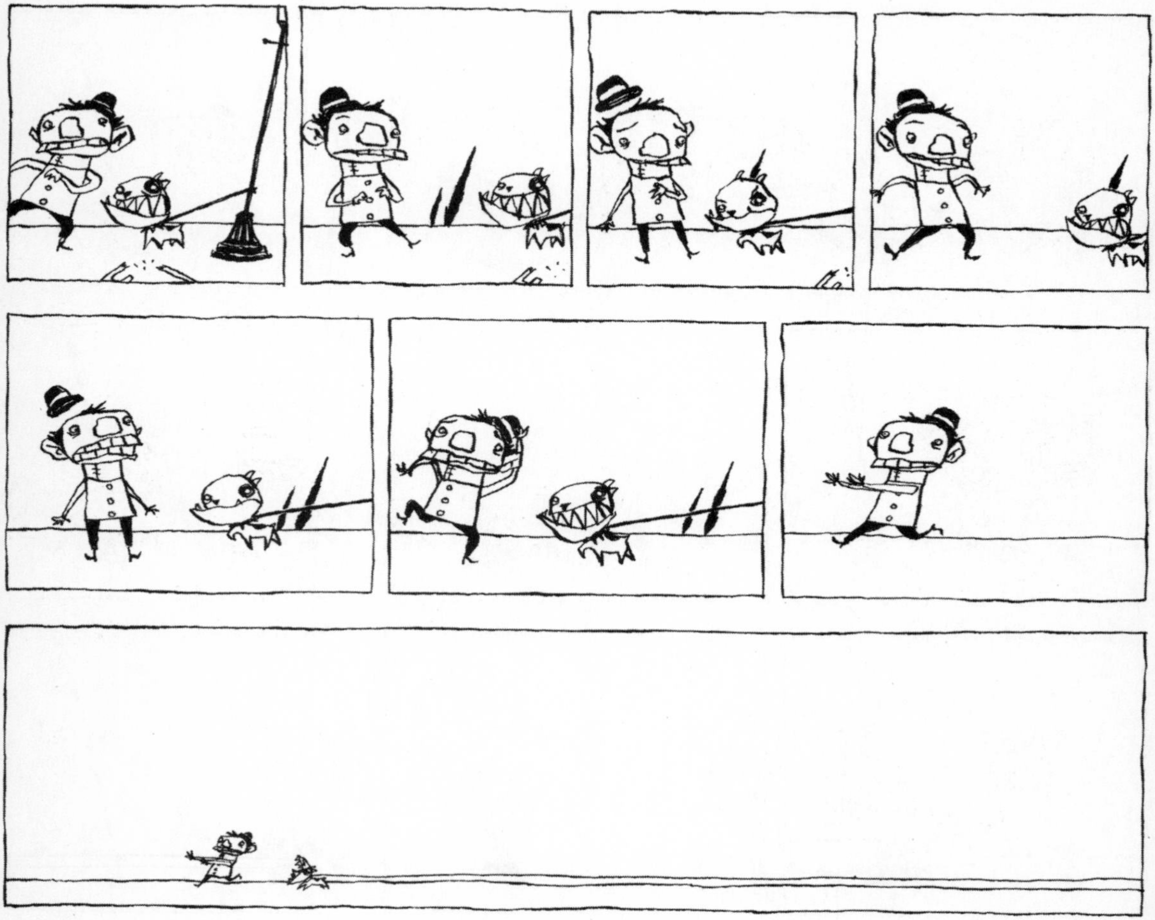

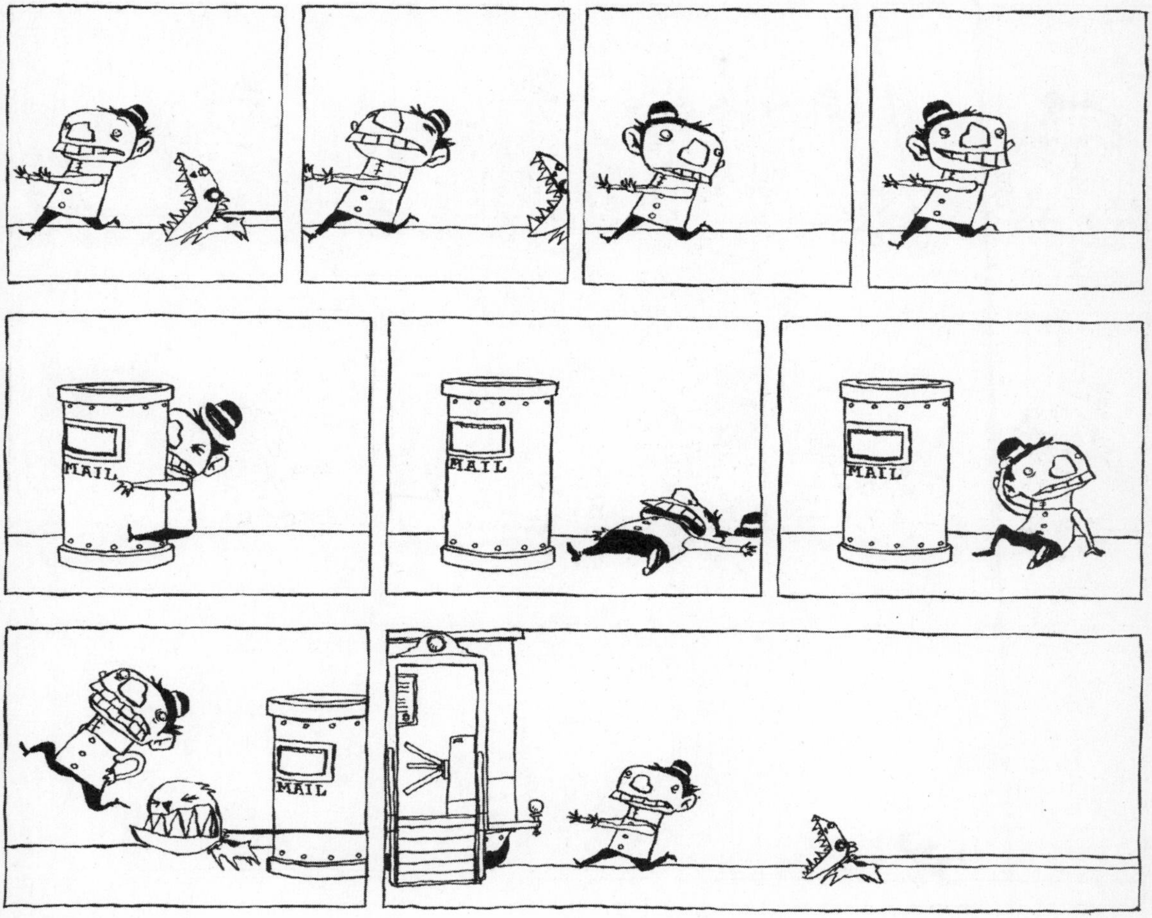
MAIL
MAIL
MAIL
MAIL

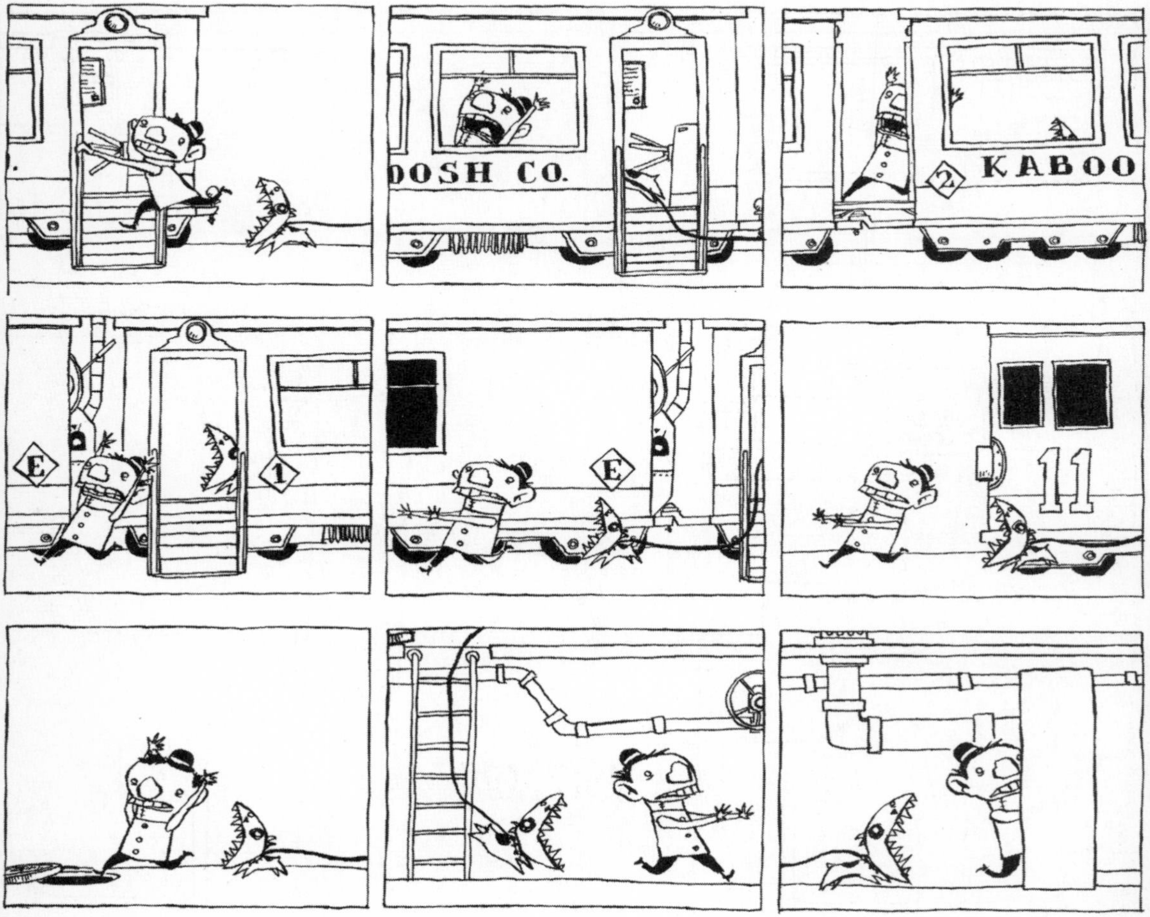
OOSH CO.
2
KABOO
E
1
E
11

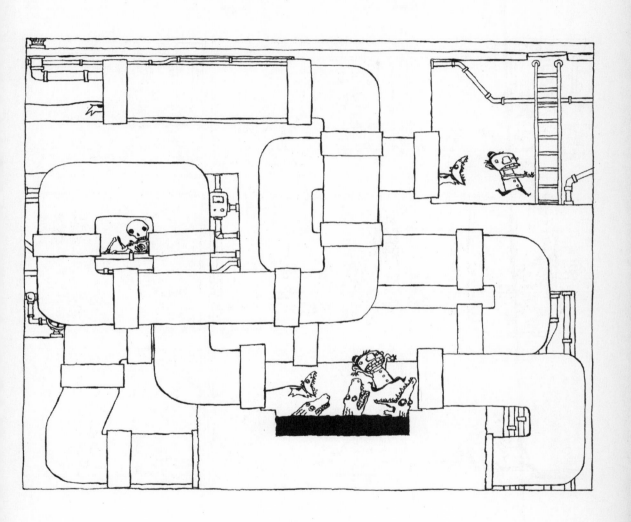

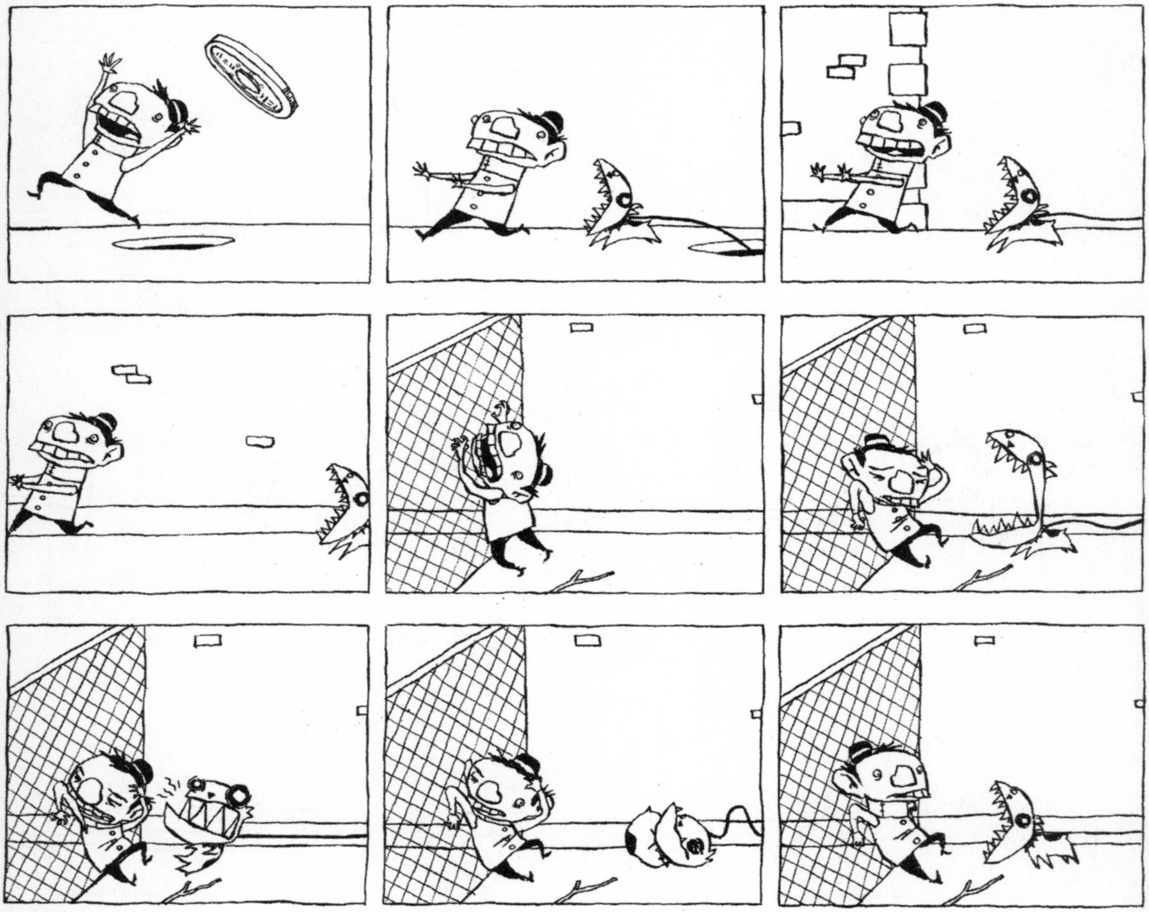

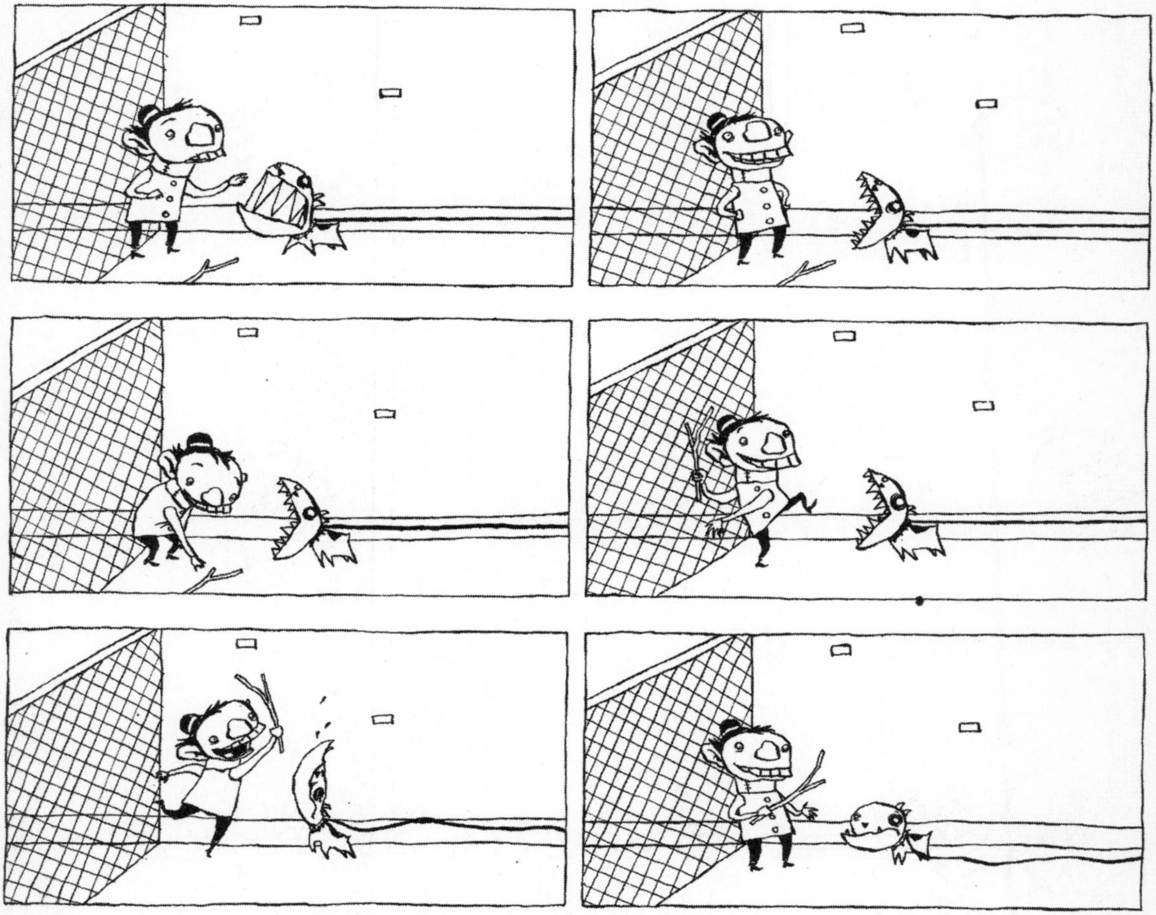

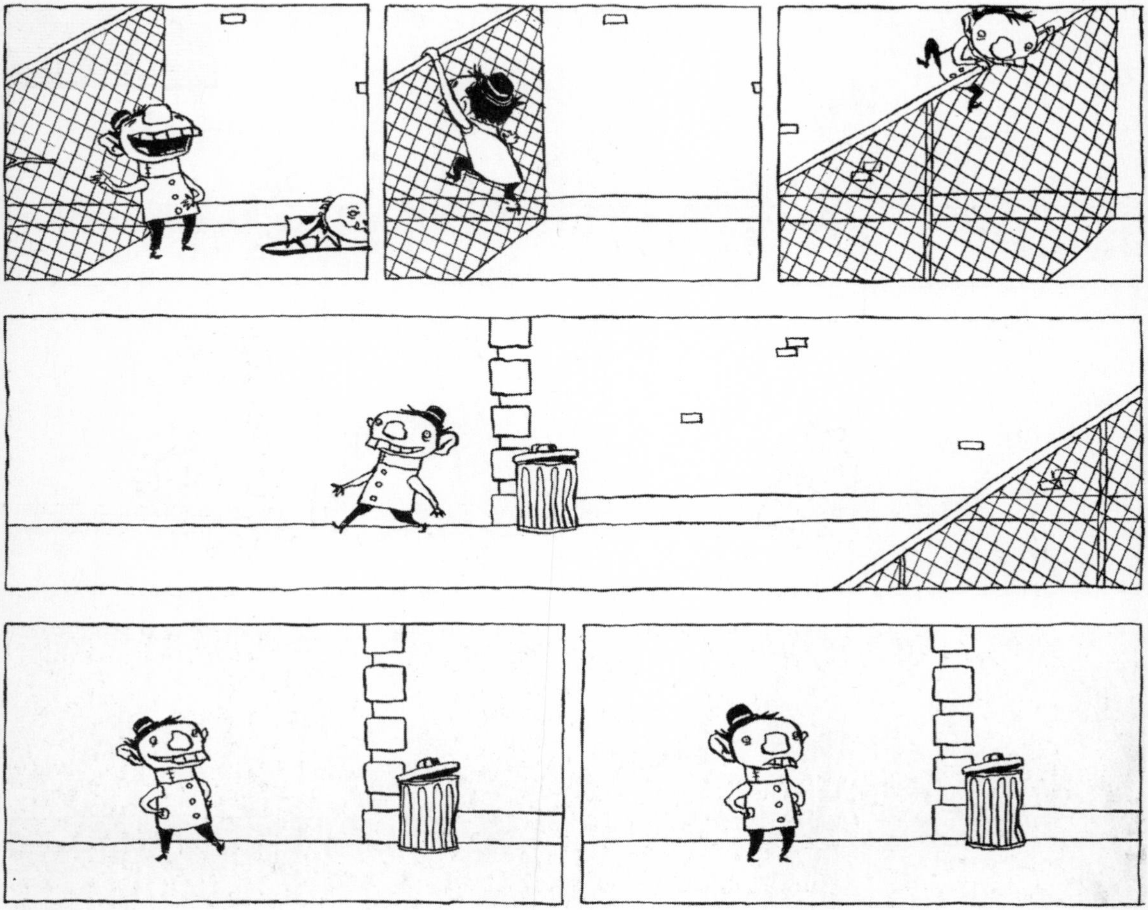

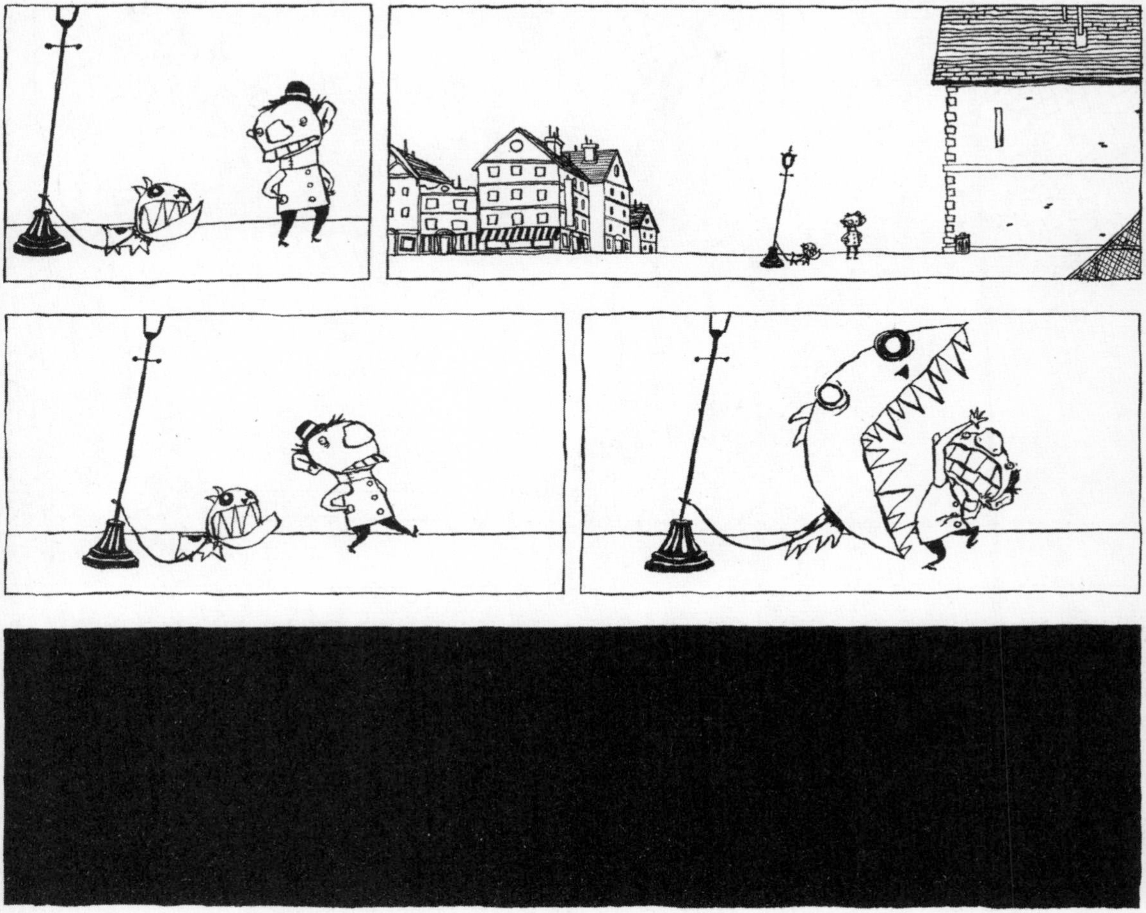

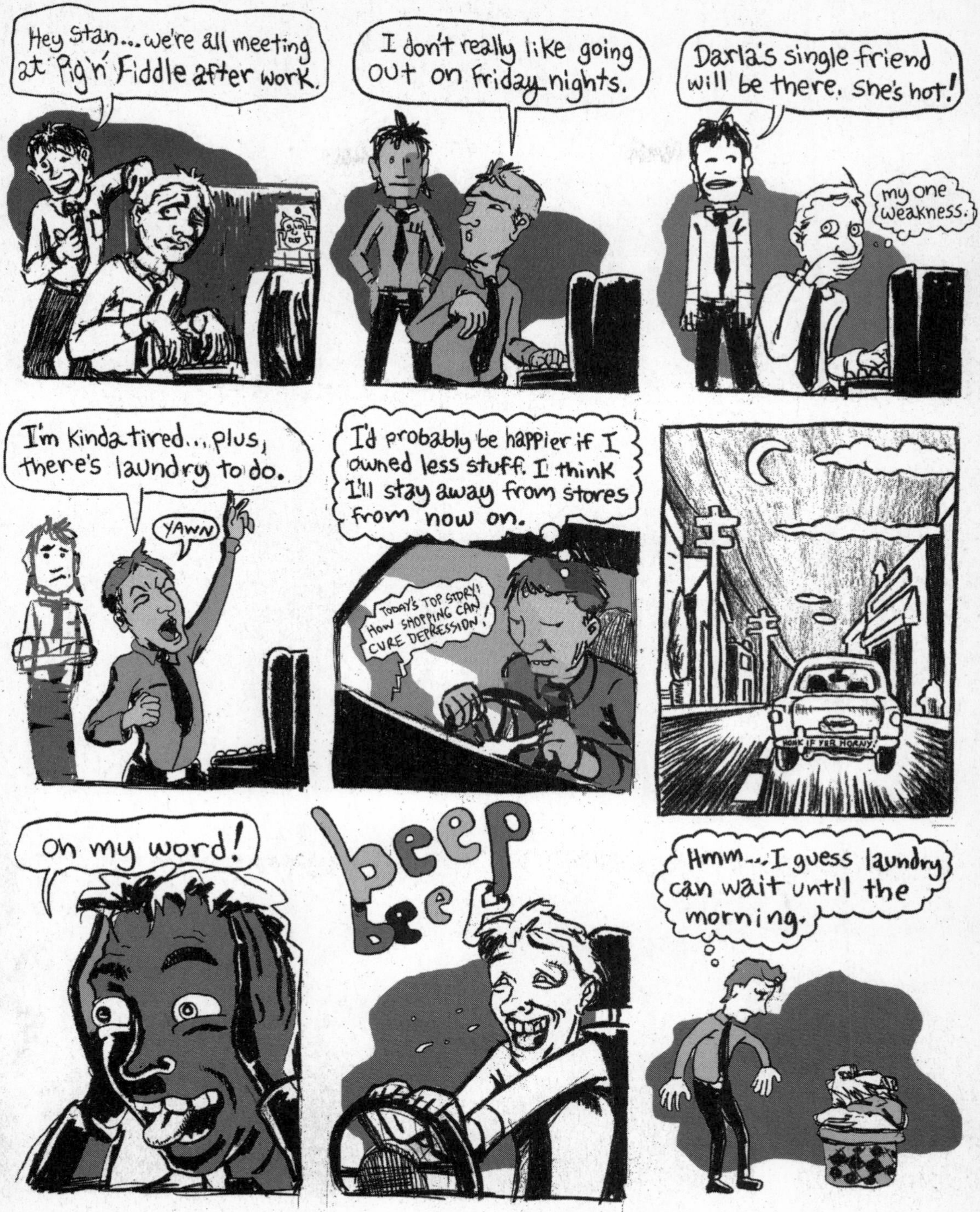

Hey Stan...we're all meeting at Pig'n' Fiddle after work.
I don't really like going out on Friday nights.
Darla's single friend will be there. She's hot!
my one weakness.
I'm kinda tired... plus, there's laundry to do.
YAWN
I'd probably be happier if I owned less stuff. I think I'll stay away from stores from now on.
TODAY'S TOP STORY! HOW SHOPPING CAN CURE DEPRESSION!
HONK IF YER HORNY!
Oh my word!
beep beep
Hmm... I guess laundry can wait until the morning.

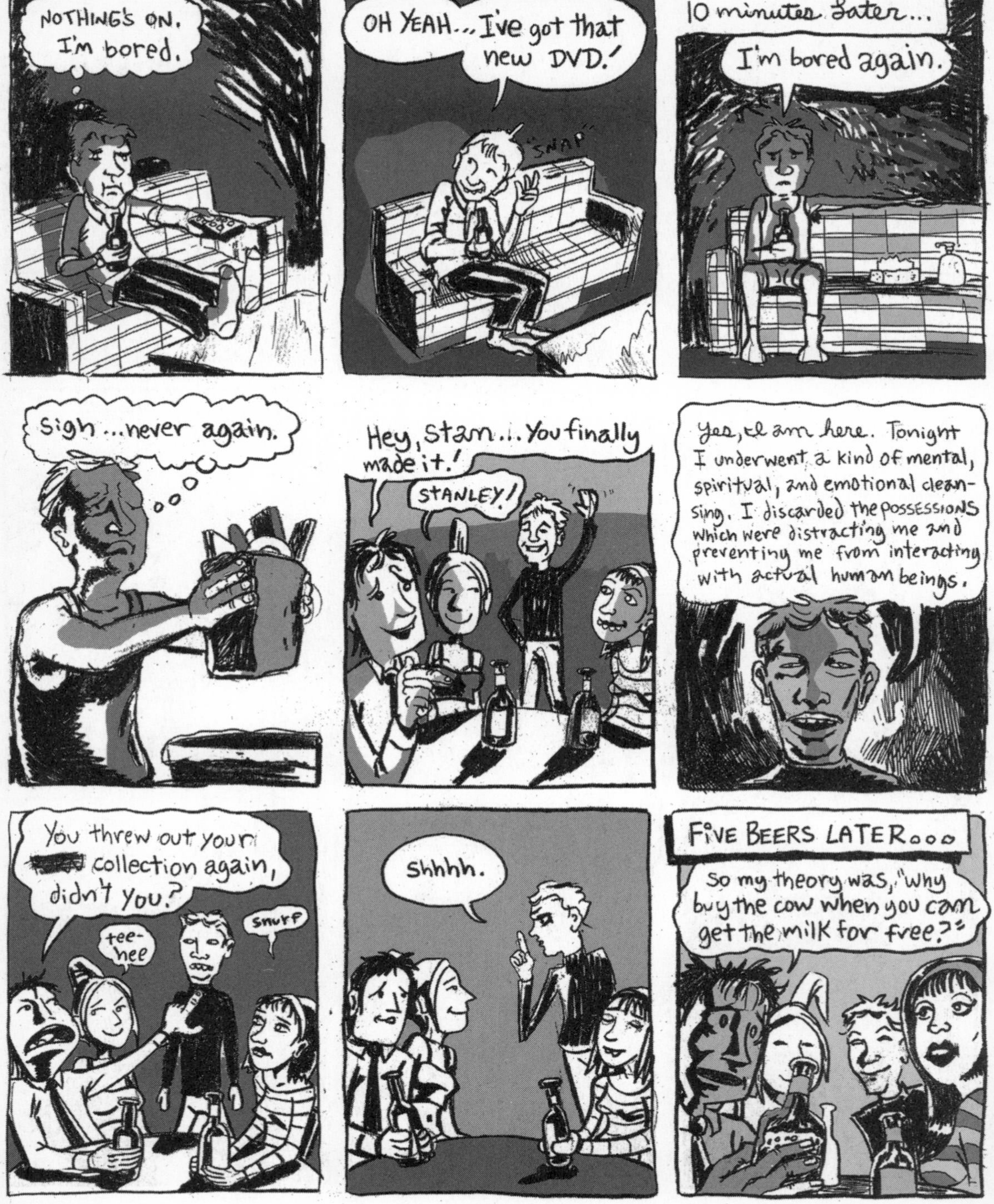
NOTHING'S ON. I'm bored.
OH YEAH... I've got that new DVD!
SNAP
10 minutes later...
I'm bored again.
Sigh ...never again.
Hey, Stan... You finally made it!
STANLEY!
Yes, I am here. Tonight I underwent a kind of mental, spiritual, and emotional cleansing. I discarded the POSSESSIONS which were distracting me and preventing me from interacting with actual human beings.
You threw out your [redacted] collection again, didn't you?
tee-hee
SNURF
Shhhh.
FIVE BEERS LATER...
So my theory was, "why buy the cow when you can get the milk for free?"

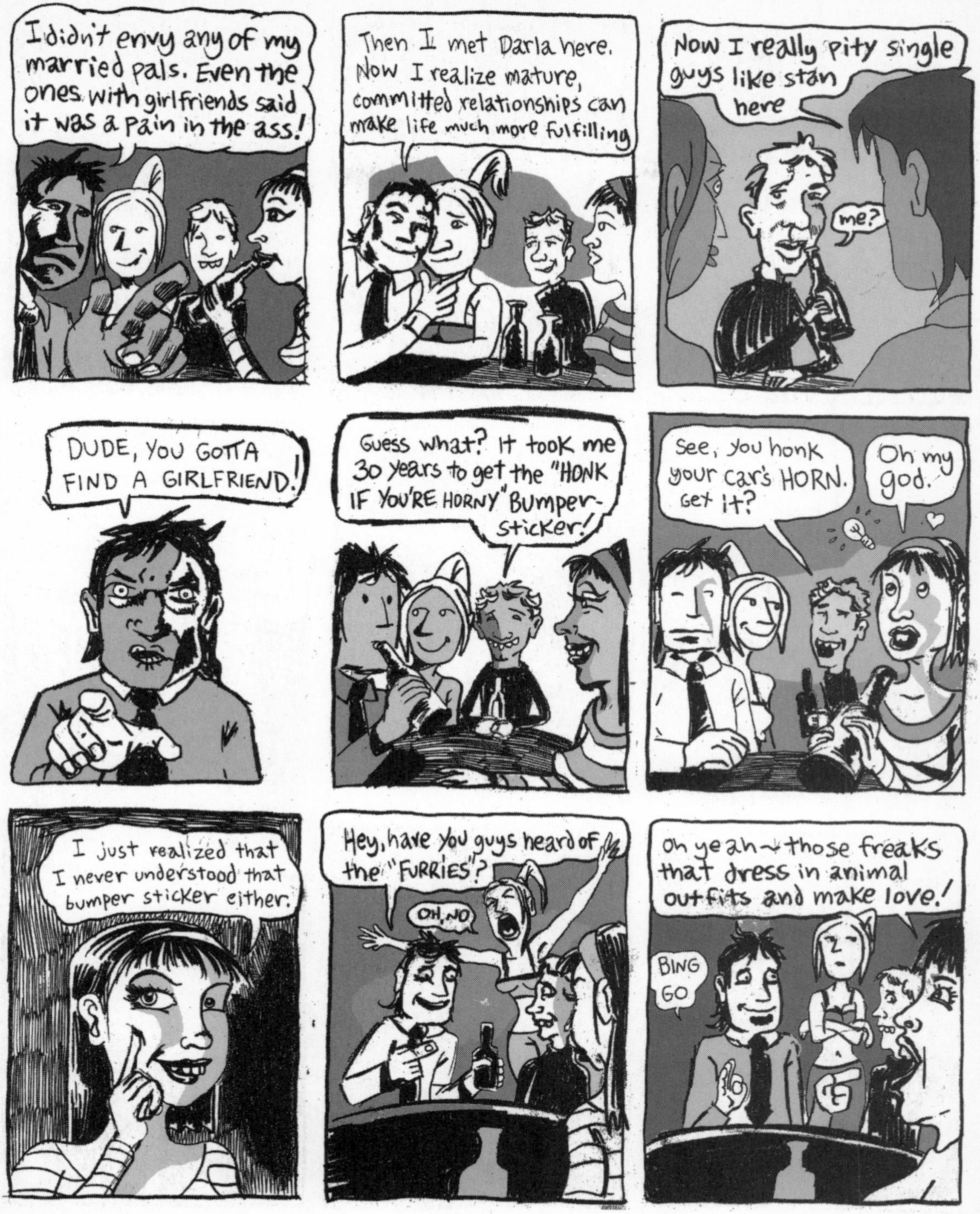
I didn't envy any of my married pals. Even the ones with girlfriends said it was a pain in the ass!
Then I met Darla here. Now I realize mature, committed relationships can make life much more fulfilling
Now I really pity single guys like stan here
me?
DUDE, YOU GOTTA FIND A GIRLFRIEND!
Guess what? It took me 30 years to get the "HONK IF YOU'RE HORNY" Bumper-sticker!
See, you honk your car's HORN. Get it?
Oh my god.
I just realized that I never understood that bumper sticker either.
Hey, have you guys heard of the "FURRIES"?
OH, NO
Oh yeah — those freaks that dress in animal outfits and make love!
BING GO

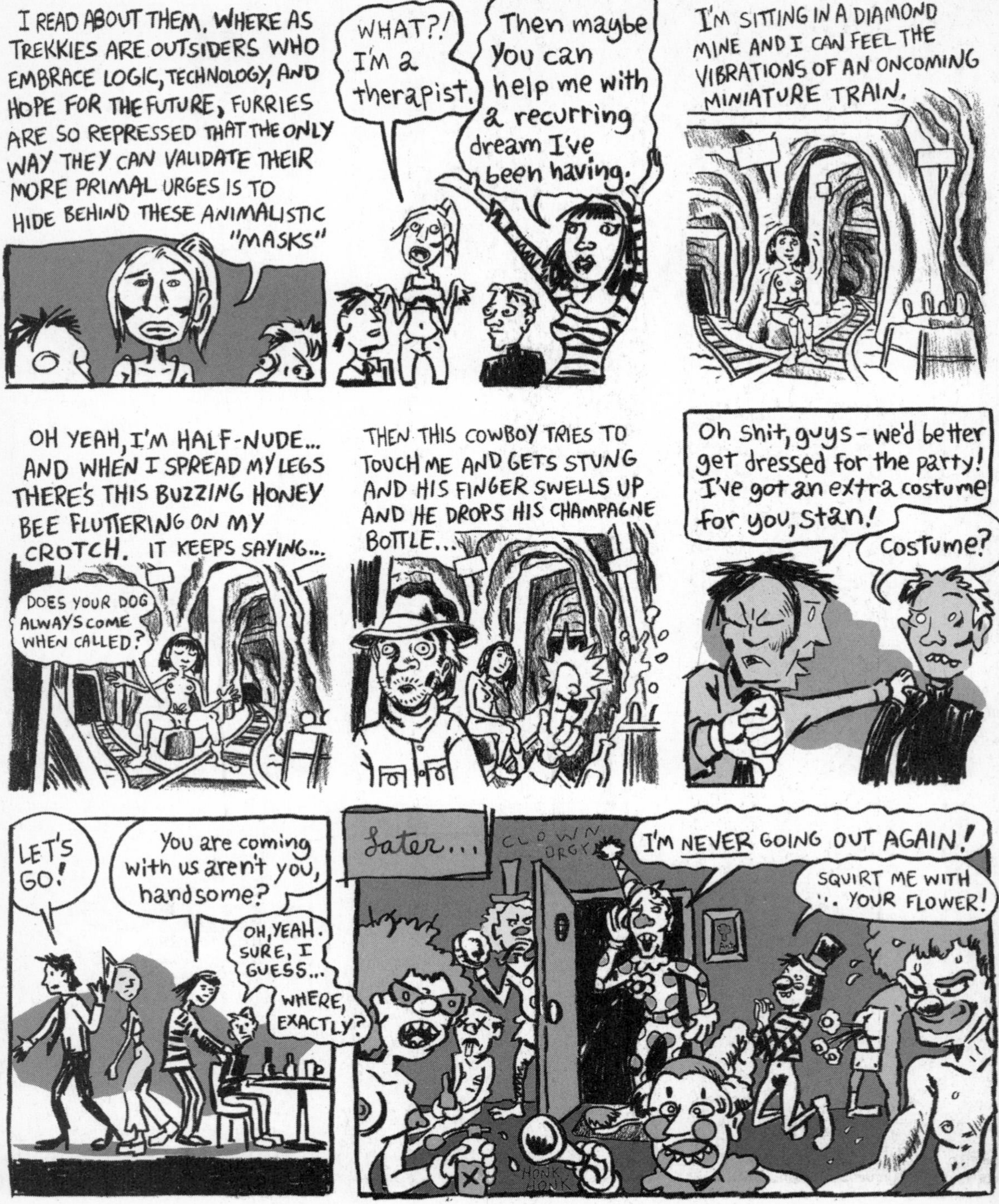

I READ ABOUT THEM. WHERE AS TREKKIES ARE OUTSIDERS WHO EMBRACE LOGIC, TECHNOLOGY, AND HOPE FOR THE FUTURE, FURRIES ARE SO REPRESSED THAT THE ONLY WAY THEY CAN VALIDATE THEIR MORE PRIMAL URGES IS TO HIDE BEHIND THESE ANIMALISTIC "MASKS"
WHAT?! I'M a therapist.
Then maybe you can help me with a recurring dream I've been having.
I'M SITTING IN A DIAMOND MINE AND I CAN FEEL THE VIBRATIONS OF AN ONCOMING MINIATURE TRAIN.
OH YEAH, I'M HALF-NUDE... AND WHEN I SPREAD MY LEGS THERE'S THIS BUZZING HONEY BEE FLUTTERING ON MY CROTCH. IT KEEPS SAYING...
DOES YOUR DOG ALWAYS COME WHEN CALLED?
THEN THIS COWBOY TRIES TO TOUCH ME AND GETS STUNG AND HIS FINGER SWELLS UP AND HE DROPS HIS CHAMPAGNE BOTTLE...
Oh shit, guys - we'd better get dressed for the party! I've got an extra costume for you, Stan!
Costume?
LET'S GO!
You are coming with us aren't you, handsome?
OH, YEAH. SURE, I GUESS...
WHERE, EXACTLY?
Later...
CLOWN ORGY
I'M NEVER GOING OUT AGAIN!
SQUIRT ME WITH ... YOUR FLOWER!
HONK HONK

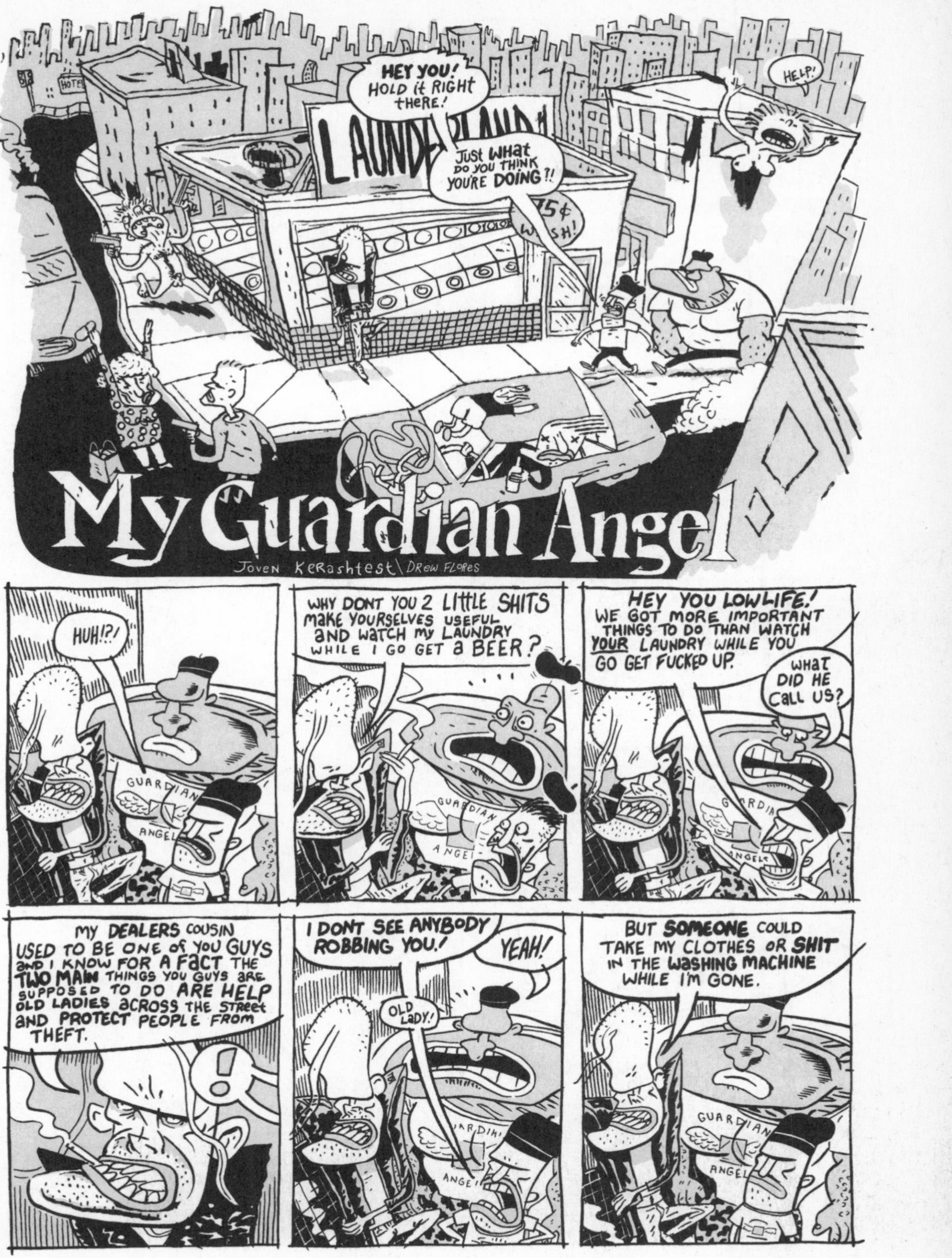
HEY YOU! HOLD it RIGHT there!
HELP!
JUST WHAT DO YOU THINK YOU'RE DOING?!
75¢
My Guardian Angel
JOVEN KERASHTEST \ DREW FLORES
HUH!?!
WHY DONT YOU 2 LITTLE SHITS MAKE YOURSELVES USEFUL AND WATCH MY LAUNDRY WHILE I GO GET A BEER?
HEY YOU LOWLIFE! WE GOT MORE IMPORTANT THINGS TO DO THAN WATCH YOUR LAUNDRY WHILE YOU GO GET FUCKED UP.
WHAT DID HE CALL US?
MY DEALERS COUSIN USED TO BE ONE OF YOU GUYS AND I KNOW FOR A FACT THE TWO MAIN THINGS YOU GUYS ARE SUPPOSED TO DO ARE HELP OLD LADIES ACROSS THE STREET AND PROTECT PEOPLE FROM THEFT.
!
I DONT SEE ANYBODY ROBBING YOU.!
YEAH!
OLD LADY!
BUT SOMEONE COULD TAKE MY CLOTHES OR SHIT IN THE WASHING MACHINE WHILE I'M GONE.

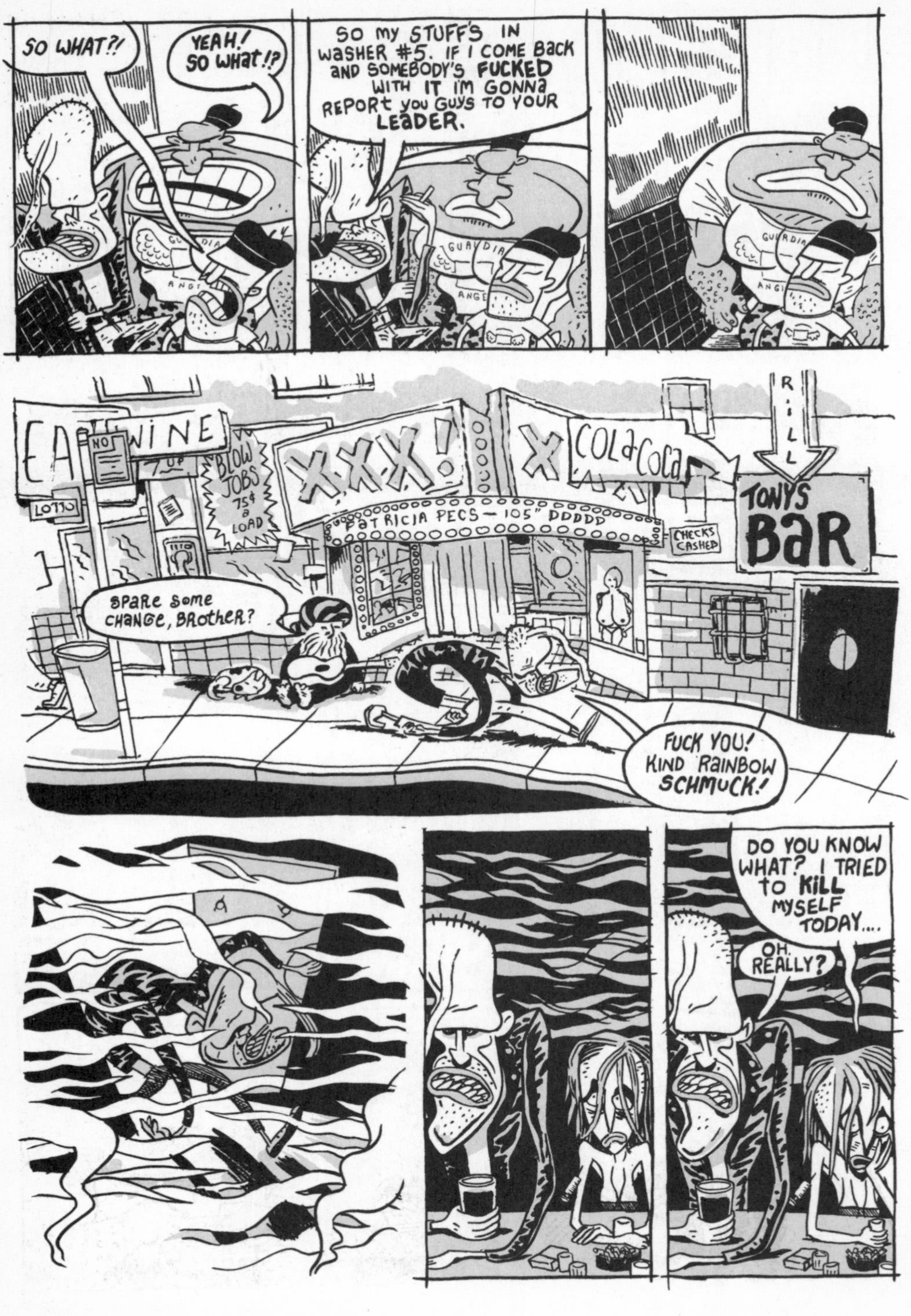
SO WHAT?!
YEAH! SO WHAT!?
SO MY STUFF'S IN WASHER #5. IF I COME BACK AND SOMEBODY'S FUCKED WITH IT I'M GONNA REPORT YOU GUYS TO YOUR LEADER.
GUARDIA
ANGE
WINE
NO
7UP
LOTTO
BLOW JOBS 75¢ a LOAD
XXX!
COLA-COCA
PATRICIA PECS — 105" DDDDD
CHECKS CASHED
GRILL
TONY'S BAR
SPARE SOME CHANGE, BROTHER?
FUCK YOU! KIND RAINBOW SCHMUCK!
DO YOU KNOW WHAT? I TRIED TO KILL MYSELF TODAY....
OH. REALLY?

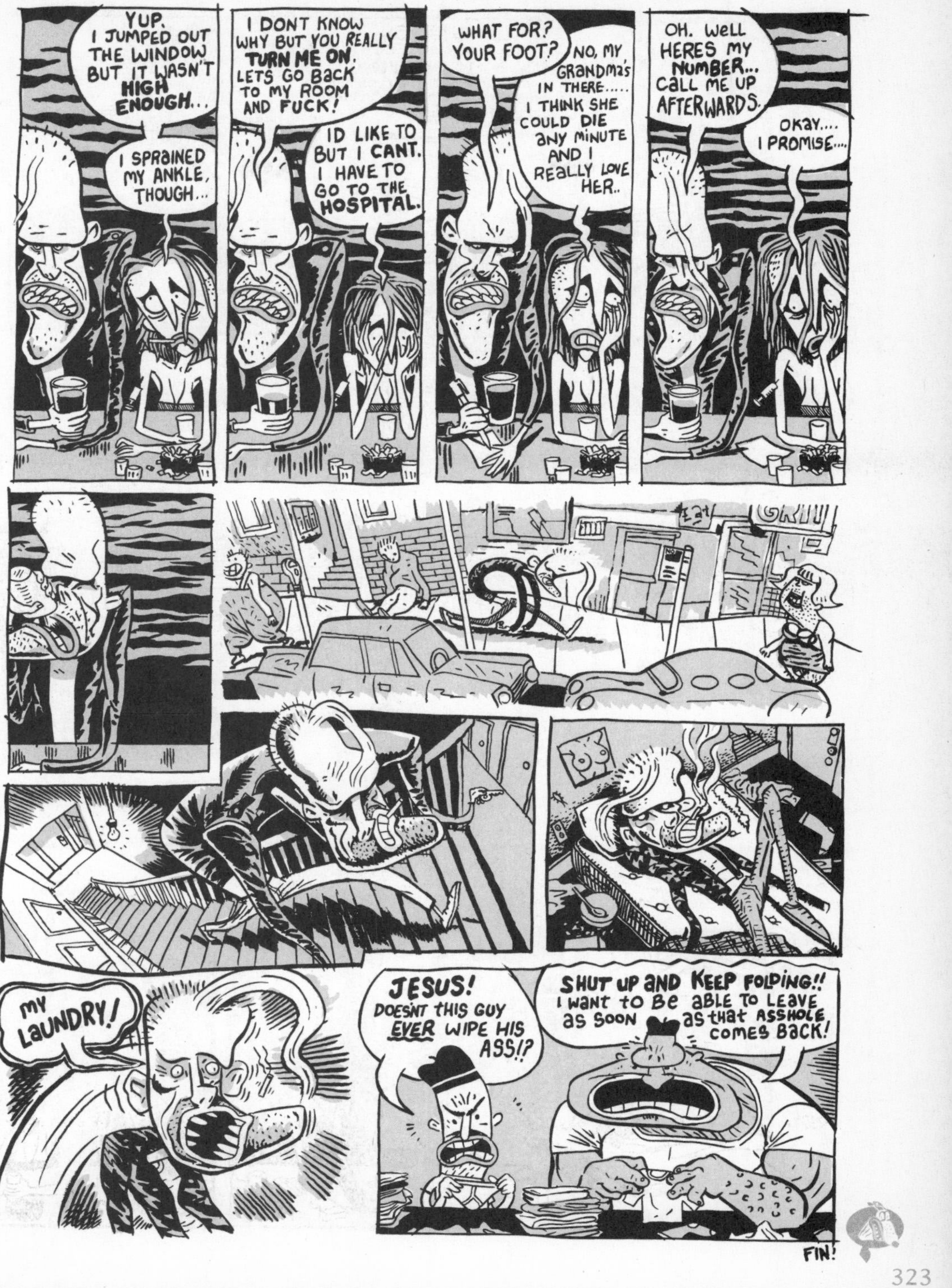

YUP. I JUMPED OUT THE WINDOW BUT IT WASN'T HIGH ENOUGH...
I SPRAINED MY ANKLE, THOUGH...
I DONT KNOW WHY BUT YOU REALLY TURN ME ON. LETS GO BACK TO MY ROOM AND FUCK!
ID LIKE TO BUT I CANT. I HAVE TO GO TO THE HOSPITAL.
WHAT FOR? YOUR FOOT?
NO, MY GRANDMA'S IN THERE..... I THINK SHE COULD DIE ANY MINUTE AND I REALLY LOVE HER..
OH. WELL HERES MY NUMBER... CALL ME UP AFTERWARDS.
OKAY.... I PROMISE....
MY LAUNDRY!
JESUS! DOESNT THIS GUY EVER WIPE HIS ASS!?
SHUT UP AND KEEP FOLDING!! I WANT TO BE ABLE TO LEAVE AS SOON AS THAT ASSHOLE COMES BACK!
FIN!

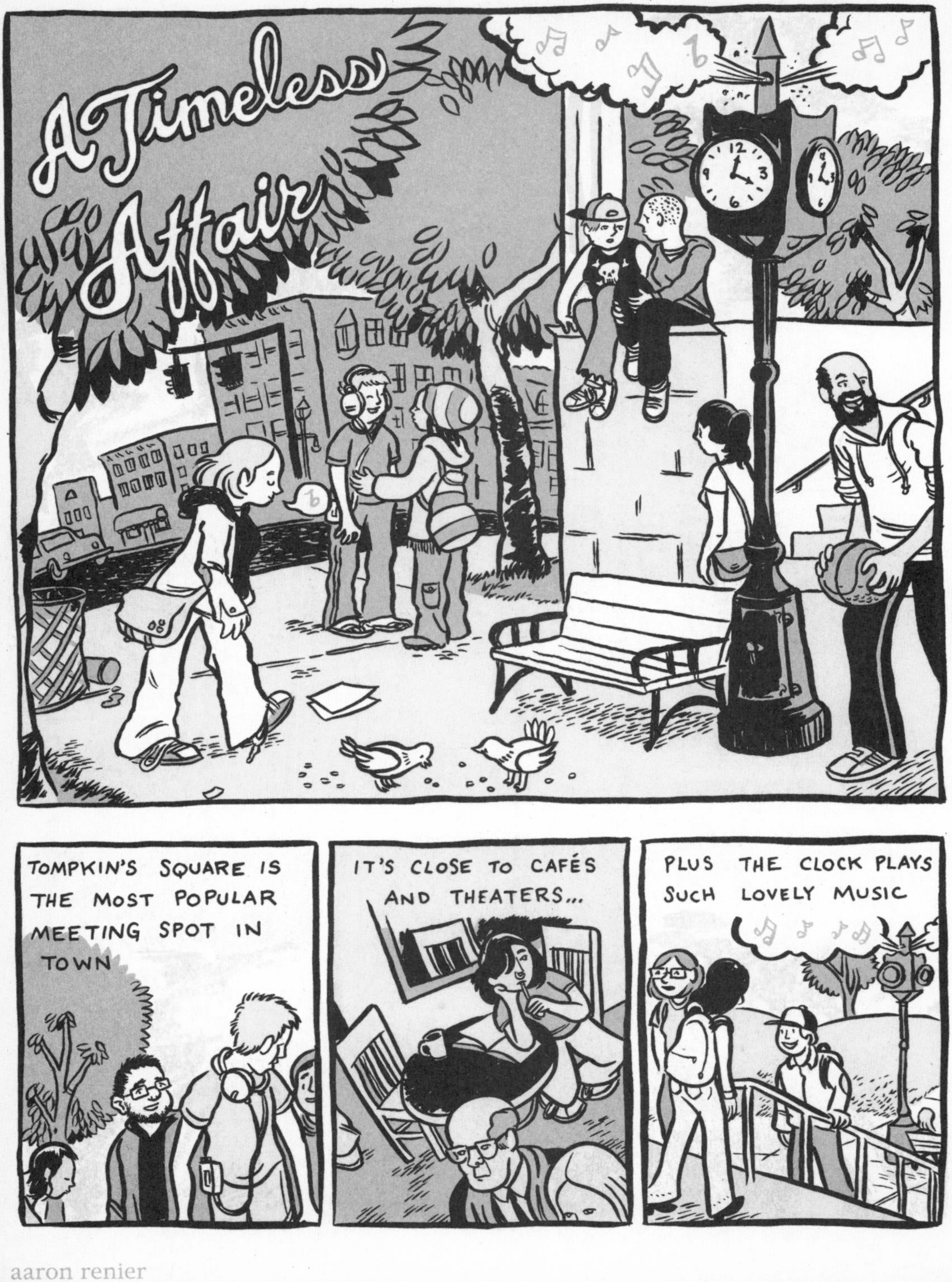
A Timeless Affair
TOMPKIN'S SQUARE IS THE MOST POPULAR MEETING SPOT IN TOWN
IT'S CLOSE TO CAFÉS AND THEATERS...
PLUS THE CLOCK PLAYS SUCH LOVELY MUSIC

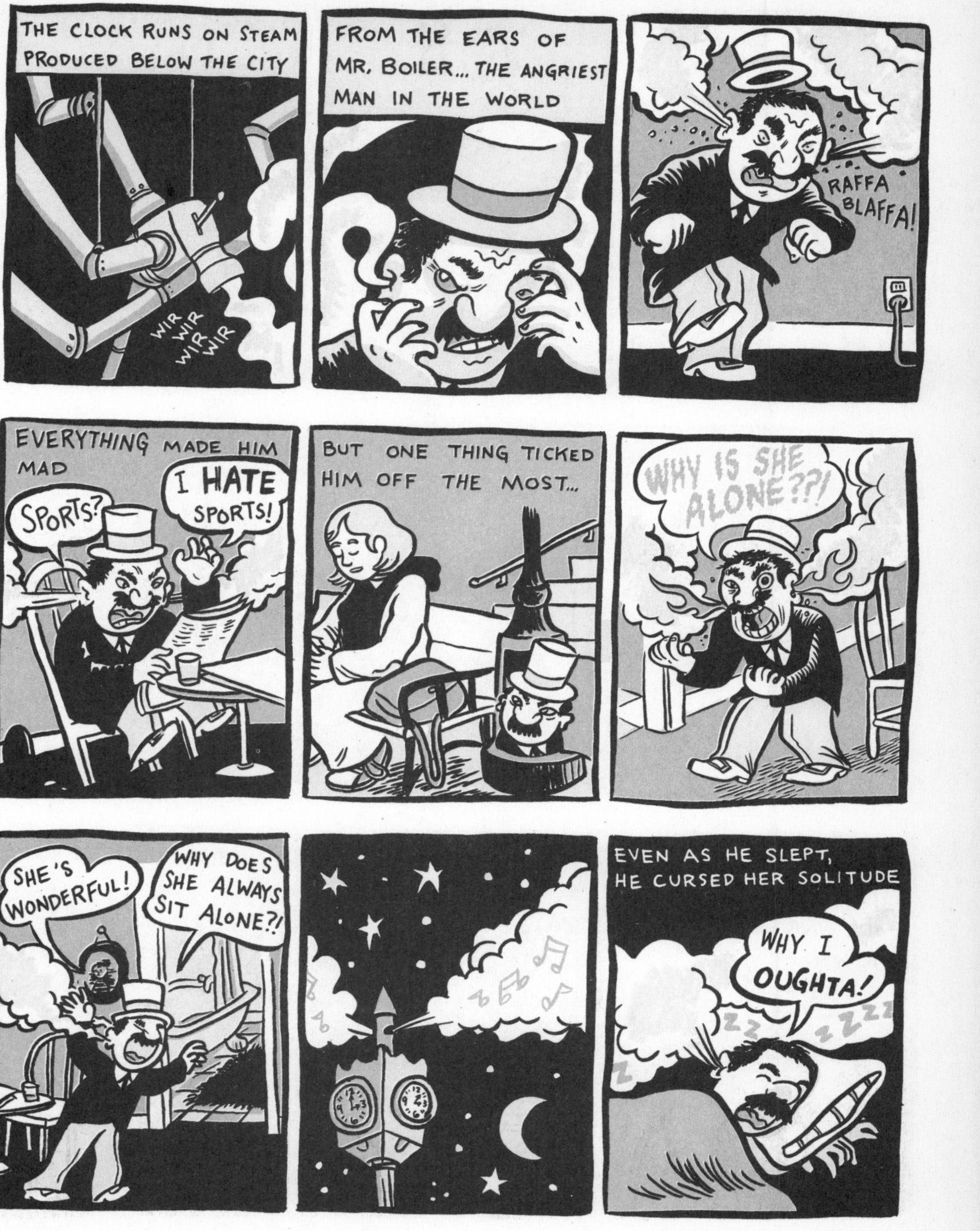
THE CLOCK RUNS ON STEAM PRODUCED BELOW THE CITY
WIR WIR WIR WIR
FROM THE EARS OF MR. BOILER... THE ANGRIEST MAN IN THE WORLD
RAFFA BLAFFA!
EVERYTHING MADE HIM MAD
SPORTS?
I HATE SPORTS!
BUT ONE THING TICKED HIM OFF THE MOST...
WHY IS SHE ALONE??!
SHE'S WONDERFUL!
WHY DOES SHE ALWAYS SIT ALONE?!
EVEN AS HE SLEPT, HE CURSED HER SOLITUDE
WHY I OUGHTA!
Z Z Z Z Z Z

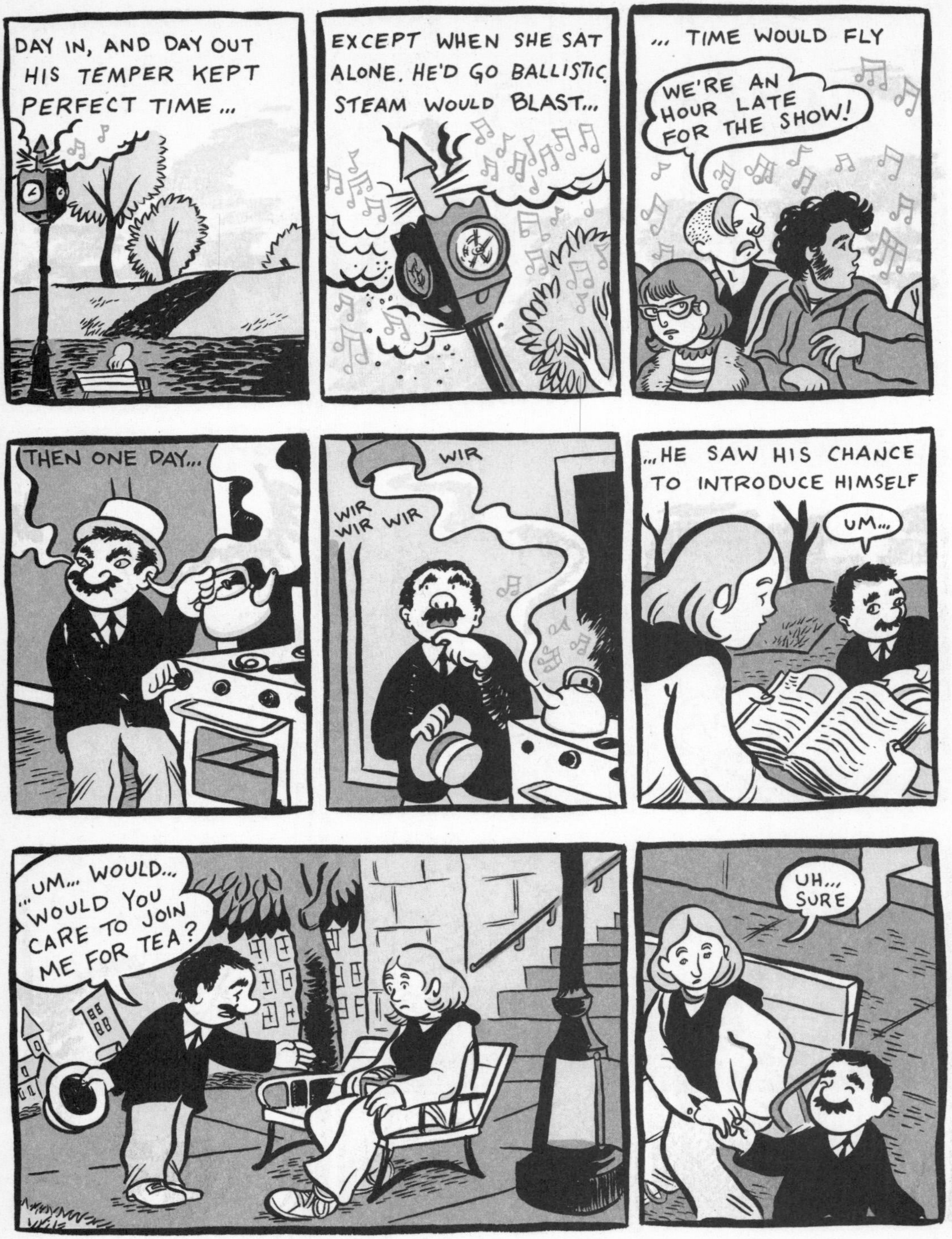
DAY IN, AND DAY OUT HIS TEMPER KEPT PERFECT TIME...
EXCEPT WHEN SHE SAT ALONE. HE'D GO BALLISTIC, STEAM WOULD BLAST...
... TIME WOULD FLY
WE'RE AN HOUR LATE FOR THE SHOW!
THEN ONE DAY...
WIR
WIR WIR WIR
...HE SAW HIS CHANCE TO INTRODUCE HIMSELF
UM...
UM... WOULD... ...WOULD YOU CARE TO JOIN ME FOR TEA?
UH..., SURE

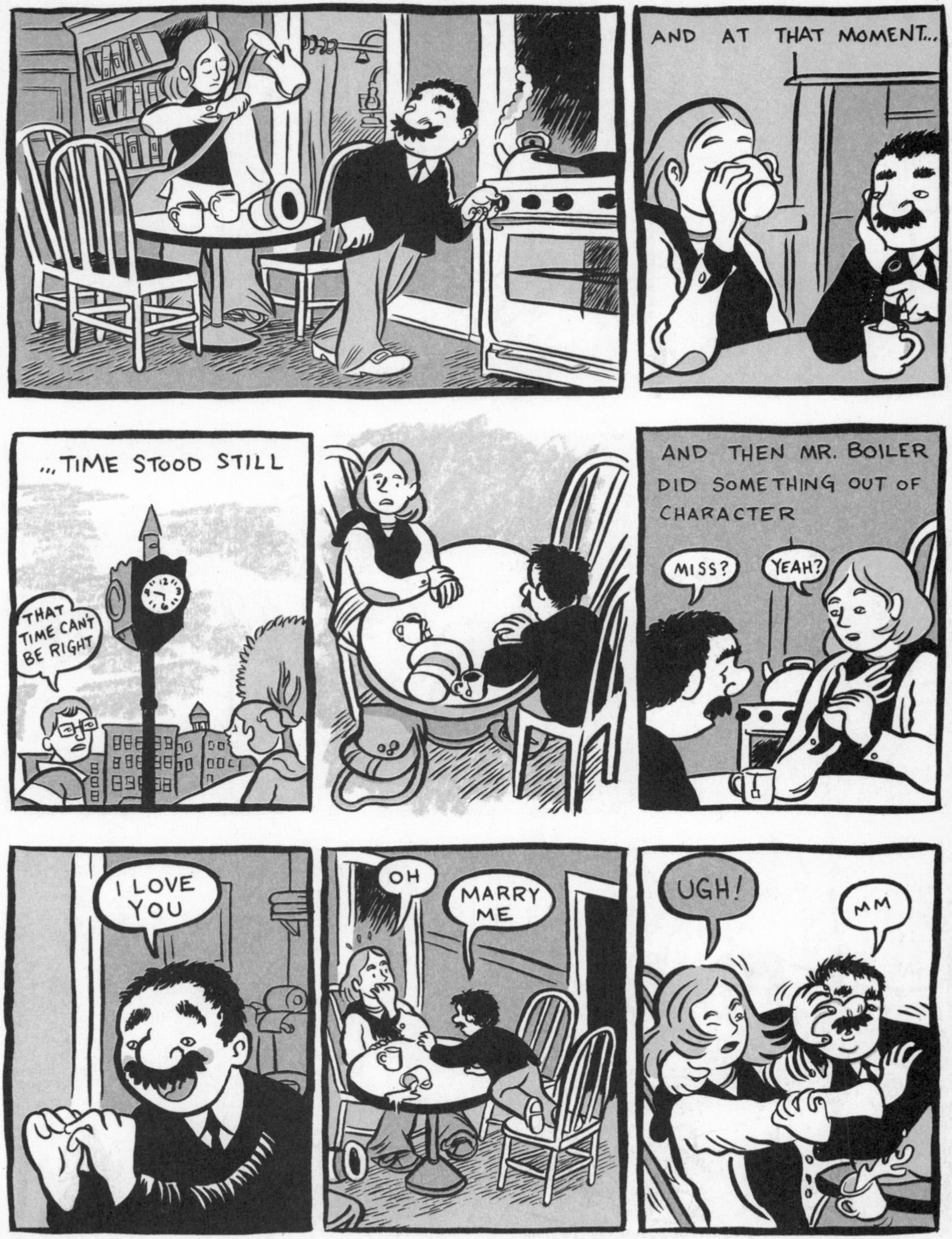
AND AT THAT MOMENT...
...TIME STOOD STILL
THAT TIME CAN'T BE RIGHT
AND THEN MR. BOILER DID SOMETHING OUT OF CHARACTER
MISS?
YEAH?
I LOVE YOU
OH
MARRY ME
UGH!
MM

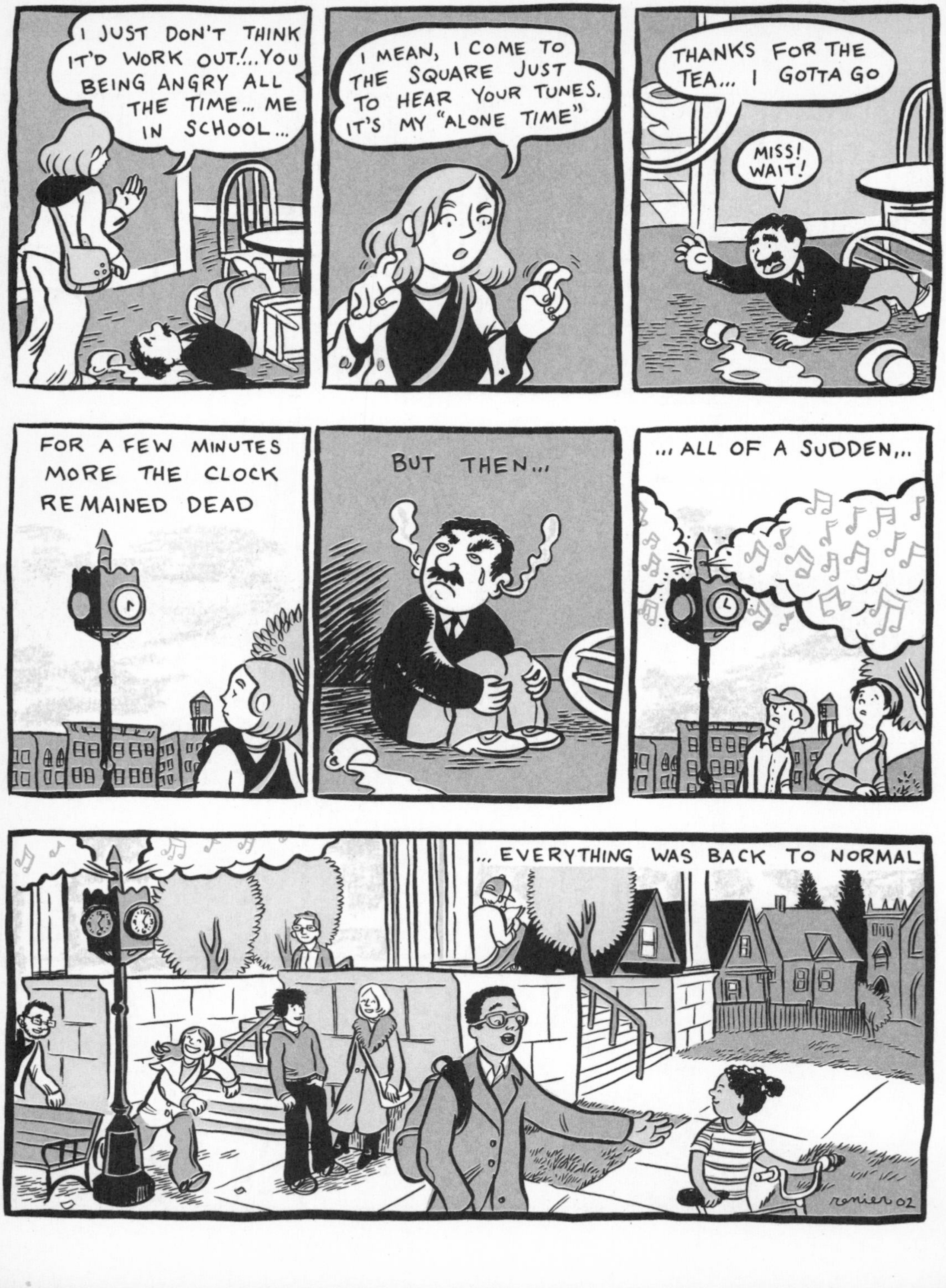
I JUST DON'T THINK IT'D WORK OUT!...YOU BEING ANGRY ALL THE TIME... ME IN SCHOOL...
I MEAN, I COME TO THE SQUARE JUST TO HEAR YOUR TUNES. IT'S MY "ALONE TIME"
THANKS FOR THE TEA... I GOTTA GO
MISS! WAIT!
FOR A FEW MINUTES MORE THE CLOCK REMAINED DEAD
BUT THEN...
...ALL OF A SUDDEN,...
...EVERYTHING WAS BACK TO NORMAL
renier 02

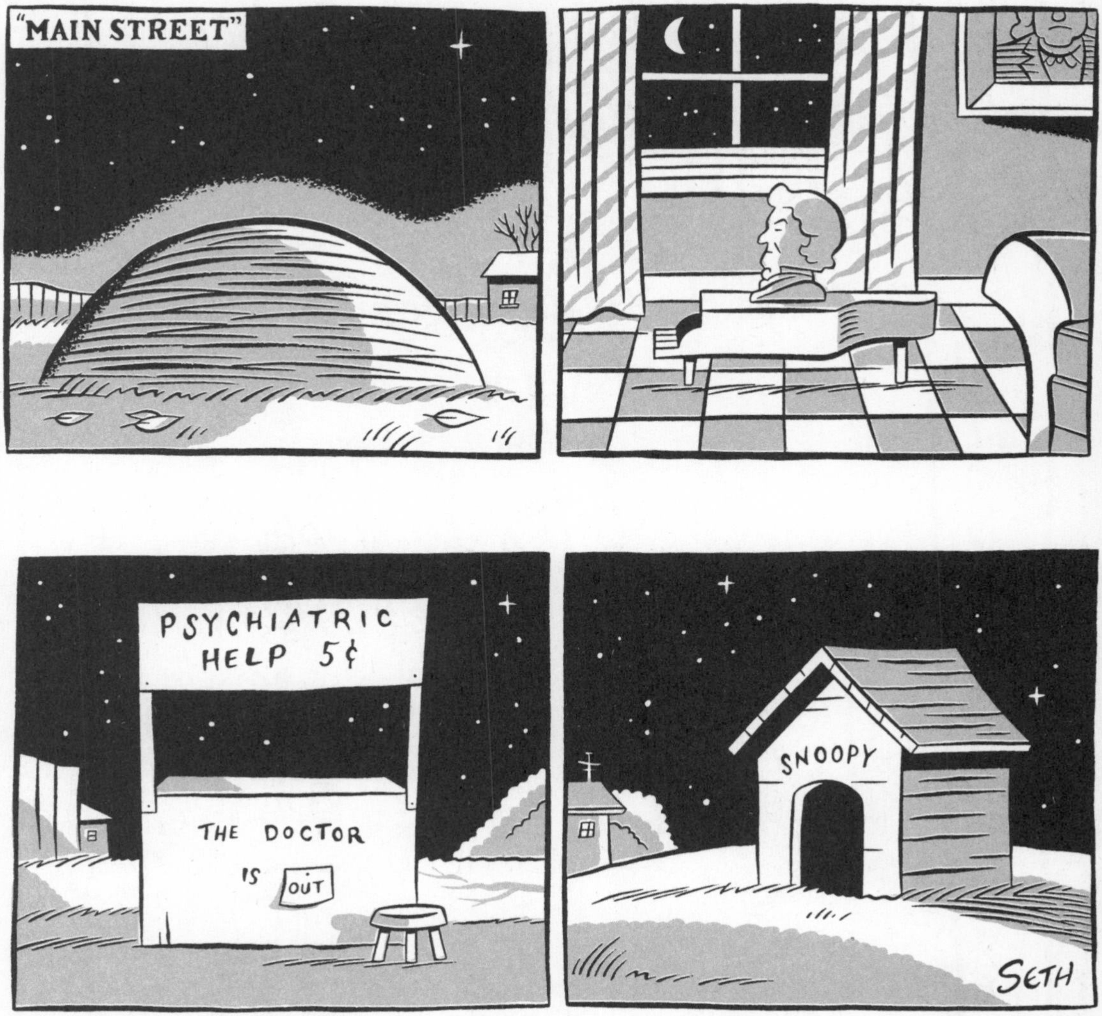
"MAIN STREET"
PSYCHIATRIC HELP 5¢
THE DOCTOR IS OUT
SNOOPY
SETH

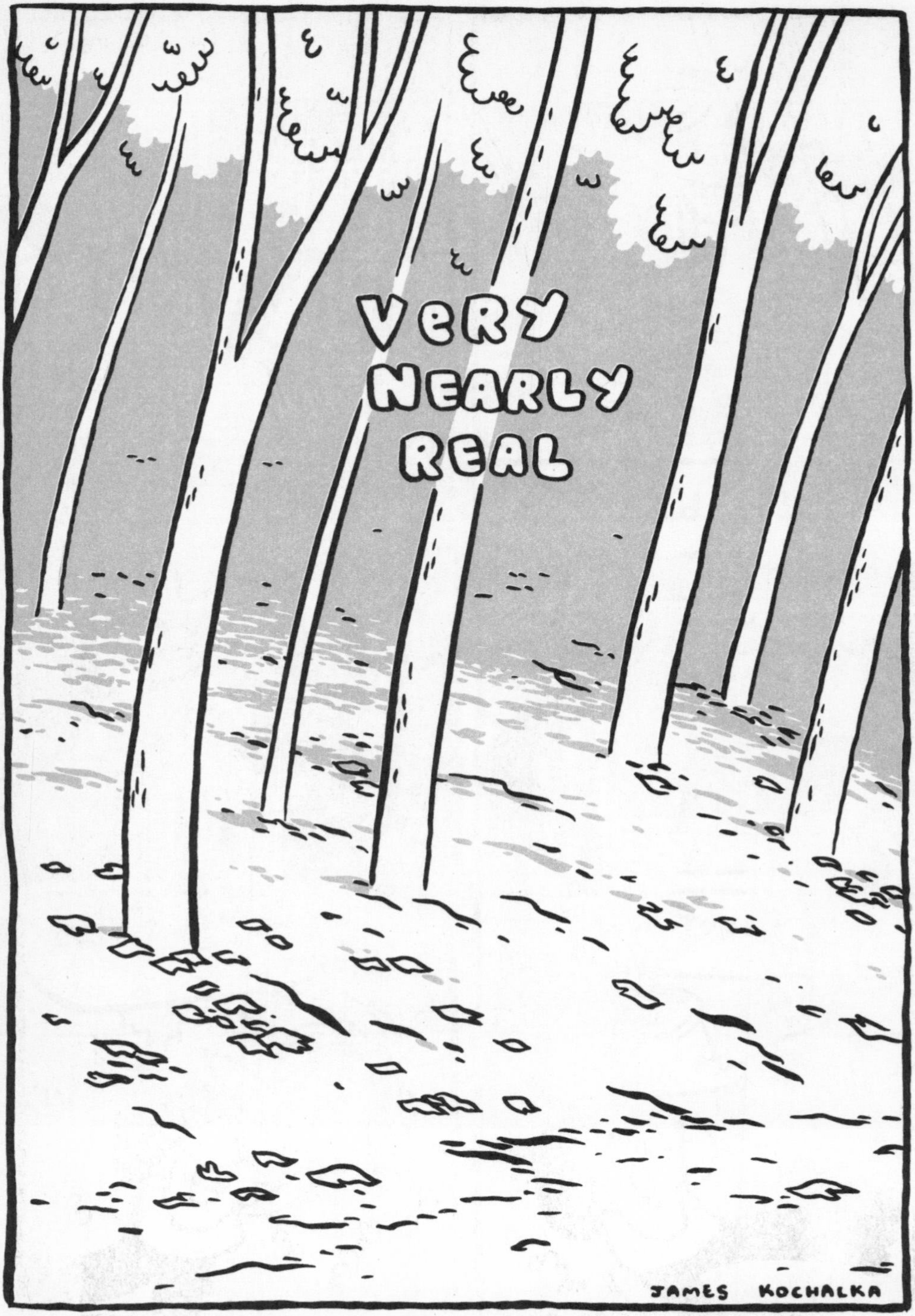
VERY
NEARLY
REAL
JAMES KOCHALKA

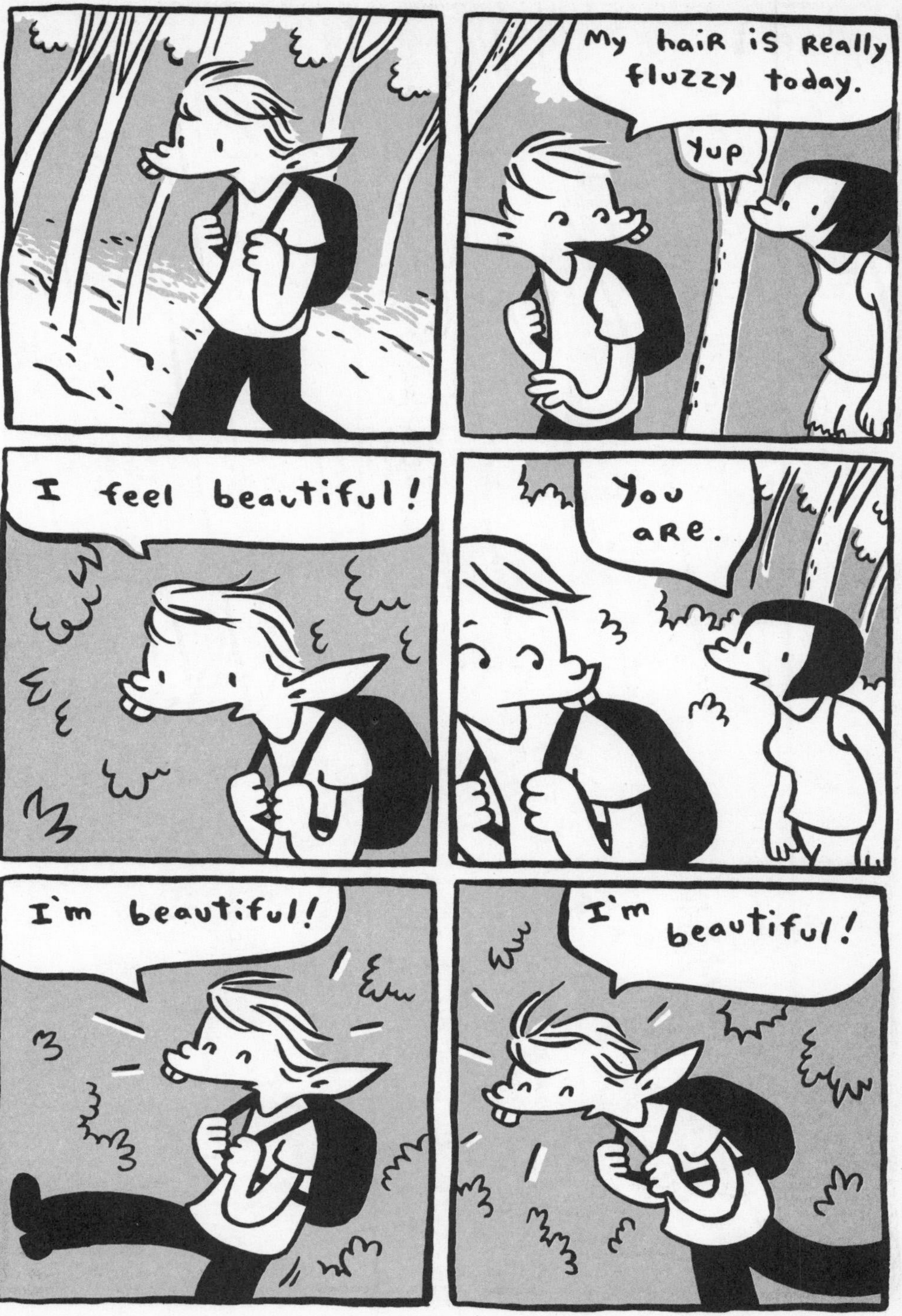
My hair is really fluzzy today.
Yup
I feel beautiful!
You are.
I'm beautiful!
I'm beautiful!

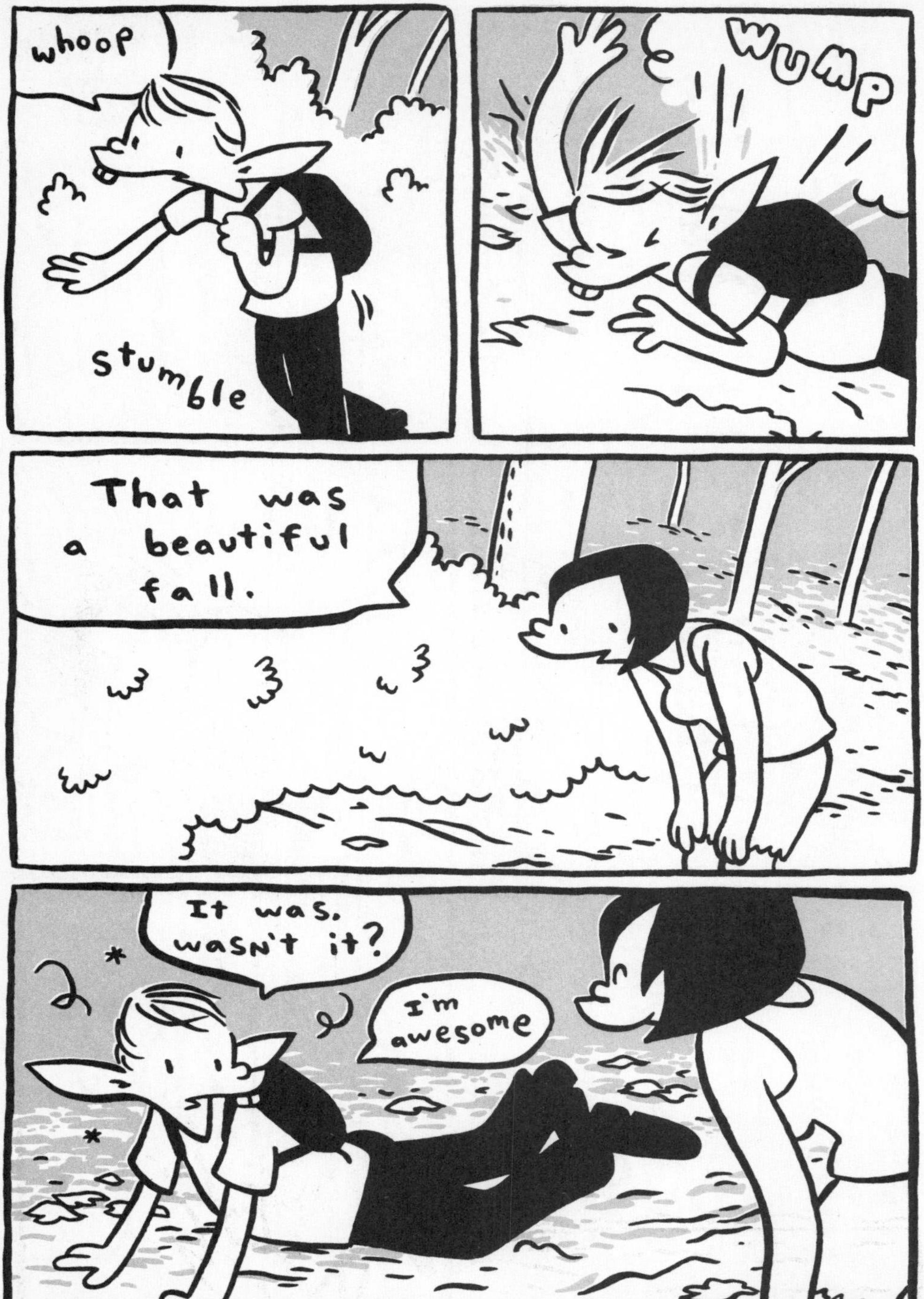
whoop
stumble
WUMP
That was a beautiful fall.
It was, wasn't it?
I'm awesome

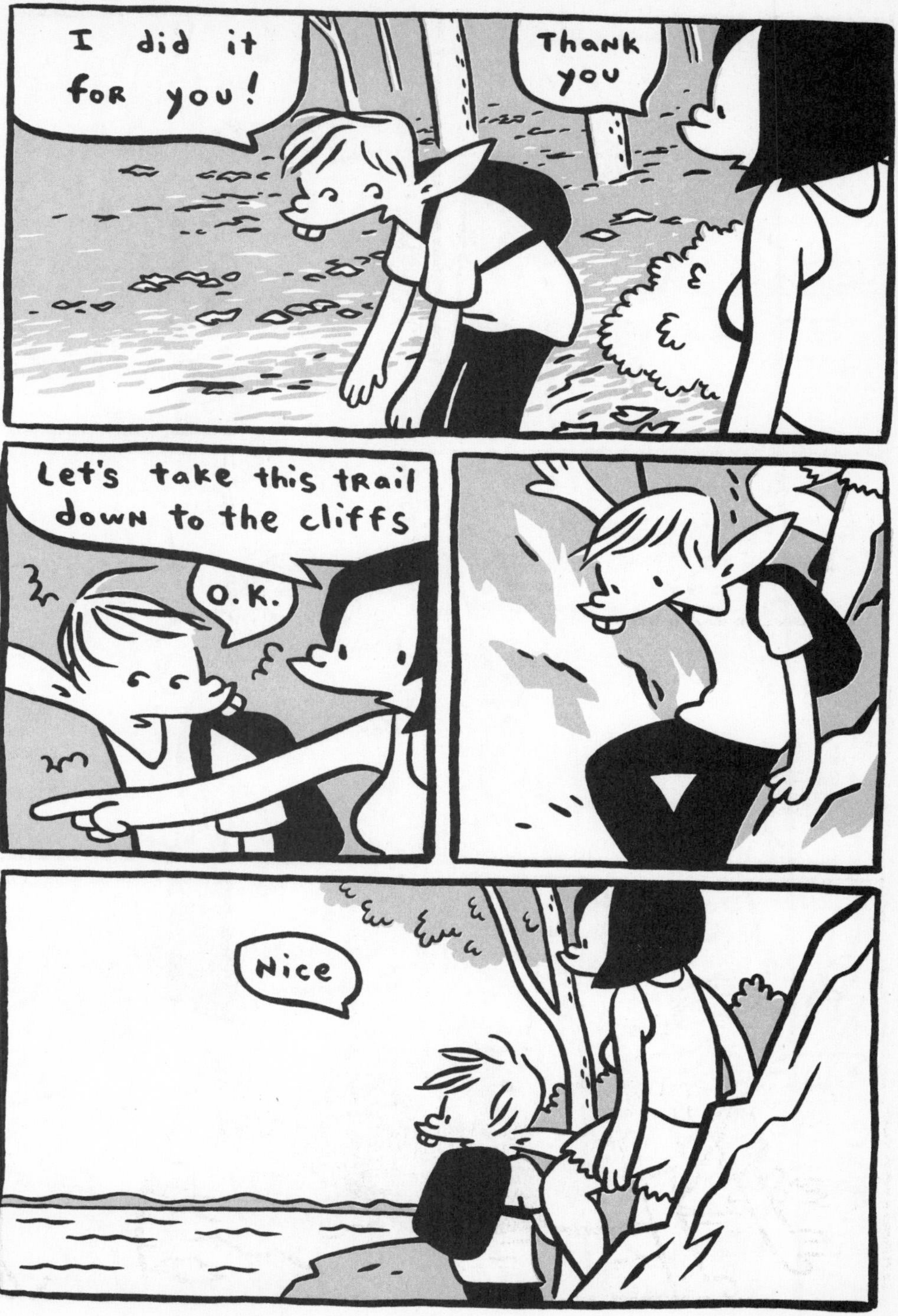
I did it for you!
Thank you
Let's take this trail down to the cliffs
O.K.
Nice

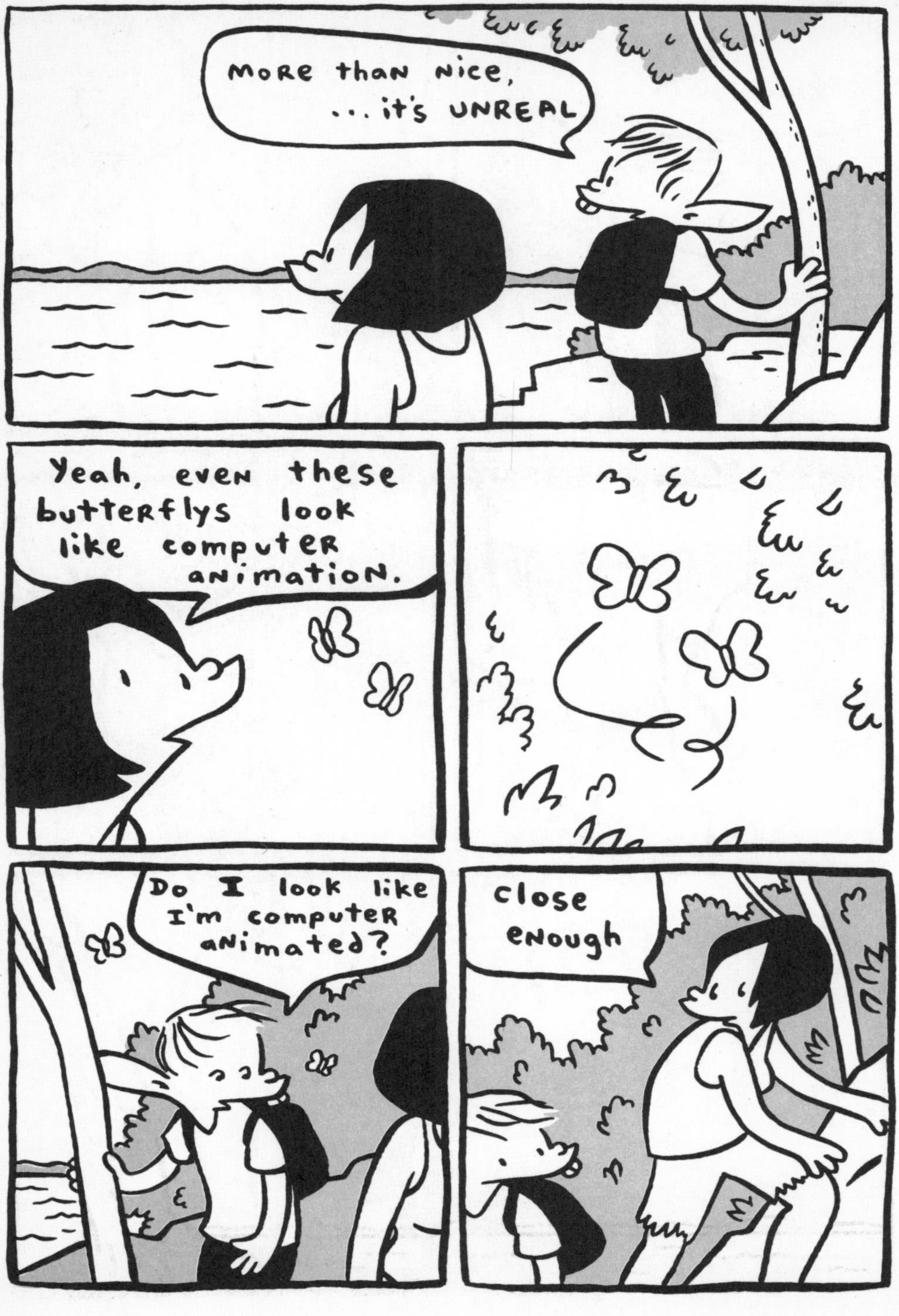
More than nice,
...it's UNREAL
Yeah, even these butterflys look like computer animation.
Do I look like I'm computer animated?
close enough

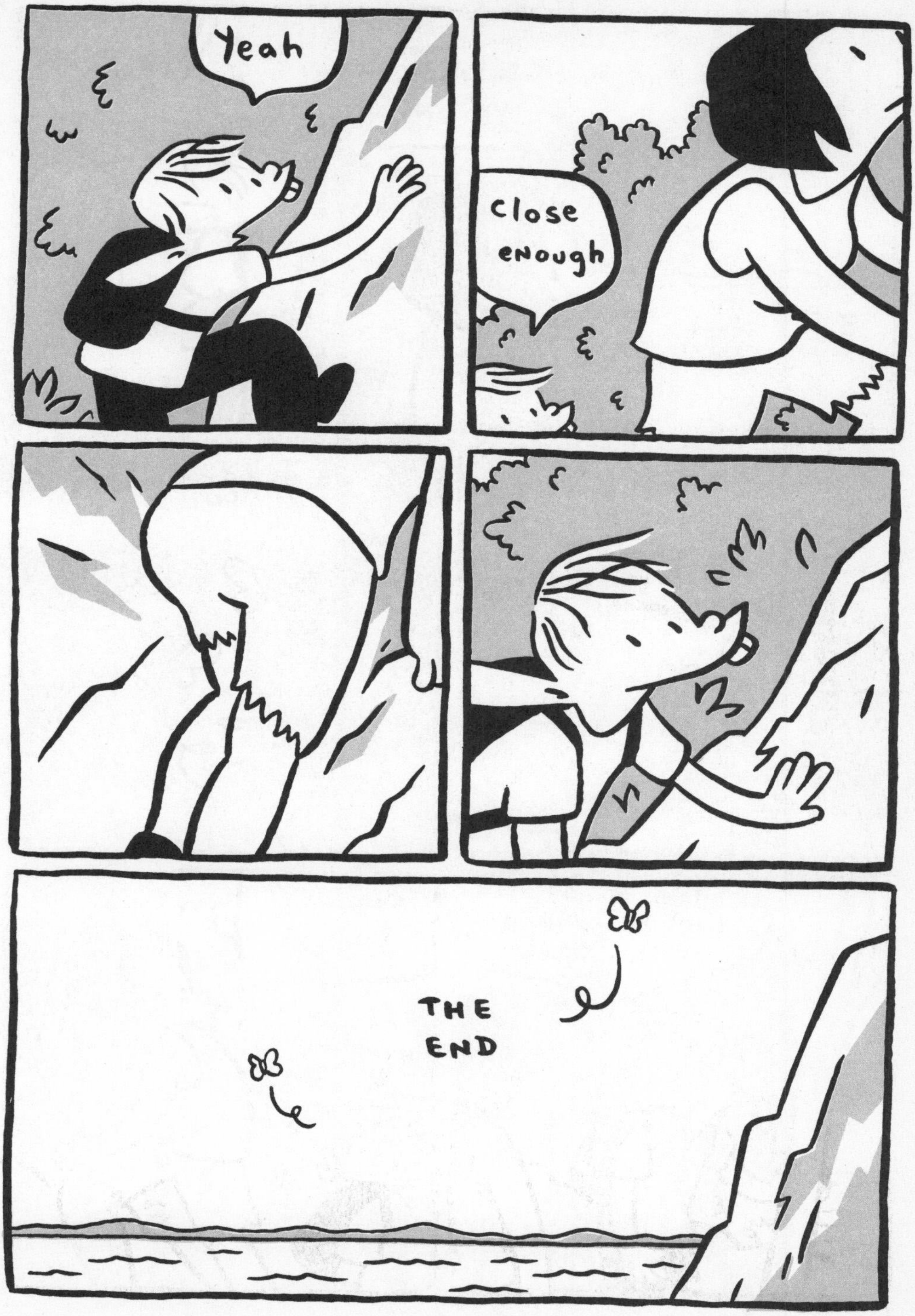
Yeah
close enough
THE END